**Toward a New International
Economic Order: Selected
Papers of C. Fred Bergsten,
1972-1974**

Toward a New International Economic Order: Selected Papers of C. Fred Bergsten, 1972-1974

C. Fred Bergsten
The Brookings Institution

Lexington Books
D.C. Heath and Company
Lexington, Massachusetts
Toronto   London

Grateful acknowledgment is made for use of material reprinted herein: chapter 3, reprinted by permission, © 1974 by the *Washington Post*; chapter 7 (from *Approaches to Greater Flexibility of Exchange Rates: The Bürgenstock Papers*, ed. by George N. Halm, copyright © 1970 by Princeton University Press), reprinted by permission of the Princeton University Press; chapters 8 and 36, © 1974 and 1973 (respectively) by the The New York Times Company, reprinted by permission; chapter 12, reprinted by permission from *Foreign Affairs* (July 1971), copyright 1971 by Council on Foreign Relations, Inc.; chapter 16, reprinted by permission from *Foreign Affairs* (October 1974), copyright 1974 by Council on Foreign Relations, Inc.; chapter 24 (originally called "Comments by C. Fred Bergsten"), © 1973 by the Brookings Institution; chapter 25, reprinted by permission from *Foreign Affairs* (Jan. 1972), copyright 1971 by Council on Foreign Relations, Inc.; chapter 32, reprinted by permission of New York University Press from *Business Problems of the Seventies*, ed. by Jules Backman, © by New York University; quote by Walter Laqueur on p. 322, © 1973 by The New York Times Company, reprinted by permission. Other chapters were reprinted by permission of their respective copyright holders: American Importers Association; *American Journal of Agricultural Economics*; A. W. Sijthoff International Publishing Co.; British-North American Committee; *Challenge*; Council on Foreign Relations, Inc.; Europa-Archiv; *Foreign Policy*: Institut für Weltwirtschaft; Quadrangle Books; *SAIS Review*.

Library of Congress Cataloging in Publication Data

Bergsten, C Fred, 1941-
    Toward a new international economic order.

    "Bibliography of the writings of C. Fred Bergsten through 1974": p. 507.
    1. International economic relations—Addresses, essays, lectures. 2. United States—Foreign economic relations—Addresses, essays, lectures. I. Title.
HF1411.B43   338.91   74-16635
ISBN 0-669-96677-0

Published simultaneously in Canada

Printed in the United States of America

International Standard Book Number: 0-669-96677-0

Library of Congress Catalog Card Number: 74-16635

Contents

List of Figures

List of Tables

Introduction

The international economic order which governed economic relations among nations with a high degree of effectiveness during the first postwar generation has been severely eroded, if indeed it has not totally collapsed. This development has contributed importantly to the growing economic difficulties faced by virtually all nations in the last few years, which at this writing has culminated in global stagflation—very slow and even negative growth, with rapidly rising rates of unemployment, and very rapid inflation—and has raised specters of runaway inflation, collapse of the international monetary system, and even depression. In addition, history shows clearly that effective international arrangements are needed to avoid economic conflict among nations, which in turn can easily spill over into hostilities on a broad political, and even military, plane. Hence the restoration of an effective international economic order is a critical and urgent matter for both economic and political reasons.

Unfortunately, there are formidable barriers, of several types, to the construction of new world economic arrangements. First, there is a major intellectual challenge in conceptualizing the nature of the current economic problem and its underlying political framework, both of which have changed dramatically in a very short period of time. Second, there is the political problem of translating any new conceptual framework into specific proposals and implementing them. Third, for an American, there is the need to assess the impact of such proposals on the United States —which largely created and maintained the previous postwar system, then was primarily responsible for its ultimate collapse, and remains by far the most important single country in the world economy—to see if they serve its national interests, properly and hence broadly defined. Fourth, it is necessary to analyze the impact of such proposals on the interests of all other major groups of countries as well, to see if they have a chance of being accepted internationally and hence provide a pragmatic base for new global arrangements.

Since leaving the U.S. Government in mid-1971, I have attempted to contribute to these four aspects of the process by analyzing the overall nature of the international economic problem, the several functional aspects of international economic relationships—international monetary affairs, trade, foreign investment and natural resources (including oil)—and its several geographic components, primarily U.S. economic relations with Europe and with the "Third World" of developing countries. This volume pulls together a number of my previously published articles on each of these topics, some of which appeared originally as testimony before Congressional committees, as chapters of collections of essays, as newspaper items, or as papers in foreign publications, and hence may not have been widely available. Several of the papers have been revised to fit the present format.

Four basic themes emerge from these writings. The first, which is featured in part I but appears in virtually every chapter of the volume, is the overwhelming reality of economic interdependence among literally all of the non-Communist countries in the world, including the United States.

The second is the need to anticipate problems well in advance. Bad policy most frequently results when governments are surprised, and react hastily and defensively. I have therefore sought to flag the emergence of new trends in a variety of areas, most of which have subsequently occurred, including:

—The basic change in the objectives of the *foreign* economic policies of most industrialized countries as a result of inflation moving up alongside, or even for a time replacing, unemployment as their cardinal *domestic* economic problem (see especially chapters 1 and 9)

—The related threat of trade wars of *export* controls (see especially chapter 10)

—The likelihood of additional commodity cartels a la OPEC (see chapter 18)

—The desirability of flexible exchange rates, and the concomitant downgrading of the international roles of the dollar, from the standpoint of the national interests of the United States (see chapters 4 and 7)

—The emergence of a Deutschemark zone in central Europe (see especially chapter 23)

—The resurgence of protectionism in the United States in the early 1970s (see chapter 12)

—The onset of "voluntary" export restraints as the principal protectionist device to limit imports (see chapter 11)

—The perils to fundamental U.S. economic and foreign policy interests of the Nixon-Connally economic offensive of August-December 1971 (see chapters 25 and 26)

—The possible onset of international investment wars in the 1970s a la trade wars of the 1930s (see chapter 16)

The third theme is the demonstrable value of international rules and institutions to limit both the economic and political problems caused by economic conflict among nations. To this end I have proposed reforms which would seek to further institutionalize international economic interdependence in the areas of international money (part II), access to supplies (chapter 10), foreign direct investment (chapter 16), and overall relations between the industrialized and the developing countries (part VIII). I argue that such regimes are in the national interests of the United States in money (especially chapter 4), access to supplies (chapters 10 and 28), trade generally (part IV), and investment (part V).

The fourth theme is the need for effective leadership in both anticipating the problems of the world economy and pressing for solutions to them. The United States can no longer provide such leadership alone, nor need it do so (part I, chapter 4 for international money, and chapters 12 and 13 for trade). But it should certainly avoid destructive international economic policies (chapters 25-28), and position itself through proper domestic policies (chapters 13-15 for trade, 27-31 vis-a-vis the developing countries) and internal organization (part IX) to participate in constructing a new order. Europe must play a major role in such a construction (chapters 21 and 24), but Germany rather than the Common Market may be the most promising partner (chapters 22 and 23). A number of the developing countries will also have to play a substantial role (chapters 27 and 28).

In all of my work, I have sought to help develop the new international economic order which is needed to assure both world prosperity and world peace. The objective of this volume is to add further to that process.

**Part I
The International Economic
Order: An Overview**

1
The International Economic Framework To 1980

The Collapse of the Old Order

The international economic framework of the first postwar generation has clearly dissolved.

The international monetary system is no longer based on fixed exchange rates and the dollar, as ordained by Bretton Woods. The international trading system is no longer characterized by non-discrimination and a focus on import barriers, as ordained by the GATT. Many developing countries no longer need "foreign aid," and many of the former recipients are now becoming important aid donors. Thus both the basic rules and institutional framework of past international economic relations have become largely inoperative.

The old order collapsed because of fundamental changes in its underlying premises. The large and increasing economic interpenetration of national economies, coupled with the increasing role sought by governments in pursuing national economic and social objectives, sharply increased the domestic political importance of international economic issues around the globe. The onset of detente has simultaneously reduced the importance of security issues and the political dependence of other countries on the United States, and hence has lifted the security blanket which in earlier years often stifled economic disagreements. As a result of these two trends, economic issues are rising toward the top of foreign policy agendas everywhere. The relatively depoliticized economic order of the past—dubbed by Richard Cooper a "two-track" system within which economic issues were left to economic officials and a widely accepted set of international rules[1]—thus became increasingly unviable.

At the same time, the United States is no longer the world's dominant economy, and no longer can or should hold an economic umbrella over the rest of the world. Japan and several European countries, particularly Germany, have moved up alongside the United States as global economic powers. The shift from commodity surpluses to commodity shortages has greatly enhanced the economic and therefore political power of countries throughout the "Third World"; the oil producers are the most obvious

Excerpted from a paper prepared for a meeting of the Commission on U.S.-Latin American Relations in New York in June 1974 and published in *The Americas in a Changing World* (New York: Quadrangle Books, 1975).

examples, but the same conclusion also applies to producers of a long list of commodities ranging from bauxite to bananas. So the political base of the international economic system has also undergone radical transformation.[2]

The result is a fluid, multipolar world political system within which is evolving an even more fluid, multipolar world economic order. New options have been opened for many countries, particularly those relegated to an inferior position in the first postwar generation. But new constraints on national action also have emerged, due to the high degree of international economic interdependence, particularly for those positioned most powerfully in the previous hierarchy. In this new setting, what will be the economic and political bases for international economic relations?

The New Bases of International Economic Relations

The most important economic change affecting international relations is the *ascendance of inflation* as the primary economic (and perhaps political) problem in virtually every industrial country.

At least since the Great Depression, unemployment has been the cardinal economic (and often political) problem in most countries. Countries have thus sought to use their external economic policies to help deal with domestic unemployment. This called for maintaining undervalued exchange rates or at least avoiding their overvaluation, erecting barriers to imports, and subsidizing exports. It meant buyers' markets for most goods at most times. It led to vicious international economic conflict in the 1930s, as countries sought to export their unemployment to each other. As a result, the postwar international economic order aimed primarily to stop such practices: the IMF sought to avoid competitive exchange-rate depreciations, the GATT sought to bar import restrictions and export subsidies, and the IBRD plus other aid arrangements tried to boost purchasing power throughout the world.

Now, however, for the first time in at least 45 years, inflation has at least moved up alongside unemployment as the cardinal economic problem faced by at least the industrial countries. As a result, the objectives of countries' foreign economic policies are being reversed. They now seek to export their inflation, rather than their unemployment.

This means they want to appreciate, rather than depreciate, their exchange rates—as many countries have sought to do during the last four years. It means that they will unilaterally reduce their barriers to imports—as many have been doing. It means they may even place controls over exports, rather than subsidizing them—as many industrialized and developing countries have done in the recent past.[3]

In addition, much of our present inflation cannot be explained by the traditional references to excessive aggregate demand. Nor does it appear to yield much to wage-price controls. It thus appears that supply shortages and bottlenecks, at all stages of the production process, ranging from raw materials through intermediate processing to final manufacturing capacity are *a* if not *the* most important problem for some time to come. As a result, sellers' markets have supplanted buyers' markets for a wide range of both primary and manufactured products.

Because this shift in emphasis is so new, few if any international rules or institutions are aimed at dealing with the new kinds of conflict among nations which it may engender. There are no barriers to trade wars of export controls to parallel the barriers to trade wars of import controls. There are no agreements, even in principle, regarding access to supplies to parallel the elaborate machinery for assuring access to markets. Inflation has become a global problem but no foundation, even of a rudimentary sort, exists for a constructive international response to it or even to limit the damage it could cause to relations among nations.

A second focus of international economic arrangements in the years ahead is likely to be *economic security*.

The postwar economic system, created of course by the industrialized countries (primarily the United States), aimed primarily to maximize efficiency. Its instruments were the freest possible flow of trade and capital movements. Ironically, it was then only the developing countries which fretted over their *dependencia* on outsiders.

Now, however, economic security is challenging efficiency as the goal of economic policies throughout the industrial world as well. Higher levels of income permit deviation from the previous focus of maximizing efficiency and growth; indeed, higher premia *can* be placed on stability and certainty in such a milieu. The growing number of economic targets sought in most countries induces governments to seek ways to reduce the often disruptive effects of external events which they cannot control, and to assure themselves access to those external resources which can help them meet their internal targets. The oil crisis has of course brought home most clearly the importance of economic security.

The quest for economic security is both consistent and inconsistent with the new focus on fighting inflation. It is consistent in that quests for assured new sources of raw materials, for example, will trigger both an increase in their global availability—hence reducing prices—and provide security for those with clear access to them. But it is inconsistent in that some countries may have to accept even higher prices to assure supplies, as has already happened under some of the bilateral arrangements for oil negotiated by Japan and several European countries.

A tension between efforts to fight inflation and to promote economic security will thus be an important factor in international economic relations in the years ahead. Indeed, countries will seek to pursue both simultaneously, as with "Project Independence" for oil in the United States. Therein may lie both new opportunities and new conflicts for relations among particular countries.

One major implication of both these economic changes is the *dramatic change in the North-South power relationship*. As already noted, inflation implies that buyers' markets have become sellers' markets. The quest for economic security places a premium on those who have the resources to which secure access is sought. Thus many of the developing countries, including most of those in Latin America, have suddenly become "have" as well as "have-not" nations.

The transformation is obvious for the commodity producers: e.g., Brazil for soybeans and iron ore, Chile for copper, Peru for fishmeal, Guyana and Jamaica for bauxite, Venezuela and Ecuador for petroleum. But it may also be true for manufactured products, because only the developing countries have the surplus labor available to significantly boost their output of such products without adding further to the spiral of inflation. Hence countries which possess both raw materials and unemployed labor—which is the case for virtually every country in Latin America —may be in a position to achieve major gains in the international economic environment which is likely to prevail into the relevant future.

Another key development is the *demise of the process of European unification*. Europe's effort to develop an "economic and monetary union" has totally failed, and most key European currencies are floating independently. The Common Agricultural Policy has become largely irrelevant as inflation has carried world farm prices well above CAP prices. Even the customs union has been badly jarred, most recently by the Italian import deposits. The European countries have obviously taken basically unilateral courses on energy and other raw materials. And the demands of the British government for "fundamental renegotiation" of its membership in the Community could sharply accelerate the disintegration of Europe.

The fundamental problem is that there now exists no rationale for European unity which is politically saleable within Europe. The old fears of Soviet aggression and Franco-German hostility are virtually gone. Europe is not the right grouping to cope with most international economic issues, which require collaboration with, e.g., raw materials producers or the United States and Japan. Neither "independence from America," nor "saving the Germans from themselves," nor fears of Soviet *political* aggression ("Finlandization"), which are sometimes offered as new rationales for Europe, are likely to fill the gap.

This development further increases the fluidity of the world economic and political scene, in two ways. It obviates the development of a European "pole" in world affairs, so it becomes ever harder to envisage the "trilateral" (U.S.-Europe-Japan) management of world affairs advocated by some. And it confirms that the European countries will be competing among themselves around the world.

This picture of fundamental change in the underlying premises of international economic arrangements is completed by reference to several more familiar trends. Detente is likely to continue sufficiently to limit any recrudescence of Cold War and rigid alliance systems dependent on coalition leaders (the United States and USSR) for security or even survival, yet is unlikely to proceed anywhere near the superpower condominium levying "law 'n order" on the rest of the world as feared by some developing countries. The "new nationalism" is likely to continue to grow, with countries throughout the world increasingly pursuing their own goals —including independence from undue external influence—in their own ways. Transnational actors, such as the multinational firms but many others as well, are likely to continue to play growing roles in international economic affairs and hence generate periodic tensions with nation-states.

The Evolving Economic Order

These fundamental developments have already triggered a number of basic changes in international economic arrangements, and suggest further directions in which the evolution will progress.

International monetary relations are now based on flexible rather than fixed exchange rates for most industrial countries. The new system has worked successfully to eliminate some of the balance-of-payments disequilibria (especially the U.S. deficits and Japanese surpluses) which fouled the previous system, and have kept markets open and functioning despite the pressures of huge capital flows and the dramatic rise in oil prices. Flexible rates are almost certainly with us for the indefinite future.

The monetary side of the system is also evolving rapidly, but its direction and ultimate destination are less clear. The dollar will continue to be the most important single currency for some time to come, but the Deutschemark and several other currencies, to lesser extents, are financing an increasing share of international private transactions and rising in importance as international reserve assets. In addition, an increase in the official price of gold now appears inevitable. And most national authorities continue to espouse the Special Drawing Rights of the IMF as the primary reserve asset of the future. So the perennial issue of the financial base for the international economic system—which in the late 1960s had clearly seemed headed toward reliance on SDRs—remains unresolved, and has become further complicated by the resurgence of gold and the growing strength of additional national currencies.

Concern has been expressed in some quarters that the international monetary system, including the new system of flexible exchange rates, will be severely strained and perhaps even fractured by the money flows triggered by the sharp increase in oil prices. To be sure, individual countries such as Italy and India do now face severe payments problems. The increase in oil prices adds significantly to the inflation problem highlighted above, and the constant threat of production cutbacks intensifies the quest for economic security.

But the oil money has been recycled successfully, at least so far, to those industrial countries which need it to finance their payments deficits. No country has sought to competitively depreciate its exchange rate, partly because of the inflationary consequences of doing so. The Euro-currency markets, which will intermediate most of the reflows, have grown by 50 percent in some recent years and appear quite able to continue to do so in the future. There are even some signs that the oil producers (particularly Venezuela and Iran) are beginning to recognize their responsibility to channel at least some of their new-found wealth to the poor countries on easy terms. Any projection in this area must be cautious, and major problems certainly exist for a number of individual (particularly non-Latin American developing) countries, but the results so far and the outlook suggest that no international monetary collapse is likely.

International trade relations have been focused on commencing a new multilateral trade negotiation (MTN) to further liberalize (particularly non-tariff) barriers to imports and perhaps draw up new rules to govern commercial relations among nations. Such efforts will probably continue, and—together with the way in which the various schemes of generalized tariff preferences are actually implemented—are of particular interest to the developing countries. However, they may be derailed for a while by the failure of the U.S. trade bill and/or the inability of a disintegrating Europe to come up with either joint or national positions.

In addition, these traditional issues have become much less important than in even the recent past. As noted above, the new focus on inflation has led many countries to liberalize unilaterally their barriers to imports. It provides protection against resort to new import barriers.

But it also induces countries to apply export controls and aggressively use their leverage as sellers, including through the formation of new producer-country commodity cartels. Hence a major focus of international trade policy in the coming years will be access to supplies, which could lead both to a spate of new arrangements for specific commodities and new international trade rules. The Mondale Amendments to the Trade Reform Act (and the similar Chiles Amendments to the Export Administration Act), supported by the Administration, reveal that such a process is already well underway in U.S. trade policy.

International investment issues are also rising in importance. The international production of multinational enterprises (MNEs) far exceeds the flow of international trade, yet most countries are still groping their way toward national policies on the issue and no international rules or institution to govern them exist at all.

It is clear, however, that most host countries—including virtually all those in Latin America, with ideologies ranging from Brazil to the Andean Pact—are positioning themselves to negotiate terms of entry for the MNEs which will increase the benefits thereof for the host countries: more jobs, more exports, more local ownership, more capital inflow and less repatriation of earnings, better technology and more local research and development, etc. Such arrangements are often quite satisfactory to the MNEs and are unlikely in and of themselves to choke off much investment—except when carried to extremes, as in India and perhaps the Andean Pact —especially as the requirements are often coupled with tax and other incentives to the firms.

But this shift of benefits to host countries may often come at the expense of home countries, particularly the United States, whose *national* interests are not represented in the negotiations between host country governments and MNEs. Viewed from one perspective, such negotiations thus represent a new means of transferring resources to developing countries. Viewed from another perspective, however, they can only intensify the pressures against MNEs in the United States, which are already sizable, and threaten the maintenance of a liberal U.S. policy toward outward direct investment.

Indeed, this whole pattern of emulatory national policy to both attract and regulate MNEs, and the likely reactions thereto in the United States (and perhaps other home countries), suggest an uneasy parallel with the evolution of trade policies in the interwar period. Countries then sought to manipulate to their national advantage the major avenue of international exchange, trade, and in turn triggered emulation and retaliation which finally degenerated into trade warfare when the Great Depression plunged national economies into deep despair. No such cataclysm is foreseeable today—although a Great Inflation might have unpredictable consequences along similar lines. But the same kind of trend appears to be developing with regard to national policies toward the main vehicle of international exchange today, investment. As the GATT was created to avoid the recrudescence of the interwar experience with national trade policies, international accords may now be needed to prevent such developments in the investment area.

Finally, *foreign aid* arrangements have also undergone dramatic change. The United States is no longer the chief donor, and even the absolute level of its help has declined as the old rationales wane and no new consensus has developed. New donors, both oil producers and other previous recipients (e.g., Brazil, Iran), are becoming increasingly important. Multilateral institutions are now channeling the bulk of the assistance flows. Alternative sources of help—the private capital markets, "new OPECs," the SDR link, the seabeds—have either already appeared or have important potential. Several previous recipients no longer need help. Many of those who do need different kinds. At the same time, a small but important number of countries in the "Fourth World" need assistance even more than in the past.

Each of the major components of international economic relations has thus already changed dramatically, in view of the fundamental transformations outlined earlier, and further evolution will clearly occur.

Notes

1. Richard N. Cooper, "Trade Policy is Foreign Policy," *Foreign Policy* 9 (Winter 1972-73).

2. For a more detailed analysis see C. Fred Bergsten, *The Future of the International Economic Order: An Agenda for Research* (Lexington, Mass.: Lexington Books, D. C. Heath and Company, 1973), expecially pp. 2-8 [chapter 2 in this volume].

3. A worst-case scenario could of course envisage active efforts by countries to export unemployment and inflation simultaneously through the application of export and import controls in different sectors, and even through multiple exchange rates. Such international policies could derive from a globalization of stagflation at low levels of "stag" and high levels of "flation."

2 The Future of the International Economic Order

The Salience of the Issue

International economic issues have always been important to the domestic economies of most countries, and have featured heavily in the formulation of overall foreign policies. However, the breadth and depth of international economic interpenetration which has now developed in virtually all countries, and the reactions to it in virtually all countries as well, are accelerating so rapidly that international economic relations among nations have moved onto a qualitatively new plane of both economic and political importance. In addition, international economic issues have until quite recently been relatively unimportant in economic terms to the two superpowers, the United States and the Soviet Union, ever since they became the largest economies and political powers in the world. And the effect of international economics on international politics had until recently been overshadowed by the protracted security crisis which extended for more than half a century from Sarajevo through Vietnam.

This new importance of international economics, in both economic and political terms, is likely to grow continuously into the foreseeable future. And the political-economic trends which are likely to affect the world economy differ appreciably from those encountered in the 1950s and even most of the 1960s: the deep and accelerating interpenetration of domestic economies, the tensions which have resulted between groups which benefit from these trends and groups which bear their costs, major shifts in economic power among the national actors in the international economic system, the emergence of new national and transnational actors, and the reduction in the relative concern over security interests.

As a result of all these developments, the monetary and trading systems which governed international economic relations during the first postwar generation have collapsed. The international monetary system is no longer, in practice, based on fixed exchange rates and gold. The international trading system is no longer, in practice, based on steady reductions in barriers to trade, nondiscrimination, and tariffs. International economic relations have reached a crossroads, and we cannot now tell whether in the

This chapter appeared originally as pages 2-8 of *The Future of the International Economic Order: An Agenda for Research* (Lexington, Mass.: Lexington Books, D.C. Heath and Company, 1973).

11

immediate future the world will resume the postwar path toward greater freedom for international economic transactions, replicate the proliferation of restrictions of the interwar years, or find some new middle course. We do know that the Bretton Woods and GATT systems provided the foundations for a generation of economic peace, but could hardly be expected to govern a world economy so radically different from the one for which they were constructed. Any new system must be built on very new underlying circumstances.

First, the interpenetration of national economics is increasing dramatically, and all signs indicate that this trend will continue to accelerate unless it is consciously checked by national policies. The magnitudes have become enormous: annual sales of perhaps $400 billion by the foreign subsidiaries of multinational firms; energy import needs of perhaps an additional $50 billion in the industrialized countries alone by 1980; a U.S. balance of payments deficit of $30 billion in a single year; reserve gains of almost $3 billion by a single central bank in a single day.

Between 1950 and 1971, world exports increased over fivefold in value and now exceed $300 billion; over the past decade, trade has grown at an average annual rate of 10 percent—much faster than world income. The flow of international services, such as tourism, has increased even faster. Still more impressive has been the growth of international capital flows, ranging from direct investment through portfolio movements to shifts of liquid balances—despite the proliferating panoply of controls designed to check them. The production process has become nearly as mobile among nations as trade in the goods which are produced. Technology and management expertise are frequently "exported," rapidly diffusing acquired knowledge. Even labor has become internationally mobile in some regions (especially Europe and the Mediterranean) and some sectors (especially management and skilled professions). Virtually all sectors of virtually all economies now rely heavily on external transactions.

The United States remains the least reliant of all market economies on international transactions, but its engagement in the world economy has grown dramatically. Exports have become essential to U.S. agriculture and to many sectors of U.S. industry, and hence responsible for millions of American jobs. Imports have become critical to the United States, in two senses: in some sectors, especially oil and meat, the United States has sought increases to help fight inflation (and it may soon depend on imports to meet much of its energy and other raw material needs), while in other major sectors, such as textiles and steel, it has limited the rise of imports because of their impact on domestic jobs and profits. An important share of U.S. corporate profits now derives from the foreign sector, and foreign investment by U.S. firms may have wide-ranging effects on domestic employment and other key economic variables. The international role of the dollar has become so large that it can significantly affect U.S. monetary policy, and liabilities to foreigners have become a sizable part of the U.S. national debt. The dollar has been devalued twice, after almost forty years of a fixed parity, with important consequences for U.S. jobs and prices. So the United States has at last joined the rest of the world in depending on the world economy for an important share of its own national wealth and prosperity.

Second, the sharp increase in international transactions, both in absolute magnitudes and as a share of total economic activity, has coincided with a steady proliferation of the economic and social policy objectives sought by most nation-states through their governments. Societies now demand more equitable distribution of income and increases in a vast array of social services as well as stable growth. Achievement of these objectives calls for increasingly effective control by nation-states of their own destinies.

But such control may frequently be undermined by external influences of precisely the type which are increasing so rapidly. The integration of the world economy causes both secular and cyclical fluctuations to be transmitted between countries more quickly, and to a much higher degree, diminishing the effectiveness of domestic policy instruments. Foreign ownership of capital may erode national economic control, and is widely perceived as doing so. This confluence of international interpenetration with proliferating national policy objectives is what differentiates the present from the pre-1914 period; that other great era of international economic exchange certainly had the former, but it was virtually devoid of the latter and hence conflict between international and national goals seldom arose.

Thus the contemporary world economy confronts centrifugal as well as centripetal forces, both of unprecedented scale and rising pace. One result has been deep tension within individual countries between the benefits of economic interpenetration to some sectors and its costs to others. Indeed, effective national sovereignty often seems far more threatened by economic interdependence at this stage of history than by losses of territory to hostile invaders. International integration often seems to threaten national disintegration.

Third, because nations and sectors within nations are now more affected by international economic relations than ever before, national and sectoral views on these issues have become increasingly politicized. Because some nations and some sectors gain from economic interpenetration while others lose, or gain less, these political views are in turn increasingly polarized. Groups (including countries and groups of countries) who feel they are paying for the benefits derived by others from international transactions seek to reject economic interdependence. Conflicts between nations as they pursue competing internal goals thus become even more likely. The most extreme manifestation of this trend is the ardent support of some elements of organized labor in the United States for the erection of a virtually impenetrable wall around the U.S. economy, shutting out imports of goods and people and shutting in exports of capital and technology. But the pressures exist elsewhere, and are rising rapidly. There is a risk, of sufficient possibility to merit attention, that governments could lose control of events—as they did politically in 1914 and economically in 1929-1932—with unpredictable and possibly disastrous results for the world economy and international politics.

Fourth, foreign policies around the world must therefore focus increasingly on economics if only because of their increased economic importance and the internal politicization and polarization of views which have resulted. In fact, key economic issues have already in recent years risen at least temporarily to the top of bilateral and multilateral political agendas (e.g., British entry into the European Communities, textile trade and overall economic relations between the United States and Japan, military offset between the United States and Germany, the systemic crisis of August-December 1971 among the major trading countries).

But this conclusion is buttressed further by several key trends in international politics. The intensity of the Cold War has clearly receded, and perceptions of its intensity have receded even further. With external threats reduced, if by no means eliminated, security concerns will decreasingly determine overall relations among political allies within the East and especially the West, and between East and West. Coalition leaders will be less able to use their security leverage to maintain economic cooperation from their allies, and many of those allies will be less restrained in surfacing their economic disagreement with coalition leaders. In the case of the West, the resurgence of Japan and Western Europe as major economic powers, and potential political powers as well, reinforces this likelihood. The nudging aside of the security blanket has exposed intra-alliance economic discord, and adds to the thrust of economic issues toward the top of international political agendas. Indeed, we shall later see that the complex relationship between security and economic concerns in this new milieu is one of the issues which most needs new research.

Fifth, these problems are further complicated by the emerging importance of new actors of two types—additional countries, and nonnational entities. The Communist countries are just now beginning to enter the world economy, and their inclusion raises a whole set of new issues which will be discussed in detail later as a prime focus for new research. A number of Third World countries are commencing a major role in the world economy, for a variety of reasons: they may possess a strategic resource (e.g., the oil countries, but many others as well), or they may be rapidly bridging the gap between developed and less developed and becoming important in world trade and investment patterns (e.g., Brazil and Korea). Transnational actors, including multinational corporations and the network of banks which make up the Eurodollar market, must now be considered independently along with the national states within whose jurisdictions they reside. All of these changes add to the complexity of the international economic order, and complicate both its economic interactions and the power relationships which affect its politics.

Finally, due to all these economic and political changes, the United States will no longer hold an economic umbrella over the other non-Communist countries (and questions are raised as to how long it will continue to hold a nuclear umbrella over their security as well). For most of the postwar period, sizable U.S. payments deficits and trade concessions served both U.S. and global interests. Now they serve neither, and willingness to continue them has been abandoned by both the United States and most other major countries. Foreign policy begins at home; thus the United States—like Britain in the late 1920s—can no longer sacrifice at home, e.g., by accepting the unemployment consequences of an overvalued exchange rate, to stabilize abroad even if its leadership wanted to do so.

But this reduction in the role of the United States has produced a leadership vacuum in the world economy. The international economic power—a concept which itself needs much research, as will be noted later—of the expanded European Community and Japan has been growing rapidly. Both are approaching the United States in their ability to achieve their international economic objectives, and both outstrip the United States on some key measures of international economic power. The global economy is thus dominated by three major actors, one of whose relative power is probably still greatest but waning, with the other two gaining rapidly.

However, neither Europe nor Japan has yet demonstrated a political capacity to utilize its economic power constructively. This is partly because each is engaged in an internal evolution of historic dimensions—the broadening and deepening of regional integration in Europe, the turn from quantity to quality in the economic orientation of Japan. They are able to block change, but have yet to lead. At the same time, the United States is uncertain about the role it should play in a world it can no longer dominate but in which it continues to have enormous economic and political stakes.

The results so far are twofold, The old international institutional framework—a monetary system based on fixed exchange rates and the dollar, a trading system led by a United States devoted to the principles of free trade and nondiscrimination—has broken down. Indeed, that framework will have been turned upside down if the United States now actively joins the mercantilist race for trade and payments surpluses, as seems quite possible. Second, there is stalemate in the efforts to achieve a new and stable system to replace the old, and even to settle immediate specific issues, be they citrus trade or the creation of Special Drawing Rights. Such a stalemate—unlike nuclear statemate, which is stabilizing—may be very dangerous. The potential for either constructive cooperation based on true equality, or destructive competition in an environment of mutual hostility, is greater than ever before.

The world has never before encountered such a dilemma. The economic systems which provided relative stability in the past were based on the hegemony of a single country (the United States in the postwar period), a confluence of goals among at least the major countries (the decade or so preceding World War I), or both (the "gold standard" dominated by the United Kingdom in the nineteenth century). When the hierarchy has been uncertain (the whole interwar period), and/or when goals were in conflict (the 1930s, due of course in large part to the failures of internal economic policies), the systems have failed. The present configuration of relatively equal major powers pursuing goals which often conflict, which is already central to the collapse of the postwar system, is perhaps the most difficult from which to create a durable and stable international economic order. It is uncomfortably reminiscent of the U.S. failure to seize its opportunity to succeed Britain as world economic leader after World War I. However, it is far more difficult even than that closest historical analogue—both conceptually and politically—because there are now two new powers instead of one and because Europe and Japan now almost match the economic power of the United States, whereas the United States clearly surpassed Britain's material capacity in the 1920s and its failure was "only" one of resolve.

But a major effort must be made to construct a new order, for the alternative could be severe economic loss and serious political disharmony. Indeed, we have already stood close to that brink. Confidence in the entire fabric of international economic cooperation nearly collapsed in late 1971, when it took four months to resolve the crisis triggered by the United States actions of August 15. Throughout the world, investment plans and economic projections plummeted. The British prime minister refused to meet the American president at the summit to discuss high politics until the United States took steps toward ending the economic suspense. The crisis was overcome with little time to spare, and partly due to fortuitous circumstances. But the monetary and trading systems which had provided the structure of the international economic order—and which had been dying at least since 1967—were finally buried in the process, and we do not know what will take their place.

To be sure, even the worst breakdown in economic relations now conceivable would be far short of total disaster. Governments now know how to prevent depressions, so a repetition of the 1930s is virtually impossible (though we can be less confident that governments know how to avoid a "great inflation"). Each country has such stakes in the world economy that major trade wars seem politically unreal. Breakdown has been averted despite all the pressures cited, and efforts to achieve basic reform are at least haltingly underway. Even the deterioration now observable is of fairly short duration, and may prove to be merely a temporary aberrant. Indeed, it is clear that international economic exchange has continued to grow rapidly despite all the crises, new controls, and cries of alarm—and we shall see later that there is need to test the hypothesis that any new "system" at all is really required to manage the world economy. It is thus possible to be far too gloomy.

A sober outlook for the future does suggest continued tensions, however, and the possibility of accelerating and more serious crises if countries continue to pursue the "new mercantilism" in support of a proliferating host of conflicting "internal" objectives. This in turn conjures up images of the national efforts of the 1930s to export unemployment (or inflation and other problems) to one's neighbors—with consequent threats to world peace and prosperity. The absence of functioning monetary and trade systems would seem to increase the probability that countries will act in such a way, by obviating any effective constraint on their behavior from international law and functioning institutions, and stimulate equally dangerous responses from others. The apocalypse here is not nuclear war, but it could be exceedingly costly in both human and material terms. The biggest losers, in relative terms, would probably be the developing countries, much of whose future development depends on an open world economy in which they can avoid wasteful policies such as protectionist trade measures, undervalued exchange rates, and industrialization strategies based on import substitution. So the importance of the subject seems assured for the relevant future and we turn now to its component parts.

3

Interdependence: Now a Cold Reality

In early 1973, the international economic outlook appeared reasonably clear. The dollar was weak and continued to depreciate. The yen was powerful and Japan's competitive position appeared invincible. Most countries had "been forced" to adopt flexible exchange rates, but wanted to return to fixed parities and would soon be able to do so. The Committee of Twenty would shortly negotiate a reformed monetary system. To avoid the widely perceived threat of a relapse into protectionism, the major countries would soon begin a new multilateral negotiation to further liberalize international trade. The great boom of 1971-73 was coming to an end, but "soft landings" were expected in most quarters.

The world political environment also seemed clear. The European Communities had broadened their membership and announced ambitious plans for further integration. Atlantic relations would be smoothed in the widely heralded "Year of Europe." East-West trade looked likely to grow rapidly in the wake of detente. The Third World remained docile. The world was at peace, now that the United States was finally out of Southeast Asia.

Incredible as it seems, each of these "standard forecasts" turned out to be almost entirely wrong. The dollar has become the world's strongest currency, with the U.S. trade and payments balances in healthy surplus. Japanese reserves have declined by over $6 billion and the yen is depreciating rapidly. Floating exchange rates are here for the indefinite future. The Committee of Twenty is completely stalemated. The outlook for meaningful trade negotiations is highly uncertain. As for the threat of protectionism, the House of Representatives just passed an impressively liberal trade bill by an overwhelming majority and country after country has been unilaterally reducing barriers to imports. The virtually unforeseen problem of access to supplies, most notably oil but ranging far beyond it, has become the dominant issue of international economic policy. And the real threat of a global recession looms in the wake of the Arab oil cutbacks and price hikes.

Politically, the Common Market has stagnated and even shows signs of disintegration. The "Year of Europe" deepened U.S.-Europe differences instead of repairing them. U.S. economic relations with the Communist countries received a major blow from the House action to deny them

This chapter originally appeared in the *Washington Post*, January 13, 1974.

19

most-favored-nation tariffs and export credits, and from the threat to detente itself posed by Soviet action in the Middle East. The power of many countries in the Third World is rising rapidly, with exporters of products ranging from bauxite to coffee organizing to emulate the successful cartelization by the oil countries. Peace was shattered in the Middle East, with a continuing threat of U.S.-Soviet confrontation.

What lessons for the future can be learned from this rapid and wholesale turn of events? The yearend energy crisis accelerated all of them, but all were already well under way. So deeper answers must be sought. One is simply that the pace of both economic and political change has become incredibly fast. Another is that international economic interdependence is now a cold reality, and that the U.S. economy is dependent on external events in a number of key areas. Still another is that exchange-rate changes can work effectively and fairly quickly, as in the U.S. and Japanese cases, to eliminate international financial imbalances.

But there is a much broader lesson. For almost 50 years, unemployment has been the dominant economic problem for most of mankind. As a result, countries have tried to use their foreign economic policies primarily to export unemployment: by depreciating their exchange rates or at least avoiding appreciations, erecting barriers to imports to protect threatened industries, and subsidizing exports.

Now, however, inflation may have replaced unemployment as the dominant economic problem in most of the industrialized countries. Raw materials, food, productive capacity, capital and skilled personnel may well remain in short supply. The growing market power of oligopolists —countries producing raw materials, multinational firms, aggressive labor unions—will intensify price pressures. The political unacceptability of unemployment, and the growing multiplicity of economic and social targets throughout the world (more equitable income distribution, elimination of regional disparities, better education and health care, cleaner air and water, etc.), will keep demand high and growing.

As a result, countries will increasingly seek to use their external economic policies to export inflation rather than unemployment. Precisely such efforts have appeared with increasing frequency during 1973.

At least three countries—Germany, The Netherlands, and Norway— revalued their currencies explicitly to fight internal inflation.

Japan sold billions of dollars to hold up the price of the yen, in large part to contain domestic prices, but finally yielded to a 6.7 percent de facto devaluation last week, which tends to make Japanese goods more competitive in international markets. The Japanese need to earn more foreign exchange to pay for the more expensive oil imports.

Other countries lowered their barriers to capital inflows so that their currencies would rise in value. The United States suddenly decided that the dollar had depreciated enough, welcoming instead its strengthening in the last few months. In response, the major European countries sought to stop the dollar's rise, to avoid the inflationary effects of any further depreciations of their own money. Competitive appreciation seems to have replaced competitive depreciation as the primary motive of international monetary policy in most industrialized countries.

The same policy reversal can be observed in trade. Country after country—the United States, Japan, Germany, traditionally protectionist Canada and Australia—has unilaterally reduced import barriers to fight inflation. This is particularly significant in light of the expected multilateral trade negotiation, because countries normally husband their restrictions pending the reciprocal "concessions" which are exchanged in such a session. Another significant indicator is that, for the first time in history, a body of the Congress—responding to the fact that a vote for import restraint is a vote for inflation—has passed a trade bill more liberal than submitted by a President.

Indeed, trade policy has been completely reversed and export controls are now the dominant issue. The Arab oil actions are only the most obvious case. Producers of numerous other raw materials have taken similar steps, and more are organizing to do so as well. So have numerous producers of foodstuffs, most notably the United States. And export controls are increasingly likely to be applied to manufactured goods, particularly those which are needed to increase production of the materials and agricultural produce which are themselves in short supply.

In short, the world has moved from concern over shortages of demand to concern over shortages of supply—of raw materials, food, and even many manufactured products. Will the United States sell its coal to Europe? Or its oil drilling equipment to Japan? With inflation rates soaring everywhere, and with output and employment also threatened by the supply shortages, the magnitude of these concerns is building rapidly.

This new clash of fundamental national interests, which encompass security as well as economic considerations, raises the specter on the world scene of nationalistic beggar-thy-neighbor policies at least as vicious as those which occurred in the 1930s. The Arabs (with oil) and the United States (with soybeans) have shown that export controls can "work," in the short-term perspective which dominates most political decisions, just as the British deflected depression for a while in the 1930s with devaluation and trade barriers. Indeed, stagflation at high levels of both "stag" and "flation" could create an even nastier world in which countries sought to export both inflation and unemployment through different policy measures for different sectors of their economies.

But such measures are as likely to lead ultimately to disaster, perhaps accelerating a "Great Inflation" and making it a source of major discord among nations, as did their historical predecessors in deepening the Great Depression and generating international conflict. Yet there are no international rules or institutions which meaningfully address these issues, let alone provide an agreed framework in which to deal with them. They are not even on the agenda of the present trade and monetary talks. There is no national leader, like the United States at the end of World War II, to create a new order and assure its implementation. Indeed, the U.S. reversion toward mercantilism, the stagnation of European integration, and the abject appeasement of both Europe and Japan at the first sign of oil trouble raise serious doubts about the feasibility of cooperative management by the major industrialized powers.

But such cooperation is the only conceivable basis for structuring a new world economic order at this time, and concrete steps are needed in both the trade and monetary fields. Export controls are justified in some cases, as are import controls. But, at the minimum, export controls need to be strictly regulated as import controls have been regulated in the past. This requires new international rules and procedures, to limit such controls to situations which can be strictly justified and to deter unwarranted actions by threatening international retaliation against unjustified restrictions—be they Arab oil embargoes or American soybean controls. It also requires new domestic rules and procedures, to assure that all interested parties are heard before action is taken. Far more radical steps, such as joint management of world supply for particular products and long-term contracts to share available output on some agreed basis, may also prove necessary.

On the monetary side, significant progress has already been made. Flexible exchange rates have worked well so far, in several respects. They have enabled the world economy to weather such a storm as the year-end energy crisis without compounding it through a monetary crisis, with countries losing and gaining billions daily in futile efforts to defend fixed parities. They have permitted the elimination or phasing down of artificial impediments to trade and finance such as U.S. controls over capital exports and the two-tiered gold system, and there is no evidence that they have retarded desirable trade or capital flows. They have provided a means of accommodation to global inflation and an energy crisis, which have made national balance of payments positions both certain to diverge more than in the past and most uncertain as to where they will wind up, which is much less damaging than any conceivable alternative.

Further steps are needed, however, to build a new monetary system. In the present world of "floating exchanges," most countries in fact manage their rates unilaterally through direct intervention in the exchange markets and other policy measures. Such national practices can obviously conflict, leading both to market disruption and political hostility. In a world threatened by nationalist efforts to export inflation or unemployment, such conflict could accelerate dramatically—particularly if both inflation and unemployment rise as much in the near future as is now expected in many countries. Multilateral surveillance of exchange rates, with agreed rules governing national actions and international sanctions against offenders, thus becomes an urgent need.

In the face of these needs, the Committee of Twenty has completely bogged down. It agreed in early 1973 to paper over the fundamental differences among its most powerful members, by agreeing on such inoperative concepts as "fixed but adjustable parities" and "floating rates in particular situations," and has made no progress since. Indeed, it did not even hold a substantive meeting in Nairobi, and some of its leading members are already admitting that the July 1974 deadline for reform set at that time is also inoperative.

**Part II
The International Monetary
System**

4

The Outlook for the International Monetary System

The international monetary system will be reformed. The present regime is unstable and cannot prevail for long. The issue which now faces the nations of the world is whether reform will be negotiated and rational, or result solely from the interplay of market forces and the uncoordinated exercise of national economic and political power. If the latter course prevails, new instabilities will result and the underlying problems which were evident long before the crises of 1971 will remain unsolved. The United States has a major national interest in the shape of the coming reform because of its major impact on the future of the American economy and foreign policy.

On August 15, 1971, the United States placed the world on a virtually pure dollar standard by suspending indefinitely the convertibility of the dollar into U.S. reserve assets. The exchange-rate realignment of December 1971, negotiated at the Smithsonian, strengthened the prospects for maintaining that dollar standard in the short run by sharply improving the competitive position of the United States. But two paradoxes dominate the effect of these dramatic events on the future of the international monetary system.

The first paradox is that the inauguration of the pure dollar standard in 1971 was the culmination of a long-term process through which the international roles of the dollar were increasingly markedly even as the international political and economic power of the United States, relative to other countries, was waning markedly.

The postwar monetary system is now in its third phase. The first phase lasted through 1958, when only the dollar among major currencies was convertible into other currencies and into the reserve assets of the issuing country. The second phase lasted from 1959 until August 1971, when the currencies of all major countries were convertible both into one another and into their own reserves. The third phase began in August 1971, when the dollar alone among those major currencies became inconvertible into the reserves of its issuing country—though, through the actions of the private markets and other countries, it remained convertible into other currencies. So the dollar has moved from being the only *convertible* major currency to being, at least in part, the only *inconvertible* major currency.

This chapter appeared originally as pp. 5-23 of *Reforming the Dollar: An International Monetary Policy for the United States*, Occasional Paper No. 2 (New York: The Council on Foreign Relations, September 1972).

27

The evolution through these three phases clearly indicates a declining power position for the United States, relative to other major countries. This decline can be readily explained.

The political power of the United States—and hence its ability to induce foreign "cooperation" with its monetary approach, such as the explicit German agreement in 1967 to forego any future conversions of dollars into U.S. gold in return for the maintenance of American troop levels in Europe—has been declining steadily as the Soviets achieved nuclear parity, as fears of major international conflict receded, as military might became less relevant for settling political and especially economic issues, and as other countries restored their political strength.

Three of the key economic underpinnings of foreign confidence in the dollar were eroded by actions of the United States. U.S. price stability gave way to rapid inflation in the late 1960s. The ratio of U.S. foreign assets to foreign liabilities declined steadily as a result of steady U.S. payments deficits, and especially as its current account surplus declined sharply. And the United States itself began to levy controls on the international use of its currency. One measure of the sharp decline in U.S. power is that only 23 minor countries followed the dollar devaluation in 1971-72, whereas virtually all countries would have done so as recently as two or three years earlier.

Simultaneously, other countries found ways to reduce American power. They cut its advantage of size of joining forces (as in the European Community) and achieving faster rates of economic growth (in Europe, and especially in Japan). They built their reserves to a point where Japan and Germany alone now outstrip the United States on this central measure of power, and where the EC as a unit has reserves several times greater than American reserves. The EC countries eliminated some of the technical advantages of the dollar by narrowing the width of the margins around their own exchange rates. And other countries exploited their abilities to adjust their external positions in a system based on fixed exchange rates far more effectively than could the United States.

The paradox is that the international use of the dollar increased more rapidly in the second period than in the first, and more rapidly thus far in the third period than in the second. A declining U.S. power position in both political and economic terms coexisted with increasing international roles for the dollar.

The second paradox is that the U.S. moves of August 1971, though they apparently enthroned the dollar as the center of the monetary system, had instead the real effect of beginning the end of its international reign.

The devaluation itself represented the end of an era dating from 1934, in which a fixed price for the dollar dominated thinking on international money, just as the British devaluation in 1931 ended an even longer era for sterling, after which its international role could never be restored. Since the most important single requirement for an international currency is widespread confidence in the future fixity of its price, this change alone strikes a major blow at the prospects for any international roles for the dollar. It starkly revealed the new U.S. desire to intervene actively to change the exchange-rate structure to benefit U.S. competitiveness. It indicated that benign neglect is dead, that the United States will no longer be the balance wheel of the world economy. International money has become internally politicized in the United States. Other countries must now count on a much more aggressive U.S. international economic policy. Hence they can be less confident that their dollar balances will remain aloof from the vicissitudes of world mercantilist competition, and must reckon with the possibility that the United States may seek future devaluations of the dollar as well. The act is no longer forbidden. It is crucial to remember that the United States destroyed the existing international monetary system in August 1971 because it decided that devaluation served its national economic interests, not because of any collapse of confidence in the dollar by other countries, as so long predicted by Professor Triffin and others.

In addition, the new inconvertibility of the dollar into U.S. reserve assets sharply reduces the willingness of foreign monetary authorities to hold dollars in their reserve portfolios since inconvertibility of all reserve assets, except for a negotiated asset such as Special Drawing Rights (SDR), is essential to their acceptability. All other major national currencies are convertible into their own reserves, and both gold and SDRs are fully convertible into national currencies. It is true that real convertibility for all foreign dollar reserves had become a practical impossibility long before August 1971, but some conversions were possible (and took place well into 1971); the U.S. had extended exchange-rate guarantees, through the swap network and sales of "Roosa bonds," to about 15 per cent of foreign official dollar balances; and even the nominal convertibility of the dollar was politically important to other countries as it provided them with a basis to resist internal political charges that they were recklessly risking the national wealth. One immediate manifestation of the new dollar inconvertibility has been a series of measures by foreign authorities to resist new dollar accruals through applying additional controls against dollar inflows, thereby directly reducing the international use of the dollar and further undermining its attractiveness. The sharp decline in private foreign use of the dollar is based partly on fears that foreign monetary authorities may go even further in this direction in the future.

The United States also undermined the future of the dollar in August 1971 by using up its "financial deterrent"—its persisting ability to *threaten* dollar inconvertibility—on which an important part of its international monetary power has rested. The real effects of this "deterrent" were never as awesome as the psychological fear thereof, and the world has indeed gone on. The Emperor had fewer clothes than many thought. But the threat of using the deterrent provided much leverage for U.S. monetary demands in the past, even as recently as March 1968 when it helped win foreign approval for moving toward gold demonetization through instituting the two-tiered gold system. It will never do so again.

Finally, the U.S. actions were sufficiently cataclysmic to trigger basic change in the monetary system. Inertia is the ruling force in financial matters, both within and among national economies. Change is exceedingly difficult to foment. It took the floating of sterling in 1931 to finally undermine British financial dominance of most of the world, at least two decades after the bases of that dominance had disappeared, and sterling remains widely used today even though it is the most likely of all major currencies to depreciate steadily. The piecemeal U.S. actions of the 1960s eroded the roles of the dollar marginally, but never shook the world enough to change them drastically. The U.S. moves of August 1971, which were very similar to the British moves of September 1931, did so.

So the present dollar standard is deeply unstable. Its political and economic underpinnings have been eroding over time, and were jarred decisively by the very same policy moves which instituted it last August. Other countries, and the private markets, will no longer base the world economy on a currency which fails to meet the necessary criteria. Indeed, private international use of the dollar has been declining sharply since 1969 and is now very small in absolute magnitudes. And the European countries, rejecting the dollar as an inferior reserve asset, have agreed to settle one-half their intra-EC imbalances in gold and SDRs. But neither should the United States seek to perpetuate the present dollar standard, a move which will either continue to cripple its ability to adjust its balance of payments through changing the dollar exchange rate (the only economically effective means of adjustment which is politically possible for the United States), or raise major political problems for it. The present system cannot, and should not, last.

But the present system will disappear only as it is replaced by another. The first paradox just described, that the roles of the dollar expanded while U.S. economic and political power were declining, is explained by the absence of powerful rivals to the dollar throughout most of the postwar period. But such rivals, greatly promoted in relative strength by the U.S. actions of August 1971, now clearly exist. In the absence of negotiated change along the lines described and advocated throughout this paper, a new system will evolve through the interplay of market forces and national power positions. It is likely to be a multiple reserve currency system in which several national currencies—the mark, the yen, the Swiss franc, the guilder, and perhaps others—increasingly join the dollar and sterling as both transactions and reserve currencies. Evolution in this direction was already underway before August 1971 as a result of the weakening of the dollar and the strengthening of other currencies, and has accelerated sharply as a result of both the U.S. actions of that date and the continued financial strengthening of Europe and Japan, including, the evolution of the European Community toward monetary union. National currencies other than the dollar made up almost 30 per cent of the Eurocurrency markets, and perhaps 20 per cent of world foreign exchange reserves, by the end of 1971.

National currencies have played a major international role in all modern international monetary systems, including the so-called gold standard which prevailed before 1914. Private international transactors must have national currencies to finance international commerce and investments. National monetary authorities must have other national currencies to defend their own currencies in the exchange markets. These authorities also seek national currencies to build their reserves, because the supply of other assets—gold throughout modern times, silver in the distant past, SDRs now—is limited, and because national currencies earn interest and are an extremely convenient form in which to hold reserves. In the absence of negotiated alternatives to meet these needs, the incentives to hold national currencies are very strong. And there are few barriers to the process because countries whose currencies are held by others perceive very few risks to themselves in the early years of the process.

The monetary systems of the past were relatively stable when a single currency dominated: sterling through most of the nineteenth centruy, the dollar in the early postwar period. They were also relatively stable when several currencies co-existed within the framework of an agreed overall system: the French franc and the German reichsmark, along with sterling, within the framework of the "gold standard" during the two decades before 1914; the dollar and sterling within the framework of the Bretton Woods system during the first few years after the widespread resumption of convertibility in 1959.

But instability has reigned when several currencies competed actively outside any agreed systematic framework: the dollar and the French franc with sterling in the interwar period, and several national currencies in the recent past. The competition among reserve assets has also included gold throughout all of these systems, adding to instability except before 1914 and since 1968 when it too was part of an explicitly or implicitly agreed overall framework.

There is thus nothing inherently unstable in the international use of several national currencies, nor indeed of multiple reserve assets. In principle, their use can be regulated by agreement. But such regulation is extremely difficult to achieve, particularly when no single country among the several involved can dominate the system (as the United States continued to do immediately after 1959), and when all countries actively pursue competitive economic objectives (unlike before 1914). And I shall argue that the same negotiating efforts which would be needed to achieve this kind of regulation could produce a far superior international monetary system.

Indeed, the multiple reserve currency system was seriously considered by governments as well as outside observers in the early 1960s—and rejected by all as the worst possible approach to reform. The existence of so many competing assets, convertible into each other, is virtually certain to produce frequent "runs" from whichever asset looks momentarily weaker into whichever one looks momentarily stronger. Uncertainty about any single key currency would cast doubt on the entire system, and hence jeopardize even those other key currencies which faced no fundamental problem. The growth of the international use of each currency would be totally unregulated; thus the growth of world liquidity would be completely uncertain—perhaps excessive and inflationary at some times, inadequate and deflationary at others. The widespread international use of their currencies would either inhibit countries from using the exchange rate to adjust their balance-of-payments positions, thereby producing more controls over international transactions and fundamental disequilibria leading to major problems later, or else add to systemic instability and political problems when parities did change. (This would add to the probability, already strong, that pervasive controls will be the primary means of "adjustment" under a system which is reformed *de facto* rather than through negotiation, adding greatly to its instability.) These negative judgments were proved right even within the limited confines of the existing "multiple reserve currency" system as recently as 1968, when the decision of numerous sterling area countries to "diversify" their reserves led to a run on the *U.S.* gold stock via their drawdown of *British* dollar balances. In short, a multiple reserve currency system would replicate all the problems of the past "gold exchange standard" several times over.

Yet, in the absence of a negotiated alternative, such a system is now virtually certain to emerge. We have already noted the insatiable demand of private international transactors for national currencies and of national monetary authorities for more and "better" reserves, and the decline of the dollar as already outlined. The third requisite for a multiple reserve currency system is the presence of new reserve currencies, which is provided by the recent ability of other countries to meet the key currency criteria effectively.

The European Community, as a unit, is a far larger factor than the United States in international economic transactions. Germany alone rivals the United States in total exports, and Japan is rising fast. The reserves of both countries exceed the reserves of the United States. There is widespread confidence that the several currencies mentioned as potential key currencies will remain stable, and are indeed likely to appreciate in value over time. All have appreciated recently, and none has devalued since the early postwar period. Since none of them faces heavy external liabilities, their liquidity ratios are extremely favorable. Capital markets are rapidly becoming adequate in all these countries, partly as a result of the decision of the EC countries themselves to use each others' currencies for intervention purposes. The economies of these countries are growing faster than that of the United States, and their outlook for price stability is no worse. Some of them resist foreign use of their currencies, but the existence of the Eurocurrency markets makes it impossible for them to do so effectively. Political power is far less important to international economic position in a world of détente than in a world of Cold War, and so the relative political weakness of these countries is less an inhibition now than in earlier years. The EC as a unit and Japan individually are relatively self-sufficient economically and can thus inspire confidence that they will not be unduly buffeted by external events. And the history of the international use of national currencies clearly demonstrates that the process is self-reinforcing, especially in its early years, so that we can fully expect the increased intra-EC use of European currencies to further strengthen the probability of their use by countries throughout the world.

The Bretton Woods system provides no barrier to this evolution. It has never been able to control the overall amounts of international liquidity creation, even with the creation of SDR in 1970-72, and has no more power to block the development of new key currencies than it had to block the development of the dollar in earlier years. In addition, its rules for adjustment of national balance of payments disequilibria are in total disarray —ignored completely by the floats of May 1971, August 1971, and June 1972, and the adoption by the Group of Ten of wider exchange-rate margins at the Smithsonian.

Another route to reducing (but by no means eliminating) the inherent instability of a multiple reserve currency system would be true monetary integration of the European Community. Such integration could provide a single European currency for international monetary purposes instead of the several (sterling, marks, guilders, and perhaps others) which will otherwise become increasingly important. Yet a single European currency is at least a decade away, even on the most optimistic reading of that process. And it is uncertain whether the EC will achieve even the modest improvements in its internal monetary organization, such as the creation of a European Reserve Fund to pool at least some of its members' reserves, which could dampen at least the intra-European instability that a multiple reserve currency system would promote. Indeed, the present halfway state of European monetary integration adds to the probable development of a multiple reserve currency system, by promoting the international use of several European currencies and thus accelerating the self-reinforcing process, without any concomitant safeguards to check the instabilities that will result. In fact, the rivalries among European currencies which are likely to develop in such a system could render the process of European monetary and economic integration even more difficult than it already is.

In the absence of rapid progress toward negotiated international monetary reform, there is thus a strong probability of rapid evolution of unstable, de facto monetary reform. This outlook heightens the need for negotiated reform, which was well evident even before the crystalizing actions of 1971.

The first global reason for reform is simply that the international monetary system is not effectively performing its basic task: maximizing the contribution which international economic activity can make to the advancement of national economic and political objectives. The enormous growth of world trade and financial movements has concealed the shortcomings of the system, but they have become ever more apparent in recent years. Having achieved the primary postwar economic objectives of currency convertibility and a liberal trading system, the world must now turn its attention to improving the mechanisms which helped enable it to do so. There are risks of continued unwinding of the previous achievements unless this is done.

National economies are constrained unnecessarily by the absence of an effective adjustment mechanism and by periodic shortages or excesses of world liquidity. Exchange-rate changes are by far the most effective adjustment measure, particularly in "dilemma cases" where the needs of the internal economy call for macroeconomic policies that would exacerbate the external disequilibrium rather than promote its elimination. However, they are exceedingly difficult to execute within the present system. Excessively deflationary and inflationary policies are thus frequently pressed upon countries by external considerations. To avoid the adverse internal effects of such policies, there is increasing resort to controls over international transactions. The controls generally have small welfare costs themselves, but they rarely help solve the underlying payments problem. They ususally permit exchange-rate disequilibria to cumulate and *increase* the welfare costs of the adjustment that is ultimately required.

The other frequent response to payments pressure is exchange-rate changes outside the safeguards of the system. When this occurs, there is a strong tendency for deficit countries to overdo them in order to avoid an early repetition of the entire unhappy cycle. Since no rules govern these moves, other countries are justifiably concerned over their own position and tend to emulate for self-protection. The proliferation of controls, the tendency toward excessive depreciations when parity changes are made, and the absence of international rules to regulate such changes raise serious problems of trade policy and other political matters, in addition to problems for the monetary system itself. In short, the prevalent adjustment mechanism is basically faulty.

These shortcomings were partly obscured for most of the postwar period because the United States neglected its trade position and payments deficits. These deficits and laissez-faire policy toward its trade balance provided an economic umbrella—not unlike the nuclear umbrella which it raised in the defense area—under which other countries could achieve their basically mercantilist goals of increased reserves and trade surpluses. In August 1971, however, the United States joined the mercantilist race with a vengeance; and underlying American politics suggest that it will stay on this course, even if not as aggressively as in the first manifestation of the change. At an earlier time, when the United States retained its dominant power position the system might have adjusted to the change in American goals by simply accommodating them, by forcing others to modify *their* goals. Now, however, the clash of national goals coexists with a relative equality of national capabilities. As a result, the need for an improved adjustment process has become both much more urgent and much more difficult to achieve.

Liquidity uncertainties render the situation doubly dangerous. Partly because the adjustment process is weak, countries know that periodically they will have to face sizable deficits in their payments position without reserves sufficient to finance them, or perhaps even to give them time to adjust in an orderly way. This heightens the caution surrounding domestic policies and the proclivities toward controls and competitive exchange-rate depreciations. The problem is deepened by the resultant desire of most countries to achieve payments surpluses, to build their reserves against the day when they face deficits. International flows of liquid capital now assume tremendous size, despite the panoply of controls which seek to limit them, so that huge reserves are needed to guard against rapid exhaustion of countries' financial resources. A few persistent surplus countries, at the other extreme, fear that liquidity creation will be excessive and force them to "use" the weak adjustment devices; accordingly, they seek to limit the growth of reserves, adding further to the pressure on the system and on the majority of its members.

The second global reason for reform is that the system is not effectively performing even its minimum task: avoiding disruption to ongoing international economic activities. The frequency of international economic "crises" is both high and accelerating. Even the crises prior to August 15, 1971, none of which seriously disrupted the global flow of economic activity, levied high costs on individual countries. But when the crisis of the fall of 1971 was no closer to solution three months after the U.S. triggered it on August 15, the world moved perilously close to a breakdown of confidence in the future of international economic cooperation. Such confidence, rather than any particular system derived from the cooperation, is the real international underpinning of postwar economic prosperity. As a result, this particular crisis undermined investment plans and fostered uncertainty around the globe, and would have levied major economic costs on all countries had it not then moved promptly to resolution. But all of the crises reinforce the system's inadequacies, reduce the proclivities of individual countries to place high value on adhering to it, and add significantly to the omnipresent pressure for beggar-my-neighbor trade and payments restrictions which erode the liberalization of both that were achieved earlier in the postwar period.

If all the crises had occurred for the same reason, they would be less disturbing since some single reform could then prevent their recurrence. However, they have occurred for very different reasons and therefore point to the need for sweeping change. June 1972 reminded us of the effects of huge international movements of liquid capital, and the inadequacy of the adjustment process. August 1971 vividly demonstrated the inadequacy of the adjustment process, especially when the U.S. balance of payments is directly concerned, as well as the instability of the roles of the dollar in the system and the effects of unregulated liquidity creation. May 1971 pointed to the need for wider exchange-rate margins, for better coordination of at least the timing of national economic policies, and for more comprehensive international machinery to deal with interest-sensitive capital flows. The trauma of sterling from 1961 through November 1967; the DM problems of 1961, 1968-69, and 1971; and the franc difficulties of 1968-69, all highlighted the need for improved means to adjust national parities. The Canadian floats of 1950-62, and 1970 to the present, reveal the need for international rules to govern exchange-rate changes when they do take place. The systemic upheaval of late 1967 and early 1968—which led to the institution of the two-tiered gold system, the final agreements on Special Drawing Rights, and the Basel arrangements for sterling—displayed vividly the instability arising from the existence of several competing reserve assets, and the inadequacies of the existing liquidity mechanism, as did the 1960-61 difficulties with gold, to a much lesser degree. Moreover, the events of 1967-68 had already focused the inadequacy of the adjustment process, particularly when the U.S. balance of payments is involved. So had the minicrisis of late 1964-early 1965, which also showed that the system was even vulnerable to purely political maneuvering by a middle power.

Each of these problems is likely to foster more crises if left unsolved. Each succeeding crisis is likely to be larger in magnitude, in view of the growth of internationally mobile funds and the increasing market knowledge of international opportunities. Each is likely to increase the probability that truly serious economic and political problems will result. Even if this probability were small in absolute terms, it can no more be ignored by responsible policy-makers than can other possibilities with equally small odds. (For instance, the small probability that the U.S.S.R. will attack Western Europe has not undermined allied determination to maintain NATO, nor American determination to spend huge amounts of money to maintain a credible nuclear deterrent.)

Third, the present system is likely to generate ever more serious political problems among its members. There is no agreement on how to control the trade-off between adjustment and liquidity in the system as a whole, on what modes of adjustments should dominate, or on how liquidity should be created. There are highly divergent national attitudes toward these issues based on fundamental differences in national goals and capabilities.

Some countries, such as Germany, fear inflation more than unemployment due to their traumatic historical experiences with inflation, it having been their major postwar problem; some, such as the United States and United Kingdom, have a greater fear of unemployment in light of their own historical and recent experiences. Some countries, most clearly the Netherlands and Switzerland, want adjustment to occur via changes in domestic economic policies because they are so open to international transactions that exchange-rate changes and controls will disrupt their economies even more; some, such as the United States but also France and probably Japan in the future, far prefer adjustment via the exchange rate and controls because they are so independent of international transactions that adjustment via the domestic economy would be far more costly to national objectives. Some countries, such as France, Germany, and Japan, have traditionally used their foreign economic policy for essentially mercantilist ends—seeking both trade and payments surpluses—while others, such as the United States and the United Kingdom, have preferred to invest abroad and take more imports rather than build reserves and seek larger trade surpluses.

Some of these differences in national goals are now being reduced in a stabilizing way. For example, all industrialized countries are now forced to a major concern over inflation, even when higher unemployment is required to combat it. But some differences are being reduced in a destabilizing way. The United States (and United Kingdom) have joined the mercantilist race. All countries are now increasingly prepared to adopt controls over international transactions, which will bottle up, but not solve, fundamental disequilibria. And both Europe and Japan are becoming less reliant on international transactions—Europe through the steady expansion of the Community and Japan as its internal growth outstrips its trade growth —which makes international restrictions less costly and thus tempts both to pay insufficient heed to preserving an effective monetary system, in addition to helping qualify them to play key currency roles.

National capabilities are also converging. I have already noted that Europe and Japan have reduced the U.S. size advantage by amalgamation and rapid growth, and that the reserves of both far exceed the reserves of the United States. Because they are becoming less reliant on international transactions, Europe and Japan have more power to remain aloof from external economic pressures. Fundamental changes in world politics enable them at the same time to remain more aloof from the politcal leverage of the United States.

Potential conflict among national goals and greater equality among national power positions are both growing rapidly, and dominate the functioning of the international monetary system. Surplus countries generally attempt to force deficit countries to initiate adjustment, but no surplus country has the power to force adjustment unless a particular deficit country loses reserves below a level which it views as its absolute minimum. Deficit countries try to force surplus countries to initiate adjustment—and U.S. deficits have certainly contributed to foreign exchange-rate, and perhaps even price-level, adjustments. But the United States does not have sufficient power to force such changes, as was amply demonstrated by the refusal of France to adjust at all in 1971 except as a result of American actions fully acceptable to it and negotiation at the highest political level. Surplus countries fearing inflation want deficit countries to adjust by deflation, while deficit countries facing unemployment want surplus countries to inflate or revalue. Despite the agreement on SDRs, total changes in world liquidity remain completely unregulated and subject to constant conflict between surplus and deficit countries. Some countries are perfectly willing, some are even eager, to finance their surpluses by accruing dollars, thereby obviating adjustment pressure on the United States, whereas other countries are not only unwilling to do so themselves but deplore this abstention by others from forcing "discipline" on the reserve center.

Liquidity creation and adjustment initiative are thus determined largely by the exercise of the naked power which accompanies economic importance and/or key-currency status. Obviously this is unsatisfactory for all who do not possess such power and tempts others to seek "equality." But it is also unsatisfactory for the wielder of the power, since it induces widespread hostility abroad. In this instance, such hostility could produce non-cooperation with U.S. efforts to adjust the exchange rate of the dollar. More broadly, it would of course affect all relations among the countries involved, as it did on two notable occasions in 1971. In May, Senator Mansfield seized upon the German float as "an action directed against the dollar" finally to bring to the floor his amendment to halve American troops in Europe—and lost by only eight votes. In November, Britain's Prime Minister Heath refused to meet with President Nixon to discuss the President's forthcoming trips to Peking and Moscow, until the United States called a meeting of the Group of Ten to negotiate a solution of the deepening international economic crises.

Even the potential for determining economic issues through the exercise of pure power, which will always prevail in the absence of a clearly understood alternative, will tend to induce hostility. Such problems have become particularly acute with the development of a sizable disparity between the declining world political and economic roles of the United States, and the increasing international use of the dollar and the resultant U.S. involvement in virtually every foreign monetary crisis. The very uncertainties as to the outcome of the power struggle, which derive from the changes in national capabilities, multiply the risks to the system (and hence to all countries, including the most powerful) of relying on such unregulated interplay.

Who initiates adjustment is only part of the issue of the distribution of the costs of adjustment, although it is a large part because domestic political costs are clearest where a country has acted itself. But at present there is absolutely no agreement among nations on how to share this "burden." In practice, excessive pressure generally rests on the deficit country because its power to avoid initiating action declines as it loses reserves. Once again, *force majeure* carries the day.

A final political effect of the inadequate adjustment and liquidity mechanisms is the likelihood of pervasive national controls over international capital movements and trade, and unregulated exchange-rate moves. Any such steps impinge directly on national economic welfare in other countries. The resulting conflicts among nations will grow in importance as economic interdependence opens national economies increasingly to international exchanges, and as foreign economic policy becomes a larger element in overall foreign policy considerations.

The adjustment-liquidity trade-off, and the methods by which adjustment is achieved and liquidity created, are thus resolved in today's international monetary system largely by the exercise of national power. Yet the nature of this power is frequently unclear. Is it based on a country's reserve level? On its current balance-of-payments position? On the size and strength of its underlying domestic economy? On its overall political and military position in the world? In any given circumstance, different factors dominate the outcome. It is then completely unclear if individual payments problems will even be resolved, let alone *when* or *how* resolution will occur.

The lack of predictability in the system raises major problems for the United States. Will the United States be able to undertake, and carry through, effective adjustment measures of its own if it wants to do so? Will next year's deficit be financed by the accumulation of dollars abroad? Or will the countries which run surpluses demand U.S. reserve assets whether or not this country is in deficit? Will some of the "overhang" of outstanding dollars descend? Will the United States be affected by a crisis caused by the unwillingness of some other country to adopt effective adjustment measures? The uncertainties are equally intolerable for other countries, whose greater economic reliance on international transactions magnifies the potential danger for them of the system's instability.

The uncertainties are particularly acute and potentially troublesome during a period, such as the present, when international power relationships are unsettled. Hegemonial periods—such as those dominated by the United Kingdom in the early nineteenth century and the United States in the early postwar period—are relatively free of uncertainty. Non-hierarchical periods—such as the interwar years, when the United Kingdom lost its leadership role and the United States and France competed for the right of leadership without expressing much willingness to accept its responsibilities—are particularly dangerous. They call for maximum international cooperation to resolve the underlying uncertainties, treading between the Scylla of attempting to preserve an anachronistic hegemony and the Charybdis of passing power to those unprepared to exercise it effectively.

We are now in such a period. United States dominance of the non-Communist world is over, both politically and economically, for the international and domestic reasons outlined. This global need to align power realities with the actual functioning of the international monetary system highlights the unique U.S. interest in reform. An American effort to maintain dollar hegemony, beyond the time when others were resigned or even pleased to accept such dominance because of the true power position of the United States, courts disaster. Other currencies are gaining strength relative to the dollar. The costs of the dollar's international roles are already extremely high and will continue to rise, and the benefits will decline as the decline in relative power of the United States renders others less willing to finance its deficits by accruing dollars, and forces it toward an ever weaker bargaining position in monetary matters. The uncertainties in the system, particularly as they affect the United States, will multiply. The constraints on its policy will tighten, and its ability to force on others the solutions favorable to itself will recede. Crises will become a more severe threat to both the United States and the system as a whole. Ultimately, the United States would have to negotiate changes in the dollar's roles from weakness—with a more costly outcome for it as the clear result.

This is the major lesson for the United States from the historical experience of the United Kingdom. An unwillingness to recognize that fundamental changes in Britain's world position precluded any possibility of maintaining sterling's pre-1914 role disastrously pervaded British economic and foreign policy for more than forty years, from the return to a grossly overvalued gold parity in 1925, which promptly produced mass unemployment, through the abortive effort to avoid devaluation during 1961-67. Sterling's lame duck position contributed significantly to the sterling crises which have permeated the postwar period with sizable costs both to Britain and to the entire system. When finally forced to negotiate the international roles of its currency in mid-1968, Britain did so with its back to the wall and emerged with arrangements which maximized the costs to itself and minimized the benefits. It was an object lesson in the absence of foresight —by both Britain and the rest of the world—and a victory for inertia predicated on unanalyzed nostalgia.

The United States could never be constrained as badly by the roles of the dollar as was Britain by the roles of sterling, even if past errors were to be repeated. Being much bigger, the American economy is far less dependent on the world economy; the United States could therefore retreat to isolationist economic and even foreign policies; and the rest of the non-Communist world will probably continue to rely much more heavily on the United States for broad security and political support than did Britain's allies after the Napoleonic period. But the difference in degree should not mask the similarity in kind, and it cannot hide the absolute magnitudes of the problem which could develop for the United States and the world.

The international roles of the dollar are central to each of these problems. They are the means through which U.S. financial dominance is displayed daily. They are the mechanisms through which U.S. deficits are financed by others, whatever the others may think of the U.S. policies which contribute to the deficits. They represent a national means of creating international money, with a double bite politically because the dollars must be accepted and held by other countries to complete the transactions which "favor" the United States. The dollar overhang represents a threat to the stability of the entire system and characterizes the impotence of others to elicit "equal action" from the United States. In view of the undesirability of changing the official price of gold and SDR, the fixity of the dollar price in terms of gold and SDR provides a strong argument that all exchange-rate changes should be initiated by other countries, further symbolizing the dominant central position of the United States. And others view the international roles of the dollar, including its impact through the Eurodollar market, as enhancing the ability of the United States to export inflation or deflation to the rest of the world, forcing them to share the internal adjustment of the American economy.

But the roles of the dollar also levy major costs on the United States. It now pays over $1 billion annually in net interest costs on the outstanding balances; foreign dollar holdings must rise by at least this much each year for the dollar's roles to provide *any* net financing for the U.S. balance of payments. It does not control its own exchange rate and is thus sharply limited in its ability to adjust, particularly since the only real adjustment alternative to exchange-rate changes—domestic deflation or a different mix of domestic monetary and fiscal policies—are unacceptably costly for the United States because international transactions make up such a small part of its total economy. At the same time, the U.S. has inadequate power to force others to adjust through changes in their exchange rates or any other means; overvaluation of the dollar can result and cause major trade policy problems, giving impetus to such recrudescent protectionist pleas as the current Burke-Hartke bill, as well as the monetary problems just cited. The United States has to meet numerous criteria to preserve its key currency roles, some of which—such as where it locates on its deteriorating Phillips curve, which characterizes its trade-off between unemployment and inflation, and the need to build its key liquidity ratio by running a current account surplus—may tilt its policy priorities from where they would otherwise be. The roles of the dollar give the United States the major responsibility for managing the international monetary system, but its relative power no longer enables it to do so effectively—and it might be tempted to maintain a greater world role, to check the decline in its power, than would otherwise be desirable. The uncertainties of how to finance recurring deficits, and the possibility that parts of the overhang may collapse, coupled with the weaknesses of the adjustment process, can constrain both domestic economic policy and U.S. foreign policy.

In short, there are compelling reasons from narrowly American standpoints, as well as from the global standpoint, for thorough reform of the international monetary system.

5

Convertibility for the Dollar and International Monetary Reform

What is "Convertibility?"

The U.S. dollar remains convertible into all other foreign currencies. Private money markets throughout the world remain willing to sell other currencies for dollars. Virtually all central banks continue to buy dollars in exchange for their own currencies in order to keep their parities from appreciating at all or, in the case of those countries whose exchange rates are floating, from appreciating too rapidly. The dollar thus continues to play a major role in private international finance and as a reserve asset in the portfolios of foreign central banks. It is "inconvertible" in only one very special sense: it cannot be exchanged by foreign monetary authorities into the reserve assets of the United States (which consist primarily of gold and Special Drawing Rights).

The United States is not the only country which does not now stand ready to convert its own currency into its national reserves, as called for by the Articles of Agreement of the International Monetary Fund. The same is true for any country whose exchange rate is floating, such as the U.K. and Canada for some time—and the currencies of both, like the dollar, are convertible into other national currencies in the exchange markets. Indeed, almost any currency will almost always be "convertible" in the private markets (including black markets) at *some* (usually a fluctuating) price. The dollar would itself be a freely fluctuating currency now if it were U.S. policy which determined the outcome, since the U.S. is intervening very little in the exchange markets.

Prior to the widespread adoption of floating rates in March 1973, however, the case of the dollar was unique in that it alone combined inconvertibility into national reserves *and a fixed exchange rate*. If a majority of the other major countries return to pegging their currencies to some par value (or "central rate") declared to the International Monetary Fund, or even if they adhere to some *de facto* peg through "dirty floating," this situation would recur. (If freely floating rates become permanent for most countries, convertibility of currencies into national reserves will become a dead issue:

This chapter originally appeared in C. Fred Bergsten and William G. Tyler, eds., *Leading Issues in International Economic Policy: Essays in Honor of George N. Halm* (Lexington, Mass.: Lexington Books, D.C. Heath and Company, 1973), pp. 99-114.

43

this paper assumes that it will not.) We shall henceforth refer to this unusual phenomenon as "market convertibility."[1]

Such a situation could not now arise for any currency other than the dollar. All other countries actively use their reserves when they seek to maintain fixed exchange rates,[2] selling their reserves (buying their own currencies) to keep their rates from depreciating and adding to their reserves (selling their own currencies) to keep their rates from appreciating. If they stopped doing so, their exchange rates would float outside the agreed margins around their fixed parities.

Most of this intervention, throughout the postwar period and still today, has been affected through their buying and selling dollars. There was thus no need for the United States to intervene actively in the exchange markets, with U.S. reserves, to maintain a relatively fixed exchange rate for the dollar. Other countries did so for the United States in the course of maintaining their own exchange rates against the dollar. Thus a relatively fixed exchange rate for the dollar is compatible with U.S. abstention from the foreign-exchange market because of the intervention currency role of the dollar.

One result of this system was that virtually all foreign countries held sizable working balances in dollars,[3] while the United States held virtually no working balances in foreign currencies.

A second result was that the system functioned smoothly. There can be only $N-1$ exchange rates in a world of N currencies. If all N countries sought to achieve an independent exchange rate, the system would be overdetermined and could not work. United States abstention from the exchange markets, however, meant that only $N-1$ countries were seeking to achieve the $N-1$ exchange rates. There were no important problems of coordination, and the market itself readily produced a consistent set of exchange rates.

A third result was that other countries controlled the exchange rate of the dollar. Other countries intervened actively in the exchange markets, while the United States remained passive. The United States could change the official price of gold, but not the prices at which other countries bought and sold dollars—which set the exchange rate between the dollar and their currencies, and was a major determinant of international trade and capital flows. The Nixon Administration feared that other important countries would use this leverage to abort any U.S. effort to achieve a sizable devaluation of the dollar, so decided in August 1971 and again in February 1973 to negotiate exchange-rate realignments rather than simply announce unilateral changes of parity like other countries always have.

So the United States has traditionally abstained from using its reserves in the exchange markets. From 1934 until August 15, 1971, however, the United States declared itself ready to convert any dollars held by foreign monetary authorities into U.S. gold.[4] The postwar monetary system negotiated at Bretton Woods authorized this U.S. policy as a means by which a country could fulfill its "convertibility" obligation, as an alternative to active exchange-market intervention, and thus provided the legal foundation for the key currency role of the dollar just described.[5] One can therefore characterize U.S. postwar policy (until August 1971) as one of "passive convertibility," as contrasted with the "active convertibility" of all other countries.

There are thus three relevant types of convertibility:

1. *active convertibility* of national currencies into the reserves of their countries of issue, sanctioned by the Bretton Woods system and maintained by most countries prior to March 1973.

2. *passive convertibility* of national currencies into the reserves of their countries of issue, sanctioned by the Bretton Woods system and maintained by the United States until August 15, 1971.

3. *"market convertibility,"* as defined above, in which a currency is convertible into other national currencies at a fixed rate (within the prescribed margins) in the exchange markets but neither actively nor passively into the reserves of the country which issues it. This was the situation of the United States from August 1971 to March 1973.[6]

Why Convertibility? The Background

It is universally agreed that currencies must be convertible *into each other* to facilitate an optimum flow of trade and other international transactions. Currency inconvertibility requires the use of comprehensive foreign exchange controls, was a major impediment to international flows in the early postwar period, and remains a serious barrier to trade with the Communist countries and numerous less developed countries.

However, we have already noted that almost any currency can almost always be converted into almost any other currency at *some* price. The objective of convertibility is thus more accurately stated as minimizing the instability of the price at which conversion is assured.[7]

Until recently, there was a widespread consensus that "convertibility" thus required "fixed exchange rates"—as called for by the Articles of Agreement of the IMF. Many have tended to equate the interconvertibility of currencies with convertibility of each into national reserves, because the latter technique was used to preserve the fixed exchange rates at which the former took place.

Now there is a growing view, in both official and private circles, that exchange rates cannot remain truly fixed without spawning a proliferation of controls over international transactions, and that they will be more stable if permitted—even encouraged—to fluctuate more readily. The history of the postwar monetary system, in which the "fixed-rate" regime amounted in practice to "jumping parities fixed *until further notice*," strongly supports this view. For the purposes of this chapter the key question is: which of the three types of convertibility, for both the United States and other countries, will provide maximum support for a stable and effective international monetary system? (We again assume away the fourth possibility of *no* convertibility for any currency into national monetary reserves, i.e., freely floating exchange rates.)

At least until the middle 1960s, the postwar monetary system rested fairly successfully on the dollar. Virtually all countries maintained their exchange rates by intervening in the dollar market for their currencies. Most countries held a growing share of their reserves in dollars. The dollar provided most of the growth in both private and public international liquidity. Much more importantly, other countries were able to achieve the payments surpluses they desired because the United States was willing to run payments deficits. Foreign balance-of-payments targets, as well as exchange rates, were thus reconciled largely by the abstention from the game of the Nth country—the United States.

In such a system, it is fair to ask why the dollar needed to be convertible into U.S. assets at all. There were, however, solid economic, political, and psychological reasons.

The objective of the system was to preserve fixed exchange rates. This in turn required countries to pursue policies which enabled them to preserve their parities. The ability of other countries to convert their dollars into U.S. reserves provided an avenue—*the only avenue*—for them to signal that, in their view, U.S. policy was not conducive to doing so.

Such signals had no effect on U.S. policy at least through 1957, while U.S. reserves remained far higher than any foreseeable need to use them. Once U.S. reserves began to decline sharply, however, it had to regard reserve losses as significantly undermining its capacity to continue to play by the rules of the Bretton Woods system.

Thus the major U.S. balance-of-payments programs of the 1960s, each composed essentially of new restrictions over U.S. international transactions, followed a period of significant gold losses: in early 1961 after the short-lived breakout of the London gold price, in early 1965 after France launched its "gold war" against the dollar, in early 1968 after the massive run on the private gold market (which at that time led directly to U.S. gold losses through the operations of the gold pool). It has also been argued by close observers that the gold losses of the early 1960s were decisive in keeping U.S. interest rates higher than was desirable on purely domestic grounds, that the losses of 1967-68 were decisive in inducing key congressmen (such as Wilbur Mills) to finally support the income tax surcharge in 1968, and that the threat of massive gold losses played a major role in inducing President Nixon to finally adopt an incomes policy in August 1971. So the system of dollar convertibility has clearly had an important impact on U.S. domestic and foreign economic policy—providing pressure for "discipline" over U.S. internal policy in some cases, inducing the adoption of controls over international transactions in others.

The gold convertibility of the dollar also played an important role in its acceptability to foreign monetary authorities.[8] Some central banks held dollars solely because they bore interest, were convenient to use, represented a claim on goods anywhere in the world, and were based on the world's strongest economy. But a number of conservative central banks valued the U.S. convertibility pledge, in addition, if only because they could use it to refute international charges that they were "mindlessly financing the United States." Their views were particularly important in a fixed-rate system, because they were often the major surplus countries from whom the United States needed financing for its deficits. Gold convertibility was even important to the role of the dollar in private international finance, because the private sector had confidence that their own central banks would always be willing to buy dollars at a fixed rate. Thus it significantly helped the United States finance its balance-of-payments deficits by contributing to its ability to build up dollar liabilities to foreigners—one of the benefits of convertibility to the United States which offset the pressures on it to take actions to maintain its fixed gold parity.

Finally, the convertibility obligation provided an appearance of symmetry between the United States and other countries in a world which was highly asymmetrical. After the other major currencies became convertible in the late 1950s and early 1960s, inconvertibility for the dollar could have meant only one of two things. It would probably have meant a fixed-rate system in which the United States had the ability to finance any level of deficits through the dollar—since there was no conceivable alternative monetary base to the dollar—with no adjustment responsibilities. Such a situation would have been politically intolerable for other countries, particularly since there was very little they could have done about it—except take very destructive steps, such as the adoption of more controls and a retreat to inconvertibility for their own currencies. Alternatively, it could have meant abandonment of fixed exchange rates—which, at that time, would have been completely unacceptable to all other countries. The broad U.S. foreign policy goal of maintaining a world economic structure which promoted harmony among the non-Communist nations thus played a major role in the U.S. decision to maintain a convertible dollar, just as it had in the much earlier U.S. push to create the IMF system itself.

So dollar convertibility played a major role in the postwar monetary system. As the 1960s progressed, however, the two declined together. Dollar convertibility became increasingly nominal, as U.S. liquid liabilities grew far beyond the level of U.S. reserves into which they could in principle be converted. The system was racked by repeated crises, proliferating controls, and growing exchange rate disequilibria. The need for fundamental reform became increasingly clear.

Why Convertibility? The Future

The role of dollar convertibility in any new monetary system depends on the nature of that system.[9] It is not an objective in itself, as many Europeans (and even some Americans) implied when they suggested immediately after the Smithsonian that "the restoration of convertibility" should be accorded top priority, with other issues to be decided subsequently. Such a view in reality represented a desire to return to the system which had just been discredited, on the rather naive (or mischievous) view that the only problem had been the misalignment of exchange rates which was hoped to have been corrected at the Smithsonian—but which lasted only fourteen months.

There are three reasons why Bretton Woods-style convertibility for the dollar could not work now. First, the "dollar overhang" of $60-80 billion —the legacy of the past reserve currency role of the dollar— continues to swamp U.S. reserves of about $12 billion. Large amounts of these dollars could flow back into private hands if the current U.S. balance-of-payments position improves,[10] and large amounts are in countries perfectly willing to hold them—especially if their doing so will *keep* the United States from trying to eliminate its deficits! But enough countries are unhappy with their dollars that the United States might immediately face requests for major conversions and hence have to revert quickly to inconvertibility. The risk that this could occur would undermine from the start the stability of any system which included both the overhang and a resumption of dollar convertibility. Collapse of the contemporary sterling overhang in six weeks (after the United States had tried to get Britain to negotiate a funding operation for it) ruined Britain's attempt to restore convertibility in 1947, and we must not repeat that error now.

In addition, the existence of the overhang would mean that the United States might not acquire reserve assets when it runs payments surpluses in the future, because other countries could simply pay for their corresponding deficits by running down their dollar balances. The United States could not then agree to finance its payments deficits with reserve assets, because it could be losing reserves over time even if its annual surpluses and deficits balanced out. The United States could run out of reserves altogether even though it was, over time, in payments balance!

The private overhang could add to the magnitude of these problems. Foreign monetary authorities may be unwilling to hold dollars which they receive from the private sector, especially if they doubt that the private sector will repurchase the dollars in the near future. So definitive arrangements for both the official and private overhangs are needed to permit a restoration of dollar convertibility.[11]

Second, U.S. reserves of $12 billion are now quite small even in terms of *current* deficits which the United States might run. They are smaller in relation to annual imports, for example, than those of any other major country except the United Kingdom and Sweden.

In 1971 and 1972, the U.S. basic deficit, which includes trade in goods and services and long-term capital movements and is the best existing measure of our underlying position, exceeded $9 billion. The official settlements deficit, which adds short-term capital flows as well, was almost $30 billion in 1971 and over $10 billion in 1972. The size of these numbers should not be regarded as abnormal for any period of time as short as a year, since they represent differences between gross flows totaling hundreds of billions of dollars which can change radically in response to relatively small changes in the national economies (or exchange rates between economies) which underlie them.

Third, and closely related, the improvements made recently in the adjustment process do not yet assure that national payments imbalances will be attacked more effectively in the future. Better adjustment, by other countries and by the United States, would permit the United States to restore convertibility on a smaller reserve base. At present, however, the outlook encompasses the possibility of continued frequent, sizable, and persistent imbalances.

In my view, the United States could thus prudently agree to restore convertibility of dollars acquired by other countries as a result of U.S. basic deficits only if four conditions were met: elimination of the dollar overhang, a sizable increase in U.S. reserves, new means for handling the huge flows of liquid capital which will continue to permeate the system,[12] and a dramatic improvement in the adjustment process.[13] But should it do so even under these conditions?

The national interest of the United States calls for two basic changes in the monetary system: an improvement in the adjustment process, and a new basis for world liquidity. The adjustment process must be sharply improved, so that the United States can avoid disequilibrium exchange rates—which lead to a deterioration in its trade balance, costing jobs at home and undermining domestic political support for the preservation of a liberal trade policy.[14] This improvement must come primarily through adequate flexibility of exchange rates. Domestic deflation (beyond that needed for purely internal reasons) would simply be too costly to the U.S. economy, because the foreign sector represents such a small share thereof. Direct controls over trade flows (import surcharges and/or export subsidies) are ineffective; they are absorbed by private traders if applied for temporary periods, and are certain to trigger retaliation and emulation by others if intended to be permanent. Capital controls are ineffective unless made so comprehensive that they stifle desirable economic activity. Surplus countries could of course reduce their import barriers and controls over capital exports, but it is unrealistic to expect much adjustment from such measures.

The United States has a particular interest in being able to initiate adjustment since one can never count on other countries to take the necessary steps. Since exchange rate changes are the only economically effective means of external adjustment that is politically acceptable in the United States, their embodiment in the monetary system is very much in the U.S. national interest. Adequate steps by others, and unimpeded U.S. initiatives, can be assured only by international agreement on a set of guidelines which will indicate when adjustment should take place—and when it must be allowed to take place—backed up by international sanctions against countries which fail to comply. Such guidelines could be implemented either through discrete parity changes within a parity ("fixed rate") regime or through permission/denial for market intervention by monetary authorities within a no-parity ("dirty float") regime.

One barrier to exchange rate flexibility, and especially to initiatives by the United States to change the dollar rate, is the widespread role of the dollar in the international monetary system. The intervention role of the dollar means that other countries set the exchange rate of the dollar, as outlined in the first section of this paper. This was revealed clearly in August 1971 when the United States had to *negotiate* a dollar devaluation—and when France kept its rate (for commercial purposes) unchanged for four months despite U.S. pleas, the suspension of convertibility, and the import surcharge. Countries holding dollars in their reserves are also reluctant to revalue their dollar parities because of the reduction in the value of their assets which will result, and the United States may—as in the past—not wish to cut the value of others' holdings by its own actions. This problem would be particularly acute if exchange rates were to fluctuate more freely and more frequently, since the reserves of all dollar holders would then become much more unstable than they were in the "fixed-rate" regime of the past. More generally, the international roles of the dollar have in the past tended to promote U.S. immobilism on exchange rate issues, because of the standoff between those who wanted adjustment via the rate and those who opposed rate changes because they might undermine the capacity of the dollar to provide continued financing for U.S. deficits.

So the second major change in the system, which is necessary to achieve the needed improvement in the adjustment process, is a sharp reduction in the reserve currency role of the dollar. Fortunately, it can readily be replaced by Special Drawing Rights as the central element in official reserves. Annual creation of SDRs can provide the needed growth in official reserves, just as a special issue of SDRs can be used to consolidate the dollar overhang. Substitution of SDRs for dollars would have a number of desirable effects on both the liquidity mechanism and confidence in the system as a whole, in addition to facilitating the needed improvement in the adjustment process.

These two basic changes in the system will require fundamental concessions from other countries. They will have to agree to subject their exchange rates to international rules, and to sanctions available to the international community to back them up, as already officially proposed by the United States—though some (Japan, Germany) know it will mean broader pressure on them to let their rates appreciate periodically. They will have to agree to place Special Drawing Rights at the center of the monetary system—which will require some (especially France) to give up their hopes for restoring gold. They will have to agree to create enough SDRs annually to really meet world liquidity needs—though some (Germany, Switzerland, the Low Countries) may be more conservatively inclined. They will have to agree to a consolidation of the dollar overhang on terms which are generous to the United States. They will have to agree to a marked expansion of the swap network to recycle liquid capital movements.

More fundamentally, they will have to get used to the new notion that the United States, too, has balance-of-payments and trade-balance goals which will make it much harder for them to realize their own goals. They will have to let the United States adjust, rather than continuing the comfortable (if sometimes irritating) route of financing U.S. deficits as in the past. They will have to exercise increased responsibilities for management of the system, since the United States no longer has either the economic strength nor the internal political consensus to maintain an economic umbrella over the system as in the past.

It is inconceivable that the United States could successfully negotiate all these changes in the system without agreeing to resume convertibility of the dollar into U.S. reserve assets. A world which is asked to move toward symmetrical treatment of the United States can hardly be expected to accede without symmetrical adoption of responsibilities by the United States, as called for in its obligation under the Articles of Agreement of the IMF. There is in fact a widespread foreign desire to achieve total symmetry between the dollar and other currencies; U.S. insistence on continued dollar inconvertibility would imply total asymmetry instead. Thus a restoration of dollar convertibility appears to be a sine qua non for international agreement in the monetary area.

The alternative to a reformed system of greater exchange rate flexibility under international rules, based on SDRs with dollar convertibility, is a continuation of the status quo: proliferating controls and unregulated, competitive exchange rate changes (perhaps through dirty floats) based on an increasing variety of competing reserve assets, including an inconvertible dollar.[15] Such a "system" appears to some to be attractive from a U.S. standpoint, because no external pressure can be placed on U.S. policy through conversion of foreign dollar balances.[16] Unfortunately for the United States, however, there are two sides to the coin. In a system with no agreed adjustment rules, other countries can use their dollars to block U.S. efforts to adjust its exchange rate—and they would be particularly likely to do so if the United States insisted on staying inconvertible.

This is particularly true under the regime of dirty floats adopted by most of the major countries in early 1973, since their activities under such regimes undergo no international surveillance at present. Even before then, however, a number of countries had already adopted two-tiered exchange rates, which maximize their competitive position in international trade while making U.S. foreign investment more costly. Under French "leadership," the entire Common Market could make such a system an integral part of its new monetary union unless global monetary reform provides a better alternative. Other countries could adopt direct controls over U.S. investment inflows. They could even refuse to accept more dollars, which would severely undermine the use of the dollar for private transactions (as well as its reserve currency role) by forcing its depreciation in the exchange markets and eliminating the traditional "purchaser of last resort." Even without such steps by others, crises would be frequent because of the inadequacies of the system. Needless to say, such economic conflict would adversely affect political relationships which are vital to U.S. security concerns. No countries would have been economically strong enough or politically independent enough to contemplate such steps a decade ago, but the expanded European Community and Japan can do so now.

An inconvertible dollar world would thus jeopardize major U.S. national interests. It would also jeopardize the national interests of other countries, perhaps to an even greater degree. So the likelihood that such a world represents the real alternative—as implied in Secretary Shultz's speech to the IMF in September 1972—should help galvanize cooperative reform. Indeed, U.S. agreement to restore dollar convertibility is perhaps its major lever in the reform negotiations—which is why the Administration has been right to avoid any steps toward "partial" or "interim" convertibility prior to achieving agreement from other countries on what the United States wants from these negotiations.

What of the costs to the United States under such a restoration of dollar convertibility? The new international guidelines would call on other countries to appreciate their currencies or take other steps to eliminate their surpluses, or permit the dollar to depreciate when the United States was in payments deficit. Under the proposals of Secretary Schultz, there could apparently be no pressure on the United States to restrain its domestic economy—the guidelines would always permit a U.S. devaluation if the United States was in deficit. My own view is that the United States (and other countries) should devalue only when an external deficit coincides with significant internal unemployment. This would leave open the possibility that foreign dollar conversions would place the United States under pressure to restrain its domestic economy when inflation rather than unemployment was the key domestic problem. In such instances, however, restraint would be desirable for purely internal U.S. reasons anyway—so the dollar conversions would help provide a *needed* dose of domestic "discipline," as they did in 1968 (and perhaps in 1971, depending on one's view of the desirability of the Nixon wage-price restraints). In short, the United States has to risk being forced to adjust by others—though only when it should do so anyway—in order to be assured that it will be able to adjust when it wants to.

Professor William Fellner, in a recent article on a related subject, agrees that a resumption of dollar convertibility would require giving the United States "extra-large" contingency reserves, the need for which would, however, be mitigated by greater exchange rate flexibility. However, he opposes returning to dollar convertibility, suggesting that the United States instead meet foreign concerns by guaranteeing the purchasing power of dollars held by foreign monetary authorities.[17]

Professor Fellner argues that dollar convertibility would not help solve any of the problems facing the monetary system, and fears that it could actually impede the functioning of a reformed system by reviving the notion that the United States could be forced by a "reserve squeeze" to deflate its domestic economy. He regards this as both impossible to achieve and undesirable if it were achieved. Hence dollar convertibility would perpetuate a delusion which would divert attention, and policy action, away from the needed increase in flexibility of exchange rates and undermine the needed improvement in the adjustment process.

It is undoubtedly true that, as Professor Fellner fears, some surplus countries will always try to avoid having to initiate adjustment by pressuring some deficit country to do so. And it is true that dollar convertibility could encourage them to include the United States in such efforts. As noted above, however, such pressure might on some occasions actually help the United States do what it should do anyway. But, more broadly, this possibility strongly reinforces the need for the United States to insist—as a condition of its resumption of convertibility—on firm guidelines which indicate when surplus countries must initiate adjustment, and vigilant implementation of those guidelines (including the use of sanctions against offenders) after they are agreed. A system operating effectively under such rules is in fact the only way to obviate the risk cited by Professor Fellner.[18]

Active or Passive Convertibility?

I have advocated that the United States resume converting dollars into U.S. reserve assets under a reformed international monetary system which satisfied U.S. national interests. A remaining question is whether such convertibility should be carried out in the passive manner of the past, or through active U.S. intervention in the exchange markets a la all other countries.

The distinction between active and passive market intervention should not be confused with the distinction between an active and passive parity policy. I have argued above that the United States should actively change its parity, against some "ultimate" *numeraire* (preferably SDR). But it could do so while remaining entirely passive in the exchange markets. The choice between the two types of intervention policy rests on additional considerations.

A passive U.S. intervention policy was entirely consistent with the dollar-based system of the past, and supported U.S. interests. United States abstention from the markets assured that the N currencies would be linked consistently through $N-1$ exchange rates without any need for active coordination. The United States let other countries set the "exchange rate of the dollar" because it preferred financing to adjustment. The dollar as intervention currency could fluctuate only one-half as much against any other currency as could two other currencies against each other,[19] so was likely to be more stable in the exchange markets (even assuming no parity changes) than any other currency and thus the most attractive currency for foreigners to hold (all other things equal). The total margins were so narrow that the United States gave up very little by accepting this limitation on its own flexibility. The system required the monetary authorities of other countries to explicitly take the onus of actively seeking conversions into U.S. reserve assets if they wanted to get rid of their dollars; which many were reluctant to do for political reasons as well as for fear of being blamed for contributing to systemic instability; all other countries, by contrast, lost reserves through the impersonal play of market intervention. The British could only suspect "the gnomes of Zurich," but the United States could explicitly finger the Bundesbank.

An active U.S. intervention policy might be more consistent, however, with a reformed system which sought effective adjustment (including adjustment initiated by the United States) instead of lots of financing (mainly through the dollar). The United States may no longer be willing to let other countries set the exchange rate of the dollar: within the widened margins which must be part of any new parity-based regime—at least the 4 ½ percent which prevailed after the Smithsonian Agreement, compared with 1 ½ percent in practice before then, and preferably much more—the United States would gain a great deal of added adjustment potential, and freedom for its internal monetary policy, if the dollar could flex as much as any other currency. The reduced U.S. zeal for dollar financing of deficits reduces the importance to the United States of forcing other countries to take active initiatives to trigger conversions, and the importance of this procedure would be eliminated completely if the United States agreed to full asset settlement of its deficits as part of the new system. From the U.S. standpoint, the potential for improved adjustment may be worth more than the reduced potential for financing. Indeed, the proposals of Secretary Shultz at the IMF meeting suggest that the present Administration has reached such a conclusion.

An active U.S. intervention policy would call for significant technical changes in the exchange rate mechanism, however. Additional currencies would have to start playing significant intervention currency roles, as the United States began intervening with them. This would in turn require new rules to avoid destabilizing shifts among holdings of them. Active coordination would now be needed, at least among the major countries, to avoid conflicting market intervention.

It is clear that such a system would be less efficient and more cumbersome than the single-currency system of the past. World trade and investment can be financed more cheaply via a single currency. The cost to multinational firms of holding liquid balances can be minimized by holding them in a single currency.[20] Indeed, it is impossible to completely eliminate the "asymmetry" through which the dollar plays a far greater international role than any other currency (even if it were desirable to do so).

However, other currencies will naturally be financing an increasing share of world transactions as the economies on which they are based become more equal to that of the United States. It appears that all parties favor an effort to move toward a multicurrency intervention system—the United States because it would get better adjustment, the others because they would get greater symmetry between their currencies and the dollar. And new modes of coordination among the key countries will have to be part of any new adjustment process anyway, either to oversee market intervention in a world of floating rates or to prompt needed parity shifts in a regime of "stable but adjustable" parities. From the United States standpoint, the best outcome would be a sufficiently firm agreement on new adjustment rules so that a continuation of the intervention currency role would not deflect any needed changes in the exchange rate of the dollar.

Conclusion

A resumption by the United States of convertibility of the dollar into U.S. reserve assets must be seen in the context of the fundamental reform of the international monetary system which is needed. Such convertibility would be redundant in a system of freely fluctuating exchange rates. In any return to a parity-based regime (perhaps implemented by "dirty floats"), the United States can prudently restore convertibility only if basic changes are made to improve the adjustment mechanism, eliminate the problem of the dollar overhang, assure adequate amounts of world reserves through the SDR mechanism, and deal effectively with liquid capital movements. Such changes, which are very much in the national interest of the United States, can be negotiated only if the United States agrees to restore convertibility as part of the package. Thus the United States should agree to do so as part of a negotiated reform package. It should continue to resist agreeing to any interim or partial convertibility in the meantime, which would reduce its bargaining leverage. The choice between the active and passive methods for implementing U.S. convertibility in the new regime depends on whether the other major countries decide that it is worthwhile to give up the economic benefits of relying on a single currency to achieve greater symmetry with the dollar.

Notes

1. The IMF has never reached a legal decision as to whether a country must maintain a fixed exchange rate to qualify as a "convertible currency" under its Article VIII. See J. Keith Horsefield, *The International Monetary Fund 1945-65*, Vol. I, p. 480. In practice, a number of countries have of course floated their exchange rates without losing "Article VIII status."

2. Within margins on either side of their parities, which were widened from ±1 percent permitted by the Article of Agreement of the IMF to ±2 ¼ percent in the Smithsonian Agreement of December 1971.

3. Excepting only the members of the sterling area and French franc zone, which followed the same process with sterling and francs instead of

dollars. In turn, the U.K. and France defended their parities in the dollar market.

4. With the institution of the two-tiered gold system in March 1968, the United States excluded from that policy any dollars acquired by foreign monetary authorities from selling their gold into the private gold markets.

5. The IMF Articles require that a member country maintain convertibility of its currency only for current account transactions. This distinction is virtually impossible to implement in practice, and has not been used by any Fund member—although almost all have availed themselves of the corollary permission to apply controls to capital transactions while generally abstaining in recent years from controls on current account transactions.

6. Numerous other distinctions can be made: nonresident vs. resident convertibility, current account vs. total convertibility, etc. The discussion in the text is limited to the distinctions which are most relevant for broad policy. For more detailed discussion see Gottfried Haberler, *Currency Convertibility* (Washington, D.C.: American Enterprise Institute, 1954).

7. This consideration has dominated the discussion of convertibility in the IMF throughout its history. See, e.g., Margaret G. de Vries and J. Keith Horsefield, *The International Monetary Fund 1945-1965*, Vol. II, pp. 75-76. Convertibility would of course fail to enhance the flow of international economic transactions if it could be achieved only by applying controls which directly limited those very transactions themselves, e.g., through misguided efforts to preserve "fixed" exchange rates.

8. It must always be remembered that the dollar was the *only* major currency which was convertible until 1958 (except for the Canadian dollar, whose exchange rate floated freely after 1950).

9. Haberler, op. cit., p. 23, made precisely the same point in 1954 when he argued that the Europeans should restore convertibility of their currencies (into other currencies, of course) only if they adopted flexible exchange rates to assure that the convertibility could be maintained.

10. Incidentally, I foresee a smaller reflow of this type than do many others because I observe a sharp rise in the use of several European currencies for private international purposes and expect it to continue, buttressed by the efforts of the Europeans to create an internal monetary union.

11. There are several proposals for how to do so. The most popular is the creation of a special issue of SDRs into which foreign monetary authorities could convert unwanted dollars. The United States would then pay interest on the dollars to the IMF, to enable it to pay interest on the new SDRs. The United States might also amortize the dollars over a long period of time, although there are strong arguments against its doing so. This

58

scheme would change the composition, but not the level, of world reserves. It is opposed by some who fear that the SDR is too new to be created in such sizable amounts at this time. This objection could be met by creating a new IMF debt instrument into which the dollars could be converted, instead of SDRs, as proposed by the Monetary Committee of the Atlantic Council, *To Modernize the International Monetary System*, September 18, 1973, pp. 22-24. A wholly different approach is for bilateral funding of the overhang through the conversion of liquid dollar reserves into nonmarketable Treasury securities, but the maturities usually mentioned are far too short to provide a real solution to the problem.

It is doubtful that all countries will agree to consolidate all of their dollars. Thus any such new arrangement must be optional, and will leave some overhang outstanding. In all probability, those dollars will have to remain inconvertible into U.S. reserves even if all foreign dollars created by new U.S. deficits are made convertible. This creates significant but solvable technical problems. (See C. Fred Bergsten, *Reforming the Dollar: An International Monetary Policy for the United States*, Council on Foreign Relations Paper on International Affairs, No. 2, September 1972, pp. 64-68.)

The private overhang could be handled along with the official overhang by making dollars now held by private foreigners eligible for similar conversion into SDRs (or new IMF instruments, or nonmarketable Treasury securities) if they moved into official reserves. If the shifts were viewed as temporary, they could properly be handled by swaps among the central banks as in the past.

12. I would prefer that any renewed convertibility of the dollar (and other currencies) be limited to deficits in the U.S. basic balance, with short-term capital flows recycled through an expanded swap network. Convertibility could also encompass all international transactions and be based on deficits in the official settlements balance, however, in which case U.S. (and everybody's) reserves would have to be much bigger; but I would regard it a mistake to focus on the official settlements balance because this would call for exchange rates to change, and/or huge reserve movements to take place, as a result of liquid and often reversible capital flows.

13. Which does not call for freely flexible exchange rates, in which convertibility of the dollar (or any other currency) into U.S. reserves assets (or the reserves of any other country) would be redundant. My specific proposals for each aspect of reform can be found in my *Reforming the Dollar: An International Monetary Policy for the United States*, pp. 48-88.

14. A significant part of the AFL-CIO pressure for the Burke-Hartke bill can be traced directly to the job losses resulting from the increasing overvaluation of the dollar in the late 1960s.

15. Some observers have referred to the "system" which has existed since the U.S. suspension of convertibility as a "pure dollar standard." This is wrong, however, because of the rapid growth in the international use of several other national currencies (primarily the DM but also the Swiss franc, guilder, and yen) as both reserve assets and private transactions currencies. The present "system" thus looks increasingly like a "multiple reserve currency standard," probably the least stable alternative which has been seriously studied.

16. There are three possible ways the United States could seek a dollar standard: by *force majeure*, as at present; by offering gold-value guarantees on all foreign dollar reserves, which would mollify those countries (probably a majority) which cared only about the valuation of their reserves but not those (a small but powerful minority) which also cared about the U.S. policies which produced U.S. deficits; or by undertaking policies which would make the dollar the most attractive asset in the exchange markets, which however could levy enormous costs on the U.S. economy. Only the first is mentioned in the text, because it now appears by far the most likely candidate of the three.

17. As noted in footnote 16, however, guarantees would meet only the asset-valuation concern of foreign dollar holders; they would not meet foreign concern over U.S. policies. See William Fellner, "The Dollar's Place in the International System: Suggested Criteria for the Appraisal of Emerging Views," *Journal of Economic Literature* 10, 3 (September 1972); 735-56. He does not indicate explicitly whether his analysis relates to convertibility on the official settlements or basic (or some other) balance, but his context makes it clear that he assumes the former.

18. Professor Fellner makes several other interesting points in his article. He argues that there is no need for the United States to initiate exchange rate changes, because "equiproportionate disequilibrium of the other countries relative to the United States—with balance among them—would be very rare"; hence it would usually make more sense for other countries to initiate parity realignments. I have argued elsewhere (op. cit., p. 40), to the contrary, that both U.S. adjustment interests, and systemic interests in a better adjustment process, would be served by the United States becoming a *frequent* initiator of parity changes. This is because such changes are far easier to implement here than in other countries, given their far smaller impact on the domestic economy, and because (for the reasons stated in the text, p. 50) they are by far the most efficient way for us to achieve adjustment of our balance of payments. Professor Fellner may be right about the rarity of equiproportionate U.S. disequilibria, but they have occurred twice in the recent past and the same phenomenon holds true (if to a lesser extent) for all countries. It is true that

an active U.S. parity policy would force other countries to make adjustments among themselves, as indeed happened in the fall of 1971, but a passive U.S. parity policy would risk continued inaction by everybody even under a new set of rules and intentions.

Professor Fellner also notes the problem of deciding whether shifts of foreign-held dollars from private into official hands are temporary or permanent, and hence whether they should be recycled, on the one hand, or should trigger asset settlement and/or adjustment on the other. This is a real problem only if the new system is based on the official settlements balance, however, and adds to my case for focusing instead on the basic balance.

19. Each nonintervention currency was allowed to fluctuate by one percent on either side of its intervention currency. Thus two nonintervention currencies, each fluctuating by one percent against the dollar *in opposite directions*, could fluctuate by two percent against each other. The dollar could never be farther than one percent from any other currency.

20. Henry Wallich, "The Monetary Crisis of 1971—the Lessons to be Learned," the Per Jacobsson Lecture of 1972, p. 14.

6

International Monetary Reform: A Viewpoint from the United States

The world stands today on a pure dollar standard. The dollar is the dominant currency in private financial transactions throughout the world. It is thus the currency in which national monetary authorities must carry out the bulk of their intervention in the exchange markets. Yet the United States will not convert dollars into U.S. reserve assets, does not intervene in the markets to maintain the new dollar parity, and will not offer exchange-rate guarantees through the swap network or Roosa bonds as in the past.

Thus other countries have only the choice between holding any dollars which may accrue to them, or taking action themselves to eliminate such dollar holdings through appreciation of their own currencies or erection of controls against capital inflows. The elimination of the overvaluation of the dollar, brought about by the exchange rate realignment agreed to on 18 December 1971, eliminated one major threat to the economic viability of this pure dollar standard. Success of the current U.S. effort to bring its internal inflation under control, relative to inflation in the other major countries, would eliminate the other major threat. Indeed, the world role of the dollar had been continuing to expand rapidly anyway—despite the relative decline in U.S. world power, mismanagement of the U.S. domestic economy in the last half of the 1960s, the persistence of sizable deficits in the U.S. balance of payments and growing overvaluation of the dollar, the creation of an alternative reserve asset in Special Drawing Rights, and despite even the suspension of gold convertibility and devaluation. It is little wonder, then, that the dollar standard option should now look quite viable.

Superficially, this situation appears quite attractive from the standpoint of the United States. There is no external constraint on U.S. domestic economic policy. There is no pressure to tighten the present controls over capital outflows and government expenditures abroad in order to protect U.S. reserves; they could even be lifted with impunity. Indeed, the United States can now avoid the political risks of taking *any* adjustment initiatives, acting only when—as on 15 August 1971—there is domestic political *gain* in doing so. It is quite likely that preservation of this new status quo will

Paper originally prepared for a conference on Europe and the Evolution of the International Monetary System held in Geneva in January 1972, and published in Alexander K. Swoboda, ed., *Europe and the Evolution of the International Monetary System* (Leiden: A W. Sitjhoff, 1973), pp. 35-47.

61

become increasingly appealing in the United States as its implications become more widely understood.

Nevertheless, it would be a disastrous error for the United States to seek to keep the world on a pure dollar standard. Such dollar hegemony is politically, and therefore economically, impossible for the longer run without over-all U.S. political and economic hegemony—which no longer exists, and will not be achieved again in the future. Other major countries would simply not accept U.S. financial domination in a world where they have already demonstrated both their ability and their desire to be full partners in endeavors ranging from negotiations with the Soviet Union through management of collective defense to determination of the amount of annual additions to world reserves. Europe, at least, would seek an alternative to the dollar and monetary duopoly could develop in the most destructive possible manner. Even if Europe *failed* to find a viable alternative for a while, the resulting acrimony would plague and indeed jeopardize economic, and eventually political, relations across the Atlantic.

But neither should the United States be willing to shoulder the responsibilities incumbent on a single key currency country, and to accept the resultant sacrifices of its own national sovereignty, without the requisite power and the "cooperation" of other countries which comes only with political domination. The great lesson for the United States and the dollar from the similar historical experience of the United Kingdom and sterling is to foresee in time the need to reduce gradually the world financial role of its key *currency* to maintain an equilibrium with its over-all world position as a key *country*. Such foresight is difficult, since tradition dies hardest in matters monetary and simple inertia prolongs the international status of a currency far beyond the dictates of the objective situation.

Better Adjustment

However, major changes will be needed in the monetary system to induce the United States to give up the benefits of the currently prevailing pure dollar standard and to resume dollar convertibility and its other international monetary obligations. Even greater changes will be needed if the United States is to agree to finance future deficits, in at least its basic balance of payments, with reserve assets as other countries are generally obliged to do. The most important change is the institution of an effective adjustment mechanism. Heretofore, from the standpoint of the United States, the adjustment system has been fatally marred by two paradoxes.

First, the United States has the least open economy to international transactions in the non-Communist world. It is thus the country in which exchange-rate changes have the greatest comparative advantage among alternative adjustment techniques. From the standpoint of maximum economic efficiency and political feasibility, the United States should perhaps even adjust its exchange rate *more* frequently than the other major countries. Yet, in large part because of the international roles of the dollar, the United States is the one country which has been unable to unilaterally change its own exchange rate at all.

Second, the United States has run persistent balance-of-payments deficits and has been continually exhorted "to put its house in order"; yet, the exchange-rate changes initiated by other countries prior to 1971 produced a steady *upvaluation* of the dollar. This is because the monetary system generally has placed great pressure on deficit countries to adjust, but little pressure on surplus countries to do so, and because it has discouraged small parity changes in favor of large changes to occur only when "fundamental disequilibrium" has clearly developed. The result has been a quadruple bias against the dollar: currencies frequently succumb to the pressure to devalue, but infrequently to the pressure to revalue; devaluations tend to be larger than necessary, to prevent speculation; against further devaluations of the same currency; any single devaluation tends to induce additional devaluations by other countries, because they both fear for their competitive positions and find it politically easier to devalue in company with others; and revaluations tend to be smaller than necessary, since countries are even less fearful of pressures for additional revaluations than they are susceptible to pressures to move upward in the first place.[1]

Thus the United States has been unable to initiate effective adjustment itself, and its adjustment needs have often, and on balance, been affected perversely by the initiatives of other countries. The new adjustment mechanism will have to effectively resolve both problems to be acceptable to the United States.

It can hope to do so only by incorporating an internationally agreed set of criteria indicating when exchange rate changes are needed, which all countries—including the United States—will have both the right and responsibility to honor under penalty of sanctions applied by the international community as a whole against flagrant violations. The basic rule should be that exchange rates change to resolve "dilemma" cases: revaluation when a country runs a payments surplus with its domestic economy near full employment, devaluation when payments deficits coincide with high unemployment. Domestic macroeconomic policy, of course, continues to be the proper remedy for "non-dilemma" cases: internal expansion in response to domestic unemployment coupled with payments surpluses, internal disinflation in response to excessive domestic inflation coupled with payments deficits.

In any given situation it may be difficult to distinguish between "dilemma" and "non-dilemma" cases. This is particularly true when domestic economies suffer from the purely internal dilemma of high unemployment and rapid inflation, as several now do. A schematic set of guidelines to deal with these more complex cases, which distinguishes between the proper responses of relatively open and relatively closed economies, can be found in Table 6-1.

The difficulty of implementing such guidelines, even if they were agreed upon, should not be underestimated. Indeed, countries would be able to challenge the international assessment of their situation, or could try to convince others that actions already taken are adequate. Nevertheless, any meaningful guidelines would point clearly to the major problem cases which could disrupt the system (and the internal economy of the country in question) if left unattended, for instance the extreme undervaluation of the Japanese yen for an extended period prior to August 1971. Such guidelines, implemented through strong IMF leadership and backed by the threat of action by the entire international community, could have promoted adequate yen revaluations in plenty of time to help forestall the need for actions such as those taken by the United States on August 15.

Some will view this proposal as utopian, with its apparently dramatic transfer of sovereignty from national authorities to the international community. To this charge, there are three simple answers. First, it is the only way to achieve an effective adjustment process—without which the world economy will continue to suffer repeated crises with an ever-growing risk of serious breakdown. Second, the system is already evolving quite rapidly in this direction. The amount of the British devaluation of 1967 was, to a large extent, an internationally negotiated figure; the amounts of the German revaluation and French devaluation of 1969 had been largely negotiated at the Bonn conference in late 1968; and the U.S. devaluation of 1971 was of course completely negotiated. The present proposal simply seeks to substitute timely negotiations based on internationally agreed criteria for these crisis-forced negotiations which involve a host of *ad hoc* judgments. Third, it has happened before. Robert Triffin's proposals for creating an international money were labelled utopian in the late 1950s for the same reasons, yet Special Drawing Rights were negotiated less than a decade later. Changes in similarly dramatic scope, again transferring apparent sovereignty from national to international hands, are needed in the adjustment arena now just as they were needed and then implemented in the liquidity arena in the past.

Elimination of the Problems of the Overhang

Even with such new rules, however, effective adjustment in the future could be frustrated by a major legacy of the past—the dollar overhang.

Table 6-1
Guidelines for Economic Adjustment[a]

Economic situation	Open or closed economy	Demand policy	Selective policy	Exchange rate
(1) Full employment, rapid inflation, payments deficit (classic "non-dilemma" case)	Both	Restraint	(Manpower policy)	—
(2) Full employment, stable prices, payments deficit	Open	Restraint	Manpower policy	
	Closed	—	(Incomes policy)	Devaluation
(3) Full employment, rapid inflation, payments surplus (classic "dilemma" case)	Both	—	(Manpower policy)	Revaluation
(4) Full employment, stable prices, payments surplus	Open	Expansion	Manpower policy	Revaluation
	Closed	—	Manpower policy	Revaluation
(5) Unemployment, rapid inflation, payments deficit	Open	—	Incomes policy	Devaluation
	Closed	Expansion	Incomes policy	Devaluation
(6) Unemployment, stable prices, payments deficits (classic "dilemma" case)	Both	—	(Incomes policy)	Devaluation
(7) Unemployment, rapid inflation, payments surplus	Open	Expansion	Incomes policy	—
	Closed	—	(Manpower policy)	Revaluation
(8) Unemployment, stable prices, payments surplus (classic "non-dilemma" case)	—	Expansion	(Incomes policy)	—

[a]Parentheses around a particular policy mean that the need for it is uncertain, and would depend on the circumstances of the particular country at the particular time.

Conversions of outstanding dollar reserves into U.S. reserve assets, or even dollar shifts among foreign monetary authorities, could distort current payments patterns. Thus they could trigger undesirable exchange-rate changes, or prevent desirable changes, or both. Shifts of dollars between private and official hands could have the same effects. In the process, the overhang would continue to foster well-known confidence problems and jeopardize the aggregate level of world liquidity by posing an omnipresent threat to the existing level of U.S. reserves.

In addition, the United States should be able to add to its gross reserves when it runs surpluses in its basic balance of payments in the future. If the United States is to finance future *deficits* in its basic balance with reserve assets, which it should agree to do upon implementation of reforms along the lines proposed here, it will need larger reserves. Indeed, the U.S. ratio of reserves to imports is now below that of seven other members of the Group of Ten, and of most other industrialized countries. (See Table 6-2 for details.) Without disposition of the overhang, however, the United States could easily find itself financing its deficits by selling reserve assets and financing its surpluses by a rundown of foreign dollar holdings. Such a situation could obviously not persist for very long, even if the United States were in basic balance—or even surplus—over time. Indeed, a ten-year average of zero basic balance for the United States comprised of five years of $4 billion surpluses and five years of $4 billion deficits, financed in such a way, would virtually wipe out U.S. reserves even if SDRs were created at an annual rate of $4 billion throughout this period and allocated on the present basis of IMF quotas.

Elimination of the problems of the dollar overhang thus constitutes a second prerequisite to monetary reform from a U.S. standpoint. This can be done in at least three different ways: elimination of the entire overhang via mandatory conversion by all countries of all of their reserve (as opposed to working balance) dollars into SDRs (or a new international account); mandatory conversion for the Group of Ten countries, with no provisions for reserve dollars held by others; or voluntary conversion for all countries combined with a clear understanding that any dollars retained in national reserves were forever inconvertible into U.S. assets.

The first approach is by far the neatest and most elegant. Nevertheless, it would require forcing all countries to convert all of their reserve dollars, which might be unacceptable to many of them and hence jeopardize passage of the necessary amendments to the Articles of Agreement of the International Monetary Fund.

The second would presumably be easier to negotiate since it disregards dollar reserves held by countries outside the Group of Ten. This would, however, leave at least $10 to 15 billion outstanding, preserving that much of the dangers cited above. It might also leave unresolved the disposition of

Table 6-2
Reserve Adequacy of Group of Ten Countries

Country	Reserves (in millions of dollars)	Months of imports covered
(1) Switzerland	6,549	12.0
(2) Japan	14,100	8.7
(3) Germany	16,957	6.4
(4) Italy	6,666	5.1
(5) France	7,310	4.4
(6) Canada	5,072	4.0
(7) Belgium	3,424	3.4
(8) United States	12,130	3.2
(9) Netherlands	3,609	2.8
(10) United Kingdom	5,013	2.6
(11) Sweden	998	1.7

Data are for 30 September 1971 except for Japan and Canada, where they are for 31 October 1971.

the dollars that later moved to the Group of Ten countries. Politically, it would create two sharply different classes of dollar holders by making a new option available only to some of the rich.

However, both national choice over reserve portfolio composition and equivalent treatment of all countries can be maintained, while eliminating the monetary problems of the overhang, through a two-part "optional consolidation". First, a special issue of SDRs could be authorized for conversion of all reserve assets (including sterling and gold, as well as dollars) outstanding at the time of the agreement. Following the lead of the Basel arrangements for sterling, the authorization should cover dollars and sterling held privately at that time as well; they could otherwise move into official reserves and cause the problems outlined above, so they too should be eligible for consolidation into the special issue of SDRs if they move into official reserves and the authorities do not wish to hold onto them.

Second, countries could elect to retain some or all of their dollars or other assets, but these could be used in the future only to finance payments deficits—*à la* the SDR "needs test"—and would no longer be convertible into other assets via the key currency countries. (Countries would presumably keep working balances in dollars, which by definition would be used only to finance their payments deficits.) The United States would no longer automatically convert "old" dollars into gold, or gold into dollars. The option to convert into the special issue of SDRs could be exercised by a particular country either at once or in the future. It could be exercised by the country holding a particular asset at the time of the agreement, or by a country acquiring it later through the settlement of payments imbalances.

The restrictions on the use of the dollars prior to conversion into the special issue of SDRs would render them harmless to the system and to the United States; delayed conversion would thus be feasible. Whether the reserve dollars were retained or converted into the special issue of SDRs, they would be removed as a problem for the United States and for the monetary system as a whole.

The major drawback of this approach is its technical complexity, particularly since it would probably be linked with optional arrangements for "new" dollars acquired from future U.S. basic deficits. ("New" dollars could either be converted into U.S. reserve assets immediately, or retained in inconvertible form by countries which preferred to do so. They could, however, still be converted into U.S. assets if they subsequently shifted to countries which did not wish to hold them and so would not necessarily provide lasting financing for U.S. deficits.) The technical problems are nevertheless manageable and are simply part of the much closer international cooperation which must exist at all levels, from statistics to high policy, in the future. This is the only approach which deals comprehensively with the problems of the overhang while permitting countries to maintain sovereign control over the composition of their reserve assets.

Two specific aspects of any consolidation scheme are of particular importance to the United States: the disposition of the dollars converted into the special issue of SDRs and the interest-rate provisions. The dollars could be retained by the IMF and redeemed by the United States with its reserve assets, wither on a fixed schedule or whenever it ran payments surpluses; retained indefinitely by the IMF as interest-bearing "consols"; or returned to the United States and eliminated altogether. In considering these issues, it must be remembered that the United States will undertake an obligation to guarantee the gold value of all SDRs created to consolidate outstanding dollars, in marked contrast to the present situation where very few dollar reserves even carry exchange-rate guarantees.

U.S. amortization of the overhang could have a severe deflationary effect on the world economy. It has already been noted that the United States will need to build its reserves. Any dollar repayment obligation would thus add to the magnitude of the payments surpluses targeted by the United States. Reconciliation of the essentially mercantilistic trade and payments objectives of most other nations has been very difficult in the past, with the United States playing an essentially passive and accommodating role; it will become extremely difficult even with the United States aiming for small surpluses to build its reserves; and it could become unmanageable if the United States aimed at sufficiently high surpluses to achieve the desired reserve growth *plus* pay off debt. It is quite possible that $30 billion will be consolidated, so that even a 50-year amortization schedule would add $600 million to the annual U.S. payments target. (The

British surplus target might also have to rise by $100 million to pay off the $5 billion of sterling which could come in.)

In addition, there is no one to redeem any gold converted into the special issue of SDRs, so an amortization requirement for reserve currencies would require different treatment of the different assets now outstanding. It would also create "backing" for these SDRs (as would even IMF holding of U.S. "consols"), and hence raise questions and technical problems concerning the absences of "backing" for the regular SDRs.

Most important, the other countries will by definition be getting an asset which they prefer to the "old" dollars. There is thus no reason from their standpoint, or from the standpoint of the system, why the United States should amortize. The only argument for amortization is that the United States should not "get away with" the past appropriation of real resources from the rest of the world accomplished through its payments deficits. The answer to this is that many of these dollar holdings were the result of foreign demand (for reserves and exports) rather than of U.S. supply, so others *wanted* the United States to take some of those resources; that many of the dollars which *were* supply-generated resulted from expenditures in the global interest, ranging from the Marshall Plan through NATO; and, most importantly, that the United States will assure against the re-creation of a new overhang by agreeing to finance its basic deficits in the future entirely with reserve assets.

The United States would thus strongly prefer the third approach—total retirement of the consolidated dollars—and has good grounds for doing so in terms of the interests of the system as well as of its more narrow national interests. Indeed, the United States might prefer to remain inconvertible, or to take its chances with the overhang at the risk of going inconvertible again, rather than to accept arrangements even as superficially generous as the 50-year repayment schedule mentioned above in addition to the gold-value guarantee attached to the specially created SDRs.

On the interest-rate issue, there are five basic approaches. The first is to treat the new SDRs as "initial allocations", on which no interest is paid. The second is for the United States to pay the IMF amounts sufficient only for it to pay interest to the holders of the new SDRs at the current SDR interest rate of 1 ½ per cent, or some new (presumably higher) rate which would apply to all SDRs. The third is for the United States to pay the IMF amounts equal to the "normal" U.S. debt service burden on the consolidated dollars—this "normal" rate being equal to current U.S. market rates on the debt instruments which were originally consolidated, or to some "average" current U.S. interest rate, or to some average U.S. debt service level in the past, or simply to some negotiated rate agreeable to all—with this rate passed on to the holders of the special SDRs, and with lower rates continuing to apply to regular SDRs. The fourth is for the United States to continue its "normal" payments, with the present (or some other lower) rate prevailing for all SDRs, the difference being used to amortize the dollar "principal". The fifth is for some new use to be found for this difference.

All of these approaches are consistent with returning the consolidated dollars to the United States, as just proposed. The special issue of SDRs would be treated as a "net use" of SDRs by the United States and a "net acquisition" by other countries, with interest paid through book transfers as under the present SDR scheme. The Fund need not actually hold any dollar instruments.

Avoiding interest payments altogether on the new SDRs would of course maximize the financial savings to the United States, and be extremely attractive to it. However, there would be technical problems in treating these SDRs as "initial allocations" rather than as "net use" by the United States, and attempting to do so would intensify the opposition on moral grounds to the entire consolidation scheme.

The alternative of increasing the interest rate on all SDRs to equate it fully or at least more nearly with the interest rate on dollars has serious disadvantages. Countries will gain a gold-value guarantee by converting their dollars into SDRs and can hardly expect to receive an equally high interest rate as well. In addition, higher interest rates on "net acquisitions" of SDRs would make payments surpluses even more attractive than they are now, and payments deficits even costlier; it would hence exacerbate the adjustment bias of the system against deficit countries, whereas a key objective of the needed adjustment reforms is to eliminate or at least reduce this bias. It is doubtful that such a proposal could even receive serious consideration in the IMF since enough countries probably anticipate deficit positions over time to block the amendment to the Articles of Agreement which would be necessary.

The alternative of paying a higher interest rate on the special issue of SDRs than on regular SDRs is also undesirable. It would actually require creation of a totally different asset, to avoid insuperable technical problems when the SDRs shift hands, and thus undermine rather than enhance the movement toward reliance on a single international asset for world liquidity.

The two viable choices are thus (a) U.S. payments to the Fund equal to the interest rate paid to SDR holders, at or near the present 1 ½ per cent, or (b) higher U.S. payments based on some notion of a "fair" burden for the United States, with a decision as to how to use the difference. For reasons already outlined, there is no utility in using the difference to "redeem" the U.S. debt. The most promising method for using it, and the most likely to develop strong political support, is to seize this opportunity to forge a link between the SDR system and development finance. The difference could be granted to the World Bank to augment the lending capabilities of its International Development Association. Consolidation of $30 billion, with

SDR rates remaining at 1 ½ per cent and U.S. interest obligations set at 4 ½ per cent, would generate $900 million annually for development. The "burden" of this aid would be shared by the previous holders of the dollars—who would give up their interest earnings in return for the gold-value guarantee and systemic effects of the SDRs—and the United States—which would actually be paying the interest and might otherwise have seen its interest burden reduced. Some of the lower income countries may have to be bribed to go along with an overall reform program such as is outlined here and this interest provision seems the best way to do so consistently with the basic monetary needs of the industrialized world.

Enough Reserve Growth

The third U.S. requirement for monetary reform is assured expansion of international liquidity at a pace sufficient to enable countries to achieve their own reserve-growth targets without taking reserves away from each other, and without relying on the dollar. Anything less would undermine two of the basic objectives of these over-all reforms: the elimination of the present asymmetrical pressure on deficit countries to take most of the adjustment initiatives and a reduction of the role of the dollar in the system.

In addition, such aggregate liquidity growth through non-dollar means is the only way for the United States to achieve its new objective of reserve increases. The United States would want liquidity growth to be even larger if it had to amortize the consolidated dollars—instead of their being retired, as proposed above—in order to avoid major new pressures on the world economy.

A number of studies, in addition to the actual decision on the first allocation of Special Drawing Rights, indicate that world reserves should rise by at least 5-6 per cent annually. At current rates of world inflation, this amounts to real growth of only 1-3 per cent, and suggests that even higher nominal growth may be necessary.

Such growth should be achieved wholly through creation of SDRs. The SDR creation will have to be larger than the desired increase in reserves, however, since 30 per cent of each country's SDR holdings must now be "reconstituted" within five years and hence represents medium-term credit rather than "owned reserves". (It would be preferable to abolish reconstitution altogether and to introduce several other changes in the SDR rules to improve the "moneyness" of the asset and further reduce the distinctions between it and other reserve assets.) New rules will also be needed to assure that increases in other reserve assets—mainly dollars but also gold, and sterling and other national currencies—do not throw total reserve growth off course as in 1970-1971.

The last reform concerns the need for new mechanisms to deal with the huge movements of liquid capital which will continue to pervade the system, despite their being dampened by the widening of exchange-rate margins. The United States has a particular interest in this aspect of reform because the vehicle currency role of the dollar assures that such movements will lead to dollar accruals to foreign monetary authorities whenever the flows are away from the United States. (The United States could not possibly be expected to finance such movements from its reserves, and the previous discussion of U.S. asset financing has therefore been confined to U.S. *basic* deficits.)

The liquid flows could be checked directly, but effective controls would have to cover a wide range of international transactions comprehensively and thus bear significant economic costs. The best remedy is to sharply expand the swap network to offset the effects of these flows on national reserves. The network should be greatly enlarged, perhaps to $50 billion from the present $11 billion for a starter, to credibly cover any possible level of flows. Maturities of swaps should be longer, perhaps 18-24 months relative to the present standard of 3-6 months, since it often takes that long to eliminate the interest-rate differentials which trigger the flows. And the swaps should carry full exchange-rate guarantees instead of the partial guarantees which exist at present.

Conclusion

With these four fundamental improvements in the monetary system, the United States should be willing to resume full convertibility of the dollar into U.S. reserve assets and all of its other international monetary obligations. It should also be willing to see the dollar continue to serve as a transaction and intervention currency for all who wish to use it—and even as a reserve asset for those who want it under the restricted conditions outlined. Most important, the United States should be willing to commit itself to finance all future deficits in its basic balance of payments with reserve assets. Without such reforms, the United States will be sorely tempted to try to preserve the pure dollar standard which has existed since 15 August 1971.

Fortunately, the same reforms are in the interest of other countries as well. At a minimum, they would bring the United States and the dollar back into the system. Beyond this, however, all countries would gain from improving the adjustment process, eliminating the problems of the dollar overhang, and assuring adequate international liquidity. It is hard to see how such goals could be accomplished except through greater flexibility of exchange rates and creation of enough Special Drawing Rights. Both of these steps would, moreover, accelerate the progress toward cooperative international management of the monetary system to replace the dollar hegemony and/or disorganized multipolar scrambles for power of the recent past. The bases for rapid progress toward reform thus appear to be present in the national interests of all countries, and the great need is to get on with it.

Note

1. For a more complete analysis, see the author's "The United States and Greater Flexibility of Exchange Rates" in *Approaches to Greater Flexibility of Exchange Rates: The Burgenstock Papers,* arranged by C. Fred Bergsten, George N. Halm, Fritz Machlup, and Robert V. Roosa and edited by George N. Halm, Princeton, N.J., Princeton University Press, 1970; especially pp. 68-70 [chapter 7 in this volume, pp. 82-83].

7

The United States and Greater Flexibility of Exchange Rates

The United States is by far the most important single country in the international monetary system, and the dollar is the key currency of the system. It is difficult to imagine any significant change in the system that is unacceptable to the United States. Any proposals for change, such as those for increasing the flexibility of exchange rates, must, thus, be tested for their effect on the United States alone, as well as for their broader effects on the system as a whole.

This paper will attempt to assess those effects. It will avoid repeating the general analyses of greater flexibility of exchange rates, except where necessary to clarify a particular point regarding the United States and the role of the dollar. It will refer throughout to "greater flexibility of exchange rates" without citing specific schemes, lumping together the crawling peg and the wider band except where explicitly differentiating between them.

Two major considerations are often cited as militating against any possible interest in greater flexibility on the part of the United States.

The first relates to adjustment and runs as follows. Removal of the present presumption against exchange-rate changes would generate greater movements of exchange rates. This would produce more depreciation than appreciation because of the greater pressures on deficit than on surplus countries, because of the general reluctance of countries to lose reserves or risk deterioration of their competitive positions, and because it would lead to a relaxation of the "discipline" of fixed rates. These exchange-rate movements would take place against the dollar, because of its role as the pivot currency of the system. The dollar would, thus, become increasingly overvalued and the competitive position of the United States would steadily deteriorate.

The second relates to confidence and liquidity. The dollar is now widely held as a reserve currency and an intervention currency by foreigners. One important reason for its attractiveness is the widespread perception of the stability of its price in terms of other currencies. (Its price stability in terms of gold is also important for some monetary authorities.) Increasing flexibil-

The research underlying this paper was carried out during 1967-68 while the author was a Visiting Fellow at the Council on Foreign Relations, for whose support he expresses deep gratitude. The views expressed herein are wholly personal and in no way represent the official views of the Government of the United States. The paper was originally published in George N. Halm, ed., *Approaches to Greater Flexibility of Exchange Rates: The Bürgenstock Papers* (Princeton, N.J.: Princeton University Press, 1970), pp. 61-75.

ity of exchange rates would destroy this stability and, hence, jeopardize both future increases in foreign dollar holdings and the huge volume of outstanding dollar assets. Introduction of such flexibility could, thus, preempt an important source of financing for any future balance of payments deficits of the United States and generate immediate demands for conversion of outstanding dollars into American reserve assets, neither of which would appeal to the United States.

There are several immediate answers to these propositions. In terms of stability alone, the dollar—as the pivot currency—would be able to fluctuate only half as much vis-a-vis any single currency as would any other currency. It would remain as stable as gold and SDRs because both would retain a fixed relationship to the dollar under the probable techniques for implementing greater flexibility described below. And "discipline" would probably decline more in other countries than in the United States, in view of the relatively small effect of the American international financial position on its overall economy, so that the depreciation of other currencies might simply offset their increased rates of inflation and leave the dollar, even more clearly than today, as the leading candidate for stability over the long run.

More importantly, the two considerations cited contradict each other. If American adjustment is prejudiced by depreciations against the dollar greater than would be called for by relative price changes, the resulting appreciation of the dollar with regard to a weighted average of all other foreign currencies could only result from foreign willingness, or even desire, to increase their dollar holdings. In turn, this appreciation—or even a widespread perception that such appreciation was likely—would increase the attractiveness of the dollar as a financial asset. It would, thus, enhance the likelihood that dollar accruals by foreign nations would provide financing for any American payments deficits prompted by the appreciation of the dollar.

Conversely, any actual or expected net depreciation of the dollar beyond what would be called for by relative price changes—which might stem from foreign distaste for dollars and, in turn, discourage foreign holdings—would, of course, contribute to an improved competitive position for the United States and, hence, would probably lead to an improvement in its balance of payments. The United States would, thus, need less balance-of-payments financing and, particularly if pushed into surplus, could readily liquidate outstanding dollar holdings.

The United States would, thus, benefit from either the adjustment or the confidence-liquidity effects of greater exchange-rate flexibility. The more it would benefit from one, however, the less it would benefit from the other. And the United States would certainly prefer greater adjustment to further financing, in view of their relative effects on the long-term stability of the system. One basic issue throughout this paper will be the net effect on the United States of the trade-off between the two.

The Interests of the United States

The United States has interests both broad and narrow in the international monetary system.

Because of its broad objectives in economic and foreign policy, the United States has a major stake in the maintenance of an effective monetary system. This means a system that minimizes the impediments to international transactions. More specifically, it means a system in which countries are assured of sufficient liquidity to finance imbalances of payments while adjusting any underlying imbalances through policies consistent with their other legitimate national objectives.

Effective adjustment must, of course, be predicated on effective domestic economic policies. However, these policies may not be implemented soon enough to restore equilibrium by themselves. And adjustment must also be possible in those "dilemma" cases where policies required to regain external equilibrium run counter to those needed to meet domestic objectives. Selective controls over international transactions, which have been used increasingly in recent years, are almost always ineffective in restoring equilibrium and—after their inevitable proliferation—must give way eventually to other measures in any event. In addition, they can cause serious problems for economic and foreign policy and will do so increasingly if reliance upon them continues to grow. The broadest interest of the United States in the monetary system would, thus, be served by an improvement in the use of exchange rates to help accomplish effective adjustment.

The narrow interest of the United States is difficult to distinguish from this broader interest. Improvement in the system as a whole means less risk to foreign holders of dollars and to those who rely heavily on the Eurodollar market to meet ongoing business needs, as well as to the United States. This has been dramatically demonstrated since March 1968 by the effect of the two-tier gold system, adopted essentially for reasons of system-wide confidence, in reducing the potential threats to the dollar.

In addition, it is as much for international as for national reasons that the United States must be able to adjust any disequilibrium in its own payments position both gradually and by means consistent with its domestic objectives. Elimination of an American deficit through rapid domestic deflation would generate repercussions of recession throughout the world, as well as create unacceptable social, economic, and political problems at home. Elimination of an American surplus through rapid domestic inflation could set off a global wave of price rises. And the United States can use the policy-mix approach only to a limited extent, because it would trigger a sharp escalation of interest rates throughout the world, and because increased interest rates in the United States worsen the American balance of payments, by sharply increasing payments by the United States to foreign holders of dollars, as well as help it by attracting capital inflows (if rate increases in the United States are not fully offset by increases in foreign interest rates).

Most uses of restrictions by the United States are likely to be ineffective in achieving adjustment, simply postponing the need for more definitive action and, therefore, increasing the magnitude of the steps needed later. An improvement in the exchange-rate mechanism might, thus, help adjust any disequilibrium between the United States and the rest of the world if it provided for an earlier and, hence, more gradual attack on the problem. Such an improvement could bring broader benefits as well, since restrictive action by the United States for payment reasons encourages additional controls and protectionist sentiment in the United States and elsewhere in the world.

The Options for Greater Flexibility

These general conclusions must be tested against the specific manner in which limited flexibility would operate in practice. Theoretically, there are six possibilities.

(1) The dollar could remain convertible into gold at $35 per ounce with all other currencies free to fluctuate more freely in terms of the dollar. This makes eminent economic sense, since only $N-1$ currencies can possibly fluctuate consistently in a world of N currencies (or currency areas). It would represent the smallest change from the present system, in which discrete parity changes and the limited flexibility that exists within the present margins take place in terms of the dollar, and would, thus, be the most likely to win widespread acceptance. The following analysis will focus on this option.

(2) All other currencies could be free to fluctuate more freely in terms of the dollar with the United States no longer converting dollars into gold on demand at $35 per ounce. This would mean adoption by the United States of "current account convertibility" as defined in the Articles of Agreement of the International Monetary Fund.[1] The United States would then intervene in the exchange markets, if necessary, with foreign exchange obtained through sales of its reserve assets or borrowings. This approach would appear as more of a change from the present system than would Option 1, although in practice it would not be very different. It would, however,

probably introduce the additional complication of requiring negotiation of a Reserve Settlement Account, into which monetary authorities could deposit their dollars and perhaps other reserve assets in exchange for SDRs or some other international asset, to cushion the political implications of the abandonment of gold convertibility.

(3) A currency other than the dollar could become the pivot of the system, with all other currencies, including the dollar, free to fluctuate more freely with respect to it. This is not a practical option at present because no other currency is a plausible candidate for the center role. On a more limited scale, however, one or several currencies might become key currencies for a certain geographical region and, thus, move toward sharing the dollar's international roles.

(4) All currencies, including the dollar, could be free to fluctuate more freely in terms of gold with market intervention carried out in gold. (Gold could also become simply the numeraire of the system with intervention continuing in dollars and the two-tier system continued. In practice, however, this is virtually the same as Option 2.) This would require reintegration of the official and private markets for gold through abandonment of the two-tier system, including legalization of private gold holdings in the United States and elsewhere. It would greatly enhance the role of gold and reverse the highly desirable evolutionary trend away from reliance on gold for monetary purposes.

Implementation of this approach would almost certainly require a massive initial increase in the price of gold, to enable present holders of dollars to acquire enough gold to use for intervention purposes without completely draining the reserves of the United States and other large holders. In addition, such a return to reliance on gold—buttressed by the relative stability that gold might then be perceived to enjoy relative to the dollar —would increase the desire of monetary authorities to hold their reserves predominantly in that form, and would make them unwilling to accept reductions in their holdings to make intervention balances available to others.

Such an increase in the price of gold is overwhelmingly objectionable on both economic and political grounds. In addition, under this option the value of world reserves would be subject to sizable fluctuation, as the price of gold and of any national currencies held in reserves fluctuated relative to each other, thus injecting a new element of instability into the system. This approach will not be considered further.

(5) All currencies, including the dollar, could be free to fluctuate more freely in terms of Special Drawing Rights with market intervention in SDRs. (Like gold, SDRs could become the numeraire with intervention continuing in dollars. This too would mainly change the cosmetics of the system.) This approach is only a theoretical possibility at present, since

SDRs can be held only by monetary authorities. Any extension of its use to include the private sector would have to avoid replicating the problems caused by the dual character of gold prior to March 1968. It will not be considered further in this paper.

(6) The concept of market intervention could be abandoned altogether, replaced by frequent clearing of balances among central banks. This would be akin to the mechanism that actually operated among the members of the European Payments Union. Under it, central banks could accumulate all other currencies with an assurance that any net balances would be converted periodically. Thus, there could be no need for an intervention currency. Applied on a global scale, this approach would be extremely cumbersome, and will not be considered further.

Greater Flexibility and the Dollar

How then would a pattern of greater flexibility of exchange rates be likely to operate in the near future?

It must first be noted that only a few currencies would in practice probably wish to crawl or fluctuate within a wider band. Most countries would probably continue to peg their exchange rates within the narrow (or no) band to the major country to which their economies were closely related.[2]

For example, a de facto dollar area—which might include such major countries as Japan and Canada—could emerge. Such an area already exists in practice, but would become more apparent if countries continued to peg to the dollar rather than exercise their new option of letting their exchange rates flex.

The logic of the European Community suggests that it would seek to retain fixed exchange rates among its member states. This would require a major stride forward in their economic integration, or a willingness for large-scale financing among the members, or both. It might also require some technical innovations that might lead to use of one or their currencies as per Option 3. (At a later stage of EC integration, of course, they might adopt a common currency that could play such a role.) On the other hand, each member could continue to intervene with dollars, but at an intervention level designed for the Community as a whole.

If the United Kingdom were to remain outside the EC, the sterling area might live on with exchange rates of its members fixed internally and sterling fluctuating more freely relative to the dollar. Its membership might shrink, however, with several countries moving into the dollar area instead.

If Japan decided to flex relative to the dollar, a yen area in the Far East could develop along similar lines. "Member countries" would probably accomplish this by continuing to intervene with dollars, but at intervention points in line with those of the yen.

In fact, it is precisely between these broad areas that improved techniques of adjustment are needed to deal with the disequilibria that may have existed in the postwar period. The United States and the sterling area have been in persistent deficit, often simultaneous with underutilization of domestic resources. The EC has been in persistent surplus, and Japan may now be achieving such a position, often simultaneous with excessive levels of demand pressure. (Of course, some or all of these imbalances may not have represented disequilibria, reflecting as they did the conscious policy decisions of a great number of countries.) The following analysis assumes that only a few major exchange rates would actually move more freely, although most of the analysis could be applied to the broader case as well.

However many currencies were actually to fluctuate more freely, the dollar would almost certainly remain the pivot of the system. Monetary authorities in each of the fluctuating countries would define their currencies in terms of the dollar and intervene in the exchange markets in dollars, as they do at present. This would have several implications for the United States.

First, the United States would remain largely passive with regard to market intervention.

Second, there would be no commonly regarded "exchange rate of the dollar." Such a rate could be determined only implicitly, by calculating a weighted average of all other exchange rates. Rates of all other currencies (or key currencies or currency areas) would be commonly defined as their price in terms of dollars.

Third, the dollar could fluctuate vis-a-vis any single currency only half as much as could any other currency. Assuming flexibility as in Option 1, there would continue to be no fluctuation in the gold-dollar or SDR-dollar prices. The dollar, gold, and SDR would all be equally stable.

Fourth, passiveness on the part of the United States would obviate the international coordination problems that could be caused if the monetary authorities of the key currency country and the monetary authorities of other countries had different ideas about the proper exchange rates between their currencies.

It is striking that all of these features also exist in the present system, indicating how little in practice would be the changes due to limited flexibility. They would probably become more obvious, however, under a system where some other currencies were in fact fluctuating more freely.

Effects on Adjustment

A passive intervention policy would certainly not mean that the United

States would be indifferent to the exchange-rate movements that occurred in a world of greater flexibility. The reasons were stated at the outset of this paper: the United States could get either more adjustment or more financing, and would prefer more adjustment. And the greater opportunity for exchange-rate changes could produce a tendency toward depreciation of other currencies relative to the dollar, which would steadily impair the competitive position of the United States.

The United States could not get much worse off in this regard, however. Under the present system, there is a quadruple bias against the dollar, against which all exchange-rate changes take place:

payments pressures prompt or force devaluations, but seldom prompt or force revaluations;

revaluations tend to be smaller than necessary since countries are even less susceptible to fears of a need for additional revaluation than to pressures to move upward in the first place;

devaluations tend to be larger than necessary to prevent speculation on further devaluation, although this effect may be offset for major countries by their desire to avoid triggering responsive devaluations by others;

any single devaluation generates pressures on other countries to devalue, both because of legitimate fears over loss of competitive position (exacerbated by the tendency for the initial devaluations to be excessive) and because devaluation is easier to justify politically if done in response to a like movement by another country.

Under the present system, American payments deficits have, to a significant extent, been caused by these biases toward devaluation against the dollar. In the 1950s, the American balance of payments suffered from the excessive and widespread devaluations of 1949 (coupled with the maintenance of controls elsewhere). In the early 1960s, it suffered from the excessive French devaluations of the late 1950s, the inadequate German (and perhaps Dutch) revaluation in 1961, and the failure of other surplus countries (such as Italy and Austria) to revalue at all. All four aspects of the bias against the dollar thus played an important role in the development and perpetuation of the deficits of the United States.

The United States has, thus, had to maintain a much better record of price stability than virtually all other countries just to avoid losing its international competitive position. The United States did hold its share of world export markets during its period of amazing price stability in the early 1960s, which was however probably maintained at some cost in terms of domestic unemployment. But this analysis suggests why at least this indicator of the competitive position of the United States did not improve, even during a period when sharp increases in outflows of capital obviously provided some direct boost to exports.[3]

Each of the four biases should be removed or at least mitigated if greater flexibility of exchange rates were to work in practice as outlined in theory:

It would be based on rules or presumptions under which a surplus country would have the same responsibility to permit appreciation of its currency as a deficit country would have to permit depreciation of its currency.

The same rules or presumptions would assure that the amount of the appreciation was sufficient to remove the disequilibrium.

The system should reduce the amount of currency depreciations.[4] First, it would make an earlier start on the removal of disequilibrium and would, therefore, normally reduce the extent of the adjustment needed. Second, and more important from the standpoint of the dollar, the rules should provide countries with a high degree of confidence that depreciation could continue until a new equilibrium rate was reached and, therefore, reduce the need to overshoot the mark. This effect would be re-emphasized by the knowledge that depreciation could begin again if necessitated by the onset of a new disequilibrium.

It should reduce the "follow-the-leader" tendency to devalue, because any rate could begin to move as soon as disequilibrium became apparent. This is partly because greater flexibility would to some extent de-dramatize and de-politicize changes in rates.

In terms of adjustment, the United States would, thus, benefit to some degree simply from the reduction in the amounts of depreciation of other currencies and perhaps in the number of such depreciations. This suggests that the United States should prefer a symmetrical system of greater flexibility to an asymmetrical system that permitted only upside flexibility. The great benefit for the United States, however, would come from the elimination—or any reduction—of the revaluation-devaluation asymmetry of the present system and the shift in the moral burden of responsibility to adjust that would accompany it.

The Effects on Dollar Balances

It seems clear that private holdings of dollars would continue to rise with the need to finance international transactions under a system of greater flexibility. But a major question concerning the interest of the United States in such a system is whether it would lead monetary authorities to seek to disgorge their present dollar holdings, or avoid dollar accumulations in the future, or both of these.

We can identify a number of reasons why monetary authorities hold dollars in their reserves. (These reasons differ among countries due to different weightings of economic and political objectives and different degrees of economic ties with the United States.) Most basic are the opportunity for interest earnings and convenience of holding an asset widely useable without a need for conversion. Monetary authorities will take advantage of these opportunities, however, only if they are confident that convertibility, particularly into other national currencies, but also into other reserve assets widely used in the system, will be preserved with little risk of capital loss.[5]

The outlook for American balance-of-payments performance is critical to whether such confidence can be maintained, both for its current effect and because of its impact on the ratio of American liquid assets to external liabilities. Rates of domestic price increase and overall economic growth are in turn central to the outlook for payments equilibrium. Other important factors that led to foreign official dollar holdings are the overall political and economic role played in the world by the United States; gross capital outflows from the United States; the continued presence of adequate financial markets; relative aloofness of the American economy, and, hence, the dollar, from external disturbances; and avoidance of controls on the use of the currency.

The basic criterion had two components: continued convertibility and little risk of capital loss. For countries that continued to peg their currencies to the dollar, there would of course be little change from the present situation. The better adjustment of any American disequilibrium, which should derive from greater flexibility, should better assure all countries about the continued convertibility of the dollar and reduce even further the possibility of a change in the price of gold, the only financial reason why monetary authorities may have been uneasy over their holdings of dollars. And by helping the United States to adjust, greater flexibility would eliminate the need for the present controls over some international transactions by the United States and the possibility of tighter controls in the future —improving still further the attractiveness of the dollar.

On the other hand, the value of the dollar in terms of a weighted average of other currencies would depreciate, relative to the same price in the present system, if this adjustment conclusion is correct. This decline would be very slow, however, under any of the variants of greater flexibility now being considered, and would not of itself, probably, have much negative effect on holders of dollars. In absolute terms, of course, such a weighted average value of the dollar could be appreciating. Despite recent problems, the United States has a better long-term record of price stability than any other country, and few would bet against the dollar over the long haul. And the relatively closed nature of the American economy makes the dollar more susceptible to appreciation because policy in the United States is less likely than policy in most countries to be motivated by concern about the balance of payments and by overt mercantilism.

The major problem would come if one or two of the fluctuating currencies exhibited a strong bias toward appreciation relative to the dollar. (The mark and the yen might represent such cases.) Two questions must then be asked: Would any of these other currencies meet the requirements for key currency status sufficiently to draw balances away from the dollar? Could the United States or the appreciating country avoid such shifts through interest rate policy?

Sterling seems to be the only other currency that meets the wide range of requirements for key currency status, and long-term trends suggest that sterling is unlikely to appreciate steadily against the dollar. Germany's financial capabilities are improving rapidly, but its exposed geographic position and absence of a world political role—which is one major reason why its authorities continue to be completely negative about assuming any key currency role—make it doubtful that the mark could take much business away from the dollar. A promising possibility would seem to be some linkage between the UK's financial capabilities and still-global interests and the Continent's economic weight and potential political power, but there appears to be little movement toward such a merger even in the context of possible British entry to the Common Market.

The Swiss authorities are even more adamantly opposed to a key currency role for their franc, and they are quite right in view of the smallness of their economy and its extreme sensitivity to external transactions. Finally, although Japan shares a certain economic resemblance to Germany, it is much less far along the road both financially and politically.

We have already noted that the opportunity for yield is an important factor that induces foreign monetary authorities to hold dollars. Any anticipated depreciation of the dollar, even in terms of a single other currency, could thus be offset by increasing that yield. And Willett shows that (1) any interest rate constraint in the crawling-peg system is likely to be less than under the present system and (2) that the constraint is not very great in absolute terms once the initial stock adjustment, which could, however, be quite prolonged, has taken place. He also notes that any net constraint that remains due to the crawling peg could be reduced further by a greater widening of the band.[6]

It would thus appear feasible for the United States to use interest-rate policy to induce increased dollar holdings or to deter movements out of the dollar if it wanted to do so to help meet its international financial objectives. Given the assumptions that there could be no more than one or two other currencies that could attract shifts from the dollar, however, it would probably be far more efficient from the standpoint of the system as a whole if those other countries were to adapt their interest-rate policies to the need to prevent destabilizing shifts. This is because of the impact of American interest rates on all other countries, given the weight of the United States in the world economy, and because of the relatively closed nature of the American economy and, hence, the disproportionate effects on its domestic economy (and on the world economy) of the required change in interest rates. Such policies could, therefore, properly be made part of the amended rules of the game.

Political Considerations

Finally, what of the politics of a system in which other currencies moved more freely around the dollar, enhancing the appearance of the dollar as the lonestar of the system and its bastion of stability?

First, I have already noted that the system in practice would not differ very much from the present system. Second, only a few currencies could in practice be expected to fluctuate more freely. All other countries would retain their present fixity (to the dollar or some other currency) just as the dollar would retain its fixity (to gold). Third, the continued tie of the dollar to gold would continue to exercise its present degree of discipline on the United States, while all other countries would gain an additional degree of flexibility in their adjustment policies.

Most important, however, is the fact that the present system brings little real pressure to bear on the United States. The major surplus country, Germany, agreed publicly in 1967 not to buy gold from the United States. Some others follow a similar policy in practice, and there is a widespread perception that the United States, if confronted with demands for large gold conversions, would suspend the gold convertibility of the dollar rather than suffer further large losses of reserves.

If this is true, other countries have to add to their dollar reserves or initiate adjustment on their own when the United States is in official settlements deficit. They could, therefore, only gain from acquiring an additional policy instrument to fend off unwanted dollars in a more efficient way than the present mechanism for changing exchange rates. At the same time, the United States would benefit from the increased responsibility of other countries to permit adjustment and their increased moral obligation to hold dollars if they did not.

In addition, greater flexibility of exchange rates would "bottle up" inflation or deflation to a greater extent within its country of origin. This would reduce the possibility that Europe would have to "import inflation" from the United States or that the United States could "export unemployment" to the rest of the world.

There is one other probable political gain to other countries vis-a-vis the United States in such a system. Given the relatively small impact of foreign transactions on the economy of the United States, it is highly doubtful that the United States will ever permit balance-of-payments developments or foreign authorities to exercise overriding influence over its domestic policy. However, the exchange rate of the dollar has a relatively small impact on the American economy. American authorities should, thus, be prepared to accept much greater foreign influences over the exchange rate than over its domestic policy. Any system that increased the influence of exchange rates in the adjustment process should enhance the influence of foreign developments and foreign authorities.

If the political appearance of a fixed dollar in a world with several major currencies fluctuating around it were unacceptable, despite all these factors, one remedy would be to move to Option 2. The United States might accept a change in its obligations under the (revised) Articles of Agreement of the IMF by pledging to intervene in the exchange markets to defend the exchange rate of the dollar—within the wider band, or by regulating the rate of the crawl. This would mean that the United States would no longer pledge to convert foreign official dollars into gold at a fixed price (and vice versa), but would, rather, accept the same obligation now accepted by all other IMF members. Because the elimination of gold convertibility might cause unease among some monetary authorities—both those who now hold dollars and those who now hold gold—such a step would probably have to be accompanied by the creation of a Reserve Settlement Account, which would permit conversion into SDRs (or some other international asset) of any present reserve assets no longer wanted under these conditions.

In practice, such a system would require little, if any, intervention by the United States. As long as the dollar retained its intervention currency role, other countries would *ipso facto* maintain the dollar within its limitations as they carried out their own obligations under the Articles of Agreement. (In fact, intervention by the United States would create a redundancy problem unless any such intervention was limited to the time when exchange markets abroad were closed because of time differentials.) The system would thus operate in a manner virtually identical to Option 1.

The main difference would be the substitution of a dollar legally subject to the same rules as all other countries for the present system of gold-dollar convertibility. As a result, there would no longer be any foreign pressure on the United States by direct conversion of dollars into gold or threats thereof. There would seem to be less occasion for any such pressure, in any event, if my conclusion is correct that greater flexibility would improve the likelihood of adjustment to any payments disequilibrium between the United States and the rest of the world. If it were deemed necessary to create a Reserve Settlement Account to smooth the transition to this system and to determine the future relationship among the various reserve assets, that would be another difference—and one that would certainly complicate and slow the adoption of greater flexibility.

Conclusion

The foregoing analysis suggests that there are no overriding reasons why the United States should oppose greater flexibility of exchange rates. The arguments so far advanced against an American interest in such a system do not stand up to analysis. In fact, any of the technically feasible approaches to such an evolutionary change would appear to offer some advantage to the United States—both in terms of its broad interest in an effective international monetary system and its narrower interest in its own international financial position.

The interest of the United States would be maximized if the rules or presumptions that governed any increase in flexibility were to eliminate or even reduce the present "quadruple bias" against the dollar, which makes adjustment extremely difficult for the United States. If other countries were unwilling to commit themselves irrevocably to upside fluctuations when market forces suggested them, however, the United States could still expect to gain adjustment benefits from the changes in the rules affecting currency depreciations. It would, thus, benefit more from a symmetrical system of greater flexibility than from an asymmetrical system that permitted only upside flexibility, although it could of course expect significant benefit from the asymmetrical system alone.

If others were unwilling to commit themselves to upside fluctuations, of course, the dollar would face even less risk of confidence problems and both the foreign countries and the United States would want to keep open the option of foreign accumulations of dollar inflows as at present. If a confidence problem were perceived to exist under any of the greater flexibility variants, it could be handled by introducing appropriate rules for interest-rate policies by countries whose parities were expected to crawl steadily upward, by American interest-rate policy, or by a sufficient widening of the band.

The United States should, thus, have in mind some particular proposals that would maximize its advantage if included in the rules or presumptions of any new system of greater exchange-rate flexibility. Acceptance of these proposals would make it most clear that the adoption of such a system would be in the interest of the United States.

Fortunately, these changes would also seem to be in the interest of the other major countries. They would gain an additional policy instrument for use in adjusting their own payments positions, although they might prefer less firm rules on upside rate changes in order to preserve their present option of accumulating dollars rather than adjusting. They would gain even more than would the United States from the improvement in the overall system, in view of their greater reliance on international transactions. They could lose little of substance vis-a-vis the United States, since they do not now bring substantial pressure on it to adjust. The various approaches discussed in this volume should, therefore, be suitable for serious international discussion.

Notes

1. It could also mean abandonment by the United States of *any* convertibility obligation. However, this would probably not produce a system of limited exchange-rate flexibility, at least not of the negotiated type being discussed in this volume.

2. This means that any negotiated system would probably have to permit such continued pegging. It would also, however, have to assure that enough currencies actually fluctuated to avoid aborting the basic objectives of the adoption of greater flexibility. One reconciliation would be to make greater flexibility optional for all countries but with prior understandings, at least among the members of the Group of Ten, as to which rates would actually fluctuate in practice.

3. This analysis also suggests why most foreign monetary authorities were willing to accumulate dollars to finance a large part of the American deficit during this period. The dollar accumulations provided an umbrella for their own rapid growth and the elimination of their restrictions on international transactions in two ways: they provided a rapid increase in international liquidity and they enabled the rest of the world, on balance, to avoid adjustment, thereby improving its competitive position against the largest factor in the world economy—the United States itself.

4. There is a contrary view that greater flexibility would induce wage increases and, hence, increase the amount of depreciations. The point is certainly arguable, but it is also arguable that relatively small and frequent rate changes will be more easily absorbed by labor, since they would become more routine, and be less shocking, than large discrete parity shifts.

5. They may also be interested in stability per se rather than risk of loss. I have noted earlier, however, that under Option 1 there would be no change from the present equality of stability of the dollar and its two chief

reserve asset rivals, gold and SDRs. Under Option 2, some might perceive gold or SDRs to be more stable, although others might react oppositely.

6. Thomas D. Willett, "Short-term Capital Movements and the Interest-Rate Constraint Under Systems of Limited Flexibility of Exchange Rates" in Halm, ed., *Approaches to Greater Flexibility of Exchange Rates: The Bürgenstock Papers* (Princeton, N.J.: Princeton University Press, 1970), pp. 283-94.

8 Oil and the Cash Flow

Arab oil earnings will rise by $65 billion this year, the amounts will get even bigger in following years, the balance-of-payments positions of the consuming countries will plunge into the abyss, the international monetary system will collapse, the Arabs will buy up all our companies—so goes the refrain heard frequently since the dramatic increase in oil prices in December.

There are indeed extremely serious consequences of the oil crisis:

Inflation has spiraled upward; recessions are possible if governments mistakenly cut back aggregate demand to cope with shortages of supply; countries producing other raw materials have been encouraged to emulate oil exporters; a few of the poorest countries will suffer serious deprivations, and political tensions deriving from the energy problems could intensify among countries.

But the international monetary situation adds relatively little to the problem. No industrial country will go bankrupt. The monetary system will not collapse. The prophets of financial doom simplistically compare the increase in each country's oil bill with its existing monetary reserves. They note that United States imports will rise by $15 billion and that its reserves are $12 billion, and conclude that the United States cannot pay—even for one year.

Such observations are absurd. First, they ignore that a sizable share of the increased earnings of the oil-exporting countries will be spent on imports from the industrial world. Some oil countries will spend virtually all of their increased earnings themselves; all are rapidly revising their development strategies and military plans to do so. Some will lend their money to others who will quickly spend it.

So even the trade balances of the industrial world will not decline by more than, say, half of the increase in its oil bill this year. Those trade balances will be even better in subsequent years, as any further increases in oil countries' earnings are more than offset by their increased imports. (Indeed, the United States appears to have already reached its new plateau of oil imports in April at an annual rate of $27 billion, but was in surplus in over-all trade as exports reached an annual rate of almost $100 billion.)

Second, the prophets of doom confuse the balance of trade and the

---

This chapter originally appeared in the *New York Times*, June 3, 1974.

balance of payments. They ignore the simple but central fact that the oil exporters must invest in the industrial world any of their increased earnings that they do not spend. The Arabs will not bury the money in the ground. Thus, there can be no deficit in the balance of payments of the industrial world as a whole.

To be sure, the flow of money from the Arabs will not necessarily go to individual industrial countries in amounts that precisely match the decline in the trade balance of each. Some industrial countries may wind up with a sizable surplus; others may have deficits.

But this problem is solvable solely through action by the industrial countries themselves to recycle the money to where it is needed. Much financial recycling will take place through normal market forces. Some can be handled by government borrowing in the private capital markets.

The Eurocurrency markets—those that lend a variety of currencies from European centers—have grown as rapidly in several past years as they will have to grow now and the United States capital market is now fully available with the abolition of controls. Together, they can handle the vast bulk of the money on their own, and are in fact doing so even as the full amount of the higher oil earnings is now being invested.

The rest of the money can move through such existing intergovernmental institutions as the swap network among central banks and the International Monetary Fund. Indeed, such backstopping will be needed for any individual borrowers whose creditworthiness comes under doubt in the private market. But Italy is the only such case to date.

In any event, no special cooperation with the oil exporters is needed in this area. It helps for the International Monetary Fund to borrow from them to help finance members' deficits, but there is no reason to give the oil exporters better terms than other lenders.

Doubts are sometimes raised about the plausibility of such smooth handling of the oil money. First, it is feared that the money, like the oil itself, will be "politicized." But it is highly doubtful that the Arabs will try to promote monetary instability by shifting their funds from place to place. Once invested, the very size of the funds will make it increasingly difficult for the Arabs to liquidate quickly without incurring substantial losses. If they were to make such shifts, the money could readily be recycled through the swap network.

Second, it is argued that some industrial countries may be unwilling to accept the needed shift in the structure of their balance-of-payments positions. It is certainly true that all of their trade balances will deteriorate and be offset by increases in capital inflows. But such a situation might well be sustainable indefinitely since the capital inflow will by definition continue as long as the trade imbalances do. And it is certainly sustainable for the interim period until energy conservation and the development of new sources of oil and alternative forms of energy are brought into play to change the energy situation at its roots.

Third, some industrial countries fear that many of their companies will be taken over by the oil producers. They need not. Most of the oil countries will soon find ways to spend most of their income on goods and services. And since they have decided to nationalize most of the foreign business concerns within their boundaries, they are quite unlikely to seek majority control of firms within the boundaries—and legal jurisdiction—of others. Even if they wanted to, they do not have the manpower to exert much effect on the operations of very many firms anyway. So the present pattern of diffused and highly liquid portfolio investment in a wide range of financial assets is likely to persist.

Finally, the proposed solution to the monetary problem requires the industrial countries to agree on at least a broad pattern of exchange-rate relationships among them, around which the financial flows can be recycled. It will be tricky to reach such agreements, which amount to taking oil out of each country's balance of payments for the purpose of determining exchange rates.

However, there was already evidence of progress toward such agreements before oil prices soared. They are a necessary component of any stable monetary system for the future, and were thus already at the top of the agenda for monetary reform. And history clearly shows that the alternative of competitive exchange-rate depreciations will not work.

It seems clear from the series of official pronouncements on the subject that all countries have recognized these facts and that this latest crisis —like most past crises—will speed rather than derail needed monetary reform. There is good reason for confidence that the mistakes of the nineteen-thirties and the nineteen-sixties can be avoided in resolving the latest international monetary crisis.

**Part III
World Trade**

9

The Future of World Trade

The future of international trade must be viewed against the backdrop of several sweeping and inter-related changes in the world economy and, indeed, world political relationships. First, structural inflation is fast replacing structural unemployment as the cardinal concern of economic policy in virtually every industrialized country. Second, completely new international monetary arrangements are rapidly evolving. Third, the GATT system of rules and institutions which governed world trade reasonably well for the first postwar generation has virtually collapsed. Fourth, the reduction of worldwide political tensions, particularly between the United States and the leading Communist powers, has both opened the political door to expanding East-West trade and removed the security blanket which heretofore had frequently smothered economic disputes among alliance partners both East and West.

The first two of these changes, for reasons which I will elaborate shortly, suggest a renewed impetus toward the liberalization and expansion of world trade. The implications of the third and fourth changes are not as clear, but they—and several other deep-seated trends—could strengthen the omnipresent pressures of restriction and even contraction of world trade. It is impossible to predict which set of forces will eventually dominate. I have in earlier but still recent analyses expressed deep pessimism about the outlook for world trade policies.[1] This paper, however, will focus on those new developments which augur positively for the future of world trade: global inflation and monetary reform.

Inflation and World Trade

Inflation has moved to the top of the political agenda in virtually every industrialized country. Germany, in view of its historical experiences with inflation and its postwar success in avoiding unemployment, led this trend. But it is now true even in the United States, which until quite recently had remained relatively impervious to the problem. And it has not become just

Adapted from a paper originally prepared for a conference on The International Division of Labour in Kiel, West Germany in July 1973 and published in Herbert Giersch, ed., *The International Division of Labour: Problems and Perspectives* (Tubingen: J. C. S. Mohr, 1974), pp. 543-54.

97

the chief *economic* issue; the reduction of Cold War tension, and in the United States the end of the war in Vietnam, have moved it to the top of the overall *political* agenda as well.[2] It is likely to stay there even in the event of mild recessions, because they are not likely to dampen inflation back to acceptable levels. I refer throughout to *structural* inflation, of course, not simply the traditional cyclical inflation which is far less a problem because of its responsiveness to changes in aggregate-demand policies.

Strong evidence for this trend can, of course, be adduced from the dramatic shifts in the internal economic policies of numerous major countries, such as the adoption of tough incomes policies by extremely market-oriented governments in the United States and the United Kingdom. But more important for this paper is the strong evidence which can also be adduced from the dramatic shift in foreign economic policies of many major countries as well.

Countries often seek to fight unemployment by erecting import controls, subsidizing exports, and maintaining undervalued exchange rates. Such policies, of course, reached their zenith during the depression of the 1930s, but they were also seen frequently, if less blatantly and to less extreme degrees, throughout the first postwar generation. Conversely, countries can seek to fight inflation by promoting imports, erecting export controls, and maintaining overvalued exchange rates. Indeed, import liberalization can play a major role in fighting inflation by increasing the availability of goods and, more importantly, by breaking down noncompetitive practices and generating major pressures for increased industrial efficiency.[3] Since anti-competitive forces are a key factor in the growing importance of structural inflation, the policy tool of import liberalization may now be more important than ever before. In any event, it is clear that this set of anti-inflationary policies has now displaced the former set of anti-deflationary policies as the dominant approach to foreign economic policy in almost every major industrialized country.

Unilateral, non-reciprocal import liberalizations to fight inflation have become frequent occurrences. The United States has abolished its import quotas on oil and meat, and doubled its quotas on dairy products. The President of the United States, in his Trade Reform Act of 1973, has sought Congressional approval for unilateral reductions of U.S. tariffs explicitly to counter domestic inflation. Canada and Japan have reduced tariffs and raised quotas. Australia, traditionally one of the most protectionist of developed countries, has unilaterally cut its tariffs by 25 percent. Germany, as part of its anti-inflationary effort of early 1973, sharply liberalized its quotas on imports from socialist countries—the only component of its imports over which it has unilateral control, the rest being subject to joint decisions of the Common Market. And the E.C. Commission has proposed that all members of the Community cut their tariffs by 30 percent to fight inflation jointly, a proposal which was reportedly rejected only because it would weaken Europe's position in the forthcoming multilateral trade negotiations.

These unilateral import liberalizations have almost certainly had a far greater impact on the level of world trade than the very small number of new import barriers which have been imposed in the recent past. In the United States, for example, there has been only one new commodity "favored" by a decision to raise import barriers since 1968.[4] Indeed, all of this unilateral liberalization raises the question of the importance of the multilateral trade negotiations now scheduled to begin meaningfully in 1974. Preparation for such a negotiation could even dampen the trend toward unilateral tariff cuts and quota increases (or abandonment), as countries fear to "give up something for nothing" rather than trade concessions on a reciprocal basis, as noted in the E.C. case above. It is thus particularly noteworthy that there have been so many unilateral steps, when a multilateral negotiation was clearly pending.

Indeed, the pendulum has now swung so far that export controls have replaced import controls as the most divisive issue of world trade policy. The U.S. limits on exports of soybeans and several other commodities, including some non-agricultural commodities, have been the most notable, but Canada and several other countries have taken similar steps. Several of the oil-producing countries, notably Kuwait and Libya, are also restraining critical exports (through limiting production) for reasons which are related but which also go beyond the battle against inflation.

Similar trends can be observed in international monetary policy. Germany was the leader, revaluing first in 1969 and numerous times since *in an effort to fight domestic inflation*—after many years of rejecting calls to take precisely such steps in order to restore equilibrium in its *external* accounts. Numerous other countries, including Canada from mid-1970, have followed the German example. In virtually every case, the existence of an external surplus justified the move.

The most interesting case is that of Japan in early 1973. Throughout the first half of the year, Japan kept its exchange rate from depreciating by selling $1 billion of foreign exchange per month. A priori, this constituted a massive violation of the "system" of freely floating exchange rates in place among the major countries at the time; no other country intervened in the exchange markets on a scale that was at all comparable. Did the Japanese action constitute a competitive appreciation of the yen, undertaken to enable Japan to stockpile imports (as it did) as a hedge against further price rises and eventual depreciation of its currency? Or was the outlook for the Japanese balance of payments over the next year or so sufficiently strong that it was proper to hold the rate up to avoid needless fluctuation? The question can never be resolved definitively, but the phenomenon of a country actively blocking any depreciation of its currency in the face of such massive reserve losses during a regime of floating exchange rates is certainly unprecedented in the history of international finance.

The new focus on inflation may also carry important implications for policies toward multinational corporations. Inflation is countered by foreign investment which speeds the transmission of comparative advantage and increases world efficiency, but may be accelerated by foreign investment which permits global cartelization of particular industries.[5] The Federal Trade Commission in the United States, for example, has concluded that competition can be restored in the U.S. photocopying market only if Xerox spins off its European and Japanese subsidiaries. Germany has declared that it is prepared to apply its new anti-cartel policy against the activities of multinationals in their *home* countries. So global anti-inflationary concerns could conceivably speed the development of policies, at both the national and international levels, to counter such effects.

Thus it is conceivable that, as a result of the advent of inflation as the chief economic concern of the industrialized world, we are witnessing a fundamental reversal in the nature of the international economic policy problem. Unilateral import liberalization and export controls may be replacing unilateral import controls and export subsidies as the norms of commercial policy. Competitive exchange-rate appreciation, or at least non-depreciation, may be replacing the previous problem of competitive devaluation and non-revaluation. Such policies, carried out on a unilateral basis, are no more likely to succeed, over any sustained period of time, than did their precursors. The international trading and monetary rules are not geared to these problems today, but must be for the future if they are to handle adequately the real issues which are likely to arise.

A second cause of structural inflation is the growing shortage of numerous primary products, the price effects of which will probably be intensified by the increasing market power likely to be exercised by a growing number of producing country cartels to boost further their terms of trade.[6] Prices have skyrocketed, and will stay far above previous levels, for copper, bauxite, lead, zinc and a host of raw materials. World demand for meat and other high-protein foods is rising sharply as incomes rise, and dramatically increasing demand both for meat itself and for high-quality feed. These trends have major implications for the trade and development policies of the developing countries.

These countries may have gone too far in emphasizing *industrial* exports to cope with their balance-of-payments problems. Indeed, many developing countries should re-orient their export strategies to take advantage of the major structural changes which are now apparent in the markets for a wide variety of primary products, including foodstuffs, feed, and numerous raw materials. For example, Brazil has already become the world's second largest producer of soybeans, and soybeans will shortly replace coffee as its leading earner of foreign exchange. Brazil and other producers of soybeans are thus the major beneficiaries of the U.S. export controls.

The merits of this strategy are reinforced by its implications for unemployment in the developing countries. No conceivable increase in exports of manufactured products could meet their job needs. At the same time, much agricultural output is highly labor intensive, or can be made so. Countries with widely sought raw materials can insist that the materials be processed locally, further contributing to the reduction of their unemployment. All these new emphases would also help the developing countries achieve another of their goals, a reduction in their reliance on foreign-based multinational firms.

Developing countries should, of course, continue their efforts to expand their production and exports of manufactured goods, where it proves efficient to do so. Indeed, the outlook for increased liberalization of trade policies in the industrialized world, already outlined, improves the prospects for such exports. But the dramatic changes in outlook for world trade in primary products strongly suggests that many developing countries should re-think the exclusive focus of recent years on manufacturing, particularly in cases where it was pursued at admittedly high costs in terms of inefficient utilization of domestic resources. Taking these two trends together, I am highly optimistic about the outlook for the exports of the developing countries in the 1970s.

In sum, the advent of structural inflation to the top of the agenda of economic policy concerns is likely to have four major effects on world trade. First, it will probably raise the level of trade, as countries seek imports to help deal with their domestic problems more than they restrict exports for the same purpose. Second, it is likely to skew the structure of trade toward "Ricardo goods" because of shortages, toward standardized manufactured ("Heckscher-Ohlin") goods because of the importance of costs, and away from Product-Cycle goods, which are closely linked to foreign direct investment and may even in some cases contribute to global cartelization. Third, it is likely to increase the share in world trade of trade between the industrialized and developing countries, since the latter are major sources of both Ricardo and Heckscher-Ohlin goods, and since most Product-Cycle trade takes place among the industrialized countries. Fourth, because rates of inflation may differ more among countries in a world with higher average rates of inflation, it may increase imbalances in national trade and payments positions. We thus turn to the most promising remedy for that problem, the newly evolving international monetary system.

International Monetary Reform and World Trade

International monetary arrangements are in the process of shifting from a disequilibrium system to an equilibrium system. The Bretton Woods regime featured financing of imbalances rather than their adjustment, particularly in the case of the persistent U.S. deficits and European (plus, more recently, Japanese) surpluses financed by the growth of foreign-held dollar balances. The exchange-rate realignments of late 1971 and early 1973 should eradicate the imbalances of the past, however, and the increased flexibility of exchange rates which is likely under any new system should go far to maintain equilibrium.[7]

The new monetary system will have several implications for world trade. First, it will reduce the propensity to export and increase the propensity to import of several countries, notably Germany and (for a shorter period of time) Japan, whose industries have developed behind the protection of undervalued exchange rates. Import growth into Japan may be further accelerated by Japanese foreign direct investment to serve the home market, motivated inter alia by changes in cost considerations deriving from the exchange-rate changes. (Both Germany and Japan should be readily able to accept and even benefit from the changes, as it will help them combat inflation and, in the case of Japan, facilitate the desired shift in national policy toward "quality of life" concerns.)

Second, the new monetary system will have the opposite effect in the United States, whose exporting and import-competing industries were hobbled for at least three years by overvaluation of the dollar. This effect will be reinforced by the encouragement provided by the exchange-rate changes to American firms in numerous industries to invest at home rather than abroad. Third, by more promptly rectifying payments imbalances and thereby preventing the development of large trade imbalances, it should help pre-empt widescale support for protectionist efforts.[8]

It is impossible to predict whether these changes, taken together, will have much net impact on the level of world trade.[9] The third factor mentioned, however, does suggest a reduction in the probability of a sharp increase in protectionism—particularly when taken in combination with the advent of inflation as the chief structural problem of concern to economic policy in most industrialized countries, as discussed above. So it reduces the likelihood of a significant cutback in even the growth of world trade and inter alia reinforces the optimistic outlook for export opportunities for the developing countries forecast above.

The monetary changes could also have an impact on the structure of world trade. They should promote Heckscher-Ohlin trade, by promoting more rapid transmission of cost-sensitive production (as in the case of Japanese foreign direct investment). And they should dampen the growth of Product-Cycle trade, by reducing the incentives to U.S.-based foreign direct investment which has been a major element therein.

The Future of Trade Policy

What policy guidance do all these trends provide? One of the most disturbing features of this discussion has been confusion over the objectives of trade policy. Some observers have sought to use trade policy to combat domestic unemployment, particularly in the developing countries. Others have wanted to use it to reduce foreign exchange gaps, or redistribute income, or achieve national economic independence.

These observers seem to have forgotten two of the fundamental lessons of the theory of economic policy: that a single policy instrument cannot efficiently be used to pursue such a variety of policy targets, and that no international policy (such as trade policy) can succeed if it seeks to benefit a single country (or group of countries) at the expense of another country (or group of countries). No one even mentioned the traditional target of trade policy: the maximization of economic efficiency.

There are understandable reasons from the recent past why some countries, or at least key groups within certain countries, would reject this traditional focus. Under a disequilibrium monetary system, a country might well impose import barriers and seek non-reciprocal import liberalization from others to offset the effects of an overvalued exchange rate on domestic jobs and its balance of payments. Under a system "stacked" against primary products, the developing countries might also reject the theory and practice of liberal trade.

Now, however, the disequilibrium monetary system is being replaced. The outlook for primary products is exceptionally good. And the accelerated importance of inflation heightens the value of using whatever policy tools may be available, such as trade policy, to combat it.

Indeed, the case for so doing may be greater than ever before. In the period prior to World War I, governments accepted few responsibilities for economic policy and hence did not face the targets-instruments dilemmas of today. The cardinal problem of peacetime economic policy since 1918, in most countries for most periods of time, has been unemployment or the fear thereof. It is only now that a shortage of policy instruments (relative to government targets) combines with an emphasis on fighting inflation, which reinforces the traditional case for using trade policy to that end. International monetary policy, primarily the exchange-rate mechanism, can then be used to deal with external payments imbalances.

Indeed, there is no alternative. Developing country exports would have to rise by $20 billion—25 billion to solve their unemployment problem through trade. But this could produce only two general equilibrium out-comes. If the result were a *net* increase of such magnitude, a huge trade surplus for the developing world would result. This would require the developing countries to become net exporters of capital to the indus-trialized countries on a large scale, and would certainly trigger widespread protectionist responses there. Dismay was near-universal when the United States, in late 1971, sought a swing of one-half as much spread over many more countries.

On the other hand, the increase in developing country exports could be matched by a rise in their imports. In this case, however, the ultimate effect is simply an increase in the overall level of trade, which is the operational objective of using trade policy to maximize efficiency in the first place.

To be sure, a few small countries can get away with policies to improve their trade balances (and reduce domestic unemployment) at the expense of others. And it is certainly proper to boost net exports through external (primarily exchange-rate) steps when facing overall balance-of-payments difficulties; indeed, doing so enables countries to avoid stop-go internal policies for payments reasons which is the chief impact of the external sector on domestic unemployment.

But countries will have to rely primarily on domestic macroeconomic policies to cope with unemployment and growth and look to trade policy to help combat inflation with the exchange rate to preserve external equilib-rium. This does not mean blindly leaving all trade flows to market determi-nations. Government intervention will often be needed to counter market imperfections, including those raised by multinational corporations and other governments. The world may soon need an international incomes policy, especially when organized labor in the United States realizes that it cannot fight international economic interdependence with Burke-Hartke bills and instead joins the trend toward multinationalization of labor as a counterweight to multinational business—which could leave no represen-tation for the non-multinational public. But the assignment of trade policy to economic efficiency generally means reducing barriers to international trade and factor flows, as a presumption underlying world economic pol-icy.

Notes

1. See my "The Future of U.S. Trade Policy", *American Journal of Agricultural Economics*, Vol. LV, Menasha, Wisc., 1973, pp. 280, sqq. [Chapter 13 in this volume]—*Idem*, "Crisis in U.S. Trade Policy", *Foreign Affairs*, Council on Foreign Relations, Vol. XLIX, New York, 1970/71, pp. 619 sqq. [Chapter 12 in this volume].

2. Even including the Watergate issue, which raged at its height when this paper was written. This reference recalls a Watergate story which is relevant because of its German content and its relationship to the dynamic theory of comparative advantage. Congressman Matsunaga from Hawaii, who is of Japanese descent, has argued that the Watergate problem developed because President Nixon employed German instead of Japanese advisers. The Japanese now have better electronic devices. And, when Japanese fail, they commit hara-kiri.

3. See the excellent paper on this topic by Herbert Giersch, "Freer Trade for Higher Employment and Price Level Stability", in: *Toward A New World Trade Policy: The Maidenhead Papers,* edited by C. Fred Bergsten, Lexington Books, D.C. Heath and Company (Lexington, Mass.: 1975.)

4. The item is rubber sneakers from Korea, under a "voluntary export restraint" arrangement announced in mid-1973. Even on this item, which is relatively small in trade terms, export growth will continue at 20% annually. In addition to oil, meat, and cheese, mentioned in the text, the United States has in this period decided to end its escape clause duties on carpets and glass. Numerous industry requests for import protection, as in shoes and a number of other escape clause cases, have been turned down by the President and the Congress. The decision to restrain imports of synthetic and wool textiles was made in 1968, though not implemented until 1971; the "voluntary" restraints on steel announced in early 1971 extended an existing arrangement; and the imposition of a tariff quota on stainless steel flatware in 1970 simply restored a practice which had existed for several years until 1967.

5. For a sharp distinction between "trade-creating" and "trade-diverting" investment, see Kiyoshi Kojima, "A Macroeconomic Theory of Foreign Direct Investment", in: *Toward a New World Trade Policy, op. cit.*

6. C. Fred Bergsten, "The Threat From the Third World," *Foreign Policy*, 11, New York, Summer 1973 [chapter 27 in this volume].

7. For an analysis of these changes and detailed proposals for reform see: C. Fred Bergsten, *Reforming the Dollar: An International Monetary Policy for the United States*, Council on Foreign Relations, Council Papers on International Affairs, New York, 1972.

8. The overvaluation of the dollar played a major role in the growth of protectionist pressures in the United States in the late 1960s and early 1970s. See Bergsten, "Crisis in U.S. Trade Policy", *op. cit.*

9. Some analysts would add a fourth effect, arguing that trade flows will be deterred by the very existence of flexible exchange rates. There is no evidence from recent experience to support this view.

10 Completing the GATT: Toward New International Rules to Govern Export Controls

The "New" Problem of Export Controls[1]

Introduction

The primary economic concern of the first postwar generation was unemployment. Hence, the primary concern of foreign economic policy was access to foreign markets, to help countries generate jobs at home and export levels sufficient to avoid serious balance-of-payments deficits and the resulting need for restrictive internal policies. The primary focus of international trade policy in this period was thus import controls: the reduction of existing quotas and tariffs to provide increasing access to foreign markets, and the avoidance of new barriers to such access.

This postwar focus grew originally out of the experience of the interwar period, during which countries tried to export the unemployment which they suffered during the Great Depression by aggressively raising tariffs and applying import quotas. A consensus emerged that the imposition of such controls had in fact brought little benefit to any individual country, but had deepened and broadened the Depression for all. This had in turn contributed importantly to the massive problems faced by many national economies, especially in Europe, which were an important cause of the Second World War. Thus, international arrangements to protect the world against national import barriers were deemed an integral part of the postwar security as well as economic arrangements.

In addition, unemployment stemming from inadequate demand for domestic production was the primary economic concern of most countries at most times after 1945. In the early postwar years, most countries other than the United States also faced worrisome balance-of-payments deficits. So, there was serious risk that countries would periodically seek to erect barriers to imports, to boost employment in particular domestic industries or to limit their total purchases from abroad, despite the resulting problems for the world economy and international security. The General Agreement on Tariffs and Trade (GATT) rules and institutional arrangements sought

---

This paper was originally prepared for a meeting of the British-North American Committee in Gleneagles, Scotland in June 1974. It was published in November 1974 by the British-North American Committee; sponsored in the United States by the National Planning Association.

primarily to deal with this set of problems: by reducing existing import barriers, limiting the impact of any import controls which were adopted, and channeling the disputes triggered by such controls into established forums in order to minimize the likelihood that they would generate major political disputes among nations.[2]

It is often forgotten, however, that access to foreign supplies has sometimes overshadowed, or at least equalled, access to foreign markets among the external economic concerns of nations. Thus, export controls have been of great concern in at least three periods since World War I: the early years after 1918, the late 1930s and the early postwar period running through the Korean War.[3] They usually represented national efforts to export inflation and the effects of shortages, especially of raw materials, just as import controls represented national efforts to export unemployment and the effects of excess production.[4]

Export controls, perhaps even more than import controls, have important security as well as economic implications. We shall shortly see that the major purposes of export controls include holding on to key products (such as food and fuels) to protect a country's own security, denial of the benefits of trade to political adversaries, and the extension of such benefits to allies. Indeed, controls applied for precisely such purposes during the periodic scrambles for resources among countries have frequently been cited among the causes of both world wars. The British export tax on coal, levied in 1901, hit Germany hard and added importantly to the rising tension between them.[5] The U.S. export controls against Japan, along with the long list of export controls erected by most European countries, both reflected and accelerated the disruption of overall relations leading to World War II.[6] Throughout the postwar period, the United States and (to a lesser extent) its allies have used export controls to try to limit the military and economic capabilities of the USSR and other communist countries. And the limitation of oil exports by the Arab producers in late 1973, in an effort to change the Middle East policies of the United States and virtually every other country in the world, has dramatized the issue of "access to supplies" more than any other single event.[7]

Numerous study groups and international organizations, particularly the League of Nations, tried to formulate international rules to deal with export controls in the interwar period.[8] Indeed, Senator Mondale would be surprised to learn that his amendments to the Trade Reform Act of 1974, which call for the United States to initiate negotiations to develop international rules to govern export controls and would authorize the President to retaliate against controls placed on exports to the United States by other countries, sound very much like the proposals made by Secretary of Commerce Herbert Hoover to deal with very similar issues in 1926! The proposed International Trade Organization, which was rejected by the

Congress of the United States in the late 1940s, referred fairly extensively to export controls.[9] Article XI of the GATT explicitly prohibits export quotas, and the GATT did tackle the issue in the early postwar period.[10]

Despite these efforts, no effective framework of rules and institutional arrangements to deal with the trade policy problems arising from export controls has ever existed, and none exists today. The GATT articles provide numerous exceptions to the prohibition of export quotas in Article XI and, in practice, this prohibition has been a dead letter. The GATT explicitly permits export taxes. Thus, there is no international deterrent to national export controls, nor is there a forum into which to channel disputes triggered by such controls. If export controls were to become quantitatively or qualitatively significant, they would thus be even more likely to produce international conflict than import controls, which are subject to very explicit international rules.

The Purposes of Export Controls

In fact, the use of export controls is becoming very widespread. Many countries have employed one or another form of such controls in the recent past. For example, the United States has sharply limited, for varying periods of time, its sales of soybeans, a number of other farm products, metal scrap, and timber. Both Japan and the United States have *de facto* limited or even embargoed exports of fertilizers and other chemical products, particularly petroleum-based intermediate goods. Brazil has checked its exports of coffee, leather and beef. Export taxes have appeared on Latin American bananas. The most dramatic move was the oil embargo by the Organization of Arab Petroleum Exporting Countries (OAPEC, the Arab group within OPEC), which was intended to block all shipments to the United States, the Netherlands and a few other countries. Canada has adopted legislation enabling it to apply export controls much more readily in the future, and the U.S. Congress is seriously considering similar changes in U.S. legislation. There are dozens of other examples.

These measures have been undertaken for a variety of reasons,[11] which are summarized in Table 10-1:

1. To *avoid "unacceptable" domestic price rises*. The U.S. restrictions on agricultural exports in 1973 were adopted for this purpose. From its inception in 1949, the U.S. Export Control Act (since 1969, the Export Administration Act) has permitted export controls "to protect the economy from the excessive drain of scarce materials and to reduce the inflationary impact of abnormal foreign demand"; this consideration motivated most of the U.S. export controls of the early postwar period, but

Table 10-1
Purposes and Methods of Government Export Controls (some country and product examples)

Method / Purpose	Quantitative Restrictions on Exports[a]	Taxes on Exports	Quantitative Restrictions on Domestic Production[b]	Taxes on Domestic Production[b]
1. Restrain domestic prices	U.S.—soybeans, 1973 U.S.—logs, 1973[c]		NA	NA
2. Reinforce domestic price controls	U.S.—fertilizers 1973-74[d] EEC—wheat and rice, 1973	EEC—various agricultural products (sugar, rice, cereals, etc.) 1973-	NA	NA
3. Increase export earnings from the controlled product	Philippines—coconut oil, 1974	Panama, Honduras, Costa Rica—bananas, 1974	Kuwait, Libya, Venezuela—oil, 1974	Jamaica—bauxite, 1974
4. Seize earnings generated by other countries' import controls	Several European countries, 1930s	Netherlands—several products, 1932		
5. Conserve limited resources	(requires massive stockpiling)	(requires massive stockpiling)	Kuwait—oil, 1971-	
6. Promote domestic processing of the controlled product	Pakistan—leather, 1962 Canada—amendment to Export and Import Permits Act, 1974	Brazil—coffee, 1965-		

7. Avoid shortages	U.K.—copper scrap, periodic			NA
8. Raise government revenue	NA	Thailand—rice, longstanding	NA	Several oil producers—longstanding
9. Limit other countries' military and economic potential	U.S. and COCOM—to communist countries, 1949- ; U.K.—textile machinery, 1930s to mid 1950s			
10. Change other countries' foreign policies	Several oil exporters, 1973-74		Several oil exporters, 1973-74	
11. Reduce balance-of-payments surpluses[e]	Japan—20 industries, 1971	Germany—all products subject to export rebates, 1968-69		
12. Head off import controls ("voluntary" export restraints)[e]	Japan—textiles, 1956-			

NA—Not Applicable.

[a]Including embargoes.

[b]Not strictly an "export control". See discussion in text.

[c]Implemented by Japanese "voluntary" import restraints.

[d]Export controls were informal.

[e]Not covered in this study. See footnote 11, pages 148-49.

became insignificant by the late 1950s.[12] If one important exporting country applies controls for this purpose, other exporting countries may emulate the step to prevent the sharp increase in their sales which could otherwise result; the United States has justified its controls on steel scrap exports on precisely these grounds,[13] and numerous countries placed controls on their exports of feedgrains after the United States did so in June 1973.

2. To *reinforce domestic price controls*, which often exempt export prices and hence encourage foreign sales.[14] In 1973-74, the United States came very close to applying export quotas for this purpose in a number of industries (e.g., petrochemicals, some of which sold for three times as much abroad) but chose each time to decontrol prices instead. Sometimes the price controls to be reinforced apply to an entire sector; the European Community has recently been applying export taxes to a wide range of farm products to keep their prices from rising to the much higher levels prevailing in world trade. In the original negotiations to form the GATT, New Zealand successfully insisted on an exemption for export controls to buttress domestic price controls because it used them so widely for this purpose. As inflation remains a major problem for most countries, there will probably be increased resort to price controls; hence, there will be continued pressure to use export controls in support thereof.

3. To *improve the terms of trade of the producing country*, or at least keep them from declining, by forcing up world prices for its commodity exports. This can be done unilaterally by a single country strong enough in a given market to do so, or by a group of producers acting together, or under a commodity agreement including both producers and consumers (as in several existing agreements), for a product in which the price elasticities of world demand and supply are low enough that total revenues can be increased through export controls. Recent efforts include the limits on coffee exports by a number of producing countries, mainly in Latin America, and the taxes placed on banana exports by several Latin American countries. Similar steps are likely in a wide range of additional commodities.[15]

4. To *capture for exporting countries the scarcity rents generated by other countries' import controls*, which would otherwise accrue to importers in the countries which apply the import controls. This manifestation of the effort to boost a country's terms of trade through export controls appeared widely in the 1930s because of the growing use of import controls during that period.[16]

5. To *conserve limited resources*, especially for countries reliant on a single commodity. This may improve their terms of trade over time, and usually is based on a judgment that earnings from future production of the commodity will exceed earnings from investments made with the proceeds of current sales. This objective is usually pursued through production

cutbacks rather than export controls, however, as has been the case for several years with Kuwaiti and Libyan oil; to do it solely via export controls would require massive stockpiling and hence a heavy additional financial burden.

6. To *develop domestic processing industries* rather than exporting raw materials. Export restrictions support this process by assuring the access of domestic producers to inputs, which may at times be scarce at any price, and by reducing the costs of those producers. The controls may also enable domestic producers to achieve scales of production needed to render them efficient in world markets. For example, Brazil has restricted leather exports to permit growth of its own shoe industry and green coffee exports to boost its production of soluble coffee. A much broader use of this approach can be foreseen in the future as, for example, the oil exporting countries insist both on refining their crude and using the resulting feed-stocks to build local petrochemical industries, and the bauxite exporters insist on local alumina production. These uses of export controls can sometimes be justified by analogy to the traditional "infant industry" case for import controls. They improve the overall terms of trade of the producing country, by increasing domestic value-added and hence capturing some of the profits previously made by "downstream" countries. In addition, they bring other benefits such as increased employment.

7. To *avoid physical shortages* which might cause unemployment and unacceptable levels of economic activity. Japan stopped selling petroleum-based synthetics to other East Asian processors while it feared interruption of its own petroleum supply. A future and longer-term variant of this theme may be export controls to avoid "frittering away" the output undertaken expressly to minimize the international vulnerabiltiy of particular countries, such as the rapid expansion of the U.S. coal industry foreseen under "Project Independence."

8. For *revenue reasons*. Export duties (like import duties) were a major source of government revenue for ancient Greece and Rome, and for Britain and other major European powers until the middle of the nineteenth century. This motive is far less prevalent today, though it remains important for some developing countries.

9. To *limit the military and economic capability of other countries*. The best examples are the widespread controls applied by the noncommunist industrialized countries (especially the United States) against the communist countries through most of the postwar period.[17] Exports to belligerents are of course often rigidly controlled during wars.

10. For *foreign policy reasons*, in an effort to induce the denied consumer to change his policy. The oil embargoes against the United States, the Netherlands and a few other countries in 1973-74 were of this type. This and the previous objective are closely related; the main differences are

whether the efforts are long-term or short-term, and whether they seek to change the basic orientation of the targeted country or one specific aspect of its foreign policy. Both objectives can be promoted by using export controls both negatively and positively, by denying sales to adversaries and favoring certain countries in the allocation of short supplies; the United States used both techniques during World War II and the postwar reconstruction period, as did the Arab oil suppliers with their three categories of customers during the winter of 1973-74.

The Causes of the Renewed Outbreak of Export Controls

The renewed outbreak of export controls derives from a series of fundamental changes in the contemporary world economy. The first is the ascendance of inflation as the primary economic concern in most industrial countries. Inflation plays a central role in most of the specific rationales for export controls. Many of the export controls established in recent years sought explicitly to preserve resources for domestic use. The price controls which in turn spawn export controls are adopted to counter inflation. Primary-producing countries are encouraged, in some cases almost forced, to pursue every possible avenue to expand their own export earnings because of the increase in the cost of their imports triggered by world inflation—in essence, to index themselves,[18] in addition, these countries can be more confident of the success of such efforts in an inflationary world which—partly because of the general mistrust of paper money—has turned the buyers' markets of the past into sellers' markets for most commodities.[19] The unemployment effects of physical shortages could be more easily countered by expansionary macroeconomic policy in a less inflationary environment, and hence would be less likely to trigger export controls. Even the foreign policy leverage of export controls is enhanced by inflation, which increases the impact on the consumer of any effective denial.

In a world of "stagflation" or "slumpflation," with both high unemployment and high inflation, countries might of course seek to export both problems to each other by applying *both* export and import controls (in different sectors). And some of the reasons for adopting export controls relate very little to inflation. Primary-producing countries will always want to improve their terms of trade (and raise domestic employment) by further domestic processing, and may frequently use export quotas and/or export taxes on raw materials to that end. For example, Canada amended its Export and Import Permits Act in May 1974 explicitly to authorize export controls "to ensure that any action taken to promote the further processing in Canada of a natural resource that is produced in Canada is not rendered ineffective by reason of the unrestricted exportation of the natural re-source.'' The Canadian government made clear its intention to use such controls, if necessary, as part of Canada's overall industrial policy. Numerous other countries have instituted similar policies, formally or informally, and it is virtually certain that many more will also do so. Indeed, increased local processing is a major theme in the development strategies of primary-producing countries, and they are using their increased power in world commodity markets to pursue it.

In addition, fears of physical shortages will periodically prompt export controls to prevent unemployment. And controls motivated by foreign policy objectives need bear no relation to the business cycle. History bears out this diversity of motives: export controls were important in the early 1920s as countries tried to protect themselves against price declines stem-ming from excess supply and in the late 1930s as countries positioned themselves against the coming conflict, as well as in inflationary periods such as the Korean War and the present. Thus, export controls are likely to represent a trade policy problem whether or not inflation remains a major problem of domestic economic policy around the world, though they will be even more prevalent if inflation does persist—which is quite likely.

Several other fundamental changes in the world economy reinforce the conclusion that the problem of export controls is here to stay. Virtually every government in the world is accepting an increasing array of economic and social responsibilities. It is no longer adequate to promote full em-ployment, growth and reasonable price stability. Governments must also actively pursue such objectives as regional balance, more equitable dis-tribution of incomes and environmental quality. Thus, they are constantly seeking additional policy instruments to enable them to meet their addi-tional policy targets.

To do so, they particularly seek levers to deal with external economic events. The interpenetration of national economies has become so perva-sive that external events represent both a major threat to the achievement of internal goals and a major opportunity, if harnessed properly, to promote those internal goals. The combination of increasing governmental in-volvement in economic life and increasing international economic inter-penetration virtually assures national efforts to employ more actively the whole range of conceivable foreign economic measures.

The likelihood that export controls will be an important part of this growing arsenal of external measures is enhanced by the prevalence of inflation, as already discussed. It is also enhanced by the growing impor-tance to all countries of economic security. The cutback in Arab oil produc-tion in late 1973 shocked virtually every noncommunist country into realiz-ing how dependent it had become on events outside its borders. But the tendency toward seeking economic security was already well underway, as a result of such trends as the achievement of high income levels (which enable countries to afford the cost of buying more economic security and makes it worth more to them, relative to efficiency, than in the past because added marginal income becomes less important) and the growing role of multinational enterprises (which threaten the decision-making autonomy of the governments of both host and home countries). Export controls are likely to proliferate in such an environment as consuming countries seek to promote their own security through increased domestic production (even at higher prices, à la Project Independence), the output of which they will not want to "fritter away" through exports, and as suppliers realize that their leverage is enhanced by consumer concerns to avoid disruption.

The final structural change which promotes export controls is the repoliticization of world economics. Throughout the first postwar generation, international economic policies were largely subordinated to broad security considerations. A "two-track" system existed under which "high politics" (mainly security matters) usually dominated "low politics" (mainly economic matters), and these "low politics" were largely handled apolitically within a structure created to support the security objectives of the United States, which dominated the system. Trade concessions were exchanged for trade concessions, not for political favors, and retaliation against violations of the trade rules were limited to the trade area.[20] To be sure, national power played a major role in constructing this system itself and underlay the resolution of specific disputes; but most economic problems were solved within the existing institutional framework and without any overt brandishing of economic carrots and sticks, and economic and political power were seldom used to pursue objectives in the other domain.

Now, however, the rules and machinery which permitted such depoliticization of economics have broken down. The U.S. economic offensive of August-December 1971, and the Arab oil offensive of October 1973-March 1974, illustrate the two aspects of this change: the increased use of raw economic power to pursue economic objectives, and the increased use of economic power to pursue security objectives.

The U.S. actions signaled the final collapse of the postwar system of international economic rules and institutions, centered on the IMF and GATT. Yet, it was this system which had provided the channels for settling international economic disputes through largely nonpolitical means. Its demise virtually assures the repoliticization of economic disputes. We can expect continued and even accelerated use of naked economic power, particularly from those whose economic power is rising rapidly, as countries seek to achieve their economic objectives in a world largely devoid of effective rules and institutional barriers thereto.

The Arab actions directly repudiated the bifurcation of the past by linking security and economic issues tightly and pervasively. Underlying this breakdown of the previous "two-track" system, which had already begun well before the Arab measures, are three fundamental factors: the increasing importance of international economic relationships to virtually all countries, which increases their vulnerability to the economic actions of others; the end of the Cold War, which had held a security blanket over most economic disputes in the interest of avoiding disruption of the alliance relationships which were deemed by virtually all countries as of overriding importance; and the development of massive economic power in the hands of countries which have little military power, and hence can only pursue their security objectives effectively by linking the two issue-areas.[21] Hence, we can foresee continued, and perhaps even accelerated, use of economic measures for foreign policy reasons, particularly by countries whose major international leverage derives primarily from their economic capabilities.

For a wide variety of deep-seated reasons, national use of export controls is thus likely to remain frequent.[21a] Hence, international action should be undertaken to do something about them if they seem likely to cause international problems.

The Economics of Export Controls

Are they likely to do so? Export controls represent an additional policy instrument, which governments are forever seeking as they try to realize an increasing variety of economic targets. But their effectiveness in achieving their different objectives is a complex matter.

The most straightforward objective, as we have seen, is to limit domestic inflation by placing quantitative restrictions (including total embargoes) on foreign sales of a particular commodity or group of commodities. This will obviously reduce the price of the commodity itself. But if export earnings dip as a result of the quotas, and if the country involved has a flexible exchange rate, its currency will depreciate (or appreciate less). This will *add* to the inflationary pressures it faces. The net impact of the export controls on the country's rate of inflation depends *inter alia* on the price elasticity of foreign demand for the controlled commodity (which determines the change in the controlling country's export receipts) and the relative weights of the commodity in the country's (a) overall price index and (b) total exports.

In many cases, the price elasticity of foreign demand for the commodity may be sufficiently low that most foreigners will pay the higher price triggered by the cutback in available supplies. The value of export receipts for the commodity will then not decline; it may even rise and reinforce the anti-inflationary effect of the export control itself. But this result obviously could not occur for a total embargo; the smaller the cutback in the volume of sales, in fact, the more likely is such an outcome.

In addition, price elasticities of demand—and price elasticities of supply of the same commodity and of potential substitutes for it—are usually lower in the short run than in the longer run; the shorter the duration of the export controls, the less likely that the controlling country will suffer a decline in its total export receipts.[22] Finally, the greater the share of the world market for the commodity held by a country (or group of countries) controlling exports, the less likely it is to suffer a decline in total export revenues. The export controls most likely to avoid reductions in export earnings, and hence most likely to be undertaken, are thus those exercised (a) for a limited period (b) in a commodity with few substitutes (c) by a country or group of countries which largely dominate the world market —like the United States for soybeans, and OPEC for petroleum.[23]

Of course, export controls might be pursued even if the criteria necessary to avoid losses of total export revenues were not met: to avoid physical shortages leading to unemployment, to reinforce domestic price controls, to conserve resources, or for national security or foreign policy reasons. But the use of export controls for these purposes will become increasingly expensive over time if the criteria are not met, and export earnings decline as a result of the controls. Indeed, countries began to stop using export taxes as a major source of government revenue when they became aware of the reduction in total sales which usually resulted, and most export taxes now used for revenue purposes are quite small as a result.

When the criteria are met, a country can raise its total export revenues through export controls. Indeed, this is often the explicit objective of such policies. However, it is not the end of the story. If the country involved has a flexible exchange rate, its currency will appreciate as a result of the increase in export earnings. Hence, demand for its other exports will decline and its own demand for imports will increase, except in the unusual case where the price elasticities of both demand and supply are quite low for most of them as well.

If a country were running at full capacity and inflation were its overwhelming policy problem, it would presumably welcome this exchange-rate appreciation as reinforcing the anti-inflationary effect of the export controls themselves. Through more sophisticated reasoning, it might welcome the gain in its real national welfare deriving from the appreciation of its exchange rate even if its trade balance remained unchanged at the new equilibrium level.

However, export- and import-competing industries adversely affected by the exchange-rate appreciation stemming from export controls for a single sector can usually be expected to object strenuously to the policy. This consideration reinforces the likelihood that most uses of export con-

trols will be both short-lived and undertaken in highly inflationary conditions when their contribution to the "national interest" can be most
strongly defended. It also suggests that such controls will most likely be
used by countries heavily dependent on the commodity involved, and thus
relatively unconcerned about the repercussions on the rest of their
economies, and countries whose exchange rates are not floating freely, so
they can accumulate reserves with their increased earnings from the controlled commodity rather than see their currencies appreciate.[24] The oil
countries and most other countries which are mainly primary producers
meet both of these criteria. The United States, the primary-producing
countries of Western Europe and Canada do not, because of their more
diversified economies and floating exchange rates.

A different approach is required to analyze the economic effects of
export controls adopted to promote the development of domestic processing industries. If processing can be carried out as efficiently in the
primary-producing country as abroad, there need be no concern about
elasticities and market shares for the product itself since there will be no
change in the final price of the processed commodity. The producing
country will gain jobs, tax revenues and foreign exchange earnings in the
industry involved with no fear of losing sales of the product in question.
There may not even be any loss to the private firms involved, at least over
the longer run, if they are able to carry out the change in the locus of
processing without idling plants previously used. (The losses would accrue
to the workers, treasury and balance of payments of the country which had
previously been the site of the processing.) Such situations may well exist
in practice; firms have often chosen to process in countries other than the
source of the raw material because they wanted to minimize their foreign
exposure in general—preferring to invest as much as possible at home
—and their vulnerability to actions by the country owning the raw material
in particular.

Even in this case, however, the primary-producing country will experience an appreciation in its exchange rate—if its rate is flexible—due to its
added export earnings. Hence, jobs and exports will be threatened in other
industries, as outlined above. Whether the country wants the increase in
processing thus depends on whether it wants changes in its economic
structure. Increased processing usually means more jobs and more technological spinoff. On the other hand, it requires more energy and may
increase pollution. A country's decision on using export controls to promote domestic processing has to take account of all these considerations
—even when the product can be processed as economically at home as
abroad.

There are many cases, however, where current industry patterns are
quite rational in economic terms. Thus, a country which insists on more

processing risks some loss in its overall market position, because of its higher costs. It would then have to consider the price elasticities of demand and supply and its market share, to assess the likely impact on its total revenues, along with the potential gains (jobs, tax receipts, increased value-added) from the increased processing.

Of course, it is always possible that domestic processing will *become* efficient after a time even if it is not as efficient as foreign processing at present. The promotion of such processing through controls on the export of inputs can then be justified on traditional "infant industry" grounds.

In addition, domestic processing has frequently been deterred by high effective tariffs on the processed products—due to a low or zero duty on the raw material itself, coupled with a substantial duty on the processed product—in the consuming countries. In such cases, export controls may actually promote world efficiency. They may even get the consuming countries to lower or eliminate their duties on the processed product, so that market forces will become freer to determine the proper location of the different parts of the industry.

This analysis suggests that the economics of export controls place some important limits on their effective use, at least for some countries for some commodities over prolonged periods of time. Nevertheless, there are many cases where they can serve important national objectives. And countries may often fail to recognize the limitations cited here, and hence apply export controls even when they are in fact not likely to achieve what is intended. When export controls are applied, their effect is to export domestic inflation (or unemployment) to another country by limiting its supplies of the controlled product, or at least to raise fears of such a result.

The Problems Raised by Export Controls

Hence, every country affected by the export controls of others must view them as a threat to its own national objectives, at the same time it recognizes that the ability to employ such controls presents it with a new policy instrument. Even those countries not directly affected by another country's particular export controls will recognize that other export controls by the same or another country, which might be encouraged as a result, would hurt them. The net judgment of any country about the desirability of a world open to export controls, as compared with a world in which their use is restrained or even barred, will thus derive from a complex of considerations.

In the first instance, national positions may derive from countries' assessments of their net positions with regard to potentially controllable products—those which they buy, and those which they sell. Export controls are applied most frequently to primary products, and such products best meet the conditions just outlined under which the net effects of export controls are most likely to be beneficial to the controlling country. So, countries will first look to their net positions in primary products in assessing their attitude toward export controls. On this consideration, one can distinguish three sets of countries:

1. Heavy net importers of both agricultural products and industrial raw materials, such as Japan and most countries in Western Europe. These countries would presumably like tight restraints on export controls, and it was at European initiative that a ban on new export controls was included in the one-year "standstill agreement" announced by the OECD countries in June 1974 to avoid destructive national responses to the energy crisis.[25]

2. Large net exporters of both agricultural products and raw materials, such as Canada, Australia and a number of resource-rich developing countries. These countries might seek to avoid international constraints on national action to control exports. Indeed, many of them have already applied some export controls, and Canada and Australia strongly resisted the restriction on export controls included in the OECD "standstill agreement."

3. Countries which are net exporters of farm products and net importers of raw materials, or vice versa, such as the United States and Brazil. The intermediate position of these countries can lead to an ambivalent attitude toward international regulation of export controls. The United States itself has applied such controls in several cases, but the government has resisted strong internal pressures to do so in several important cases (e.g., wheat and cotton) and opposed export controls adopted by others.

Once countries begin to think seriously about the long-term implications of a world free for the application of export controls, however, their positions will be determined by far more complex considerations than their net commodity position.

First, many long-run economic interests of commodity-exporting countries themselves will be *hurt* by export controls. Actual use of such controls triggers reductions in demand for the product by consuming countries, and production of substitutes for the item controlled in both the importing country itself (as in oil) and in other exporting countries (as in soybeans). Even the fear of future controls can trigger such responses, by driving up the prices of future contracts and inspiring policy efforts in consuming countries to reduce their future vulnerability. The resulting loss of sales, in addition to its obvious effect on jobs and output, will weaken the controlling country's exchange rate over the long run, adding to its inflationary pressures, even if there is no such effect in the short run. The major beneficiaries of the U.S. export controls on soybeans, since Japan was willing to sign long-term contracts worth $1 billion to assure itself of alternative sources. And OPEC has sharply accelerated the search for new oil, alternative sources of energy and means to conserve energy demand by (a) demonstrating that its members are unreliable suppliers and (b) pushing prices up so far so fast.

Second, even countries which are net exporters of commodities rely on imports for a large number of key products. This is particularly true for the smaller primary producers, such as Canada and Australia. Indeed, the United States is in a stronger position than most other countries on this self-sufficiency criterion because it produces a wider range of its primary needs and can develop substitutes for some of those it does not now produce. But even the United States is dependent on imports for a number of key products, notably but going well beyond oil. So, even those countries most likely to profit by applying export controls can be hurt by the application of export controls by other countries.

Third, the issue cannot be limited to primary products. Exports of some intermediate inputs and finished goods—for example, fertilizers and steel products—have already been controlled. And there has been intense political pressure in the United States for similar action on many more manufactured products, such as petrochemicals. It is true that substitute suppliers are usually easier to find for manufactures, but the costs to consumers could still be very high in the short run. In this area, of course, the most industrialized countries are in far stronger positions than countries (including Canada and Australia) which sell mainly primary products.

Fourth, each nation must consider the broad international ramifications of a world open to export controls. Export controls for a primary product spawn export controls on the products processed from it. They spawn defensive export controls by other suppliers of the same product, seeking to protect themselves from the demand diverted to them by the initial controls. They spawn export controls on other products, as other countries observe the success of the first country and seek to recoup the costs thereof to their own positions. This process ratchets world inflation further upward.

In addition, a world open to export controls further increases the likelihood of the formation of producer-country cartels, by implicitly sanctioning one of their chief policy tools. At the same time, it could trigger unilateral retaliation; the support in the United States for the Mondale amendments, whose primary focus is to promote new international rules to limit export controls but which would also authorize the President to retaliate against such steps, was motivated largely by resentment against OPEC and desires to avoid being "held up" by other commodity sellers.

Furthermore, export controls—far more than import controls—can in some circumstances produce results repugnant to our humanitarian instincts. The most obvious case is controls on food sales, which can lead to severe malnutrition and even starvation if imposed when world food supplies are tight—which is precisely when they are most likely to be imposed. There is a real risk of such occurrences in a world free for export controls, because food shortages appear to be a real possibility[26] and domestic political pressures, at least in the United States, suggest that any food made available for export under a regime of controls would go to cash customers rather than the neediest countries, which might not be able to pay for them immediately (if ever).

Finally, a proliferation of export controls could lead to new international monetary problems. The maintenance of import controls by some countries in the past (e.g., Japan) helped bring them large balance-of-payments surpluses, which placed increasing pressure on the deficit countries (especially the United States and United Kingdom) and the monetary system itself. Successful export controls could also help produce payments surpluses, at least temporarily, again adding to the pressures on deficit countries and the entire monetary system—as the OPEC actions have done so dramatically through their buildup of "petrodollars."

In short, widespread resort to export controls could trigger the same cycle of emulation and retaliation which resulted from the widespread resort to import controls in the 1930s—when there were no international rules or institutional arrangements to govern that type of commercial policy. World inflation could thus spiral upward, as world depression once spiraled downward. International political tension could rise sharply, both due to the cycle of emulation and retaliation itself and because consuming countries will scramble increasingly for bilateral deals with particular suppliers—intensifying suspicions and animosities among the consuming countries and emboldening the producing countries to move even further—in the absence of new multilateral rules to govern export controls.

Yet, there is a real risk that countries will continue to adopt new export controls, as they have been doing rapidly in recent years (and as they did in some previous periods). Some may simply not understand the risks of so doing, as outlined here. Some may think they can "get away with it," avoiding retaliation or other adverse repercussions because they are small or because they are so large that others will fear to offend them. Some will put overwhelming priority on meeting immediate policy problems, even when they recognize the long-run costs of the action. The same kinds of problems have always applied to import controls, but it took the disastrous experience of the 1930s to develop a meaningful consensus that they were wrong and some countries continue to apply them to this day.

There is thus a strong case for a new international framework to deal with export controls. We turn now to some possibilities for such rules and arrangements.

124

New Rules to Govern Export Controls

Objectives

Any new rules to govern export controls would aim fundamentally to combat world inflation, enhance the economic security of all nations, avoid the politicization of this particular economic issue, and minimize this particular source of friction among nations. Like those existing GATT rules which seek to govern the use of import controls, a set of rules on export controls would have four immediate goals:

1. To deter producing countries from erecting export controls except in clearly defined and justified circumstances.

2. To reinforce that deterrent by providing a basis for concerted response by the world trading community.

3. To limit the scope and duration of those controls which are actually applied.

4. To provide an international framework into which disputes triggered by export controls can be channeled when they are actually applied, to reduce the likelihood of unilateral reactions and emulation/retaliation cycles.

Previous Efforts

The concept of international rules governing access to supplies goes back at least to Woodrow Wilson's Fourteen Points, one of which was officially interpreted to "contemplate fair and equitable understanding as to the distribution of raw materials."[27] The Gini Report to the League of Nations in 1921, which was endorsed by the League's Provisional Economic and Financial Committee, called for intervention by the League to place states "as it were, at the bar" when they adopted restrictive export duties; the Committee added that it was "undesirable particularly [that such measures] be so prolonged or altered as to change their character from being acts of precaution or defence to degenerate into measures of economic aggression." The World Economic Conference of 1927 recommended that exports of raw materials should not be "unduly burdened" by export duties, that such duties should not place processing countries "in a position of unfair inferiority," and that such duties "should never discriminate between different foreign destinations."[28]

Twenty-nine countries signed the draft Convention on Import and Export Prohibitions and Restrictions which emerged from the 1927 conference, and two agreements abolishing export prohibitions on specific products[29] went into effect among eighteen countries in 1929. The Convention itself was actually brought into force for seven countries, including the United States and United Kingdom, but all withdrew by 1934.

The final interwar effort was undertaken by the Raw Materials Committee of the League in 1937, on the basis of whose recommendations the Economic Committee proposed a series of principles which would have banned "export prohibition or restriction" except where provided for under an *international* agreement. (This same principle was the basis for the chapter on commodity agreements in the charter of the International Trade Organization, ITO.) Even then, such controls should "be administered in such a way as to provide consumers with adequate supplies of the regulated material" and "to prevent, so far as possible, the price of the regulated material from rising to an excessive height . . . ."[30] The official U.S. view was that "action in this field should be as far-reaching and effective as proves to be possible."

In the Atlantic Charter signed in August 1941, Roosevelt and Churchill maintained the interwar focus on access to supplies by proclaiming that one of the key postwar aims was "access, on equal terms, to the trade and to the raw materials of the world." And, as already noted, Article XI of the GATT explicitly rules out export quotas as well as import quotas. Indeed, the drafters of GATT considered inserting a complete prohibition on export restrictions, and the United States supported that approach. Furthermore, both the European Economic Community (EEC) and the European Free Trade Arrangement (EFTA) agreements provide for a general elimination of export restrictions.[31] So, there has also been postwar interest in, and some movement toward, international regulation of export controls.

In practice, however, the GATT and other global economic institutions have been totally ineffective in dealing with the issue. The GATT permits export taxes, and increases therein unless existing taxes are explicitly bound.[32] And there are numerous exceptions to the ban on export quotas. Such controls are permitted:

"To prevent or relieve critical shortages of foodstuffs or other products essential to the exporting contracting party."

To conserve "exhaustible natural resources if such measures are made effective in conjunction with restrictions on domestic production or consumption."

In conjunction with price controls on raw materials.

For national security purposes.

Thus, many of the most important export controls adopted in recent years might well have been justifiable under the GATT rules. The United States would have argued that its controls on soybean exports were needed "to prevent critical shortages." The Arab members of GATT would have argued that their controls on oil were "necessary for the protection of their essential security interests." Canada would have had no need to justify the increase in its export tax on oil, nor the several Latin American countries their imposition on export taxes on bananas. The present GATT rules thus provide so many "outs," permitting export quotas and taxes, that they are virtually useless; it appears impossible to improve the situation simply by implementing the existing articles more faithfully.[33] And GATT members are not even required to notify the organization of their use of export controls, and consult other countries about them.

The only serious GATT effort to implement its rules on export controls came in 1950.[34] The Contracting Parties adopted a report of a working party on the subject, which concluded that four types of export restrictions "appeared to fall outside the exceptions provided in these Articles [of the GATT itself]" and hence were illegal:

1. Those used to get other countries to relax their import restrictions.
2. Those used to get other countries to relax their export restrictions "or otherwise to obtain an advantage in the procurement from another contracting party of such commodities."
3. Those used to "protect or promote a domestic fabricating industry."
4. Those used "to avoid price competition among exporters."

On this interpretation, three types of export controls recently used or contemplated would be illegal. The second point would seem to rule out any retaliatory export restrictions (even by those hurt by export controls permitted by the rules). The third point would ban export controls used to develop or support domestic processing. (The first point reinforces this prohibition, by barring such controls even when processing is artificially shifted downstream by high effective duties in importing countries.) The fourth point could apply to OPEC and all other commodity cartels. In addition, the OPEC embargoes on the United States and several other countries clearly violated the most-favored-nation cornerstone of the GATT system. Nevertheless, the GATT has done nothing to deal with any of these problems—nor any of the other problems raised by export controls.

Thus, the existing GATT framework achieves none of the four objectives stated at the outset of this chapter, which should be pursued by any international rules and institutional arrangements to govern export controls. Far-reaching new international agreements would be necessary to fill this vacuum completely. Of course, less ambitious objectives could be served by more modest agreements. The following discussion of what should be done will start with those points which seem most central, and hence required even in a minimal agreement. It will then proceed toward those points which would be needed to round out a comprehensive scheme, and which might evolve over time if they could not all be agreed at the outset. Most of the rules regarding export controls are analogous to those which now exist regarding import controls, or are being proposed to modify the present arrangements in that area.[35]

New Rules: Some Tentative Proposals

1. The minimum requirement is for *international notification of, and consultation on, the imposition of any new export controls*. There is now no such requirement, and the shock effects of export controls—and reactions thereto—are greatly intensified as a result. The creation of formal diplomatic procedures, to provide at least a minimum of prior notification, would help defuse reactions. The effect would be still greater if affected countries were given a chance to record their views before the action was implemented. And the compilation of export control practices by a single center, and their periodic publication, would highlight the increased tendencies to use such controls and hence their potential importance.

Even these minimum steps would provide some deterrence to unjustified export controls. They would expose such actions to international view and reaction. If they forced delays in implementation, they would provide time for countervailing forces to develop. And their very existence would strengthen the position of opponents of such measures (both in and out of governments) within individual countries. All three developments would improve the probability that controls would only be applied when truly needed.

At the same time, there is a risk that advance consultations on the application of export controls would increase public awareness of the possibility and trigger speculative purchases of the commodity being discussed, which might intensify the problem and *increase* the likelihood that controls would be applied. However, close observers of most commodity markets keep well abreast of government thinking anyway and would probably know when export controls were being contemplated. And this problem is no different than the anticipation effects generated by international consultations on changes in exchange rates, import controls and limitations on capital flows—all of which are required under long-standing international agreements. As in these cases, markets could be closed while the consultations proceed, with tight time limits imposed on the process, or any measures actually implemented could be made effective from the date they were first *proposed* (instead of the date on which final *agreement* was reached). And if countries began to adhere faithfully to such consultation requirements, the absence of consultations in particular cases might well reduce speculation from levels that would otherwise develop.

In addition, efforts could be made to develop international understandings on a product well in advance of any need for actually controlling its export. This would be like the standby agreements which potential borrowers at the International Monetary Fund negotiate well in advance of any actual need to draw the money (which are in fact often never activated). Such advance discussions would also help prod national governments to improve their own efforts to forecast commodity problems and develop plans to head them off, instead of letting themselves be caught off-guard and hence reacting defensively and often ineffectively or even destructively.

One could go further than notification and consultation on *new* controls by requiring that all *existing* export controls also be notified and brought into conformity with whatever new rules were agreed, as is required under the new Arrangement Regarding International Trade in Textiles. This would avoid "rewarding" countries for having moved before the rules were set up, and would deter the imposition of controls while the rules were being negotiated. But it should not be pushed so far as to risk breaking up the negotiations, since the major objective is to avoid new problems in the future rather than to undo controls imposed in the past.

2. A second step would be to subject to *multilateral surveillance* any proposals for new export controls, and the way in which any such controls put in place were actually administered. This could be done by the regular GATT machinery.[36] Or it could be done by a committee devoted solely to export controls, like the committee newly created solely to monitor restraints on textile trade. The usual questions would arise concerning the composition of the surveillance committee, its degree of independence from national governments, the authority of its findings, and other matters. Primary-producing countries should participate actively in such a committee, in view of its potentially major impact on them both as exporters and importers.[37]

3. Such surveillance could be based solely on *ad hoc* judgments concerning individual restrictions as they were adopted. It is much more likely, however, that creation of a surveillance committee would have to be accompanied by an agreement which *defined the conditions permitting export controls*.

It is both unnecessary and politically unrealistic to seek to bar all export controls. Indeed, some may be justifiable economically and acceptable politically. However, it is extremely hard to know where to seek to draw the line. Such controls are adopted for a broad range of reasons, as we have seen. In a given situation, the motivation for a move may be unclear—and may be obfuscated rather than clarified by the official statements of the government taking it. So, the issue of who interprets the motives of export controls, like the issue of who decides whether "injury" exists sufficient to justify import controls under Article XIX of the GATT, must be considered along with formulation of the principles themselves. The multilateral surveillance group just proposed should be the primary organ.

4. There will have to be a *national security exception to any limits to export controls*. However, one principle widely espoused of late, at least in the industrialized countries, is that export controls should not be applied for foreign policy purposes. And United Nations Resolution 2625 (XXV) of the 1970 General Assembly, entitled "Declaration of Principles of International Law Concerning Friendly Relations Among States in Accordance With the Charter of the United Nations," states that "no state may use or encourage the use of economic, political or any other type of measures to coerce another state in order to obtain from it the subordination of the exercise of its sovereign rights and to secure from it advantages of any kind."[38]

But export controls have been applied throughout the postwar period by the United States and its allies (to lesser extents) explicitly to try to limit the military and economic capabilities of the communist countries. And the Arab oil producers would certainly justify their production cutbacks and embargoes of 1973-74 as the only way they could affect the Middle East negotiations, which they regarded as central to their security.

A deep philosophical issue underlies the question whether the political use of export controls (or other types of economic actions) should be banned by international law. All previous international economic rules have included an exception for national security purposes, or the equivalent. And even bans on the use of economic controls for economic purposes have represented either self-denying ordinances by countries which were powerful *both* militarily and economically, and which exempted from many of their requirements those countries which were weak both militarily and economically, or obligations imposed by the strong (in both senses) on the weak (in both senses). The GATT itself included both elements: self-denial by a powerful United States (and, to a lesser extent, United Kingdom), imposition by the United States on the weakest members, and some of both for most of the Western Europeans.

Now, however, the fundamental changes outlined earlier in this paper are creating a class of countries which are economically strong though, at least for a while, militarily still weak.[39] This asymmetry of power raises fundamental issues. Why should the economically strong deny themselves the use of their only lever of world power, when it is obvious that the militarily strong will not refrain from using military force when they deem it necessary to pursue their national interests? Even if one were to grant that economic power can be used to pursue economic objectives, why should it be barred from the political arena when the principle of comparative bargaining advantage clearly suggests using whatever elements of strength maximize a country's overall position—especially since trade wars, bad as they are, are certainly preferable to real wars?

These problems have already arisen in the relations between the United States, on the one hand, and Western Europe and Japan, on the other. Economic power has increasingly provided a source of comparative advantage for the latter, and the asymmetry between their economic and military power has grown steadily. These developments have contributed importantly to the repoliticization of international economic relations, as described in the first section of this chapter, as Europe sought political ends through its economic power and the United States sought economic ends through its political power. Nevertheless, the asymmetries among these countries are far less than among the countries with new "commodity power" and other economic leverage but little military power, on the one hand,[40] and the military powers which are increasingly reliant on them in the economic area, on the other.[41]

There are two types of responses to these asymmetries: the primary producers can be granted more political power, on the basis of their increased economic power, or the consumers can seek to weaken the economic power of the producers. The rules on export controls envisaged here would pursue both paths, by giving the producers a far greater role than ever before in international economic decision making and by providing a basis for concerted responses to this particular use of their power by the consuming countries.

But should, and can, the political use of export controls be banned in any new set of international rules? It may turn out that unbridled use of "commodity power" for political, or even economic, purposes will prove so costly for all countries that such a system of restraints on national action will be accepted as widely in this area as it is with regard to military force, import controls and competitive devaluations. At this point in time, however, there are at least three barriers to banning the use of economic measures, such as export controls, for political purposes. First, for the reasons just cited, consuming countries are uncertain about the legitimacy of moving decisively against such steps by producing countries, who after all are simply employing the major (or sole) lever of international power available to them. Second, consuming countries may want to keep open the possibility for unilateral actions of their own—especially if, like the United States, they are in the intermediate position of exporting as well as importing large quantities of primary products. Third, the new wielders of commodity power are unlikely to quickly give up their newly found clout. So there is probably little chance of adopting any firm rule in this area.

It must always be remembered that trade or other international economic rules cannot be used mechanically to deal with issues of high politics. Efforts to do so usually destroy the rules rather than solve the political problem; such destruction of the rules will in turn undermine the economic system and, hence, in fact intensify political problems. Indeed, it is almost ludicrous to imagine trying to use the GATT to stop the Arabs' use of the "oil weapon" in the Middle East conflict.

Any effort to develop new rules to govern export controls should thus not be based primarily on hopes of "stopping OPEC," in the sense of avoiding Arab efforts to use oil for political reasons. Rather they should be based on trying to deal more effectively with the whole range of *economic* problems triggered by export controls—including OPEC efforts to raise oil prices through this device—with their *indirect* spillover into politics. Success in this effort, albeit more limited, would represent a major accomplishment. And the use of export controls for "national security" purposes should be subjected to the notification, consultation and surveillance procedures to avoid egregious abuses.[42]

5. The economic criteria would not, however, be much easier to handle than the "political" criteria. The objective is to prevent countries from trying to export their inflation (or other problems) to others. At the same time, it is widely accepted that sovereign states have first call on their own resources. Both principles would be consistent with a rule that *export controls would be allowed only when the failure to adopt them will result in "serious injury or the threat thereof" to the economy of the country involved*.

This approach is similar to the injury test for import controls, except that the latter permits the imposition of barriers when imports "cause or threaten serious injury" to an individual industry rather than an overall economy. The broader criterion is proposed for export controls because the primary goal of the new rules is to halt efforts to export inflation, whose harmful effect is on an entire economy rather than differentially on a single segment of it. Indeed, an individual industry may benefit from a shortage in its supply of inputs, by applying its usual percentage markup to the higher costs which it experiences, while the economy as a whole loses. So, the injury test should apply to the overall economic impact of not imposing export controls, except in cases where physical shortages threaten severe unemployment in particular industries if raw materials or intermediate inputs are exported.

The proposed test would be hard to apply in cases where the controls were proposed to avoid domestic price increases, even when actual inflation was observable, because of the difficulty in judging (a) the causal impact of the exports of the commodity in question and (b) because of the feedback effects of the export controls on the country's exchange rate.

However, such a test of "export injury" would be no harder to apply than the traditional test of "import injury" in assessing whether import flows have caused unemployment.[43] In both cases, economic phenomena—price rises and unemployment—can be observed. But, in both, analytical judgments must be made on the causal impact of foreign trade—and, in practice, policy judgments must be made of the overall impact on international relations of accepting or rejecting a proposal by an individual country to apply a certain export control.[44]

In the case of a "threat" of either inflation or unemployment, the difficulties of analysis are of course compounded by the uncertainties of forecasting the flow of both trade and the usual host of domestic economic variables. This would be an important issue, because countries might frequently seek to justify export controls aimed at boosting their terms of trade, or developing domestic processing capacity, by arguing that they would suffer from increased inflation or unemployment (or both) if they did not do so.

Detailed rules thus appear neither more nor less feasible to govern export than import controls. In both cases, national and international judgments have to be made on individual proposals for action within a broad framework of agreed principles. Case law would develop over time, and help provide the predictability which helps decision making in both governments and private sectors.

6. This approach would place heavy emphasis on procedures, both within each country and at the international level, to assure that all viewpoints were carefully considered. As with import penetration, however, there might be times when export surges threaten "market disruption" and call for speedier action. Indeed, the disruptive effect of the Soviet wheat deal on U.S. inflation was probably far greater than the disruptive effect of Japanese textile imports on U.S. unemployment. So, there should probably be a *market disruption clause* under which governments could short-circuit the usual rules and procedures. They should be required to justify the action subsequently under the injury test, however, and be subject to the standard limitations on duration to be discussed shortly. It need not be feared that such a clause would obviate the importance of the general requirement for advance consultation, because export controls to promote domestic processing or to improve terms of trade could seldom, if ever, be justified as a response to "market disruption."

7. *Export controls should be permitted for "infant industry" purposes*, in clearly defined circumstances, to protect the supply (and perhaps the price) of inputs to developing processing industries which can be expected to become competitive over time. "Infant industry" protection via import controls has traditionally been accepted as one of the few cases where

deviations from free trade can be justified on economic grounds. It is therefore curious that the GATT has no explicit exception for tariffs or import quotas on these grounds. The absence of such rules means that there is no precise analogue in the existing GATT arrangements to the exception proposed here for export controls.

This exception should apply automatically in cases where it can be determined that processing of a commodity is shifted "downstream" artificially by high effective duties (or other import barriers) in a consuming country. In other cases, judgments would have to be made about (a) the long-run viability of the "infant industry" without the protection of export controls, and (b) whether export controls are needed to help it through infancy.

8. Having decided when to permit export controls, the next step is to decide what type of controls should apply. Should the *new rules differentiate between quantitative export controls and export taxes*?[45] As noted at the outset, both are being used by primary producers to the same end. Theoretically, they can be made to have identical effects on trade flows.

Present GATT rules permit export taxes (and import tariffs) while, in principle, prohibiting quantitative restrictions (on both exports and imports). Economists generally favor market-oriented controls when controls are needed at all, to minimize distortions.[46] Taxes are easier and less costly to administer, and there is less likely to be pressure to retain them from a bureaucratic apparatus with vested interests. The proceeds of export taxes usually accrue to the general government budgets of the exporting countries, which in principle is preferable to letting windfall benefits accrue to private firms or government monopolies, as generally occurs under quantitative controls. And discouraging quotas would *ipso facto* have the desirable effect of discouraging total embargoes.

For these reasons, the traditional preference for taxes over quotas, when controls can be justified at all, appears to hold for exports as well as imports. However, the Constitution of the United States bars the use of export taxes by that country.[47] In addition, quotas may be the only effective way to check exports quickly and with some degree of predictability in several of the circumstances where controls may be justifiable. So, it would be impossible to ban export quotas altogether. But countries applying quotas should have to fulfill the extra obligation of justifying the use of that particular device instead of an export tax.

9. A far more complex question is *whether to try to cover domestic policy measures which have effects identical to export controls*. Countries can limit foreign access to their supplies by cutting production, as the oil countries have done, or boost their terms of trade by raising taxes on domestic output, as several bauxite countries have done. Even if countries

agreed to strict limits on export controls, they could often achieve the same purposes through such "domestic" measures.

The GATT does deal with such possibilities on the import side. It explicitly rules out taxation and government regulations which discriminate against imports relative to domestic production. Such "national treatment" was regarded by the United States, during the negotiation of the GATT, as one of the "indispensable minimum of subjects" which must be encompassed in any meaningful trade agreement.[48] However, exports are explicitly exempted from the "national treatment" requirements of the GATT.

The logic of preventing evasion of rules governing external policies through the use of internal policies is compelling. Indeed, the Jamaican increase in taxes and royalties on bauxite output is precisely equivalent to an export tax, since all Jamaican bauxite is exported. At the same time, there is widespread acceptance of the principle that sovereign nations have first call on the use of their natural resources. This issue would therefore be one of the toughest to negotiate in developing any new set of rules. Its inclusion would be highly desirable, but insistence upon it should not be permitted to block all agreement since agreement on rules limited to export controls would still represent major progress over the status quo.

10. Any use of export controls should be *strictly limited in time and/or tied to domestic adjustment measures*. At least two classes of export controls might be envisaged. One class would be strictly temporary. It would include controls justified by "market disruption," usually due to a sharp jump in foreign demand. And it would include controls fostered by a domestic crop failure, reparable incapacity at a particular plant or plants, or some other presumably temporary phenomenon. Standard time limits might be set on all controls of this class, to avoid abuses, or might be different in each case as agreed by the surveillance body depending on the nature of the problem.

The second class of controls would be of longer duration, and stem from more fundamental imbalances. As a result, they should be permitted only if the controlling country agrees to undertake domestic measures which the international surveillance body judges to be adequate to assure that the controls can in fact be phased out over a period of years (again, either a fixed number or set case-by-case). If the United States had wanted to prolong its controls on soybean exports and been able to justify them at all under the injury test, for example, it could probably have satisfied such an adjustment requirement by its decision to increase sharply its production acreage for succeeding crop years. Likewise, subjecting export controls employed to reinforce domestic price controls to such a requirement would have the desirable effect of prompting the country involved to focus clearly on the need for a clear schedule to terminate the price controls, and to use the time which they bought to boost domestic output of the controlled products.

The "infant industry" controls for promoting domestic processing industries would also have to be phased out over time. Their time limit could be set equal to the second class just discussed, set case-by-case, or subject to a fixed but separate (presumably longer) duration than applied to either of the other classes.

Their remains the issue of truly long-term controls, where there is no possibility of "real adjustment" in view of physical shortages and/or the judgment of the country involved that such a policy will maximize the return from its resources over time. However, such policies are much more likely to be implemented (as for oil in Kuwait and Libya) by production limitations rather than export controls; otherwise, massive stockpiling would be required. Thus, this issue would almost certainly have to be treated under commodity arrangements rather than by the new trade rules per se.[49]

11. This possibility, however, highlights the issue of *"reverse dumping."* A producing country (or group of countries) might restrict supply for some time, either through production or export controls, and then cut prices sharply—by increasing production and exports—to retain its market share when the substitutes triggered by the earlier price hikes were about to enter the market. This is the reverse of traditional dumping, where an exporter sells cheap to bankrupt competitors in the importing country and then raises prices drastically after establishing his monopoly position. It is a very real issue, and is one major reason why many U.S. companies are reluctant to invest heavily in domestic coal and other substitutes for imported oil unless the U.S. government assures them a floor price against the possibility that the oil producers will undercut them after their investments have been made. As with dumping itself, neutralization of such practices by the governments of countries injured by them should be an integral part of any new rules governing export controls—and the desirability of deterring such actions further enhances the desirability of bringing as many countries as possible into the new regime governing export controls.

There will be difficulties of interpretation in this area too, however. A skillful producer or cartel could disrupt the market for infant import-substituting industries simply by altering the level of its export (and probably production) controls continuously. And complications could arise if some consuming countries opted for domestic substitution while others did not: U.S. companies which *used* petroleum inputs and competed in world markets would hardly welcome the application of "reverse dumping" duties against cheap oil imports, to protect the investments of other U.S. companies made under "Project Independence," if their European and

Japanese competitors were importing such oil freely. One cost to the United States of buying economic security, against the risks of depending too heavily on foreign oil, might thus be either a depreciating exchange rate or payment of compensatory export subsidies to companies using the more expensive domestic energy inputs.

12. Just as there could well be "reverse dumping," there could be import subsidies provided by governments—to get more goods to fight inflation—which would justify the application of *"countervailing export controls."* Many countries have been unilaterally reducing, or even eliminating, their import barriers during the past year or so to fight inflation; for example, the United States has done so for meat and sugar, and Japan and Australia have reduced their duties across-the-board. If countries went further and subsidized imports, export controls would clearly be justified if the induced exports injured the supplying country by accelerating its inflation or inducing unemployment there through shortages of inputs, just as countervailing duties are justified on the import side if foreign export subsidies increase an importing country's unemployment.[50] International codes to govern import subsidies might be negotiated, along with international codes to govern export subsidies which have frequently been under international discussion but never yet produced meaningful agreement.

13. The last two points raise the broader issue of *compensation and retaliation*. One approach would be to require compensation, or permit retaliation, for *any* resort to export controls. This would be analogous to the present GATT rule governing import controls; it would presumably maximize the international pressure against such controls, and the strength of anticontrol forces within each country. If drawn to cover "voluntary" import restraints as well as explicit export controls, it could avoid the gaping loophole which has in recent years gutted much of the GATT's effectiveness in restraining import controls by permitting "voluntary" export restraints.[51]

The alternative would be a "two-track" system, such as has been proposed to reform the GATT rules on import controls.[52] No compensation would be required if the country could justify its controls under the international rules—meeting the injury test (or the national security or infant industries exceptions), limiting their duration and, for longer-term controls, presenting an acceptable domestic adjustment program. Compensation/retaliation would be limited to steps taken outside the international rules, which can of course be expected to occur periodically. This approach would pursue the less ambitious, but perhaps more realistic, goal of seeking to induce countries to conform to agreed international norms rather than refrain from trade controls altogether.

Table 10-2
Four Proposed Classes of Export Controls

	Justified*	Not Justified
Short-term (including "market disruption")	Neither compensation nor retaliation	Compensation or retaliation
Long-term (including adjustment plan)	Neither compensation nor retaliation	Compensation or retaliation

*Must meet injury test, or "national security" or "infant industry" exceptions. See text for exceptions.

It was suggested under point number 10 that export controls might be justified either for short-term periods (and hence require no accompanying adjustment program) or for longer durations, in which case an acceptable adjustment plan would have to be part of the package. Under the "two-track" system suggested here, either type might be justified and hence avoid compensation/retaliation. But either type might also fail to meet the approval of the international surveillance body, either because it did not meet the injury test or, in the case of a longer-term control, because there was no adequate adjustment plan. There would thus be four possible sets of export control actions, as depicted in Table 10-2.

14. Closely related to the choice between these options is *the nature of the compensation and retaliation which could result*.

It would probably be impossible to assure compensation for the creation of one export control by the reduction of other export controls by the country in question, as is done with import restrictions. Export controls are not nearly as widespread as import controls, and the impact of one new example might swamp the impact of all existing controls maintained by the same country—a very unlikely occurrence on the import side at this point in economic history. Thus, there would be little scope for direct compensation. In addition, the inflationary circumstances which are most likely to spawn a new export control would often make it extremely difficult for the country taking the action to reduce any of its other export controls simultaneously.

Compensation could be kept within the trade area, and thus institutionally intact within national governments and the GATT, if the country creating a new export control were required to compensate by reducing its import controls on a like amount of trade. In some cases, this approach might be appealing to some countries injured by the export controls.

European opposition to any prolonged U.S. limits on soybean exports, for example, might be at least partly mollified by suspension of "Buy American" requirements or reductions in U.S. chemical duties, including the American Selling Price (ASP) system of customs valuation. And export-oriented countries like Korea and Taiwan might readily accept compensation of this type.

However, the approach is not very promising in general. As already noted, some of the countries most likely to apply export controls are those whose "commodity power" is their major asset; hence, they are unlikely to have a market or sufficient attractiveness to offset the damage to other countries by increasing access to it. Even more important, relaxation of import controls in what is often, by hypothesis, an inflationary environment is unlikely to provide much real help to the countries hurt by the export controls; it could even be viewed as adding a further anti-inflationary benefit to the country applying the new export control! For example, Japan's response to the U.S. soybean controls would hardly have been mollified by reductions in even the most sensitive U.S. import controls, such as the "voluntary" restraints it had imposed on Japanese exports of textile and steel, because the same inflationary circumstances which prompted the U.S. action were also present in Japan and were already holding Japanese exports below their permissible limits. And the least developed countries, which are often hurt worst by export controls, could seldom take much advantage of freer import markets anyway.

In addition, compensation for export controls through relaxing import controls raises problems of timing. It usually takes some time for a country receiving trade compensation to actually utilize it, since new investments may be required to expand production sufficiently to take advantage of the increase in market access. Yet, under the rules proposed so far, many uses of unjustified export controls—which were therefore subject to compensation or retaliation—would probably be quite short term. Meaningful compensation via reductions in import barriers could thus be provided only by countries which adopted long-term export controls—for example, to boost their commodity prices or to protect infant processing industries—which they could not justify under the new rules. The problem is then compounded once more by the fact that the countries likely to adopt such export controls are mainly primary producers, most of which are developing countries loathe to reduce their import barriers and in fact exempted from doing so under most present circumstances through Part IV of the GATT, which enshrines the principle of nonreciprocity for developing countries.

Thus, retaliation is likely to play a far bigger role than compensation in dealing with unjustifiable export controls. In 1926, Secretary of Commerce Herbert Hoover proposed the following list of retaliatory measures, most of which were used at one time or another during those years, against the spate of commodity cartels which were developing.[53]

1. Antitrust prosecution under U.S. law. Between 1912 and 1928, suits were brought against the Brazilian coffee cartel, Mexican sisal combine, Franco-German potash syndicate, Canadian asbestos corporation, and Dutch quinine monopoly.

2. Diplomatic representations. France and Germany were threatened with upward tariff adjustments in retaliation against the potash syndicate.

3. Closing the U.S. capital market to them. This was done in 1925 against the potash syndicate and Brazilian coffee cartel, but they raised the money elsewhere.

4. Creation of buyers' cartels to meet the sellers' cartels. Such a cartel was set up in rubber, but a bill to legalize similar deviations from the antitrust laws never passed the Congress.

5. Conservation of U.S. use of cartelized products, especially rubber.

6. Government assistance to spur new output, both in the United States and in new foreign areas; this was pursued for rubber, coffee and potash.

7. Research to develop substitutes, especially for natural rubber.

All of these proposed steps have a familiar ring today. The last three are in fact components of "Project Independence" in the United States, and are usually viewed not as "retaliation" in terms of commercial policy but rather as adjustment to the new economic situation triggered by the controls (and hence, implicitly, acceptance of them). The first four steps are retaliatory, however.

In addition, present U.S. law (and the GATT) permits retaliation against export controls on one product with import controls against another product from the same country. This would have been ineffectual against many of the key oil producers, who sell only oil.[54] But it could be very effective against the great bulk of the primary-producing countries, which are seeking to industrialize as well as exploit their possession of raw materials.[55] Indeed, a direct response to unjustifiable uses of export controls to promote domestic processing industries would be increases in import barriers against the processed products of those very industries —which, since such export controls would result in a subsidy for the protected processing industry by lowering the cost of its inputs, would be conceptually equivalent to a traditional countervailing import duty. Despite the scope which such a provision might provide for protectionism of the traditional type, it should thus probably be included to help deter export restrictions.

The list of possible retaliatory steps is broadened in the Mondale amendments to the Trade Reform Act:

—export restrictions, including quotas and embargoes by the United States (as some proposed the United States should do, with food, against the oil embargo);

—cutoffs of economic aid, military aid, credits, credit guarantees, and investment guarantees;

—prohibition or restriction of U.S. private investments, direct or indirect, and "transfers of technology."

Thus, in practice, there is much wider latitude for retaliation against export controls than for compensation for them. A variety of responses could be tailored to individual country situations, thereby increasing the deterrent value of the entire scheme.[56]

A key question is whether retaliation would have to be agreed and implemented multilaterally.[57] Multilateral sanctions are of course preferable, both to avoid bilateral political confrontations and to maximize their effectiveness—or even make them effective at all.[58]

Yet, it may prove particularly difficult to reach agreement on retaliation in the area of export controls, in view of the sharply different degrees of national dependence (especially among the otherwise most powerful consuming countries) on those raw materials which are the most likely candidates for control. It would be unfortunate to let the whole enterprise fail over disagreements on retaliation, even though any new rules would be far stronger if supported by agreed retaliatory provisions.[59] At the same time, the whole objective of formulating international rules on export controls is to multilateralize the issue. So, the rules should authorize concerted retaliatory action with the recognition that national retaliation might occur, in practice, in unique cases.

15. This discussion leads directly to the question of whether the traditional *most-favored-nation (MFN) approach* should apply to the new rules governing export controls themselves. One of the few agreed points in the earlier international discussions of export controls was that they should be nondiscriminatory. And among the few steps against export controls ever taken in GATT were three charges against the *discriminatory* use of such controls.[60] In addition, requiring MFN treatment—even for export controls which could be justified under the national security exception—would be an indirect way of barring such political steps as the OAPEC embargo against the United States and several other specific countries.[60a]

An objection to the MFN approach for export controls is that the inflation (or other problem) which triggers the need for them may be generated by one or a few particular foreign countries. One example is the sudden entry of a new, sizable purchaser into the market, as with the Soviet grain deal. Another is that a buying country is inflating more rapidly than the rest of the world and hence not "sharing the burden" of limiting demand pressures in a more general sense.[61] A third is speculative buying, such as the alleged Japanese stockpiling of numerous commodities in 1973 and early 1974. Similar situations on the import side—e.g., charges that the Japanese "flooded a market" or built excessive productive capacity which could only be employed by "dumping exports" (e.g., in steel)—have in recent years led to many doubts about whether the MFN rule should continue to apply in all circumstances on that side of the trade equation. And the existing GATT rule covering allocation of materials in short supply requires "equitable" rather than "nondiscriminatory" treatment.

All three kinds of "disruptive" purchases could, however, be effectively checked under an MFN approach which simply set an early enough base period against which to gauge the export quotas. This would keep the extra demand of the newcomers, excessive inflaters and speculators from entering the calculation—even if they had signed long-term contracts, by applying *force majeure* to those contracts. It would favor traditional purchasers, which is proper.

In addition, it would be desirable to avoid actual reductions in export levels. So, any export controls should be implemented through a nondiscriminatory limit to the percentage growth over (or, if rollbacks are permitted, percentage reduction from) the actual levels of sales in the most recent "representative period."

16. A related question is whether *any new international rules would be applied to nonsignatories*. This issue arises in two ways. Could export controls proscribed among signatories still be applied against nonsignatories? Could signatories retaliate jointly against export controls applied by nonsignatories?

Assuming current GATT membership, an affirmative answer to the first of these questions would permit continuation of the current U.S. and allied export controls against the USSR, China and some other communist countries (though not Poland and Romania, which are now members of the GATT) even without invocation of the national security exception. Such a rule might enhance the inducement to these countries to join the GATT, so should be retained; if countries need not join international organizations to receive their benefits, there is little incentive to accept the responsibilities that go with membership.

The second question—could signatories retaliate against nonsignatories?—is tougher. Most OAPEC countries and many other primary producers do not belong to the GATT, so even the most comprehensive set of GATT rules might not bind them legally to avoid using export controls unless they were to join that organization.[62] However, international law generally recognizes the right of nations to respond in kind to aggression committed against them by other nations. Export controls are a form of economic aggression, so retaliation—to an extent commensurate with the aggression itself—would appear justifiable against nonsignatories. Countries which agreed to retaliate together against export (or other economic) controls, whether adopted by signatories or nonsignatories to their agreement, would in essence be practicing collective economic security.

An alternative to applying the new rules against nonsignatories would be to incorporate the rules in a more universal international organization. An obvious candidate would be the United Nations. It has, of course, been debating the issues of resources and access to them, and it has steadily been seeking to apply international law and sanctions against offenders.

This approach, however, would forego using the technical expertise and long-standing conventions of the GATT. Much more importantly, because of the basic orientation of the United Nations and the nature of its delegations, it would risk intensifying the politicization of the issue rather than achieving the desired depoliticization. This problem is heightened by the presence of the major communist countries in any UN proceedings. They cannot yet be meaningfully integrated into efforts to regulate economic relations among essentially market economies, because their prices (and any external manifestations thereof, such as "tariffs," "exchange rates," and "export duties") bear little relationship to the market. Thus, their presence could only divert attention and cause disruption. A further pragmatic consideration is the dim view held in most industrial (and many developing) countries of the likely success of UN efforts to deal effectively with economic issues. And UN Resolution 2625 (XXV), cited above, which purports to bar the use of economic measures for foreign policy purposes, has never even been mentioned—let alone implemented—as a possible response to the oil crisis.

None of these problems is inherent, nor rules out the United Nations as a forum for regulating export controls. Indeed, some primary-producing countries might more readily engage in such a new approach if it were institutionalized in the United Nations rather than the GATT. But most industrial countries would appear far more likely to accept new commitments if they were to be implemented under a familiar institutional rubric which had been at least moderately successful in the past.

A better alternative would thus be to seek to draw the widest number of countries into any new GATT arrangements. This has already been done for the proposed Multilateral Trade Negotiations (MTN). More than 20 non-GATT (primarily developing) countries have indicated their intention to participate and have in fact joined the Trade Negotiating Committee which is charged with preparing ground rules for the MTN. These countries could have no objection to the voting arrangements of the GATT, as it embraces the same one country-vote rule as does the General Assembly. Indeed, it is the United States which has most vehemently objected to the voting rules of the GATT, as contrasted with the weighted voting of the IMF and the International Bank for Reconstruction and Development

(IBRD) and the veto privilege of permanent members of the Security Council of the United Nations. At the same time, much GATT business is accomplished outside the formal voting arrangements and the developing countries feel—often quite rightly—that their interests are not adequately represented in the process. Hence, it is essential to include them fully at all stages in this particular negotiation, which is fully justified by their economic strength.

Trying to broaden the GATT seems the best approach when the issue is viewed in strategic as well as tactical terms. Any effort to negotiate new rules to govern export controls should strive to include those countries most likely to apply such controls, since the major value of these (like any international) rules is as a self-restraining ordinance which deters disruptive national actions. This means that participation must be sought from those countries most likely to try to wield "commodity power," which are both developing countries with no other international leverage and those primary producers with a far broader range of economic (and political) capabilities, such as the United States, Canada and Australia.

Hence, such rules are likely to be most effective if they apply to the widest possible membership, which in turn requires that they be developed and applied in ways that truly serve the interests of the several groups of countries. There can be no exemption for less (or even least) developed countries, as there is from the standard rules governing import controls (in Part IV of the GATT). And proceeding with a limited group of industrial countries such as the OECD membership, as is sometimes proposed for dealing with import barriers, would be decidedly second-best (although it would at least provide a basis for joint reaction to export controls adopted by outsiders).

The whole objective of the exercise is to minimize the use of export controls and defuse the resulting threat of political confrontations. It is unlikely to get off the ground if it implied confrontation from the outset. Indeed, the heavily dependent importing countries in Western Europe and Japan might not even go along with a system which permitted implementation of international rules against nonsignatories. Nor can such rules descend on the world community from decisions made by one or even a few countries, as did the original GATT. The substantive need for the widest possible participation to make the rules work blends almost indistinguishably with the need for wide agreement to negotiate the rules in the first place.

17. A final issue is the *liberalization of existing export controls*. One of the basic thrusts of the original GATT agreement was to liberalize existing import controls. It would also be desirable to negotiate reductions in existing export controls.

Export controls, however, are not nearly as widespread now as were import controls when the GATT was originally negotiated. In addition, any liberalization of existing export controls would presumably require compensation to countries doing so, and we have seen the difficulties in finding ways to provide such compensation. Thus, the main thrust of any new rules would be preventative, not redemptive.

The fact that most nations have not yet adopted firm policies on the issue should, in fact, make it easier to negotiate such rules. All signatories would in effect bind themselves against new export controls except where such controls could be justified internationally.[63] No systematic reduction of existing barriers thus seems to be either needed or feasible in the context of the new trade rules.

Reaching Agreement on Rules to Govern Export Controls

The proposed set of rules would achieve the objectives set down at the outset of the preceding section. They would permit the use of export controls for national security purposes and "infant industry" protection, and to avoid serious injury (or the threat thereof) to national economies. But they would otherwise be proscribed.

The proscription would be backed by the requirement that any country adopting an unjustified export control had to provide adequate compensation or, more likely, accept any of a number of types of economic retaliation. Nonsignatories of the agreement could be subjected to such retaliations, broadening the scope of the deterrent, although every effort would be made to maximize membership in the new regime. Retaliation would also be authorized against "reverse dumping" and against import subsidies, in the form of import duties and "countervailing export controls," respectively.

When controls were justified, their application would be subject to agreed time limits and, for longer-term controls, the presentation of an acceptable domestic adjustment program. And they would require advance notification and consultation, undergo multilateral surveillance both at their initiation and throughout their subsequent application, have to be administered through export taxes rather than quotas whenever possible, and apply on a most-favored-nation basis. Such a regime would seem to provide a reasonable chance that export controls could be relatively depoliticized, and avoid unilateral reactions and emulation/retaliation cycles.

In looking at the tactical issue of reaching agreement on such rules, it must be remembered that the basic problem of assuring access to supplies goes well beyond any limits on export controls. Access to supplies can be limited by controls over domestic *production*, and several of the motives for producer-country action outlined earlier in this paper suggest widespread use of production controls instead of, or in addition to, export controls. Indeed, the problem of access to foreign supplies raises fundamental questions:

1. *Must* a country extract resources from its territory which other countries want, or can it conserve them for the future (as Kuwait and Libya have been doing with their oil for several years)?
2. Must it *sell* all or at least some share of its current output, or can it stockpile everything (perhaps to keep prices up, as Brazil did with a recent coffee crop)?
3. If it does sell, must *foreigners* get some "fair" share of the output on "equal terms" (as implied by current GATT rules)?
4. If exports are permitted at all, must *all* foreigners be treated equally (as called for under the present GATT most-favored-nation approach)?

Any comprehensive arrangements to "assure access to supplies" must therefore probably encompass commodity agreements as well as rules limiting the use of trade controls. Buffer stocks, agreed production levels and perhaps other arrangements to preserve agreed volumes of trade and price ranges would be needed.[64] The nature of the decision-making machinery on all these issues would be a central concern to all negotiating parties.

Thus, from an intellectual standpoint, commodity agreements and new trade rules must be viewed together in dealing with the problem of access to supplies. But they must also be viewed in tandem from a negotiating standpoint, because together they might provide the basis for a package which served the interests of the several different groups of countries.

The primary producers currently possess considerable "commodity power." But most of them quite properly remain uncertain about the long-term outlook for the prices of their primary products—especially after the sharp declines in many prices in mid-1974. They know that efforts to boost their returns now, through "new OPECs" or any other contrived means, risk triggering reductions in demand and production of substitutes which will cost them money in the longer run.

In addition, most of these countries want to reduce their dependence on primary products, even if commodity prices are likely to remain strong indefinitely. Industrialization means more jobs, more knowledge and less dependence on the fluctuations of a few markets, and raises economic security through diversification.

The desires of the consuming countries for assured access to supplies at reasonable prices could thus be traded against the desires of the primary-producing countries for (a) assured prices for their commodities and (b) accelerated industrialization. Implemented perhaps in the context of the MTN, the following package would promote the economic security of both buyers and sellers:

1. Commodity agreements for individual primary products, to encompass floor prices (for the producers) and assured volumes of output and perhaps ceiling prices (for the consumers).[65] There might be some merit in negotiating an overall framework for commodity agreements first, to be applied subsequently to a growing list of specific products.

2. Sector arrangements which reduced tariff and nontariff import barriers of particular interest to the primary producers, as part of the general trade liberalization of the MTN, to increase their access to the markets of the industrial countries. This would include reductions or elimination of tariffs on processed goods, to foster increases in value-added in the producing countries and eliminate some of the artificial inducements to downstream processing. It could also encompass significant liberalization of the generalized tariff preferences extended to developing countries, both by loosening the "safeguards" which are not placed on preferential imports and by increasing the lists of eligible products. And it might include technical assistance, sales of technology and other aid to developing countries to help them take advantage of their increased access.

3. Negotiation of the rules proposed in this paper to govern export controls which would probably require amendment of the GATT.[66] Amendments are already needed to modernize many other parts of those arrangements, which is only natural now that a generation of massive structural change has occurred since they were devised. Thus, any new rules to complete the GATT by effectively covering export controls would, properly, be considered alongside modifications in the rules to govern import controls and other issues of trade policy.

Such a program might seem expensive for consuming countries since it would entail guaranteeing floor prices for individual commodities, budgeting adequate funds for adjustment assistance for workers (and perhaps firms) dislocated by the increased imports of processed and other manufactured goods, and perhaps some additional flows of foreign assistance. But the advantages of pursuing the effort are also very high:

1. The increased economic security of assured access to supplies.

2. Avoidance of the costs of the alternate routes to such security: developing domestic alternatives, and cutbacks in use of the products.

3. Reductions in prices from levels that might otherwise be reached, through agreed ceiling limitations.

4. And, in the broadest sense and probably most importantly, avoidance of the economic (and perhaps political) conflicts which could develop in the absence of a new international framework for these issues: both between consuming and producing countries, and among consuming countries as they "struggle for the global product."[67]

There would thus seem to be a basis for the negotiation of far-reaching changes in the total package of conventions governing world trade, one important part of which would be a new set of international rules and institutional arrangements to cover export controls. Such negotiations could in fact provide an entirely new basis for world commercial relationships, as did the creation of the GATT itself a generation ago. Indeed, that historical precedent demonstrates the possibility of achieving meaningful international agreement on even the seemingly most intractable issues —such as the use of export controls at the present time.

New rules to govern export controls would complete the GATT, and in so doing help reduce the risk of new international economic conflict. They would thus, at the same time, help make the world safe for economic interdependence and enable all individual countries—the industrialized and the developing—to enjoy true independence within that interdependence. It is hoped that the proposals in this chapter will help promote such a process.

Notes

1. The term "export controls" will be used throughout this chapter to cover all trade policy measures adopted to affect the flow of exports directly: quantitative limitations (including total embargoes), export taxes and "voluntary import limitations" negotiated with importing countries. "Domestic" policy measures which have the same effects as direct export controls are discussed on pages 133-34 and 144-47.

2. The rules and institutional arrangements of the International Monetary Fund similarly sought to deal with efforts to export unemployment through monetary means, by making devaluations of exchange rates the last resort of a country experiencing balance-of-payments deficits, requiring international approval whenever devaluations exceeded 10 percent, and providing financial support for countries in order to limit their need to take such actions.

3. In the introduction to Robert C. Turner, *Export Control* (Ann Arbor: Edward Brothers, Inc., 1947), Halford Haskins, Director of the School for Advanced International Studies at Johns Hopkins University, wrote: "For the last five or six years, export controls were the most important single influence in the development of the foreign trade of [the United States]."

4. The United States apparently lagged behind most other countries in developing the use of export controls for general economic purposes. The most extensive study of U.S. export controls unearthed only one product

(tinplate scrap in 1936) on which the United States applied such measures before World War II. See Harold J. Berman and John P. Garson, "United States Export Controls—Past, Present, and Future," *Columbia Law Review*, Vol. 67, No. 5 (May 1967), p. 791.

5. For a striking comparison between the problems of today and those preceding World War I, see Emma Rothschild, "1914 and Today's Trade Crisis," *New York Times*, June 23, 1974.

6. See Margaret S. Gordon, *Barriers to World Trade: A Study of Recent Commercial Policy* (New York: The MacMillan Company, 1941), pp. 349-63.

7. In late 1973 and early 1974, the oil-producing countries adopted three distinct but interrelated sets of policies: cutbacks in their total petroleum production, total embargoes of sales to certain countries, and sharp increases in prices. Only the embargoes were, strictly speaking, a trade policy measure. The production cutbacks and increases in taxes levied on the oil companies (which produced the higher prices) had similar effects, however, as will be discussed later.

8. For a brief history, see League of Nations, *Raw Material Problems and Policies*, 1946. Eugene Staley wrote the original manuscript and it was completed by Klaus Knorr.

9. However, the focus of its chapter on commodity agreements was *excessive* supplies and hence *falling* prices to commodity producers. Similarly, virtually all of the efforts to create and maintain arrangements for individual commodities, prior to the last few years, were aimed at limiting declines in commodity prices and most of them foundered when it became necessary to control exports (or production) to do so.

10. GATT, *The Use of Quantitative Restrictions for Protective and Other Commercial Purposes*, 1950, pp. 5-9, which noted that ". . . since the War . . . many countries have made extensive use of restrictions on exports, in order to protect their supplies of scarce commodities . . ." (p. 3).

11. The focus of this chapter is export controls undertaken (a) by governments (b) to *limit* exports or raise export prices (c) at their own initiative (d) during peacetime. It thus excludes (a) export quotas employed by private cartels, and divisions of markets among the branches of multinational firms. It excludes (b) the *minimum* export quotas increasingly levied by host (especially developing) countries on the local subsidiaries of multinational firms, which contribute to the need for new international rules regarding foreign investment, as discussed in C. Fred Bergsten, "Coming Investment Wars?" *Foreign Affairs*, October 1974 [chapter 16 in this volume]. It excludes (c) the "voluntary export restraints adopted by numerous countries to head off import restraints in specific

industries by their customers; for an analysis of that type of trade control, see C. Fred Bergsten, "On the Non-Equivalence of Import Quotas and 'Voluntary' Export Restraints" in Bergsten, ed., *Toward A New World Trade Policy: The Maidenhead Papers* (Lexington, Mass.: Lexington Books, D. C. Heath and Company, 1975) [Chapter 11 in this volume]. And it excludes (d) wartime controls because of the very different circumstances under which they are applied, and the total impracticability of attempting to develop rules to govern such situations. The present paper also excludes export controls undertaken by surplus countries to fend off—so far, always unsuccessfully—more fundamental balance-of-payments adjustment, such as the reduction of export rebates by Germany in 1968 and the "voluntary" export restraints in a number of industries announced by Japan in 1971, or in earlier periods to avoid building up excess credit balances under bilateral clearing arrangements. And it excludes the traditional export controls perculiar to particular items such as narcotics (reasons of "health and morals"), art objects ("to preserve the national heritage") and other monetary substitutes (such as gold, silver and jewelry) to avoid circumvention of exchange controls.

12. For the history, see Berman and Garson, "United States Export Controls," pp. 830-33.

13. Statement of Special Representative for Trade Negotiations William D. Eberle before the Subcommittee on Economic Growth of the Joint Economic Committee of the Congress, July 23, 1974.

14. During World War II, however, the U.S. Office of Price Administration controlled the export prices of all U.S. products whose domestic prices were regulated, both to avoid gouging dependent foreign purchasers and to avoid any incentives to U.S. firms to evade the export quotas. This practice was continued after the War to facilitate the removal of export quotas on as many products as possible. Canada and the United Kingdom, on the other hand, did not control export prices even during the War, relying solely on export quotas instead. See Turner, *Export Control*, esp. pp. 68-70, and the explanation of the U.S. export price controls by the eminent economist who wrote and first administered them, Seymour E. Harris, "Export Price Control" in Office of Price Administration, *A Manual of Price Control* (Washington, D.C.: Government Printing Office, 1943), pp. 221-32.

15. For an analysis of this approach in contemporary circumstances, its widespread recent use, and the likelihood that it will continue to proliferate, see C. Fred Bergsten, "The New Era in World Commodity Markets," *Challenge*, Sept./Oct. 1974, pp. 34-43 [chapter 18 in this volume]. Thirty-nine commodity cartels of the interwar period are described in Eugene Staley, *Raw Materials in Peace and War*, A Report to the Tenth Interna-

tional Studies Conference, 1937, pp. 251-318. Staley also quotes Secretary of Commerce Hoover as asserting in 1926 "that there were governmentally controlled combinations in nine raw materials, of which U.S. imports in 1926 would amount to about $1.2 billion, and that twenty or thirty other commodities could be controlled by the action of one government or by agreement between two governments" (p. 128).

16. See Heinrich Heuser, *Control of International Trade* (George Rutledge and Sons, 1939), especially chapter IX. The distribution between exporters and importers of the scarcity rents generated by trade controls is analyzed in Bergsten, "On the Non-Equivalence of Import Quotas and 'Voluntary' Export Restraints" [chapter 11 in this volume].

17. It is ironic that most of the long-standing U.S. export controls have been directed *against* the Soviet Union, whereas many of the recent U.S. export controls on farm products were adopted largely because the United States sold so much of its farm output *to* the Soviet Union.

18. The most precise linkage of this type has been made by Jamaica: to offset the increase of $100-150 million in its oil bill for 1974, it forced an increase of $180 million in its returns from bauxite exports. Even the OPEC countries, which have caused an important part of current world inflation, have consistently sought to raise their oil prices—through production or export controls, if necessary—*pari passu* with world inflation.

19. Bergsten, "The New Era in World Commodity Markets [chapter 18].

20. The "two-track" system is described and analyzed by Richard N. Cooper, "Trade Policy Is Foreign Policy," *Foreign Policy* 9 (Winter 1972-73), pp. 18-36.

21. This critical problem is discussed in detail on pp. 129-31.

21a. In the United States, "The AFL-CIO has repeatedly called for effective controls on exports of farm goods, crucial raw materials and other products in short supply domestically." Statement of Andrew J. Biemiller, Director, Department of Legislation, AFL-CIO before the Subcommittee on International Trade of the House Banking and Currency Committee, April 25, 1974, p. 6.

22. However, the long-run elasticities, particularly of supply, are frequently not very high either, and may have declined quite significantly for a number of commodities in recent years. The institutional and political, as well as economic, barriers to rapid expansion of commodity supply are analyzed in Bergsten, "The New Era in World Commodity Markets."

23. The case for applying "optimum export controls" to maximize the welfare effects of exports is thus similar to the case for applying "optimum tariffs" to maximize the welfare effects of imports for a single country. However, the main purposes of export controls are not the usual form of

welfare maximization, and that analytical approach—which is of limited empirical significance anyway—will not be elaborated here.

24. Theoretically, such a buildup in reserves would expand the money supply of such countries with adverse effects on their other export- and import-competing industries similar to the effects of exchange-rate appreciation (and adding to the country's inflationary tendencies rather than helping to counter them). In practice, however, many countries can effectively sterilize such effects through active use of domestic monetary policy. Such sterilization is hardest for countries with imperfect monetary tools and those most open to the world economy, so they are less likely to employ export controls than are more closed economies with effective monetary instruments to employ export controls.

25. A number of resource-poor developing countries are also heavy net importers of both agricultural products and industrial raw materials. However, due to "Third World solidarity" and fear of jeopardizing further their positions *vis-à-vis* OPEC, even those hardest hit by the oil cartel have refrained from any criticism of OPEC and have even called for "new OPECs" and the use of "commodity power" by other developing countries—which would further hurt their own economies!

26. See, e.g., Lester R. Brown and Erik P. Eckholm, "Food and Hunger: The Balance Sheet," *Challenge*, Sept./Oct. 1974.

27. These historical paragraphs are based on League of Nations, *Raw Materials Problems and Policies*, 1946.

28. *Duties* were the primary form of trade control (for both exports and imports) prior to the 1930s, when quantitative restrictions became prevalent for the first time. Hence, they were the focus of the international discussion of access to supplies in the 1920s.

29. Hides and skins, and bones and other glue-making materials. Export controls on both sets of products had been utilized primarily to protect domestic processing industries.

30. The Committee actively discussed the creation of buffer stocks, and John Maynard Keynes proposed them a year later in "The Policy of Government Storage of Foodstuffs and Raw Materials," *Economic Journal* (Sept. 1938), pp. 449-60.

31. However, the EEC sanctioned the temporary British controls over steel exports in early 1974 and could hardly have stopped the controls on petroleum exports to the Netherlands seriously considered by several EEC members when the Arabs embargoed Holland in October 1973. Nor did EFTA halt the more lasting British controls over scrap exports.

32. Such a binding exists on exports of only one commodity from one country: Malaysian tin ore and concentrates. See note 63, page 156.

33. The most exhaustive study of the GATT concludes that "these exceptions . . . leave very little, if any, effective GATT policing of export control policies." John Jackson, *World Trade and the Law of the GATT* (Indianapolis: Bobbs-Merrill Co., Inc., 1969), p. 502. The official U.S. government position as stated by Ambassador William D. Eberle (before the Subcommittee on Economic Growth of the Joint Economic Committee of the Congress, July 23, 1974) is that "the [GATT] prohibition on export quotas is virtually worthless because the exceptions are so broadly defined."

34. GATT, *The Use of Quantitative Restrictions for Protective and Other Commercial Purposes*, 1950, especially pp. 5-6.

35. See, e.g., the sweeping proposals by Eric Wyndham-White, "Negotiations in Prospect" in C. Fred Bergsten, ed., *Toward A New World Trade Policy: The Maidenhead Papers* (Lexington, Mass.: Lexington Books, D. C. Heath and Company, 1975). Wyndham-White was Director-General of GATT from 1949 to 1967.

36. Throughout most of this analysis, I refer to "GATT" on the assumption that it would be the institutional locus of any new rules. This assumption is later relaxed, and the organizational alternatives discussed on pages 142-43.

37. Thus, the agreement of the OECD countries not to apply new export (or import) controls for the next 12 months and to consult with each other in case any such issues arise, as part of the "standstill agreement" agreed in June 1974, while extremely useful for the intended purposes, is not a desirable precedent for permanent machinery to monitor export controls. Such a limited group simply excludes too many countries which are central to an effective regime to govern export controls; see pages 142-43.

38. Richard N. Gardner, "The Hard Road to World Order," *Foreign Affairs*, April 1974, pp. 566-67. He argues that "at a minimum [new trade rules] should prohibit the use of export or other controls for political purposes," and points out that the Afro-Asian Group in the United Nations, including the Arab countries, sponsored this resolution and all voted for it.

39. Communist China, and perhaps India, are examples of countries which are militarily strong and economically weak. They raise problems for world security arrangements somewhat similar to the problems for world economic arrangements discussed here.

40. The several sources of this leverage are analyzed in C. Fred Bergsten, "The Threat from the Third World," *Foreign Policy* 9, Summer 1973 [chapter 27 in this volume], and "The Response to the Third World," *Foreign Policy* 17, Winter 1974-75 [chapter 28 in this volume].

41. For an analysis of some of these asymmetries, see Robert O.

Keohane and Joseph S. Nye, "World Politics and the International Economic System," in C. Fred Bergsten, *The Future of the International Economic Order: An Agenda for Research* (Lexington, Mass.: Lexington Books, D. C. Heath and Co., 1973), esp. pp. 121-26, pp. 131-33 and pp. 145-52. They conclude that "for the next decade, strategies of issue-linkage (i.e., between economic and security concerns) will play an extremely important role in world politics, quite in contrast to the situation during the first postwar quarter century."

42. Such as the use of this exception to justify the oil *import* quotas maintained by the United States for 14 years, which of course *undermined* rather than promoted the national security of the United States and were carried out for blatantly protectionist reasons. This case illustrates the need for any surveillance body to probe well beyond the stated rationales for national policies.

43. Present GATT rules (and the U.S. escape clause) permit application of the injury test only to imports triggered by *prior tariff concessions*. However, this limitation is under severe attack from most observers and will probably be changed, at the first opportunity, to cover injury caused by all imports, whatever their cause. On the export side, all exports should be covered from the outset; since there have been no "export concessions," there is in fact no alternative.

44. Before the issue ever rises to the international level, each individual country contemplating an export control would of course have to make a policy judgment as to whether the control promoted its national interest, taking into account the overall effects on its economy and foreign policy. This requires careful domestic procedures in each country to assure that all affected interests are considered. In the United States, such procedures should include hearings by the Tariff Commission before final decisions by the President, on the model of the existing escape clause for import relief.

45. Governments can (and often do) regulate exports by creating government corporations through which all trade in a certain product is channeled. Conceptually, however, the regulation is still affected either by controlling exports directly or by controlling domestic production. Government corporations will therefore not be analyzed separately.

46. There is nearly unanimous agreement that the present GATT provision (Article XII) permitting countries in balance-of-payments deficit to apply quotas but not surcharges to imports is anomalous and should be amended, either to permit both or to reverse the situation completely by allowing surcharges and banning quotas. In practice, all major countries adopting import controls for balance-of-payments purposes (United States, United Kingdom, Canada) during the last 15 years have in fact used surcharges.

154

47. Although it is possible that export "fees" or "licenses," which have the same effect as taxes, might be acceptable to the courts if their purpose was clearly regulatory instead of fiscal.

48. Jackson, *World Trade and the Law of the GATT*, p. 277.

49. The present GATT rules accept export controls if they are accompanied by limitations on domestic consumption as well as exports. However, there is no sign that this condition is being met by any of the oil-producing countries. Indeed, most of them are seeking additional refining capacity which requires *additional* domestic "consumption."

50. Present U.S. legislation on countervailing import duties is defective because the duties must be applied whether or not the foreign export subsidies are injuring any U.S. interests; the United States must now offset foreign subsidization of U.S. consumers even when no other Americans are hurt!

51. See C. Fred Bergsten, "On the Non-Equivalence of Import Quotas and 'Voluntary' Export Restraints," in Bergsten, ed., *Toward A New World Trade Policy* [chapter 11 in this volume]. Examples of "voluntary" *import* restraints are Japan's agreement in 1973 to limit its purchases of U.S. logs in order to eliminate the risk of U.S. application of export controls to that commodity, and the 10 percent reductions in Japanese and EEC imports of feedgrains from the United States announced in August 1974 to reduce the pressure for U.S. export controls on those products.

52. See Anthony M. Solomon, "A New Import Safeguard Mechanism," in Bergsten, ed., *Toward A New World Trade Policy*.

53. Eugene Staley, *Raw Materials in Peace and War*, A Report to the Tenth International Studies Conference, 1937, pp. 129-31.

54. However, particularly if carried out jointly by the bulk of the industrial countries, such measures could have hurt those large oil producers (Indonesia, Nigeria, Iran, and Venezuela) which do export other products. In addition, any such retaliation would have had a major psychological impact on the oil producers by jeopardizing their overall relations with consumers, which are extremely important at least to Saudi Arabia (because of its fervent anticommunism) and to Iran (because of its exposed geographic position), an appropriate response to *their* use of economic power to achieve foreign policy aims.

55. Particularly if it included retaliation against imports of services as well as goods. For example, revoking the validity of U.S. passports for travel to Jamaica would probably be the most effective form of U.S. economic retaliation against a Jamaican bauxite embargo.

56. Eberle, in his statement before the Subcommittee on Economic Growth, indicated that "the actual method of retaliation could be geared to

the situation and would range in severity from minor administrative measures to major trade and financial actions."

57. At one stage during their development, the Mondale amendments would have authorized the President to retaliate unilaterally only *until* there existed the multilateral agreement on export controls which the amendments call for, after which time "the President *shall* exercise the authority conferred on him . . . in conformity with such provisions." The House of Representatives added such a two-stage approach to the authority it would give the President to use trade policy measures—primarily import controls—against countries which do not act effectively to adjust their balance-of-payments disequilibria, on the hope that international monetary reform will at some point produce agreed rules for multilateral sanctions.

58. Gardner, "The Hard Road to World Order," p. 568, argues that all retaliation should be multilateral.

59. Disagreement over the same issue was a major impediment to negotiating international monetary reform in 1972-74. The United States insisted on explicit rules to govern the balance-of-payments adjustment process, with multilateral sanctions to back them up. Most of the other industrial countries opposed both specific rules and sanctions. So, little progress has been made in negotiating improvements in the monetary system. For one set of proposals to resolve this problem see the concluding chapter of C. Fred Bergsten, *The Dilemmas of the Dollar: The Economics and Politics of U.S. International Monetary Policy* (New York: Council on Foreign Relations, forthcoming 1975).

60. By Pakistan against India in 1948, by Czechoslovakia against the United States in 1949, and by India against Pakistan in 1952.

60a. There is also the issue of whether customs unions and free trade areas should continue to be exempted from any new MFN rule for export controls, as they are from all present GATT MFN rules under Article XXIV. The issue has immediate practical significance, because some of the current export controls of EEC countries (e.g., on copper, aluminum, and lead waste and scrap) apply only to nonmembers.

61. A consideration raised by William Diebold, Jr. in his statement before the House Subcommittee on Foreign Economic Policy, May 8, 1974, p. 10.

62. Only Kuwait among the OAPEC countries is a full member, though the GATT applies *de facto* to Bahrein and Qatar. Some of the major non-Arab oil exporters, such as Indonesia and Nigeria, are also full members of GATT. So are such other past, current or possible users of export controls as Australia, Canada, Guyana, Jamaica, Malaysia, the United States, and Zaire.

63. There is one example of a binding of export controls under the GATT. In the late 1940s, Malaya and Singapore bound their taxes on exports of tin ore and concentrates, relative to their taxes on exports of smelted tin, for as long as the U.S. government refrained from subsidizing U.S. tin smelters. For this and other references to present GATT rules and practices, see Frieder Roessler, "Access to Supplies: The Role GATT Could Play," *Journal of World Trade Law*, forthcoming 1974. Roessler places primary emphasis on bindings against new export controls, partly because such an approach would obviate any need to amend the GATT itself.

64. In the case of food, new international reserve stocks (and aid programs) are needed to protect the poorest countries against severe deprivation as well as to limit price fluctuations for all buyers and sellers.

65. Both floor and ceiling prices might be subject to change, over time, by negotiation and/or through indexing them to some world price index. Some developing countries are now proposing the even more ambitious approach of linking changes in aggregate export and import prices in order to protect their terms of trade. This amounts to international indexation, and would be extremely difficult to apply in practice. Would efforts be made to adjust prices of *individual* products to right any imbalance which developed, and if so how would the products be chosen? Or would cash grants be made to offset imbalances, and if so where would the money come from? Nevertheless, consuming countries may have to face this issue if they want to assure access to supplies.

66. Amendment of GATT might be avoidable if that were deemed desirable. A "Code of Export Conduct" could be negotiated which was not inconsistent with the GATT, but which provided more stringent standards than the current articles; such a procedure was followed with the Antidumping Code. Another alternative would be to seek a GATT waiver for such a code, if it appeared to be inconsistent with the Agreement, as was done for the Generalized System of Preferences (for the developing countries).

67. See Helmut Schmidt, "The Struggle for the Global Product," *Foreign Affairs*, April 1974. Schmidt is, of course, now Chancellor of the Federal Republic of Germany.

11

On the Non-Equivalence of Import Quotas and "Voluntary" Export Restraints

Introduction

Until the 1930s, tariffs were the dominant instrument of commercial policy. From the 1930s until the 1960s, quantitative import restrictions (QRs) acceded to that role. Since the early 1960s, "voluntary" export restraints (VERs) have moved up alongside both.[1]

Economists have analyzed the similarities and differences between tariffs and QRs.[2] But there has been no systematic effort to compare the economic and political effects of VERs and QRs, on the erroneous view that they are virtually identical.[3] This chapter will make such an effort.

Countries have restrained their exports for several reasons. A prominent motive has been national security, which throughout the postwar period has sharply limited the willingness of the United States (and Western Europe and Japan, to much lesser extents) to export to communist countries products that might strengthen their military capabilities. More broadly, exports have been restrained to deny the benefits of trade to importing countries, as with the embargo on oil sales to Italy maintained for a while by some League of Nations members in 1936, the embargo on sales to Rhodesia mandated by the United Nations in 1967, and the withholding of oil exports to the United States and Holland by Arab oil-producing countries in late 1973. A third motive has been the preservation of certain commodities for domestic consumption and to try to fight internal inflation, the traditional "short supply" criterion, which has recently prompted the United States and several other countries to limit their sales of a variety of agricultural and other products. A fourth is a conscious effort by an exporting country (or group of countries) to exploit an oligopoly position in a particular commodity market, as recently accomplished by the Organization of Petroleum Exporting Countries (OPEC). Individual industries or firms have also limited exports for oligopoly reasons—that is, through a division of markets among the subsidiaries of a given multinational firm or among independent firms in an industry that is cartelized internationally.

All of these types of exports restraint are initiated by the exporting

This chapter was originally prepared for a conference on world trade policy in Maidenhead, England in April 1973 and published in C. Fred Bergsten, ed., *Toward a New World Trade Policy: The Maidenhead Papers* (Lexington, Mass.: Lexington Books, D.C. Heath and Company, 1975).

157

country in pursuit of its own interests. They are presumably not welcomed by the importing country. They are *not* the subject of this chapter.[4]

I deal here with those export restraints that are adopted, by a country or by an industry, ostensibly[5] because of the problems the exports are causing for the country (or countries) *to* which they are flowing—and which are, therefore, perceived as a substitute for other actions, including restraints by the importing country of the same trade, to deal with those problems. Thus they are seldom voluntary, and I enclose the word with quotation marks throughout to indicate as much.[6] Such restraints are usually adopted in response to industry-specific pressures, as in the prominent cases of textiles and steel in the United States. They may also be adopted across a wide range of industries, in response to aggregate balance-of-payments or trade-balance pressures, as an alternative to exchange-rate changes (including revaluation by the surplus country) or import surcharges by the deficit country, as was announced by the Japanese in late 1972. Most of my examples will be drawn from VERs on sales to the United States, although the United States has by no means been alone in arranging such restraints in recent years.

VERs are limitations on export sales (a) administered by one or more exporting countries or industries (b) on the volume or value of their sales (c) to a single foreign market or several markets, or (rarely) the world as a whole, (d) triggered by pressure from the government or industry of the importing country or countries (e) carried out either bilaterally or within a multilateral framework (f) sometimes explicitly authorized or guided by domestic law, and sometimes not. There are thus numerous permutations among specific VER arrangements.[7]

A major distinction is between those VERs that are administered solely by the exporting country and those where the importing country uses back-up QRs to assure that the restraints are effective. In the U.S. case, the steel VER, negotiated between the U.S. government and the foreign industries, fits the former category.[8] So does the bilateral cotton textile VER negotiated with Japan in 1957, the precursor of the multilateral "Long-Term Arrangement on Cotton Textiles" (LTA), which governed the bulk of world trade in cotton textiles from 1962 through 1973. The LTA and its successor, the "Arrangement Regarding International Trade in Textiles," which commenced all-fiber coverage in 1974, fall into the latter category for the United States under Section 204 of the Agricultural Adjustment Act, which authorizes U.S. quotas once there exists a multilateral arrangement under which "a substantial volume of world trade" is covered by VERs. It also covers meat, under the Meat Import Act of 1964, which requires the president to trigger quotas if certain import levels—which therefore *de facto* set the VER ceiling—are exceeded.[9]

Indeed, some observers argue that this latter group of restraints should

Table 11-1

Major U.S. Imports Subject to Voluntary Export Restraints and Import Quotas: 1971

(In millions of dollars)

	VERs	QRs
Petroleum		3,278
Sugar		813
Dairy Products		70
Total		4,161
Cotton Textiles	590	
Synthetic and Woolen Textiles	1,840	
Steel	2,009[a]	
Meat	598	
Total	5,037	

[a]1969 figure, excluding several categories of steel products covered by the VERs. Thus the figure for total VER coverage should be somewhat higher. In 1973, the total coverage approximated $2.3 billion.

Source: Stephen P. Magee, "The Welfare Effects of Restrictions on U.S. Trade," *Brookings Papers on Economic Activity* 3: 1972, edited by Arthur M. Okun and George L. Perry, p. 662. © 1973 by the Brookings Institution, Washington, D.C. Reprinted with permission.

be viewed as QRs rather than VERs, because ultimate control rests with the importing country. Such a contention is only partly true. Even when the importing country has such control, it may choose not to exercise it in particular cases even when the VER ceiling is pierced, as has frequently been true with U.S. imports of particular categories of textiles. Thus the ceiling on imports, which is certain under QRs, is not certain even under VERs backed up by QRs. Even more important for the analysis of this chapter, the exporting country organizes the market under VERs even when they are backed up by QRs—and may even do so more efficiently by virtue of the QR threat standing behind its own VER. I will distinguish between these two types of VER when necessary in the analysis but will maintain the fundamental distinction between VERs and QRs.

There is no complete record of VERs, past or present, and hence no way to judge their aggregate importance in world trade.[10] In 1971, however, as shown in Table 15-1, more U.S. imports were covered by VERs than QRs. VERs covered well over $5 billion—about one-eighth—of all U.S. imports. There were three major QRs (oil, sugar, dairy products) and four major VERs (cotton textiles, synthetic and woolen textiles, steel and meat), as well as a number of both covering minor products.

The importance of VERs relative to QRs has grown since 1971. In mid-1973, a new VER was announced to cover exports from Korea to the United States of "certain rubber and plastic footwear."[11] The VER on meat was suspended, but was to be reinstated in 1975, and the elimination of the QRs on oil and sugar were much more important quantitatively. There were also signed a large and growing number of VERs on sales of a variety of products, mainly from Japan and a few other countries in the Far East, mainly to Western Europe[12] and Canada. And the new "Arrangement Regarding International Trade in Textiles" extended the scope for VERs to all textile fibers for all countries.[13]

The Relative Effectiveness of VERs and QRs

VERs and QRs can be set at identical levels of trade.[14] If such equivalence were actually achieved, the losses in economic efficiency caused by each would be equal. However, the differing natures of the two instruments virtually assure significantly different outcomes in practice, in terms of both the actual degree of restraint and the distribution of effects among exporting countries. In addition, VERs and QRs would produce different distributional effects between the importing and exporting countries involved in the restraints even if their aggregate effects were identical.

VERs are inherently less effective in achieving import restraint than QRs, for several reasons.

First, it is technically more difficult for most countries to control exports than imports. Most countries still have comprehensive import control machinery, while few have comprehensive export controls. In most cases, effective export control thus relies on truly cooperative behavior from the industry or the creation of a completely new government apparatus.[15]

Second, this technical problem is compounded by asymmetrical motivations. Most export restraining countries do not really want to restrain. Indeed, they will often hope that the announcement of the new VER, along with some minimal attention to carrying it out in practice, will avoid action by the importing country. Even if the countries want to do so, their industries can often evade the efforts (as through transshipments, discussed below). Most import-restraining countries and industries, on the other hand, do want to maintain effective controls.

Third, and perhaps most important, VERs rarely cover all suppliers. They are usually sought only from the chief producers of "market disruption." The sales of small suppliers, or even large suppliers whose export growth is modest, or the occasional country that just won't agree (e.g., Canada in steel) remain uninhibited. The sales of these non-restrainers are in fact likely to be stimulated, both because of the limits on supply from restraining countries and because they will want to establish the highest possible level of sales against which to base the restraints they naturally fear they may be induced to accept in the future.[16] Companies in restraining countries may foster such developments by investing in new production facilities in non-restraining countries, as Japanese textile firms have done throughout Northeast and Southeast Asia.[17] QRs, on the other hand, are almost always global in their coverage, although discriminatory quotas —such as those levied by European countries against Japan and in favor of the overseas associates of the EC—are not unknown.[18]

Substitution by non-restraining countries can occur readily, because many of the industries that are most likely to become subject to pressures for import restraints embody simple technology and relatively unskilled labor. Textiles are the classic example, where production facilities in non-restraining countries have been set up very quickly to supplement sales from countries that accepted VERs. U.S. imports of cotton textiles from non-restraining countries, mainly Hong Kong, rose from $3.6 million in 1956 to $108 million in 1960, while the Japanese VER held its sales virtually constant. The same kind of geographical shifting in synthetic textiles accelerated after the United States extracted VERs from the four principal suppliers (Japan, Korea, Taiwan, and Hong Kong) in 1971.

Fourth, sales from restraining countries can be augmented by trans-shipments through non-restraining countries, including non-producers (or very small producers) of the product in question. This adds to the technical difficulty of actually controlling exports, even with the most sincere efforts on the part of the restraining government.[19] When U.S. meat prices soared in the early 1970s, for example, meat from Australia entered the United States via Canada in response to the price incentives to Canadian meat importers generated by the VER.[20] And Japanese steel has apparently entered the United States via Canada and Korea. QRs are of course applied at the border of the importing country; they encounter no such problems at all if the quotas are allocated on a global basis and can stop transshipments even under country quotas through strict rules of origin.

Fifth, VERs may actually *raise* the level of imports in some years. VER levels are usually negotiated annually, even when within the framework of a long-term agreement. Thus they are usually based on some negotiated growth factor over the actual results of the previous year. QR levels, on the other hand, are more likely to relate to a fixed base period. Thus a shortfall of exports in any VER restraint year, below the maximum permitted for that year, could reduce a country's allowable sales in all succeeding re-straint years.[21] So countries may treat their *maximum* VER levels as *minimum* targets to be reached.[22] For example, European steel shipments to the United States might have fallen even more than 29 percent below restraint levels in 1970 in the absence of the steel VER, in view of the massive pressure of European demand on European steel-producing capacity. For similar reasons, there was widespread industry surprise that total U.S. steel imports in 1973 fell only 14 percent below 1972.[23] And the Japanese administrative apparatus for implementing the textile VERs, at least in the early years of the cotton restraints, penalized firms for not filling their quotas.[24]

Sixth, VER agreements are particularly likely to be ineffective during their last year. In the general absence of backup QRs or other sanctions on non-compliance, the incentive to exporters to restrain is further reduced. Even a provision for deductions from future VER levels has proven difficult to implement. Such "last years" can occur frequently. The meat restraints were annual. The steel VERs had durations of three years. So have many of the bilateral arrangements on cotton, woolen, and synthetic textiles. Only the first international arrangement on cotton textiles, which provided the umbrella over the cotton bilaterals, lasted even five years. On the contrary, terminal dates are seldom if ever set for QRs.

Finally, the terms of VERs are almost certain to be looser than the terms of QRs simply because they are subject to negotiation with the exporting country, in terms of such key variables as the overall level of restraint, the tightness of coverage of individual categories, shifting among categories, carryovers into previous and succeeding years, and so forth. Indeed, this is one of the major advantages of the VER alternative for the exporting country. From the standpoint of the importing country, the greater looseness reduces further the effectiveness of the import controls, relative to QRs, in limiting imports.

It is also frequently argued that VERs are less effective than QRs in restraining imports because they are politically easier to remove and thus likely to be of shorter duration.[25] It is true, as already noted, that VERs require frequent renewal while legislated QRs usually carry no termination date. But there is little evidence from U.S. experience that VERs come off more readily than QRs. It is true that the steel VER was permitted to expire in 1974. And the meat VER disappeared temporarily in recent years, but it was backed up by a U.S. quota law so the president in fact waived the back-up QR as well as the VER. But VERs may turn into QRs (as in oil) or into quasi-QRs (VERs backed up by QRs, as in cotton and now synthetic and woolen textiles), and their terms may tighten with renewal as in steel. And any QRs implemented under escape clause procedures, rather than legislated by Congress, do carry time limitations (though they can be renewed indefinitely). Finally, the recent unilateral U.S. import liberalization steps have focused more on QRs, with the elimination of the oil and sugar quotas and the expansion of dairy quotas, than on VERs.

The crucial issue determining the retention of both VERs and QRs is the balance of domestic political forces supporting and opposing them. Seen in this context, there is one important structural reason why VERs might last longer than QRs. VERs produce no overt compensation or retaliation. Thus they avoid any costs to other industries in the importing country, and avoid one important source of political opposition relative to QRs, where compensation and/or retaliation normally occurs.[26] Liberal trade interests thus develop sufficient power to terminate VERs only when price concerns become dominant, as recently in meat. They derive no support from other producing interests who, in seeking a termination of QRs, want termination of the compensation that reduced their own protection or the foreign retaliation that limited their own exports.

A related effectiveness question is whether VERs or QRs can be implemented more quickly.[27] That issue is also indeterminate. VERs have to be negotiated with other countries, QRs legislated by Congress or implemented through the lengthy procedures of the escape clause (Tariff Commission plus the president) or national security provision (study by the Treasury, formerly by the Office of Emergency Preparedness, and action by the president). In some cases, the executive has enough leverage with other countries to implement VERs quickly. However, many countries are becoming increasingly resistant to VER requests—note the reticence of Korea and Taiwan, as well as Japan, which balked at synthetic textile VERs for more than two years.

In sum, VERs clearly restrain trade less than QRs. This is of course a disadvantage to the industry seeking protection in the importing country, and an advantage to importers and consumers there as well as to the industry of the exporting country. (The advantage is greater for the former, because they benefit from continued imports from non-restraining countries.) Its effect on the overall balance between VERs and QRs can only be determined after the discussion of other considerations to which we now turn.[28]

Distributional Effects

Any increase in trade barriers reduces consumers' surplus. In Figure 15-1, which portrays the effect of an increase in prices from Pw to Pus due to the imposition of a new trade barrier, the reduction equals PwSRPus. Area E represents the transfer from U.S. consumers to the U.S. government, which results if the increase in barriers takes the form of a hike in the American tariff.[29]

A QR or VER, having the same effect on the level of imports, would under conditions of pure competition also raise prices from Pw to Pus.[30] However, there would be no transfer of revenue to the U.S. government unless it were to auction off quota tickets, which is not done under any existing QR. The disposition of the "tariff-equivalent revenue" of area E is thus indeterminate under a QR or VER. It will be shared between U.S. importers and foreign exporters, each of which will strive to maximize his share of the total.

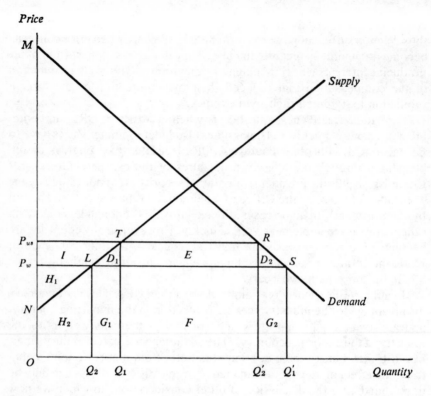

D_1, D_2 = Production and consumption deadweight losses, respectively;

E = Government revenue deriving from a tariff, or "tariff-equivalent revenue" in case of QR or VER:

$G_1 + F + G_2$ = Quantity imported in absence of restriction;

H_1 = Producers' surplus without restriction;

$H_1 + H_2$ = Level of domestic production under free trade;

$I + H_2$ = Producers' surplus with restriction;

MSP_w = Consumers' surplus without restriction;

MRP_{us} = Consumers' surplus with restriction.

Figure 11-1. The Economic Effects of Trade Restrictions.

There are two plausible bases on which this division might take place. One is the relative concentration of market power on the buying and selling sides of the trade. An oligopolistic industry selling to a competitive market of importers might well be able to capture most of area E, while an oligopsonistic set of importers buying from a market of competitive sellers might also be able to do so.[31]

A second possible explanation relates to the administration of the controls. Under QRs, the importing country organizes the market and assigns quotas. It may assign the quotas either to domestic importers (as in oil) or to exporting countries (as in sugar). If importers get the allocations, they should be able to capture most of the scarcity premia triggered by the restraints. On the other hand, under quotas allocated to exporting countries *or under VERs*, even when the VERs are reinforced by QRs in the importing country, the exporting country organizes the market and should be able to gain a predominant share of area E. In essence, restricting trade from the supply side strengthens the ability of the seller to maximize; restricting trade by a similar amount from the demand side strengthens the ability of the buyer to maximize.

The two explanations can be combined. The exporting country would be in the strongest position to maximize its share of area E if its export industry was relatively concentrated and if it also administered the controls, as via VERs. The importing country would be in the strongest position if its buying power was relatively concentrated and if it administered the controls via QRs allocated to domestic importers. The results would be less predictable if the criteria were mixed, especially under duopoly conditions where both the buying and selling sides of the market were heavily concentrated.[32]

Empirical work in this area is scarce. The evidence that does exist, however, suggests that administration of the controls largely determines the distribution of the tariff-equivalent revenue, at least in industries where neither oligopoly nor oligopsony dominates. The fact that VERs themselves foster added concentration in the exporting industry in question, as appears to have occurred in both textiles and steel, reinforces the dominance of this factor.[33] There would thus seem to be a significant difference between the microeconomic effects of VERs and most QRs.[34]

The clearest evidence comes from the oil, textile, and steel restraints. Under the oil QRs, "quota tickets" were allocated to U.S. importers. Some holders of these tickets exchanged them for domestic oil, instead of actually importing foreign crude or petroleum products, "which enables them to realize about the same value as they would receive from selling the ticket."[35] The imputed price of the tickets was basically determined by the difference between the U.S. and world price for oil (PusPw in Figure 15-1).[36] Hence the reduced U.S. consumers' surplus was captured by other Americans, through the operation of the quota system.[37] The oil industry is about equally concentrated on the selling and buying sides, so it appears that it was the retention of administrative initiative by the United States that determined the distributional effects.

Similarly, under the textile VERs in Japan and several other countries, export quotas are allocated to domestic firms largely on the basis of their historical market shares. Some of these quota holders sell some of their allocations to firms that will actually export to the American market.[38] The price of the tickets, again, presumably reflects most or all of the scarcity premia generated by the import restraints.[39] MITI has tried to assure this outcome in Japan by rejecting applications for export licenses when offer prices are too low, by penalizing firms whose prices are too low in the determination of quota allocations in subsequent years, and by providing bonuses in succeeding quota years for firms that most expand their total receipts.[40] Thus the textile exporters capture most of area E. The textile industry is highly competitive on both the exporting and importing sides, so it is again quite plausible that the administrative initiative is determinative. Indeed, this particular VER has had a self-reinforcing distributional effect by promoting greater cartelization of foreign textile industries, as larger firms have bought out smaller ones explicitly to get their export quota allocations.[41]

However, U.S. textile importers and retailers report that they apply their usual markups to the cost of the VER ticket as well as to the usual, pre-quota price of the textile goods. They regard the tickets as an additional cost to them, on which they must pay import duties, financing charges, agents' fees, and so forth. If they cannot pass on this markup to their customers, their demand for the goods in question and hence the price of the VER tickets will decline. Since their combined markups may raise the final price of the product to consumers by a factor of three to six, the distribution thereof is central to the distribution of the overall scarcity premia. Some of it clearly goes to other Americans: the duty on the VER ticket component of the import price to the U.S. government, whatever share of the financing is provided by U.S. banks, and so forth. Some of it may go to foreigners other than the sellers of the product or the quota tickets, such as agents and other middlemen who operate on a percentage basis. These institutional arrangements render much more difficult any analysis of the geographical distribution of the price increases stemming from VERs, at least in the case of textiles.[42]

Foreign steel originally penetrated the U.S. market in significant quantity, in the late 1950s, because of interruptions of domestic supply resulting from strikes by U.S. steelworkers. It increased its U.S. market share further during each succeeding strike, or period of stockpiling by U.S. steel users who feared future strikes. But it always maintained most of its newly won share of the U.S. market, and even increased it further, after domestic production resumed. (The data are in Table 15-2.) The main reason was price, which became determinative after American producers learned (from necessity) that the quality and reliability of foreign steel was comparable to domestic production.[43] This competition from foreign steel was a major factor in the relative stability displayed by steel prices in the United States throughout the 1959 to 1967 period, despite the high degree of concentration of the U.S. industry. The U.S. steel industry admits as much.[44]

Table 11-2

Steel Mill Products: Shipments, Exports, Imports, Apparent Supply, and Steel Trade Balance

(In millions of net tons)

Year	Net Domestic Shipments	Exports	Imports	Apparent Domestic Supply	Imports as Percent of Apparent Supply	Steel Balance of Trade Millions of tons	Amount (millions)
1957	79.9	5.3	1.2	75.7	1.5	+4.2	+$577
1958	59.9	2.8	1.7	58.8	2.9	+1.1	+372
1959	69.4	1.7	4.4*	72.1	6.2	−2.7	−150
1960	71.1	3.0	3.4	71.5	4.7	−0.4	+152
1961	66.1	2.0	3.2	67.3	4.7	−1.2	+41
1962	70.6	2.0	4.1*	72.6	5.6	−2.1	−60
1963	75.6	2.2	5.4	78.8	6.9	−3.2	−163
1964	84.9	3.4	6.4	87.9	7.3	−3.0	−127
1965	92.7	2.5	10.4*	100.6	10.3	−7.9	−670
1966	90.0	1.7	10.8	99.0	10.9	−9.1	−788
1967	83.9	1.7	11.5	93.7	12.2	−9.8	−877
1968	91.9	2.2	18.0*	107.6	16.7	−15.8	−1,532
1969	93.9	5.2	14.0**	102.7	13.7	−8.8	−946
1970	90.8	7.1	13.4	97.1	13.8	−6.3	−948
1971	87.0	2.8	18.3*	102.5	17.9	−15.5	−2,060
1972	91.8	2.9	17.7	106.6	16.6	−14.8	−2,190

*Year of steel strike, or threat thereof due to negotiation of new labor contract.
**First year of steel VER.
Source: American Iron and Steel Institute, U.S. Department of Commerce.

This price stability deteriorated rapidly with the inauguration of the steel VER in 1968. In response to the VER, European and especially Japanese steel producers radically changed their pricing strategy. They no longer sought to achieve and maintain growing shares of the U.S. market through price competition. Indeed, they explicitly priced their steel at a small discount below comparable U.S. steel—to compensate for "quality differences"—and raised their prices *pari passu* with each price rise by U.S. companies. Thus the difference between the U.S. and world prices for steel virtually disappeared, which clearly indicated that the foreign companies were reaping virtually all of the increase in price triggered by the trade restraints.

International trade in steel is highly concentrated on both the selling and buying sides. Thus it is likely that the administrative arrangements of the controls largely determined this outcome. Despite the high degree of oligopoly maintained by virtually all national (or regional, in the case of the EC) steel industries within their domestic markets, price competition clearly did take place among them through foreign trade before the imposition of the VER. U.S. wholesale prices for iron and steel rose by 28.4 percent from 1967 through 1972, compared with a rise of less than 18 percent in wholesale prices of all industrial commodities,[45] after rising less than the aggregate price level in the earlier period. In addition, a U.S. district court has recently suggested that the steel VER probably violated the Sherman Antitrust Act and hence is illegal under U.S. law, thereby implying that trade was not so restrained before the VER. So there is strong evidence that the steel VER has sharply reduced competition in the entire U.S. steel market, and that the foreign producers have reaped most of the benefit from the higher prices of their sales into the United States.

The few estimates made by other authors support the view that foreign suppliers pick up most of the reduction in U.S. consumers' surplus when other countries administer the restraints, under VERs or QRs (sugar) that are allocated on a country basis, while Americans do so when QRs are allocated to them on a non-country basis by the U.S. government. Mintz[46] has estimated that the U.S. loss of "tariff-equivalent revenue" (area E in Figure 15-1 under a QR or VER system) to foreigners is negligible in the case of oil; about $300 million under the sugar QR, which as noted earlier is biased toward foreign suppliers because it is they who receive the quota allocations; and $53 million in 1970 for meat, where "the higher price paid under the quota...goes to the foreign exporters since the quotas are allocated to them." Magee[47] estimates that foreigners capture at least 66 percent of this "revenue" in steel, or about $175 million at the 1971 level of trade. He agrees with the above analysis on textiles, which suggests that foreign suppliers gained over $600 million in 1971 from the reduction in U.S. consumers' surplus. He attributes a loss of tariff-equivalent revenue of only $2 million to the dairy quotas, which are administered by the United States. Magee concludes that "loss of tariff-equivalent revenue accounted for almost a third of the U.S. social loss due to quotas [sic]," an outcome which is primarily attributable to administering two of the major restraints via VERs rather than via QRs allocated to U.S. importers.

Large amounts of money are thus involved in the allocation between Americans and foreign suppliers of the reduction in U.S. consumers' surplus triggered by VERs and QRs. The ability of foreigners to capture a much greater share of this total under VERs may play a major role in explaining why they are willing to accept such restraints, even at the cost of limiting the potential growth of volume of their sales.[48] Indeed, this phenomenon represents a significant degree of compensation to the restrained sellers—which is a politically more desirable form of compensation to the government of the exporting country than tariff cuts on some of its other exports, since the compensation accrues to the same people hurt by the restraints.[49]

Most businessmen, placing a high utility on reducing the variance of their sales and hence the possibility of overproduction (or underproduction, which may be psychically as well as financially costly in terms of lost opportunities), like nothing better than a predictable market, especially if they can dictate prices in that market. This phenomenon is particularly marked in industries that are already heavily oligopolized, such as steel, and may explain a good deal of the willingness—even eagerness—of the European and Japanese steel industries to restrain their exports to the United States.[50] Of course, it is far easier for an industry to cartelize in this fashion if it can point to a request for restraint from the importing country and conjure up worse consequences if it fails to do so. Under the blanket of the LTA, the Japanese may even have introduced quotas on some cotton textile items "for purposes of reducing competition among Japanese exporters and suppliers, (which) tended more to frustrate foreign buyers who were benefiting from the competition."[51] Correspondingly, the national cost of import restraints to the United States will tend to be significantly larger under VERs than under QRs, per dollar of deadweight loss, because of the loss of tariff-equivalent revenue in addition to the deadweight losses.[52]

A second distributional issue relates to the array of costs and benefits among the different supplying countries. VERs are usually applied only by the fastest growing suppliers, while QRs usually apply to all suppliers. Thus any small suppliers left outside the VER network obviously prefer VERs. Indeed, their market opportunity will be enhanced by the restraints on their largest competitors, and they will have an incentive to build their sales rapidly to hedge against the risk that they will subsequently be brought under the VER, or that the VER will turn into a QR.

Figure 15-2 modifies Figure 15-1 to depict this effect. A QR of $Q_2Q'_2$ would leave potential new suppliers with no scope for increased sales. A VER placing the same limitation ($Q_3Q'_3$) on traditional suppliers, however, would enable new suppliers, whose costs exceed those of the traditional suppliers but are less than those of suppliers in the importing country, to sell $Q'_3Q''_3$. Hence the U.S. price would rise only to P_{ns}, and the efficiency losses to the United States would be less than under QRs (only $D_1 + D_2$). Area 1 would be the "tariff-equivalent revenue" contested between traditional suppliers and U.S. importers. Area 2 would be the loss of consumers' surplus relative to the free-trade alternative, which would however represent an increase in consumers' surplus relative to the QR alternative.

The largest supplier of a given product may also benefit from import restraints. Any such restraints tend to lock in market shares, and hence limit the scope for market penetration by new foreign suppliers who are also covered by the restraints.[53] QRs do this most completely because they cover all suppliers and may even benefit the strongest suppliers further if the quotas are allocated on a first-come first-served basis. But most VERs cover at least the several leading suppliers rather than just the single leader.[54] Thus the major losers among the exporting countries from VERs,

170

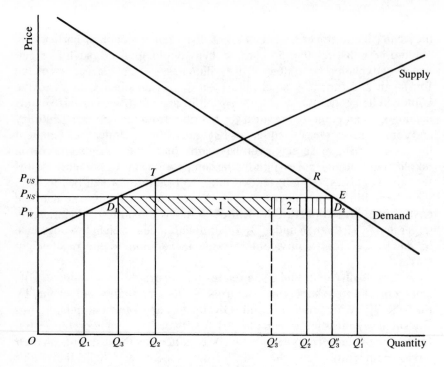

D_1, D_2 = Production and consumption deadweight losses, respectively;
1 = "Tariff-equivalent revenue" due to restrictions on traditional suppliers;
2 = Increase in consumers' surplus relative to QR alternative, due to imports from non-restrained countries.

Figure 11-2. The Economic Effects of QRs and VERs.

relative to QRs, are likely to be the rapidly growing intermediate suppliers—who find the industry leader locked into his superior base even though he is no longer the most dynamic producer and their newly emerging competitors completely unrestrained. Korea and Taiwan in synthetic textiles are prototypes. The acquiescence of covered suppliers to the multilateralization of textile VERs into the LTA and its successor arrangement was motivated in part by precisely these kinds of concerns, though multilateralization was of course basically promoted by the United States and other importers to increase the coverage of the overall restraint program.

Trade Policy Effects

VERs have several important effects on U.S. and world trade policy: the possibility that their implementation can satisfy the protectionist demands of individual industries and thus avoid import restrictions in additional industries by avoiding altogether the legislative process, which would otherwise be triggered as those protectionist industries sought QRs and which is the only likely route to widespread protectionism in the United States; the related erosion, by the same token, of domestic and international rules and procedures for determining trade policy; and their impact in adding to the erosion of the most-favored-nation (MFN) principle.

Some liberal traders view VERs as "less bad" than QRs because of their lesser degree of trade restrictiveness, as outlined above. However, VERs and QRs may not really be alternatives if consideration is limited to a single industry. Few if any industries would seek protection via VERs if they thought they could obtain QRs. The U.S. administration argued that it had to negotiate a steel VER in 1968, but there was little risk that steel QRs would have been legislated at that time. A different administration made the same case for synthetic textile restraints in 1969, yet Congress failed to vote such quotas in 1970 despite eight months of effort. Any "advantages" that liberal traders might see in the greater flexibility of VERs might thus be more than offset by their greater ease of implementation in the first place.[56]

But VERs may well be "less bad" than QRs in terms of overall U.S. trade policy. For example, Congress might have passed a protectionist trade bill in 1970 had steel and meat not "been taken care of" with VERs in 1968. Abolition of the steel and textile VERs might well trigger major efforts by those industries, and leaders of their unions, to get legislated QRs. Such efforts could tip the political balance in the United States toward a protectionist trade bill.[57] And any such bill would almost certainly include quotas going far beyond steel and textiles, because Congress appears to oppose favored legislative treatment for particular industries threatened by imports.[58]

It is also true that VERs can help clear the way for trade liberalization. The first cotton textile VER with Japan, in 1957, made possible a four-year extension (the longest to that time) of the Reciprocal Trade Agreement Act and hence the Dillon Round of trade negotiations.[59] The Kennedy administration was able to assure Congressional support for the Trade Expansion Act, and hence the Kennedy Round, by first nullifying the opposition of the textile industry by negotiating a more comprehensive VER on cotton. The Nixon administration had no chance to achieve a liberal trade bill in the early 1970s, to authorize it to participate in a further round of trade negotiations, until it again satisfied the textile industry with a synthetics VER (and perhaps the steel industry by extending the steel VER). So, in trade policy terms, the relative merits of VERs and QRs must be considered in the overall context that exists at any given time rather than simply in terms of the different impact of the two approaches on the single industry in question.

The second trade policy issue is procedural. There are three major routes to import restriction in the United States. One is via existing law, which authorizes protection in cases of (a) "injury or threat of injury" from imports under the escape clause, (b) jeopardy to the national security, or (c) external threats to domestic agricultural support programs. Each of these authorizations lays out detailed procedural steps to assure that all interested parties will be heard before a decision is made.[60] The second is via new Congressional legislation, which by its nature triggers the airing of all sides of an issue both in public hearings and among Congressmen with different constituencies. The third is VERs, where no procedural requirements apply.

Democratic decision making is obviously fostered when provision is made for the input of all relevant considerations. VERs violate this basic principle. Industry representatives dominate the discussion, and financial support for political campaigns (as in textiles) and other acts of political back-scratching can easily dominate the outcome. No other voices may be heard at all—particularly if, like exporters and especially consumers, they are ineffectively represented within the government itself. So the interplay of national interests that attends all trade policy issues is least permitted to enter the decision-making process on VERs.[61] Indeed, as already indicated, the absence of such procedures may have actually led the government to violate the Sherman Act in negotiating the steel VER.

A similar, and related, loophole exists in the international trade rules. Article 19 of the GATT covers "Emergency Action on Imports of Particular Products" and applies only to increased imports resulting from "obligations incurred by a contracting party under this Agreement, including tariff concessions . . . ," none of which relates to export restraints. Thus most observers conclude that the GATT does not cover VERs. But Article 11, aimed at the "General Elimination of Quantitative Restrictions," clearly states that "no prohibition or restrictions other than duties, taxes or other charges, whether made effective through quotas, import or *export licenses* . . . shall be instituted or maintained on the importation of any product . . . *or on the exportation or sale for export* of any product . . ." (with the exception of agricultural, classification, or short-supply controls).

In practice, however, the GATT has exercised no jurisdiction over VERs.[62] Indeed, it has implicitly sanctioned both the cotton and all-fiber textile VERs by providing the forum within which they were multilateralized. Aside from textiles there has been no international guideline at all to which national laws and policies on VERs must conform. In turn, this has permitted the domestic situation just described in the United States. There is no requirement that an importing country seeking VERs provide compensation to the restrainer, or accept retaliation. As a result, an importing country can seek VERs for the benefits of a single industry without concern for any direct consequences for other industries. Both the procedural vacuum and the absence of other-industry effects add greatly to the ease of implementing VERs relative to QRs.

A final trade policy issue stems from the usual limitation of VER coverage to the major supplying countries, whereas QRs generally apply to all suppliers. The U.S. request for synthetic and woolen textile VERs, for example, was addressed solely to Asian countries although European countries supply a larger share of the U.S. market for some of the items covered.[63] The steel VERs covered both Japan and the Common Market,[64] but excluded Canada, some Europeans (e.g., Sweden and Austria) and some Asians (e.g., Korea and Australia). On the other hand, the meat VERs covered all major suppliers (but did exclude minor suppliers Canada and the United Kingdom). No firm conclusions can thus be drawn about the importance of this factor, and VERs do not seem to be promoting the formation of trade blocs. As long as the MFN rule continues to cover QRs (and tariffs), however,[65] VERs will provide a policy instrument that can be used in a discriminatory manner and thus heighten tensions between particular countries or geographic regions.

The Comparative Politics of VERs and QRs

VERs are alleged to raise fewer international political problems than QRs because of their greater flexibility, avoidance of repercussions on industries other than the one restrained (by avoiding compensation or retaliation under the GATT rules), and avoidance of spillover into broader issues of trade policy. My analysis of the economic effects, especially on this last point, tends to support the contention. And there have certainly been occasions when VERs were truly voluntary and hence raised no serious political problems. A recent example is steel where, as indicated above, the European and Japanese industries were as happy as the U.S. industry to eliminate the only arena in which they had previously been forced to compete.[66]

Some recent cases, however, are much less clear. Japan withstood major and accelerating U.S. efforts to induce it to adopt synthetic and woolen textile VERs from early 1969 until October 1971, when the United States applied the crudest and most blatant pressure to finally achieve Japanese acquiescence. Korea, Taiwan, and Hong Kong were equally unyielding over this period. Spain has wholly rejected U.S. efforts to induce it to accept VERs on shoes, and Italy has been unwilling to restrain on shoes unless Spain did.

Indeed, the United States suffered exceedingly high political (and economic) costs from pursuing the synthetic-woolen VERs so relentlessly with Japan. Part of the cost was the intangible but very real adverse impact which it had on overall U.S.-Japan relations, both because the Japanese felt they were simply being asked to redeem a campaign pledge made by President Nixon, which had no economic justification, and because President Nixon felt that Prime Minister Sato failed to deliver a VER after twice promising to do so. It is highly likely that the antipathy that the president developed toward these Japanese "betrayals" played an important role in his neglecting their sensitivities while dropping the "Nixon shocks" of July and August 1971 on Tokyo.[67]

More tangibly, the U.S. textile effort deflected the attention of both countries from the truly critical economic problems that were building up between them throughout 1969 to 1971: the mounting Japanese trade and payments surpluses, globally and with the United States, and the continued Japanese restrictions on imports (and capital inflows) that accelerated protectionist sentiments in the United States. The heavy costs associated with the international aspects of the New Economic Policy of August 1971 might have been avoided had these far more serious problems been addressed earlier, but the textile dispute kept them on the back burner.[68]

At the same time, the Japanese government proved unable or unwilling to force its textile industry to restrain. Hence it seemed finally to prefer that the United States take decisive action, so that it would avoid domestic political blame for "caving in to the American demands." U.S. QRs would probably have been less damaging to overall U.S.-Japan relations than the VERs that eventuated, particularly if they had been levied in 1969, but even had they been passed as part of a Mills bill in 1970 *without other protectionist elements*—which is precisely the legislation that the administration sought throughout the second half of 1970.

Any generalizations in this area are extremely hazardous. The relative desirability of VERs and QRs, in broad political terms, hinge on four factors: the political importance in the exporting country of the industry whose restraint is sought, the attitude of that industry toward restraint, the degree of overall national self-assertiveness (especially vis-à-vis the United States) in the country being asked to restrain, and the importance of that country to the United States. Politically, it is probably better for the United States itself to act via QRs versus a politically powerful industry that opposes restraint in a self-assertive nation of high importance to U.S. foreign policy. VERs would be more likely to minimize political costs if they were adopted by a politically weak industry that was willing to accept restraints (or even welcomed them, for the reasons outlined above, like the Japanese and European steel industries) in a relatively non-nationalistic society of lesser political importance to the United States. The attitude of the industry from which restraint is sought is probably the single most important factor. Of course, the degree of control sought will always be a major factor, as it was with Japan in 1969-71.

A second important international political implication of VERs is their discriminatory nature. As indicated above, most VERs cover only the most important supplying countries. Hence they deviate from the MFN rule that was installed at the center of the postwar trading system largely for political reasons. They carry especially high costs for those "middle countries" who have become significant enough to be covered under VERs but, unlike most leading suppliers, still have the internal dynamism and the market scope to grow a good deal more.

These considerations have related particularly to the relations between Japan and the other industrialized countries. Japan has been by far the major target of VER pressures, due to its phenomenal export success in a variety of industries. The United States has been a major applier of such pressure. But Europe has always done so as well, would doubtless have done so even more in the absence of its maintenance of discriminatory QRs against Japan on some of the same products, and is perhaps doing so even more rapidly now with the rapid rise of Japan's sales as it tries to diversify its export markets.

Yet Japan has also probably been more sensitive about foreign discrimination than has any other major country, particularly with regard to American policy.[69] So maximum discrimination and maximum sensitivity about discrimination have combined to heighten the political tensions surrounding VERs. The inclusion from the outset of the synthetic and woolen textile VER of Korea, Taiwan, and Hong Kong helped alleviate its discriminatory connotation, but an Asian bias clearly remained since no serious effort was made to exact similar restraints from several major European suppliers.

On the other hand, QRs raise problems with a larger number of suppliers precisely because they are not discriminatory. In the case of synthetic and woolen textiles, for example, U.S. quotas on European exports would clearly have damaged the Atlantic relationship at the same time that they relieved some of the strain on the Pacific relationship. So VERs may enable the importing country to avoid political problems too. It should also be noted that QRs, while usually less overtly discriminating than VERs, can also encompass discriminatory aspects: the allocation of U.S. sugar quotas to foreign countries, while based in principle on actual shipments in the 1963-64 base period, were in fact altered significantly in response to lobbying activities, and large and/or nearby countries are usually favored de facto by first-come first-served quotas that are allocated to domestic importers for other products.

The LTA on cotton textiles tried to resolve the discrimination problem by placing VERs within a multilateral framework within which importing countries "guaranteed" restraining exporters that other exporters would be covered as well. The meat VER tried to do so by including virtually all suppliers. So discrimination is not inherent in VERs, and can be avoided in several ways if it is deemed sufficiently important in particular cases. And discriminatory use of QRs may rise in the future, if the prohibition of such treatment is excised from the GATT as many observers now propose. Even if QRs are not overtly discriminatory, they can be used de facto to bite hardest on the most rapidly growing suppliers simply by setting an early base period against which all countries are permitted similar percentage increases. So the two may not differ too much on this count in the future, with the important political difference that the discrimination of VERs is overt while the discrimination of QRs can be much more subtle, and indeed be treated as non-discriminatory under the international rules. The desire of the importing country to achieve effective restraint and the desire of the covered exporting country to avoid discrimination (for both economic and political reasons) both suggest, of course, that VERs should either be generalized or QRs used instead.

Conclusions and Policy Recommendations

Barring significant changes in international and national trade policy and practices, efforts by importing countries to negotiate VERs are likely to continue to proliferate. This is certainly true in the United States.

Congress clearly likes VERs. The Meat Import Act of 1964 explicitly authorized negotiated VERs as an alternative to its mandatory QRs. The Mills bill of 1970 authorized the VER alternative in all of its QR provisions. The Trade Reform Act submitted by President Nixon in early 1973 made a similar proposal, which became law in the Trade Act of 1974. Even the Burke-Hartke bill would permit VERs to supersede the QRs that it sought on virtually all U.S. imports.

The executive also likes VERs. It would certainly prefer their flexibility to the mandatory nature of any QR legislation. It usually has a penchant for avoiding the limiting and time-consuming procedural requirements of present law. Individuals within the executive branch can pursue their special interests with such an under-the-table policy instrument. VERs enable any administration to play favorites both at home and abroad.

The analysis of this chapter suggests that VERs should be brought fully within the same domestic and international legal and procedural requirements that govern QRs. This would mean making them subject to Article 19 of the GATT, or any new "safeguard" provision which emerges from new international negotiations, and to the criteria and procedures of the escape clause in the United States. Action to do so is quite urgent in view of the strong prospects for their further proliferation.

VERs are far easier to implement than QRs because they are now subject to no domestic or international procedural restraints, and because they involve no other domestic interests through compensation or retaliation requirements. They restrict trade less than QRs, but there is no evidence that they are likely to be of shorter duration. Hence, on balance, their availability outside any legal or procedural constraints is quite likely to increase the degree to which international trade is restrained.

VERs may also raise even greater international political problems than QRs. Exporting countries are becoming increasingly reluctant to adopt VERs, which tendency can be expected to grow with the continuing decline of relative U.S. political and economic power and the accelerated sense of independence in most potential VER countries. Exporting countries, particularly Japan but also others throughout Asia and Latin America, will grow increasingly resentful of discrimination as their world role grows.

There is one case, of course, where VERs do not raise international political problems: where they are actually welcomed, or even sought, by the "restraining" industry to boost its oligopolistic position. By that very token, however, the VERs significantly exacerbate inflation in the importing country if, as is frequently the case, QRs are not likely to eventuate in their stead. In addition, the distributional effects of VERs add to their costs relative to QRs in the importing country. These effects argue against VERs for reasons of both global trade policy and national self-interest in the country seeking import relief.

Under present trade policies and practices, however, VERs provide two benefits relative to QRs. By providing the United States with an alternative to legislation to limit imports in particular sectors, they avoid the risk that protection will be accorded far more widely. And by permitting the exporting country to organize the restraints, they provide compensation within the restricted industry—the kind of compensation most needed by the government of the restraining country and most saleable to the "compensating" industry in the importing country. It is particularly important for the United States to be able to extend such compensation during periods when the president has no Congressional authority to provide compensation through lowering import barriers in other industries, as was the case from mid-1967 until the end of 1974.

Both of these benefits of VERs could be retained without VERs themselves, however. First, the United States should amend its escape clause so that it will be effective in permitting temporary QRs (or increased tariffs) for industries that are injured by imports. There is a widespread consensus in the United States that the escape clause has been too tight to deal with legitimate problems of import injury since 1962 and that it should be loosened by (a) eliminating the link between imports and previous tariff concessions and (b) requiring that imports be only "the primary" or "a substantial" cause of the injury rather than "the major" cause. These changes, which were in fact made by the Trade Act of 1974, should revitalize the escape clause, with its careful procedural safeguards, as a fair but effective avenue for import relief. Hence it would obviate the need for industries to seek legislated QRs to provide them with import protection, and the need for the executive to pursue VERs to avoid the wider manifestations of such Congressional action.

Once the criteria of such a modified escape clause were met through its standard procedures, the availability of VERs rather than QRs to provide the temporary import relief could be beneficial. The choice between the two instruments would turn basically on two issues: (1) whether the United States wanted to discriminate overtly among foreign suppliers, which is done more easily with VERs, and (2) whether it wanted to compensate the exporting country by letting it seize the scarcity premia generated by the VER itself or by extending trade concessions on other products. There would be policy advantages in retaining such flexibility once the VERs were brought within the same legal limitations as QRs—which was *not* done by the Trade Act of 1974, leaving the VER loophole intact.

Second, all such VERs and QRs (and increased tariffs) should henceforth take place within the framework of a new "import safeguard" mechanism negotiated internationally and embodied in an amended Article 19 of GATT. Such a mechanism should encompass the features recommended in the Rey Report: limited duration for all restraints, a declining degree of protection throughout their lives, and accompanying domestic programs to assure that they will in fact turn out to be temporary. In my view, even safeguards of this type should require compensation from the importing country and authorize retaliation by the exporting country, in the absence of satisfactory compensation, to assure that it will be no easier, from an international standpoint, to use the new safeguards than it was to use the old ones.[70] However, it should be possible to grant "compensation" within the restrained industry itself by letting the exporting country administer the restraints via VERs or by assigning QR allocations to each supplying country (as the United States has done with its sugar quotas).[71] This new type of compensation should not be granted when it would foster cartelization, however; in such cases, the traditional approach to compensation (via other industries) should be used instead.[72]

Third, developing countries should receive tariff preferences (preferably zero duties) for any of their exports to industrialized countries limited by VERs (or QRs) under the new safeguard mechanism. This would maximize their opportunity to expand their market shares at the expense of industrialized country exporters under non-country QRs and would at least help them fill the quotas allocated to them under either country QRs or VERs, without exceeding the aggregate level of imports sought by the importing country. It would also enable developing countries to improve their terms of trade at the expense of the treasury of the importing country, by charging sufficiently higher prices to capture the revenue formerly collected as customs duties. These gains would at least partially obviate the high costs of trade restriction to such countries, which would be particularly important under the proposed new trade regime in which (geographically non-comprehensive) VERs would by virtue of their being subjected to procedural limitations be used much less frequently, relative to (geographically comprehensive) QRs, than in the past. However, the U.S. Trade Act of 1974 explicitly *rejects* preferences for goods covered by VERs or QRs.

Each of these three changes in U.S. and international trade policy is desirable in its own right. It is suggested here that taken together, they would also turn VERs from an under-the-table device that permits countries to avoid both domestic and international trade rules into an acceptable, and perhaps useful, commercial policy instrument in the future. Benefits of both an economic and international political nature would flow to a variety of countries as a result.

Notes

1. To be sure, VERs have also existed since the 1930s. For an interesting short history see Stanley Metzger, *Lowering Non-Tariff Barriers* (Brookings Institution, 1974). Interwar VERs, such as those on French imports of Dutch and Italian agricultural goods and British, German, and Belgian manufactured goods, are discussed as "bilateral quotas" in Heinrich Heuser, *Control of International Trade* (George Routledge and Sons, 1939), especially chapter IX.

2. See especially Jagdish Bhagwati, "On the Equivalence of Tariffs and Quotas," in Robert E. Baldwin and others, *Trade, Growth and the Balance of Payments* (Rand McNally, 1965), pp. 53-67; the comments thereon by Hirofumi Shibata, "A Note on the Equivalence of Tariffs and Quotas," *American Economic Review*, Vol. LVIII, No. 1 (March 1968), pp. 137-42; and the reply by Bhagwati, "More on the Equivalence of Tariffs and Quotas," ibid., pp. 142-46. For the critical differences that result in a dynamic model see Mordechai E. Kreinen, "More on the Equivalence of Tariffs and Quotas," *Kyklos*, Vol. XXIII-1970-Fasc.1, pp. 75-79, and Ingo Walter, "On the Equivalence of Tariffs and Quotas: A Comment," *Kyklos*, Vol. XXIV-1971-Fasc. 1, pp. 111-2.

3. The only exceptions I could uncover were Shibata, *American Economic Review*, in three paragraphs, and brief references to their different distributional effects in Richard E. Caves and Ronald Jones, *World Trade and Payments: An Introduction* (Little, Brown & Co., 1973), p. 289, and Robert Stern, "Tariffs and Other Measures of Trade Control: A Survey of Recent Developments," *Journal of Economic Literature*, Vol. XI, No. 3 (September 1973), p. 870.

4. Most of them are analyzed in C. Fred Bergsten, *Completing the*

GATT: Toward New International Rules to Govern Export Controls (British-North American Committee, 1974)[chapter 10 in this volume].

5. I inject here the caveat "ostensibly" because we shall soon see that VERs bring sufficient benefits to exporting countries or industries that, in some circumstances, they may actually be welcomed by those countries or industries.

6. The term "orderly marketing agreements" avoids this problem, but "voluntary export restraint" is less inaccurate and understood more widely so I use it in this chapter.

7. There are also numerous trade-restraining agreements that have the same effect as VERs. An example is the Automotive Products Trade Agreement of 1965 between the United States and Canada, under which the United States essentially limited its exports of automobiles and parts to Canada by promoting growth in Canadian production of those items—to avoid a perceived threat that Canada would impose its own limitations on automotive imports in the absence of some such U.S. action. And multinational firms may sometimes be permitted to invest in a host country only if they limit the imports of the new subsidiaries from the parent firm. The sharply different institutional features of such arrangements differentiate their effects from the straightforward VERs under consideration here, however, and they are excluded from the analysis.

8. The U.S. government denies playing any formal role in the arrangements, and its position is supported by the absence of any U.S. machinery to back up the VERs. However, it clearly negotiated them with the foreign industries in 1968 and again in 1971.

9. Unless the president waives the quotas themselves for overriding "national interest" reasons, as he did in 1972, 1973, and 1974.

10. Even a complete list of VERs and their trade coverage would not provide a satisfactory basis for assessing their significance because of the familiar problem that the volume of trade is *reduced* as the VERs (or QRs) are *tightened*. For a partial listing of the widespread use of VERs through the early 1960s see Gardner Patterson, *Discrimination in International Trade, The Policy Issues 1945-1965* (Princeton University Press, 1966), pp. 295-6. For a detailed discussion of interwar VERs see Heuser, *Control of International Trade*.

11. Press Release #183, Office of the Special Representative for Trade Negotiations, June 19, 1973. Imports of these shoes, primarily sneakers, were valued at about $40 million in 1972.

12. An EC Commission working party has reportedly listed 55 cases in which Japan has introduced VERs "in the hope of avoiding restrictions by the Community." *Journal of Commerce* (August 3, 1973), p. 9. And additional Japanese VERs on sales to Europe (e.g., television sets to Britain and tape recorders to Italy) were announced after that date.

13. A new area for the growth of VERs may occur in East-West trade. The U.S.-Soviet commercial agreement of 1972 calls for VERs by the exporting country in any product where the importing country declares unilaterally that "market disruption" has occurred.

14. There are of course other similarities between VERs and QRs, that will be ignored in this analysis. For example, either type of restraint on trade to a single market deflects trade in the restrained product into other markets; but there is no systematic difference between VERs and QRs in this regard.

15. For a fascinating account of the complex machinery that the Japanese government and industry associations had to create to administer the original cotton textile controls, see John Lynch, *Toward An Orderly Market: An Intensive Study of Japan's Voluntary Quota in Cotton Textile Exports* (Tokyo: Sophia University, 1968), especially chapter 6.

16. For example, the share of U.S. steel imports obtained by non-restrainers doubled, from 12 percent to 23 percent, between 1969 and early 1973. This issue is discussed in Caroline Prestieau and Jacques Henry, *Non-Tariff Trade Barriers As a Problem in International Development* (Private Planning Association of Canada), especially p. 158.

17. Evasion of VER limits is not the only motivation for Japanese foreign direct investment in textiles. Indeed it is conscious Japanese policy to upgrade Japan's industrial base by exporting its lowest wage, lowest productivity industries—such as textiles—particularly if they are also major polluters and heavy users of energy. One implication is that the Japanese textile VER may have become unnecessary even from the standpoint of the U.S. textile industry, which view is supported by the failure of the Japanese to fill their quotas in many commodity categories in recent years.

18. There are also numerous proposals to relax the non-discrimination rule, which has governed QRs throughout the life of the GATT, in the future. Such proposals are made by Anthony Solomon in Chapter 16 and Eric Wyndham-White in Chapter 19 of C. Fred Bergsten, ed., *Toward a New World Trade Policy: The Maidenhead Papers* (Lexington, Mass.: Lexington Books, D.C. Heath and Company, 1975), and in the U.S. Trade Act of 1974.

19. Warren Hunsberger, *Japan and the United States in World Trade* (Harper and Row, for the Council on Foreign Relations, 1964), p. 323, called this "The most serious administrative difficulty" of the cotton VER in its early days.

20. The response of the U.S. government provides a fascinating anecdote in the history of trade controls. Overruling all of his advisors who had concluded that this Canadian loophole had to be plugged, both to implement faithfully his policy of limiting meat imports and to be fair to suppliers

who could not take advantage of it, President Nixon in early 1970 refused—due to the rise in meat prices—to authorize the imposition by the United States of QRs on meat imports from Canada. As a result, the VER limits were sharply liberalized at the first opportunity to accommodate (rather than stop) the transshipments.

21. This "problem" could be avoided by basing restraint levels on a constant *share* of the market in the importing country, to be monitored *ex post*. In practice, however, both QRs and VERs are almost always defined in absolute volume or dollar terms.

22. The tighter the VER restraints, in terms of barring carryover of shortfalls from one year to the next and shifting of allowables among restrained categories, the more likely is this result.

23. *Journal of Commerce* (February 22, 1974), p. 6. Meyer Bernstein, for many years Director of International Affairs of the United Steelworkers of America, attacks the steel VER as perverse on precisely these grounds (see Chapter 14 of Bergsten, ed., *Toward a New World Trade Policy*).

24. Lynch, *Toward an Orderly Market*, p. 157.

25. Hunsberger, *Japan and the U.S. in World Trade*, p. 364 and Patterson, *Discrimination in International Trade*, p. 298.

26. I include the modifier "overt," because VERs may provide compensation to the restraining country *within* the industry being restrained and because they may levy costs on the importing country in terms of its broader economic and even political relations with the country on which export restraint is urged. These issues are discussed in the text.

27. As distinguished from the more important question of whether VERs or QRs are more likely to be adopted *at all*, which is discussed in the section on "Trade Policy Effects."

28. There is no way to generalize about the relative effectiveness of VERs and tariffs. But Shibata, "A Note on the Equivalence of Tariffs and Quotas," p. 141, is clearly wrong in stating that "the protectionists are essentially indifferent between quotas and tariffs," for the reasons pointed out by Kreinen, "More on the Equivalence of Tariffs and Quotas": an increase in demand in the importing country leads to increased domestic production and/or prices under quotas, but (at least partially) to increased imports (with smaller price rises) under tariffs.

29. Area I represents the transfer to American producers. Areas D_1 and D_2 are the production and consumption deadweight losses that reflect the reduction in efficiency generated by the increased tariff.

30. Bhagwati, "On the Equivalence of Tariffs and Quotas." See also Rachel McCulloch and Harry G. Johnson, "A Note on Proportionately Distributed Quotas," *American Economic Review*, Vol. LXIII, No. 4 (September, 1973), pp. 726-32, who demonstrate that the price-quantity

equilibrium "does not depend on whether consumers or producers receive the import licenses." When competitive conditions do not exist, this equivalency between a tariff and quota may break down; for a survey of the literature, see Stern, "Tariffs and Other Measures of Trade Control," pp. 868-70. The present discussion focuses solely on the differential distribution of benefits under QRs and VERs, whose overall effect on price and import levels is assumed to be equivalent.

31. As suggested by Shibata, "A Note on the Equivalence of Tariffs and Quotas," pp. 139-42.

32. When retail prices are frozen, as they were in the United States under Phase I and Phase III ½ of the Nixon incomes policy in 1971 and mid-1973, foreigners should be able to seize any increase in the scarcity premia caused by trade restraints even under QRs. This is because increases in the "landed cost of imports," though one of the few exceptions permitted from the freeze, can be passed on only dollar-for-dollar. Thus all increases in scarcity premia accrue to the foreign seller (assuming no illegal kickbacks to the U.S. importers to circumvent the freeze). Similar results occur under any type of price controls for any increases in the scarcity premia that exceed the price increases permitted by the controls. I ignore this case in the analysis in the text.

33. For textiles, see the discussion in the text. For steel, *Economic and Foreign Policy Effects of Voluntary Restraint Agreements on Textiles and Steel*, A Report by the Comptroller General of the United States, March 1974, p. 24, concluded that the ". . . 1969 arrangements reduced competition among Japanese steel companies." Heuser, *Control of International Trade*, p. 121 concluded that "combination (oligopoly) . . . undoubtedly receives a new impetus from the practice of bilateral quota restrictions (VERs)."

34. Another issue is whether consumers really get the "consumers' surplus." The more concentrated an industry, on either the selling or buying side (or both), the less likely are they to do so. For example, a reduction in trade barriers in a monopsonistic industry may simply increase importers' profits. This issue arises irrespective of the nature of the import restraint in place or being removed, however, and hence is not treated in this chapter. Anticipating the conclusion to be reached shortly in the text, it does suggest that, in the real world, the effect on consumers of a trade restriction can range across a wide spectrum: from 100 percent of the theoretical consumers' surplus in a highly competitive industry where trade is restrained via a VER, to nothing in a highly concentrated industry regardless of the method of control.

35. Cabinet Task Force on Oil Import Control. *The Oil Import Question* (Government Printing Office, 1970), p. 86.

36. Pro-rationing of U.S. domestic production of course played a major role, along with the import quotas, in preserving this price differential.

37. Auctioning rather than allocating the quota tickets would also "assure that the benefit of permitted low-cost imports is fully realized by [the public of] the importing country," Cabinet Task Force on Oil, ibid. A similar issue arises under VERs with regard to distributing the benefits within the exporting country. Export quota tickets could be auctioned or sold at a fixed price, as was done by the Dutch government on its restrained level of butter exports to France in the 1930s (Heuser, *Control of International Trade*, p. 114) instead of allocated free.

38. Lynch, *Toward an Orderly Market,* p. 157, reports that Japanese firms were assessed fines by the Japanese government under the cotton VER if they did not use all of their export quotas, so had an incentive to "transfer" their tickets instead. (On the other hand, their quotas were determined on the basis of each previous year's sales so they had an even greater incentive to actually fill their quotas, as indicated above.) There are unverified industry reports that quota tickets have been sold by holders in one restraining country to sellers in a second restraining country.

39. Richard Ward (Director, Foreign Buying, Montgomery Ward), "Remarks to Republican Task Force on International Trade," January 29, 1972, reports that the price of export "tickets" often amounted to $2.50-4 per dozen units, raising the price to U.S. importers by 10 percent or more. Industry sources report more recently that the premia often amount to 15 to 30 percent of the ex-quota prices, Comptroller General's Report, pp. 26-27.

40. Lynch, *Toward an Orderly Market,* pp. 152, 156, indicates that price levels of actual sales were accorded a 30 percent weighting in the formula for determining future quotas.

41. The seizing of the scarcity premia by foreign textile producers can also be inferred from the findings in G. C. Hufbauer, Naygara Aziz, and Asghar Ali, "Cotton Textile and Leather Exports: What Cost Foreign Exchange?" *Pakistan Development Review,* Vol. IX, No. 3 (Autumn 1969), pp. 330-3. They conclude that "profits on some exports are so large that the goods could be sold abroad at a gain to the manufacturer, but at a loss to the nation."

42. The Comptroller General's Report, pp. 26-28, concluded that only about one-third of the price increase induced by the quotas went to foreign suppliers while the rest went to U.S. importers and retailers. In discussing the interwar VERs, Heuser, *Control of International Trade,* pp. 115, 118, points to such a division of the scarcity premia between exporting and importing countries under VERs. He notes that French retailers, who first opposed the VERs bitterly, proposing QRs instead so that *they* could reap the scarcity premia, soon accepted them because they began to get enough

of the induced price increases to offset the effect on their profits of the reduced volume of trade.

43. The latest evidence of the importance of price in this industry is the shift back to U.S. steel by a number of U.S. steel users in the wake of the 1971-73 exchange-rate changes, through which the Japanese yen and German mark (including its 1969 revaluation) have both appreciated sharply against the dollar.

44. Stewart S. Cort (Chairman of Bethlehem Steel and spokesman for the U.S. steel industry), Statement before the House Ways and Means Committee, June 7, 1973, p. 18: "Production costs are not the determining factor in steel export prices of foreign producers. They frequently price the product to get into our market to achieve domestic economic objectives." Cort used this argument to support protection for U.S. steel, charging predatory pricing by foreign companies. In so doing, however, he clearly recognizes the reduction in prices to U.S. steel users from such imports; foreign sellers covered by the VER hardly need to cut prices "to get into our market."

45. *Survey of Current Business* (January 1974), pp. S-8, S-9. This difference narrowed in 1973, but almost wholly because of the effect of the explosion of fuel prices on the all-commodity index. Kurt Orban, president of a steel-importing company and president of the American Importers Association, has testified before Congress that "the true market price [of steel] has risen much more, because of all kinds of hidden increases." See his statement on the Trade Reform Act of 1973 before the House Ways and Means Committee, May 14, 1973, p. 6. To be sure, factors other than the VER have affected U.S. steel prices in recent years, and high demand for steel in foreign markets held U.S. imports even below VER levels in 1969. Nevertheless, the close correlation between institution of the VER and the dramatic acceleration of U.S. steel prices, relative to other U.S. prices, strongly suggests that the restraints are a major cause thereof.

46. Ilse Mintz, *U.S. Import Quotas: Costs and Consequences* (Washington: American Enterprise Institute for Public Policy Research, 1973). Her estimates cited in the text are drawn from pp. 78, 40, and 76, respectively.

47. Stephen P. Magee, "The Welfare Effects of Restrictions on U.S. Trade," *Brookings Papers on Economic Activity 3; 1972*, pp. 671-4.

48. At least some of the interwar VERs seem to have been negotiated for precisely this reason. See Heuser, *Control of International Trade*, p. 112.

49. Still another alternative would be a lump-sum payment (e.g., foreign aid) from the United States to the exporting country in lieu of the higher prices it could charge under the VER. Rachel McCulloch, "Import

Quotas and Resource Allocation'' (unpublished Ph.D. thesis, University of Chicago), pp. 54-56, has demonstrated that both the monopolist and the importing nation can improve their welfare through such arrangements. However, such compensation would require fiscal appropriations in the United States, whereas one of its basic objectives in pursuing the VER route is precisely to avoid the legislative process (see text discussion), and it remains unclear how importers could be prevented from exploiting the scarcity premia themselves. Such a lump-sum payment, of $375 million, was apparently pledged by the United States to get Korea to agree to the VER on synthetic textiles in 1971; a "U.S. Embassy official" in Korea is quoted to that effect in the Comptroller General's Report, p. 29.

50. Striking evidence of this eagerness was recently provided as a by-product of the suit filed against the steel VER by Consumers Union. Early in the legal proceedings, it appeared that questions might be raised about the standing in court of Consumers Union to prosecute the case. Efforts were thus made to find steel importers or end-users of steel in the United States to join the suit. Despite major efforts, including discussions with importers who had publicly complained of shortages of steel resulting from the VER, not a single additional plaintiff could be found. All expressed fear that they would suffer retaliation from their foreign suppliers if they made such an effort—despite the fact that the suit sought to eliminate the restraints that had been "forced on" those very suppliers by the U.S. government!

51. Lynch, *Toward an Orderly Market*, p. 195. Hunsberger, in *Japan and the U.S. in World Trade*. also notes the irony of U.S. promotion of cartelization of the Japanese textile (and later, steel) industry after its major effort to break up the *Zaibatsu* after World War II. See also the commentary by Komiya following Chapter 15 of Bergsten, ed., *Toward a New World Trade Policy*.

52. On the other hand, as noted above and in Figure 15-2, the decrease in imports and hence deadweight losses—areas D_1 and D_2 in Figure 15-1—are usually less under VERs than QRs.

53. The U.S. textile restraints have probably perpetuated the life of parts of the Japanese textile industry, for example, that might have moved abroad more rapidly had they not been assured a particular share of the U.S. market.

54. Japan has been frequently singled out, however, as in many of the VERs on sales to Europe and in the original cotton textile VER with the United States in 1957.

55. The U.S. textile industry vetoed a U.S. government proposal that might have produced U.S.-Japanese agreement on a very tough

synthetics-woolens VER in December 1970 because they still thought that the Mills bill, with its all-fiber QRs, might become law.

56. George Ball, *The Discipline of Power* (Little, Brown & Co., 1969), p. 193, has noted that voluntary agreements, "since being too easy to work out, have tempted hard-pressed government officials to yield to industry pressure."

57. For an analysis of that balance, see Chapter 20 of Bergsten, ed., *Toward a New World Trade Policy.*

58. The "Byrnes basket" provision of the Mills bill of 1970, which would have presumptively triggered QRs for any industries that met certain numerical criteria and which passed the House of Representatives, is the latest evidence of such a view. The president and Congress agreed on the desirability of textile QRs in 1970 but could not agree on whether other industries should receive similar treatment and hence no action resulted.

59. Hunsberger, *Japan and the U.S. in World Trade*, p. 355.

60. The procedures may not always be totally effective in achieving that purpose. Nevertheless, they do provide a basis for the consideration of all relevant viewpoints.

61. In his assessment of the textile and steel VERs, the Comptroller General, p. 33, reported that "We did not find evidence that responsible agencies had made this assessment [of the costs and benefits of import restraint, and of different methods of achieving a desired level of restraint]. Restraints continue without regard to current or prospective conditions."

62. Patterson, now Deputy Director-General of GATT, indicated in *Discrimination in International Trade*, p. 298, that VERs "do not legally violate GATT rules."

63. There was also a request to Israel, a minor supplier, that never produced any results.

64. One early "benefit" to the United Kingdom of joining the EC was the entry of its steel exporters into the steel VER.

65. Except where superseded by the GATT authorization for customs unions and free-trade areas, and the "transitional" arrangements of article XXXV that continue to provide a justification for Europe's discriminatory barriers against Japan.

66. The Commission of the EC formally expressed unhappiness about the steel VER, but no national governments voiced displeasure. Lynch, *Toward an Orderly Market*, p. 193, also believes that the original postwar Japanese cotton VER in 1956 was at least partly voluntary: "The Japanese wanted peace, and an end to a messy campaign that may possibly hurt their business and name at a time when they still had an international inferiority complex. The enticing offer of compromise and a chance to bury one more

unpleasant memory of the late Pacific war were tempting tidbits that the Japanese finally accepted.'' The "messy campaign" of course means that the Japanese, even in this case, were not acting wholly on their own initiative.

67. For a detailed and absorbing analysis see I. M. Destler, Haruhiro Fukui, and Hideo Sato, *The U.S.-Japan Textile Negotiations of 1969-1971: A Study in Bureaucratic and International Politics* (Brookings Institution, forthcoming).

68. In May 1969, before Secretary of Commerce Stans made a major trip to Japan, the National Security Council was presented an options paper that analyzed the four major problems in U.S.-Japan economic relations: their bilateral payments imbalance, Japan's import restrictions, Japan's investment restrictions, and textiles. The paper concluded that the United States would have to clarify its priorities among the four issues in order to make any progress at all and recommended the ordering just indicated. The president was unwilling to set any priorities, however, the practical effect of which was to focus most of the U.S. policy effort on textiles.

69. See Chapter 12 of Bergsten, ed., *Toward a New World Trade Policy*.

70. For a contrary view see the two-track import safeguard mechanism proposed by Anthony M. Solomon in Chapter 16 of Bergsten, ed., *Toward a New World Trade Policy*. He would exclude compensation and retaliation in cases where countries adhered to the new international rules and require such treatment only when they violated those rules. This approach is conceptually sound, but could lead to frequent action outside the new rules due to the internal political temptation to impose new restrictions without a clear requirement for compensation/retaliation and the strong possibility that a country applying safeguards, especially a powerful country like the United States, could then successfully "justify" its actions as coming fully within the new framework whether in fact they did so or not.

71. A further wrinkle could be for the *government* of the exporting country to auction off the export quotas or levy an export tax, seizing the scarcity premia generated by the trade restraints for its public as a whole rather than letting them accrue to the protected industry. The same reasoning suggests that an importing country should auction off QRs (to a large number of buyers) so that its public will gain back the cuts in consumers' surplus generated by the quotas, rather than handing price increases as well as quantitative protection to the injured industry.

72. Implementation of this principle could prove difficult. Is cartelization strengthened more by giving more market power to an industry that is already heavily concentrated, as in the steel VER, or by providing an impetus to cartelization in an industry that is highly competitive, as in the

textile VERs? Guidelines would have to be developed to indicate when each type of compensation would be appropriate.

Part IV
United States Trade Policy

12 Crisis in U.S. Trade Policy

Since 1962, U.S. trade policy has been moving steadily away from the liberal trade approach which had characterized it since 1934 and which has been the objective of every administration since that time.

In 1962, the Trade Expansion Act passed the Congress with the largest majority in the history of the trade agreements program and led to the Kennedy Round of trade negotiations. Since 1962, however, the number of U.S. industrial imports subject to quantitative restrictions, including "voluntary restraint" by foreign suppliers, has risen from seven to 67—a number which will shortly exceed the total of any other industrialized country, and whose restrictive impact is undoubtedly greater than the liberalizing effect of our tariff cuts in the Kennedy Round. And Chairman Wilbur Mills of the Ways and Means Committee—who helped pilot the 1962 law to its overwhelming passage—commented last year that the Trade Expansion Act would have been unlikely to attract 50 votes on the House floor in 1970.

The shift has come along an accelerating trend line. In 1964, Congress passed the Meat Import Act—the first legislated import restrictions for a major industry in the postwar period. There were attempts in 1964 and 1965 to negotiate voluntary restraint agreements covering U.S. imports of woolen textiles. The modest trade bill submitted by the Johnson Administration in 1968, whose only significant liberalizing feature was its request for repeal of the American Selling Price system of customs valuation (ASP), was never even reported out of the Ways and Means Committee; and the Administration decided that it had to negotiate voluntary restraint agreements on steel and meat to avoid turning the bill into widespread protectionist legislation. And the Nixon Administration sought to negotiate voluntary restraints on synthetic and woolen textiles throughout 1969 and 1970.

The most dramatic evidence of the shift in Congressional and public opinion developed in 1970. The so-called Mills bill, which would have levied quotas on all textile and shoe imports and tariff quotas on two minor products, passed the House of Representatives by a vote of 215 to 165. It would also have sharply increased the likelihood of additional import restrictions by a drastic loosening of the escape clause. It would have relegated adjustment assistance—the most constructive alternative to im-

Appeared originally in *Foreign Affairs*, July 1971, pp. 619-35.

port restrictions—to such a subordinate position that the concept would have been totally discredited.

The bill's only concessions to liberal trade policy were its hedged repeal of ASP, and a provision that the President could waive the import restrictions if he deemed them against the national interest. The Senate Finance Committee passed a bill similar in its restrictive features, omitting ASP repeal. Only the adjournment of the 91st Congress precluded the passage of a new trade law along these lines.

The question is whether the trend will continue, with more products covered and less presidential flexibility to avoid them, or whether it can be reversed so that momentum toward trade liberalization can be renewed. If it cannot, history amply demonstrates that further slippage away from free trade is probable.

II

Two major arguments have supported a liberal U.S. trade policy in the postwar period. The first is the standard economic case for free trade: the improvement of our economic wealth and income by exchanging goods which we can produce most efficiently for goods which can be produced more efficiently by others. Imports help moderate inflationary tendencies and maintain competitive pressures on U.S. industry. Freeing of trade reduces the discrimination against the United States inherent in regional economic arrangements elsewhere in the world, notably the Common Market and European Free Trade Association; this both protects our exports and reduces the incentive for American firms to invest behind the trade barriers of those groupings.

It is also argued that free trade on balance creates jobs in the United States, because of the famous paradox that our exports use more labor than would be necessary to produce at home the goods currently imported, but primarily because we continued to run a surplus of exports over imports. And it is also argued that freer trade supports a continuation of the trade surplus and thus helps our balance of payments.

The economic argument was never sufficient by itself, however, to support a liberal trade policy for the United States. Trade has simply represented too small a share of our total economy, especially on the import side where the benefits are widely diffused among consumers. The trade surplus argument was always phoney: any restrictions on U.S. imports would be fully or largely offset, in trade balance terms, either by our compensation on other imports or a loss to our exports from foreign retaliation; it would be irrelevant to the outcome whether our trade balance started from a surplus or deficit position.

Though the economic argument was always marginal, it was generally regarded as positive by the major political groups in the United States. But it was the foreign policy case which provided the real impetus for liberal trade policies in the United States in the postwar period. Expanded exports were an essential component of the reconstruction of Europe and Japan, and a liberal U.S. trade policy was therefore an essential corollary to Marshall Plan aid. Later, freeing of trade was seen as a key to forging an Atlantic partnership between the United States and Europe, thereby to contain communism. Our interest in keeping the lower-income countries free from communism, and their obvious need for increased markets abroad to complement our capital and technical assistance programs, also required liberal trade policies. In submitting the Trade Expansion Act, President Kennedy went so far as to state that, ''Our efforts to maintain the leadership of the Free World thus rest, in the final analysis, on our success in this undertaking.''

Today, neither the economic nor the foreign policy argument for liberal trade commands much support in the United States. More disturbingly, they have lost support for reasons which appear to be deep-seated rather than subject to rapid reversal. Most disturbingly, they seem likely to continue to lose support in the years ahead unless new policies are developed and pursued both here and abroad.

III

The most important shift in the U.S. political constellation on trade policy is organized labor's move to the protectionist camp. This shift cannot be explained simply by high unemployment. Labor was becoming more protectionist even as unemployment was dropping steadily after 1962, and had adopted a completely protectionist stance when unemployment stood at its post-Korea low in early 1969. A return to overall full employment alone cannot be expected to bring organized labor back to the liberal trade camp, though it could of course only help.

In its role as a factor of production, labor can adopt either of two courses. It can be essentially dynamic, supporting rapid change with the objective of increasing national output and hence overall welfare— accepting, as a price, the occupational and personal dislocations which must inevitably accompany rapid change. Or it can adopt an essentially static attitude, giving up income but avoiding many of the costs of dislocation.

Organized labor now seems to have chosen the second approach, at least concerning foreign trade. Organized workers have apparently achieved sufficient income levels that the movement as a whole has become more interested in avoiding shifts of geographic location, seniority rights, local interests, etc. than in seeking higher real incomes elsewhere. The dramatically improved competitive position of other countries has of course had an important effect on this decision. Protectionist trade policies on the part of labor may be an inevitable consequence in a highly developed country where foreign trade plays a small role in the overall economy, and which faces tough foreign competition.

This decision by organized labor has been promoted by the accelerated pace through which international trade and investment transmit technological change. The dislocations of dynamism may be acceptable up to a point, but unacceptable beyond. As the most visible embodiment of such rapid change, the multinational corporation has become a special target of organized labor; and it must be recognized that these corporations command factors of production—capital and management—which are much more mobile internationally than is labor, and which thus appear across the bargaining table as invincible and unfair competitors.

Lawrence Krause has identified another underlying cause of organized labor's change of position—its decreasingly representative nature as the overall U.S. labor force grows primarily in the services rather than goods-producing sector.[1] Most goods producers are unionized and most services producers are not. The trade policy impact of this development is critical because workers in the services industries can only gain from free trade; and only the goods producers can lose from free trade, since few services can be traded internationally.

Moreover, labor has not moved quickly enough in organizing the fast-growing high-technology industries as those industries have developed their share of the U.S. economy. This factor is also crucial for trade policy, since it is the high-technology industries which can compete effectively—a recent study shows that they produced a $9 billion trade surplus in 1969—and thus have a great interest in liberalizing international trade. The non-technology intensive industries, which cannot compete well—registering a deficit of over $5 billion in 1969—and thus want protection, are grossly overrepresented in the labor movement.

The single most potent political group in the country has thus turned against the economic case for a liberal U.S. trade policy. It is unlikely to return shortly and, in fact, may become increasingly protectionist as the international transmission of technological change accelerates even further. Organized labor may become even less representative as our major economic growth continues to take place in the largely unorganized services and high-technology industries. Even a reduction in the national rate of unemployment is unlikely to turn the tide. The next question is whether there are countervailing forces which appear likely to take up the economic case for liberal trade to offset this swing.

A logical candidate is the consumer. Protectionist legislation would have a more adverse impact on consumers than most of the legislation to which their representatives have devoted so much attention, and they would be among the major gainers from free trade.

There are two new economic factors, of particular concern to consumers, which argue strongly for their mobilization in this regard. First, recent studies have discovered changes in the structure of U.S. unemployment which mean that a given level of aggregate unemployment corresponds to much sharper price rises in the United States than was the case even ten years ago—the "Phillips curve" has moved sharply against us.[2] Second, at the present cyclical point of our economy, high unemployment coexists with the persistence of inflationary pressures. These new structural and cyclical situations make it exceedingly difficult for macroeconomic policy to cope effectively with inflation. Selective anti-inflationary policies, such as increased imports, have therefore become even more appealing than usual as a means to moderate price rises.

To date, however, consumer groups have not mobilized effectively on trade. This is largely because most of these groups are dominated by organized labor, and thus focus on the sharper costs of job losses from imports than their more general but widely diffused benefit in moderating prices. The shift toward a services-producing economy gives at least theoretical promise that consuming groups will begin to play a stronger role in support of liberal trade, either because they will influence organized labor in that direction or because the impact of organized labor will decline along with its failure to reflect accurately the composition of the labor force.

There is a curious paradox concerning the impact of inflation on the politics of trade policy, however. As just indicated, price rises increase the desirability of imports as a means to check inflationary pressures and thus should call forth the voice of consumer interests. But increased inflation also reduces the international competitiveness of U.S. industries closest to the competitive margin, and thus increases their protectionist pleas. The net impact on trade politics of changes in the rate of inflation is thus indeterminant, and may be essentially neutral. We cannot count on reductions in the present rate of inflation as contributing decisively to the political base of support for a liberal U.S. trade policy, though a return to full employment together with relative price stability would probably help appreciably.

A second possible countervailing force are the multinational corporations; their Emergency Committee for American Trade was a major force against the Mills bill in 1970. They gain greatly from international trade, since they can then use their various bases of production to sell anywhere in the world and thus increase their profits. Their effects will become more pervasive as more firms go multinational.

However, these same corporations lose least from trade restraints, since their variety of production bases means that they can avoid trade restrictions better than most by simply producing in or near the markets which they serve. Their greater concern is thus with maintaining freedom for their international investments rather than free trade. In addition, relationships with labor and domestic industries seeking protection have reduced the zeal with which some of them have supported liberal trade policies.

The multinational corporations can therefore be expected to continue to support freer trade, but whether their support will be concentrated enough to countervail the protectionist pressures is uncertain. If foreign retaliation against U.S. restrictions began to take the form of action against U.S. investments, their support for freer trade would undoubtedly increase, since exports would then become relatively more important to them.

Third, smaller industrial exporters—which would gain from reductions of trade barriers and suffer from foreign retaliation against U.S. import restrictions—should also oppose the projected trends. However, most of these smaller firms sell only a small share of their output abroad, and they account for only a small share of the political clout of U.S. business.

Agriculture is the U.S. political bloc with the greatest interest in achieving liberal world trade. About one-fourth of all U.S. farm produce is exported, and the share exceeds one-half for several key crops. Agriculture can be expected to continue to support freer trade, though its political importance will continue to decline as its share of the total U.S. labor force continues to fall. And the vigor of its support is being increasingly undermined by agricultural policies in the rest of the world.

IV

Support for continued liberal trade policies on foreign policy grounds has also been sharply eroded. This is primarily due to the neo-nationalist views which counsel that we turn away from world involvement, and which are deep-seated and likely to continue to grow. They are particularly acute in the trade field, because trade more directly affects particular U.S. interests than do most other aspects of foreign policy—even military programs affect most Americans only indirectly, via the budget—and because of widespread views that the behavior of our main trading partners justifies a protectionist shift in the United States.

It is true, of course, that any need for the United States to help support the economies of the other industrialized countries through expanding our imports from them disappeared long ago. More broadly, however, the generally reduced fear of a threat to our security from the communist world—in the industrialized or lower-income countries—renders our society increasingly unwilling to inflict economic pain on important groups to promote our overall foreign policy; one of President Kennedy's main arguments for the Trade Expansion Act was the need to counter the "communist aid and trade offensive," and the theme of anti-communism ran throughout the message in which he proposed it.

Neo-nationalism in trade policy is characterized by repeated charges that the United States has given away, in purely commercial terms, much more than it has gotten in past trade negotiations. It is widely believed that America has done so to assure the success of successive trade negotiations, and thus achieve broad foreign policy objectives. As a result, the Congress has developed deep doubts that any administration can be trusted to negotiate "fair" trade arrangements—and is thus extremely reluctant to extend trade liberalizing authority. A corollary belief is that the United States does not insist that other countries live up to their international obligations in the routine daily business of international trade relations.

Here, too, the future looks even more difficult than the past. Non-tariff distortions now probably rival tariffs as barriers to trade, and national policies in new areas (such as protection of the environment) will add to the list. In view of their disparate nature and subtle effects, these distortions are very hard to measure. Our analyses of the trade effects of tariffs have always been unsatisfactory, but at least they could be made. But it will be exceedingly difficult to demonstrate convincingly that the United States—or anybody else—will have gotten true commercial reciprocity from a negotiation on non-tariff distortions. It may then become even harder to convince Congress of truly reciprocal bargaining by the Executive branch in the future.

A tough trade policy stance by the Executive, producing fair treatment for U.S. commercial interests from the more routine business of trade relations, is thus an essential precondition for any new Congressional grant of trade liberalizing authority and any major new international trade negotiation. Such a policy will itself create foreign policy problems, though presumably of lesser magnitude than those that would be caused by the protectionist trends which the policy would seek to avoid.

The foreign policy case for a liberal U.S. trade policy has also been undercut by the practices of our major trading partners. The Mills bill could have been characterized as sharply escalating an international trade war, but not as starting one.

There are three major problems which concern the trade policies of the European Community (EC). The most important is the Common Agricultural Policy (CAP), which sharply increases production through the maintenance of price levels well above world prices, with no production controls. World trade in the commodities covered by the CAP is affected in two ways: imports are restricted through variable levies which fully protect Community producers against the lower prices of outside suppliers, and exports are subsidized to sell abroad some of the induced surpluses.

The CAP has a highly significant impact on U.S. trade policy through its impact on our own agricultural community. As already noted, U.S. agriculture is now the sole major political bloc here which strongly supports liberal trade. However, restrictions on agricultural imports by other countries—of which the CAP is the most restrictive and covers the major foreign market—reduce agriculture's support for liberal trade and undermine its position badly.

The second Common Market problem is its preferential trade arrangements with its former colonies and, more importantly, the semi-developed countries surrounding the Mediterranean. The trade impact of these arrangements on America is not yet clear, although individual problems are already jeopardizing the support of particular industries for liberal trade policies.

It is clear, however, that the arrangements violate at least the spirit of the most-favored-nation principle of the General Agreement on Tariffs and Trade (GATT), under which all member countries are to benefit from tariff reductions extended by any other member country. They thus undercut supporters of the most-favored-nation principle and liberal trade generally. The Community moves also support those who would have the United States work out its own preferential deals, especially in Latin America and perhaps East Asia. The resultant world of large trading blocs would probably add impetus to the protectionist movement.[3]

Third, the Community's nascent industrial policy could pose new problems if it were to restrict the activities of U.S. companies, including their subsidiaries in Europe. There has already been a proposal for preferences in EC government procurement for companies controlled by Community nationals in sectors where the governments have helped finance research and development, which would represent both a non-tariff barrier to trade, and discrimination against foreign investors. There could certainly be more such steps, since one of the basic objectives of the industrial policy is to create European-wide companies which can compete more effectively against the U.S.-based multinational firms. If an EC industrial policy were to become significantly restrictive against both foreign investors and imports, the major adverse impact would be on the U.S. multinational corporations—precisely the group which has continued to support liberal trade for the United States more strongly than any besides agriculture.

All of these Community trends are likely to continue in the future, particularly if the EC successfully expands its membership to include the United Kingdom and the other applicants. In broad terms, a new Community of Ten would want to take steps to distinguish it as "Ten." More specifically, the agricultural restrictions would then include another major market; Britain has already begun to raise its price levels and accompanying import restraints. Preferential arrangements would be extended to some of the former Commonwealth countries, and all of these arrangements would of course then include trade with the Ten. Even more important, expansion of the Community virtually assures that new preferential arrangements will be worked out with other European countries unable to obtain full membership, bringing a large volume of additional trade within the discriminatory grouping. And the industrial policy may become one of the next major Community efforts, of particularly great interest to the British in view of their competence in various high-technology sectors and their desire to improve their competitive position against U.S. firms.

The difficulties which these developments raise for maintaining political support for a liberal trade policy in the United States among affected economic groups are exacerbated by growing doubts that the United States will obtain any significant political advantages from European economic integration—the basic rationale for U.S. support for the whole enterprise. This view usually focuses on the apparent lack of political spill-over from the economic steps, and is stimulated by the likely association of the European neutrals—which could only impede progress toward political unity.

Just as the economic view often ignores our large and growing volume of trade and investment with Europe, however, this political view seems to assume that a common European defense and foreign policy could have been expected to develop in a decade, and that the plans and progress already made toward European monetary integration are not the most profoundly political of steps which could be pursued by sovereign nations. Nevertheless, the broad foreign policy doubts exist and add to the problems raised by the EC economic policies themselves.

The Japanese situation raises three important problems which add to the bleakness of the outlook for a liberal trade policy in the United States. First, the pace of Japanese liberalization, though quickening now, has lagged far behind liberalization in the other industrialized countries. Second, there is a widespread view that administrative practices and the business-government collusion of "Japan, Incorporated" will continue to prejudice the trade opportunities of outsiders whether or not explicit barriers remain. Finally, barring a sizable revaluation of the yen, Japan's competitiveness will probably continue to grow and thus keep Japan in the forefront of protectionist attacks in the United States whatever the policies which it pursues.

The final foreign policy problem is the lower-income countries. There still remains a generally sympathetic view in the United States toward their need to expand their export markets, but that consensus is beginning to change. Textile imports from Taiwan and Korea are regarded as equally dangerous as textile imports from Japan. Imports of electronic components and other relatively sophisticated products from subsidiaries of U.S. companies in Mexico, Taiwan and elsewhere are of increasing concern to those U.S. firms and workers with which they compete. If U.S. firms continue to expand their activities in these countries, essentially to take advantage of lower labor costs in producing standardized products, their lower-income status may be increasingly ignored by wide segments of opinion in the United States as trade policy toward them develops.

V

Finally, the protectionist shift is partly a reaction to the relatively pure free-trade approach of the Trade Expansion Act itself. Its major impact was its changes in the escape clause, the traditional safety valve for meeting the temporary but legitimate problems periodically caused for entire U.S. industries by imports. Precisely at a time when world economic competition was becoming much tougher, with the creation of the Common Market and the full emergence of Japan, the escape clause was tightened significantly.

During the 1950s, Presidents Truman and Eisenhower imposed escape clause restrictions on an average of twice yearly, and it was a credible alternative for industry complaints even when they faced less foreign competition. But between passage of the Trade Expansion Act in 1962 and 1968, there were no escape clause actions. The strength of the U.S. economy in this period would probably have reduced the number of cases in any event but the strictures of the Act, its interpretation by the Tariff Commission, and the Administration's efforts to avoid any disruptions of the Kennedy Round negotiations effectively voided the escape clause as an avenue for import relief.

The Trade Expansion Act also included the major conceptual breakthrough of providing for adjustment assistance to individual firms and workers injured by imports—a new alternative to import restrictions which could both zero in on specific problems and avoid disrupting international trade relationships. It enabled organized labor to support the Trade Expansion Act.

However, the adjustment assistance provisions were drawn so tightly, and interpreted so stringently, that not a single case of adjustment assistance was authorized through 1968. The present Tariff Commission and Administration have changed this situation as rapidly as possible, certifying adjustment assistance for 11 firms and over 15,000 workers and budgeting almost $250 million for it in fiscal year 1972. However, from a political standpoint, the administration of the program for its first six years has discredited the entire concept—though it remains the most valid alternative to import restrictions yet conceived.

VI

Some would disagree with this analysis, and suggest that the situation today differs little from 1961. At that time, protectionist pressures also looked very strong. But a major presidential initiative in the very next year carried the largest majority of any trade legislation in the history of the United States.

It could happen again. But today differs sharply from 1961. At that time, Europe and Japan had just emerged as true competitors to the United States in the world economy; today, they exceed or equal us in a wide range of sophisticated product lines. Perhaps the most startling perception of change comes in remembering that one of the five "fundamentally new and sweeping developments" on which President Kennedy based his case for the Trade Expansion Act was "the need for new markets *for Japan* and the developing countries." We are unlikely to base a trade initiative today on the need to provide new markets for Japan.

In addition, the Trade Expansion Act was sold largely on foreign policy grounds—as the most important tangible step in the U.S. effort to create an Atlantic partnership with Europe, and thus to continue to contain communism. No such grand design exists today. It is extremely dubious that foreign policy considerations would suffice to carry such an initiative now. Finally, organized labor's shift has come wholly since 1962.

In analyzing developments in 1970, some have also suggested that the near-miss of protectionist legislation was due primarily, if not solely, to the Administration's support of textile quotas when its effort to negotiate "voluntary" export restraints with Japan broke down. This position undoubtedly affected the legislative situation deeply last year, and accelerated the success of protectionist efforts. It provided support for the concept of protectionism. It forced the Administration into an ambivalent posture on trade policy, despite its liberal positions on virtually every other trade issue, which is particularly important because the President is in by far the best position to take all of the factors affecting trade policy into account —including its diffuse but crucial economic benefits and its foreign policy implications, as well as its sharp economic costs to particular groups—and thus base his position on the overall national interest.

However, the problem is much deeper than any single industry, and the basic situation would be as outlined—whatever position was taken by President Nixon on textiles in 1968-70. And it should be remembered that

Candidate Humphrey made the same pledge as did Candidate Nixon, and that the textile industry would have powerfully affected developments through the Congress in any event.

VII

The development of U.S. trade policy along the lines described above could have a profound impact on overall U.S. foreign policy.

Trade policy uniquely pervades U.S. relations with all major areas of the non-communist world. Trade and related economic issues are already among the most important between the United States and Europe, and will become more so as the European Community continues to replace America as the single most important entity in international economic relations. Trade already heads the list of U.S.-Japan problems, as the textile issue demonstrates. Economic issues dominate relations between America and Canada. Expansion of trade is one of the greatest needs of the lower income countries, so U.S. trade policy will have a major bearing on our overall relations with Latin America, Asia and Africa—particularly since the level of U.S. economic assistance is unlikely to rise dramatically in the period ahead. And even our relations with the communist world would not remain unaffected if we helped resuscitate long-buried Marxist shibboleths by permitting economic confrontations in the West both to undermine Western unity and tempt individual non-communist countries to seek new economic, and therefore political, relations with the communist world.

The foreign policy impact of a restrictive U.S. trade policy would go far beyond dollars and cents, important as they are. Throughout the postwar period, the United States has largely been viewed as a generous country, which makes mistakes but whose mistakes are usually made in following policies intended to help the world as a whole as well as the United States itself.

Continued U.S. leadership of this type is probably no longer needed. In view of our pressing domestic priorities and the changing perception of our national interests by many Americans, it could probably not be sustained domestically at this time. But a lurch all the way to crass mercantilism could have a devastating impact on foreign perceptions of the United States.

Another key quality of U.S. foreign policy throughout most of the postwar period has been its predictability. In a crunch, others could usually count on the United States to provide the anticipated support or to seize a constructive leadership role. A posture of uncertainty in such a crucial area would also undermine U.S. foreign policy. The deliberations on the Mills bill in 1970, for example, spanned almost nine months with the outcome uncertain into the final two weeks—and with the uncertainty resumed when the new Congress convened. And the unpredictability could spread well beyond trade, since U.S. interest groups, hurt by foreign retaliation against our own import restrictions, would undoubtedly seek to retaliate themselves, perhaps by seeking to reduce U.S. troops in Europe.

The importance of trade policy to overall U.S. foreign policy will undoubtedly increase over the next few years. First, the economic interdependence of nations is increasing rapidly and protectionist steps by our country will thus have an ever larger economic, and therefore political, impact on other countries. Second, the economic content of overall U.S. foreign policy is likely to grow as these economic exchanges rise and as we reduce our direct military and political involvement around the globe. Third, the basic objective of present U.S. foreign policy is to forge new and mature partnerships with other areas of the world; many other countries rank trade policy very high on their priority lists, and it will be impossible to create true partnerships if we fail to heed these most crucial concerns of theirs.

Throughout the postwar period, U.S. trade policy—indeed, all U.S. foreign economic policy—has primarily served to promote overall American foreign policy objectives. The realities of the 1970s require that the "economic" component achieve a much greater share of the foreign economic policy equation. But there are those who wish to make overall foreign policy the handmaiden of foreign economic policy, and there is a strong risk that trade policy will come to dominate overall foreign policy disastrously. It is in this sense of steady erosion—not necessarily of abrupt cataclysm—that it is proper to speak of a trade policy crisis in U.S. foreign policy.

VIII

This picture is extremely pessimistic concerning U.S. trade policy, and therefore concerning a key element of overall U.S. foreign policy. Several new policy directions are necessary to reverse this trend, and even more sweeping changes may be required as well.

First, any administration will have to defend U.S. commercial interests vigorously around the world, including placing people who comprehend the importance of these economic problems in key positions in the U.S. foreign policy machinery. Credible policies in this direction are necessary, at a minimum, to avoid having Congress take trade matters increasingly into its own hands. Beyond that, it appears to be a sine qua non for any administration to receive authority from the Congress to embark on new trade liberalizing negotiations. This course itself will have important foreign policy costs, confirming the general thesis that U.S. foreign policy will undoubtedly be eroded by U.S. trade policy in the years ahead.

Second, adjustment assistance must be resuscitated politically to forestall new restrictions to meet import problems. It will probably have to become available at an earlier point in the adjustment process, more quickly after the problem is perceived, in bigger amounts, and in more innovative forms.

Third, increased flexibility of exchange rates would ensure earlier correction of payments imbalances among national economies. They would thereby relieve the political pressure on marginal industries which can compete only if equilibrium exchange rates exist, and avoid trade balance shifts which provide support for protectionist pleas. The United States has a particular interest in improving the exchange rate mechanism because the biases of the present system promote undervaluation of other currencies against the dollar.[4]

Fourth, a liberal trade policy will have to be rebuilt with new political constituencies. Workers in the services industries, and who have major export interests, might decide that their interests differ from the organized labor movement on trade policy. Consumer groups might mobilize. The strong support of agriculture must be maintained. U.S. firms with direct and indirect (especially foreign investment) interests in freer trade must play a greater role. Foreign policy interests must resume their efforts on behalf of tough but liberal trade policies.

Even with such constituencies, however, it is uncertain whether any administration would be able to mount sufficient domestic support to launch a new initiative for freer trade—possibly the only way to avoid further slippage in the protectionist direction. It may well be asked, however, why America should once again have to take such a lead—as it has in every one of the numerous postwar GATT trade negotiations which culminated with the Kennedy Round.

The European Community has already become the major factor in world trade; with the expansion of its membership and the expected conclusion of additional preferential arrangements, it alone will account for almost one-half of world trade. Japan has been a major cause of today's trade problems. Foreign trade is more important to both Europe and Japan than to the United States. As several Congressmen are reported to have said, "Let a trade war come—we'll win it." There would, of course, be no winners in a trade war, but it is probably true that—in an economic sense, at least—we would lose least.

It therefore appears that the Community or Japan, or both, should take the next major international trade initiative. A logical time might be when the expansion of the Community is definitely achieved, since protectionist sentiments in the United States would otherwise rise precisely at that time in expectation of new threats to our commercial interests.

We should be under no illusion that it will be easy for the Community or Japan to take such a trade initiative. But the whole concept of shared responsibility for world leadership is most likely to develop first in such an area where their interests—and their relative power—provide a strong incentive for them to do so.

Faced with such an initiative from abroad, the United States would have only two choices—to turn its back on the world, or cooperate in launching an effort to resume the postwar movement toward trade liberalization and hence avoid the broad international problems which would arise in its absence. The political problems cited throughout this article would not permit an easy response but the odds are heavy that, in such a situation, the American answer could only be positive.

No other step could so dramatically display both the full maturation and outward-looking nature of the new Europe and Japan, indelibly marking their arrival as major powers on the world scene—and at the same time confirming the wisdom of the unremitting support extended to them by the United States throughout the postwar period. Such a sequence of events could turn the tide of global trade policy, at once arresting the protectionist push and moving to preempt the greater problems which will arise tomorrow if they are not headed off today. And the passing of the mantle of world leadership in such a crucial field would mark the most concrete evidence yet that we have moved beyond the postwar period, and that shared leadership is indeed possible in the 1970s and beyond.

Notes

1. See Lawrence Krause, "Trade Policy for the Seventies," *Columbia Journal of World Business*, Vol. VI, No. 1 (January-February 1971).

2. See George L. Perry, "Changing Labor Markets and Inflation," *Brookings Papers on Economic Activity 3: 1970*.

3. See Theodore Geiger, "A World of Trading Blocs?" *Looking Ahead*, Vol. 19, No. 3 (April 1971).

4. See C. Fred Bergsten, "The United States and Greater Flexibility of Exchange Rates," in Bergsten, Halm, Machlup, Roosa, eds., *Approaches to Greater Flexibility of Exchange Rates: The Bürgenstock Papers*. (Princeton Univ. Press. 1970) [chapter 7 in this volume].

13 Future Directions for U. S. Trade

The Setting

The United States now faces a clear choice between alternative trade policies. On the one hand, the AFL-CIO and some others actively support unilateral U.S. imposition of a new regime of comprehensive import quotas. If erected in the form which these groups presently propose, the Burke-Hartke bill, the new regime would *reduce* U.S. imports by at least $11 billion from the 1971 level and limit their growth to a fixed share of U.S. consumption thereafter.[1] Any such cutback in U.S. imports would cut back U.S. exports by at least a like amount, in view of foreign income effects, overt retaliation, and emulation by other countries of the U.S. moves. Thus the decline in world trade would be roughly double the size of the U.S. action—about 8 percent of world trade in 1971.[2]

The Burke-Hartke bill is highly unlikely to become law in its present extreme form. But a new "orderly marketing" regime, which would limit future import growth to some given share of the U.S. market, implemented either by the U.S. or through the favored new technique of "voluntary export restraints" by foreign suppliers, is a distinct possibility.[3] Indeed, the U.S. has been applying such restraints in several key industries over the past decade (cotton textiles, meat, steel, synthetic and woolen textiles, stainless steel flatware, etc.), and such a generalized approach would in one sense represent a culmination of present trends.

On the other hand, the U.S. Administration and numerous private groups have been actively calling for new international negotiations to resume the earlier postwar effort to reduce national barriers to world trade, and to devise new international rules and mechanisms to govern those barriers which will continue to exist in the future. This approach is partly motivated by the traditional economic desire to eliminate foreign barriers to U.S. exports, and partly by the traditional foreign policy desire to use economic negotiations as a functional means for expanding global cooperation.

It is primarily motivated, however, by the realization that trade policy is dynamically unstable and that a theoretical third trade policy alter-

This paper was originally presented at a joint meeting of the American Economic Association and the American Agricultural Economics Association in Toronto in December 1972 and published in the *American Journal of Agricultural Economics*, May 1973, pp. 280-88.

native—maintenance of the status quo—is untenable. Protectionist pleas by special interests can be countered only by trade liberalization in pursuit of the general interest. Steady movement toward trade liberalization is necessary to halt the acceleration of the trend toward increasing trade restrictions, and a new liberalizing initiative of sizable proportions might be required at this time in view of the strength of the protectionist pressures. If more proof of this eternal verity were needed, it is provided by the impressive success of U.S. special interests immediately after the completion of the Kennedy Round in obtaining new import protection (steel, meat, the pledge on synthetic and woolen textiles by both Presidential candidates in 1968 which culminated in new restraints in 1971) and altering the overall thrust of U.S. trade policy (severe tightening of the administration of antidumping and countervailing duty laws, the import surcharge of 1971, the near passage of the Mills bill in the face of Administration ambivalence in 1970).

Indeed, the primary impact of the Kennedy Round on world trade flows was not its tariff cuts. Its major achievement was in providing governments around the world with a broad international initiative of sufficient political importance to enable them to reject the entreaties of particular domestic groups which sought trade restrictions that would have rendered its completion impossible. Again, the U.S. evidence is clear: demand for the restrictions which were implemented after 1967, as outlined above, grew rapidly during the 1960's despite steady growth of profits to record levels and steady decline of unemployment to post-Korea lows. They probably could not have been forestalled without the simultaneous presence of a major trade-liberalizing initiative, and they can certainly not be forestalled now with the far less satisfactory state of our domestic economy and external economic position.[4] It is even highly unlikely that individual industries can any longer be "bought off" by restrictions limited to them alone, in view of the political pressure for "equitable treatment" of all. Precisely this view motivated the "Byrnes basket" provision of the near-miss Mills bill of 1970, making eligible for import quotas all products where imports satisfied certain numerical criteria—a total of $7 billion of trade at that time.

In the absence of new trade liberalization, new trade restrictions are therefore likely in the United States. The implications for world agricultural trade are obvious. Farm trade attracts even more protectionism than industrial trade. It has firmly resisted the trade liberalization of the earlier postwar period, and was virtually untouched even by the Kennedy Round. It is thus clear that a major overall trade-liberalizing negotiation will be necessary to provide a framework for negotiation of any significant new liberalization of farm trade, since the U.S. could get major foreign concessions on agriculture only by extending concessions of its own in the industrial sector. (It is barely possible that the U.S. could get minor agricultural concessions in return for concessions on its own dairy imports, though the official position of the EC is that the dairy quotas are illegal under the GATT and thus the EC will pay nothing for their removal.) Further slippage away from liberal trade policies, whether through a discreet (or indiscreet) measure like the Burke-Hartke bill or through slippage into a policy vacuum, would probably lead to additional barriers to farm trade—at least in Europe, through new preferential deals on particular commodities and extension of the Common Agricultural Policy itself to additional products.[5] Johnson [5] points out the sharp differences for agriculture of these two potential trends in trade policy: under free trade, an increase of $5 billion in North American exports of grain and oilseeds alone, with much return of land to cultivation and highly favorable efforts on farm profits and jobs, in contrast to stagnant exports if there is no trade liberalization (and, I would add, probably some cutback if new restrictions were erected instead).[6]

The ultimate choice between the highly polarized alternatives could be very close, and I hazard no forecast of the outcome at this time. It seems that it will turn on five key issues, to be discussed below.

The Link to International Money

All theories of international trade which conclude that maximum freedom of trade maximizes world welfare rest on a variety of assumptions. One of these assumptions is the existence of equilibrium exchange rates. The absence of a monetary system which provides a mechanism for assuring equilibrium exchange rates thus severely jeopardizes the economic case for free trade. It certainly undermines political support for freer trade by eroding the competitive position of industries in countries with overvalued exchange rates and thereby generating additional desires for protection.[7] This is the real link between trade policy and international money.

Until recently, however, the U.S. has not sought an equilibrium exchange rate for the dollar. Indeed, the international monetary policy of the United States throughout the postwar period—until August 15, 1971—was aimed primarily at assuring financing for U.S. payments deficits, primarily through the key currency roles of the dollar. The adjustment mechanism in the dollar-centered monetary system was in fact biased against the United States, and the dollar actually appreciated against a weighted average of the other major currencies during the 1960's despite the persistence of U.S. payments deficits.[8]

Some observers argue that the dollar had become overvalued by the late 1950's. Others view the overvaluation as occasioned solely by the inflation associated with the Vietnam war. Whatever the timing, however, it is clear that a fundamental contradiction pervaded U.S. foreign economic policy: the U.S. sought to lead the world toward freer trade but made no effort to lead the world toward a monetary system which produced equilibrium exchange rates.[9]

Perhaps ironically, the victim of that contradiction was the United States itself. In August 1971, the U.S. decided that it *wanted* to adjust its exchange rate—largely for domestic reasons but also in belated realization that it had to do so to restore the prospects for a liberal U.S. trade policy.[10] However, it found itself confined by a monetary system which made it very difficult for the U.S. to devalue, the only economically effective means of adjustment which would be politically acceptable in the relatively closed U.S. economy. It was thus caught in its own policy contradiction.

The U.S. was able to evade this contradiction until 1971 for two reasons. In the 1950's, it faced little serious international competition. Throughout the 1960's, its internal economy boomed; profits rose to record levels in 1966 and stayed there for several years, and unemployment dropped steadily toward the post-Korea low achieved in early 1969. Only in the 1970's has the U.S. come to face simultaneously real international competition and an unsatisfactory internal economic situation.

This is why the United States pushed so hard for the Smithsonian and early 1973 exchange-rate realignments and has begun to push for fundamental reform of the international monetary system. The basic aim of those proposals is to improve greatly the balance of payments adjustment process, by placing major international pressure on both surplus and deficit countries to move promptly and in adequate magnitudes to rectify any imbalances which they develop. Achievement of such a new monetary system, to help avoid any sizable or sustained disequilibrium in the exchange rate of the dollar in the future, is a necessary condition for the avoidance of further U.S. trade restrictions.[11] Tangible results from the Smithsonian and 1973 realignments, in terms of improvement in the U.S. trade balance, are also necessary to demonstrate the effectiveness of the exchange-rate approach.

The Trade Balance and Level of Trade

The second key issue is whether U.S. trade policy should focus on the trade *balance* or on the *level* of U.S. trade.

One American point of view is that the other major countries should be willing to grant non-reciprocal trade concessions to the United States, to help the international adjustment process which finds them in trade and payments surplus and the U.S. in trade and payments deficit. Former Treasury Secretary Connally openly espoused this view, confusing the appropriateness of minor trade concessions in the context of an overall effort to restore short-term payments equilibrium (as in the fall of 1971), if countries choose to extend them rather than revalue their exchange rates further, with the inappropriateness of sizable nonreciprocal concessions in a negotiation over the long-term level of trade barriers which, as noted above, must proceed on the assumption that the monetary system will achieve balance of payments equilibrium

Another school of thought reasons that the U.S. can afford to agree to a "reciprocal" reduction of trade barriers only when its trade balance again becomes strong, for four reasons. First, "reciprocity" in tariff negotiations has traditionally been defined, very crudely, as equality in the products of the average percentage cuts in duties times the volume of trade affected.[12] For example, "reciprocity" is achieved between two countries if each reduces its duties on $1 billion of trade by an average of 10 percent, or if one reduces duties on $2 billion by an average of 5 percent while the other reduces duties on $500 million by an average of 10 percent.[13] This school feels that price elasticities of demand for imports are higher in the United States than in other countries, so that equiproportionate tariff cuts from the relatively equal tariff levels that now exist in the major countries would have an adverse effect on the U.S. trade balance.[14]

Second, whatever the static effect on price elasticities, this school argues that the U.S. cannot afford "reciprocal" trade cuts at the present time because it is so uncompetitive in world markets that the dynamic effects of reducing trade barriers will be unfavorable to the U.S. trade balance. On this argument, the U.S. should avoid any new trade liberalization until it has first established a better underlying foundation of productivity growth and control of domestic inflation.[15] This school of thought was promulgated by the Kennedy Administration in the opposite direction, when it argued that the Kennedy Round would help solve the U.S. balance of payments problem by enabling the U.S. to capitalize on its highly competitive international position to increase further its trade surplus (and reduce unemployment at home in the process).

The third part of this argument is that U.S. energy imports will rise by about $25 billion between now and 1980, making its trade position that much more difficult to balance. And the final strand is that "U.S. negotiators are always soft," because the U.S. always wants to bring negotiation to a successful conclusion for broad political reasons and hence are outdone in purely commercial terms by their foreign counterparts. The U.S. trade balance is thus bound to suffer from whatever is finally agreed.

In my view, there is some intellectual merit in each of these viewpoints. There is a place for nonreciprocal trade liberalization by countries running balance of payments surpluses, if they choose to adjust in that way. A much more sophisticated definition of "reciprocity" is clearly needed, as will be discussed below. The U.S. will certainly have to improve its competitive position to assure avoidance of trade balance deterioration as a result of new trade liberalization, especially in light of pending increases in energy imports, and will be unable to do so if other countries hamstring U.S. exports in the two areas where they are strongest—agriculture, as Europe particularly is already doing, and high-technology goods, where the industrial policies that Japan, Europe, and Canada are in different stages of developing could have similar effects. And the U.S. did extend nonreciprocal trade concessions, at least in the early postwar period, due to broad political reasons which it (correctly) deemed of overriding importance at the time.

None of these considerations, however, should dominate U.S. trade policy. The objective of trade policy should continue to be maximization of the welfare effects of international commodity flows. This may call for increasing or reducing the level of flows at any given time, for reasons we will come to shortly, but it is independent of trade balance considerations.

The appropriate trade balance for a country can be determined only by the needs of its overall balance of payments, which may call for changes in the trade balance in either direction at any given time. Over time, the trade balance needed for payments equilibrium may change in response to structural changes in other parts of the balance of payments, e.g., the sharp and steady rise in U.S. income on its foreign direct investments. In addition, the external payments positions of virtually all countries fluctuate between surplus and deficit several times within a decade; we often forget that Japan was in payments deficit as recently as 1966-67, and the U.S. was in payments surplus as recently as 1969. And the competitive position of an individual country can change very dramatically between the start of a trade negotiation and the completion of the liberalization resulting from it. The Kennedy Round, for example, spanned a full decade which started with the U.S. in a dominant competitive postwar position and actively *seeking* new markets for Japanese exports, and ended with a sharp reversal between those two countries. Finally, reductions in trade barriers probably reduce the flow of foreign direct investment, some of which is motivated by the need to get behind such barriers. This has some effect on trade flows; helps the balance of payments of a capital-exporting country such as the U.S. in the short run and hurts it in the long run; and has indeterminate effects on both the trade and payments balances at any given point in time.

Any major negotiation on trade barriers, however, sets the level of world trade restrictions for many years. Since it would be impossible even to tell which countries should benefit in trade balance terms from nonreciprocal concessions and which countries should extend them, let alone the magnitudes of such targets or even how the dynamic trade effects of liberalization would work out, the trade balance could hardly be the focal point for trade negotiations. Indeed, most countries can only win internal political agreement to reduce their import barriers by pointing to the equivalent gains to their exporters which are inherent in a "reciprocal" negotiation; it is inconceivable that European governments would, to put it provocatively, "sacrifice their farmers so that American multinational firms could continue to buy up Europe." No country could be sufficiently confident of its future payments position to negotiate consciously a decline in its trade balance in such a context.

Nevertheless, there is need to link the trade balance and trade policy in an operational way. Indeed, the monetary reform proposals of the United States do so by suggesting that countries have the option of adjusting their payments surpluses by unilaterally reducing trade barriers instead of revaluing exchange rates. The problem with this idea is that such a step would reduce the bargaining position of any such country in the next round of international trade negotiations and might reduce the incentive of other countries to pursue additional trade negotiations in the future. The Schultz proposal thus needs to be amended in two ways: countries would get credit in the next trade negotiation for trade liberalization undertaken earlier for purposes of payments adjustment, and they could restore their previous barriers if they moved clearly into payments deficit before the next round of trade talks (in which case they would get credit only for the duration of the temporary liberalization). If there is any role for trade policy measures in the adjustment arsenals of deficit countries, it is for surcharges applied across-the-board to all imports for a temporary period of time; those who seek quota protection for particular commodities to help the balance of payments are still another school of thought, but one not worth serious discussion.[16]

Reciprocity

Two aspects of the problem of reciprocity require discussion. On the technical level, new concepts are needed to replace the crude techniques applied in the past to tariff reductions. Wholly new techniques will be needed to measure "reciprocity" in the reduction of nontariff barriers, of which quantitative restrictions are the simplest but still raise difficult problems. The objective in all cases must be to quantify the changes in trade flows which are likely to result from particular changes in trade restrictions, to give countries a much sounder gauge than they have had heretofore of whether the outcome of their bargaining over trade barriers will in fact be truly reciprocal expansion of trade flows in both directions. Such improvement may have to be limited to equalizing the static effects of changes in barriers, since the dynamic effects are so much more difficult to measure,[17] but that would still represent major progress.

A further technical problem is how to handle limits to import growth, such as the Burke-Hartke proposal for restricting imports to a fixed share of U.S. consumption. Retaliation in the past (as in the "chicken war" of 1962-63) has always related to actual rollbacks in trade, not limits to its growth. The problem could become particularly important in any new negotiation if new "safeguard" clauses are adopted along with cuts in tariffs and nontariff barriers. The simplest approach would be to extend the principles of the past by letting Country B place quantitative limits on a magnitude of its imports from Country A similar in both regards to the limits placed on its exports by Country A—emulation rather than retaliation in the conventional sense.

Such a search for better estimation techniques would further complicate a negotiation which already promises to be quite complicated. Countries would haggle endlessly over the accuracy of contending elasticities and over formulas for converting nontariff barriers to tariff equivalents. Improvement over past practices will almost certainly be needed, however, to achieve agreement on "reciprocal" liberalization among the major traders of today, all of whom are intensely concerned about their trade balances and may prove unwilling to liberalize at all unless they are assured of a "neutral" effect. And I indicated above that I see merit, not demerit, in extended (even constant) negotiation among the major trading countries.

This problem of adequately defining "reciprocity" was avoided in the past largely because the United States *was* willing—rightly, in my view—to accept liberalization which was not fully reciprocal from the standpoint of the U.S. trade balance in the short run.[18] The U.S. did so both because it was confident that its competitive ability would enable it to offset quickly any static economic losses with dynamic gains,[19] and because it had a major foreign policy stake in seeing that each of the succeeding trade negotiations concluded successfully. As in the monetary case, however, both the economic and international political situations have reversed; the U.S. will now insist on full reciprocity in short-term trade balance terms.[20] U.S. trade policy, and the outlook for international economic cooperation, are thus again hampered by the legacies of a successful past. Because the traditional concept of "reciprocity" has been discredited in the U.S. through its "misuse" in the past, a new concept will probably be needed if political support is to be generated for a new round of liberalization.

The more substantive aspect of reciprocity is whether the U.S. should offer concessions in the industrial sector in an effort to obtain concessions in the agricultural sector. It has been estimated that net U.S. exports might rise by $3 billion if all agricultural trade barriers were removed, although this figure omits consideration of sugar (and a few commodities of minor trade importance) and thus may overstate the likely impact.[21] However "reciprocity" were defined, this would of course require reductions in barriers to industrial trade which would increase net U.S. imports of such products by similar amounts.[22]

First-round economic welfare considerations would of course support this kind of intersectoral reciprocity. But there are offsets. Consider domestic job effects. Farm exports are highly capital-intensive, and even their sharp increase under free trade would produce relatively few jobs. The increased industrial imports, many of which would be in lower skill industries, would by contrast be much more labor-intensive and eliminate far more jobs. To be sure, domestic macroeconomic and manpower policies could recoup the lost jobs, but the costs of doing so—including budgetary and other inflationary effects—have to be set against the welfare gains of the freer trade.

Long-term trade balance considerations might also be negative. On the one hand, there is a case for such a deal because the U.S. appears to have a clear comparative advantage in agriculture, which is now largely unexploited, whereas it might well continue to lose ground on the relevant industrial items even without a further reduction of U.S. trade barriers. On the other hand, trade in most industrial items would tend to grow faster over time than trade in agricultural products. If the net result was to force future devaluations on the U.S., additional negative welfare effects would offset the original gains from improving the allocation of resources. These structural considerations suggest that the welfare effects of such a trade could be negative in the U.S. even if it achieved true reciprocity in trade-balance terms.

Whether the U.S. should seek to trade industrial for agricultural concessions also turns on domestic political considerations. There are four political arguments which favor it: further solidification of the support of the farm bloc for liberal trade, the demonstration effect of tangible rewards for a community which has maintained a liberal trade stance, the view of the farm trade in return for industrial concessions in the Kennedy Round, and the great importance to overall U.S.-European relations (and hence to the world economic order) of getting meaningful European concessions on an issue which has been a focal point of the growing U.S. antagonism toward Europe.

There are two political drawbacks of making such a trade. One is the problems it would raise with the U.S. agricultural producers now protected by import barriers (mainly in the dairy, sugar, and beef industries), whose short-term interests would have to be sacrificed to minimize the net concessions granted on industrial trade. The second is those industrial interests whose protection would be reduced further to compensate for the foreign concessions on agriculture—which is particularly important because none of the favorable job effects would accrue to the unions which would suffer most of the unfavorable job effects and because these very unions are the leaders of the whole present protectionist push.

On balance I would go for the trade on both economic and political grounds, because the welfare effects are probably close to neutral and because I place high priority on the political importance of breaking the present U.S.-EC conflict over agricultural trade. However, I fear that neither the European nor Japanese will give us the choice. Europe is not sufficiently interested in U.S. concessions on industrial trade to make the tough internal decisions which would be necessary to liberalize the CAP and does not seem to understand that new restrictions on such trade will probably result if forward progress is not made. Indeed, in joining the Community, Britain has raised its duties on farm imports and lowered its duties on industrial imports—giving the U.S. reciprocity opposite to what is suggested here.

Internal Adjustments to External Disturbances

Another assumption underlying the policy conclusions of classical trade theory is full employment. In the U.S., however, excessive unemployment has existed frequently throughout the postwar period. It certainly does so now and adds to the difficulties of pursuing a liberal trade policy.

But the problem is not just the aggregate rate of employment. The AFL-CIO supported the Trade Expansion Act in 1962 when the rate was 5.5 percent, but had become protectionist by 1969 when the rate had dropped to 3.5 percent. A major factor is changing value preferences. Most American workers have now entered the lower middle class and achieved income levels at which they place much higher emphasis on job stability, relative to higher wages, than they could afford to do in the past. Reluctance to give up community, home, schools, and church may dominate the opportunity for marginally higher income, particularly in the absence of vesting of pensions and transferability of other fringe benefits from one job to another, for individual workers and for the labor force as a whole. American labor thus increasingly resists change—particularly change emanating from abroad, which is "different" in at least its susceptibility to successful resistance (and may also be substantively different due to the accelerating pace at which it is taking place). This attitude is greatly reinforced by the bureaucratic interests of the AFL-CIO, which knows that structural change of the U.S. economy means movement out of the highly organized, traditional manufacturing industries (such as steel and textiles) into the highly unorganized, modern high-technology and services industries.

This increasing resistance to change clashes head-on with the increasing pace of change itself. A mix of two approaches will probably be needed to cope with this clash, if a complete restrictionist relapse is to be avoided. Of critical importance will be a vastly improved adjustment assistance program, especially for workers displaced by imports. Adequate compensation and effective retraining and relocation programs will be necessary components of any such effect. Unfortunately, the record of manpower programs to date—not only in the United States, where they are now prime candidates for budget cuts, but in countries such as Sweden which have much longer and more comprehensive experience with them—is not encouraging.

The other approach is to slow the pace at which disturbances occur by limiting the permitted growth of imports. It is quite likely that new mechanisms will in fact be required to "safeguard" against any massive dislocations at least from new trade liberalization that takes place. Agreement on how they might work was the major area of progress recorded in the recent Rey Report to the Secretary-General of the OECD [6, pp. 83-84]. One aspect of that proposal was that application of any such safeguards "should be accompanied by action to bring about domestic adjustment so that the use of the safeguard mechanism will in fact be temporary," linking the two approaches in order to avoid undue reliance on new controls.

The Foreign Reaction

The final ingredient needed to avoid a continued and probably accelerated restrictionist trend in U.S. trade policy is a cooperative stance by other countries, in two senses. First, they will have to tolerate a much tougher U.S. trade policy than they have experienced in the past. The U.S. has already begun to administer its antidumping and countervailing duty laws with increased vigor and to bargain much harder over the level of particular concessions than it has in the past—not to mention the excesses of the fall of 1971. This will be necessary to erase the legacy of the "soft positions" of the past and to establish sufficient credibility for any Administration to win Congressional and public confidence in its ability to negotiate major new trade liberalization without "selling out the U.S. interest." At a minimum, it is clear that other countries can no longer look to the U.S. always to take the lead in launching negotiations and in making concessions to break logjams so that the negotiations will succeed. Indeed, as both the largest world trader and the largest problem for world agricultural trade, Europe should exercise a special responsibility for launching new trade talks.

Second, other countries will have to be willing to make concessions on issues of real importance to the United States, such as the level of agricultural support prices in Europe and real market access in Japan. They may also have to be willing to renegotiate some of the basic GATT rules which govern both trade flows and trade relations, to make them more relevant to present conditions. For example, the MFN rule may need to be modified, to require compensation for trade diversion inherent in the new kinds of "free trade areas" represented in the EC's Mediterranean policy and to permit discrimination against countries which cause particularly severe trade and/or balance-of-payments problems. New rules are needed to cover issues not now treated in the GATT, or treated inadequately, but which have become sufficiently important to warrant some such international treatment (e.g., foreign direct investment and multinational corporations, environmental protection policies, regional and other industrial policies, export subsidies).

To be sure, it will be intellectually and politically difficult for these countries to make the needed adjustment in their views. It is hard to reverse the momentum of a generation, and the signs that they will do so are not promising at present. Yet they must realize that the very foundations of the international economic system are at stake, that their actions will have major effects on U.S. internal politics, and act accordingly.

Fortunately all countries have a common long-run interest in avoiding new trade wars, which would disrupt both their domestic economies and world politics, and in working together to construct a new international economic order and to deal with such joint problems as energy imports and multinational firms.[23] The new tripolar economic world which is now dominated by the United States, the expanded European Community, and Japan provides them with plenty of scope for shifting coalitions in search of particular short-term goals. The U.S. and Japan together oppose Europe's discriminatory restrictions against Japanese exports and its proliferating preferential arrangements. The U.S. and Europe together oppose Japan's continued import restrictions and unbridled export surges. Japan and Europe together seek to eliminate some present U.S. trade barriers, certainly wish to avoid new U.S. restrictions, and probably join in opposing the U.S. effort to free world agricultural trade. As long as these coalitions shift from issue to issue, they could form a stable basis for moving ahead on liberalization through a series of high-level policy trade offs.[24]

Conclusions

It will obviously be difficult to achieve major progress on all the issues discussed in this paper within even the next few years. If the conditions outlined do not overstate what is needed, one must conclude that the outlook for reversing the trend of U.S. (and world) trade policy is dim. If this is true, the best that can be hoped for is minimizing the creep of additional restrictions while progress is made on the several needed fronts.

The early commencement of international negotiations on a limited range of issues, even in the absence of new Congressional authorization for the U.S. to liberalize, is one of the necessary steps. But even such negotiations are unlikely to produce much change in world trade in agricultural products.

The outlook for freer trade in farm products is thus close to nil, in at least the short run, with a far greater probability of increased protection as internal policies, especially in Europe, continue to distort the markets for agricultural output.

Notes

1. The bill also proposes severe new limitations on foreign direct investment by American firms. Though related to trade, and contributing to the protectionist trade pressures because they accelerate the pace of change occasioned by trade flows, foreign investment raises a host of different issues and will not be dealt with in this paper.

2. The Burke-Hartke formula would of course produce a greater reduction of world trade in absolute terms from the levels which would have been reached by the time of its enactment, and the percentage decline would be larger as well because *all* growth beyond the 1965-69 base period for items brought under quota would be rolled back.

3. For a complete analysis of the underlying economic and political changes which raise such a spectre, see Bergsten [1].

4. Hence it is unfortunate that the EC, in the communique issued after its recent summit meeting, called for the next round of trade negotiations to be concluded by 1975. Aside from the impossibility of moving that fast, in view of the wide range and complexity of the issues involved, it would be undesirable to do so because the shield against new restrictions would then again be quickly dropped.

5. Foreign retaliation against new U.S. import controls, or emulation thereof, might well hit U.S. agricultural exports, since protectionist forces in several key countries are strongest in agriculture and the U.S. has important comparative advantages in that sector. However, this would probably be a strategic error for the countries involved, assuming their goal was to get the U.S. to reverse its policy. This is because it would play directly into the hands of organized labor, cutting U.S. exports in a capital-intensive industry which is totally unorganized by the AFL-CIO and thus levying little offset on U.S. labor to their gains from restricting labor-intensive imports.

6. It is possible, of course, that farm trade will continue to expand whether or not farm trade policy is liberalized (or even if new restrictions are implemented). This paper addresses only the policy issues and makes no effort to assess net developments in farm trade over the coming years.

7. By stimulating excessive allocation of resources to export and import-competing industries in countries with undervalued rates, it also makes it harder for such countries to agree to revaluations—which would surrender their enhanced competitive positions.

8. For a theoretical explanation of the bias, see Bergsten [3, pp. 68-69]. The dollar appreciation amounted to 1.5 to 5 percent, depending on the method of calculation and the precise time period chosen.

9. So perhaps the Treasury Department should at least share the blame usually leveled at the State Department for "selling out U.S. economic interests."

10. It must never be forgotten that it was the desire of the U.S. to adjust, not any Triffinesque collapse of the dollar overhang, which motivated the international aspects of President Nixon's New Economic Policy in August 1971. See Bergsten [2, pp. 200-204].

11. Many Americans believe that such a system must be firmly in place before the U.S. can resume pursuing a liberal trade policy. This would mean a continued drift toward protectionism, since it will probably take some time to install formally the new regime. I do not share this view on timing, though it is admittedly tempting to try to use the threat of protectionism to speed the pace of the monetary talks. I believe that steady progress toward agreement on the needed reforms, plus their ad hoc implementation in individual cases in the interim, should suffice to lay a foundation for new trade liberalization—which itself would not begin to be implemented until a similarly distant point into the future.

12. Preeg [7, esp. p. 132 and note 20]. He notes that additional considerations were often factored in on an ad hoc basis but that the basic formula was as stated in the text.

13. "Reciprocity" has thus been defined in terms of changes in *absolute* trade levels. Some observers, including Government officials, have however erroneously viewed "reciprocity" as meaning equal *percentage* rises in each country's exports and imports. This would increase the level of all existing trade surpluses and deficits and move away from, rather than toward, payments equilibrium. Thus it would certainly not be acceptable to deficit countries. Nevertheless, this view seems to be widely held in the U.S., strengthening the policy conclusion of some that trade liberalization is in the U.S. interest when the U.S. is running a trade surplus but is not when (as now) it is running a trade deficit.

14. Unfortunately, none of the economic analysis to date on price elasticities by country is sufficiently reliable to base policy on. One of the most elaborate efforts, Houthakker [4], provides tentative support for this school of thought by deriving a U.S. price elasticity for imports (adjusted for serial correlation) of -1.03 and much lower elasticities for all other

major countries except Canada and Denmark. A host of other issues, such as "disparities" between the dispersion of individual tariffs around the averages in the different countries, complicates the matter further.

15. These factors are important in the competitiveness of agricultural as well as industrial products. See Sorenson [8, pp. 819-820].

16. The United States has also proposed the use of import surcharges by the international community, or by individual countries, as sanctions against surplus countries which refuse to take steps to eliminate their surpluses. Such "sanctions" will always in fact be applied by someone; the U.S. import surcharge of August 1971 was such a step against Japan. The issue is whether they will be applied by individual countries outside any international framework, or by the international community as a whole. I would strongly prefer the latter.

17. For example, no one negotiating the Kennedy Round, even at its conclusion, could have foreseen the deterioration of U.S. competitiveness due to its internal inflation in the immediately succeeding years.

18. Similarly, the willingness of the U.S. to eschew adjustment of its balance of payments position enabled other countries to achieve their trade (and payments) balance goals more easily. However, it is interesting to note the recent rejection of the Supplementary Chemicals Agreement to the Kennedy Round by the EC, on the grounds that the EC would now lose from the deal in trade balance terms. In this case, at least, U.S. negotiators apparently made a magnificent bargain for the United States, since one must view the U.S. gain in this deal against the massive deterioration in the *overall* U.S. trade balance since 1967.

19. This probably goes far to explain why U.S. labor supported free trade in the past, but does not now: they used to perceive that increased trade meant *more* jobs, whereas now they perceive that it means *fewer*.

20. Of course, the real gain to the U.S. from trade liberalization is the welfare benefit of reducing present restrictions plus, since trade policy is dynamically unstable, the avoidance of welfare (and international political) costs imposed by the new restrictions which would otherwise take place.

21. West [9, pp. 19-20]. Johnson [5] estimates an increase of $5 billion in gross exports of U.S. *and Canadian* grains and oilseeds; he makes no net calculation for the U.S., but his data confirm the broad magnitudes of the West estimate.

22. Most analysts agree that farm trade can be liberalized only through efforts to align domestic farm policies, rather than attacks on barriers to farm trade per se. I abstract here from the method by which farm trade is liberalized.

23. A further international political complication is that the less developed countries may oppose a new multilateral trade negotiation, even

though they would not be required to extend reciprocal concessions, because it will erode the value of their newly won tariff preferences. This position is extremely short-sighted. On the one hand, the preferences are not very meaningful in economic terms (and the U.S. has not even extended any). On the other, the economic health of the LDCs rests fundamentally on healthy economic relations among the DCs. If a major new trade negotiation is needed to avoid continued slippage toward a world of trade restrictions, the LDCs—who need market access for their exports even more than do the DCs—would be among the major beneficiaries.

24. See Yalem [10, pp. 1051-1063], for an analysis of international political tripolarity which is broadly relevant to these considerations of international economic tripolarity.

References

[1] BERGSTEN, C. FRED, "Crisis in U.S. Trade Policy," *Foreign Affairs* 49:619-635, July 1971. [Chapter 12 in this volume.]

[2] ——, "The New Economics and U.S. Foreign Policy," *Foreign Affairs* 50:199-222, January 1972. [Chapter 25 in this volume.]

[3] ——, "The United States and Greater Flexibility of Exchange Rates," in *Approaches to Greater Flexibility of Exchange Rates: The Bürgenstock Papers*, ed. George N. Halm, Princeton, N.J., Princeton University Press, 1970. [Chapter 7 in this volume.]

[4] HOUTHAKKER, H. S., AND STEPHEN P. MAGEE, "Income and Price Elasticities in World Trade," *Rev. Econ. Stat.* 51:111-125, May 1969.

[5] JOHNSON, D. GALE, "The Impact of Freer Trade on North American Agriculture," *Am. J. Agr. Econ.*, May 1973.

[6] OECD, *Policy Perspectives for International Trade and Economic Relations*, 1972.

[7] PREEG, ERNEST N., *Traders and Diplomats*, Washington, The Brookings Institution, 1970.

[8] SORENSEN, V. L., AND D. E. HATHAWAY, "The Competitive Position of U. S. Agriculture," in *United States International Economic Policy in an Interdependent World*, Washington, Government Printing Office, 1971.

[9] WEST, QUENTIN M., "World Trade Prospects for U. S. Agriculture," *Am. J. Agr. Econ.* 54:827-833, Dec. 1972.

[10] YALEM, RONALD P., "Tripolarity and the International System," *Orbis* 15:1051-1063, Winter 1972.

14

A Trade Policy for the United States

The Purpose of U.S. Trade Policy

Inflation has replaced unemployment as the cardinal economic problem facing the United States, and it may well have already become our primary political problem as well. Prices continue to rise rapidly despite the downturn in economic growth and increase in unemployment. There is little sign that even the *rate* of price increase will abate significantly in the near future. There is widespread fear, from observers from a variety of schools of economic and political thought, that the United States may soon join the growing ranks of countries suffering from double-digit inflation.

Traditional policies of restraining demand and applying direct controls to prices and wages have not checked inflation, and would now probably make it worse. Thus U.S. economic policy is much more difficult to conceive and manage than at any previous time in the postwar period. Even if one does not agree that inflation has become our most important economic problem, it is clear that it is here for the indefinite future and is being caused by new and perhaps structural, rather than simply cyclical, factors.

The objectives of U.S. foreign economic policy are dramatically altered by this new internal economic situation. In the past, like all other countries, the United States has sought to use its external policies primarily to avoid increases in domestic unemployment. Barriers were erected to protect industries threatened by imports. Exports were subsidized. Overvaluation of the dollar was opposed, since August 1971 with a vengeance.

But now that inflation has become so serious, and so resistant to traditional policy measures, U.S. foreign economic policy must be geared at least in large part in that direction. Such a policy would facilitate imports, to increase the supply of products available in our economy. It would reject any new barriers to imports. It would end subsidies to exports, which drain resources away from our economy.[1] In short, it would reverse much of the thrust of our previous foreign economic policy. Fortunately, the dramatic improvement in our balance of trade and overall balance-of-payments position, and the strong outlook for both despite the sharp increase in oil

Originally presented as testimony to the Senate Finance Committee during its hearings on *The Trade Reform Act*, Part 4, April 3, 1974.

prices, permit pursuit of such approaches without fear of falling again into the costly pitfalls of an overvalued dollar à la 1969-71.

Such a use of non-traditional policies to fight inflation is particularly important at this time. The traditional resort to restraining aggregate demand could raise unemployment to unacceptable levels, and—as in 1970-71—would probably not even curtail inflation much, since the root of the problem lies elsewhere than excess demand. Wage-price controls have also failed, at least in the ways tried recently, and probably made things worse. So there is an urgent need to adopt a whole series of more selective policies to fight inflation without raising unemployment. The foreign economic policy I advocate today could be an important element in any such strategy.

The Administration has taken a number of steps in this direction, in recognition of the new economic situation. Import quotas on petroleum and meat have been lifted, and the quotas on dairy products significantly raised. Subsidies on agricultural exports have terminated. The appreciation of the dollar has been supported by official intervention, and its depreciation resisted.

It is noteworthy that numerous other countries, faced similarly by a steady acceleration of inflation and unable to cope with it by traditional policies, have taken similar steps. Several countries (e.g., Germany, Netherlands, Australia, Norway) have revalued their exchange rates explicitly to fight inflation, even when their payments positions were not in surplus. Several (e.g., Japan, Canada, Australia) have unilaterally cut their tariffs for the same purpose, despite the imminence of a multilateral trade negotiation in which are to trade "concessions" on a "reciprocal" basis and hence would have traditionally husbanded their import barriers with great vigilance. And a great number, ranging from the United States on soybeans through Brazil on cotton and leather to the United Kingdom on iron and steel, have embargoed or severely limited exports.

Thus there clearly is scope to use foreign economic policy to fight inflation. In addition, it is clear that the United States must be prepared to counter the efforts of other countries to export their inflation to us through such measures as export quotas. We must also be prepared to counter the inflationary effects on us of the policies of other countries, even when adopted for other reasons—as with the cutbacks in production, and selective embargo, by the oil producers.

Because this set of problems is so new, however, it is virtually ignored in both the legislative basis for U.S. trade policy and the international arrangements which seek to regulate world economic relations. The Trade Reform Act cannot ignore needed improvements in dealing with the traditional problems of trade policy, such as adjustment assistance for workers dislocated by imports, and I will comment briefly on some of those issues

227

later in my statement. But the primary goal of any new legislation should be to enable U.S. trade policy to cope with the primary international economic problems of today: inflation at home, and the inflationary impact on us of the policies of other countries.

The Trade Reform Act

There are several ways in which the Trade Reform Act should be amended to this end. Some changes would deal with the risk that other countries will seek to deny us access to their resources, and some would deal with our own policies which might impede such access.

1. *The Mondale-Ribicoff Amendments should be added to the legislation.*

The basic purpose of these amendments is to foster the negotiation of new international rules to govern export limitations, just as international rules have governed import limitations throughout the postwar period. If the import precedent were followed, countries would have to justify internationally any resort to export limitations, apply them only for temporary periods, and provide compensation to countries injured by the move or accept retaliation from them—which is why the amendments quite properly would also authorize the United States to retaliate against unfair export controls levied by others.[2] No international rules could be expected to work perfectly, of course, but their existence would almost certainly deter precipitate resort to export controls.

As a result, the United States would face less risk from the actions of other countries. That risk is very real, as long as inflation continues and shortages tempt suppliers to limit exports, both to permit domestic consumption of their own resources and to raise world prices for their output. At the same time, such rules would lessen our own temptation to resort to export controls except when they were clearly and justifiably needed.

To assure that we did so only in such cases, it is essential that domestic procedures be specified which would permit all interested parties to express their views on the desirability of export controls. In addition, when the United States faces export restrictions by others, such procedures should be required both on the desirability of retaliation and on the means of any such retaliation. I recommend that such procedural requirements be added to the Mondale-Ribicoff Amendments.

In short, the world should negotiate new rules and institutional arrangements to prevent trade wars of export controls, just as it negotiated the GATT after World War II to prevent trade wars of import controls. National efforts to export inflation are no more likely to succeed in the long run than past national efforts to export unemployment, but they could wreak havoc in the interim and raise major problems for both national economies and overall relations among countries. The negotiation of such new arrangements should be a priority U.S. objective in the forthcoming multilateral trade negotiations, as called for by the Mondale-Ribicoff Amendments.

2. *Section 123 of the Act, which authorizes the President to suspend import barriers to restrain inflation, should be expanded.*

As already noted, both the United States and numerous other countries have taken a number of ad hoc measures in this direction. Such steps make eminent sense. They increase the supply of available goods and hence counter inflation in a fundamental way—unlike the artificial restraint of inflation through price controls, and opposite from the shortages of goods and acceleration of inflation triggered by import controls.

In the United States, barriers to imports were raising our consumer prices by at least $20 billion as recently as 1971. Fortunately, that cost has been reduced by lifting of the oil and meat[3] quotas. But sizable costs remain from the whole array of tariffs plus the remaining quota restrictions on textiles, steel, dairy products and several smaller items.

Section 123 of H.R. 10710 would authorize the President to reduce tariffs and increase the level of import quotas to restrain inflation. This is a major and highly desirable innovation in U.S. trade law. However, the authorization is limited to 30 percent of total U.S. imports at any given time and a duration of five months for any product, and excludes any agricultural products under import quota.

I recommend that all of these restrictions be struck from the Trade Reform Act. All imports should be subject to elimination of all tariff and non-tariff impediments, for a period to be determined by the President. (If time limits are deemed necessary, they should run for at least two years to encompass the boom phase of the normal business cycle.) Domestic groups which might be injured by such actions are fully protected by Section 123(b)(1), which requires the maintenance of existing import barriers for any products where injury might result from their reduction.

3. *Section 331 should be amended to require injury to a U.S. party before countervailing duties must be levied against the export subsidies of a foreign government.*

As already noted, the use of export subsidies is declining around the world as countries seek to export their inflation rather than their unemployment. Nevertheless, some export subsidies remain and more may occur in the future. Thus the United States needs a clear policy to cope with them.

However, in an inflationary climate there will be many instances in which the United States should welcome the benefits to its consumers provided by foreign export subsidies. Hence it should countervail against the subsidies only if they clearly injure the workers and firms which compete with the subsidized imports. Such a policy has traditionally been followed with regard to dumping of products by foreign firms, which also subsidize U.S. consumers.

Regrettably, Chapter 3 of Title III of the Trade Reform Act does not incorporate an injury test for the application of countervailing duties. In fact, for the first time it would authorize countervailing against duty-free imports, with an injury test only when required "by the international obligations of the United States." I recommend that an injury test be required for any application of countervailing duties, on dutiable and non-dutiable goods, so that U.S. inflation can be reduced by foreign export subsidies except where U.S. producers of competitive products would be injured in the process.

4. *Title V should be liberalized to further facilitate imports from the developing countries.*

The developing countries are a major potential aid to U.S. efforts to fight inflation. Unlike virtually all industrial countries, many of them have unutilized labor which could be profitably employed if markets existed for their output. Thus there is a natural fit between our need for more goods and their need for more jobs.

In addition, many of these developing countries control the supply of key primary products. They are much more likely to seek to raise the price of these commodities, *increasing* our inflationary problem, if they are unable to meet their own needs for jobs and export earnings by developing their manufacturing sectors.[4] Hence our own anti-inflationary effort could be doubly boosted if we increase our imports of manufactures from the Third World. And recent international discussions suggest that we and the other industrial countries may *have* to provide more access to our markets for the manufactured goods of the developing countries if we are to win their acceptance of new rules to govern our access to their raw materials.

Title V of the Act seeks to do so by authorizing generalized tariff preferences for such products. However, several key limitations to that authorization are now included. The President is required to take into account a number of factors in determining whether imports from particular developing countries are even eligible for preferences, including their actions toward U.S. investments. At least 35-50 percent of the value of the imported product must be produced in the beneficiary country itself. Products subject to import quotas would not be eligible. Preferences would be lifted wherever eligible imports reached a level of $25 million or 50 percent of total U.S. imports of the item—both tiny amounts of U.S. consumption of virtually every product—unless the President explicitly decides "that it is in the national interest" to continue the preferences.

I recommend that all of these limitations be eliminated. Any value-added requirement should at least encompass value added in *all* eligible developing countries, not just the country exporting the final product. Products subject to import quotas, such as textiles, *should* be eligible for preferences; indeed, these preferences would run less risk of causing injury to domestic interests than preferences for any other products by virtue of the existence of the quantitative limits. Most important, any ceilings on preferential imports should be much higher—and it would be far better to avoid ceilings altogether, as in the original U.S. preference plan proposed by President Nixon in 1969. The standard escape clause, particularly as modified by this Act, would provide the needed safeguards against injury to U.S. workers or firms resulting from an excessive growth of preferential imports—which brings me to my final point.

5. *Further improvements in the adjustment assistance program are needed to maintain the anti-inflationary trade policy which I have proposed, because of the problems occasionally caused for particular groups of workers by import flows.*

Even in an inflationary climate, where increased imports are clearly in the national interest, equity requires governmental assistance to those particular groups—particularly workers, but sometimes firms or even entire industries—which may on occasion be injured by those same imports. Indeed, the enhanced importance for the United States of unimpeded access to imports enhances the importance of an effective program of adjustment assistance because the only alternative to deal with such injury, restrictions of the imports themselves, is so obviously undesirable. Thus I strongly support the preference expressed for adjustment assistance over import relief in several sections of Title II, the several requirements that industry efforts to adjust be carefully scrutinized in determining whether to grant import relief or to maintain such relief after it is initially granted, the numerous requirements that consumer interests be considered in any determination regarding import relief, and the authorization of Congressional vetos of any new import quotas enacted by a President.

In addition, H.R. 10710 would reduce the need to resort to import restrictions by significantly improving the adjustment assistance program. However, further improvements are highly desirable and can be implemented at quite modest cost:

—The bill provides that workers laid off due to increased imports would receive 70 percent of their previous weekly wage for the first 26 weeks of unemployment, and 65 percent for the remaining 26-65 weeks of eligibility. This level of benefits would represent a significant cutback in the take-home pay of many workers, and should be raised to 80 percent for the duration of eligibility.

—The proposed program provides no fringe benefits. Such benefits, particularly health and life insurance, add perhaps 15-40 percent to the real income of most workers. The Federal Government could easily keep such insurance going during the periods of worker eligibility by paying the premiums previously paid by their employers.

—To achieve real adjustment and limit costs, early warning of possible trade-induced dislocation is needed. The Government, working closely with private industry and labor, should create a systematic program for detecting new areas where increased imports will lead to problems and which will give them prompt attention.

—Adjustment assistance should be available to import-impacted communities, as well as groups of workers and firms.

—A new Office of Adjustment Assistance should be created in the Executive Office of the President to run the program. Its administration is otherwise too diffuse to be operated with maximum efficiency.

Conclusion

With the proposed changes, along with its other provisions, the Trade Reform Act could take the lead in addressing U.S. foreign economic policy to the problems of the relevant future. It could play a particularly important role in combatting inflation. It could provide means to deal effectively with any job losses caused by increased imports. And it would place the United States in an excellent position to negotiate new trade rules which would both promote our national economic interests and further the prospects for global economic cooperation—a vital necessity in today's world of unquestionable economic interdependence. My final recommendation is that the Committee report the amended bill as quickly as possible, and push for its early adoption by the entire Congress.

Notes

1. The DISC legislation has apparently done little to spur exports, and has significantly reduced Government revenues. In addition, there is no need for such selective export subsidies in a world of flexible exchange rates. And, even had it worked as planned, it would have no place in the current inflationary environment. *The Trade Reform Act should repeal DISC, or at least authorize its suspension with a clear instruction to the Administration to do so until the basic economic situation changes once more*. It is sometimes argued that we should use the "leverage" afforded by DISC to negotiate an end to the export subsidies of other countries, but I will note later that such foreign subsidies help us fight inflation and should be welcomed unless they injure particular U.S. groups—in which case we can and should countervail against them.

2. *I recommend that this authority be limited to instances where there is international agreement to do so under the new international rules, once those rules are put in place*. This would be precisely analogous with Section 122(c)(3) of H.R. 10710, which requires that any import barriers to protect the U.S. balance of payments must be consistent with any new international rules agreed to govern the balance-of-payments adjustment process.

3. It should be noted, however, that the meat quotas have only been "suspended"—not terminated. Since meat takes about three years to produce, the major foreign suppliers cannot be expected to undertake the expansion of output needed to restrain *U.S.* meat prices unless they have long-term assurances of access to our market. Thus *repeal of the Meat Import Act of 1964 should be incorporated in the Trade Reform Act*.

4. See C. Fred Bergsten, "The Threat From the Third World," *Foreign Policy* 11 (Summer 1973) [chapter 27 in this volume] and "The Threat is Real," *Foreign Policy* 14 (Spring 1974) [chapter 19 in this volume].

15

Economic Adjustment to Liberal Trade: A New Approach

Introduction

The Chamber of Commerce supports a liberal trade policy for the United States. The Chamber in fact believes that liberal trade is now more important to our national interest than at any time in the postwar period, for both economic and political reasons.

Economically, the United States is likely to continue to face persistent problems of both high unemployment and inflationary pressures. The Chamber rejects the notion that unemployment can be reduced to acceptable levels only by pushing inflation to unacceptable levels or vice-versa. However, skillful public policy is needed to solve the two problems simultaneously.

Fiscal and monetary efforts provide much of the policy response, but it is too much to expect that they can do the job alone, particularly since each problem is caused in part by structural difficulties rather than inappropriate levels of aggregate demand. Selective measures are thus needed as well. One such measure is the present program of wage-price controls, which is necessary at this time but which violates the basic precepts of the free market that are essential to the continued success of the American economy. The controls should thus be phased out as soon as possible.

But a number of other selective measures both conform to the precepts of the market and offer the possibility of major help in fighting unemployment and inflation. One is free trade. Import restrictions levy heavy costs on our economy. Tariff and quota restrictions were raising prices to our consumers by close to $20 billion per year before the administration wisely liberalized the oil and meat quotas to help fight inflation. They undermine our competitiveness, by raising costs to our producers and by shielding important sectors of our economy from the stimulus of foreign competition. They do not save jobs; indeed, they cost American jobs by triggering foreign barriers to our exports and by retarding the historic and natural evolution of our economy into ever more efficient and higher-wage indus-

Prepared by the Task Force on Adjustment Assistance, U.S. Chamber of Commerce, C. Fred Bergsten, Chairman, and published in *Trade Reform*, Hearings before the House Ways and Means Committee on the Trade Reform Act of 1973, May 1973, Part 3 of 15, pp. 894-906. This chapter also appears as Chapter 17 of C. Fred Bergsten, ed., *Toward a New World Trade Policy: The Maidenhead Papers* (Lexington, Mass.: Lexington Books, D.C. Heath and Company, 1975).

tries. Indeed, the Chamber believes that new import restrictions would deal a devastating blow to the American economy and undermine over time both our standard of living and the basic economic system on which our nation is based.

At the same time, foreign barriers to trade continue to impede the U.S. economy by restraining our exports in industries (including agriculture) where we possess marked comparative advantages. These barriers cost us high-paying jobs and reduce the competitive incentives to our firms and workers. Our major national interest in their reduction can be realized only within the framework of an international negotiation in which all major countries agree to renew their progress toward freer trade.

A second selective approach, which can help combat both unemployment and inflation, is manpower policy. The skill mix of our labor force can of course never mesh precisely with the needs of the shifting patterns of production; there will always be some unemployment. But effective manpower programs can reduce the level of unemployment by equipping workers to fill available jobs. They can reduce inflation by increasing the productivity of our labor force and by reducing the costs of unemployment compensation. Indeed, they can represent a highly productive investment in the future of our nation.

Similar in principle to manpower training is assistance to smaller firms that also need help in adjusting to the rapid changes triggered by modern economic forces such as foreign trade. Their contribution to our overall economy can be promoted if they can be helped to improve their competitiveness in their present industry or shift their resources into more promising endeavors.

Freer trade, manpower programs, and industrial assistance are integral components of the foreign economic policy that the Chamber believes must be pursued by the United States in the 1970s. Each is highly desirable in its own right, as just indicated, and the relationship among them is straightforward. Freer trade causes dislocation for a few in order to benefit all. The personal hardships that result are often severe and must be alleviated. Those who are hurt by a policy that is thus pursued in the general interest should be compensated adequately for their losses, and the opportunity should be seized to enable them to increase their contribution to the national welfare. The Chamber is confident that the benefits of such a foreign economic policy to our nation far exceed its costs, as will be demonstrated later.

The Chamber also wishes to emphasize the importance of freer trade to the foreign policy of the United States. Economic issues now play a central role in U.S. relations with virtually every country in the world, especially our closest allies in Canada, Europe, and Japan. New U.S. trade restrictions could severely injure those relations. Steady progress toward freer trade could smooth them. Since amicable U.S. relations with both Europe and Japan are an essential component of continued improvement in our relations with the Soviet Union and China, a successful and cooperative U.S. foreign economic policy will play a central role in realizing our hopes for a generation of peace.

A New Program of Economic Assistance

The concept of "adjustment assistance" to workers and firms displaced by imports was embodied in the Trade Expansion Act of 1962. The Chamber believes that the program authorized by that Act, however, is wholly inadequate for the following reasons:

1. It generates little real adjustment to economic change for dislocated workers, providing only temporary supplements to unemployment compensation.
2. Its assistance commences long after dislocation has occurred, and it delivers this long-delayed assistance far too slowly.
3. Its level of compensation to workers for their loss of jobs is inadequate and frequently amounts to less than one-half their previous earnings.
4. The program provides no help whatsoever for communities.
5. There is no high-level governmental attention to the program, and no central direction to it.

None of these problems are inherent in the concept of adjustment assistance. The Chamber believes that each of them must be solved in order to construct a program of economic adjustment that will enable the United States to pursue a liberal trade policy in the 1970s, and that such a program can be devised. It believes that such a program must compensate those whose skills are rendered unprofitable by trade for their losses *and*, more importantly, help them adjust into new endeavors. The Chamber offers the following proposals to that end.

1. Eligibility

Under present law, firms and workers are eligible for trade adjustment assistance only if a majority of the Tariff Commission concludes that they are suffering serious injury (or are threatened with serious injury) and that the major cause of their injury is an increase in imports, which was in turn triggered in major part by U.S. tariff concessions. This formula has proved exceedingly restrictive. It ignores the vast bulk of our imports, since they are not caused by U.S. tariff concessions. It is often difficult to prove conclusively that imports are the major cause of a particular dislocation. There has been no basis for helping those affected indirectly by imports, either as suppliers to firms directly affected or living in communities whose "gross community product" is retarded. The procedures for determining eligibility and extending benefits are so cumbersome that severe delays in both are inevitable. And there has been reluctance to determine eligibility, both at the Tariff Commission and in the White House, because the identity of the criteria for "adjustment assistance" and for protection from imports under the escape clause has raised the spectre of trade wars any time that assistance is provided—although the intent of the legislation was to authorize such assistance as a clear alternative to import quotas and tariff increases.

The Chamber recommends a basic change in the eligibility criteria:

1.1 *Workers employed continuously by a firm for more than six months should be presumed to be eligible for assistance if layoffs affect a significant share (perhaps 5 percent) of those engaged in producing a product in which total domestic output and the output of their particular firm have declined, and imports of a like or directly competitive product have increased, over a representative period of time (perhaps the latest twelve months for which data are available compared with either of the two previous twelve month periods, or an average of those two periods).*

1.2 *Firms would be presumed eligible if their own output and total national output of the product declined while imports rose, and for certain forms of assistance when there was serious threat of such developments, if the product represented a substantial share of the total output of the firm, unless the imports were generated by the firm itself.*

The combination of these two changes—reduced domestic output and increased imports for both workers and firms—of course implies a rise in the ratio of imports to domestic production. This approach is superior to formulas that would trigger assistance solely on the basis of some given increase in the import/domestic production ratio, however, because such increases frequently take place for products for which total demand is growing rapidly.

1.3 *Firms, and workers thereof, whose output declined and 50 percent of whose output represented inputs to product lines that met this new injury test themselves would also be eligible; other supplying firms could become eligible if they could demonstrate that their own problems were substantially due to the effect of import competition on their customers.*

In all of these cases, a "product" would be defined narrowly in order both to permit help for small groups of workers and, conversely, to avoid paying benefits to those for whom they were not justified.

1.4 *Communities would automatically be eligible when a significant share (perhaps 5 percent) of their total workers have been declared eligible for the program themselves. Communities could qualify in any event by demonstrating that their own problems were substantially due to the effect of import competition..*

1.5 *In all of these cases, there would thus be a presumption that injury existed and eligibility for assistance established when rising imports and reduced output coincided. The presumptions could be challenged by the administering authority in cases where it felt that imports were not a substantial cause of the dislocation,* as could often be the case for firms where poor management (including failure to anticipate competition from imports) was the crucial factor.

Indeed, cases can be envisaged where workers of a firm would receive full benefits whereas the firm would not be eligible. Particularly for workers, however, the presumption would be realized in most cases.

Under the Automotive Products Trade Act of 1965, an analogous formula was used to provide assistance for the dislocations caused in the course of the restructuring of the North American automobile industry under the U.S.-Canada Automotive Agreement of that year. Under that arrangement, the legal presumption was never challenged and the eligibility criteria of the adjustment program were regarded by all parties—the unions, workers, firms and U.S. government—as a complete success. The Chamber is confident that the approach can work successfully for U.S. trade policy as a whole.

Under the program proposed here, the criteria would encompass dislocations caused by imports both from foreign-owned firms and from the foreign affiliates of U.S. firms. It is recognized that there are problems of comparability between the present U.S. data for imports and domestic output and that improvements in these data are needed for a wide variety of purposes, but the technical problems have been met so far and can be met in the future.

2. Speed of Delivery

At present, there are two routes to obtaining "adjustment assistance." Under the escape-clause procedures, firms and workers in an entire industry can obtain help. The process in this case takes up to six months in the Tariff Commission; a subsequent decision by the president, which may take 90 days; subsequent certification of individual firms and workers by the Departments of Commerce and Labor, respectively; and delivery of the benefits through specific agents. When individual firms and groups of workers apply for assistance, they must undergo scrutiny by the Tariff Commission for 60 days; presidential consideration if the Tariff Commission vote is tied, as has frequently been the case; certification by the relevant department; and then delivery. In both cases, interminable delay has been the rule.

The proposed changes in adjustment assistance eligibility criteria (we are proposing no changes in the criteria for tariff increases, or the applications of quotas, under the escape clause) would themselves go far to speed the delivery of assistance. The simple correlation between declining output and increasing imports would be easy to verify, particularly in comparison with the complex investigation of "serious injury" and two-stage causality under present law. The dissociation between the new criteria for economic adjustment and the criteria for imposing new import restrictions would relieve concerns that the former might trigger the latter, and hence remove another impediment to a speedy delivery process.

Further steps are needed, however, both to anticipate and hence avoid dislocation caused by trade flows and to assure prompt relief when dislocation does occur. Early warning of impending dislocations is needed well before firms begin to slide competitively. The government, which now enters the adjustment process far too late, can help in this process by improving its analytical capacity. To do this, however, the government must get close and continuing advice from those directly affected, who are likely to first pick up the signals of impending change—the firms themselves.

Recommendations to improve speed of delivery are as follows:

2.1 *The government should actively contact firms (and trade associations) to keep abreast of their judgments concerning trade trends, and inform firms of problems that appear to be developing.* (A two-way process is needed, however, so that the information can be effectively utilized.)

2.2 *Firms should actively consult the government to check out their own individual views as they make their future investment and marketing plans.*

Such information should be particularly helpful for smaller firms, who usually suffer most from import dislocation. Acting as a broker, the government could assure the confidentiality of information of commercial importance to individual firms. In the consumer goods industries, where imports have been rising sharply, retailers—who are frequently in the best position to spot changing patterns of production and hence pending economic dislocations—should be consulted.

The objective would be to develop and share information on the outlook for foreign competition in the U.S. market, in an effort to spot emerging trends better than could be done by individual firms on their own. Firms would then have an earlier opportunity to adjust on their own and avoid import dislocation.

2.3 *The Chamber also recommends that firms be eligible for technical assistance from the government, on both a grant and reimbursable basis, when the administering authority determines in advance of the actual manifestation of any injury that they face a "threat of serious injury" from imports.*

The concept of a "*threat* of serious injury" is encompassed in the present "adjustment assistance" legislation, but it has been interpreted to require that the threat be imminent. Under the propew approach, it would encompass a much longer lead time than has been required heretofore.

The primary responsibility for early warning to workers rests with private firms, however, because it is they who face the pressure of increased competition and must make decisions to respond to it. Many U.S. firms already give such warning, and many agree to do so under their management-labor arrangements. Several countries require their companies to give a minimum amount of prior notice, which ranges from four to sixteen weeks, to workers who are to be laid off.

2.4 *The Chamber views it as the responsibility of U.S. firms to give the maximum possible advance notice to workers whom they will be laying off and to provide them with full information concerning the available benefits under the proposed program. It urges all firms to comply with this principle.*

In combination with the speedy delivery of benefits permitted by the new assistance criteria and promoted by the new administrative machinery to be discussed below, and the improvement in compensation and adjustment aids to be discussed next, these early warning mechanisms should go far to assure workers that they would have both the time and the means to transit from present to future employment with minimum personal disruption. Indeed, early action by firms to preempt import penetration would, if successful, obviate any dislocation to workers at all. The proposed program, taken in its entirety, should thus significantly reduce their resistance to import-induced change.

3. Compensation Benefits for Workers

Under present law, workers declared eligible for "adjustment assistance" receive 65 percent of their previous wage *or* 65 percent of the average manufacturing wage, whichever is less. These benefits are not taxable.

There is no compensation for lost fringe benefits. Present benefits thus range from about 40 percent of previous net earnings (for workers with above-average wages and large fringe benefits) to as much as 70 percent of previous net earnings (for those workers with higher tax liabilities than fringe benefits and below-average wages), with most clustered about 50 to 60 percent.

The Chamber agrees with the judgment of the House Ways and Means Committee, the entire House of Representatives, and the Senate Finance Committee, as recorded in their passage of the Trade Act of 1970, that these levels are inadequate. Workers have invested considerable time, and often money as well, in acquiring their skills. Time, and often money, will always be required to reemploy or replace those skills to rebuild the worker's earning capacity. Individual workers should be adequately compensated for losses imposed on them by government policies, such as liberal trade, which are pursued because they serve the overall national interest.

The House and the Senate Finance Committee, in 1970, voted to provide eligible workers with 75 percent of their prior earnings, or 75 percent of the average manufacturing wage, whichever is less, non-taxable.

Proposals for compensation benefits for eligible workers are as follows:

3.1 *The Chamber believes that 75 percent is a reasonable level of compensation and recommends that it replace the present level (with a ceiling of an annual rate of $12,000 for any individual worker).*

However, the Chamber feels that it is inequitable to penalize a worker because his wage is higher than the national average for manufacturing. Every worker should receive a like proportion of his previous wage—75 percent, on this recommendation.

3.2 *There should thus be no alternative calculation based on the national average.*

The resource cost of these benefits would of course be simply their excess above the level of unemployment insurance that virtually all displaced workers would otherwise receive.

3.3 *For those few workers affected by imports who are not covered by unemployment insurance, the assistance program would have to finance all benefits.*

Salaried workers, as well as those who are paid an hourly wage, would of course be eligible.

Fringe benefits now comprise a major part of a worker's income; they average about 15 percent beyond money wages for all workers but amount to as much as 30 to 40 percent for some. An important share of these benefits is not transferable as the worker moves from one firm to another, unlike the case in many countries, which greatly increases his reluctance to do so. Indeed, there is no way to provide compensation for a number of important fringe benefits, such as guaranteed overtime pay and seniority rights, even if it were deemed desirable to do so. A number of the most important fringes, however, represent health and life (and perhaps disability and other) insurance whose lapsing could levy heavy costs on a displaced worker and his family. There should be no reduction in the level of benefits available to displaced workers under these plans.

3.4 *The Chamber thus recommends that the government assistance program pick up whatever premiums the companies had previously been paying, at the group rate prevailing before the worker was laid off, to enable all dislocated workers to maintain in full their insurance plans.*

3.5 *In cases where workers were enrolled in local plans that could not be maintained, if they moved elsewhere to train or pursue jobs, they could join the insurance plans for employees of the governments of the states to which they had moved for the temporary period in question.*

Some other important fringe-benefit problems, such as vesting of pensions, may be met by changes in the relevant legislation that are already under consideration. Older workers, who often find it particularly difficult to find a new job, could get added benefits as will be outlined below.

4. Adjustment by Workers

The Chamber believes that economic adjustment to liberal trade should focus most heavily on helping workers adjust into fruitful new occupations as quickly as possible.

4.1 *Workers would thus have to be actively seeking employment to receive any of the compensation benefits just described.*

Workers receiving benefits would cease to receive them once they were offered suitable jobs.

4.2 *Workers would also have to apply for retraining programs to qualify them for suitable jobs, that were identifiable as available, to use the skills when they were trained for them, and join those training programs as soon as openings developed.*

These two requirements would assure that the enhanced level of compensation benefits promoted, rather than deterred, the likelihood that the trade-impacted worker would find new employment as soon as possible. The higher the level of employment in the economy as a whole, the less need would of course exist for the actual payment of compensation benefits— although structural problems will always exist even when aggregate unemployment is very low.

Under present trade adjustment assistance, a worker can receive compensation benefits for 52 weeks plus 26 additional weeks if he is undergoing retraining plus an additional 13 weeks if he is over 60 years of age. The Chamber believes that this period may be too long for some workers, and—in the absence of the "accept suitable employment and apply for retraining" requirement included here—reduce the incentives for them to seek new jobs. At the same time, it recognizes that the average duration of unemployment of workers who have received trade "adjustment assistance" in the past is ten months. This compares with the national average of one and a half to three months, which fluctuates with the level of aggregate unemployment. It also recognizes that appropriate retraining programs are not always available immediately and may take some time to complete. It is to be expected, of course, that workers displaced by imports—who generally come from industries that are less productive than the industries employing the "average worker," much of whose "unemployment" is due to voluntary quits as he moves from job to better job—will suffer periods of joblessness far longer than the average.

It should be recalled that the requirement exists for an eligible worker to accept an offer of a suitable job or to apply for retraining for a job that will be available to use his new skill.

4.3 *The Chamber therefore recommends that the full compensation benefits as outlined above be paid for the durations specified in the present act, except that the extension period for workers in training programs be increased from 26 to 52 weeks.*

This extension will enhance the likelihood that such training will have a full opportunity to provide real adjustment for them.

4.4 *Workers 55 or older would be eligible to receive the same benefits.*

It is often much more difficult for their older workers to obtain new jobs, however, even with retraining, both because employers are frequently reluctant to hire them and because these older workers may be less adaptable themselves. And experience demonstrates that the number of older workers laid off due to imports constitutes a large share of the total problem.

The Chamber therefore recommends that older workers be offered the alternative of early retirement, with immediate commencement of benefits (at the level otherwise available at age 62 for those retiring before 60, at the level available at age 65 for those retiring at 60 or over) under their private pension plans and the Social Security and Medicare systems.

4.5 *The additional costs of such early retirement would be reimbursed to the private firm or Social Security system by the new government assistance program.*

Real adjustment into new positions will often require retraining and relocation to areas where new jobs exist, in addition to proper incentives to workers to seek and accept such jobs. Such steps can be most effective in reducing the costs of dislocation if they are initiated as early as possible in the dislocation process. Thus proposals have already been made to assure early warning of pending dislocations, to require entry into training programs for workers to qualify for the proposed compensation benefits, and to provide financial incentives (the additional period of compensation benefits) for those workers who are dislocated to stay in retraining programs. The narrow "product" definition of the eligibility criteria also enhances the potential for adjustment, by enabling workers producing the impacted product to receive (presumably on-the-job) training to fill a new position with the same (multi-product) firm. More specific measures are also needed, however, to reduce hardships to individuals and the costs to society as a whole of unemployment triggered by trade flows.

A successful adjustment program for trade-dislocated workers requires four key components. The first is early attention to the problem. Part of the success of the Office of Economic Assistance in the Department of Defense in helping whole communities adjust to cutbacks in defense expenditures can be traced to its early knowledge of developing problems. It would be difficult to replicate as much early warning in the private sector, of course, since the Defense Department usually knows where defense cuts are coming. Nevertheless, the suggestions already made to provide early warning of pending problems would permit much earlier triggering of adjustment efforts, including efforts to preempt the dislocation from occurring at all. (Such early warning would also assure timely commencement of compensation benefits when they become necessary.)

The second requirement is that job training be geared to jobs that will in fact be available when the training is completed. This suggests a focus on on-the-job training, under which the new employer receives government payments for each new worker hired during the training period.

4.6 *To utilize effectively both the on-the-job and institutional programs, sharp improvements are needed in the federal-state employment service and computerized job-worker matching, including better statistics on "jobs available" and continuous updating of job definitions.*

4.7 *All dislocated workers should receive sharply improved counselling services to bring workers and jobs together.*

The counselling should be of the type that facilitated the adjustment of workers laid off when Studebaker folded in 1964.

4.8 *Workers should be authorized to use private counselling services approved by the government, but under its continuing surveillance, and be reimbursed for the costs thereof.*

A final requirement is conscious effort by the employment service to pinpoint emerging job opportunities, preferably in the same or neighboring geographical areas, that will be available to job trainees. Job searches by the employment service for the relatively small number of workers displaced by imports might be a particularly useful area in which trade adjustment could be a pilot program for broader manpower programs in the future, as advocated at the outset of this report, since major improvements in the federal-state employment service would have to be a major part of such improvements. The effort could draw on the successful computerized job placement system maintained by the Department of Defense to direct retiring defense personnel into civilian employment.

Third, adequate training programs are needed. There is much present criticism of the effectiveness of current manpower training programs. Few of the present government programs bearing that name, however, have aimed at the kind of adjustment discussed here. Most of them have been adjuncts for the poverty program, aimed at the most disadvantaged and least skilled of all Americans. Even so, a number have achieved real adjustment—even in extremely difficult circumstances, such as Appalachia. Specific programs for specific circumstances have worked—the Studebaker and Armour reconversions and the Defense Department programs to smooth the adjustment to reductions in defense spending in Wichita and dozens of other locales. Manpower programs have worked effectively in other countries, where they have received a higher priority from national governments, have had longer periods of experience from which to learn, and have operated within a context of low unemployment. Such programs have worked in individual states in our country in that they have attracted firms by training workers to meet the firms' specific job needs.

4.9 *Trade-dislocated workers should be eligible to participate in all present programs, and the new counseling programs must assure that workers will be aware of all alternatives available to them.*

The most important reason why the Chamber is confident that current training programs can achieve adjustment to trade dislocations, however, is that the workers displaced by trade flows are far superior to the participants in most current manpower efforts—who are essentially recipients of poverty help. Trade-impacted workers have been working, often for many years and even decades. This means that they have demonstrated work skills. Even more importantly, they have a proven desire to work—the work ethic is clearly alive in this group. They are thus likely to be highly employable relative to the average participant in current manpower training programs, many of whom have little work experience or education. (A possible exception is older workers, for whom special compensation provisions have already been suggested.) They are superior to the average unemployed worker, who is a new entrant to the labor force or re-entrant to it after periods of absence that are often quite extended.

There is thus real reason to expect that trade-impacted workers, if given appropriate help including proper incentives, will be able to adjust effectively into new occupations. We believe that the proposals made in this report will strongly enhance that possibility. We see little risk that the proposals would create disincentives to work: the compensation benefits represent a cutback from previous earnings, their duration is limited in time, no benefits are available unless the worker meets the job test and applies for retraining. The workers involved would have already demonstrated their desire and ability to hold the job. Indeed, serious efforts to train the relatively able workers dislocated by trade flows could provide valuable lessons for the broader manpower programs that, as indicated in the introduction to this report, can play a major role in helping to win the fight against inflation by upgrading the skills of our national labor force.

Fourth, adequate relocation reimbursement is needed. Efforts should be made to avoid the need for workers to move geographically to obtain new employment, because of the disruption of their lives that results. The community assistance programs discussed below should help meet that objective, as should the inducement to multi-product firms to shift workers displaed from prokng their trade-impacted product to producing more competitive items. However, geographical moves will be needed in some cases.

4.10 *The costs of such moves should be completely financed by the trade adjustment program.*

This assistance would be similar to that in the Amtrak settlement promulgated by Secretary of Labor Hodgson in 1970 as part of the creation of our new national passenger railroad system. This includes the search process for a new home and the loss to the worker, if any, of selling his old home in a depressed market or breaking an apartment lease. The Homeowners Assistance Program of the Department of Defense, and the forebearance authority of HUD, could be mobilized to assist this effort.

4.11 *All dislocated workers, not just heads of families, should be made eligible for relocation expenses.*

In making all of these proposals, the Chamber is aware that some observers argue that special adjustment programs for trade-impacted workers are illogical, because these workers are no different from those Americans dislocated by other changes, of purely internal origin, that affect our economy. In response, it would note that Congress has judged for over a decade that special adjustment to trade dislocation is needed; the only issue would seem to be the effectiveness of that adjustment program. In addition, however, the Chamber supports the judgment of Congress.

The trade adjustment issue will have to be faced head-on in the near future in the context of trade legislation alone. The costs of an adequate liberalization of compensation benefits (such as unemployment insurance benefits) for workers dislocated by all types of economic change, and a total new manpower program, are widely regarded as excessive under present conditions. Perhaps most important, a pilot project along the lines suggested could try out the needed new approaches in a policy area in which much greater knowledge is necessary. The Chamber thus feels that it is sound policy to propose a special program for trade-impacted workers.

5. Adjustment by Firms

This report has stressed the need for reformed economic adjustment for workers, because the Chamber believes that management should itself generally be responsible for the response of firms to dislocation from imports (as other disturbances) and that the responsibility of government to provide assistance is thus primarily to workers. There should be no compensation benefits for firms. Indeed, firms that fail to adjust to competition from imports, either by improving their ability in their present product line or by shifting to a new product line, may have to go out of business entirely.

There is often a need to help smaller firms really adjust, however, as provided for under present trade legislation. Changes should be made in the application of that legislation to firms to parallel the changes already proposed for workers. Depending on the particular case, the objective of the assistance should be to help the firm restore competitiveness in its present industry or adjust into a new line of endeavor. Despite the limited nature of the experience gained so far under the existing program, it appears that both objectives can be achieved.

The most necessary improvement in aid to firms is increasing its timeliness. Firms must adjust rapidly to avoid major losses that may undermine their positions for years, or even lead to total collapse. Most of the failures to promote firm adjustment under the present program can be attributed to its slowness to identify a problem and then provide the available assistance. Early help is more effective and cheaper as well.

The needed speed-up should be achieved through liberalization of the criteria for eligibility and an improved delivery system. As already proposed, new approaches to early warning and technical assistance to firms facing a threat of future injury could play a critical role in preempting dislocation from imports for firms (and through them for their workers), if expert management consultants were employed at an early stage to analyze the firm's problem and propose a plan of action.

The criteria for eligibility (1.2) after most import injury has occurred would be similar to those proposed for workers: *an increase in imports coupled with a decline in output, both by a firm and nationally for the given product, if the product represented a significant share of the firm's output, would make the firm eligible for assistance with discretion to the administering authority to challenge the presumption of injury if it felt that imports were not a substantial cause of the dislocation.* Firms and workers in those firms should in fact be encouraged to apply for help together; the use of similar eligibility criteria will promote that objective.

The benefits available to firms in present legislation include eligibility for tax loss carrybacks for two years beyond normal practice, preferential access to government credit, and technical assistance to help them achieve a viable business position. These aids to adjustment should be maintained, but several should be added.

5.1 *Government guarantees should be extended—for a fee—to enable eligible firms to obtain credit from private sources.*

This recommendation, which would possibly save money for the government, requires two changes from present law.

5.2 *The interest rate on guaranteed loans should not be tied to the borrowing rate of the Treasury.*

The Treasury is obviously a far better credit risk than firms threatened by import competition.

5.3 *Guarantees should cover 100 percent of the private loans (instead of the present 90 percent ceiling) if they were arranged sufficiently early in the adjustment process to provide high promise of saving the firm.*

5.4 *Technical assistance, including consideration of mergers and sales of a firm's assets, should be expanded through additional use of private consultants approved by the government and under its continuing surveillance, at the earlier instances made possible by the new system of early warning, the new criteria, and the improved administration.*

6. Adjustment by Communities

Communities are not eligible for "adjustment assistance" under present law. Yet many of the most severe dislocations caused by trade flows fall on those affected indirectly—the firms and people who provide services and inputs to the firms and workers who compete internationally. Indeed, communities may wither even if firms and their workers affected by imports successfully resist the new competition by moving elsewhere. The problems of direct suppliers would be met by the proposals made above for them to become eligible for all of the new adjustment benefits. Action is needed at the community level, however, to meet the problems of many others.

Communities should therefore automatically be eligible for aid under the new program when a significant share (perhaps 5 percent) of their workers themselves had become eligible under the new criteria applicable to them. Even if these particular workers found jobs elsewhere, their eligibility would enable the community in which they were laid off due to trade dislocation to receive benefits—providing a means to deal with the local problems caused by "runaway plants." *Other communities could apply for eligibility on the grounds that imports were a substantial cause of their problems.*

6.1 *Eligible communities should then receive attention of the type carried out successfully by the Office of Economic Adjustment in the Department of Defense, in recent years on behalf of the President's Inter-Agency Adjustment Committee, for over 160 large and small communities* (including entire counties) *impacted by changes in defense spending since 1961.*

The primary thrust of this effort is to help affected areas mobilize their own resources effectively, and by doing so attract private resources from outside the area to add to the adjustment. (In Wichita, for example, $40 million of federal funds played a key role in attracting $700 million of private money.) The Department of Defense sends teams of experts into impacted areas to analyze their problems and devise rehabilitation efforts. Local leaders—from business, labor, and other groups—are brought together to agree on a plan of action, assign responsibility for its implementation, and monitor the follow-through.

6.2 *Financing from ongoing government programs should be available under the new trade adjustment program as well.*

Agencies such as the Small Business Administration have provided key seed money in some cases, but the primary emphasis would be on technical assistance of all types, to help the communities realize their own potentials for adjustment.

7. Administration

This report has stressed the need for major improvement in the administration of the program of economic adjustment for those firms and workers who suffer dislocation as a result of the maintenance of a liberal trade policy by the United States. The present program is badly fragmented; delay and lack of coordination are inherent. The Tariff Commission must first find injury from imports. In industry-wide cases brought under the escape clause, the president must then determine whether adjustment assistance is the proper remedy. (He may also break ties in cases limited to specific firms and groups of workers.) Individual firms must be certified as eligible by the Secretary of Commerce, and the process has been extremely clumsy and prolonged. Individual groups of workers must be certified by the Secretary of Labor. There is no early warning, and no early action.

7.1 *A single agency is needed to administer the adjustment program under tight time limits specified in the authorizing legislation.*

It would be responsible for the participation of the government in the new system of early warning, economic analysis, eligibility findings, packaging of appropriate benefits, delivery of benefits to firms and communities, monitoring, evaluation, publicity of results, and accountability to the president and Congress. (Benefits to workers would continue to be delivered through the local Employment Service, under close surveillance from the Trade Adjustment Agency.) Such an integrated approach would permit early attention to emerging dislocations and rapid delivery of the new and liberalized help to meet them.

Such an agency could closely link, in time and in the decision-making process, determinations of eligibility and packaging of benefits—instead of the sequential process of the present program, which has proved to be ineffectual. It would build on previous experience, which suggests that the best-managed government programs are those of specialized agencies with unitary purposes—and that the worst of all worlds, adopted so far for "adjustment assistance," is to attempt to manage a unitary program by parceling out various aspects to a combination of old-line agencies and regulatory commissions. To insure full coordination of the assistance program with overall foreign economic policy, its director should be made a member of the Council on International Economic Policy (or any successor body created to coordinate foreign economic policy). To insure full coordination with overall economic policy, including structural adjustment efforts, he should also be a member of the Council on Economic Policy.

The Chamber shares the general distaste for new government agencies. Nevertheless, they may have to be created when a particular need arises. The Chamber believes that domestic adjustment to trade flows represents such a case.

7.2 *The Chamber recommends the creation of a new government agency independent of all existing departments.*

The agency would be along the lines of the Export-Import Bank or the Federal Home Loan Board. It would operate with a small cadre of top-flight administrators, manpower specialists, business and financial analysts, and economists.

7.3 *In view of the long-run and continuing nature of the adjustment problem the new government agency should operate under a multi-year authorization.*

7.4 *The policy direction of the agency, within the framework legislated by the Congress, should be set by a mixed board comprising the relevant government officials* (e.g., at present, Assistant to the President for Economic Affairs, Assistant to the President for Human Resources, Secretary of Labor, Secretary of Commerce, Special Representative for Trade Negotiations) *and representatives from the private sector* (including labor union officials and corporate executives).

The Costs of the Proposals

The maximum resource cost of the proposed program is estimated at about $300 million in its first year of operation. By its tenth year, the resource cost could rise to about $350 million annually as the early retirement benefits accumulated for older workers who took advantage of them. If present procedures are continued, the budgetary cost to the federal government would be $100 million per year higher as it replaced the state unemployment insurance funds in paying compensation benefits to trade-impacted workers (or reimbursed the funds for their payments of unemployment compensation to such workers in cases where the trade assistance program did not move quickly enough to provide payments as soon as the workers were laid off). This is simply a substitution of one payment for another with no inflationary effect on the economy, however, since the workers would have received the unemployment compensation anyway. In addition, there would be offsetting resource gains (including tax payments) in productivity of the retrained workers and the reduced likelihood that they would ever again require unemployment compensation.

Detailed analysis of the experience of 1967-69 suggests that 60,000 annual job layoffs were directly attributable to increased imports. Imports increased very rapidly in those years, and domestic output of the imported products did not decline in all cases; so this number may err on the high side as a guide to eligibility for trade assistance in the future. On the other hand, the size of the labor force has increased since then. But 60,000 appears to be a reasonable estimate of the maximum number of workers who might be eligible for benefits under the new program as a direct result of import flows.

Educated estimates suggest that another 20,000 layoffs annually could be attributed to the indirect effects of import increases. Under the liberalized criteria proposed, the annual number of workers laid off due to trade flows could thus number about 80,000. The following calculations will be based on this number, implicitly assuming that none of the 80,000 find new jobs on their own. This is obviously unrealistic. Only 65 to 75 percent of the workers eligible under the Trade Expansion Act have actually sought help, and the percentage of workers seeking help under liberalized criteria would undoubtedly be smaller because this group would include far better workers—who would find new jobs quickly—then were eligible under the restrictive approach of the present law. The estimated costs would thus be adequate to cover a much larger number of displaced workers (probably 100,000 or more) if some did find work on their own, as they certainly would, and are undoubtedly biased toward erring on the high side.

The Department of Labor estimates that 17.5 percent of the dislocated workers could quickly find on-the-job training, with the government compensating their new employers at the average current rate of $60 per week for an average of 26 weeks. Thus, 14,000 workers would require little or no compensation benefits, at a cost to the government of about $22 million per year.

The other 66,000 workers would receive compensation benefits. The average manufacturing wage is now approaching $140 per week, 75 percent of which is $105. Unemployment insurance benefits already average $62 per week, however, so the supplementary trade benefit is only $43. To this must be added a maximum of $10 per week for government takeover of the health, life, and other insurance premiums previously contributed by the firms that laid off the eligible workers. The net economic cost of the compensation benefits is thus about $53 per week for the 66,000 workers.

It is estimated that the average duration of benefits will be 26 weeks. Under the assistance provisions of the Automotive Products Trade Act, the average duration was 20 weeks. This program took place in 1967-68, however, when aggregate U.S. unemployment was low and declining, and covered auto workers whose productivity (and hence potential for finding new work) was above average. It is probably too low a figure for the future program.

On the other hand, the 30-week average of the present trade "adjustment assistance" program is probably too high. Most of its experience came during 1970-71, when aggregate unemployment was very high. In addition, the workers who finally became eligible under the tight criteria of the present law are probably less productive, and hence less employable, than the average trade-impacted workers. And the early warning provision of the new program would permit an earlier start on searches for new jobs and retraining, so that fewer workers would now need the maximum duration of benefits. Thus an average benefits period of 26 weeks per worker over an entire business cycle under the liberalized criteria appears reasonable and again likely to err on the high side. The annual cost of compensation benefits to workers could thus average about $90 million.

This figure represents the *additional* payments to laid off workers above the unemployment insurance benefits they would receive anyway and is thus the best measure of the real resource cost of the new program. Under the present trade adjustment program, the federal government, out of trade assistance funds, reimburses the state unemployment insurance funds for all unemployment insurance benefits paid out to these workers. Most estimates of the cost of a new trade adjustment assistance program *include* this reimbursement, which would total about $100 million for the number of workers here estimated to receive compensation benefits due to trade dislocations. (In the new approach proposed here, of course, the emphasis on early warning and early action would often enable the trade assistance program to pick up the benefits for many workers as soon as they were laid off, so standard unemployment compensation would never enter the picture.) Whether or not such reimbursement is continued, however, the real resource cost of the program is limited to the *additional* benefits that it makes available.

In addition to on-the-job training, the proposed program would include institutional training. The Department of Labor estimates that 13 percent (10,000) of these dislocated workers can benefit from such programs. The programs cost the government about $2,000 per worker, so add about $20 million to the annual bill.

The Department of Labor estimates that relocation costs would amount to about $250 per worker, and that 20 percent of dislocated workers (16,000 annually) will relocate. This adds $4 million to total program cost.

Acceleration of Social Security benefits requires reimbursement to the Social Security Fund of about $2,600 per worker per year. The Department of Labor estimates that 20 percent of all dislocated workers (16,000) are 55 years or older, so this aspect of the program would add about $20 million to its total cost in the first year if even one-half of those eligible opted for early retirement. This reimbursement to the Social Security Fund would have to be paid for each worker for each year prior to the year in which he would have normally retired—probably an average of about 5 years later. By the tenth year of the program, the cost of this provision could thus rise to about $100 million annually—again assuming that one-half of all eligible workers opted for early retirement. Small additional expenditures would be required to reimburse individual firms for the early commencement of retirement benefits to workers with private pension plans.

The total cost of the proposed program for workers would thus be well under $200 million in its first year, and rise to a long-run equilibrium level of no more than $250 million annually after ten years. About 10 percent of all dislocated workers would be over 55 years old and are assumed to take advantage of the early retirement option. About 30 percent would benefit from on-the-job and institutional training. The rest would be able to find new jobs without such programs, assisted by the improved counselling or simply due to the inducements provided by the job test and the limited duration of compensation benefits, within an average period of six months.

It is extremely difficult to estimate costs for firms and communities. The relatively few firm cases to date have cost about $2 million each. Some of the proposals made above would actually reduce government costs per case, by substituting loan guarantees for loans, and promoting earlier—and hence cheaper—help. On the other hand, the new eligibility criteria may well produce more cases. Until experience is gained with the new program, it will be impossible to say how much it might cost. The same is of course true of the completely new program for communities. The Chamber therefore proposes an initial budgetary ceiling of $100 million for the two together, with that figure to be adjusted in future years in the light of whatever experience is gained to that time. The total annual resource cost of the proposed program would thus rise from a maximum of about $300 million in its first year to a maximum of about $350 million in the longer run.

The annual costs to the economy of the Burke-Hartke import quotas would rise from at least $4.5 billion in its first year—$3.4 to 6 billion from the rollback of imports, $1.1 billion from the proportional quotas—to $5 to 10 billion (the $3.4 to 6 billion from the rollback, plus $3.5 to 7 billion from the proportional quotas, whose cost rises as time passes) in later years.[1] The annual costs to the U.S. economy of present trade restrictions, both here and in other countries, average $7.5 to 10.5 billion (and are rising over time). All of these costs are economic, and very conservative because standard economic analysis cannot capture dynamic and monopoly effects. The estimates do not even attempt to include the incalculable costs of such trade measures to U.S. foreign policy and to our national security. If the proposed new program of economic adjustment to liberal trade were instrumental in permitting an elimination of present restrictions as well as avoiding the Burke-Hartke quotas, its benefits would thus amount to $15 to 20 billion per year plus the avoidance of major national security difficulties, compared with its resource costs of $300 to 350 million per year.

Conclusion

The Chamber believes that the benefits of the proposed program far outweigh its costs. Indeed, the Chamber believes that the liberal trade policy which this program makes possible is essential for U.S. economic welfare and for the maintenance of our national security. It believes that the proposed program will work, building as it does on a number of precedents in different areas that have existed for many years, and may in fact provide a basis for much more extensive structural adjustment programs in the future that could play an even greater role in promoting the efficiency and growth or our economy. The Chamber urges the early adoption of such a program by the Congress, as part of legislation that will establish a new and constructive U.S. trade policy for the 1970s and beyond.

Note

1. Stephen P. Magee, "The Welfare Effects of Restrictions on U.S. Trade," *Brookings Papers on Economic Activity 3: 1972.*

**Part V
Foreign Direct Investment
and Transnational
Enterprises**

16 Coming Investment Wars?

Canada will now permit new foreign direct investments only when they bring "significant benefit" to Canada. The determination of "significant benefit" is explicitly to be a policy decision of the cabinet, based on five criteria: the contribution of the proposed investment to "the level and nature of economic activity in Canada," including employment, use of Canadian components, and exports; the degree and significance of Canadian participation in the enterprise; the effect on productivity, technological development and innovation in Canada; the effect on industrial competition; and the compatibility of the investment with the economic and industrial policies of the national and provincial governments.

The following scenario thus becomes almost inevitable. The Canadian cabinet will approve a large and controversial U.S. investment. Nationalist opposition will charge a sellout of Canadian interests. The government will respond that the investment brings "significant benefit" to Canada.

But Canadian politics will not permit the simple assertion of "national interest" by the governing party. Opponents of the investment (and of the governing party) will enumerate the alleged injury it brings to Canada. The government will be forced to counter by specifying the benefits which, in its view, outweigh the disadvantages. It will thus publicly reveal, for example, that the investment will bring x thousand additional jobs and y million dollars of additional exports to Canada.

International conflict becomes certain at this point. The AFL-CIO will charge that the x thousand jobs have been exported from the United States to Canada, validating its case against foreign investment by U.S. firms. The Treasury Department will charge that Canada has diverted the y million dollars of exports from the United States, weakening the U.S. balance of payments and the dollar. One virtually certain result is intensified U.S.-Canadian hostility. Another, which is a theme of this article, is an intensification of political pressure in the United States against all foreign investment by American firms.

Such overt efforts by Canada to capture an increasing share of the benefits of foreign investment would by themselves have a significant impact on U.S. policy, because Canada remains by far the largest single recipient of U.S. investment and because the rapid flow of communications between the two countries assures that adversely affected American in-

Appeared originally in *Foreign Affairs*, October 1974, pp. 135-52.

terests will become aware of the situation. But the new Canadian policy is only illustrative of one of the basic global trends of the 1970s. Virtually every country in the world which receives direct investment—which means virtually every country in the world, big or small, industrialized or developing, Communist or non-Communist, Left or Right—is levying increasingly stringent requirements on foreign firms.

The objective of these policies of host countries is to tilt the benefits brought by multinational companies as far as possible in their favor and to minimize the costs to them which can be associated with such investments. Few countries any longer ask the simplistic question: "Do we want foreign investment?" The issue is how to get foreign investment on the terms which are best for them, and indeed to use the power of the firms to promote their own national goals.

Host countries are adopting a variety of strategies to achieve this objective. Most are applying much more sensible general economic policies, and thus removing such sources of windfall profits for the firms —and losses for the countries—as overvalued exchange rates and undervalued interest rates. In addition, most are seeking to position themselves as strongly as possible to negotiate better deals on the whole range of relevant issues with applicant firms. They list broad criteria for judging specific applications, require detailed statements from applicant firms on the effects of their proposals, and then seek the best mix of benefits they can achieve without deterring the investor. This effort of host countries to negotiate maximum benefits and minimum costs from foreign investors will shortly become the focus of the entire international debate about multinational firms.

II

Efforts by host countries to maximize their returns from foreign investors are, of course, nothing new. There are four features, however, which differentiate the present markedly from the past. First, virtually all host countries are now adopting such policies, whereas only a few did so before. Second, the policies themselves are becoming more evident and explicit and hence will attract increasing attention in the home countries of the firms, particularly the United States.

Third, host-country objectives are now much broader and deeper. Governments throughout the world are accepting responsibility for an increasing number of economic and social objectives—such as regional equity, better income distribution and the development of indigenous high-technology industries—in addition to the traditional macroeconomic goals of full employment, growth and price stability. Developing countries are also seeking to reduce unemployment directly rather than assuming that it will fall automatically with economic growth.

Thus governments are seeking additional policy instruments, to meet an increased number of policy targets. With the explosive acceleration of international economic interpenetration, external forces can hinder—or assist—the successful use of traditional domestic policy instruments. Multinational firms, as the chief engine of interpenetration, represent both a major threat to the success of internal policies and a major opportunity for help. Host countries are thus virtually compelled by their own political imperatives to seek to exert a maximum impact on the detailed behavior of almost all incoming direct investments.

Fourth, host-country efforts are now far more likely to succeed because of fundamental shifts in the world economic and political environment that have put many host countries in a far stronger position than before. They have large and rapidly growing markets, especially when they are members of regional arrangements, such as the European Community or the Andean Pact, which discriminate against imports from outsiders. Many represent highly productive, lower-cost "export platforms" from which multinational firms can substantially improve their global competitive positions. Those possessing key raw materials are in a particularly strong position, both with companies in the extractive industries themselves and with companies which use the materials;[1] producers of raw materials have now demonstrated the ability to get together to promote their common interests, rather than compete with each other to the benefit of outsiders. And the indigenous talent that has emerged in even the least developed, as the result of a generation of economic growth with heavy emphasis on advanced education, enables host countries both to perceive accurately their national interests and take maximum advantage of their stronger positions. Outside help in negotiating with the firms is also increasingly available for those countries which still need it. So the firms can no longer dictate, or even heavily influence, host-country policies as they may have done in the past; the *dependencia* syndrome, under which foreign and domestic elites collude against the national interests of host countries, is rapidly disappearing.

In addition, host countries now have a far wider array of options in pursuing their objectives. Not long ago the multinational firm was the only source of large-scale capital, advanced technology and superior management. Not long ago the United States was virtually the sole source of large chunks of investment capital, technological know-how and marketing skills. Not long ago security considerations devolving from the cold war enabled the United States to dominate its allies, most small countries, and the international rules and institutions which governed world economic relations.

Now, however, the multinationals have lost much of their power because the attributes which they once monopolized, and which could only be obtained in package form, can be increasingly "unbundled"—capital obtained in the private markets, technology licensed from a variety of sources, management hired directly. Increasing numbers of European and Japanese companies offer formidable competition for American multinationals—and are often willing to invest on terms more generous to host countries, to make up for their delayed emergence on the world scene. Capital, technology and other skills can be bought in Europe and elsewhere, as well as in America. With the onset of détente, host countries large and small no longer fear to cross the United States by challenging U.S.-based firms and the international economic environment which helped them flourish in the 1950s and 1960s. Multinational firms based in the United States, recognizing these basic changes and with their own international exposure greatly increased by virtue of their rapid global expansion, complete the circle by seeking in virtually all cases to accommodate to the new leverage of host countries and by eschewing the backing of the U.S. government.

In short, sovereignty is no longer at bay in host countries. To be sure, the degree of this shift in power differs from country to country, and from industry to industry. It is virtually complete in most industrial host countries and some developing countries as well, and is well underway in many other developing countries. Only in a few countries—industrial as well as developing, and indeed including the United States itself—have new host-country policies on foreign investment not yet begun to emerge.

The shift in power and resulting policy is further along in extractive than in manufacturing industries. Within manufacturing, it is further advanced for low-technology investments and those aimed at the local market than for high-technology investments and those which use the country as an "export platform." But the trend appears inexorable.

III

What about the effects of this trend on home countries—that is, the countries from which investment comes, via multinational firms based there—in particular the United States? Before addressing that question, we need to take a closer look at the specific requirements being levied on the multinational firms.

These requirements derive from the policy objectives of the host countries. They differ in degree from country to country, but fall into three broad categories: domestic economic objectives, foreign economic policy objectives, and national control over the local subsidiaries of the foreign-based firms.

In the first category, the most direct requirement is job quotas for nationals. This has both a quantitative and a qualitative aspect. Developing countries with high rates of aggregate unemployment simply impose overall job requirements. Indonesia requires that 75 percent of all employees of foreign-based firms be Indonesian within five to eight years; Nigeria and Morocco sharply limit the access to alien labor of such firms. In both industrial and developing countries, such job requirements are often part of "regional policies": Canada, France, Iran, the Netherlands, and the United Kingdom, among others, offer major incentives to enterprises to bring jobs to "depressed areas." (In some countries, regional authorities themselves add to the list of requirements.) In addition, layoffs may be forbidden (Italy, some recent cases in France) or made very costly (Germany, Belgium), so that the firm is locked tightly into any level of employment which it initially recruits.

Qualitative job requirements are prevalent in both industrial countries and the new middle class of semi-developed countries. Argentina requires at least 85 percent of management, scientific, technical and administrative personnel to be Argentine. Singapore judges investment applications partly by the ratio of skilled and technical workers to be included in the work force. An increasing number of industrialized countries, particularly in Europe, are requiring the firms to carry out locally both a significant share of their total research and development and some of their most advanced research. Training of local workers is another requirement, aimed at both more and better jobs.

Two measures used to pursue both domestic and foreign economic objectives are "value-added" and "anti-concentration" requirements. To avoid becoming mere entrepôts for foreign firms, developing countries will now often require domestic production of a certain share of final output. This promotes the employment objective, both in the new industry itself and in those local industries which supply it; and furthers its balance-of-payments objective by raising the net foreign exchange return from the investment.

To avoid excessive industrial concentration, which can lead both to higher prices at home and to an impaired competitive position in world markets, some countries—particularly more developed ones—either reject foreign investments (especially take-overs) which would create excessive market power or let them proceed only if steps are taken to guard against such an outcome. Germany, the United States and Canada are particularly concerned with this issue.

Many developing countries are pursuing a similar aim through different means. Some multinational firms have traditionally limited or excluded competition among their own subsidiaries (and the parent) by dividing up world markets for each of their products. One result is that subsidiaries in particular countries are barred completely from the export market, or limited to a particular region. Global competition may be reduced as a result, and the export (and hence total production) opportunities of the country hosting the hobbled subsidiary are certainly reduced. Led by the Andean Pact, developing host countries are banning any such limitations on the distribution of local production by the subsidiaries (and by other tie-in clauses that would restrict the subsidiaries' use of the parents' technology).

Host countries are now promoting balance-of-payments objectives in several ways. A special target has been the trend in most multinational firms toward local financing, a practice which both limits the inflow of capital and diverts scarce local capital.

From 1957-65, for example, only 17 percent of the investments of U.S.-based firms in Latin America originated outside the host country.[2] From 1965 until early 1974, U.S. policy actually promoted the trend toward local financing by limiting (first voluntarily, then mandatorily from 1968) the capital outflows of U.S. firms—but not their actual investments. Now a reaction has set in. Australia was one of the first countries to require external capital to come with the firm, largely in retaliation against the U.S. capital controls. Many hosts now require external financing for foreign investments, and others achieve the same purpose by limiting subsidiaries' access to domestic capital. On the other side of the capital account, a widening array of countries (e.g., Brazil, India, the Andean Pact) limit tightly the repatriation of capital investment and even profits.

Requirements that the investing firm export a sizable share of output are even more important, because they go directly to the location of world production, jobs and the most sensitive aspects of each country's external position. Andean Pact countries will permit foreign investors to avoid divestiture only if they export more than 80 percent of their output outside the group. Mexico permits 100 percent foreign ownership only if the firm exports 100 percent of its output. India requires foreign investors to export 60 percent of output within three years. Practically every host developing country—and many host developed countries—attach very high priority to the export criterion.

As with jobs, the export requirement is qualitative as well as quantitative. Many countries are seeking to upgrade and diversify their export base, and so require foreign investors to push the processing of raw materials or the assembly of components a stage or two further than might otherwise occur. A particular objective is building high-technology exports.[3]

Some efforts are still being made to get foreign firms to replace imports as well. Canada recently barred a major U.S. computer company from competing for government contracts unless it helped Canada achieve balanced trade in that sector, by replacing imports as well as exporting.

However, host countries are increasingly emphasizing exports because such a focus permits larger-scale production, greater efficiency, and more jobs and growth for the longer run. The shift requires more explicit policies toward the foreign investor and more affirmative action by the firms (especially if the host country is to avoid the costs to its wider objectives of excessive export subsidies and undervalued exchange rates). In addition, larger production runs by the subsidiaries mean greater potential conflict with the economic interests of the home country. This issue well illustrates the increasing clashes among countries which may arise.

Finally, virtually all host countries are seeking majority (if not complete) ownership of local subsidiaries of foreign firms. Many are seeking a major share in day-to-day management as well. The objective is to increase the likelihood that the subsidiary will respond positively to the national policies of the host country rather than to the global strategy of the corporate family, headquartered in the United States or another home country, and perhaps to the global strategy of the government of the home country as well.

Some of these host-country policies treat the multinational firm differently from local companies, though many do not. The main point, however, is not whether the policies are discriminatory. The significance is their clear intent to shift toward the host country the package of benefits brought by the foreign firms. To the extent that they do so successfully to an important degree, they trigger a potentially important new source of international conflict. To the extent that they do so through measures which produce results different from market-determined outcomes, there is increased justification for such clashes and even greater likelihood that they will occur.

IV

The firms themselves may have little or no objection to these host-country policies. They may be relatively indifferent, within fairly broad limits, as to where to locate sizable portions of their production and how to finance it.[4] They may quite easily accommodate to host-country requirements on a majority, if not all, of the issues raised. The alacrity with which many firms have accepted the exceptionally detailed and far-reaching conditions imposed by Communist host countries is the most dramatic example, but the phenomenon is common. If too many firms do not play, a host country will sense that it has pushed too hard and retreat on the least important of its concerns, until it finds the mix that will maximize its interests.

The cooperativeness of the firms is promoted by the newly powerful positions of the host countries, as outlined above. It is often further accelerated by specific inducements. Some of the most frequent are favored tax treatment, export subsidies, "location grants," within the context of regional policies, subsidized training of local labor, prohibitions of strikes, preferred access to local credit, and protection against imports.

These considerations round out the strategies of the host countries. To maximize their returns, they must not only harness the activities of the firms but assure that the investments actually proceed. Thus they utilize the traditional mix of carrot and stick. The greater the incentives, the further the firms will, of course, tilt toward complying with the requests of their hosts.

Thus, a second broad trend is toward collaboration between the multinational firms and their hosts, and greater distance between the firms and their home governments. Few firms any longer appeal to their home government for support against host governments even in cases of outright nationalization, let alone to deal with the growing array of economic and political requirements which they face. Some firms, particularly in the natural resources industries, seek to limit the leverage of host countries by blending together capital from a variety of countries and selling their output forward to buyers in a variety of countries, to increase the problems for the host if it takes extreme action.[5] But even this strategy does not deter the achievement of the host's primary objectives; indeed, it may promote them by enhancing the inflow of external capital and assuring a diversified export market. And most firms, in recognition of the current balance of power, are in fact cooperating fully with their hosts. The oil industry is the most obvious recent case in point, but the trend is certainly widespread.

This analysis differs sharply from the picture painted in the recent debates in the United Nations and elsewhere, where the developing countries (and even some developed countries) continue to attack the alleged alliance against them of multinational firms and home-country governments. The difference can be explained partly by the usual lag in perceptions of overall bargaining power by the bargainer who is catching up step by step; partly by the dominance of the rhetoric by politicians whose perceptions are shaped by images, rather than by the technocrats who are implementing the new policies; partly by the zeal of the developing countries to stick together, which requires them to adopt the position of the weakest among them; and perhaps mainly by the overwhelming tactical advantage of keeping the home countries tagged as defenders of the multinations and aggressors against host-country interests. As in the case of raw material prices, some of the traditionally have-not countries suffer from intellectual lag and others find it highly convenient to maintain the rhetoric of the past though it no longer bears much relation to reality. Their tactics can succeed as long as the home countries fail to recognize what is really happening. But reality in the field of foreign direct investment cannot be submerged much longer.

V

The main impact of these new global trends is on the home countries of the multinational firms. It falls most heavily on the United States, the largest home country by far.

If host countries are achieving an increasing share of the benefits brought by multinational firms, someone else is receiving a decreasing share. As just outlined, this "loser" is seldom the firms themselves; indeed, they may gain more from the incentives than they lose from the requirements. In some cases, countries which are neither home nor host to the company may lose—as when a Brazilian subsidiary of a U.S. firm competes with German sales in the world automobile market.

But the United States, as the home country, may frequently be on the losing side of the new balance in two senses. Host-country inducements to American firms may attract economic activity and jobs away from the United States, in some cases without economic justification. Traditionally, the United States has forcefully opposed policies which discriminated against foreign investors; now it increasingly finds its national interests threatened by policies which discriminate in favor of those firms. And host-country requirements may skew the results of U.S. investments against the overall U.S. national interest.

To be sure, many foreign direct investments represent non-zero-sum games: as in all classical market behavior, world welfare improves. It is also conceivable that all parties benefit from some of those investments. Some host-country measures may also help home countries, such as the United States; if a host country breaks up the global allocation of markets by a multinational firm, the home country may benefit more from lower prices than it loses in oligopoly rents. And some host-country policies (such as placing a few directors on the boards of subsidiaries) essentially bring them psychic rather than financial income, and have no adverse impact on anyone.

However, there is always the issue of how to divide the benefits even when all parties do gain. Indeed, there may be losses to the United States (through the firms) even when more economically sensible host-country policies increase world welfare by eliminating or reducing market imperfections which profited the firms in the past. Most important, many investments are largely indifferent to location and hence are close to zero-sum games; in such cases a decision that is one party's gain *is* another party's loss. Furthermore, world welfare may actually decline as a result of some foreign investments, such as those induced primarily by host-country tax preferences and those which increase global market concentration, even though host countries gain from them. So there is great latitude for home countries to lose when host countries successfully tilt the benefits of the investment package in their own direction.

The balance-of-payments aspects are the clearest case in point. Existing world demand for a product may often be relatively fixed in the short run, especially for the processed goods and high-technology items which countries are avid to produce. Thus there is a limit to world exports. If Brazil requires General Motors to export a certain share of its production in order to remain in business (or to retain its favored tax treatment), U.S. automotive exports may decline even though no such shift was dictated by purely economic considerations. Similarly, the U.S. capital which Brazil requires General Motors to use to construct its plant may not be automatically offset by other capital inflows into the United States. Similar shifts in benefits can occur with respect to jobs, technology or other economic aspects of investment whose outcome is altered by host-country policies.

The effects of shifts in ownership and management control imposed by host countries are more subtle, and more difficult to trace. In the past, control of foreign natural resources by U.S. companies generally increased the likelihood that those resources would be available to the United States in a crisis; now, however, the seizure of effective control by most host countries has rendered the United States as uncertain as all other countries in this area. Increased host-country control renders the firms less susceptible to the extraterritorial reach of the U.S. government. And shifts in effective control reduce the likelihood that the United States will derive monopoly rents or other benefits from the overseas activities of U.S. firms.

Such shifts of investment-induced benefits from the United States to host countries may, from many points of view, be desirable. They may distribute world income more equitably. They may reduce some of the tensions which have clouded interstate relations heretofore, because host governments felt inferior to the firms and hence susceptible to ill treatment by them.

However, these shifts may not always be so benign from the standpoint of the home country. Indeed, the United States now finds itself in a most peculiar position. Negotiations between U.S.-based multinational firms and host countries are having an increasingly important bearing on the national interests of the United States. The interests of the host countries are represented through their governments. The interests of the firms are represented directly. But the third major actor in the drama is at present wholly unrepresented.

In the past, some observers would have brushed off this apparent asymmetry on three counts: that U.S.-based firms could be counted on to represent U.S. national interests explicitly, or at least advance them inadvertently; that the United States was so powerful economically that any costs to its economy would be easily absorbed (and perhaps welcomed officially in view of U.S. support for economic development elsewhere); and that any such costs would be quite small anyway in view of the insensitivity of the U.S. economy to external events and the marginal economic importance of foreign investment.

Each of these considerations has now changed dramatically, as part of the change in the overall economic and political environment noted in Section III.[6] Many "U.S.-based" firms have become truly multinational and thus, quite logically and defensibly from their standpoints, pursue a set of interests which may not coincide closely with any of several concepts of U.S. national interests. Indeed, as discussed above, many firms now respond much more clearly to host-country interests, because those host countries have both achieved a much stronger position vis-à-vis the firms and articulated far more clearly than home countries what they expect the firms to do.[7] In their constant quest for legitimacy and acceptance, the firms will naturally slide toward those who care most about their activities and who direct policies at them most explicitly.

And it is obvious that the U.S. economy is not so healthy that it can blithely ignore the effects of a phenomenon as large as direct investment. Such investment now accounts for more than 20 percent of the annual plant and equipment expenditures and profits of U.S.-based firms, and both numbers are rising rapidly. The corporations and the AFL-CIO agree that the phenomenon has an important impact on U.S. jobs and the balance of payments (though they disagree whether that impact is positive or negative). The United States is increasingly affected by world commodity arrangements, the structure of world markets and changes in exchange rates, all of which are influenced importantly by multinational firms.

It is thus both undesirable and completely unrealistic, in both economic and political terms to anticipate continued abstention by the U.S. government from involvement in the foreign direct investment activities of U.S.-based enterprises. The British government has for several years made foreign exchange available to U.K.-based firms only if they can demonstrate that their foreign investments will benefit Britain's balance of payments, through exports and profit remittances. The Swedish government has had similar restrictions, and has just passed legislation which will also enable it to block foreign investments by Swedish firms which hurt its economy or foreign policy. Japan and, to a lesser extent, France have also traditionally used a variety of government levers to try to assure benefits to the home country from the foreign activities of their firms. So the United States is virtually alone, among home countries, in not playing an active role toward foreign investment by national enterprises.

As in host countries, the issue will not be whether or not to permit foreign investment as a general rule. Nor will it primarily focus on the simplistic U.S. concerns of the past: "prompt, effective and adequate" compensation for nationalized properties, avoidance of barriers to U.S. investment or discrimination against it, codes of conduct to legitimize the firms. The issue will sometimes be whether to permit a specific investment. But it will primarily be the terms on which investments proceed, and the equitable sharing of the resulting impact on the national economies involved.

VI

As the United States seeks to fill the empty chair which currently marks most international discussion of its foreign direct investment, the likelihood of international conflict will rise sharply. For at stake is nothing less than the international division of production and the fruits thereof. Indeed, "the kinds of techniques used by governments both to attract and to constrain multinational firms sometimes look like the largest nontariff barriers of all."[8] Unless host countries cease their efforts to tilt the benefits of investment in their own direction, which is unlikely (and undesirable unless accompanied by other steps to help them achieve their legitimate objectives), the clash of these particular national interests could become a central problem of world economics and politics.

Over the coming decade, international investment policy could therefore replicate to an unfortunate degree the evolution of international trade policy in the interwar period. At that time, trade was the dominant source of international economic exchange. As governments accepted increasing responsibility for the economic and social welfare of their populations, particularly with the onset of the Depression, they sought to increase their national shares of the international benefits which resulted from trade. Other governments would not accept such diversion, and either emulated the moves of the initiators of controls or retaliated against them. There were no international rules and institutions to deter and channel such conflict. The result was trade warfare, and the deepening and broadening of the Depression.

Some observers fear that another depression looms on our contemporary horizon. Others wonder whether a Great Inflation, which in my view is more likely, will similarly lead countries desperately to pursue nationalistic measures in an effort to export their problems and insulate themselves from external pressures. Either cataclysm would greatly intensify the problem under discussion. Indeed, the national clashes outlined here might already have arisen much more frequently had not the postwar world economy progressed so successfully until recently.

Even without such extreme underlying conditions, however, the struggle for the international location of production will almost certainly continue to grow in both magnitude and impact on all countries concerned. Foreign direct investment and multinational enterprises have now replaced traditional, arms-length trade as the primary source of international economic exchange. As indicated throughout, host countries are increasingly adopting explicit policies to tilt in their directions the benefits generated by those enterprises. The impact of these efforts may turn out to be even greater than their trade predecessors of the 1930s, both because the economic interpenetration of nations is now more advanced than in the 1920s and because governments now pursue so many more policy targets.

Indeed, the U.S. government has already begun to voice opposition in international forums to the tax subsidies and other incentives which artificially lure U.S. firms to invest abroad, and the changes in U.S. taxation of foreign income proposed by the Treasury Department in April 1973 were largely aimed at countervailing such practices. Much stronger U.S. reactions can be envisaged over the next few years. The original AFL-CIO attack against foreign investment by American firms, as embodied in the Burke-Hartke bill, was based on ambiguous aggregate data and a handful of unrepresentative individual cases. Hence it made little headway. The efforts of the Treasury Department to limit direct investment outflows in the middle 1960s were similarly stymied by ambiguities over the effect of the outflows on the balance of payments.

But now labor, those concerned with the balance of payments, and the many other opponents of multinational enterprises will have a much stronger case: the shifting of benefits from the United States to host countries *through the overt policy steps* of those host countries. Such groups will ask how the U.S. government can sit idly by and let such shifts occur, just as similar American groups have since the 1930s—correctly and usually successfully—insisted that the U.S. government retaliate against the efforts of other countries to tilt the benefits of trade through subsidizing exports to the United States, blocking imports from the United States, or other measures of commercial policy which injured U.S. economic interests. And there are no domestic or international rules and procedures through which to channel such protests, like those developed for trade after World War II to avoid a repetition of the interwar experience.

The problem is further exacerbated by the subtlety and variety of inducements offered, and requirements levied, by host countries. A tariff or import quota is easy to see, and is usually known publicly. But a regional investment grant can be negotiated privately with a firm, and portrayed as "purely domestic" in any event if exposed. Export or job quotas, which are by their nature negotiated on a case-by-case basis, are even less obvious. The universal call for "transparency" of the operations of multinational firms must be joined by a call for transparency of the policies of many host countries toward those firms.

VII

The scenario envisaged at the outset of this article can thus be concluded as follows. After the Canadian government approves the proposed investment, because it transferred x thousand jobs and y million dollars of exports from the United States to Canada, the U.S. government—under intense domestic political pressure—decides to retaliate. It seeks to bar the particular investment, either directly or by declaring that the foreign tax credit will not apply to its profits.

Either approach, however, requires legislation. Congress, probably supported by any Administration in power, properly decides that such legislation should cover the overall issue of foreign investment rather than a single case or even a single country. The legislation clearly derives from a foreign action to pull jobs and exports away from the United States, and more examples of such actions, by a growing list of host countries, are added to the debate each day. The whole discussion may even take place with unemployment rising and the trade balance slipping. Thus the new legislation slaps a licensing requirement on all foreign investment eliminates the tax credit altogether, except perhaps for investments where host countries avoid levying any requirements on U.S.-based firms.

Canada and most other host countries of course stick to their guns, being unable politically to back down in favor of multinational firms and at the dictates of the U.S. government. Foreign-based multinationals quickly begin to fill the void, and the United States begins to lose the many advantages conferred on it by the foreign investments of U.S.-based firms. Many of these firms then seek to "leave the United States," but the Treasury pursues them. In the end, as in the trade wars of the interwar period, the results include open political hostility among nations, a severe blow to the world economy, and a shattering of investor confidence.

Hopefully, the world will learn from its past mistakes and prevent this scenario from ever occurring. To do so, host countries should limit their efforts to skew the activities of multinational firms, perhaps by following the Australian example of insisting on "no adverse effects" rather than the Canadian example of requiring "significant benefit." But many will not do so unless some other power countervails the power of the firms. Nor will many of them, particularly the developing countries, do so unless they find other ways to meet their legitimate national aspirations.

It follows that home countries, particularly the United States, should take steps to help developing host countries achieve their goals in less disruptive ways. Such measures should encompass trade policy, commodity arrangements, and foreign assistance.[9]

More narrowly, home countries will also need tools that can be used to counter efforts of host countries that go beyond reasonable norms. For example, legislation increasing taxation of the foreign income of American corporations to offset tax inducements offered by host countries would be a precise analogy to present laws, in the trade field, that provide for countervailing duties against export subsidies by foreign governments. And a mechanism is needed to deal with individual cases where problems arise, analogous to the present escape clause in the trade area providing for temporary protection where U.S. interests are injured by particular import flows.

But such measures by home countries could simply lead to a series of retaliatory and counter-retaliatory steps between them and host countries. Thus international investment wars will be prevented only by the adoption of a truly new international economic order, just as the trade wars of the 1930s were prevented from recurring in the postwar period only by the creation of a new international order based on the GATT, the IMF, the World Bank and American leadership.

The new order will have to include international rules governing investment itself, to limit the jousting for benefits between home and host countries and to provide a channel for the disputes that will inevitably arise among them, however ambitious the preventive rules. It will have to limit the power of the firms in ways acceptable to host countries, and provide alternative means for the latter to reduce domestic unemployment and expand exports. Multinational enterprises have a vital interest in the creation of such a new order, because they will otherwise be caught increasingly in the struggle between host and home countries; it will no longer be possible for them to side with home countries due to the weakness of the hosts, as in the 1950s and early 1960s, nor with hosts due to the inattention of the home countries, as in the late 1960s and early 1970s.

There are already many reasons to begin the construction of a new international economic order to replace the order of the first postwar generation, which has collapsed: the globalization of inflation, international monetary instability, the growing use of export controls, the scrambles for oil and other natural resources, the dire needs of the resource-poor countries of the "Fourth World" and the abilities of the new "middle class" of semi-developed countries to help in assisting them.

The threat of investment wars adds another crucial issue to the list for global economic reform. Fortunately, this particular threat has not yet become acute. There is time to deal with it carefully and constructively, instead of waiting for a series of crises to force hasty reaction. To begin to do so would both defuse the emotional issues raised by the existence and spread of multinational enterprises, and begin to apply the tested principles of international rules and cooperation to one of the major new features of the postwar world economy.

Notes

1. See C. Fred Bergsten, "The New Era in World Commodity Markets," *Challenge*, Sept.-Oct. 1974 [chapter 18 in this volume].

2. Ronald Müller, "Poverty Is the Product," *Foreign Policy*, Winter 1973-74, pp. 85-88.

3. This emphasis on high-technology exports may affect a country's balance of payments less than its industrial structure. In a country whose exchange rate is floating, such as Canada, any increase in the exports of the promoted sector will produce upward movement in the currency, which will tend to limit exports (and increase imports) in other sectors.

4. For an excellent analysis of this range see Paul Streeten, "The Multinational Enterprise and the Theory of Development Policy," *World Development*, Vol. 1, No. 10 (October 1973). He counsels host developing countries to marry cost-benefit analysis of their own needs to bargaining-power analysis of how far they can push. However, he views many host countries as weaker in their relations with multinationals than do I.

5. See Theodore H. Moran, "Transnational Strategies of Protection and Defense by Multinational Corporations: Spreading the Risk and Raising the Cost for Nationalization in Natural Resources," *International Organization*, Vol. 27, No. 2 (Spring 1973).

6. And elaborated in C. Fred Bergsten, *The Future of the International Economic Order: An Agenda for Research*, Lexington, Mass., Lexington Books, D.C. Heath and Company, 1973, esp. pp. 1-8 [chapter 2 in this volume].

7. This in turn reflects a far clearer appreciation by host than home countries of the effects on them of multinational firms, and thus a far clearer idea of the ends to which they might want to harness foreign investors. There has been much more extensive analysis of the effects of foreign investment on host countries than of the effects on home countries, a situation which a forthcoming book on U.S. policy toward such investment by the present author, Thomas Horst and Theodore Moran seeks to help balance.

8. A. E. Safarian and Joel Bell, "Issues Raised by National Control of the Multinational Corporation," *Columbia Journal of World Business*, Winter 1973, p. 16.

9. See C. Fred Bergsten, "The Threat From The Third World," *Foreign Policy*, Summer 1973 [chapter 27 in this volume].

17

Foreign Direct Investment in the United States

Introduction

The United States is the world's second (to Canada) biggest host country for foreign direct investment (FDI), as well as the world's biggest home country for firms making such investments. But the historical experience of the United States with FDI is overwhelmingly as a home country rather than as a host. Even the large foreign investments which promoted our economic development prior to World War I were primarily of a portfolio nature, and some American firms were already at that time beginning to expand abroad. In the period since World War II, FDI by U.S. firms has of course been one of the chief features of the international economy, whereas investment in the United States by foreign-based firms has begun to expand rapidly only in the past six or seven years.[1]

I begin with this comparison because the relationship between the home-country and host-country roles of the United States is central to all consideration of the latter. At the analytical level, we still know very little about the effects on the United States economy and foreign policy of FDI abroad by American firms despite their obvious importance, the close scrutiny to which they have been subjected in recent years, and the wide range of attacks leveled against them. The United States still has no explicit policy toward FDI by U.S. firms; it simply continues to apply a series of ad hoc measures, each adopted to deal with some other problem through FDI. And we are, naturally, much further from being in a position to come to grips comprehensively with the issues raised by the much more recent and quantitatively less important issue of FDI in this country by foreign-based firms.

Asymmetries Between FDI By and In the United States

We do know, however, that there are marked asymmetries between FDI by U.S. firms and FDI in the United States by foreign firms:

—The United States is the world's largest economy and U.S. firms are

Originally presented as testimony to the International Finance Subcommittee of the Senate Banking, Housing and Urban Affairs Committee in its hearings on *Foreign Investment in the United States*, February 21, 1974.

generally larger than foreign firms. As a result, U.S. firms usually play a much more important role—individually and as a group—in the countries in which they invest than do foreign-based firms in the United States.

—The U.S. market remains the most sophisticated in the world, and hence the leading site of product and process innovations. FDI in the United States by foreign firms is thus usually "upstream" in terms of the product cycle, while FDI abroad by U.S. firms is usually "downstream." As a result, much foreign investment in U.S. manufacturing appears to be motivated by a desire to get in on U.S. technology, partly to help foreign firms compete better in their home markets, whereas U.S. firms invest abroad largely to exploit technological advantages which they have already developed.[2] One result is that the U.S. subsidiaries of European firms do a great deal of research and development themselves, with a high measure of independence from their parents, whereas most R & D by U.S. firms continues to be done at home.[3]

—U.S. firms may invest abroad to take advantage of lower labor costs, whereas no investment in the United States is likely to be motivated by that factor.

—A very high percentage of FDI in United States manufacturing consists of takeovers rather than the construction of new plant and equipment. The sizable increase in European FDI here in 1969-70, relative to 1966-68, was wholly accounted for by acquisitions.[4] From 1946 through 1967, about 60 percent of the European affiliates here were accomplished through takeovers, compared with 25-40 percent of the number of U.S. affiliates abroad[5] and only 10-15 percent of the value of all U.S. FDI in Europe.[6] One recent study found that 25 of 40 European subsidiaries recently established here took the acquisition route.[7] This tendency might be further accelerated, perhaps greatly, if the oil producing countries were to invest any significant share of their increased earnings in U.S. firms, because they obviously have neither the manpower nor the technology to build new plants; any "direct investment" which they undertood would almost have to come via takeovers.[8]

It would thus be erroneous to simply extrapolate our thinking about FDI by U.S. firms to FDI in the United States by foreign-based firms. The significant differences cited, plus others which might well appear in future analyses, call for independent judgments about the effects of inward FDI on the United States and what U.S. policy toward it should therefore be.

Policies of Other Host Countries

At the same time, it is instructive to note that virtually every other country in the world has adopted explicit limitations on incoming FDI. Such limitations appear to be growing rapidly around the world,[9] in developed (e.g., Australia, Canada) and developing countries alike. They take very different forms, but appear to have a common theme: the effort by each host country to maximize *its national share* of the package of benefits brought in by a foreign-based firm (e.g., jobs, export earnings, capital, learning) and to minimize the costs to it which can also be part of that package (e.g., jeopardizing national economic security, deflection of national economic and social goals, repatriated earnings, draining off scarce national talent). Indeed, new Canadian legislation declares that it will henceforth be the policy of that country to accept only FDI which *helps* the Canadian economy, which is quite different from rejecting only that FDI which is deemed to *hurt* the nation. The trend noted is true even for some of those host countries which are also major home countries of multinational firms: France (the third largest home country, by value of FDI), Japan (seventh largest, and fastest growing), and increasingly the United Kingdom (second largest).[10]

This trend poses several important issues for U.S. policy. As a home country for much of the FDI which is the target of such policies, can the United States simply leave the outcome to bargaining between the firms and the host countries? (In oil, this has obviously not worked out very well—but it continues.) More directly to the point of today's session, should the United States remain virtually the *only* host country which does not play at least some role toward incoming FDI by foreign-based firms as a matter of general policy?[11] Or is the United States so big, and foreign firms relatively so small, that we need not be concerned?

The Impact of Incoming FDI on the U.S. Economy

To answer this question, two aspects of incoming FDI must be analyzed. First, what is their impact on the U.S. economy? Do they create jobs? Do they add to welfare and check inflation by increasing competition, or do they accelerate inflation by adding to the global strength of oligopolies? Do they help the balance of payments, by bringing capital with them and perhaps substituting for imports, or hurt it by repatriating earnings and improving their competitive positions against U.S. firms in world markets? Do they enhance our economic security, by diversifying sources of supply, or jeopardize it because their "centers of decision"—to seize a phrase widely used in Europe to describe American multinationals—are abroad?

To answer these queries, one must determine what would happen in the absence of the FDI. Would a U.S. firm make the investment instead? Would another foreign firm? Or would the investment not be made at all? The differences under these three alternatives, on the criteria just listed, would provide a reasonably comprehensive picture of the economic costs and benefits of FDI in the United States.

Needless to say, such analysis is extremely difficult to carry out in practice. Data limitations are severe, and one can never be too confident in judging "what would have happened otherwise." Some progress has been made in applying this approach to U.S. FDI abroad, however, and more work is in progress. But I am aware of no effort to apply such analysis to FDI in the United States; it should be attempted, to provide a better basis for judging the economic impact of the phenomenon.

A priori, one must be skeptical that incoming FDI provides much benefit for the U.S. economy. New plant and equipment expenditures by foreign firms *which would not otherwise be undertaken by U.S. firms* are unlikely ever to loom large in the U.S. economic picture, in the aggregate or even in particular industries. Even when such investments are made, their benefits to the U.S. economy appear quite marginal:

—Much foreign investment here is financed originally by borrowing in the United States and subsequently through funds generated internally, so there is relatively little capital inflow to help the balance of payments.[12] The share of such investment financed internally may rise even further now that the Interest Equalization Tax and FDI regulations, which inhibited some forms of such financing, have been terminated.

—Little FDI here appears to substitute for imports, in view of the asymmetries cited earlier and the fact that most foreign firms need to maintain their export markets in order to maintain efficient production scale in their home plants.

—As already indicated, takeovers constitute a large share of FDI here, at least so far, and one of the few conclusions widely shared by observers of FDI is that takeovers are the least beneficial type thereof for host countries.

The overriding consideration appears to be that, unlike U.S. firms, few foreign firms are likely to undertake FDI here to marry their existing technological superiority with lower costs. Instead, they are seeking new technology here despite higher costs. The gains of the investment to the United States, as a host country, are thus unlikely to be sizable.

There are certainly exceptions to this generalization. A Japanese steel mill and German chemical plant have recently brought new jobs to depressed areas in the United States. Pechiney introduced new methods for processing aluminum. It is possible that some FDI here could add to price competition, e.g., if Volvo and Volkswagen set up local production of automobiles—although it is also possible that proximity would instead increase their *de facto* collusion with the U.S. auto industry. As with the general phenomenon of FDI, few generalizations hold up very far and an eclectic policy approach probably makes most sense.

This conclusion is buttressed by the fact that FDI in the United States is unlikely to levy significant economic costs on us either. The *dependencia* syndrome which dominates fears of incoming FDI in other countries, developed as well as developing, simply has no place here in view of the magnitudes involved. The balance of payments is unlikely to suffer significantly if the present pattern continues, even over the longer run, because very high percentages of earnings are reinvested rather than repatriated. Continued vigilant application of U.S. antitrust laws by the Department of Justice—which is, tellingly, often cited by foreigners as a U.S. barrier to investment here—should preclude undue market concentration stemming from foreign investments. Two potential costs have recently moved to the forefront, however, and deserve consideration.

Two New Concerns

The first is the possibility of sizable investments in U.S. firms by oil-exporting countries, particularly those few Arab countries with huge oil reserves and small populations. As already noted, their "direct investments" could only take the form of takeovers of existing firms because they have neither the manpower nor the technology to build new plants here or elsewhere; indeed, they will continue to rely on foreign firms to manage the bulk of their domestic industry even as they fully take over the ownership of their own oil and diversify their economies.

I personally doubt that much of this "direct investment" will actually take place. The Arab countries have a great deal of economic leverage over the United States (and the other consuming countries) at this point in time. They would be unlikely to hand us the leverage which would come through placing sizable and obvious shares of their wealth within our jurisdiction, particularly since they have just demonstrated their own distaste for foreign majority ownership—even ownership which, unlike their own potential takeovers, brought with it valuable resources over a long period of time—by nationalizing most of the foreign firms they could get their hands on. In addition, any rapid efforts they might make to take over U.S. firms would run up the price of the firms' stock appreciably, and make the investment much more questionable in purely financial terms. And the similar fears which were being raised about the Japanese just a year or two ago have proved groundless, at least so far. The Arabs might very well buy sizable blocks of stock of individual U.S. companies, but I regard the likely patterns to be distinctly minority positions held through intermediate nominees and acquired over extended periods of time.

Nevertheless, there is a possibility that majority takeovers could occur. Such takeovers would bring little benefit to the U.S. economy. It is true that such takeovers would in theory provide additional capital to the bought-out shareholders which might then be invested usefully elsewhere in the U.S. economy, but I see no reason to go through the extra step of the takeover when there is every prospect that much of the Arab money will wind up in the same places through normal market forces anyway—with similar effects on our balance of payments. In either case, the money will not go to capital-short industries which really need help. Indeed, it is widely agreed that takeovers in general carry few benefits for the host countries, and this would be particularly true for investors who brought little to the firm in terms of management or other skills.

I doubt that such investments would bring significant economic costs either, but subtle problems could arise. A Japanese takeover of Chrysler, for example, could lead to charges that imports of Toyotas were being facilitated and intensify pressures for U.S. import restrictions. An Arab takeover of U.S. energy firms could lead to charges that they were subverting either "Project Independence" or "Project Interdependence," in favor of continued dependence on Arab oil.

Such charges would seldom stand up intellectually, but I cannot be very confident that their psychological and political effects would be costless. At precisely the time when major efforts are underway to reduce hostility and the sense of confrontation between oil producers and consumers, as will likely be necessary for some time to come, takeovers by them of U.S. firms could instead fan the flames.

Thus I certainly see no case for new U.S. incentives to attract such investments. Any such U.S. effort would quickly be emulated (and probably topped) by other industrialized countries, so the only effect would be further revenue transfers to the Arabs. Indeed, it might be prudent to erect a new general policy to prevent or at least screen all foreign takeover bids, rather than respond ad hoc and emotionally to individual cases which might arise in the future.[13]

The second recent concern is that FDI in U.S. raw materials—coal, shale oil, etc.—could siphon off U.S. resources for the benefit of other countries and prevent our achieving a capacity for energy independence. It is certainly true in theory that, if left to market forces, investment in these resources by foreign firms could (a) reduce such U.S. investment, because the U.S. firms would fear creating excess supply which would not provide them with adequate return, and (b) increase the likelihood that U.S. output would be exported in future periods of shortage.

In practice, however, I doubt either outcome. The priority at this time, and probably for some time to come, must be to increase world supply of all energy sources as rapidly as possible. It will be some time before firms will have real reason to fear energy gluts. Even so, it is quite possible that U.S. energy policy will protect the firms against the falling prices which would accompany such gluts, as recently hinted by Secretary Shultz, in order to generate the massive investments now needed.

In addition, the United States will never be truly independent in the energy (or any other) field as long as the other national economies with which we have become so intertwined remain dependent, as recognized by Secretary Kissinger when he focused on the theme of Project *Interdependence* at last week's energy conference. Energy sharing will be an essential part of such a program, as offered by Kissinger at the conference, and it will make little difference whose investment is involved. And, in the event of dire catastrophe—such as a future oil embargo against the United States which had real impact—the U.S. Government could apply temporary controls on exports of U.S. energy resources whether the firms affected were owned by Americans or foreigners; other countries will understand this possibility when making their investments in the first place, but it should certainly be made explicit in any inter-governmental discussions on the subject.

Thus I see no reason why the United States should ban, or even limit, FDI in U.S. energy resources. This is particularly true when we recall that the United States clearly wants U.S. firms to be able to continue looking for such resources throughout the world, at least part of which will be exported to the United States. This brings us to the final component of our analysis: the intimate relationship between U.S. policy toward increasing FDI here and the policy of other countries toward U.S. FDI there.

The Relationship Between U.S. and Foreign Policies Toward FDI

As already noted, the United States is the second biggest *host* country for FDI as well as the biggest *home* country of multinational firms. In addition, it continues to be the most outspoken advocate of freedom for international capital flows, including FDI. Along with its usual weight on all international issues, particularly economic issues, these factors assure that any policies it decided to adopt toward incoming FDI would have an important effect on the policies of other countries—particularly other industrial countries, which host the bulk of U.S. FDI—toward *their* incoming FDI, much of which is based in the United States.

Thus the United States must weigh carefully the policy repercussions of any new measures it might take in this area. If the United States continued to seek free access abroad for U.S. firms, it could hardly place serious restraints on incoming FDI.

If it began to take a more eclectic view toward FDI by U.S. firms, however, as I have suggested elsewhere, it could quite consistently take a similarly eclectic view toward the reverse flows. As indicated above, virtually all other host countries have already adopted explicit measures to govern incoming FDI. Thus the United States would only be "catching up" if it decided to do so. Although few investment flows would probably ever be restrained, in practice, I believe that the U.S. Government should certainly have the authority to do so on a case-by-case basis. To provide such authority, I propose enactment of an "escape clause" for such investment, like the escape clause which has existed for many years in the trade field, under which any U.S. party (industry, firm, group of workers, or the government itself) which felt that it was (or would be) injured by an investment could seek to block or limit that investment by testing its case against specified criteria through specified procedures—probably focused on the Tariff Commission—which assured that all interested parties would be heard.[14]

Conclusions

1. Our knowledge of foreign direct investment in the United States remains quite limited. I recommend that this Subcommittee (a) sponsor legislation to increase sharply the manpower and budget in the U.S. Government responsible for compiling data on the subject and (b) promote a comprehensive, non-governmental research program to analyze comprehensively the costs and benefits of such investment for the United States.

2. The United States has relatively little to gain, in a direct economic sense, from incoming direct investment. I therefore see no case for the adoption of fiscal or other incentives to promote such investment. If such encouragement were ever to be provided, it should in practice be extended only as part of a negotiated package with the foreign investors which assured commensurate benefits to the United States—the practice now followed by virtually every other host country.

3. Virtually all other host countries have long since adopted explicit policies to govern incoming foreign direct investment. I recommend that this Subcommittee sponsor legislation which would create an "escape clause" for such investment, as outlined above. Once the United States had adopted such a policy, of no incentives to inflows and a mechanism for case-by-case reviews thereof, the time would probably be propitious for launching an effort to draw up international rules to avoid conflicts among national policies in this area. This would replicate the evolution of international trade policies during the postwar period.

4. There is widespread agreement that takeovers are likely to be the

least useful form of foreign direct investment, and it is conceivable that takeovers of major U.S. firms could become a real possibility. I therefore recommend that the Subcommittee explore the possibility of sponsoring legislation which would at least set up a screening procedure for that particular type of activity, in addition to its being subject to the more general "escape clause." Since I see little benefit to the United States from takeovers of foreign firms by U.S. companies, I am not concerned about triggering similar policies in those few countries where they do not already exist.

Notes

1. I make no effort here to predict the future magnitude of such investment. However, much of its sharp jump in 1973 was due to (1) the sharp devaluation of the dollar from August 1971 through July 1973, (2) the sharp increase in fears of a protectionist swing in U.S. trade policy dating from the near-miss of the "Mills bill" in 1970 and the strong push for Burke-Hartke legislation in 1971-72, and (3) the huge increase in monetary reserve holdings in Japan, Germany and most other countries which prompted some of them to drop their barriers against foreign investment by their firms and even to encourage such activity. All three of these factors have now changed dramatically: (1) the dollar has strengthened markedly since July 1973, wiping out much of the second devaluation (of February 1973) as well as the subsequent market depreciation; (2) the House passed a relatively liberal trade bill, and Burke-Hartke pressures have subsided noticeably; and (3) virtually all countries are again husbanding reserves due to the increase in their oil import bills.

2. Arnold W. Sametz, *The Foreign Multinational in the U.S.*, Salomon Brothers Center for the Study of Financial Institutions Working Paper Number 9, Oct. 1973.

3. Lawrence G. Franko, *European Business Strategies in the United States* (Geneva: Business International, 1971), reported that 70% of the European companies which he sampled did R & D in the United States.

4. H. E. Ekblom, "European Direct Investments in the United States," *Harvard Business Review*, July-August 1973, p. 22.

5. United Nations, *Multinational Corporations in World Development* (New York, 1973), table 36, p. 186.

6. A figure of 10 to 12% "in recent years" is cited in Sidney E. Rolfe and Walter Damm, eds., *The Multinational Corporation in the World Economy* (New York: Praeger Publishers, 1970), p. 81. The 15% figure comes from 1963-68 and is cited by Rainer Hellman, *The Challenge to U.S.*

Dominance of the International Corporation (New York: Duneller, 1970), p. 257, who also lists a large number of these takeovers in 1969-70 on pp. 172-74.

7. J. D. Daniels, *Recent Foreign Direct Manufacturing Investment in the United States* (New York: Praeger, 1971), p. 62.

8. It could also be argued that the European penchant for takeovers will decline in the future, by analogy with the trend of U.S. FDI in Europe which was itself heavily oriented toward takeovers 15-20 years ago to get an original foothold but by now has progressed to a focus on expansion of existing plant. This view draws support from the Survey of FDI in the United States in 1973 just published by the Conference Board, which indicated that only 18% of those investments represented takeovers. The structural differences cited in the text, and the unusual and temporary factors operating in 1973 and outlined in footnote 1, raise strong doubts about this analogy, however.

9. With the notable exception of Japan, which is liberalizing from one of the most restrictive base levels in the world, and Germany, which continues to avoid controls although it has moved in a few specific cases to deter takeovers and does require registration of incoming investments.

10. The United Kingdom has placed a series of increasingly stringent requirements on incoming FDI. See Economist Intelligence Unit, *The Growth and Spread of Multinational Companies*, 1971, pp. 58-63, and Hellman, *op. cit.*, pp. 143-45.

11. The United States does limit FDI in a few specific industries on the basis of *ad hoc* laws passed long ago, and some states provide incentives to foreign investors, but no legislation or even policy applies to it in general at the national level.

12. Ekblom, *op. cit.*, p. 146, concludes that "European business in the United States is substantially self-financing . . . ."

13. Hellman, *op. cit.*, p. 172, notes that "Contrary to the governments of numerous European countries, the U.S. Government does not distinguish in its policy on foreign investments between new investments and joint ventures on the one hand, and the acquisition of existing firms on the other."

14. For details of my proposal to adopt a similar U.S. "escape clause" vis-a-vis *outward* direct investment by U.S. firms, and the rationale for such a policy, see the *Journal of Finance*, May 1973, pp. 457-62.

**Part VI
Natural Resources**

18 The New Era in World Commodity Markets

Many countries that produce primary products are now making intensive efforts to boost their earnings from these commodities. Increasingly, these countries have sought to maximize their market power by forming cartels. The success or failure of these "producers' associations" will have a major bearing on world economic conditions, particularly inflation, and on international political relationships for the foreseeable future.

The Effort to Cartelize

Joint action has now been taken by producing countries in at least seven major commodities since I first predicted this trend over a year ago (in "The Threat from the Third World," *Foreign Policy*, Summer 1973 [chapter 27 in this volume]):

—The twelve leading oil exporters, operating through the Organization of Petroleum-Exporting Countries (OPEC), have raised their returns by a factor of ten and, for a period, significantly limited world production.

—The seven leading bauxite exporters formed the International Bauxite Association (IBA). Immediately thereafter, Jamaica forced a sixfold increase in its earnings. Other members are now beginning to follow suit, and further price rises may well be in store. Bauxite is, of course, the major raw material in the production of aluminum.

—Six leading phosphate producers have tripled their prices, with further increases likely. Phosphate is a major input to fertilizers and detergents.

—Four leading copper producers, through the Intergovernmental Council of Copper-Exporting Countries (CIPEC is its French acronym), have announced that they will seize a greater share of the marketing of copper; expand the membership of CIPEC to increase its market power; and work directly with the producers of potentially substitutable metals to reduce the risks of cartelization to each.

—The tin producers, through the International Tin Agreement, are seeking a 42 percent increase in the guaranteed floor price maintained by their buffer stock. These countries operated an effective producers' cartel before World War II.

Originally appeared in *Challenge*, September-October 1974, pp. 34-42.

—The leading coffee producers, through a series of interlocking marketing companies and stockpile-financing arrangements, have seized control of world coffee prices. They were confident enough of their success to let expire the International Coffee Agreement, through which they had previously sought the help of consuming countries to block price reductions.

—Five of the leading banana producers, through the Organization of Banana-Exporting Countries, have levied sizable taxes on banana exports to boost their returns.

In addition exporters of iron ore and mercury have been meeting regularly. The four major tea producers have sought to coordinate marketing and establish a floor price, and at least once reached agreement on production quotas. There are numerous other primary products, including tropical timber, natural rubber, nickel, tungsten, cobalt, columbium, tantalum, pepper and quinine, for which effective collusion among producing countries is distinctly possible. For some of these commodities, producer organizations, such as the Association of Natural-Rubber-Producing Countries and the Asian Pepper Community, already exist.

The primary producing countries have also taken several broad policy steps to support their commodity interests. Over two dozen of them have established ministries of natural resources. In an effort to legitimize their activities, they succeeded in including in a resolution adopted May 2 by the Special Session of the UN General Assembly, a call for "all efforts . . . to facilitate the functioning, and to further the aims, of producers' associations, including their joint marketing arrangements." To date, they have rejected all calls for new international rules to limit the use of export controls. And even Canada and Australia were most reluctant to accept the one-year moratorium on export controls encompassed in the "stand-still agreement" on trade barriers agreed by the OECD countries in June.

The measures employed so far by primary producers have taken many different forms—decreed prices, production cutbacks, selective embargoes, increased royalty payments, negotiated prices, direct market intervention, stockpiling, export taxes. Their objectives also differ: sharp increases in receipts from the commodity itself, protection against price declines, greater price stability, conservation of a depleting resource, more domestic processing, more local control over the industry, changes in the foreign policy of consuming countries. Some have clearly succeeded, at least so far (oil, coffee, phosphates); others have faltered at an early stage (bananas); for still others, it is too early to tell (bauxite, copper, tin). The importance of the products differs greatly; little sleep will be lost over a banana cartel, but many of the commodities are vital to modern industry and account for significant portions of consumers' market baskets. It is absolutely clear that such efforts are being made for an increasing array of products, and that more efforts are likely. What will determine their success?

The Successful Cartel

First, demand for the product must be relatively insensitive to price changes, that is, a higher price must neither excessively reduce final demand for the product nor trigger much substitution by alternative commodities. Second, supply of the product must also be relatively insensitive to price changes. This can occur because of actual physical shortages or technological monopolies, but such situations are quite rare. In virtually all cases, maintaining an artificially limited supply requires that most of the commodity be under the control of a small number of countries; it is even better for the cartel if a single country can dominate the market at the margin. The third requisite for success is that the potential colluding countries must be able to get along with each other.

These criteria appear to be met for a wide range of primary commodities. In the short run, demand for most metals and agricultural products is clearly very insensitive to price change. For commodities such as copper, aluminum and tea, a price increase of 10 percent would reduce the amount demanded by only about 2 percent. A 10 percent price increase for coffee and cocoa would bring about a 4 percent drop, and for tin, about a 5 percent decrease in demand.

The opinion is widely held that demand is significantly more responsive to price changes in the long run. At best, however, the "long run" is very long indeed. It takes six to seven years, for example, to bring a new copper mine into production and as much as ten years for some other metals. But how do we get to the "long run" anyway?

Massive investments are necessary to generate an efficient expansion of supply, and they are very lumpy in nature. Because mines must be run near full capacity to be efficient, they will be developed only if the investors can count on a sustained level of high returns for the indefinite future. In purely economic terms, this is highly uncertain because of the traditionally very cyclical nature of demand for materials. In addition, there are other uncertainties which make it unlikely that these investments will be made as readily as in the past. New resource development often must be undertaken in countries which are likely to limit the freedom of the investing firm once the capital and technology are in place. And these countries include Canada and Australia as well as the developing nations. The host country may even take such extreme measures as expropriating the company's property or joining a cartel and limiting output. The difficulty in getting government insurance for such risky ventures deters investors even further. Finally, both within the United States and abroad, the high cost of environmental requirements, probable loss of previous tax advantages and the likelihood of renewed price controls add greatly to the uncertainties.

The cartels themselves can further reduce the likelihood of major new investments in nonmembers, investments which could erode the cartel's position over time. To do so, their members must pursue subtle, and moderate, marketing strategies in raising their prices; and they must find that optimum price at which they can maximize their returns without triggering new investments. Indeed, if price rises are produced by cartel action rather than by underlying economics, there is always a strong possibility that the cartel will reduce its prices to choke off potential competitors. The fear of such "reverse dumping" is in fact a major deterrent at present to new investments in petroleum substitutes in the United States in the absence of governmental guarantees.

New cartels are in fact likely to adopt such strategies in light of the experience of OPEC. OPEC's actions clearly show that a cartel is likely to trigger a search for substitutes for its output if it pushes prices too far too fast (especially if it also demonstrates its unreliability as a supplier by cutting production and embargoing some buyers). So new OPECs are likely to adopt a more moderate and hence more successful approach.

In addition, the likelihood of substitution of alternative commodities for a cartel's product is sharply reduced if the prices of these commodities are rising as well. This has been the case in the recent commodity boom, either through natural market forces or parallel action by producing countries. For example, natural rubber suddenly became a candidate for cartelization when the price of synthetic rubber climbed dramatically in response to the rise in oil prices. It is thus particularly significant that representatives of IBA attended the latest meeting of CIPEC, since aluminum and copper are substitutable in many products from a technical standpoint.

The production processes for many end products are simply too fixed, both technologically and in terms of the proprietary interests of individual firms, to shift to new inputs without massive economic inducements. Even during World War II it took several years to develop synthetic rubber, and the efforts to produce substitutes for chrome and manganese, even of low quality and high cost, never did succeed. So, for a variety of reasons, it would be very risky to assume that "the market" will abort cartelization efforts even over the "long run."

It should also be noted that some producers' cartels might not be deterred even if members foresaw long-term substitution. Iran is pushing hard for OPEC to maximize oil prices now precisely so that it can diversify its economy and reduce its vulnerability to such substitution. Jamaica's Prime Minister Manley publicly based his action to boost bauxite receipts on that nation's "urgent" short-term needs and "reports [that] the time may not be too distant when technological progress will begin to yield substitutes for bauxite." Indeed, Harry Johnson long ago pointed out that it might be quite rational for developing countries to maximize in the short run even at the expense of future earnings.

As we noted, for a cartel to be successful, it must be able to limit the supply of its product. There are many cases where a few countries exert tight control over the supply of a basic commodity. The IBA countries account for about 75 percent of world bauxite exports. The four leading tin producers account for about 80 percent of noncommunist tin output, and an even larger share of exports. The CIPEC countries provide well over half of world copper exports and will probably expand that percentage by broadening their membership. Three countries provide 70 percent of world exports of tropical timber. These numbers, and the similar figures for other key commodities, are particularly impressive when we recall that they significantly exceed the shares of the four or five leading OPEC producers in world oil trade.

Furthermore, for a number of commodities, a single key country is in a position to exercise market dominance, as does Saudi Arabia in oil. Morocco is doing it in phosphates. Brazil is doing it in coffee. Malaysia could do it in tin and natural rubber and Nigeria in cocoa, and Jamaica can probably do it in bauxite. Similar situations exist for several commodities that are quantitatively less important, such as cobalt, for which the dominant producer is Zaire, and columbium, mined principally in Brazil. Such capacity for price leadership by a single country simplifies the procedures needed to regulate a market.

As for the requirement that cartel members be able to get along, it is true that there are a few potential cartels which might be deterred by political differences. Three countries provide virtually all the world's exports of soybeans, but the United States, People's Republic of China and Brazil are unlikely to form a SOYBEC. The Soviet Union and South Africa are unlikely to collude overtly on platinum or chromium ore, though both are natural oligopolies. (Even in these cases, however, parallel market action could quite easily have similar effects.)

But there is little if any hostility among most of the key suppliers of heavily concentrated commodities. Indeed, many have no reason even to talk to each other except for their similar resources: Malaysia and Bolivia for tin, Chile and Zambia for copper, Jamaica and Australia for bauxite. The absence of a common enemy, as was Israel for the oil-producing Arab states, probably does rule out the use of new OPECs for noneconomic purposes. But there is no political discord to block economic efforts by most of the potential cartels.

Oil Is Not the Exception

Contrary to my argument, there are those who assert that oil and OPEC represent a unique case which cannot be duplicated. This argument stresses the "shared political values" (that is, the enmity toward Israel) of the

OPEC countries; the existence of monetary reserves large enough to permit them to take the risks associated with cartelization; the greater insensitivity of the demand for oil (and perhaps its supply) to price changes; the vertically integrated, oligopolistic market structure created by the multinational oil companies; the greater economic strategic importance of oil; and the lesser susceptibility of the key OPEC countries to economic retaliation because of their small populations and hence small economic needs.

The Middle East politics ignited by the Yom Kippur War clearly prompted Saudi Arabia, the dominant oil supplier, to cut production temporarily. But the OPEC countries had more than tripled their 1970 earnings before the war broke out. And policy toward Israel had very little to do with the massive increase in oil prices last December—sponsored by Iran, which has been consistently pro-Israel, and Venezuela, which cares little about the Middle East conflict.

Most important, many if not all of these price hikes will continue to stick even though Saudi Arabia has restored its production to the pre-October 1973 level. And they will also stick despite the deep political *hostilities* among the Middle East oil countries over proper policy toward Israel, control of the Persian Gulf, and several key boundaries. The Yom Kippur War may have triggered the oil action that demonstrated to OPEC its own strength, but that genie is now out of the bottle and, in view of the massive economic gains to all member countries, is most unlikely to be capped again whether or not permanent peace comes to the Middle East.

Sizable monetary reserves do not distinguish OPEC either, although here again the initial Saudi move may have been influenced by its considerable wealth. But most OPEC members, including Iran, actually possessed very small reserves *before* they undertook the 1973 actions. In fact, the members of many other potential cartels (such as Malaysia and Brazil) are much stronger financially than were many OPEC countries, and much less dependent on the commodity in question.

Even more important, it is unclear that poverty breeds caution in this area. Jamaica has acted to boost its annual bauxite revenues by $180 million because its oil import bill has risen by a like amount and its reserves are low. Successful cartelization offsets *low* reserves, so the issue becomes how much "risk" is really involved.

A related argument is that production cutbacks in other primary products would generate unacceptably high unemployment, even if they were successful; such an outcome would supposedly differ sharply from the situation for oil, since the petroleum industry is capital intensive and the largest producers have small populations. But production of many other commodities is also very capital intensive, and the proceeds of successful collusion could be used to create many more jobs through the promotion of labor-intensive industries.

Economists simply do not know enough about the price sensitivity of supply and demand for different products to make firm judgments on the alleged difference between oil and other commodities, especially since all present estimates derive from earlier periods when both the structure of demand and the organization or markets differed greatly (as will be explained below). Some, such as Hendrik Houthakker, argue that the demand for oil is in fact quite responsive to price in any event. And there are certainly plenty of physical reserves of oil, so there is no reason to believe that the responsiveness of its supply *in purely economic terms* is less than for other commodities.

In addition, as indicated above, the responsiveness of many other commodities appears very low in the short run and may even be quite low in any relevant "long run." However, it is certainly true that stockpiles exist for a few commodities, though recently many of them have been run down. It is also true that recycling is possible for some commodities (though there is still not much known about the technology or the economics of the recycling process). Thus it may turn out that the supplies of some commodities may respond much more favorably to price increases than was the case for oil.

But if so, we cannot know it now. Market actions will, as always, be based on *ex ante* judgments rather than *ex post* analysis. In practice, the issue of cutting demand and triggering substitutes will probably turn on whether the new OPECs are wise enough to learn from OPEC's own major blunders (blunders, at least, from the standpoint of a maximizing cartel) in raising prices too far too fast, demonstrating their unreliability as suppliers by cutting back production and using their commodity power to gain influence over the foreign policies of their consumers. If they show such wisdom, new OPECs may succeed over the longer run far better than OPEC itself.

It is certainly useful for a cartel among nations to inherit an oligopolistic market structure from private industry. But oil is not the only product for which this kind of market structure exists; bauxite is a precise parallel. The producer country levies higher taxes and royalties on the firms, which in turn recoup these losses through higher prices to end users or diversion of revenues fron the treasuries of consuming countries. In addition, there are many ways to implement oligopoly power other than through multinational firms. Again, the oligopoly is helpful but not necessary for success, and it is not peculiar to oil anyway.

Oil is certainly more important, both quantitatively and qualitatively, than any of the other commodities under discussion. Yet this would seem likely to trigger *more* resistance to OPEC than to its offspring, since any moves by the latter can be more readily absorbed or offset. The difference in importance has little impact on the *nature* of the action which is possible for different products.

Finally, it is certainly true that the oil-rich desert countries were peculiarly invulnerable to economic retaliation. But many of the key oil producers—Iran, Nigeria, Venezuela, Indonesia—were acutely vulnerable to economic retaliation. Even the desert countries would have been loathe to face the political consequences of economic countermeasures by the consumers, though the economic effects of such steps were limited. So their so-called invulnerability explains very little. Indeed, overt action by the rich and powerful against the poor and weak is probably politically infeasible in the 1970s and beyond, so that no producers' cartel need fear it.

Thus it is very doubtful that oil is different in any qualitative sense. Indeed, many other OPECs look much *easier* to organize and maintain. OPEC had to pool twelve countries to control 80 percent of world oil exports, but fewer countries are usually involved in production of other primary products. Most OPEC countries are heavily dependent on oil, and cartelization was especially risky for them. Other commodity producers are more diversified. OPEC could politicize oil and threaten the world economy; its successors will have an easier task because their products are less important. And economic and political differences among OPEC countries seem much sharper than those among other potential cartelizers. So new OPECs seem at least as likely as OPEC itself.

What Has Changed?

The new international situation does not involve physical shortages. The limits-to-growth projections of the Club of Rome are misleading, since physical reserves appear adequate for all important primary products for the relevant future. Instead, the new likelihood of producers' cartels is explained by changes in demand patterns, increases in the market power of producers, and increases in their perceptions of this power.

First, the advent of high rates of inflation, seemingly for the indefinite future, adds dramatically to the structural demand for commodities. Secular inflationary expectations generate higher, perhaps much higher, levels of business demand for inventories. The erosion of confidence in paper currencies triggered by rampant inflation, possibly accelerated by the widespread adoption of flexible exchange rates, has induced widespread shifts into real assets, primarily commodities (and land). Indeed, many of these commodities—particularly those traded on commodity exchanges— have now taken on a quasimonetary function. They have become more like gold and silver, which have always played both an industrial and a monetary role, and their prices will reflect monetary as well as industrial demand as long as inflationary expectations remain high.

In addition, rampant inflation spurs the investment demand for commodities. Real interest rates are rendered quite low by double-digit price rises, and that reduces the attractiveness of fixed-yield assets and makes credit to finance commodity purchases cheap. The plight of equities stemming from inflation has accelerated commodity investments.

These additions to demand have converted buyers' markets into sellers' markets for a wide range of primary products. Since the higher commodity prices further intensify inflation and vice versa, "commodity spiral inflation" may now have come to supplement price-wage inflation as a lasting feature of the world economic scene. Moreover, fears of new OPECs probably add to all these types of anticipatory buying.

Studies made at the National Bureau of Economic Research show that downturns in commodity prices have consistently led downturns in the economic cycle by one to five quarters throughout the postwar period (see Table 18-1), and that the average lead time of five to six months has been one of the more accurate indicators of coming slumps. This is why many observers began to predict a bursting of the latest commodity boom in early 1973 when the global economy began to slow down.

Yet commodity prices accelerated dramatically throughout 1973 and did not turn down, even temporarily, until the second quarter of 1974—about eighteen months behind schedule. They boomed even in the face of the first quarter's sharp *reductions* in GNP in the United States, Japan and the United Kingdom, and very slow growth everywhere else. A lesser though significant deviation from the historical trend was also evident around the 1969-70 downturn. (The *only* previous such deviation occurred in 1951-52. It was much shorter than the recent one, and was even less than the deviation of 1969-70, which was almost ignored at the time.) So the explosion of prices of primary products in the recent past cannot be explained by the latest worldwide economic boom, though it obviously added significantly to the picture, nor can it be passed off simply as a recurrence of the Korean War experience. More lasting changes seem to be at work. At the same time, the likely increase of worldwide economic growth in the period immediately ahead adds to the probability that commodity prices will shortly resume their upward movement.

Market conditions thus provide an ideal setting for producers' cartels to inprove their earnings still further. A world of inflation also increases the likelihood that countries will make every effort to collude so they can, in a sense, index themselves against increases in import prices through the best (sometimes only) means available to them. The many unsuccessful cartel efforts of the past are simply irrelevant; the present situation gives the producers more incentive and a far greater chance to succeed.

The second fundamental change is the success of OPEC itself. In economic terms, the dramatic increase in oil prices means that other countries will try to right their own terms of trade by forcing up prices of their commodities. As already noted, it is no coincidence that Jamaica will

Table 18-1

The Relationship between Prices of Nonfood Raw Materials and U.S. Economic Growth, 1948-74

(Lead −, lag +, in no. of months)

Growth cycle		Wholesale Price Index–crude materials excluding foods	
High	Low	High	Low
July 1948	October 1949	December 1947 (−7)	July 1949 (−3)
June 1951	June 1952	October 1950 (−8)	November 1951 (−7)
March 1953	August 1954	July 1953 (+4)	January 1954 (−7)
February 1957	May 1958	December 1955 (−14)	January 1958 (−4)
February 1960	February 1961	October 1958 (−16)	November 1960 (−3)
April 1962	March 1963	July 1961 (−9)	July 1962 (−8)
June 1966	October 1967	March 1966 (−3)	January 1967 (−9)
March 1969	November 1970	August 1969 (+5)	November 1970 (0)
March 1973		May 1974 (?) (+14)	
Mean lead or lag, excluding 1973-74		−6	−5
Correlation coefficients with leads in leading index, excluding 1962-63 and 1973-74 (all significant at 0.5 level)		0.93 0.82*	0.52

*Highs and lows.

Source: Geoffrey H. Moore, "Prices During Business Cycles," paper presented at a Roundtable on Inflation held by the Conference Board, Montreal, January 22, 1974.

earn from its bauxite actions an amount virtually equal to the increase in its oil bill. This is the most direct form of international indexing against inflation.

The success of OPEC has dramatically raised the primary producers' perceptions of their market power. Indeed, it is almost impossible for a primary producing country in a position to try cartelization *not* to do so today in view of the success of OPEC, the burgeoning list of emulators, and the strident commodity rhetoric. How can Chile face Jamaica if CIPEC cannot equal IBA?

In addition, the oil situation shows that a concerted response by consuming countries is highly unlikely. The scramble for "special deals" by virtually all oil consumers continues to encourage OPEC efforts, a lesson not lost on OPEC's potential successors. Finally, there have been rumors that OPEC might help its offspring directly by buying commodities or financing producers' stockpiles—a rumor more likely to be true for products directly involving an OPEC country, such as Indonesia's tropical timber, or, shortly, Iran's copper.

Third, the producing countries are now in a far better position to pursue their own national interests effectively. In the past, both production and marketing were left largely to multinational rules and institutions created and maintained by the United States and other industrial countries.

Now, however, the postwar success of economic development throughout the world, particularly its emphasis on advanced education, has created cadres of exceptional indigenous talent in virtually all developing countries. OPEC was reportedly conceived in a bar in Cambridge, Massachusetts, and every country now has its full quota of graduates from prestigious institutions. The sizable resources of the firms can with impunity be forced to serve the host country rather than vice versa. Indeed, in oil and bauxite the firms have become tools of the producer countries. One result, as noted above, is the reduced likelihood of new investments which would undermine the cartel's prospects.

Concomitantly, the political leaderships in most developing countries are now well past the stage of nationalistic rhetoric and political adventurism. They are focusing primarily on the hard realities of economic and social welfare and are looking to every possible device—like commodity cartels—to achieve it. Both the new capabilities and the current focus of national leaderships have sharply raised the market power of most primary producers.

At the same time, the rules and institutions which focused on market solutions to maintain the international economic order during the first postwar generation—and provided an eminently hospitable environment for large multinational firms—have largely eroded. The United States can no longer exert decisive leadership to that end. It can no longer effectively protect the "rights" of multinational firms, and indeed its policy makers have increasing doubts as to whether trying to do so would promote U.S. national interests anyway. In the resources industries, all these developments mean a much weaker position for the firms, much of whose leverage disappears once they sink their capital and technology into the foreign subsoil.

Thus there are structural changes which sharply tilt the balance of power in commodity markets. The producing countries have new capabilities. The firms are weaker. The consuming countries can no longer dictate either the structure of the system or its daily operation; and they are in disarray among themselves. Both the politics and the economics of commodity relations are now wide open.

Resources Diplomacy

It is of course impossible to generalize about all primary products at every moment in the future. Firm judgments can rest only on intensive analysis of the economics and politics of each. Policy responses must be based on assessments of the costs of possible cartel action compared with the costs of the possible responses by consumer countries.

But individual commodity developments, like all economic and political events, take place within a framework of broad and fundamental trends. The trends outlined in this article, many of which appear to represent lasting shifts in both the economic and political environments, suggest that "commodity power" and "resources diplomacy" will be with us for the relevant future.

If the cartels succeed—and, for a time, even if they do not—they will produce higher prices throughout the world. They can disrupt individual industries. They will raise the specter of interruptions of supply, deterring needed investments (at various stages of production as well as in the commodities themselves) and adding to the risk of political enmities in the already uncertain world. They will further impoverish the resource-poor developing countries, and add at least marginally to the balance of payments problem of some industrial countries as well. They could trigger more scrambles for position among the largest consuming countries and intensify the element of conflict in their relations. Hence they mark a major new factor in both international economics and world politics.

19 Oil Is *Not* the Exception

In "Oil is the Exception,"[1] Stephen Krasner disposes of most of the potential differences between oil and other commodities. He concludes, however, that there are two distinguishing features which set oil apart: the flush foreign exchange positions of the oil producers, which enable them to afford the risks of cartelization, and their "shared value" concerning Israel. Neither point in fact distinguishes OPEC from potential emulators.

The Foreign Exchange Argument

The foreign exchange argument fails for four reasons: some of the key oil producers are *not* flush, some of the leaders of other potential cartels *are* flush, reserve holdings do not tell the whole story of a country's ability to risk failure in a cartelization effort anyway, and, most important, none of these considerations is very important if the likelihood of successful cartelization is high.

Iran is crucial to OPEC, as the second largest oil producer, but its reserves equal less than three months' imports and it spends virtually all of its earnings for development. So do Iraq, Algeria, Venezuela, Nigeria, and Indonesia, which along with Iran account for 60 percent of OPEC output. Yet OPEC has obviously succeeded; reserve levels thus need not be high for even the most important cartel members.

The reason is that oil was a setup for cartelization, with very little risk involved. The same situation holds for several other commodities as well. But a country can undertake even a risky cartelization effort for a particular commodity if its *over-all economic position* is strong enough to stand failure.

If its economy is solely or heavily dependent on the commodity in question, as is Saudi Arabia's on oil, the risk *is* high unless its reserve cushion is also very high. But the risks are much lower if the potential cartelizer has a highly diversified economy, and if its reserve position does not then determine whether it can undertake the effort. This is precisely why Brazil, which has developed both an impressive manufacturing base and a highly diversified range of primary exports, as well as the world's eighth largest reserves, can hold an umbrella over the coffee market now

---

Adapted from "The Threat is Real," *Foreign Policy* 14, Spring 1974, pp. 86-90

whereas it could not do so a decade ago. Colombia can even help, because coffee now provides less than one-half its export earnings and its reserves equal six months' imports. Krasner's Table II is thus misleading; it needs to be weighted by the dependence of the producing countries on the commodities in question to portray an accurate picture of how likely they are to initiate cartels.

In addition to "safe" export earnings, a diversified economic base sharply increases the likelihood that the country can borrow sizable sums from the international capital markets to supplement its reserves. The Third World obtained over $8 billion in Eurocredits in 1972, and perhaps $10-12 billion in 1973. So there is every likelihood that cartelization efforts can be underwritten by foreign loans as well as by national reserves and ongoing earnings from other exports of goods and services.

One source of financing for emulators of OPEC might be OPEC. The huge increase in oil prices obviously hobbles the development efforts of many countries in the Third World. But the Shah seems to reject the obvious alternatives of dual pricing for oil and compensatory grants to the beleaguered, because those options could undermine his own cartel and deplete his own reserves, respectively. Hence he has called on other developing countries to restore their terms of trade by raising their own export prices, and offered to help them do so. Underwriting such an effort would, in one fell swoop, establish OPEC as leader of the entire Third World and provide a handsome return on invested capital if the cartels worked.

These considerations of economic invulnerability are far more important for potential cartel leaders than rank and file members. There will always be cheating by smaller countries, as Krasner suggests, but the output decisions of one or two leaders determine whether the price umbrella can be held. How then do the potential leaders, and to a lesser extent members of other potential cartels, meet these criteria?

For tin, Malaysia accounts for one-half of world exports, has reserves which exceed seven months' imports, and relies on that commodity for only 20 percent of its export earnings. That same country accounts for 38 percent of world rubber exports, but rubber provides only one-third of its export earnings. Australia, which has announced that it will attend the organizational meeting of the bauxite "OPEC" and has spoken publicly of developing a "resources diplomacy," is a leading exporter of bauxite, iron ore, and lead, and has a widely diversified economic base and the world's ninth largest reserves. (The other bauxite producers are less affluent, but this appears to be the commodity least susceptible to substitutes and hence the least risky to cartelize, especially if the tin and copper producers move along similar lines.) Thailand is an important factor in the tin and rubber markets. Each of these commodities represents less than 15 percent of total Thai exports, and its reserves exceed eight months' imports. Each of the four main copper exporters relies heavily on that commodity, but Zambia, the largest exporter, has substantial reserves as do Peru and Zaire. There are many other similar examples. "Surfeit reserves" are not a distinguishing characteristic of great significance for the petroleum oligopoly.

"Shared Values"

The issue of "shared values"—hatred for Israel—is even more easily disposed of. OPEC is comprised of countries with sharp political *differences*. Iran has always been *close* to Israel. There remains deep hostility between Iran and Iraq, Iran and Kuwait, and Iraq and Kuwait. Iran and Saudi Arabia are leading rivals for dominance of the Persian Gulf. Libya under Qaddafi and Saudi Arabia have bitterly competed for leadership of the entire Arab world. Venezuela and Nigeria have none of the so-called "shared values."

Yet OPEC has clearly succeeded, and was in fact a highly successful cartel well over two years *before* the latest war submerged at least some of these differences. It nicely survives the failure of Iran, Iraq, Libya, and all non-Arabs to join the production cutbacks to pressure the West over Israel. There is only one explanation: the common economic gain for all participants from raising their prices and avoiding the production increases which would undermine such action—a motive which could readily trigger similar action wherever the economics permit.

Indeed, the only political prerequisite for producer cartels is the absence of overt hostility, and none seems to exist among the members of any of the potential emulators of OPEC. Few of those countries (e.g., Bolivia and Malaysia for tin, Guinea and Guyana for bauxite) have any reason even to talk to each other *except* for their common interest in maximizing their economic returns from a commodity which they happen to have in common. So "shared values" hardly set OPEC apart.

In fact, producer cartels look more feasible in other commodities than in oil. Fewer countries need to collude. Capital, technological, and marketing complexities may be more easily mastered. As already indicated, other potential cartelizers are frequently more diversified economically and less antagonistic politically. I continue to fear that oil is only the beginning, particularly in view of the dramatic demonstration effect of OPEC's success and the utter failure of the consuming countries to respond with common action of their own.

302

Note

1. *Foreign Policy* 14, Spring 1974.

20 Oil and the International Economic System in 1974: Two Scenarios

Scenario One: Severe Production Cutbacks and World Recession

By far the greatest threat in the present oil situation is that cutbacks in production levels will be sufficient to trigger supply-shortage recessions throughout the industrialized world. Under such conditions, two perilous international monetary trends could develop.

One is that a number of countries, both industrialized and developing, would try immediately to export their resulting unemployment. They could make such an effort by (a) depreciating their exchange rates, which may be easier to accomplish in the present world of managed flexibility of exchange rates than it was under the Bretton Woods system; (b) erecting barriers to imports of manufactured goods; and (c) implementing new export subsidies. The second is that countries would seek to fight their supply-shortage recessions with traditional policies of macroeconomic expansion of demand, which would accelerate inflation beyond its already rampant levels. This could in turn produce problems for the balance-of-payments positions of particular countries well beyond the problems already caused by the increase in oil prices, leading indirectly to the same kinds of international policies just cited.

It is important to recognize that such a world could develop because cutbacks in oil production caused serious *unemployment* problems in major countries, not because of any direct effects of increased oil prices on balance-of-payments positions. Indeed, balance-of-payments positions would probably be *less* adversely affected by oil prices under this scenario than under the second scenario, to be described shortly, in which price was the ''only'' problem, because the higher price decreed by OPEC would apply to a smaller volume of transactions.[1]

In my view, the possibility of such a scenario cannot be ruled out. Early political settlement in the Middle East on terms acceptable to the key oil producers (primarily Saudi Arabia, Abu Dhabi, and the United Arab Emirates; Kuwait and Libya will hold production down anyway and most other producers will expand production anyway) is uncertain. Even such a settlement would not necessarily restore adequate production levels in view of (a) the economic incentive to the major producers to restrict

Paper originally presented at the Second Tripartite Businessmen's Conference in Puerto Rico in February 1974.

303

production to maintain for the longer run the higher prices they have decreed, and (b) their calculation that oil reserves are probably worth more than any financial assets that are available to them. Nor is it very effective to lecture the Arabs about their "common stake in avoiding world depression," because in such a world there would be *even more* scrambling for their money and *even more* reason for them to keep their oil in the ground, unless this is a euphemistic warning that they face military intervention if they push too far.

Policy responses in this kind of world must keep the two chief lessons of the 1930s firmly in mind. Efforts to export unemployment via competitive depreciations and trade controls *do not work*; they simply deepen and widen the problem faced by all. And a world in which there is no national leader can rapidly fall apart under stress of this magnitude, particularly if—as was the case in the 1930s and is largely true at present—there are no effectively functioning international economic rules and institutions.

One key difference between the 1970s and the 1930s both heightens and lessens the risks of such policies. Most countries now face rampant inflation as well as the threat of recession, and would hesitate to accept the inflationary consequences—including the resulting further increase in the price of oil—of depreciating exchange rates and import barriers. However, this could lead countries *either* (a) to avoid altogether the active use of their external policy instruments, obviating the risks just cited, *or* (b) to patch together a hodge-podge of import *and* export controls which would compound the problems of the 1930s and the problems of the past year (the OPEC oil embargo itself, the U.S. controls on soybean exports, the new Japanese controls on a range of oil-intensive intermediate products, etc.). Different countries would probably choose differently, and the net outcome would be uncertain, to say the least.

One possible solution to a world of supply-shortage recession would be for the United States to resume, at least temporarily, the role which it played in the 1950s and 1960s as balancer for the world economy. Other countries would be tacitly permitted to export some of their unemployment to the United States, which itself would be less hurt by the oil cutbacks than most others and could hence best afford such a result. This could be accomplished simply by permitting the dollar to continue to appreciate in the exchange markets, or even pushing it up through official purchases of dollars by non-U.S. central banks as under the "Bretton Woods system." Such a solution would require:

—Willingness on the part of other countries to accept the inflationary effects of continued depreciation of their currencies, perhaps responding with tough incomes policies internally.

—Willingness on the part of other countries to accept (or overtly buy) dollars *which would doubtlessly never become convertible into U.S.*

reserves, and might have to be consolidated at some later point in the IMF (or bilaterally) on terms highly favorable to the United States (no amortization, low or no interest rates).

—Willingness on the part of the United States to compensate American workers losing their jobs as a result of the overall strategy, and on the part of the Administration to withstand steadfastly the protectionist pressures which might subsequently arise. (For this American, who tries to be sensitive to domestic politics in other countries as well, this seems to be the toughest and riskiest part of the package. However, it is no tougher in terms of U.S. politics than the alternative—often suggested—of sharing U.S.-produced oil directly with other countries.)

If this or other "purely economic" options turn out to be unviable, rougher counteraction would unfortunately have to be contemplated. Economic retaliation *carried out jointly by all of the consuming countries*, including the developing consuming countries, would be an obvious first step. Though leakages are inevitable, the psychological and deterrent effect of such a step might turn the taps back up. The use of force is obviously a last resort, but appears technically feasible and hence cannot be ignored . Once the Arabs turn oil into a security issue, as they have by using it to threaten a world recession or even depressions, they risk losing their comparative advantage.

Scenario Two: Price is the Problem

I fervently hope that the above scenario does not eventuate, and I believe that the odds are against it. Even if Arab production does return to levels which avoid supply-shortage recessions, however, the huge increases in oil prices still raise major problems for the world economy.

Whatever the precise numbers, which no one can accurately forecast, the massive increase in oil prices will (a) sharply accelerate inflation in an already highly inflationary world and (b) sharply increase the export earnings of the oil producers and the import payments of the oil consumers. The two problems are closely related. But, in my view, (b) is highly manageable whereas (a) raises questions about the fundamental structure of all our economies.

All other things equal, the inflationary effects of the oil price hikes alone will depress demand in economies already facing significant slowdown —though, assuming here no *additional* output effects from production cutbacks, much less than in Scenario One. One obvious result would be growing unemployment. Another could be cutbacks in investment plans, the one heretofore bullish element in the short-run world economic outlook and a vital necessity to break the inflationary spiral for the longer run.

Governments in virtually every country thus face a critical policy choice. Should they expand demand in traditional Keynesian fashion, to minimize such developments, knowing that more inflation is likely to result? Or should they follow policies of restraint, to at least limit the extent of inflation, accepting higher unemployment in return?

This is obviously an agonizing choice, one of the toughest of the post-war period. Different countries may come out quite differently, depending on local economic structures and policy preferences. But it is my bet that virtually every major country will opt for expansionary macroeconomic policies, for both economic and political reasons.

Economically, it does not make sense to respond to inflation caused by supply shortages with demand restraint. It is critical to remember that most countries already faced severe inflation *before* the oil price increases, and that supply bottlenecks range far beyond oil—including foodstuffs, other raw materials, and a wide array of manufactured products. The only lasting answer to these problems, and indeed to the energy problem itself, is new investment on a massive scale. Yet demand restraint would discourage such investment, and hence accelerate rather than restrain inflation over any relevant time horizon. Demand restraint would also heighten the uncertainties confronting businessmen, further depressing their investment plans. To the traditional argument that demand restraint might *promote* investment by reducing interest rates, I would respond that (a) the effects just cited would dominate and (b) real interest rates are already going to be very low because of the slackening of growth which will take place in any event and the massive availability of capital from the oil producers, some of which have the highest savings rates (almost 100%) of any countries in the world.

Politically, it is my guess that unemployment will continue to attract more political opposition than inflation. Politicians will therefore opt for expansion of demand, unless the economics were to act overwhelmingly in the opposite direction—which, I have just argued, is not the case. I have always looked to Germany, the industrialized country with the greatest fear of inflation, as the leading indicator in this area of policy choice and thus regard as highly significant the German shift from restrictive to expansionary policy at the first hint of serious recession.[2]

Thus I believe that most governments will, and should, opt for expansionary policies to both limit unemployment in the short run and provide part of the response to supply-shortage inflation in the long run. At least some countries, however, might try to avoid the tough choice which confronts them by following internal policies to restrain inflation and seeking to export their unemployment by undervaluing their exchange rates and erecting new trade controls, as in Scenario One. Indeed, some might try to export at least part of both their unemployment *and* inflationary problems by placing selective controls over both key imports *and* exports. This is the possibility which conjures up images of global economic conflict à la the 1930s, and has added greatly to the uncertainties of the situation and the alarms sounded by a number of world leaders. The recent devaluations by Japan[3] and France (and perhaps Britain) are cited as evidence that such a trend is already underway.

Here the analysis must link to the shift in trade balances which flow from the oil situation itself. It is obvious that the *trade* balances of virtually every industrialized country will decline, some sharply, in 1974 and beyond. This could provide countries with an excuse to undertake competitive devaluations, as just outlined, "to restore their external positions."

The critical point is that, *for the industrialized world as a whole, virtually all of the deterioration in trade balances has to be offset by improvements in capital accounts*. To the (considerable) extent that the oil producers do not spend their new earnings on imports of goods and services (including military hardware), they will invest the money abroad. Most of the money will, in the first instance, go into the Euromarkets. For national balance-of-payments purposes, however, the issue is where the money is invested *ultimately* by these financial intermediaries. To repeat, taking the industrialized world *as a whole*, virtually all of the overall effect will amount simply to a change in *the structure* of its external position: a deterioration in the current account offset by an improvement in the capital account.[4]

The story cannot end here, of course, for two reasons. First, any *individual* industrialized country may not autonomously receive back, in capital inflow, a full offset to the decline in its current account position. Second, some countries may not like the notion of altering for the indefinite future even the structure of their payments positions. So the risk of competitive devaluations and the like would still exist.

It is at this point that international financial and trade policies can, and must, intervene. First, countries must be willing to accept the structural changes just outlined. It would be nothing new for Japan, for example, which as recently as 1967 had 90-day liabilities to U.S. banks which exceeded its monetary reserves, i.e., "lived on borrowed money." Faced with rampant inflation, countries should actually *welcome* such changes as long as they do not go too far, which amount to getting real resources (including oil) in exchange for pieces of (investment) paper, a practice which many people thought was great for the United States for many years.[5]

As for the fear, often expressed in the United States, that protectionist trade policies of the traditional variety (import controls) will be inevitable as a result of any shift into trade deficit, I have two responses. The dominance of the inflation problem will continue to stop import protec-

308

tionism, as it has for the last two years, and indeed may promote further unilateral import liberalization. And a slide into trade deficit of *all* industrialized countries *together*, because of the oil situation, has very different economic and political effects than a deterioration of the trade balance of one industrialized country in favor of another industrialized country in labor-intensive industries, e.g., the U.S.-Japan experience of 1969-72. The necessary change in mental sets, to accept changes in the *structure* of each country's external position, may not come easily, but it is certainly doable—and the case for doing it is overwhelming.

Second, there exist a number of well-known techniques for dealing with imbalances in financial flows among the industrialized countries. The swap network is the most obvious. It worked perfectly in June 1967 when several Arab countries tried to "bring down the pound" by moving their money to Switzerland, from whence the Swiss recycled it immediately to London. The amounts of money were smaller, to be sure, but the principle is identical.[6] Special creations of Special Drawing Rights are another. A few countries can run down reserves, including the "dollar overhang." Governments and government entities can borrow directly in the Euromarkets, as the Italians have done frequently and the British have already been doing on a large scale. Or they can induce their private sectors to do so, as the United States has done since 1965. To be sure, a competitive borrowing scramble could result, so constant collaboration among the monetary authorities will again prove essential.

Again, I do not underestimate the practical difficulties involved in working out such collaboration. For example, in a world of floating exchange rates, agreements would have to be reached among national officials as to the "proper" relationships among currencies and the pattern of financing which was necessary to maintain them, so that, e.g., Japan's unwillingness to borrow from the United States or the Euromarkets would not be construed as "competitive depreciation." But the principles involved are clear, the premium on success is enormous, and the problem *is* manageable.[7]

These two sets of measures can wholly mitigate the balance of payments effects of the oil price rises, solving at least this aspect of the problem. It would thus obviate any excuses for competitive devaluations and new import protectionism, which is the only really "disaster scenario" which could emerge in the short run. It is thus heartening that the Committee of Twenty made statements in these directions at its recent meeting in Rome, though it is discouraging—if understandable, due to the real complexities involved—that no concrete implementing steps have yet been taken.

There is one other approach to the balance-of-payments problem which bears mention. Why not just let all exchange rates float freely, to avoid the need for new financial flows as outlined? The answer is three-fold. First, the result would be depreciation of the currencies of precisely those countries which, by definition, would be hit hardest by the oil crisis—and would thus have to pay *even more* for their oil (and all other) imports! This would hardly be desirable for the countries themselves. Second, protectionist pressures *could* be kindled in any individual country, including the United States, if *it alone* were asked to accept a shift in payments structure (trade deterioration offset by capital inflows) which cost it jobs *relative to Japan, Germany, etc.* This would be far different from the acceptance of such structural shifts by *all* key countries. Third, some countries would be suspected of intervening (directly or indirectly) in the exchange narkets, to achieve improvements in their competitive positions and hence export unemployment, even with the cleanest of floats. Constant consultations and efforts to cooperate in the ways outlined, even with their inevitable shortcomings, seem far preferable.

Conclusions

Scenarios One and Two both spell rampant inflation. But there are two significant differences between them. The real problem of unemployment and world recession is much greater in One than in Two, raising much greater risks concerning national policy responses. The apparent problems of national balance-of-payments positions are greater in Two than in One, probably in absolute terms and certainly relative to the unemployment problem.

Therefore, there is no threat of world depression, or even serious recession, if:

1. Arab oil production is restored to reasonable levels (i.e., no Scenario One). Efforts to get production restored *and to maintain the cuts in unnecessary energy consumption in the importing countries* must assume absolutely top priority.
2. The industrialized countries (i) adopt sufficiently expansionary domestic economic policies, (ii) accept the inevitable shifts in the *structure* of their external financial positions and (iii) avoid competitive depreciation (or import controls) by recycling the capital flows from the oil producers to avoid major payments disequilibria. If these steps are taken, the international financial system will readily survive.

Accelerating inflation, at least in the medium term, would then be the "only" serious result of the oil price rises. But it will be a most serious economic, social and political problem. And it is doubtlessly with us for the indefinite future. The industrialized countries must therefore also devote

their full energies to developing new programs over the longer run, preferably on a joint or at least cooperative basis, to avoid a "great inflation" and
national policies which might seek to export inflation from one country to
another.

Notes

1. This assumes that demand for oil is very price-inelastic in the short
run context of this discussion, which I believe to be true.

2. Britain appears to provide an opposite example—and is part of a
curious role reversal in which "discipline-less" Britain is fighting the
toughest anti-inflation battle in the world while "inflation-traumatized"
Germany expands at the first sign of unemployment. However, Heath's
battle is to preserve an incomes policy and hence make *expansionary*
policies possible, rather than any effort to defend a restrictive focus.

3. I should immediately indicate that I reject this view with respect to
Japan. Indeed, Japan could be accused of competitive *over*valuation for
much of 1973, fighting internal inflation by keeping the yen high through
huge sales of dollar reserves, but the present depreciation of the yen
appears fully consonant with the "rules" of the present *de facto* system of
floating exchange rates.

4. Some observers have argued that the huge volume of Arab funds will
not be manageable by the present Eurocredit institutions. I strongly disagree. The U.S. balance of payments alone fed almost $30 billion into those
markets in 1972. Tight U.S. money sucked about $15 billion out of those
markets in 1969. They have been growing extremely rapidly, while retaining needed stability. I see no reason to believe that, from their currently
much higher base, they will be unable to handle the $40-50 billion flowback
from the oil producers in 1974.

5. The other side of this coin is, of course, the reason why the Arabs
may keep the oil in the ground and we could find ourselves in Scenario One.

6. In practice, this might largely mean U.S. loans to other countries if
the United States runs a sizable overall (not trade) surplus, as I expect, as in
earlier periods when the phenomenon was called "dollar shortage."

7. Similar solutions are available for the several important developing
countries hit hard by the oil price rises and unable to recoup by boosting the
prices of their own exports, as many commodity producers will be, or by
persuading the Arabs to help them directly. It would be desirable to limit
the increase in their interest burdens, however, so the IBRD should probably adopt new techniques to handle such intermediation, including interest
rate subsidies à la the Horowitz plan.

**Part VII
U.S. Economic Relations:
The Industrialized Countries**

U.S. Economic Relations with Industrialized Countries

21

Prospects for the Atlantic World: An American Perspective

The Setting: Domestic Politics

Foreign policy begins at home. At a time when the government of virtually every industrial country is weak to an almost unprecedented degree, it should thus be no surprise that relations among them are adrift—and even regarded as in a state of "crisis" by many observers.

The normally adverse effect of domestic political problems on Atlantic relations is, moreover, exacerbated by three interrelated contemporary phenomena.

First, the unparalleled prosperity of the postwar period, and particularly of the past decade, have led populations everywhere to demand from their governments a rising level of material benefits and economic security which may now have come to exceed even the capabilities of strong governments to provide. Weak governments certainly cannot do so. Indeed, they will be prone to look for scapegoats—especially foreigners—to justify their failings instead of facing up to the impossibility of the demands.

Second, and closely related, weak governments faced by such demands have traditionally grasped for national solutions. There is no longer the comfortable luxury of some past periods, when domestic contentment was far greater, to pursue the international approaches which both take longer to achieve and are less certain to eventuate. Nor is there confidence that equally weak counterparts will come through in a constructive way.

Third, there is no widely perceived external threat to push countries toward cooperative efforts. The permanence of détente is nearly universally accepted, and Soviet policy is designed to foster that perception. Hostilities among Western countries are unthinkable. Despite the valiant efforts of John Connally and OPEC, no one seems able to replace the threats of the 1950s to coalesce either the entire Atlantic world or its European component.

So we have no right to expect very much progress in Atlantic relations. But is there, in fact, much of a problem? If so, what is it?

This paper was originally presented as part of the Christian A. Herter Lecture Series at the School for Advanced International Studies, Johns Hopkins University, in April 1974. It was first published in the *SAIS Review*, Summer 1974, and (in German) in *Europa-Archiv*, No. 16/1974, pp. 541-54.

313

What is the Problem?

It cannot be ruled out that much of any present "Atlantic problem" derives from style rather than substance.[1] The bad manners of de Gaulle and Connally obviously hurt. Kissinger has exhibited irrational pique over minor irritants, and Jobert did his worst to make things difficult.

On such a reading, more diplomatic behavior by both sides—such as we have been seeing in recent months—would go far toward smoothing relations. The reduction of rancor in the economic field which accompanied the transition from Connally to Shultz provides support for such a view.

As seen by this American, however, the problem runs far deeper. It is based on deeply rooted asymmetries which overarch the entire Atlantic relationship. Europe has bridged most, if not all, of the Atlantic economic gap, including the psychological aspects thereof such as "technology gaps," "management gaps" and the like. But it remains wholly dependent on the United States for its security. It suffers increasing doubts about the depth of the U.S. commitment to that security. It fears U.S.-Soviet condominium collusion.

This in turn produces a deep European sense of psychic dependence and hence inferiority, which undermines overall Atlantic relations. The importance of such feelings is heightened in a world polity dominated by Henry Kissinger, whose regard for other countries is well known to equate closely to the number of nuclear weapons stored in their arsenals.

Almost like Japan, Europe is thus an economic (and cultural) giant but, in the eyes of many (including Europeans) who count, a political pygmy. Unlike Japan, it cares—and the threat to its security which continues to peek across the East validates that concern. A sturdier basis for Continental neurosis is hard to conceive.

Many in the United States, at the same time, have increasing doubts about the wisdom of providing security for allies which neither support it on major international issues (e.g., the Middle East) nor pick up "a reasonable share" of the costs of doing so, particularly as their per capita incomes rise so close to its own. Respected analysts argue that traditional U.S. military objectives in Europe could be obtained with a much smaller U.S. military contingent there anyway, and that any specter of "Finlandization" is nonsense if Europe would take steps fully within its capacity.[2]

In addition to these doubts, the United States now faces a Europe which often demands to be heard as a single unit—and given the weight thereof —but which seldom can arrive at a single position. Thus the United States faces a real trilemma in constructing and implementing its European policy:

—If it waits for a common European policy, it will certainly lose much time and probably get a halting least common denominator; it may even get nothing.

—If it goes to individual countries, it will be accused of "seeking to disrupt Europe" and "belying its own stated policies."

—If it does neither, it will be accused of unilateralism and "ignoring its oldest allies."

The Year of the End of Europe

Any American (or Japanese, or Iranian) who must choose among these approaches must assess the structure of "Europe" and where it is going. Indeed, "whither Europe" is the key question underlying U.S. policy across the Atlantic today.

There has been some progress toward a "European view" on security issues. But the primary vehicle for uniting Europe, the European Community, appears dangerously close to senescence if not death.

The EC has sequentially pursued three distinct steps toward joining Europe: the customs union, the common agricultural policy, and economic and monetary union. One is dead, one is largely moribund, and even the oldest faces severe testing.

Economic and monetary union was in fact still-born. Virtually all economists warned that exchange rates could not remain fixed at this stage of Europe's economic history, and that an effort to fix them ran directly opposite to the global trend toward greater flexibility. It did not take long to prove that view correct.

Virtually from its outset, EMU was in reality a Deutschemark zone. It excluded three EC members (United Kingdom, Italy, Ireland) and included several non-EC countries (Sweden, Norway, Austria, de facto Switzerland). The distinguishing characteristic of the joint floaters was their closeness to the German economy, not their membership in the EC. The departure of France in early 1974 only clarified the situation. So the third phase of the effort to unite Europe economically, at least in the form tried so far, is dead.

It should also be noted that the demise of EMU eliminates one rationale for a European regional policy. Intra-European transfers are a necessary component of any real economic union, as are transfers among the United States. But if Britain insists on the right to change its exchange rate, unlike West Virginia, its case for getting German money declines sharply. Indeed, such money would then amount largely to outright aid—à la transfers to the developing world—rather than an alternative adjustment device. So the prospects for another potential engine of European growth have been reduced with the collapse of EMU.

The second phase of European integration—the CAP—is also largely moribund. The system of common farm prices began to collapse when exchange rates began to change in 1969, and has never really come back together. More important, world food prices have now exceeded CAP prices for most commodities for some time, so free trade in agriculture now largely prevails as between Europe and the outside world. One cannot be sure how long this situation will continue, but it may do so for some time. In that event, the enthusiasm of France (and a few others) for the Community, as a means to prop agricultural income, would obviously wane. One of the key pillars of the EC would thereby be eroded.

Finally, even the customs union itself is backsliding. The Commission sanctioned British export controls in early 1974, and seems prepared to do so at least for other energy-related products. Export embargoes on oil for the Dutch were a near-miss in October 1973. Italy and Denmark have certainly violated at least the spirit of the Community with their recent import controls. It is virtually impossible to imagine a formal cessation of the customs union, but not de facto exceptions which would add to the disintegrating trend of the European entity.

The obvious absence of joint European policies in a number of other areas caps this picture. The frantic individual response to the energy crisis, a common external threat which might have been expected to prod them together, is the most obvious. But there has been little progress toward, e.g., fiscal harmonization or a European company law. And the renegotiation of Britain's terms of membership add significant new pressures to the crumbling facade.

The demise of "Europe" has been sounded too often in the past to be sounded now with great confidence. But any observer must face seriously the possibility that the fundamental assumption on which U.S. policy toward Europe has been based for almost two decades—that Europe is uniting, and will eventually become at least a confederal entity speaking with a single voice on most issues—holds true no longer.

In my view, this crucial uncertainty goes far to explain the shortcomings of present U.S. policy toward Europe. To be sure, there are other key factors. Nixon and Kissinger prefer acrobatic solos with totalitarian counterparts (Communist or Arab), on issues of high politics where domestic public opinion has little impact, to complex dialogues with other democracies on economics and other issues where domestic coalitions must be painfully constructed. Their curious intellectual construct of a pentagonal world balance seems to require demonstration to old adversaries that friendships are no more eternal than antagonisms, and suggests kicking the recalcitrant into "big-power behavior" to round out the pentagon.

But disdain for a "Europe" which claims to be a single entity, but clearly isn't, obviously has a major impact on the present U.S. foreign policy leadership—and is likely to have an impact on any such leadership. Paradoxically, it is precisely such fundamental inconsistencies within

Europe which will in fact promote a restoration of America hegemony, by default, and heighten the likelihood that American policymakers will, out of exasperation with the alternatives, actively seek such hegemony —whereas such an outcome is allegedly the greatest fear of those most responsible for the European inconsistencies. And dismay over "whither Europe" weakens both the resolve and influence of those who have successfully pressed for close Atlantic ties in the past. Any restoration of stability in Atlantic relations must be based on a widely shared perception, on both sides of the ocean, of how that question will be answered.

The Current State of Atlantic Economic Relations

With these asymmetries at the heart of the relationship, domestic political weaknesses and real economic problems, one might except Atlantic economic relations to be in a state of constant peril. Perhaps surprisingly, I do not find this to be the case at all.

To be sure, not all of the old economic problems have been resolved. There is no explicit agreement on a new monetary system, nor a detailed blueprint on how to finance the sizable payments imbalances flowing from the increased price of oil, nor clear progress toward long-term resolution of the energy problem. The launching, let alone success, of the multilateral trade negotiations remains uncertain.

Yet there is impressive progress on the whole range of Atlantic economic issues:

—The monetary system has been dramatically reformed. Greater flexibility of exchange rates has avoided crises, kept exchange markets open, and helped eliminate the most persistent previous balance-of-payments disequilibria (especially the American and Japanese). The major countries appear headed toward agreement on ranges within which their exchange rates will fluctuate vis-à-vis each other, to provide the needed multilateral surveillance over the present system of managed flexibility. The new valuation and interest rate on Special Drawing Rights will help restore their momentum toward playing a central role in world reserves.

—The dramatic improvement in the U.S. balance of payments has stilled most debate about the dollar and charges that the United States is "exporting inflation." At the same time, the United States has become less rigid about the official price of gold.

—The Arab oil money is being recycled. Deficit countries are borrowing much of what they need. With the agreement of Europe, the United States has reopened the New York market. The swaps are being enlarged. The IMF is beginning to borrow from the oil producers, and lending to industrial deficit countries.

—Nobody has undertaken a competitive devaluation. France quickly intervened on a sizable scale to keep the franc from sliding very far after it floated, and has borrowed massively to avoid further depreciation. Japan spent about $7 billion to keep the yen up last year, so its decision to float downward a bit since early 1974 can hardly be called "competitive depreciation." The fear of inflationary consequences makes competitive depreciations unlikely.

—Only Italy has resorted to import controls, and even its restrictions were soon limited in scope. Indeed, country after country has been unilaterally liberalizing import barriers to fight inflation—despite the runup to a multilateral negotiation in which such barriers are to be traded off for "reciprocal concessions."

—As already noted, agricultural trade is now largely free of controls. U.S. demands on Europe in this area are thus muted, at least for the time being. In addition, the U.S. resort to export controls strengthens the European case for having a CAP.

—Europe and America have remained good hosts to each other's foreign investments. There are few signs that either will resort to policies in this area which would disrupt political relations among them.

—The divisive bilateral issues of a few years ago which then seemed so important, such as citrus and reverse preferences, have rightly been relegated to the back burners by both sides.

Nor is energy *per se* the great crisis for Atlantic relations which newspaper headlines still occasionally proclaim. In the short run, there is only one thing that the Atlantic countries could do about the energy crisis even if they were to adopt a wholly united front: to keep it from getting worse by avoiding competitive exchange-rate or trade policy actions. As indicated above, every country has done precisely that—despite the hostility which surrounded the entire Atlantic dialogue on energy for many months. The "special deals" which a number of European countries have sought originally produced an irate U.S. response, but both the deals and the response are diminishing in intensity as their vagueness and economic *dis*advantage become clearer—and as the United States pursues somewhat similar deals. So, again, the substance proceeds reasonably satisfactorily though the rhetoric implies deep division.

For the long run, cooperation across the Atlantic (and Pacific) could importantly reduce the costs of the energy problem to all consuming countries. On this front, a promising start was made at the Washington conference in February and appears to continue. So there is real potential for success in the energy-related areas where cooperation counts.

Thus I regard the recently high political tension over energy as reflecting the deeper psychological and security tensions between America and Europe. Energy naturally brings these tensions to the surface, for three reasons. First, energy relates so closely to security that it is an economic reminder of U.S. security dominance. Second, the United States is so much less dependent on imported oil than any European country that its superior economic security highlights a key phase of that dominance. Third, European reliance on the American Secretary of State to get oil production to satisfactory levels still further magnifies its dependence even in the geographical area most proximate to it. So energy becomes an understandable surrogate for high politics, and the tension which it triggered reflects the deeper problem at the heart of the Atlantic relationship.

Indeed, it is my view that the Atlantic countries (and Japan) are handling quite skillfully the wide array of very tough economic issues which they have been forced to face. One cannot be overconfident about the future, as even tougher issues may lie ahead: the common threat of rampant inflation; the new trade policy spinoff therof, export controls;[3] scrambles for scarce supplies of raw materials in the Third World;[4] the desirability of ongoing cooperation to develop additional energy sources; the need to develop more explicit guidelines for intervention in the exchange markets and excessive tapping of the private capital markets. But, as of now, the record is impressive and the outlook reasonably sanguine.

If the political underpinnings are so weak, how could the economic record be so good? The answer is to be found largely in the development of transnational forces which have overridden the shortcomings of governments to deal with economic issues. The economic interdependence of the Atlantic countries has progressed so far that each has an overwhelming stake in avoiding major economic problems. The unions can complain. A Connally can bellow. Politicians may succumb to their visceral, nationalist impulses. But cooperation will usually prevail simply because the costs of conflict are so high.

The transnational forces which promote such outcomes are of two types. One is the private sector of multinational firms, banks and the like. Even in the United States, the least open of any non-Communist country to external events, these groups are heavily reliant on outsiders—especially Europe—for their welfare. And even those American groups (notably labor) which espouse protectionism and oppose the transnational forces see Japan and the developing countries rather than Europe as the devil to be held at bay.

The second transnational group comprises the governmental officials working in each issue-area (money, trade, agriculture, etc.). They have by now developed such close personal ties, from the endless stream of meetings and consultations, and such a shared interest in avoiding disruption, that they can usually be counted on to attempt to promote cooperative outcomes. Indeed, the existence of transnational forces is one of the major differences between the present situation and that of the interwar period, and provides an important basis for hope that the world economy will never again slip into the calamities of former times.

The key question for the future is whether these forces are strong enough to continue to prevail. No sure answer can be given. One key determinant will be the degree to which international economic issues are politicized within each country: the more politicized the issue, the less susceptible it will be to management by the transnational forces.

The toughest recent test of the resiliency of these transnational forces came in the fall of 1971, when Connally highly politicized both money and trade and as a result both cowed the entire bureaucracy (and even the President) and stilled most of the voices of moderation in the private sector. But the two forces, working largely through Henry Kissinger and Arthur Burns, prevailed when a real breakdown of economic relations loomed in late November of that year. A similar test was launched at the Washington energy conference by M. Jobert, but has by now been let quietly die even by the French government itself.

So there is reason to believe that these transnational forces are quite powerful and quite durable, with regard to *economic* issues. This is especially under the weak governments now in place in virtually all of our countries; it would take a politically powerful or confident politician—a de Gaulle or a Connally—to override the transnational forces.

The Implications for Overall Atlantic Relations

Paradoxically, however, the very strength of these forces may weaken the Atlantic relationship on *security* issues. For if the transnational forces will keep economic relations on an even keel anyway, there need by less fear that security differences will upset that issue-area. This reduces the need for the United States to pursue security policies which assure a "positive framework" for economic issues. It also reduces the potential for linkage between the two issue-areas by any country, which despite its obvious shortcomings *can* produce resolution of security problems.

The problem of translating the economic progress into the security area is heightened by the relative absence there of similar transnational groups. Further, many of the politico-military elites continue to view international relations as zero-sum games, in contrast with the positive-sum view accepted by most economic actors. So there is real doubt that the roots of economic success will spill over into the security area.

The uncertainty of spillover also flows from the misplaced focus of European integration on economic, rather than security, issues. It is fully understandable why Europe has pursued the economic route toward unity. Political integration *was* tried first, but failed to get off the ground. The economic approach almost had to follow, in view of the impetus to form *some kind* of community to cope with the Soviet external threat and to cement the Franco-German relationship. And the original rationale for economic union was of course that it would produce political union over the longer run. Even the belated British entry to the EC was predicated primarily on political, rather than economic, considerations.

In 1974, however, Europe has (a) an economic community for which it has little real need and (b) no security or political community, which it does need.

On economic issues, each of the major European countries is clearly strong enough to stand alone on most issues, as long as the international economic structure as a whole is open and liberal.[5] Their recent actions, on every major economic issue from exchange rates to oil, clearly indicate that they *believe* they can do so. Where they do need external help—to solidify the monetary system, finance payments deficits, avoid scrambles for oil and other raw materials, fight inflation—the European stage is too narrow for effective action. Hence "Europe" is either too large or too small an entity to deal with most of the contemporary economic problems faced by the individual European countries.

At the same time, each European country benefits relatively little from the EC in economic terms. Tariffs are low everywhere, getting lower, and could be eliminated globally in one more multilateral negotiation. Non-tariff barriers exist within Europe as well as outside it. Most major EC countries now float on their own, and turn to the IMF or the Eurobond market, not the EC institutions, to finance payments deficits. As noted, world inflation has made CAP support prices largely irrelevant at least for now. It is even unclear whether the EC enhances the negotiating leverage of most of its members on international economic issues: there is no "single voice" on money or energy, the delays in reaching Community positions dilutes their international impact, and the unanimity requirement primarily strengthens the leverage of a blocking minority *within* the Community over the positions of other members. The malaise exhibited toward the EC in recent years by virtually all of its members appears to support the conclusion that they do not attach heavy weight to the benefits which it provides for them. Indeed, there now seems to be no rationale for European economic unity which is sufficiently important to the domestic politics of any major European country to justify the domestic sacrifices needed to propel it forward once more.

On the security side, the picture appears to be reversed. Each European country is clearly inferior, in terms of manpower and firepower, to both superpowers. Thus emerges a pervasive feeling of dependence. Yet there is no serious effort, let alone progress, toward political community—the one step which could go at least part way toward meeting their need—though

322

numerous plans for an independent European defense force have been formulated. The Common Market has not lead to economic union, and the likelihood that it will ever promote political community appears remote. It is hard to disagree with Kennan[6] that "No one can stop the Western Europeans . . . from seeing themselves as the helpless playthings of superior force and then governing themselves by the image they have themselves evoked," or with Walter Laqueur[7] that "for years to come America will have to . . . hope that, in the end, the instinct of survival will reassert itself and that one day Western Europe will be more than a geographical term."

Europe's Options

Europe appears to have three options at present. One is to take the "great leap forward" needed to restore momentum toward economic union, based on renewed confidence that political union would then eventually emerge. A second is to refocus the whole "European" movement on security rather than economic issues.[8] A third is simply to recognize that nationalism has prevailed, at least for the moment, and frankly jettison the rhetoric of "Europe" in a return to the nation-state approach of the past.

Each approach would have a different impact on the Atlantic relationship. A resurgence of economic Europe would essentially revalidate the economic base of Atlantic relations of the past two decades, and presumably reduce Europe's inferiority complex by restoring the path toward eventual political community. A new, direct breakthrough toward a European security community could have much the same effect, and augur well for Atlantic cooperation.

But the prospects for early and meaningful moves toward a European security community appear about as dubious as a "great leap forward" which resuscitates progress toward economic community. There is virtually no evidence that Europe would pay the price necessary to overcome its psychic dilemma for two reasons. First, there simply exists no perception of an external threat sufficient to justify the massive expenditures that would be needed. Second, Germany still doubts whether any conceivable European defense arrangement would support it as credibly and effectively as even a diluted American arrangement. Third, some other European countries continue to resist the key role for Germany which would be a necessary component of any such arrangement.

Hence there looms the strong possibility of option three: a more-or-less explicit return to a world of nation-states with the dropping, at least for now, of the concept of a *European* role in world affairs. The Common Market and the CAP would continue to exist, but all pretense of economic union and a "common European position" would be put into cold storage. As already indicated, the economics of such an arrangement would appear acceptable for at least the larger European countries.

The politics could be trickier. One result would be a further acceleration in bilateral dealings with Washington—"reverse Rapallos?"—and perhaps the emergence of a special relationship between the United States and Germany.[9] There could be some psychic cost to some important European groups, which have staked much on steady progress toward integration. Indeed, it might take virtually as much courage for European governments to renounce Europe as to move it forward, although it would be less difficult if they agreed together to do so—especially in terms of a "holding pattern" from which might emerge options one and/or two sometime in the future.

From the standpoint of Atlantic relations, *any* of the three options might turn out to be decidedly superior to the status quo. Any would remove its high degree of uncertainty. Any would solve the American trilemma cited earlier—the wait for a "European" position which seldom emerges, and does so if at all in a way which often heightens rather than reduces transoceanic tension—and hence provide a new and stronger basis for American cooperation with Europe.[10] And any might increase European security, for the alternative could in practice turn out to be " . . . a weak and divided Europe, of which the United States had washed her hands, [which] would be for the Soviet Union the best solution of all."[11]

To be sure, nothing that Europe can do will alone assure a cooperative America. But the transnational forces described above virtually assure constructive economic interaction across the Atlantic indefinitely, unless thrown off course by major breakdowns in the security area. Such breakdowns are most likely to occur if fumbling and indecision in Europe, on the basic issue of its internal organization and hence its role in the world, triggers exasperation and dismay in America.

We have recently observed quite blatantly such exasperation and dismay at the highest levels in Washington. They could quickly permeate the American body politic, and the current cooling of rhetoric—however desirable—must not be mistaken for the fundamental changes which are needed. The result of such dismay could be growing disarray and even dissolution of the Atlantic relationship. The key move is thus up to Europe.

Notes

1. See, for example, Zbigniew Brzezinski, "The Deceptive Structure of Peace," *Foreign Policy* 14 (Spring 1974), pp. 46-48, and the European "Z," "The Year of Europe?" *Foreign Affairs*, Jan. 1974, esp. p. 248.

2. George Kennan, "Europe's Problems, Europe's Choices," *Foreign Policy* 14, pp. 3-16.

3. C. Fred Bergsten, *Completing the GATT: Toward New International Rules to Govern Export Controls* (Washington, D.C.: British North American Committee, 1974) [chapter 10 in this volume].

4. C. Fred Bergsten, "The Threat From the Third World," *Foreign Policy* 11 (Summer 1973) [chapter 27 in this volume].

5. There would be a strong economic case for European economic union only to lessen the costs to each country of a world of protectionism. This was the case for the creation of the Commonwealth and sterling area to lessen the costs to each member of the import controls and competitive depreciations triggered by the Great Depression in the 1930s.

6. *Op. cit.*, p. 16.

7. *New York Times Magazine*, Jan. 20, 1974, p. 46.

8. It might be argued that both economic and political community could proceed simultaneously, and even that trade-offs between the two issue-areas could speed the process. But top policy-makers can only focus on a limited number of issues, and they are less likely to push the pooling of weapons if they are thinking about the pooling of monetary reserves. In addition, divisions over further economic efforts could well impede political progress, especially when those divisions have become as pervasive and obvious as is now the case. Finally, public opinion can usually be better mobilized to support a discrete, narrow objective than one which runs across-the-board—especially when the narrow focus is on relatively abstract security issues and the broader approach encompasses economic matters of more direct concern to most citizens.

9. C. Fred Bergsten, "Die amerikanische Europa-Politik angesichts der Stagnation des Gemeinsamen Marktes," *Europa-Archiv*, Folge 4/1974 [chapter 22 in this volume (in English)].

10. As pointed out by John Newhouse, "Stuck Fast," *Foreign Affairs*, Jan. 1973: "A Western Europe permanently bogged down is likely to present the United States with the worst of all possible worlds."

11. Michael Howard, *Survival*, Jan.-Feb. 1974, p. 23.

22

U.S. Foreign Economic Policy and Europe: The Ascendance of Germany and the Stagnation of the Common Market

U.S. Foreign economic policy toward Europe in the relevant future should focus on Germany rather than on the Common Market. This is both because the Common Market has stagnated, and because Germany has by itself become an economic colossus exercising economic dominance within Europe and major economic influence around the world. For political reasons, some of this focus on Germany will have to be carried out through Common Market institutions—but our main efforts should be directed toward Bonn rather than Brussels. Major implications for U.S. foreign economic policy derive from these conclusions.

The Ascendance of Germany

Americans have been slow to recognize the emergence of Germany as a great world economic power. German per capita income now approximates our own. German exports of manufactured goods became greater than our own several years ago, and total German exports now exceed ours. Germany will this year run a trade surplus of about $12 billion, almost twice the size of the largest surplus ever run by the United States and about one-third larger than any surplus ever run by Japan. German monetary reserves are well over twice our own. The value of the German currency has risen by more than 60 percent against the dollar over the last four years.[1]

As a result of all these developments, a Deutschemark (DM) zone is developing in Europe. A number of important countries have tied their exchange rates to the DM, because of their dependence on the German economy in a world in which virtually all other countries have decided not to declare fixed parities for their currencies. Some of these countries are members of the Common Market, but some members of the Common Market (United Kingdom, Italy, Ireland) are not yet members of the zone. Some members of the DM zone (Sweden, Norway, Austria, Switzerland de facto) are outside the Common Market.

This grouping of countries centered on Germany is often referred to as the "Common Market float," or the "joint European float," but this

Originally presented as testimony to the Subcommittees on Europe and Foreign Economic Policy of the House Foreign Affairs Committee in their Hearings on the *American Interest in the European Community* on November 8, 1973 and published (in German) in *Europa-Archiv*, No. 4/1974, pp. 115-22.

terminology confuses the issue. The membership of the group indicates clearly that it is *not* a Common Market operation. When widely recognized, this will prove embarrassing to France—and it adds one more reason why the British are likely to keep sterling floating indefinitely. It is, at the same time, an indication of the stagnation of the Common Market and the growing strength of Germany.

The German economic ascendance has also induced scores of countries around the world to start holding large portions of their international reserves in DM, and has triggered a similar rise in the DM portion of holdings of private sectors. Data are poor in this area, but the Deutsche Bundesbank (the German central bank) has reported that the DM has already far surpassed sterling as the world's second key currency, despite its own opposition to the trend and overt policy measures to check it. Despite these restrictions, at least one-fourth of all Eurocurrency transactions now take place in DM and an even greater share of Eurbond flotations are denominated in the German currency. Indeed, there is in progress a world-wide shift of currency holdings from the dollar into the DM, as it moves into the international monetary vacuum opened up by the failings of the dollar in the last several years.

This German economic power has also had major political manifestations. It was the critical inducement to Pompidou to let Britain into the Common Market, reversing de Gaulle. It has given Germany major leverage within the Common Market, since only Germany can pay for the "European" agricultural policies sought by France and regional policies sought by Britain and Italy. It has doubtless been an important element in the willingness of the Soviet Union and Eastern Europe to respond positively to Chancellor Brandt's *Ostpolitik*, and may become even more important in this context if U.S. economic relations with the Communist countries are sidetracked by political disputes. It has enhanced Germany's ability to pursue its national interests effectively in the Third World, as indicated by its recent set of far-reaching agreements with Iran on a wide range of raw materials and manufacturing projects.

This discussion of German economic ascendance is not intended to obscure the fact that Germany, like all other countries, has some serious problems too. Even with the exchange-rate changes, its GNP is only one-third of our own and its economy is much more susceptible to external events, such as the energy crisis. Its geographical exposure in Central Europe remains a potential problem, and it of course remains non-nuclear. Its desire to avoid major political confrontation with France limits its freedom of action, particularly on economic issues where the French seek a "common European position." Some economists argue that German industry, having developed in a highly skewed direction due to a decade or more of an undervalued DM, is now extremely vulnerable to any significant cutback in world growth because of the sizable revaluation which has now

taken place, and that even my economic appraisal is unduly favorable to
Germany. At least one futurist, Herman Kahn, believes that France rather
than Germany will be the leader of Europe in the decades to come.

There is not time to answer these points here, and some of them are
valid to some extent. It *is* particularly relevant to this discussion to note
Germany's desire to avoid confrontation with France, and to avoid "being
forced to choose between Washington and Paris" on specific issues. This
real German political concern must condition U.S. policy toward Europe
as a whole, and toward Germany in particular. But neither this point, nor
the others just cited, lead me to back away from the thesis of this presentation.

The Stagnation of the Common Market

At the same time that Germany is moving briskly ahead, the Common
Market is largely marking time. I say this not without understanding or
sympathy, because the digestion of the expansion of the Community's
membership and its efforts to pursue the extremely ambitious goals laid out
by Europe's political leaders at their summit meeting in October 1972 were
bound to move slowly. The United States should certainly avoid policies of
hostility toward the emerging Europe, which is probably with us to stay and
may well slowly evolve into something approaching a true economic union.

Nevertheless, no objective reading of the situation in Europe can regard
the Community and its institutions as a driving force—particularly in
comparison to the national progress of Germany. The Common Market can
agree to block the proposals of others, but it shows no capacity to fill even
part of the leadership vacuum created by the necessary (and desirable)
cutback in the global role of the United States. It is unwilling even to engage
seriously with the Japanese, despite the obvious impact of Japan on European interests throughout the world. Ardent "trilateralists," who see a new
community of the advanced nations (United States, Western Europe, and
Japan) as the core of a new U.S. foreign policy, may well have their sights
on the right goal for a decade hence and are thus playing a useful role in
beginning that process now—but they have no European "pole" to deal
with now.

There might be no need for this paper if we could wait that long. But we
simply cannot. There are too many major issues which require early attention, in the economic field alone (without even referring to a series of
security matters of at least equal urgency which, taken together with the
economic issues, raise the real threat of major U.S.-European discord in
the years ahead if they are not dealt with now):

—Restructuring of an entire new international economic order to replace the postwar system which collapsed in 1971

—Management of the new international monetary system which is rapidly evolving, largely in constructive directions but with some serious pitfalls which must be avoided

—Trade negotiations and new trade rules to govern commercial relations

—Shortages of energy and other raw materials

—Food supplies

—International investment, etc.

The Common Market, as an entity, does not even enjoy nominal—let alone real—competence on many of these issues. For cosmetic purposes, much of the apparent negotiating will have to take place with Community organs. But U.S. foreign economic policy must look elsewhere to get real action.

The Implications for U.S. Foreign Economic Policy

The United States and the Soviet Union bear a heavy joint responsibility for the maintenance of world peace and security, as a result of the national power of each. The United States and Germany, probably along with Japan, bear an equally heavy responsibility for the maintenance of world economic peace, as a result of the national economic power of each. American-German cooperation must therefore provide the basis for the response to most of the problems just cited.

In fact, such cooperation has already played a major role in world economic events during the past decade. The explicit German pledge not to convert its dollar reserves into U.S. gold, in response to a U.S. request that it do so, played a major role in saving the United States from even greater international monetary troubles in the late 1960s and postponed the collapse of the Bretton Woods monetary system. Germany led the rest of Europe in standing down the French on the decision to begin the reform of the monetary system by creating Special Drawing Rights, and got the United States to make concessions on particular details of the new monetary asset in return. The German decision to float the DM in late 1969, after the United States had sought such action from her a year earlier, and again in May 1971 signaled in a constructive way the beginning of the end of the Bretton Woods system. German willingness to let the DM appreciate significantly in value during the crisis triggered by the U.S. actions of August 1971 was the key to the entire Smithsonian Agreement, because it permitted the Japanese to revalue their currency by an even greater amount and the French and British to accept a sizable dollar devaluation. Joint U.S.-German intervention in the foreign exchange markets last summer helped reduce international monetary offset agreements with the United States (and United Kingdom) has, properly, kept balance of payments questions from distorting NATO security considerations.

Politically, it is noteworthy that virtually all of these German actions required it to either seize leadership of the Common Market as a whole, or to take the risk of openly confronting other Community members (mainly France) by going explicitly outside the Community framework. In every case, Germany "got away with it"; there was no noticeable adverse repercussion on German interests. And German economic power, and political flexibility, is greater now than at the time many of these steps were taken. While remaining ever cognizant of the German desire to avoid such intra-European problems, neither we nor they should be deterred by it from taking necessary actions.

It seems, however, that many American practitioners and observers of foreign economic policy have either failed to grasp this recent history, or have forgotten it in their mesmerization with the rhetoric and cosmetics of the Common Market. I can testify from personal experience that the United States failed to push hard for reform of the balance of payments adjustment process in 1969-70—reform which might have precluded the need for the traumatic crises of 1971 and beyond—due partly to a misplaced willingness to let the Europeans devote their energies in that area to "European monetary unification," a project whose repeated failures have now become obvious to all and whose short-run outlook is quite dim. Even now, excessive U.S. preoccupation with the "position of Europe" and disregard for the central importance of Germany seems to have edged the Germans toward the negative French stance on both monetary arrangements and trade negotiations.

Even worse, the United States has adopted overtly hostile policies toward Germany when it should have been seeking cooperation instead. The United States has frequently allowed the financially insignificant military offset issue—insignificant in balance of payment terms because Germany first held all of its reserve gains in dollars and now has revalued its currency by 60 percent against the dollar—to dominate the U.S.-German economic agenda, and even to lead to charges in Germany that the United States brought down the Erhard government in 1966. The U.S. government criticized Germany for floating the DM in May 1971, when such action greatly helped the U.S. balance of payments and actually paved the way for precisely the kinds of monetary changes which the United States soon decided to seek itself. Repeated U.S. badgering of the Germans on minor trade, especially agricultural, issues has made it difficult to maintain the kind of relationship needed to deal with really critical matters.

For the 1970s, I believe that Germany must be the focus of our economic policy toward Europe, and along with Japan the focus of our global economic policy as well. Fortunately, the United States and Germany share a number of critical interests in this field:

—As the two leading key currency countries in the world, neither of which *wants* its currency to play such a world role, we have a common interest in constructing a new international monetary order which avoids reliance on national currencies in the way that the international monetary system of the recent past relied on the dollar. Indeed, any system based on national currencies in the world of the 1970s and 1980s, where two or three major economic powers coexist, would raise grave risks of financial instability, monetary blocs and political rivalry reminiscent of the sterling-franc and sterling-dollar conflicts of the past.

—We both favor reliance in that new monetary order on exchange-rate changes to effect balance of payments adjustment, Germany because of its antipathy to direct controls and the United States because its economy is so relatively self-sufficient, in contrast to the French-Japanese penchant for controls and the Benelux-Swiss focus on internal economic adjustment. (Such exchange-rate changes could take place between the dollar and the DM zone as a whole, whether or not it comprised the entire Common Market.)

—As by far the largest national holder of dollars, Germany is in the best position to take the lead in proposing a consolidation of the "dollar overhang" on terms which would be acceptable to the United States, thereby contributing both to international monetary stability and the battle against world inflation.[2]

—As by far the two largest trading nations in the world, we both seek general trade liberalization to hold back protectionist pressures, to avoid the risk of the evolution of the world economy toward trading blocs, and to fight internal inflation, in contrast to the continuing preoccupation of many other countries with import-induced unemployment and their resulting protectionist tendencies.

—We both seek liberal rules to govern international investment flows, and indeed U.S. firms must rely on Germany to block possible Anglo-French efforts to create a "European industrial policy" which might discriminate against them.

—Because of these relatively liberal views on trade and investment, and out of necessity in the U.S. case and relative confidence in the German case, we are more likely to work cooperatively with Japan than are the other less confident and less liberal Europeans.

—And despite a multitude of problems, we continue to share perhaps the deepest bond of any two countries in the world in the security field, a relationship which is of course related closely to our ability to deal cooperatively with the array of economic problems which we constantly confront.

Conclusion

Thus both German economic power, and the confluence of U.S. and German interests on the most critical questions of international economics for the 1970s, strongly suggest that our policy focus in that direction in the years immediately ahead. We should stop carping negatively at Germany on minor issues, or where their actions cause us short-term problems. We should work constructively with Germany, on all of these economic issues, on a consistent ongoing basis.

All of this does *not* argue that the United States should forget about Japan, France, Britain, the Community institutions in Brussels or the developing countries. The new structure of world economics *and* politics requires the active engagement of many countries on many key issues in a swirl of shifting alliances which will appear extremely messy but will be the only way to do business effectively in the 1970s and beyond. And the German priority cannot be expressed too overtly, due to the risk of French (and perhaps British and other) backlash which would make the whole strategy counterproductive. As already indicated, the mode of operations will often have to encompass the Conmunity institutions. In real terms, however, our sights must be on Bonn rather than Brussels.

Notes

1. Converting at the exchange rate of 2.4 DM = $1 which has prevailed for the last three months, German per capita income in 1972 was about $5,600 compared with U.S. per capita income of about $5,500; and German exports in the second quarter of 1973 were running at an annual rate of almost $73 billion compared with U.S. exports of just over $70 billion. At the end of August 1973, German reserves were $33.4 billion compared with U.S. reserves of $14.4 billion.

2. For a simple explanation of how this could be done see my "The Dollar Overhang," *New York Times*, Op-Ed page, Aug. 31, 1973.

23

The United States and Germany: The Imperative of Economic Bigemony

There are only two economic superpowers in the world today: the United States of America (USA) and the Federal Republic of Germany (FRG). Their active joint leadership is essential for resolution of the host of immediate problems which now plague the world economy, even to avoid relapse on all continents into destructive nationalistic policies, and to rebuild a stable international economic structure. Such leadership should be exercised through a series of concentric circles of decision-making, centered on their own bilateral relationship and radiating out through the other industrialized countries (primarily the rest of the EEC and Japan) into the existing global institutions.

To restore a world of stable economic growth in the short run, America and Germany should jointly use their massive economic power—exercised primarily through cautious but steady stimulation of their own economies, the extension of financial credits, and avoidance of any new trade restrictions—to lever effective anti-inflationary policies in the rest of the world. For the longer run, they should collaborate on the further evolution of the monetary system, the needed reform of the trading system, the creation of new rules to deal with currently unmanaged problems such as international investment, and increased world economic security through reduced energy dependence on OPEC. An early start on these structural issues would greatly facilitate satisfactory resolution of the more immediate problems.

The Economic Bigemony[1]

On virtually every economic criterion, the USA and FRG stand far above all other countries:

1. German *monetary reserves* exceeded $33 billion at the end of August 1974; if the official price of gold is valued at about $127 per ounce, about 80 percent of the current free market price, they would reach almost $43 billion. American reserves nominally exceed $15 billion, or $38 billion at the more realistic price for gold. No other country even approaches these magnitudes with the higher valuation of gold (see Table 23-1).

This paper was originally prepared for the VIII American-German Conference in Bonn in November 1974.

Table 23-1
The World's Leading Holders of International Monetary Reserves
(In millions of US dollars, as of August 1974)

	With gold valued at official price ($42.22)	With gold valued at $126.66 (triple the official price)
1. GERMANY	33,131	42,885
2. UNITED STATES	15,251	38,137
3. Japan	12,903	14,653
4. Saudi Arabia	9,313	9,569
5. France	8,413	16,783
6. Switzerland	7,253	14,153
7. United Kingdom	6,842	8,714 (March data for gold)
8. Iran	6,303	6,613
9. Brazil (July)	6,162	6,274
10. Spain (June)	6,101	7,305
11. Netherlands	5,869	10,373
12. Italy	5,363	12,203
13. Belgium	5,024	8,522

Source: IMF, *International Financial Statistics*, October 1974.

2. Partly as a result, but due also to their sizable gross national products and trade flows, the USA and FRG stand at the *center of the world's two key currency areas:* the dollar area and the mark zone. Though much smaller than in the past, the dollar area still includes a majority of the world's countries—and would encompass more if France, and later the United Kingdom and Italy, were to rejoin it.[2] In addition, as the Bundesbank pointed out over two years ago, the mark has passed sterling as the second most widely used currency both as an international reserve asset and as vehicle for private transactions.[3]

3. The FRG and USA have the world's strongest *balance-of-payments positions*. Germany continues to run the largest trade surpluses known to economic history, despite the steady revaluation of the mark for five years. Despite its huge deficit on services transactions, the German current account—alone mong the major industrial countries—remains in strong surplus.

American trade is close to balance, despite being subjected to by far the largest jump (in absolute terms) in payments for oil imports. However, the traditional American surplus on services—due primarily to huge earnings from its massive foreign investments—generates a stronger current account.

No other major industrial countries even approximate this current balance-of-payments strength of the FRG and USA (see Table 23-2).

Table 23-2

Balance-of-Payments Positions of Major Industrialized Countries, 1972-1974

(In billions of US dollars)

		1972	1973	1974[a]
1. GERMANY:	Trade	8.24	15.43	20.25
	Invisibles	−7.20	−10.70	−13.25
	Current account	1.04	4.73	7.00
2. UNITED STATES:	Trade	−6.91	0.69	−2.65
	Invisibles	−1.44	2.35	1.65
	Current account	−8.35	3.04	−1.00
3. France:	Trade	1.28	1.50	−4.05
	Invisibles	−0.99	−1.65	−2.15
	Current account	0.29	−0.15	−6.20
4. Japan:	Trade	8.97	3.96	−2.70
	Invisibles	−2.35	−3.82	−5.05
	Current account	6.62	−0.14	−7.75
5. Italy:	Trade	0.05	−3.96	−10.05
	Invisibles	1.99	1.43	1.30
	Current account	2.04	−2.53	−8.75
6. United Kingdom:	Trade	−1.68	−5.78	−12.20
	Invisibles	1.87	2.07	2.45
	Current account	0.19	−3.71	−9.75

[a]Forecast by OECD Secretariat.

Source: derived from OECD, *Economic Outlook*, July 1974, pp. 44, 46.

This combination of huge reserves and balance-of-payments strength isolates the USA and FRG as the only two industrialized countries which can be major international creditors for the foreseeable future.[4] From the advent of flexible exchange rates—August 1971 for the dollar, March 1973 for most other countries—until quite recently, the importance of such creditor positions had been denigrated. Now, however, virtually every (industrialized and developing) country running current account deficits—i.e., virtually every country in the world except the oil exporters, a few other commodity producers (including Canada), and the USA and FRG—are seeking foreign loans to avoid the inflationary impact of further depreciation of their exchange rates. Thus the FRG and USA have major responsibility for the maintenance of world economic order, and possess massive international leverage because of their unique creditor positions.

4. USA and FRG *exports* are virtually identical, and far exceed those of all other countries (see Table 23-3). American exports are a bit higher in total, while German exports are higher for manufactured goods. The two countries also have by far the world's highest levels of imports (see also Table 23-3).

In addition to their financial power, the USA and FRG thus are the

Table 23-3
The World's Leading Trading Countries
(*In millions of dollars, 1973*)

	Exports (f.o.b.)	Imports (c.i.f.)
1. UNITED STATES	71,314	73,199
2. GERMANY	67,502	54,552
3. Japan	36,982	38,347
4. France	36,659	37,727
5. United Kingdom	30,535	38,847
6. Canada	26,309	24,918
7. Netherlands	24,072	24,736
8. Belgium	22,459	21,987
9. Italy	22,224	27,796
10. Sweden	12,171	10,625

Source: IMF, *International Financial Statistics*, October 1974.

world's dominant traders. This means that world trade policy will largely follow their lead toward liberalism or protectionism. Even more significant, it means that world economic growth is importantly, even decisively, affected by the growth (or decline) in their demand for foreign goods and their displacement of domestic production in foreign markets. The effect of the two dominant traders is of course more pronounced in the geographic area most proximate to each, including the EEC for Germany and Japan for the United States.

5. The FRG and USA are, over any relevant period of time, the industrial world's *least inflationary* economies[5] (see Table 23-4). This factor of course underlies the international financial and trading success of both. Such relative price stability implies that both have more room than any other major countries to maneuver their domestic economic policies.

6. The USA and FRG are the *least dependent on oil imports* of the industrialized countries (see Table 23-5). Indeed, Germany imports no more oil than the other "middle-sized" European countries, with their much smaller economies—though it is still quite reliant on imports, including imports of natural gas from Holland, in absolute terms. Thus the USA, and to a lesser extent the FRG, possess greater economic security than other countries.

7. Finally, the USA and FRG are the most significant economic markets in the world. A proper evaluation of "market significance" encompasses both total size and income per capita. These factors are best measured by GNP and income per capita, respectively. I have thus constructed an index of "market significance," which is of great importance to the weight of a country in world economic affairs in addition to the variables already

Table 23-4
Inflation in the Major Industrialized Countries, 1959-75
(Percentage changes in consumer prices)

	Annual Average 1959-60 to 1970-71	1972	1973	1974[a]	first half 1975[a]
			Change From Preceeding Year		
1. UNITED STATES	2.4	2.6	5.3	10.0	7.25
2. GERMANY	2.8	5.6	7.2	8.5	9.25
3. United Kingdom	3.5	6.7	8.6	15.0	12.0
4. Italy	3.9	5.7	10.8	19.0	18.0
5. France	4.1	6.2	7.3	14.0	14.0
6. Japan	5.6	4.9	11.8	24.75	15.0

[a]Forecast by OECD

Source: OECD, *Economic Outlook*, July 1974, p. 10.

Table 23-5
Energy Dependence of Major Industrialized Countries, 1973[a]

	GNP (billions of dollars)	Oil Imports (million barrels per day)	Dependency Ratio
1. UNITED STATES	1,295	2.2	1.7%
2. GERMANY	343	1.0	3.0%
3. France	227	1.0	4.0%
4. Japan	414	1.9	4.6%
5. United Kingdom	166	1.0	6.2%
6. Italy	134	0.9	6.7%

[a]This is obviously not the best "dependency ratio" which could be constructed, though it is certainly usable. One should properly compare oil imports with total *energy consumption*, using *1974* data to take the new price structure into account.

cited, by simply multiplying GNP times income per capita (Table 23-6). Such a procedure reveals the irrelevance of the fantastic per capita income of an Abu Dhabi, and the limitations even of the sizable GNP of the Soviet Union.

All these data indicate that the USA and FRG exceed all other countries on the key international economic criteria by a significant amount, and rank clearly as the world's only economic superpowers. Thus they possess the capability to decisively affect the world economy if they collaborate actively. Their power certainly levies on them the responsibility for doing so, if the problems of the world economy are sufficiently serious to warrant the political-psychological risks of asserting such positions of leadership.[6]

Table 23-6
GNP of Major Industrialized Countries, 1972

	Total GNP[a] (1)	GNP per capita (2)	(1) × (2)[b]
1. UNITED STATES	1,155	5,532	6,389
2. GERMANY	292	4,736	1,383
3. USSR	549	2,217	1,219
4. Japan	341	3,218	1,097
5. France	221	4,269	943
6. Canada	103	4,714	486
7. United Kingdom	152	2,731	415
8. Italy	118	2,179	257

[a]In billions of dollars, converted at March/April 1973 exchange rates.
[b]In 10^{12} dollars.

Source: derived from Department of State, *The Planetary Product in 1972*, p. 25.

The World Economic Problem

There is little need to reiterate the array of world economic problems. Global inflation remains rampant, threatening both economic prosperity and societal stability. At the same time, unemployment is rising sharply in many countries—including the USA and FRG. "Slumpflation" thus dominates the short-run outlook, and many observers fear that it will become endemic or may even collapse into another depression. The problem, already unique in economic history because it combines high inflation and high unemployment, is further compounded by the need for massive structural adjustment to the end of the era of cheap energy (and perhaps other raw materials).[6a]

Internationally, there is still no assured solution to the recycling problem. Greater stability of exchange rates remains a desirable goal, though much of the initial instability of the flexible-rate system has subsided and stability is far more likely to be found through better international management of flexible rates than through any effort to restore fixed rates. It remains urgent to avoid any revival of protectionist trade measures, which are as likely to emerge in the form of export controls—as countries seek to export their inflation—as in the traditional form of import controls.[7]

In addition to these immediate problems, the structural foundations of the postwar economic order have largely collapsed. The Bretton Woods monetary system was based on fixed exchange rates and the dollar, and neither is a viable basis for the monetary system of the future. The GATT trading system dealt with barriers to imports generally, tariffs in particular, and non-discrimination, which are no longer the primary issues or can no longer be handled in the traditional ways. There exist no international arrangements to deal with foreign direct investment and multinational corporations, one of the central features of today's world economy.[8] So there is pressing need to begin the construction of an entire new international economic order—to prevent problems over the longer run, to bolster world confidence that governments have their economic relations under control, and to point the ultimate direction toward which short-run policies should aim.

Finally, traditional security issues cannot be forgotten despite widespread perceptions of detente. Support for the economic components of detente, a major Soviet incentive in relaxing tensions, has diminished greatly in the United States. The arms race continues, and on some accounts accelerates. Nuclear proliferation again looms on the horizon.[9] A peace settlement in the Middle East remains elusive. Famine and desperation threaten a number of developing countries, including—for the first time in history—a nuclear "have-not" (India). So, as usual, economic conflict among nations could have seriously adverse effects on world peace as well as on world prosperity.

A Bigemony Strategy for the World Economy

Current international economic problems mesh almost precisely with the capabilities of the USA and FRG to do something about them.

The world faces slumpflation. The USA and FRG both face serious and rising unemployment, but have the best anti-inflationary records. Hence they have both great need to resume economic growth, and the greatest room to do so without excessively inflationary results. The USA and FRG should thus adopt sufficiently expansionary domestic economic policies to assure against any risk of severe world recession.

Each country has already taken mild steps in this direction. More is needed to restore world confidence in the future economic outlook. Such expansionary measures should be adopted quickly, because of the lags in their taking effect and the need to restore world economic confidence.

The obvious risk of any such expansionary efforts is more inflation. Here enters the unique position of the USA and FRG as international creditors. The bigemonial powers should use their leverage to assure adequate stabilization policies in the other major countries, who might otherwise use their loans to avoid such measures. In essence, the USA and FRG would finance the payments deficits of other major countries and offer them expanding markets, in return for more responsible policies in those other countries. Such a strategy would certainly be "just," in that (a) the

USA and FRG have traditionally been the least inflationary countries and (b) they would be risking more inflation internally—through their expansionary policies—in order to protect the world against deep and prolonged recession.

The third component of such a USA-FRG strategy would be their total abstention from applying trade controls, on both the import and export sides. Other countries might legitimately fear protectionist pressures in the FRG and, especially, the USA in a world where the bigemonial powers were leading the resumption of economic growth—thus consciously risking an erosion of their competitive positions through narrowing the inflation differential between them and their main competitors, and increasing the potential pressures for export controls because of higher inflation itself.[10]

In addition, the USA and FRG should take joint leadership in developing a credible "Project Interdependence to Avoid Dependence" on OPEC oil suppliers, building on the Integrated Emergency Program already agreed. They should push ahead on the cooperation already evolving between the Federal Reserve and Bundesbank to stabilize the international money markets, which is within their bilateral power because the dollar and mark are the world's two key currencies.[11] They should assure effective recycling—through whatever institutional means best enabled them to use their leverage in achieving effective economic policies from borrowing countries. For the longer run, they should lead the process of reforming the GATT and creating new international rules to govern foreign investment.

This USA-FRG leadership could be implemented through three concentric circles of decision-making. First, the bigemonial powers would develop the overall strategy in detail and negotiate any tradeoffs necessary to protect their own positions vis-à-vis each other. Second, each would attempt to "sell" the strategy to the other major industrialized countries, jointly with countries where that seemed best (Italy?) or individually (the USA with Japan?), checking back with each other any modifications required by the position of others. They would of course be alert to take advantage of initiatives taken by others, such as the leadership of Davignon in the Energy Working Group. Third, the broader steps could be implemented through existing international institutions, to engage the rest of the world, on the basis of the agreements already worked out.

This method of implementing the bigemonial leadership should improve its effectiveness, by engaging other countries at an early stage in the decision-making process. It should also reduce—or even eliminate—the political risks of bigemony to the USA and FRG themselves. But it would be a much different method than now exists, and promise far greater results, by having the two economic superpowers conceive the strategies initially and then implement them in tandem.

Other countries would benefit greatly from such a USA-FRG approach:

—A resumption of growth in the two largest world markets would afford an opportunity for other countries to adopt economic policies which would simultaneously (a) boost their output—largely to meet foreign demand—and hence avoid much unemployment, and (b) cut back the need for expansionary *domestic* policies, thereby countering inflation. This would represent a reversal of recent German economic policy, which combined stagnant domestic demand with continued growth of exports.

—They would receive large loans from the USA and FRG to finance their immediate balance-of-payments problems, to the extent that those problems were not resolved by changes in current account positions.

—More heavily dependent on energy imports than the USA and FRG, they would gain most from any programs which reduced the leverage of OPEC.

—Less able to affect international monetary and trade policies, they would benefit greatly from increased stabilization of the dollar-mark relationship and avoiding the risk of new trade barriers.

—More heavily reliant on international trade and finance, they would benefit from the commencement of efforts to restore a stable international economic order.

—The implied strengthening of the USA-FRG relationship would reduce two of the main threats to Western security arrangements, by undermining Congressional opposition to U.S. troops in Germany and destroying any Soviet hopes of serious erosion of USA-FRG ties.

To at least this outside observer, such a strategy appears simply to broaden the current European policy of the Schmidt Government. The Chancellor appears to have offered German reflation (after the current wage negotiations are wrapped up) and credits, to the Italians and French, in return for the most disinflationary policies their societies can stand. Broadening the strategy to actively engage both the United States and other non-European countries would be highly desirable.

The Politics of Economic Bigemony

Such economic leadership risks political backlash for any country. This is especially true for Germany, and it is fortunate that the Schmidt Government is far less deterred by guilt over the past than any of its predecessors—though the recent European flap over agricultural prices is a reminder of concerns about German dominance. Sharing the leadership role would ease the political strain for both America and Germany.

At the same time, a coordinated approach would make the policy more effective. This is clearly true in the negative sense, e.g., by assuring that neither Germany nor America would prematurely bail out Italy. It could also be powerfully true in the positive sense, to lever effective policies elsewhere, if the USA and FRG could collude with sufficient skill to avoid the appearances of domination which would make cooperation impossible for other governments. Indeed, with sufficient skill, the economic bigemony might be operable through the existing multilateral institutions in the same way that those institutions provided effective cover for American hegemony for two decades.

Indeed, it is the end of that American hegemony which requires a USA-FRG economic bigemony. The only successful international economic orders in history have been hierarchical, indeed hegemonial under the British in the nineteenth century and the Americans after the Second World War. The non-hierarchical systems of the twentieth century and interwar periods, in which the most powerful nations competed for world economic (and political) leadership rather than cooperating, collapsed into war as well as economic disaster.

There is no possibility of reconstituting the postwar economic order, even if it were desirable to do so, because the American domination which was its structural foundation has eroded too far. A sizable number of nations, including the rising "middle class" of developing countries with commodity power and/or rapid industrialization,[12] must be intimately involved in much of the new international economic decision-making. But such pluralism is obviously too unwieldy, and too varied in its viewpoints, to provide a basis for the aggressive leadership needed to cope with the urgent immediate problems stressed in this paper and the creation of a new international economic structure.

Thus one must seriously ponder the need for, and possibilities of, economic bigemony by the USA and FRG. It would of course be characterized publicly in much softer terms, if acknowledged at all. But the needs are urgent—and no one else can take the lead.

Notes

1. "Bigemony": an hegemony of two. The term is intended to be a bit weaker than "condominium," but much stronger than "partnership."

2. The mark zone is usually called the "European snake" or "European Monetary Union" (EMU), and portrayed as a Common Market operation, presumably for political and cosmetic reasons. The absence from the arrangement, almost from its outset, of three EEC countries (including Italy and the U.K.), and the inclusion from the outset of four non-EC countries (Norway, Sweden, Austria, Switzerland de facto) made

clear that the binding tie was dependence on the German economy rather than membership in the Common Market.

3. The OPEC countries, despite their burgeoning reserves, are not key currency candidates. The criteria for achieving and maintaining such a position are analyzed in detail in C. Fred Bergsten, *The Dilemmas of the Dollar: The Economics and Politics of United States International Monetary Policy* (New York: Council on Foreign Relations, forthcoming 1975).

4. The OPEC countries are of course also major creditors, but their policy attitudes and lack of expertise rule out their playing the kind of international economic role discussed in this paper.

5. Except for the satellite members of the mark zone, which have imported relative price stability from Germany and thus are best grouped with it for this purpose.

6. The European Community *as a group* is sometimes viewed as the potential bigemonial partner of the United States. However, the EC is not an effective decision-making entity on most issues, especially in the shorter run. Moreover, it has been retrogressing rather significantly in recent years rather than progressing; for an analysis, see C. Fred Bergsten, "Die Zukunft der atlantischen Welt. Ein Betrag aus amerikanischer Sicht," *Europa-Archiv* No. 16/1974 [Chapter 21 in this volume (in English)]. The EC can be very important in translating USA-FRG bigemony into global policy, however, as indicated in the next section.

6a. See C. Fred Bergsten, "The New Era in World Commodity Markets," *Challenge*, Sept./Oct. 1974 [Chapter 18 in this volume].

7. For an analysis of export controls and proposals for new international rules to retrain them see C. Fred Bergsten, *Completing the GATT: Toward New International Rules to Govern Export Controls* (Washington: British North American Committee, Oct. 1974) [Chapter 10 in this volume].

8. For an analysis of that problem see C. Fred Bergsten, "Coming Investment Wars?" *Foreign Affairs*, October 1974 [Chapter 16 in this volume].

9. See the articles by Senator Adlai Stevenson III and George Quester in the October 1974 issue of *Foreign Affairs*.

10. It is possible that the dollar or the mark, or both, might depreciate against other major currencies in such a scenario. This would depend on capital flows, however, and both long-term and short-term money might offset any deterioration in their current accounts due to, respectively, the more rapid growth rates and key currency status of both the USA and FRG.

11. For a detailed proposal, which includes Japan as well as the USA and FRG, see Ronald I. McKinnon, "A New Tripartite Monetary Agreement or a Limping Dollar Standard?" unpublished manuscript.

12. See C. Fred Bergsten, "The Threat From the Third World," *Foreign Policy* 11 (Summer 1973) [chapter 27 in this volume] and "The Response to the Third World," *Foreign Policy* 17 (Winter 1974-75) [chapter 28 in this volume].

24

European Monetary Unification and U.S. Foreign Policy

Both the process of European monetary unification and the eventual achievement of European Monetary Union (EMU) can have a major impact on U.S. foreign policy through their effects on domestic politics in the United States. In turn, U.S. policy can significantly affect the evolution of EMU by affecting policy attitudes within Europe. My comments will focus on the close relationships between these two sets of "domestic" politics.

EMU is the third major functional phase of European integration—the first was the creation of the customs union (CXT, for the common external tariff which best symbolizes it); the second was the creation of the common agricultural policy (CAP). The discrimination of the CXT could have seriously upset U.S.-European relations, by making American industry and labor more protectionist. But the U.S. responded positively by passing the Trade Expansion Act and proposing the Kennedy Round, and by investing heavily behind the new tariff wall, and Europe replied in kind by negotiating the Round to a successful conclusion and avoiding restriction of American investment. The CAP has seriously upset U.S.-European relations, however, by undermining the crucial support of the U.S. farm community for a liberal U.S. trade policy and (along with the European Community's preferential arrangements) by cooling U.S. enthusiasm for European unification itself by signaling Europe's disregard for the interests of outsiders. This has happened because the United States rejected the Community's offer to limit increases in its agricultural supports (the *montant de soutien* or MDS proposal) in the Kennedy Round, and because the Community has obstinately continued to expand the CAP and the preferential arrangements despite increasingly shrill American and other protests. The basic question in assessing the broad foreign policy effect of EMU is whether it will follow the CXT or CAP precedents.

It is virtually certain that major economic conflict between Europe and America would decisively undercut the ability of any U.S. administration to maintain any significant (let alone the present) level of U.S. troops in Europe.[1] Senator Mike Mansfield bizarrely saw the monetary crisis of May 1971 as an "attack on the dollar," and used it in the Senate to mobilize support for legislation requiring an immediate 50 percent cut in those

Prepared for a conference in September 1972 on European Monetary Unification and its Meaning for the United States and published in Lawrence B. Krause and Walter S. Salant, eds., *European Monetary Unification and its Meaning for the United States* (Washington: Brookings Institution, 1973), pp. 286-92.

troops. He lost by only eight votes, and only after the most intensive lobbying carried out by the Nixon administration on any single issue. Pressures for cuts in the defense budget, especially abroad, are already very severe. U.S. economic interests that would be hurt by U.S.-European economic conflict would surely seek to retaliate on issues of security, even if the administration were wise enough not to try to use its leverage on those issues to extract economic concessions, as Nye suggests it might. Such a result would obviously have a major impact on overall U.S. foreign policy.[2] The broad foreign policy costs of economic conflict were, of course, also demonstrated vividly in late 1971, when British Prime Minister Edward Heath refused to meet President Nixon to discuss the President's forthcoming trips to Peking and Moscow until the United States called a meeting of the Group of Ten (which took place in Rome) to negotiate a solution to the deepening international economic crisis.

The flash point is trade (and perhaps investment), not money. Wilbur Mills told *Der Spiegel* in fall 1972 that he could move the Burke-Hartke bill through Congress "tomorrow," if he wished. Allowing for political hyperbole on the part of Chairman Mills, it remains true that protectionist pressures now run exceedingly deep in U.S. politics, and that the process of trade deliberalization which has been accelerating since at least 1967 will accelerate even further and faster if new liberalizing trade negotiations do not begin soon.[3]

Here enters the link to EMU. A major trade negotiation is unlikely to be launched unless negotiations toward fundamental monetary reform are already under way, both because Europe quite properly wants America to play by some (presumably new) monetary rules if Europe is going to play by the trade rules, and because America also wants to be assured of an effective adjustment process before increasing still further the scope for international economic interpenetration. Indeed, the avoidance of renewed disequilibrium in the exchange rate of the dollar is a sine qua non of the avoidance of serious protectionism in the United States.

EMU could thus play a decisive role in avoiding major problems for U.S.-European relations if it expedited reform of the international monetary system—or it could play a decisive role in generating such problems if it impeded such reform. (The United States itself must of course play a constructive role in achieving monetary reform; European cooperation is a necessary but by no means sufficient condition. Here I wish to treat EMU as *the* independent variable, however, so I assume a constructive U.S. role.) It will thus have a major effect on U.S. foreign policy over the next few years.

Unfortunately, there is at least a strong possibility that the process of reaching monetary union in Europe will impede progress toward global monetary reform. Many Europeans want to move first on EMU, deferring global reform talks for at least several years, because they feel that its success will greatly enhance their bargaining position on global reform and that they will be able to take a stronger position on global monetary reform if they know its shape much more precisely.[4] This could provide decisive support for the views of the majority of European trade officials, who have little understanding of the political need to heed the U.S. call for early and meaningful trade negotiations (see the Rey Report),[5] and the majority of European, especially Community, bureaucrats, who boggle at the thought of simultaneous negotiations on EMU and global reform.

Indeed, EMU *without* global reform would not merely inhibit progress; it would almost certainly make the global monetary problem much worse. EMU promotes the international use of national currencies within the Community, as the members intervene in each other's currencies, for *both* intervention and reserve purposes.[6] But history demonstrates quite clearly the dynamic spread of key currencies once they are in circulation, and how, after that, they develop their own momentum. It can confidently be predicted that these currencies will be widely used—for both vehicle and reserve purposes—*outside* the Community as well, in the absence of negotiated reform that provides for *international* regulation of world liquidity.[7] Indeed, the data suggest that such developments are already widespread. Most EC countries say that they oppose extra-Community use of their currencies, but they are powerless to stop it in view of the Eurocurrency markets. Moreover, some do not really oppose it, viewing the expansion as one route to greater "equality with the dollar" and hence an improvement of their own bargaining position. The result would be a multiple reserve currency standard, which was seriously studied a decade ago and rejected by virtually all observers as highly unstable and the worst possible approach to monetary reform.[8] In addition, as Richard Cooper points out in his paper, U.S.-European rivalry for key currency supremacy could replicate the U.S.-British rivalry of the interwar period and exacerbate both the economic and foreign policy difficulties which would already be extremely serious.

The adjustment results could be even worse. If EMU prevented global reform, it would probably assure the further proliferation of controls over international transactions and unregulated exchange rate changes. Both would provide juicy temptations to mercantilist approaches in both Europe and America, as indeed they already have. This, in turn, would promote the highly undesirable foreign policy trends described above, as indeed it already has. Corden argues persuasively in his Princeton essay that EMU would lead to EC immobilism on global exchange rate issues, because the conflicting needs of its members will be impossible to reconcile.[9] Hence, Europe would probably not contribute to constructive exchange rate changes in the absence of new presumptive rules and an international institutional framework through which they were implemented.[10] Yet EMU would itself increase the need for adjustment reform by enabling Europe better to withstand monetary pressures from the United States, as Cooper points out in his paper.

In view of the major political and economic interests of the United States in avoiding such developments, and the serious risk that they may in fact develop, the United States has two major concerns about EMU: that its development not impede early movement toward global monetary reform, and that its eventual shape be compatible with a more viable global system. Both steps call for a major U.S. initiative toward constructive global reform at the earliest possible date.

U.S. pressure for global reform will *help* Europe achieve EMU by forcing decisions on its external manifestations which will in turn force decisions on its internal aspects. U.S. pressure for the Kennedy Round helped Europe achieve its CXT and CAP, and the absence of early U.S. pressure, or even response to the MDS proposal, let European agriculture develop in a manner which carries exceedingly high costs for most Europeans. There are no internal pressures sufficiently strong to force reconciliation within the EC of the sharp conflicts among its members on EMU issues. Indeed, external pressure for global monetary reform is the *only* force likely to do so.

But this external force must be applied in the proper way, and toward the proper ends. Much of the development of EMU so far is in *defensive* response to uncooperative pressures from the United States: massive dollar flows into Europe, efforts to preserve the key currency role of the dollar far beyond what is possible or needed in the 1970s and beyond, gyrations between "benign neglect" and Connally-style confrontation. To be sure, the United States could probably push EMU further by more such uncooperative pressures: by elimination of its present capital controls, more "benign neglect" coupled with obvious efforts to keep the world on an inconvertible dollar standard by evading global reform, and the like.[11] But recent history strongly suggests that this kind of U.S. approach could tilt the intra-EC debate in favor of the French model, based on controls and rigid parities, instead of the German model, whose focus on liberal trade and payments and greater flexibility of exchange rates is far more compatible with U.S. national interests.[12] The history of the negotiations on Special Drawing Rights is an instructive parallel, where active U.S. pursuit of an objective shared by most of the Six tilted the balance against France and achieved a result which served both global and American interests.

There is thus a strong foreign-policy, as well as economic, case for an urgent U.S. initiative on constructive international monetary reform. It is clear that the United States should not be dissuaded from seizing the initiative—as it was in 1970—by pleas from some Europeans to "wait until

EMU is on the track." Fortunately, the kind of reform which would maximize U.S. interests—greater flexibility of parities in response to presumptive rules with international sanctions to back them up, much wider margins, annual injections of sufficient amounts of SDRs, a special issue of SDRs to consolidate any present reserves held in undesired forms (including the "dollar overhang"), dramatic expansion of the quantity and quality of the swap network to recycle liquid capital flows—is compatible with the existence of either EMU or separate European participants.[13] It is incompatible only with further delay. Instead of resisting U.S. pressure for monetary reform, Europe should thus welcome it as promoting both its own internal and external policy objectives.

Notes

1. I focus on the troop level because it is the most obvious manifestation of the U.S.-European political relationship. However, the analysis applies to the entirety of that relationship.

2. I do not argue that the present (or any particular) level of U.S. troops in Europe is optimum. I do argue that their precipitate withdrawal would be highly destabilizing to world politics, and that *any* withdrawal in reaction to economic conflict—which could imply that, on security grounds, they were still needed—would have a similar effect.

3. For a detailed analysis, which holds with at least as much strength now as when it was written, see C. Fred Bergsten, "Crisis in U.S. Trade Policy," *Foreign Affairs,* Vol. 49 (July 1971) [chapter 12 in this volume].

4. I argue below that EMU is *least* likely to succeed under this scenario, despite the opposite views (or hopes) of many Europeans, because it would then lack the external pressures which are probably needed to push its members to the crucial decisions which they must make.

5. Organization for Economic Co-operation and Development, *Policy Perspectives for International Trade and Economic Relations,* A Report of the High Level Group on Trade and Related Problems, Jean Rey, chairman (OECD, 1972).

6. For example, Governor Guido Carli stated in the 1972 Annual Report of the Bank of Italy that he aimed to hold 20 percent of his reserves—$1.0 billion to $1.5 billion at that time—in other EC currencies.

7. I disagree with Richard Cooper's paper in Krause, L.B., and Salant, W.S., eds., *European Monetary Unification and Its Meaning for the United States* (Washington: Brookings Institution, 1973) on two related points. A unified European currency *would* play a larger world role than the sum of the individual European currencies, and thus might well "influence

the outcome" of whether an SDR standard eventuates. And *either* a common European currency or the sum of the individual European currencies will play a much larger role relative to the dollar than the latter do now.

8. For a much more detailed analysis, see C. Fred Bergsten, *Reforming the Dollar: An International Monetary Policy for the United States,* Council Papers on International Affairs: 2 (Council on Foreign Relations, 1972), esp. pp. 5-13 [chapter 4 in this volume].

9. W. M. Corden, *Monetary Integration,* Essays in International Finance 93 (Princeton University, International Finance Section, 1972).

10. This probability also strengthens the case for an active U.S. parity policy to make the new regime work. The basic case for such a policy, involving the "triple comparative advantage" of the United States in initiating parity changes, is developed in C. Fred Bergsten, *Reforming the Dollar: An International Monetary Policy for the United States,* Council Papers on International Affairs: 2(Council on Foreign Relations, 1972), pp. 39-41.

11. Some European economists, for example, Rinaldo Ossola, have argued that such a U.S. approach would destroy rather than promote EMU. I am dubious, in view of the political commitment of all EC countries to the idea; however, it might reduce EMU simply to negative immobilism which would block all constructive global reform. In any event, the effects on U.S. foreign policy of either destroying EMU or rendering it impotent are highly undesirable—unless we were to place achievement of a dollar standard very high on our list of international priorities.

12. Overt U.S. opposition to EMU would be even more certain to do so, as Trezise points out in his paper in Krause and Salant, eds., *op cit.*

13. For details, see C. Fred Bergsten, *Reforming the Dollar*, pp. 48-95.

25 The New Economics and U.S. Foreign Policy

In the summer of 1971, President Nixon and Secretary Connally revolutionized U.S. foreign economic policy. In so doing, they promoted a protectionist trend which raises questions about the future of the U.S. economy at least as fundamental as those raised by the abrupt adoption of wage-price controls. In so doing, they have also encouraged a disastrous isolationist trend which raises questions about the future of U.S. foreign policy at least as fundamental as those raised by the President's essentially positive and decidedly non-isolationist China initiative, Vietnam policy and negotiations with the Soviet Union. Both the U.S. economy and U.S. foreign policy for the relevant future hang in the balance.

The President decided to seek a massive improvement in the U.S. balance of payments—substituting aggressive concern for our largely "benign neglect" posture toward the deficits of the last decade. He terminated the convertibility of the dollar, shattering the linchpin of the entire international monetary system—on whose smooth functioning the world economy depends. He imposed an import surcharge, proposed both the most sweeping U.S. export subsidy in history and discrimination against foreign machinery by making it ineligible for the Job Development Credit, bludgeoned East Asia into a "voluntary" restraint agreement on textiles, and sought to extend and tighten the existing "voluntary" agreement on steel—completely reversing the traditional position of U.S. administrations in resisting protectionism and leading the world toward ever freer trade. He abandoned the essential Executive role as protector of foreign aid and joined the competition to gain domestic political credit for cutting it, contributing directly to the near-scuttling of the entire aid program in the Senate just two months later. He violated the letter and the spirit of the reigning international law in both the monetary and trade fields, reversing the traditional American role of leading the effort to strengthen the rules governing global conduct.

Most Americans, and many foreigners, can support the broad objectives enunciated by the Administration. The world economic roles of America must be reconciled with the growth to power of Europe and Japan. There must be fundamental reform of the international monetary system. There must be renewed efforts to reduce world trade barriers. The underly-

Originally appeared in *Foreign Affairs*, January 1972, pp. 199-222 (written in November 1971).

ing U.S. balance of payments has deteriorated. The yen had to be sharply revalued.

But the new foreign economic policy went much too far. It set impossible objectives, both quantitatively and qualitatively. It has been alternately pursued with violent hyperbole and supreme indifference. It appears based on some totally erroneous, and exceedingly dangerous, theory that the United States has played Santa Claus to the world for the last 25 years. It is wrong for the American economy, for it risks immediate losses of jobs and investments, as well as long-term insulation from the indispensable impulses of global competition. It courts disaster for U.S. global interests, as spelled out below. It has suffered from the American tradition of waiting too long to act, then lunging unpredictably from one extreme to the other, instead of proceeding deliberately to a new equilibrium. Its dangers increase exponentially as time passes with no resolution of at least the issues of immediate urgency which it has raised. Quick action is needed, by the United States and major foreign countries, to avoid the most serious breach in the world economy and international politics since World War II. The signs of progress in early December toward resolving some of the immediate issues are thus highly welcome.

II

The international component of the New Economic Policy was wholly unnecessary.

To be sure, America was running a large balance-of-payments deficit. The deficit was due primarily, however, to the huge international movements of liquid capital which are so prevalent in today's world economy. Such capital had moved massively out of the United States since early 1970, when U.S. interest rates declined at record speed and Europe persevered in its effort to fight inflation by maintaining tight money. It could be expected to move back to the United States just as massively when the interest rate differentials narrowed again. Indeed, precisely such inflows to the United States occurred in both 1966 and 1968-69, causing large U.S. payments *surpluses* and forcing Germany to *sell* us gold to help meet the resulting dollar *shortage*. Deficits caused by such transitory events hardly call for the counter-measures of last August.

In addition, private speculation entered the picture twice: in favor of the German mark in May, and against the dollar in late July. The floating of the mark ended the first episode. The second was due primarily to the hugely inflationary wage settlements of the summer in steel and several other key U.S. industries, and resultant fears that the United States had not only lost the battle against inflation but given up trying to fight it. This reminded us that a stable and dynamic U.S. domestic economy is the key to a sound American external financial position and world confidence in the dollar. The freeze, its successor stabilization program, and proper monetary and fiscal policies were thus the proper antidote for "the international money speculators" as well as for domestic inflation per se.

It is highly significant that there are as yet no reports that foreign holders of dollars had lost their cool before August 15th, and demanded sizable amounts of U.S. gold. There is little evidence that they would have done so at any later time which might have proved more politically embarrassing to the present Administration. Even the existence of such a risk, however, would have justified at most the suspension of gold convertibility—not the panoply of protectionist trade and isolationist aid measures which accompanied it.

Inflation, past and present, had of course eroded the international competitive position of the United States. However, structural changes in both the U.S. economy and external position have sharply reduced the size of the trade surplus needed for overall U.S. payments equilibrium since the trade surplus high of $6.8 billion in 1964. Annual income on our foreign investments has risen by over $6 billion, foreign long-term investment in the United States has risen by several billion dollars per year, and foreign capital markets are able to take a large part of the load borne almost solely by the United States at that time. All these trends continue to move in our favor. Overseas military expenditures and U.S. interest payments to foreigners have risen significantly since 1964, but both are coming down as we withdraw from Vietnam, dollars flow back to the United States, and our interest rates decline. Tourist spending and outflows of U.S. private capital have continued to rise, but not nearly enough to require a return to the 1964 level of trade surplus to achieve overall payments equilibrium.

The bulk of the deterioration in the U.S. trade surplus in early 1971 was in fact due to purely temporary factors, and our long-term shift was fully mirrored in the improved positions of just three countries: Japan, Germany and Canada. Remedial action was called for—and was already taking place. The mark was revalued by 9 percent in late 1969, and had moved upward another 8 percent since being floated in May 1971. The Canadian dollar had floated up by 8 percent since May 1970. In addition, the Netherlands, Switzerland and Austria had appreciated their currencies by smaller amounts. The full payments effects of exchange-rate changes take at least two years to appear, but the process of adjustment was underway well before August.

There did remain one big exchange-rate problem: Japan. Much of the blame for the present turmoil must be laid on its doorstep, although the standard U.S. perception of Japan today over-estimates by far both its competitive invincibility and the real trade effects of its remaining controls.

In addition, the greatest tragedy of the U.S. textile effort is that it absorbed virtually all of the attention of the two governments in their economic relations from early 1969 though mid-1971. The exchange rate and overall trade policy issues, with their much wider effects, were permitted to fester unattended. The U.S. government apparently made no serious effort before August to get Japan to meet its international economic responsibilities, though the United States demonstrated shortly thereafter—on textiles —that it was willing to apply great leverage to achieve objectives deemed of truly great importance.

Finally, political pressure was certainly mounting for protectionist trade legislation.[1] The New Economic Policy would help preëmpt a quota bill if it brings a prosperous domestic economy, reduced inflation, a significant exchange-rate realignment and greater flexibility of exchange rates, and a new credibility for administration toughness in negotiating U.S. foreign economic policy. However, except for Japan, the major exchange rates had already moved. There had been no major effort to negotiate a yen revaluation, or the needed changes in the monetary system. Negotiating credibility in trade matters could have been achieved at any time by the adoption of specific retaliatory measures against any foreign barriers which were illegally restricting U.S. exports. The Administration has announced no progress whatsoever in developing a new adjustment assistance program to cushion the domestic effects of freer trade, one crucial element in restoring a progressive trade policy. No effort to build the needed new coalition of political constituencies, to combat the concentrated push of organized labor, can be observed. The import surcharge, the other trade moves, and the rhetoric accompanying the whole effort actually foster domestic and foreign protectionism. So the new international policy is hard to justify on these grounds as well, except as an admission of total neglect in seeking similar ends through far less risky means.

There are only two plausible interpretations of the real rationale behind the international component of August 15th, aside from simple error or misjudgment. The first is that it represents a straightforward effort to export U.S. unemployment to other countries. Unemployment is our cardinal domestic problem at the moment, but exporting it to others is unacceptable in principle and cannot possibly work anyway. Indeed, precisely such an effort contributed mightily to throwing the world into its deepest depression in modern history. It is fully legitimate, of course, to seek adequate trade improvement to achieve the needed payments position. Seeking sufficient trade improvement to achieve a huge payments surplus is illegitimate, however, and the Administration target of a $13 billion swing would do just that. Seeking sufficient trade improvement to permit sharply increased U.S. capital outflows, in effect changing the structure of our balance of payments, is also unacceptable to such unlikely allies as the

AFL-CIO and the Common Market. So the excesses of the present approach connote pure mercantilism at its worst, and belie the reasonableness of its broad objectives.

The second interpretation is that the Administration concluded that the United States needs a large trade surplus to maintain its international political power. This view is true only to the extent that a surplus is needed to support a liberal trade policy, which does carry considerable political weight though making little economic sense. Such a conclusion ignores all of the empirical evidence, however: Britain was in trade surplus in only four years of the century of the Pax Brittanica, and the U.S. world role well survived the sharp decline in our trade balance in the late 1950s. In fact, a "weak" payments position has on balance promoted U.S. international objectives heretofore; at most, an equilibrium *payments* position is needed to underpin a continued active world role for the United States.

III

The New Economic Policy could produce dramatic improvements in the international monetary and trading systems, and deserves unstinting support toward those ends. But it is an extremely high-risk strategy, and could lead instead to extremely damaging effects on national economies around the globe.

The policy could easily lead to the first real international trade war since the 1930s. The surcharge and discrimination of the Job Development Credit are already having an addictive effect domestically, and will be increasingly difficult to lift as individual industries become accustomed to their protection. The arithmetic is simple: an industry now protected by the ten percent surcharge plus a ten percent appreciation of the yen will not want to swap the combination for a 12 to 18 percent yen revaluation, especially if it is now helped by the "Buy America" rule as well. And the textile and steel deals, while they may reduce the zeal with which these industries seek quotas themselves, legitimize protection for others on "equity" grounds.

The difficulty is compounded by the domestic politics of U.S. trade policy. The AFL-CIO has already begun to rally support behind the incredibly protectionist legislation which it will seek in 1972. Since organized labor has made trade and foreign investment one of its top priority issues, both parties will be sorely tempted to support such legislation at least partially in the coming election campaign—as they woo the huge labor vote, which is less committed now to either of the two major parties than in any presidential election since World War II. If the surcharge is still in effect when labor begins to push, then its permanent retention will look to many like a moderate compromise. The President himself presaged such a comparison last August, when he asserted that the surcharge was superior to import quotas—a true statement about a false choice, since no one was even thinking of trying to pass a quota bill in 1971. The only possible reconciliation is that he foresaw the surcharge as much more permanent than was implied at that time, a reading which was reinforced by his own press conference statement of September 15th. The continued retention of the surcharge, when the floats have already produced most of the needed revaluations—despite the fact that the surcharge itself brakes them—adds to the fear that it is being turned from a temporary negotiating lever and payments adjustment measure into a permanent protectionist device.

The surcharge, even on its avowedly temporary basis, has already begun to produce emulation and reaction abroad. It could not help but do so, since it directly affects jobs throughout the world. Canada, which reacts first to U.S. economic moves but often accurately forecasts countermeasures elsewhere, moved quickly to provide domestic subsidies to its exporters hurt by the move. Denmark cited President Nixon by name in justifying its own adoption of an import surcharge. Japan will probably slow its trade liberalization. The DISC export subsidy,[2] if authorized by law, will certainly be emulated. And retaliation does not require overt import restrictions abroad: quiet pressures by European governments could seriously disrupt the activities and profits of the European subsidiaries of U.S. corporations, and Japan's quasi-public purchasing agencies could sharply reduce their purchases of U.S. farm goods. If the U.S. surcharge came to be seen as a permanent feature of the international landscape, retaliation and emulation would be swift and certain, if not always open and obvious.

Beside such specific effects, the whole debate has been shifted by the Administration's moves and rhetoric. Exporting unemployment has been sanctioned. The President himself has made protectionism respectable, whereas he had previously deviated from the principles of liberal trade only for textiles, for well-understood if deplorable reasons. The broad message to Congress and the public is that the Executive, by far the most powerful—and sometimes the only—bastion against protectionism in the United States, has also switched sides.

The potential effects of this switch are magnified enormously by the vast expansion of presidential legal power to act in the trade field implied by the recent acts. Was the surcharge legal? Most lawyers had always thought it would require congressional action. Was it legal, not to mention judicious, to invoke the Trading With the Enemy Act as authority to apply textile quotas against Japan unilaterally and thus force it to "voluntary restraint"? Was it not ludicrous to call the balance-of-payments situation a "national emergency" sufficient to justify invoking that Act, when the deficit at its peak amounted to less than one percent of our gross national product and when the textile effort began more than two years earlier when our payments were in large surplus? Such an expansion of executive power will obviously create domestic political pressures to use it again and foreigners will fear that it will be precisely so used.

Continuation of the status quo threatens the world economy through monetary as well as trade effects. Truly floating exchange rates would help solve international economic problems, but the present array of "dirty floats" could seriously exacerbate them. Individual countries will be increasingly subjected to domestic pressures to reduce the appreciation of their rates or even to depreciate them against the dollar, to regain competitive advantage, and most have already acted in precisely this direction. The wholesale destruction of the international rules governing exchange-rate changes, completed by the suspension of dollar convertibility, makes this one of the easiest means to "retaliate" against the U.S. protectionist devices. We, of course, triggered the "dirty floats" ourselves, by coupling the surcharge with our suspension of convertibility. Trade wars could become full economic wars, precisely as they did under similar international conditions in the 1930s.

These reactions to such a U.S. policy could have been expected at any time. But they come at a particularly dangerous moment because of the poor economic outlook in numerous key countries: unemployment is higher in Canada than in the United States and higher relative to historical norms in Britain; much of Europe is in or headed toward recession, and Japan has experienced a sharp slowdown. The danger is particularly acute because of the uncertain economic outlook in our country, and the consequent tremendous pressure on the Administration to show results, especially in reducing unemployment, in time for the 1972 election—results whose popularity would hardly be diminished, in this period of rising isolationism, if they were achieved partially at the expense of foreigners. Aside from the principles involved, this is the worst time in the postwar period to risk such an effort—and it is hard to believe that the week-enders of Camp David would have tried it had they considered the world, rather than just the American, economy.

The uncertain outlook for the world economy heightens the need for precisely the opposite approach to foreign economic policy, both here and abroad. Mercantilist efforts to achieve full employment at the expense of others are doomed to fail, because domestic politics in all countries assure that all will play the same game. In fact, such efforts are counterproductive in meeting today's economic dilemma, because they foster inefficiency and monopoly and hence exacerbate inflation. The only effective economic policy approach is to use domestic fiscal and monetary policies to restore and maintain full employment; institute an effective balance-of-payments adjustment mechanism so that such policies will not produce intolerable external financial difficulties; and develop effective income policies and other selective measures, including maximum *liberalization* of world trade, to restrain inflation. A throwback to trade restrictions and competitive depreciations would lead just where they did once before—toward a world depression. And it would make it impossible to agree on new exchange rates, the only way to really improve the U.S. balance of payments and increase U.S. jobs.

IV

These economic effects would have a disastrous impact on U.S. foreign policy, and on our own national security.

Continuation of our military commitments to NATO have already been undermined by xenophobic rhetoric, and a tough European reaction to our moves would add dramatically to existing congressional disenchantment with present force levels. Incredibly, the Administration has contributed directly to such sentiment by again demanding better "burden-sharing," after having apparently cooled the issue less than a year earlier, and after rallying the entire foreign policy community to help defeat the Mansfield Amendment only a few months ago.

Such a reduction in the credibility of U.S. military support for Europe would threaten Chancellor Brandt's *Ostpolitik* in the short run, and push Germany toward either accommodation with Moscow or extreme nationalism over the long run. It would push all Europe toward neutralism by strengthening neo-Gaullists within all major countries there and by creating an anti-American attitude which would render pragmatic problem-solving across the Atlantic increasingly difficult. The evolution of the Common Market could easily take on a distinctly anti-American flavor, self-fulfilling the prophecies of those who have always viewed it as counter to U.S. interests and thus pitting the United States against one of the dominant political drives in Europe—now including Britain, perhaps our closest ally. It would become almost impossible for us to do business constructively with Europe in such an atmosphere, on the whole range of issues where we interact daily, from trade and investment themselves to nuclear cooperation and allied defense.

Japan, the key influence in Asia for at least decades to come, has been badly shaken internally and has already begun to reconsider whether her whole national policy should continue to be based overridingly on close ties to the United States. Canada is making the same reappraisal, though it has little alternative. The less-developed countries, which were given favored treatment under all major balance-of-payments measures previously taken by the United States, were singled out for adverse treatment—the aid cut, the new trade barriers to their most dynamic export industries, demolition

359

of any possibility of U.S. trade preferences in the foreseeable future, new uncertainties to cloud their development efforts. Even worse politically, they have no control at all over the unfolding events; they will continue to face the surcharge until the industrialized countries reach a negotiated settlement. It is no surprise that these countries see August 15th, and the subsequent events which it triggered, as further confirmation that the United States has copped out of helping them with the problems which they deem most important to their national futures. No area of the non-communist world is left unscathed by the new approach, which ignores domestic politics abroad as fully as it now caters to domestic politics at home.

Indeed, America is now pursuing two separate and contradictory foreign policies. This comes as no surprise to students of bureaucratic politics, since different people are obviously running each. But the new economic approach, coupled with the coming presidential visits to Peking and Moscow, produce the most bizarre U.S. foreign policy imaginable: war on our friends, concessions to our traditional adversaries. Even within the economic area itself, the Administration has achieved the desirable objective of moving the communist countries toward most-favored-nation treatment by the highly undesirable method of raising our duties toward everyone else. This dual policy is doubly dangerous at this time, as the new overtures have already made our friends extremely nervous—witness Japan regarding Peking, and Europe regarding the Strategic Arms Limitation Talks (SALT)—and thus heightened, not relieved, the need to take their sensitivities fully into account.

It is ludicrous for the United States to call for a new sharing of responsibility among allies, and then unilaterally unleash a bombshell which both upsets such cooperation directly and makes it more difficult, economically and thus politically, for others to contribute. Or to call for an era of greater equality among allies, and then to seek to dictate terms of settlement on the central internal political issues of others. Or to call for a liberal trading and payments system, and then break all the rules and seek to export unemployment. Or to mount a massive campaign to defeat the Mansfield Amendment and cool the burden-sharing issue, and then to provide new ammunition for the next Mansfield attempt by stridently accusing Europe of not pulling its weight. Or to call for an era of consultation, and then use public rhetoric to impugn both the motives and policies of others. Or to refer to aid as a central component of the Nixon Doctrine, and then pull the rug from under it. Or to deplore abrupt shifts in policy as unsettling, and then reverse course overnight on every fundamental aspect of foreign economic policy.

Even those who argue that the United States "would win a trade war" admit that this means only that we would lose less in economic terms than would others. Some say this is enough to deter others from lashing back, especially when they consider their reliance on the United States in security terms as well. But such restraint is almost inconceivable in major countries with self respect in today's global mood of virulent nationalism, particularly given the pressure on their leaders to respond with at least verbal toughness and thus constrain their future actions just as the tough U.S. rhetoric constrains ours.

In the short run, it is unclear which foreign policy will prevail. Protectionist economics mean isolationist politics, and vice-versa, and it is extremely doubtful that an outward-looking military and political policy can coexist for long with an inward-looking foreign economic policy. Short-term U.S. politics appear to pull in the protectionist direction at this point, but it is hard to imagine that losses of farm exports, curtailment of the overseas activities of U.S. firms, a stock market depressed in part by fears of a trade war, and deep rifts with our closest allies would produce a very impressive score even on this narrow criterion.

Even if the existing pattern of relations survives these immediate dangers, the New Economic Policy has raised fundamental questions for U.S. foreign policy over the longer term. Has the United States turned basically isolationist? Or will we be able to accommodate ourselves constructively to our reduced power position in the world economy? Has the executive branch finally given up the battle to keep isolationism at bay? Will we begin to use the leverage of our military and political position to achieve economic objectives, reversing the mode of the past when economic programs were used as much to promote our security objectives as to improve American economic welfare? Would other countries succumb to such U.S. pressure, or simply jettison our political support and hence permit wreckage of the postwar alliance system? Will we abandon the effort to preserve an open political system outside the communist world, or support the economic trends toward bloc creation and move consciously toward geographic spheres of political influence?

One specific issue will be our international monetary policy. From World War II to August 15, 1971, the United States was largely passive with respect to any deficits in its balance of payments. These deficits were of great importance in supporting postwar reconstruction in Europe and Japan, economic development everywhere, a steady trend toward trade and payments liberalization, and the avoidance of major political frictions deriving from economic conflict. Our payments deficits were an economic umbrella for the rest of the world similar to the defense umbrella provided by our nuclear deterrent—except that the economic umbrella modestly improved the economic welfare of the American people, by permitting us to consume real resources from abroad and accumulate foreign assets, while the nuclear umbrella cost us substantial sums of money. To be sure, U.S.

deficits are no longer needed for some of these purposes; for example, the invention of Special Drawing Rights (SDRs) means that the world need no longer rely on U.S. deficits to create new dollar reserves and thus avoid a new cross of gold on which economic growth might founder. But the continuing growth of private demand for dollars around the world, and demand from monetary authorities to build at least their dollar working balances, means that equilibrium in the U.S. balance of payments will equate with a moderate deficit on any of the standard accounting definitions.

It is even dubious that a "strong" U.S. balance of payments would provide a sounder basis for a proper U.S. foreign policy than the "weak" balance of payments of the past, as the Administration asserts. An active, even if not aggressive, U.S. balance-of-payments policy would completely change the basic foundations on which the world economy rests. The essentially mercantilist external financial objectives of most of the other major countries are already incompatible with each other, and have been met even partially only through U.S. acquiescence. Such acquiescence makes sense from both the U.S. and global standpoints, since we are at once the biggest single factor in the world economy and the least dependent of any nation on trade. Adoption of similar mercantilist objectives by America could make the global economic system unworkable, since no other country can or will take our place as the balancer. Other countries will have to adjust their economic thinking and behavior no less radically than those small countries in East Asia which must adjust their security thinking to U.S. withdrawals and the Nixon Doctrine. For the future, only an effectively internationalized monetary and trading system could provide the basis for a viable world economy without U.S. stewardship. We turn now to what that world might look like, and how to get there.

V

The first requirement is for America and the other major countries to assess their priorities among the wide range of issues which have been raised. For reasons already stated, early elimination of the U.S. surcharge and the related "Buy America" credit are the most important immediate targets. The United States must thus clarify what it wants in return and present its proposals to others, and the foreign response must be adequate.

Our more fundamental objective, however, must be basic reform of the international monetary system to avoid in the future the errors of the crisis-prone past and to provide the foundation for a second generation of postwar prosperity. The system needs more effective means of adjusting national payments imbalances through greater flexibility of exchange rates in order to avoid the build-up of large disequilibria including our own. It needs ways of regulating the growth of international money without excessive reliance on the dollar, and hence excessive economic and political risks for the United States, which means new reliance on Special Drawing Rights. These issues are extremely complex, and will take time to work out. A two-stage approach is called for, with the surcharge removed in the first stage and basic reform achieved in the second.

Fortunately, both the short-term and long-term needs point to a single major ingredient for the first stage: an adequate realignment of national exchange rates. On August 15th, the President made such a realignment the sole condition for removal of the surcharge, and we should abandon the new "Buy America" discrimination and the DISC export subsidy as well if we could get larger revaluations in return. Indeed, this is the only way the United States can achieve a sizable sustained improvement in the U.S. balance of payments and an increase in U.S. jobs from rebuilding our trade surplus. Realignment is also a necessary prerequisite for more basic monetary reform, since no country will agree to new rules unless it knows the starting points for all countries and since a régime of greater flexibility of exchange rates can begin smoothly only if rates are near equilibrium at the outset. Fortunately, most countries have already floated their exchange rates close to the new levels which they need to find. Widening the margins within which rates would fluctuate around the new parities, to at least three percent on either side compared with the 0.75 percent which prevailed in most countries prior to August 15th, would provide for the inevitable margin of error in setting new rates.

The second U.S. and foreign priority should be new steps to liberalize world trade, building on the recent proposals of the President's Commission on International Trade and Investment Policy and using the Organization for Economic Cooperation and Development (OECD) High Level Group already created for this purpose. Such an effort is necessary to reverse the present momentum toward protectionism, and a commitment to move should be a part of Stage One. The President has no authority to make any U.S. trade concessions at present, however, so new legislation is needed to pave the way for negotiations, as well as to demonstrate that the Administration's commitment to liberal trade encompasses substance as well as rhetoric.

It would probably be possible for the United States to get some minor nonreciprocal trade concessions in Stage One. However, they would provide little help for the desired payments swing, appear purely cosmetic, and actually undermine the credibility of the tough new U.S. approach. More important, they could cost us something on the amount of the foreign revaluations, and thus actually represent a net loss for the United States if they simply represented an acceleration of steps to be taken subsequently anyway. Because different people handle trade and monetary policy in all countries, because different institutions are involved in Europe, and because the political effects of trade changes are much more obvious and thus more difficult than monetary changes, insistence on a sizable trade package could seriously delay Stage One. Actual negotiations on trade matters —and on defense burden-sharing, for precisely the same reasons—should be left to Stage Two.

Other countries have already raised two obstacles to this two-stage approach, even if it were adopted by the United States. They insist that the United States raise the official price of gold as part of the exchange-rate realignment, and that the United States resume some form of dollar convertibility at that time as well. Both points are understandable politically: the United States should "share" in the realignment by devaluing the dollar overtly, instead of solely via the revaluations of others, and others should not be forced to remain on the dollar standard imposed explicitly by August 15th after they have accommodated to a sizable improvement in the U.S. balance of payments.

Changing the gold price is the lesser evil of the two. The maximum change envisaged is five to ten percent, which would leave the official price well below the free market price and so provide no windfall profits for speculators, Russians, or South Africans. By clearly ruling out a large increase in the price, it could even discourage gold speculation. The need for congressional action could perhaps be delayed by adopting the proposal of Senator Javits that the Treasury simply declare a new selling price temporarily, without changing the official gold parity, and that Congress tidy up the legal situation as part of the fundamental reforms of Stage Two. And a willingness to change the gold price could result in a larger revaluation package since France would probably accept a five percent appreciation against the dollar via the gold price, Germany is reluctant to move more than five percent above France, Japan wants to move no more than five percent above Germany, and Italy, Britain, and some smaller Europeans will not move at all unless France does.

The negative effects of the gold price change on the monetary system could be countered by some corollary conditions. As will be explained shortly, the United States should not resume any form of convertibility, including gold convertibility, for the dollar until the satisfactory reform of the system in Stage Two. There would thus be no U.S. gold transactions at the new price until later, when new roles for the SDRs should mitigate any psychological boost which such transactions might give to gold. The change would not be meaningless, however, since other countries could trade gold among themselves or with the International Monetary Fund (IMF) at the new price.

The unfavorable psychological effects could also be met by simultaneous agreements in principle to move SDRs to the center of the monetary system. SDRs should be the future *numeraire,* in which all currencies are defined, replacing gold and the dollar in that role; we could denominate the new dollar parity in SDRs to highlight the shift, and further reduce the risk of boosting gold psychologically through the dollar devaluation. A special issue of SDRs should be authorized into which countries could convert any reserve assets now in their portfolios which they wish to get rid of, mainly dollars and sterling, but also gold itself. There should be sufficient creation of new SDRs (at least $4-5 billion annually) in the multi-year allocation period beginning in 1973, to assure adequate reserve growth without relying on dollars or gold. The details of these steps, or of steps to reduce the role of gold directly, will clearly take time to elaborate. Agreement on the governing principles should be possible in Stage One, however, if it is necessary to take the risks associated with an increase in the official dollar price of gold.

Convertibility of the dollar into U.S. reserve assets is much more critical than the gold price for the United States, and for the system as a whole. From the U.S. standpoint the external effects of the exchange-rate changes and the domestic disinflation program will take at least two years to be felt. The anticipated reversal of capital flows could get us to an official settlements balance much faster, but premature resumption of convertibility could produce losses of a sizable portion of the remaining U.S. reserves, for purely transitional reasons, when the whole objective is to strengthen the U.S. payments position. Other countries would lose, too, given their stake in having a strong dollar in the system and their interest in avoiding hair-trigger U.S. moves in the future, which smaller U.S. reserves would promote. And it is they who want the U.S. adjustment to be spread over time to cushion their own accommodations.

On the other hand, other countries want to minimize the duration of the dollar standard onto which they were formally thrust on August 15th. Before that date, foreign monetary authorities could convert any dollar accruals into U.S. reserve assets or at least justify holding dollars to their domestic critics by pointing out their right to do so. In the face of our suspension of convertibility, they now have only two choices when the United States is in deficit: to acquire dollars, or to eliminate their own surpluses by inflating, imposing controls on capital inflows or accomplishing the same end through multiple exchange rates, or appreciating the value of their currencies. Avoidance of this dilemma is precisely why these countries should be willing to move quickly to reform the international monetary system. Since the surcharge and probably the gold price will have to go in Stage One, the resumption of dollar convertibility will be the only U.S. lever to prod any such reform. Without it, we could easily see a repetition of 1967-69, when the British-French-Germany exchange-rate realignment led to much talk of reform but removed all pressure for it, and the likelihood of an August 15th was sharply accelerated.

To be sure, other countries fear that the United States wants them to revalue and then be stuck with a dollar standard forever. Such a fear is, of course, whetted by the inward-looking economic tendencies which clearly exist, so the United States would have to display consistent sincerity in pushing toward constructive reform. Our insisting on agreements "in principle" about Special Drawing Rights in Stage One should be reassuring. It should be snapped up by the others precisely in order to maintain momentum away from a new dollar standard—especially by the Europeans, who can veto all significant decisions on Special Drawing Rights under International Monetary Fund voting rules, and hence maximize their international monetary power by promoting an SDR standard to replace it.

VI

Stage Two should comprise negotiations aimed at producing fundamental improvements in both the international monetary system and international trade arrangements. Both must be included because money affects primarily the macroeconomic problems of nations, and trade affects the microeconomic problems of particular industries within nations. The underlying political objective is to adapt world economic relations to the new underlying economic and political balance, reducing the relative role of the United States and enhancing the relative roles of Europe and Japan. The reforms must preserve the benefits of growing world economic interdependence while meeting the insistence of national authorities that they retain adequate means of control over their individual societies.

The most important monetary need is a better process through which national balance-of-payments positions can adjust. Financing is generally available only for temporary periods and limited amounts, especially for deficit countries; it is essential in avoiding excessive adjustment costs, but if used too freely will simply permit disequilibria to cumulate and thus make the inevitable adjustment all the more painful. Adjustment via domestic deflation or inflation is exceedingly costly in terms of domestic economic objectives, especially if domestic needs call for moves in the opposite direction; thus such adjustment is frequently unacceptable for internal political reasons. Controls adopted for payments reasons carry significant economic and political costs and at best suppress imbalances, delaying the need for more fundamental measures and perhaps increasing their magnitude.

Changes in the exchange rate are thus the only economically effective means of adjustment which is likely to be politically acceptable in most countries at most times. This is particularly true for the United States, where adjustment via changes in domestic policy would be extremely costly, because foreign transactions represent such a small part of our total economy. Exchange-rate changes raise political problems, too, since they produce sharp changes in income distribution within a society, but the main barrier to their use in the postwar period has been the inadequate international rules by which they are governed. As it evolved, the Bretton Woods system discouraged changes except when "fundamental disequilibria" had clearly developed. This meant that the problem was obvious for all to see. Speculators could make easy money by betting on a change with virtually no risk of even modest loss; and governments dug in defensively to avoid the admission of previous errors, "national failures," or, in the case of surplus countries, "solving the other country's problem." Particularly in the case of surplus countries, no effective pressures existed to force exchange-rate changes when needed. With regard to deficit countries, there was no sure protection against unnecessary or excessive changes. The result was a devaluation bias against the dollar, the pivot currency of the entire system.[3]

A new régime thus needs to be established, essentially to depoliticize exchange-rate movements as much as possible and to equalize the incentives to adjust for surplus and deficit countries. To do so, exchange-rate changes need to be fostered on a smaller scale, and hence occur more frequently. New attitudes on the part of national monetary authorities are essential to such a new régime, and should be readily accepted by them as providing a new policy instrument to help cope with the complex array of responsibilities which they face.

It is doubtful that such changes in attitude will suffice, however, especially to induce surplus countries to take timely action. International agreement is thus needed on four changes in the rules. The margins around exchange-rate parities need to be widened permanently, to at least three percent and preferably five percent on either side, to permit greater fluctuations and hence encourage small parity changes. The International Monetary Fund Articles need amendment to clearly permit parity changes when disequilibria are pending, not accomplished facts. The international community needs to agree on guidelines which will indicate when parity changes are needed—essentially in those "dilemma" cases when the external balance calls for a domestic economic policy which clashes with the needs of the internal economy—with a presumption that changes will take place in such cases. And sanctions should be available to the international community to apply against a country which does not do so.

Such an approach would provide effective international surveillance of balance-of-payments adjustment via the exchange rate, the policy instrument through which national economies interact. As such, it would clearly represent a new "invasion" of national sovereignty. At the same time, however, it would provide national authorities with a new policy instrument to help meet their needs. In addition, through the stepped-up process of international consultation which would be triggered by the guidelines, countries could justify their failure to change their exchange rates by pointing to other policy actions they had taken, or attempt to persuade others that their payments imbalance required no action at the time. The tension between effective international control and maintenance of national sovereignty will always exist, but such a process would provide ample scope for both as it evolved toward improving the payments adjustment process.

The second key monetary need is to reform the means by which international reserves are created and held. The dominant role of the dollar in the reserve system has raised major international political problems and created major difficulties for the United States by circumscribing its ability to change its own exchange rate. (Under any reform, the dollar will doubtlessly maintain its predominant role in financing private international transactions, and for exchange market intervention use by monetary authorities.) A return to gold would reverse the evolution of money through all history, and subject the world economy to the uncertainties of South African production and private demand. If only because of the shortcomings of the alternatives, future reliance must be placed on Special Drawing Rights.

Fortunately, there are persuasive positive reasons for doing so as well. Only via Special Drawing Rights can the international community truly manage the growth of world liquidity through a rational decision-making process. Special Drawing Rights can be used to replace reserve assets presently in the system, including dollars, which other countries may no longer wish to hold and which the United States wishes to remove as a threat to its reserves. They combine the attractiveness of a gold-value guarantee and interest earnings. And they are managed by the International Monetary Fund, providing a base for enhancing the role of the institution; this is critical for successful reform of the adjustment process. Some countries will want to continue holding reserve currencies in their portfolios, and new rules could be adopted to permit them to do so while avoiding the risk of adverse international consequences from switches among assets as has been possible in the past.

At the same time, one may fairly ask: What are Special Drawing Rights? Where does their value come from? Will they always have value? The answer is simple: their value comes from agreement among virtually all non-communist countries to accept them in settlement of payments imbalances. Countries agree to provide their currencies, or other reserve assets, in exchange for Special Drawing Rights.

The value of the Special Drawing Rights rests on international coöperation. It is thus true that they might not survive a major war, or a total breakdown of international economic coöperation. The risk of either is remote, even under the pessimistic outlook described earlier. In addition, most countries will continue to hold a "war chest" of gold—whose official price and acceptability also depends on international coöperation—against such a contingency; gold converted into the special issue of Special Drawing Rights could even be retained physically in the territory of the converter as such a hedge. So the overwhelming superiority of Special Drawing Rights to either alternative, in any situation short of international disaster, renders it by far the best choice as the monetary base of the world economy of the future.

With such reforms, the United States could agree to finance completely any deficits in its basic payments position with reserve assets. Dollar convertibility would thus be resumed on a much more meaningful basis than before August 15th, into whatever assets we chose to use when necessary. We should be willing to undertake such an obligation in view of the assured creation of adequate liquidity via Special Drawing Rights; the improved prospect for prompt adjustment by other countries, reducing the pressures on our own balance of payments; and the new capability to move ourselves via changes in the exchange rate of the dollar, the only economically effective means of adjustment which is also politically feasible in the United States. It would be disastrous to U.S. foreign policy to keep the dollar inconvertible and try to maintain a world dollar standard, if most other currencies were fixed or most countries wished to return to such a régime. And such an effort would doubtlessly trigger foreign reactions which would seriously hurt wide segments of our economy as well.

On the trade side, negotiations are needed on a host of issues. The most pressing problem is agriculture, where we should be willing to swap some of our industrial protection and our dairy quotas for reductions in the stimulation afforded European production of feedgrains and other commodities by the Common Agricultural Policy. Tariffs on industrial trade remain important, particularly in those industries where they range much higher than the national averages of six to ten percent, and should be reduced reciprocally. Specific nontariff trade distortions, such as discriminatory government procurement rules and practices, need to be eliminated or moderated.

Meaningful action, however, might require a more imaginative leap than simply extending the current style of trade negotiations to more of the existing and well-recognized issues. Indeed, the development of a whole new range of relevant topics desperately requires new international rules, or at least new modes of coöperation. The multinational corporation and international transfers of technology are subject to no international understandings, despite their tremendous importance. International cooperation in devising and implementing adjustment assistance programs could prove a necessary part of any further trade liberalization. National policies adopted for purely domestic reasons, such as environmental control and regional development, will have significant trade effects. And a major breakthrough in reversing the protectionist tide may require a quantum leap toward liberal trade, perhaps a new treaty pointing to the phased removal of all remaining tariffs and most other barriers over the next 10 to 20 years, just as the Kennedy Round could be accomplished only through the adoption of new techniques which represented such a jump a decade ago.

One way to attack the subject would be to set out consciously to restructure the General Agreement on Tariffs and Trade (GATT). The IMF Articles would be basically restructured by the monetary reforms suggested above, which would substitute a presumption of exchange-rate changes for the pre-August 15th presumption of fixed rates, and reliance on SDRs for the previous reliance on gold and dollars. There is widespread agreement that many of the key GATT rules, while appropriate when devised in the late 1940s, simply cannot be expected to cope with trade problems a generation later. And an explicit effort to reconsider GATT would meet directly the perceptions of many Americans that the international trade rules are unfair, exposing them in most cases as unfounded but providing the best possible means to air the issues comprehensively.

Investment is not covered at all by GATT. Agriculture and nontariff distortions are covered inadequately. The basic most-favored-nation rule no longer governs a majority of world trade. The rules governing customs unions did not foresee the evolution of the Common Market. The trade controls permitted to meet balance-of-payments needs are outdated. The border tax rules were based on inadequate economic theory. New means of measuring reciprocity are needed to convince skeptical legislators of the fairness of future trade concessions. Indeed, it is legitimate to speculate about whether international economic responsibilities should continue to be bifurcated, with the IMF handling money and the GATT handling trade, now that the U.S. government has forced a widespread realization of how closely they are related. The absence of a single forum in which to consider both is a serious impediment to rapid resolution of the present problem.

VII

In view of their new positions of power, their resulting claims for international economic responsibility, and the uncertainties of U.S. leadership, Europe and Japan should initiate efforts to solve both the short-run and long-term phases of the present impasse. Such a step at this time would mark without doubt their transition to true international equality in the post-postwar world, and accord them new dignity and respect which would profoundly affect world politics for the 1970s and beyond. It has now become especially urgent for Europeans to put aside their differences, some petty and personal, but even those economic and very real, and achieve sufficient monetary unity to provide the basis for a common front at least on international financial issues. Only in that way will they be able to at least respond as one to the United States and to Japan, and offer any hope of seizing leadership in order to move back from the abyss.

Unfortunately, it is doubtful that other countries can mobilize quickly enough to take the lead in meeting the ever-tightening time limit for achieving a constructive Stage One. In addition, it is the United States which has primarily plunged the world into the present perilous situation. It is thus extremely gratifying that the United States has finally begun to present proposals on which immediate action can be based. In so doing, the United States has started to clarify its own priorities among the broad agenda it has tabled for discussion, to moderate its demands, and to adopt a more reasonable—though still extremely tough—negotiating approach. Failure to do so would be one more piece of evidence that the Administration was prepared to sit indefinitely behind the surcharge and an inconvertible dollar, pandering to the most isolationist elements in American society. In view of the dangers which loom in the absence of definitive action, the change came none too soon—and must be carried through to a prompt settlement of Stage One.

Notes

1. See the author's "Crisis in U.S. Trade Policy," *Foreign Affairs*, July 1971 [chapter 12 in this volume].

2. The measure would authorize creation of Domestic International Sales Corporations (DISC), domestic subsidiaries of U.S. firms which could defer, perhaps indefinitely, corporate tax payments on their export profits.

3. See C. Fred Bergsten, "The United States and Greater Flexibility of Exchange Rates," in Bergsten, Halm, Machlup, Roosa, eds., *Approaches to Greater Flexibility of Exchange Rates: The Bürgenstock Papers*, Princeton University Press, 1970 [chapter 7 in this volume].

26 The International Implications of the New Economic Policy

On August 15, President Nixon revolutionized postwar U.S. international economic policy in at least four respects. He decided to seek a massive improvement in the U.S. balance of payments, in direct contrast to our essentially "benign neglect" posture of the previous 25 years. He suspended the gold convertibility of the dollar, removing the lynchpin of the entire international monetary system and signaling a U.S. willingness to eliminate, or at least reduce sharply, the reserve currency role of the dollar. He imposed an import surcharge, completely reversing the traditional position of U.S. Administrations in leading the world toward an ever more liberal trading system. He violated both the letter and the spirit of the reigning international law in both the monetary and trade fields, reversing the traditional U.S. role of leading the effort to strengthen the rules governing world economic conduct.

In my judgment, the New Economic Policy should have excluded both the import surcharge and the suspension of dollar convertibility—although both clearly open golden opportunities for fundamental improvements in the world economy, which I strongly support. The point here, however, is that the steps taken, and their followup, will have a tremendous impact on the overall foreign policy of the United States. The reduction in our own direct military and political involvement around the world will by itself raise issues of foreign economic policy closer to the top of our own foreign policy priority list. The continuing rapid growth of economic interdependence among nations will make economic issues even more important for other countries, in many of which they are already at the top of the foreign policy priority list because they are crucial for domestic economic success. For both reasons, foreign economic policy will become increasingly crucial for our relations with the rest of the world.

It is thus perfectly clear that mishandling of the international aspects of the New Economic Policy could have a disastrous effect on overall U.S. foreign policy, in both the immediate future and the longer run. Confirmation of the growing foreign suspicion that the U.S. has turned protectionist in its economics, and therefore isolationist in its politics, would undermine our security relationships around the world. Missteps would drastically

Originally presented as testimony to the Subcommittee on Foreign Economic Policy of the House Committee on Foreign Affairs in its hearings on *The International Implications of the New Economic Policy*, September 21, 1971.

change world views of the basic character of the U.S., its reliability as an ally, and its willingness to abide by international agreements through foul weather as well as fair. I applaud the decision of this Subcommittee of the Committee on Foreign Affairs to hold hearings on the subject—which is decidedly not "just economic."

The first need is for clarity in the objectives which we seek. At the broadest level, the President is certainly right in defining them as (a) a sizeable improvement in the U.S. balance of payments, (b) a thorough reform of the international monetary system, (c) a reduction in barriers to international trade, and perhaps even (d) a better sharing of the "defense burden" of the non-Communist world.

However, even after an allowance for the tactics of negotiation, the position of the Administration is completely unsatisfactory on the next key questions: how much improvement do we want in our balance of payments? how much can we expect to get in return for dropping the surcharge and resuming our convertibility obligations? what is the U.S. prepared to give in return for foreign concessions? The technicalities of sliding parities and border taxes will not directly affect overall U.S. foreign policy; the overall reasonableness of our targets, and our own positive contributions toward achieving the necessary changes, certainly will. Excessive U.S. demands coupled with inadequate U.S. contributions, based on some erroneous—and exceedingly dangerous—theory that we have played Santa Claus to the world for the last 25 years, would have a devastating impact on the world role of this country for the next decade and probably beyond.

The first step is to recognize that the announced objective of a $13 billion improvement in our basic balance of payments overstates our true need by at least 50%, and is impossible to realize in any event. Such a swing would almost certainly produce a $3-6 billion surplus in our official settlements position, the most meaningful measure of our short-run effects on other countries, whereas we could live comfortably with a small deficit in view of the ongoing desire of both private and official foreigners to continually build up their dollar holdings. The target is unreachable because the rest of the world could simply not stand such a drain of its reserves to the United States. (The only alternative analysis is that we would sharply increase our exports of private capital instead of running such surpluses, presumably by lifting our present capital restraint programs. However, the other industrialized countries are hardly ready to hand U.S. firms a large competitive advantage over their firms to finance U.S. "takeovers of their industries.")

The second step is to recognize that the import surcharge is simply inadequate to buy the needed revaluations, international monetary reform, trade concessions, and greater sharing of military costs. Secretary Connally's arithmetic proves the point: its temporary $2 billion impact will hardly purchase a permanent $13 billion swing plus assorted other non-quantifiable objectives. Even worse, the surcharge is an exceedingly dangerous measure because its prolonged maintenance would trigger foreign retaliation, eliminating *any* net gain to the U.S. payments position; hence reducing still further its bargaining leverage; ending any chances of achieving positive results from the U.S. initiatives; and gravely jeopardizing overall U.S. relations with Europe, Japan, Canada and the lower income countries. The surcharge was presented as a substitute for the needed exchange rate changes, in view of the inability of the U.S. to change its own exchange rate, and it must not be converted unilaterally into a protectionist trade measure. We must therefore buy quickly the most we can with the surcharge, mainly in the monetary area, and get rid of it—along with the discriminatory features of the Job Development Credit.

The third step, which derives from the first two, is to scale down our objectives for the coming negotiations, or recognize that we will have to offer additional concessions of our own to achieve all of our goals. In my view, the two primary objectives are (a) an adequate realignment of exchange rates *now* and (b) basic changes in the international monetary rules so that timely exchange rate changes will prevent the *future* development of the large disequilibria, and resulting crises, which have pervaded the entire post-convertibility period. The change in the rules is really the more fundamental goal, but a new system can start smoothly only with current exchange rates in reasonable alignment. In addition, countries will not agree to new ongoing rules unless they can see their own starting points, and the starting points of the other players. So twin exchange rate goals must dominate our strategic planning, and I will elaborate on them after a quick comment on the trade and defense issues.

The removal of foreign trade barriers should be our third priority. The Administration has simply generalized so far, but we must be specific about what we want—I would focus on reduction of the production incentives of the Common Agricultural Policy of the European Community, elimination of the discrimination against U.S. trade in the Community's existing and pending association arrangements, immediate elimination of all of Japan's remaining import quotas and Europe's discriminatory quotas against Japan, liberalization of government procurement rules in all industrialized countries, elimination of most remaining tariffs and the various export subsidy devices maintained around the world. Furthermore, we must recognize that we will never get adequate changes in any of these areas without reciprocal concessions on some of our own trade barriers—such as our quotas on dairy imports, "voluntary" restraint agreements on imports of textiles and other products, American Selling Price system of customs valuation on some imports, "Buy America" rules and proposed "DISC" export incentives.

At present, however, the President has no authority to negotiate *any* reductions in U.S. trade barriers. If we are serious about pursuing meaningful trade negotiations, it is therefore necessary for the Congress to promptly pass new trade legislation, perhaps along the lines of the Javits-Mondale-Harris bill submitted early in this session. The legislation would have to include a drastically improved adjustment assistance program, which in combination with the promised exchange rate changes and monetary reform should enable the Administration to head off the protectionist pressures which it rightly fears.[See chapter 12 in this volume for a full analysis of the depth of protectionist pressures and what to do about them.] A vigorous Administration effort to secure liberal trade legislation would also go far toward meeting the urgent need to assure a doubting world that its devotion to liberal trade includes substance as well as rhetoric. With such evidence, we should be able to insist, as one condition for removal of our import surcharge, on firm commitments by each of the key foreign governments to enter immediately into negotiations on each of these trade issues and to achieve concrete results by the middle of 1972. If other countries are unwilling to reduce their barriers, we should retaliate against them in kind—by restricting our imports of items in which they specialize.

The U.S. maintains forces abroad to help preserve the security of the United States. We help defend other countries only to the extent that so doing helps defend us. The level of these forces must be determined on strategic and budgetary grounds, not by the balance of payments. Any long-term commitment by other countries to help pay for our troops, or even offset their foreign exchange costs, would almost certainly require equally long-term U.S. commitments to maintain U.S. troops abroad at present levels—a commitment we could hardly make at this time, and should certainly never make for balance of payments reasons. The surcharge is wholly inappropriate for use in this area. There is in fact a risk that Germany, in the current negotiations with us on renewing its "military offset" agreement, will claim "credit" against its revaluation for any improvements it offers over the past. Defense is best left completely alone in this context.

I return now to the priority monetary issues. The best scenario would comprise two stages. First, the other key countries would revalue their currencies against the dollar sufficiently to produce a gain of $7-10 billion in our payments position, in return for which we would eliminate the import surcharge. Second, all would agree on basic reforms of the monetary system, in return for which the United States would return to full convertibility for the dollar. It should be possible to negotiate this package in time to announce it along with Phase II of the anti-inflationary elements of the New Economic Policy in mid-October. This timing is also appropriate because foreign countries will want to see our domestic Phase II before judging whether we are doing enough to combat inflation ourselves.

The first stage would require revaluations of 10-15% for Japan, 10-12% for Germany, and 3-6% for the rest of the Common Market and Canada. Chances for obtaining the sizeable revaluation needed from Japan would be aided by tacit Administration acceptance of the voluntary restraints already initiated by Japanese industry on non-cotton textiles, with cessation of the effort to achieve tighter government-to-government controls which is unlikely to succeed anyway. An attractive alternative to immediate revaluations would be for these countries to pledge to let their currencies float freely for 3-6 months—in contrast to the controlled "floats" now being permitted—and then set new parities at true equilibrium levels determined through the market. However, this would require both a total elimination of market intervention by monetary authorities and a complete abolition of exchange controls in such key countries as Japan and France, which is not politically feasible.

In the second stage, the international monetary rules would be changed to assure more timely exchange rate changes, reduce further the monetary roles of both gold and the dollar by clearly moving Special Drawing Rights to the center of the reserve system, create sufficient SDRs annually to meet the world's need for reserve growth, and install new devices to deal with the huge international movements of liquid capital. Such reforms are essential from the U.S. standpoint, to reconcile our world financial role with the sharp changes in our political and economic power position since the postwar monetary system was created in 1945. They would require important concessions on numerous issues by both the United States and other countries. One of the most constructive foreign moves would be agreement to monetize the outstanding $40 billion of official dollar balances by authorizing their conversion into a special issue of SDRs, with the dollars returned to the U.S. and our equivalent liability extinguished—a "reverse Marshall Plan," which would be dramatic politics without any cost to the countries involved because they would simply be exchanging one type of reserve asset for another.

Even if the Administration were to adopt this two-step approach, however, some foreign governments have already raised a major obstacle to it by indicating that the United States should raise the official price of gold as part of the exchange rate realignment. Such a requirement would be nonsense from an economic point of view, because the resulting exchange rate pattern—which determines the future flow of trade and investment—will be the same with or without such a step. The insistence is allegedly based on political requirements, in other countries, that the U.S. "contribute" to the rate realignments—which is also nonsense, because the rate changes can only take place as part of an internationally agreed package. A foreign finance minister will therefore be unable to claim that he could do nothing to prevent an appreciation of his currency by the amount of his own revaluation plus the amount by which "the U.S. devalued." One therefore hopes that U.S. adoption of the two-step approach would induce other countries to abandon any insistence on a gold price increase, to expedite the elimination of the surcharge and a return to more orderly exchange rate relations.

If they do not, the problem is that an increase in the official price would imply to many people that the evolutionary demonetization of gold had ended—particularly in view of the 'demise' of the dollar—and that gold was moving back toward the center of the international monetary system. This risk could be averted by coupling the increase in the gold price with decisions which would clearly move SDRs to the center of the system, and the U.S. should be willing to accept a small increase in the gold price in such a context.

However, such decisions on SDRs could only be part of the longer term reforms of the system, and hence would fuse the two stages of my preferred scenario. Such delay would not be costly in the monetary area, since it would be clear that negotiations to solve the problems were underway, and since we have already learned that exchange rates can float without serious economic damage. However, in view of the uncertainty of the outcome, the U.S. would probably under this scenario not want to eliminate the surcharge immediately—which could cause real trouble in the trade area. I would therefore recommend that, if we are forced to take this path by foreign insistence on an increase in the official price of gold, we now cut the surcharge in half, and pledge full elimination when the parity reform and monetary reform package is completed. Such a cut is fully justified in the Administration's own terms, since the foreign floats have already resulted in about one-half the eventual revaluation implicitly sought by the Administration. The move would be extremely important as an indicator of U.S. reasonableness and good faith in pursuing a constructive outcome for the entire enterprise, while preserving leverage for us in the ongoing negotiations.

One final word on tactics. No individual foreign country will move definitively until it knows what the other major foreign countries will do. Yet it is totally unrealistic to expect the amalgam of countries which makes up the IMF, or even the Group of Ten, to develop a common position to "offer" the United States; we have already seen how hard it is for even the closest-knit group, the European Community, to do so. In addition, it is the United States which triggered the present situation, with actions of clear illegality and dubious justification. It is therefore incumbent that the United States make positive proposals including what each country might contribute to solve both the immediate and longer run aspects of the problem. A failure to do so will be seen as one more piece of evidence that the Administration does not want to negotiate real solutions, but is content to sit indefinitely behind the surcharge and dollar inconvertibility, with the foreign policy effect mentioned earlier.

In sum, the Administration should now move immediately on four fronts. It should announce publicly that we seek a $7-10 billion (rather than $13 billion) balance of payments improvement, and forget about trying to use the surcharge to buy greater defense burden-sharing. It should convey privately to the major countries a set of specific proposals for realigning exchange rates, reforming the monetary system, and eliminating trade barriers. It should eliminate the surcharge, in return for foreign revaluations adequate to get us the $7-10 billion improvement, and foreign commitments to a reciprocal reduction of the major trade barriers by mid-1972—keeping the dollar inconvertible into U.S. reserve assets until broad reform of the monetary system is negotiated. (If foreign countries insist that an increase in the official price of gold accompany their revaluations, we should agree to do so—in the context of a satisfactory agreement that moves SDRs clearly to the center of the monetary system—but then only cut the surcharge in half at this time.) And it should submit a broad trade bill to enable us to take part in the coming trade negotiations, which Congress should then pass in this session.

Part VIII
U.S. Economic Relations:
The Developing Countries

27 The Threat from the Third World

Present U.S. policy neglects the Third World almost entirely, with the exception of our few remaining military clients (mainly in Southeast Asia). This policy is a serious mistake. New U.S. economic interests, which flow from the dramatic changes in the position of the United States in the world economy and the nature of the new international economic order, require renewed U.S. cooperation with the Third World. New policy instruments, including but going far beyond foreign aid, are needed to promote such cooperation.

Any generalizations about the Third World represent vast oversimplification. Indeed, there exists no clearly definable "Third World." I use the term only because it is widely understood as meaning all countries outside the "industrialized West" and the "Communist Empire." In those countries, four major patterns appear likely to dominate the decade ahead.

First, economic and social development is likely to be the overwhelming priority policy objective. Perceptions of the potential rewards from development are broadening and deepening throughout the world. So are realizations that such progress actually is possible. Desire for economic and social progress is thus increasingly likely to dominate internal politics.

Second, the economic goals of the Third World will go well beyond maximizing GNP. Most developing countries, along with most industrialized countries, have now learned that growth alone cannot guarantee the fundamental and politically central objectives of economic policy—full employment, relatively stable prices, equitable income distribution, and ultimately an enhanced quality of life.

Many less-developed countries (LDC's) are disillusioned with both the results of the past and its simplistic focus on a single target. Despite the impressive growth rates of the aggregate Third World in the 1960s, unemployment exceeds 20 percent in many countries. The per capita income of the poorest LDC's, which now contain half of the world population, has been growing by only 1.5 percent annually. The gap between the income of the richest 10 to 20 percent and the poorest 20 to 40 percent within many LDC's has been getting wider. There are 100 million more illiterates in the Third World now than 20 years ago, and two-thirds of all children there suffer from malnutrition.

Originally appeared in *Foreign Policy* 11, Summer 1973, pp. 102-24.

Third, the countries of the Third World will increasingly insist upon autonomous management of their own societies. They will reject dictation from outsiders of all types: foreign governments, international agencies, multinational corporations. This is partly due to the increasing self-confidence that has come from recent successes, as well as the cadres of indigenous talent which are now becoming available. It is partly due to the shortcomings which they now perceive in external "assistance" and in the models of "development" offered them by outsiders. And it is partly due to nationalist desires in the Third World to overcome a feeling of dependency on the rich.[1]

Fourth, the Third World will continue to need outside help. Few LDC's will be able to meet their economic and social needs without steady infusions of foreign exchange.

The new policy targets of the Third World and its desire for independence, however, call for significant shifts among the modes of help and the manner in which that help is extended. Third World countries will place higher priority on trade than aid, because trade brings with it less foreign influence and, in many cases, creates more jobs. They will place higher priority on borrowing in the private capital markets than on seeking foreign direct investment, because they want more labor-intensive production processes and less foreign direction than frequently accompany multinational firms. They will focus more heavily on international monetary policy, because of its critical importance for the achievement of a liberal trading regime and for a freer flow of private portfolio capital, and because it offers new opportunities for development finance without strings. Most of them will seek increased multilateralization of official aid, to maximize their own roles in the decision-making process.

The Response of the Rich

At present, the industrialized countries are responding inadequately to these Third World needs.

The Third World needs increased access to world markets, perhaps more than anything else, but protectionism is accelerating. Indeed, the attitude of the industrialized world toward LDC exports of manufactured goods has totally reversed in a remarkably short period of time—from supporting tariff preferences *for* them a few years ago, to serious contemplation of new "orderly marketing safeguards" aimed largely *against* their "low-wage" products now. The level of real aid is stagnant, and the debt servicing of some LDC's has reached the point where they are now net exporters of capital to the industrialized world. The quality of aid is declining, as most terms harden; tying alone reduces the real value of aid by 10 to

30 percent below its nominal value. There is no progress toward stabilizing commodity prices, or toward helping LDC's gain access to private capital markets.

The United States is the least responsive to Third World needs of any industrialized country at this time. U.S. help is small in quantity, and getting smaller. Its quality is declining. It often runs directly counter to the central objectives of the LDC's just outlined. It lags far behind the policies of Europe and Japan. The Administration and Congress must share in the indictment.

The United States regards developing countries both large and small (e.g. India and Chile, not to mention Indochina) solely as pawns on the chessboard of global power politics. Rewards go only to the shrinking list of explicit collaborators. Economically, the United States has been increasing its trade barriers as Europe and Japan have been lowering theirs. Europe and Japan have been extending tariff preferences to the LDC's since 1971, but the United States has yet to make good on its commitment to do so. U.S. development aid, as a percentage of national GNP, is now next-to-last among all industrialized countries. The United States delayed its latest contributions to the International Development Association and Inter-American Development Bank for over a year, inhibiting their flow of current lending. The United States has failed to contribute anything to the soft-loan window of the Asian Development Bank. It has sought to bilateralize multilateral aid, instead of multilateralizing bilateral aid as called for in President Nixon's own aid reform proposals of September 1970 and April 1971, by blocking loans from the multilateral lending institutions to countries which have expropriated private investments, even when those countries (*unlike* Chile or Peru) have compensated U.S. firms under international law. At the Stockholm environment conference in May 1972, the United States was the only major country which opposed additional assistance to LDC's to finance the costs of anti-pollution equipment which their plants would need to meet the environmental safeguards imposed on products by, among others, the United States itself.[2] And it has even abandoned its own initiative to achieve multilateral untying of bilateral aid.

Despite this catalogue of shortcomings, it must be noted that some of the present LDC focus on U.S. inadequacy is unjustified. Many people around the world continue to expect the United States to take all of the major international initiatives, even though the era when the United States could or should do so is now over. And U.S. performance is not all bad: it has taken the initiative to reform the international monetary system, and it is attempting to launch a new round of international trade-liberalizing negotiations. Healthy economic relations among the industrialized countries are critical for the fortunes of the LDC's, so these U.S. efforts to restore such relations promote major LDC interests.

384

But numerous clashes have already developed between an increasingly self-confident but still needy Third World, and a decreasingly responsive industrialized world. Such clashes are likely to become far more serious in the future. The desire for progress in the Third World, and indeed the expectation that it *will* occur, is great. Failure to achieve it will almost certainly produce major frustrations, which could in turn produce highly emotional and even irrational responses across the globe. If the frustrations are caused in significant part by the recalcitrance of the industrialized countries, or even by widespread perceptions that such recalcitrance exists, much of the response may be aimed in their direction. If any particular industrialized country is widely perceived to be the leading recalcitrant, especially if that country is the United States, it could bear the major share of that response. What risk does this involve for the United States?

The Third World and U.S. Economic Interests

The Third World retains some importance for U.S. security. But its new and major impact on the United States is economic.

Much of the impact, however, relates to the position of the United States in its triangular economic relationship with Europe and Japan. The pervasive and growing economic interpenetration among these three industrialized areas is increasingly important to the welfare of key groups in each. At the same time, it threatens the welfare of other key groups. Severe political tensions thus arise. The foreign economic policies of each area are increasingly politicized and increasingly polarized, and have become potentially explosive. They could easily come to dominate the overall relationships among the areas, if new ways are not soon found to resolve cooperatively the disputes which inevitably arise. They have already done so on particular occasions, as when the British Prime Minister refused to meet with the President of the United States to talk about high politics in late 1971 until the United States initiated steps to end the international economic crisis triggered by its New Economic Policy.

Such an outcome is now possible because the security blanket which had previously smothered such economic disputes is being steadily nudged aside. Serious intra-alliance disputes over economics could brake the progress toward East-West détente, by breaking the solidarity of the "West" on which détente in part depends. Economic conflict could thus leave us further from, rather than nearer to, a true generation of peace.

But the acceleration of international economic interpenetration, with its complex sets of costs and benefits, is not limited to the industrialized world. It is global. The U.S. stake in the Third World is growing, and the leverage of the Third World to affect the United States is growing.

Natural Resources

First, the United States is rapidly joining the rest of the industrialized countries in depending on the Third World for a critical share of its energy supplies and other natural resources. For oil alone, annual U.S. imports are expected to rise by $20 billion by the end of the decade. But it is not only much-publicized oil; accelerating imports of other raw materials will raise these figures significantly.

Four countries control more than 80 percent of the exportable supply of world copper, have already organized, and have already begun to use their oligopoly power. Two countries account for more than 70 percent of world tin exports, and four countries raise the total close to 95 percent. Four countries combine for more than 50 percent of the world supply of natural rubber. Four countries possess over one-half the world supply of bauxite, and the inclusion of Australia (which might well join the "Third World" for such purposes) brings the total above 90 percent. In coffee, the four major suppliers have begun to collude (even within the framework of the International Coffee Agreement, which includes the main consuming countries) to boost prices. A few countries are coming to dominate each of the regional markets for timber, the closest present approximation to a truly vanishing resource. The percentages are less, but still quite impressive, for several other key raw materials and agricultural products. And the United States already meets an overwhelming share of its needs for most of these commodities from imports, or will soon be doing so.

A wide range of Third World countries thus have sizeable potential for strategic market power. They could use that power against all buyers, or in a discriminatory way through differential pricing or supply conditions—for example, to avoid higher costs to other LDC's or against the United States alone to favor Europe or Japan.

Supplying countries could exercise maximum leverage through withholding supplies altogether, at least from a single customer such as the United States. Withholding is a feasible policy when there are no substitute products available on short notice, and when the foreign exchange reserves of the suppliers become sizeable enough that they have no need for current earnings.

The suppliers would be even more likely to use their monopoly power to charge higher prices for their raw materials, directly or through such techniques as insisting that they process the materials themselves. Either withholding or price-gouging could hurt U.S. security. The threat of either could pressure the United States to compromise its positions on international political and economic issues. Either would hurt U.S. efforts to combat domestic inflation and restore equilibrium in our international balance of payments.

The price and balance-of-payments effects on the United States of withholding or price-gouging by suppliers of raw materials could not be attacked through conventional policy instruments. Domestic demand for raw materials could be dampened only at the cost of additional unemployment. Foreign suppliers are outside the jurisdiction of U.S. price controls. Substitution of domestic resources would also raise costs significantly. Stockpile sales help only for a short time. Devaluations make resource imports more costly without much dampening their volume. Such actions could thus cause major new problems for the U.S. economy and international position.

Such Third World leverage could have a double bite on the United States if used discriminatorily against it, thereby benefiting the competitive positions of Europe and Japan. Such discriminatory action, triggered either by the suppliers or by our industrialized competitors, is by no means impossible. It was attempted in oil by some Arab countries in 1967 and has been actively sought at least by Italy and France in the recent past. The spectre of "cannibalistic competition" among the rich for natural resources is unfortunately a real possibility which suggests that the owners of those resources have tremendous clout.

The Third World suppliers could also cause major problems by the way in which they use their huge export earnings. Oil earnings alone could rise to at least $50 billion per year by the end of the decade. It is hard to see how more than $20 billion of the total can be spent on imports. These countries could thus add $30 billion *per year* to their portfolios seeking profitable (or mischievous) outlets. They could use the money to disrupt international money markets overtly, and we have already seen that they generate great monetary instability, perhaps without consciously trying, by pushing the world toward a multiple reserve currency system. Aimed specifically at particular currencies, they could seek to force the United States (or anyone else) to adopt policies which clashed with its national objectives of the moment—as a few Arab countries, from a much weaker financial base, attacked the United Kingdom by converting sterling balances in June 1967 and again in 1971.[3] At a minimum, the uncertain destination of these huge resources will add to the already formidable problems faced by the international monetary system, which can affect the United States quite adversely.

The oil situation is, of course, the prototype. The concerted action of the OPEC countries in raising oil prices has raised energy costs throughout the world and dramatically increased their revenues. Such extortion by the oil producers—including such "normal" LDC's as Nigeria, Indonesia, Iran, and Venezuela—is likely to continue. This economic pressure is unlikely to be reduced as a result of the takeover of the production facilities by the OPEC countries from the international companies,[4] because the countries themselves—including "opposition" politicians in each—have well learned from the companies that *each* benefits from getting the highest possible price for *all,* and that price-cutting by one would be counter-productive because it would quickly be emulated by the others to preserve existing market shares. Equally important is the fact that OPEC has shown other countries how to do it. Oil may be merely the start.

To be sure, each of the specific commodity situations presents different and complex problems. There are serious obstacles to concerted supplier action: the economic option of using substitutes for some of the commodities, the political problem of achieving adequate cooperation among the suppliers, and the risk of overt retaliation by the industrialized world (or just the United States).

But the two obstacles specific to commodity action can be largely overcome within the Third World itself. Subtle pricing and marketing strategies could boost consumer costs and producer gains significantly without pushing consuming countries to the development of substitutes, which requires heavy initial investments and start-up costs. Concerted action by copper, tin, and bauxite producers would sharply reduce the risk to each that cheaper aluminum or tin would substitute for higher priced copper, or vice versa. An alliance among the producers of coffee, cocoa, and tea could preempt substitution by drinkers around the world. Objective calculations of the benefits to all producers could provide a basis for "equitable" division of the spoils.

All that is needed to permit political cooperation is increased knowledge of the market and the potential gains from concerted action, self-confidence and leadership. Whether such action actually eventuates would seem to depend quite importantly on the policy milieu of the future. The countries involved will certainly be more likely to act if the industrialized world frustrates their efforts to achieve their goals more constructively, and if they are barred from participating effectively in global decisions which vitally affect their own destinies. They are more likely to act against the United States alone if the United States is the most obstinate or neglectful of all. Even a perception of such obstinacy or neglect, sufficiently plausible to be widely believed in both the Third World and the industrialized countries themselves, could trigger action. It would seem far better for the United States, and for all the industrialized countries, to try to preempt such risks by taking initiatives to help these countries fulfill their aspirations by more stable means.

Investment and Trade

Second, a number of Third World countries exercise major leverage over

U.S. investments. The book value of U.S. direct investment in the Third World exceeded $23 billion at the end of 1971 (about $14 billion excluding oil), and the real market value is at least twice as large. About 5 percent of U.S. corporate profits now derive from these investments. Many jobs relate directly to them. Even excluding oil, they provide over $1 billion annually for the U.S. balance of payments.

Earnings on foreign investment are particularly important to the United States because of their strategic importance for its balance of payments. Many observers expect the United States to move into a structural trade deficit of growing size by the end of the decade, with the huge flow of investment earnings paying (in foreign exchange terms) for its net imports, overseas government expenditures, and continued net outflows of private capital. Any significant cutback in investment earnings would thus require new measures to compensate elsewhere in the balance of payments, levying new costs on us. Cutbacks in imports or subsidies of exports, perhaps by further devaluations, would again raise U.S. prices and costs. New constraints might emerge for U.S. foreign policy, perhaps far more costly than the actions suggested here to avoid negative Third World action. Effective controls on capital exports to help the balance of payments in the short run would cut future income from abroad, including income on investments already made, and hence produce the same constraints in the future.

Confiscation of its investments in the Third World could thus create major costs for the United States. Much of this investment is in the same raw materials just discussed, so Third World action could affect the United States doubly (as it already has in oil) by both raising our costs and reducing our earnings. It is often argued that any foreign confiscations would eliminate new U.S. investments in the confiscating countries, along with the return on old investments, so there would be no net cost to our balance of payments. This argument of course ignores the negative effects of such action on domestic jobs, profits, and perhaps even prices.

But it is also almost certainly wrong for the balance of payments over the longer run, since virtually all foreign investments return more income to the United States—and hence provide financing for net imports of goods, etc.—than they cost us capital at the outset. In the short run, it is not clear that take-overs of one U.S. investment places a halt on new U.S. investment even in the same country; major U.S. endeavors have continued in Peru despite the take-over of the International Petroleum Company. Given the focus of multinational firms on growth and market shares, it is quite likely that investments in alternative foreign locations would supplant investments which would have taken place otherwise in the expropriating country—perhaps a little less efficiently, with lower eventual returns to the United States. It is thus highly likely that the net effect of foreign confiscation on the U.S. balance of payments would almost always be negative.

Third World countries could also adopt a variety of measures against U.S. investment, far short of confiscation, which would hurt U.S. economic interests. Expropriation with compensation would of course eliminate future earnings, and could cut U.S. exports and jobs. Requirements that the local subsidiaries of U.S. firms export enough of their output to meet targets determined by the host government, reinvest some sizeable share of their earnings, or limit their imports, could all reduce the value of the investment to the United States. The investment area provides unique opportunities for Third World action geared specifically to the United States, in view of our dominant share of foreign investment.

Third, Third World countries could undertake massive repudiation of their debts to the industrialized world if it became unwilling to negotiate "fair rescheduling" thereof. U.S. government claims on LDC's totaled about $25 billion at the end of 1971, and private claims other than direct investment added another $15 billion. Foreign payments of principal and interest on these U.S. assets were well over $2 billion in 1971. In the wrong policy milieu, the severity of the debt burden faced by many of these countries—many of which have become net capital exporters—could propel them to action to evade it. The effects on individual U.S. financial institutions, on our overall money markets, and on the U.S. balance of payments, could all be severe. Repudiation has already been threatened by a number of countries, and has been avoided only because each one has succeeded in getting its debts rescheduled as a result.

Fourth, Third World countries could create additional economic difficulties in the industrialized world by deliberately cutting the prices of their manufactured exports. The United States is already seriously concerned about the effect of imports, particularly from "low wage countries," on U.S. jobs. But these countries might feel forced to compete even more vigorously if they were unable to receive cooperative treatment for their output in major international markets, or otherwise meet their needs for jobs and foreign exchange. They would of course do so subtly enough to avoid early detection and clear "blame," and only in instances where they could expand output sufficiently to take advantage of the price cuts in the short run and where foreign demand was adequate to make the strategy pay over the long run.

Again, the United States might not be able to respond through conventional measures. Anti-dumping duties might be inapplicable, because the foreign market would so dominate internal demand in the Third World that the suppliers would simply use the export price at home as well. Suppliers could also avoid countervailing duties, even under the elastic definition of "export subsidies" now applied by the Treasury, by using devaluations (including multiple exchange rates) to effect the price cuts. The United States could always react with import quotas, but quotas would almost certainly levy high costs on the United States by limiting trade with "innocent'' countries, as well as the aggressive price-cutters, and in turn trigger retaliation or simply market-induced cutbacks in U.S. exports.

Fifth, LDC's could expand their exports by becoming ''pollution havens.'' They could ignore pollution concerns in their production processes, and perhaps even foul the world environment in the process. Some major LDC's (Brazil, for example) are in fact already inviting those industries most heavily restricted by new anti-pollution standards in the United States to come to their countries with a promise that they will be free from the anti-pollution measures that are raising production costs in the United States.

These are some of the negative steps through which countries in the Third World can seriously hurt the United States. Each of these steps has already been tried and, in particular cases, has succeeded. The United States can always adjust—but the costs of doing so will become increasingly significant.

The United States also has numerous theoretical means to retaliate against such moves. Many have already been mentioned: import quotas, denial of new private investments or foreign aid, including blockage of loans by international financial institutions in which the United States has effective veto power, even overt military intervention in cases of blatant withholding of energy supplies for purposes of political blackmail. But most of these responses are only theoretical. Any LDC which undertook such actions would do so with sufficient subtlety so that rough U.S. responses would be difficult to mobilize, especially since some domestic interests (importers, consumers, exporters, other private investors) would be hurt as a result. The thought of military intervention seems remote after the domestic divisiveness of Vietnam. And, perhaps most importantly, other industrialized countries will usually be waiting in the wings with money and long-term purchase contracts—in the same way that Japanese and European companies wasted no time entering Chile in the wake of its nationalization of U.S. firms. Neither gunboat nor dollar diplomacy will work very well for the United States in the 1970s.

Thus it is no longer clear that the United States would emerge ''the winner'' in confrontation with the Third World. Even if it were economically irrational for other countries to trigger such confrontations, however, this by no means rules them out. Individual LDC governments might be forced into such a posture by internal political imperatives even if the outcome was unfavorable to their ''true'' national interest. But the main point is that the United States would suffer significant costs even if, in some sense, it ''won'' a confrontation—by substituting high-cost shale oil for lower-cost Persian Gulf crude, or South Carolina cotton goods for Korean synthetics. In the long run, there will be no winners. Since the policy framework of U.S. relations with the Third World is likely to go far in determining whether such events occur, or even threaten to occur, U.S. interests would be greatly served by creating a framework in which they will not occur.

Management of the International Economic System

In addition, the United States needs positive help from the Third World on a number of issues. Achievement and maintenance of an effective international monetary system is critical to U.S. economic and foreign policy interests. Agreement among the industrialized countries is central to achieving such a system. But a majority of the Third World must also agree to any changes in the Articles of Agreement of the International Monetary Fund, because amendments to the Articles require a weighted majority vote of 80 percent and the support of 60 percent of all member countries —and the Third World holds about 27 percent of the weighted vote and well over one-half of the total membership. Beyond reform of the system, active cooperation from Third World countries will be needed to preserve its stability because of the financial power which they will wield in the future.

The United States also needs to move rapidly into a major new negotiation to reduce barriers to international trade, to promote its own export and anti-inflation interests and to block the accelerating protectionist trend which may otherwise fill the trade policy vacuum. The LDC's are potential U.S. allies here, because of their urgent need for access to foreign markets. Yet the Third World as a whole could impede the effort by placing overriding concern on the fact that new tariff reductions on a most-favored-nation basis would erode its own newly won tariff preferences. The large number of developing countries linked to Europe could do so to retain their own selective preferences in the Common Market. LDC's could be especially reluctant to support total elimination of tariffs, which would wholly eliminate their preferences, even though such a goal could prove necessary to dramatize the negotiations sufficiently to produce the needed political support to launch them.

Such attitudes would be a great mistake for most LDC's, since they stand to gain far greater access to developed-country markets from even a modestly successful multilateral trade negotiation than from the niggardly preferences which now exist. Nevertheless, such a view could prevail unless the Third World was confident that its interests would be met sufficiently in such a global negotiation to offset the loss—for example, by giving them preferred treatment under any new "safeguard mechanism" which could otherwise choke off their new industries anytime they began to significantly penetrate a "sensitive" developed-country market, and by providing generous preferences during the period when all tariffs were being phased out.

The United States should be seeking allies wherever possible on monetary and trade issues. It faces a stacked deck in the GATT, where the "one country-one vote" rule means that the European Community—the principal target of most U.S. attacks there—goes into every debate with a huge voting lead, given its own membership plus its numerous associated states. The LDC's have nine seats on the new Committee of Twenty. It should be possible to induce most LDC's to side with the industrialized world on oil and other resource issues, since they are heavy consumers who can afford price increases even less than we. Yet the LDC's can be expected to support U.S. interests only if the United States supports theirs. Even the toughest of recent U.S. negotiators have ignored this obvious source of potential support for U.S. international economic efforts, and indeed launched policies which drove them to oppose us. Active engagement of the Third World in such global issues would pay the additional dividend of inducing them to accept a measure of responsibility for the functioning of the entire system, rather than leaping outside it to continue and even accelerate the policy of confrontation on "the big picture" symbolized by the creation of UNCTAD as long as a decade ago.

The United States also needs the Third World to take more U.S. exports if it is to achieve the improvement now needed in its trade balance. Most of the other industrialized countries are basically mercantilist, unwilling to accept large enough shifts in their trade positions to accommodate the needed U.S. improvement, and strong enough to resist such shifts. Third World countries, on the other hand, can readily use additional imports as they pursue their development goals. Many of them can steer purchases to the United States—or away from us—if they want to, through their elaborate control machinery. They can only finance additional net imports, however, through traditional forms of concessional development finance, access to private capital on terms which render neither their debt burdens nor sovereign control of their internal economies intolerable, and new modes of development finance such as the "link" to SDR's—all of which require policy cooperation from the United States (and others). The two aspects of economic interdependence are here revealed most clearly: the interdependence among the various international economic issues of monetary policy, trade, and investment; and the interdependence among all countries, rich and poor alike.

Drug addition is a critical problem in America today. Yet any of a number of LDC's can produce enough opium to easily supply the entire addict population of the United States, and will find it politically difficult to avoid doing so unless their economies are successful enough to enable them to fully compensate their poppy growers. Further removed in time, yet perhaps as threatening to broad U.S. interests, is the need to avoid unbearable strain on our environment and resources by slowing the growth of world population—the vast bulk of which now occurs in the Third World, and which history demonstrates will be checked definitively only by the achievement of much higher levels of income. The list of issues goes on and on.

The Implications for U.S. Policy

There are thus a number of economic issues of critical importance to the United States on which it needs help from Third World countries, and where these countries could seriously impede U.S. interests. If they are unable to achieve their own priority objectives in a constructive and cooperative milieu, they may well seek to use this emerging leverage in an atmosphere of destructive confrontation. They may even use their economic leverage to pursue political goals, exploiting their own comparative advantage, in bargaining terms, and hence intensify the potential costs to the United States of noncooperation.

Third World leverage is heightened by the possibility that they will be increasingly able to play on disputes among the members of the U.S.-Europe-Japan economic triangle in the future, as they have played on disputes among members of the U.S.-U.S.S.R.-China political triangle in the past (and may again). The great economic powers will certainly strive to reconcile their most important differences, and restore a stable international economic order. Even if they succeed, however, their relations will clearly be much more competitive than in the past—because Europe and Japan now compete with the United States as economic equals, because internal U.S. economic conditions will require the United States to continue to concern itself deeply with its external economic situation, and because there will be no overriding cold war issues to submerge such conflict. And it is unfortunately possible that the major powers will fail to resolve their differences; assuring bitter competition for Third World support.

Europe and Japan have long ago realized this fact of international life, and have placed their relations with the Third World high on their list of foreign policy priorities. The Europeans are busily lining up allies throughout Africa, the Mediterranean and the old British Commonwealth, and are even signing trade pacts in Latin America. They make no effort to hide the fact that the Third World is a focal point of their foreign policy. Japan, although hindered by its own colonial past in Asia, is making similar efforts.

In such a framework, the opportunities for discriminatory action by the Third World are magnified. They can play off one consumer of raw materials against another, one private investor against another, one exporter against another—wholly or partly in return for policies favorable to their own interests. Some of this has always occurred, some does today, and some always will. But it could become a major factor, with significant effects on the United States in the 1970s and beyond, if we continue to lag behind the rest of the industrialized world in this crucial policy area.

The United States needs to pursue its interests in the Third World through three types of policies. Their basically economic nature stems from my earlier conclusions: that the priority goals of most LDC's are economic, that the major threat to the United States from the Third World is likely to be economic, and that the policy tools with which we can respond to the Third World are primarily economic. Each would work best if carried out cooperatively by all of the industrialized countries together, to share the costs and present the strongest deterrent to aggressive Third World action.

One set of policies could include explicit or implicit hands-off agreements among the major powers in the security sphere, and joint trade and aid liberalization in the economic sphere. A second type of cooperative policy, in the economic field, would aim at creating a joint defense by the industrialized countries against the potential LDC threats outlined in this article, such as a monetary system which could withstand speculative attack indefinitely by recycling footloose capital among central banks, and the presentation of joint fronts by countries which consume raw materials produced in the Third World—for a start, an Organization of Petroleum Importing Countries (OPIC) to counter the Organization of Petroleum Exporting Countries (OPEC). A third approach is to bring the Third World itself into active cooperation wherever possible; to induce it to accept the obligations which usually produce responsible behavior. U.S. policy should vigorously pursue all three approaches.

There are several different specific U.S. policies which can fit within this framework. Third World considerations should add to the U.S. interest, already strong for other reasons, for new reductions of international trade barriers. The United States should join Europe and Japan in extending tariff preferences. It should renew its effort of 1969-70 to liberalize all tariff preference schemes, and go further by proposing preferential treatment for LDC's within developed-country non-tariff barriers. It could take the lead in expanding the scope of LDC textile exports in the coming effort to negotiate a multilateral all-fiber agreement. It should seek to improve the quality of aid by getting all donors to untie it from procurement from their own suppliers, ease its terms, and channel it through the multilateral lending institutions. It could support a "link" between world monetary arrangements and development finance,[5] new understandings and perhaps rules to govern the activities of multinational firms, and perhaps a higher level of concessional aid. It should get the industrialized countries to routinize consultation with the LDC's on the wide range of international economic issues whicn affect them directly, and consciously seek to thrust them into positions of international responsibility as rapidly as possible.

Most of these measures, especially if undertaken along with the other major industrial countries, would be very cheap. Tariff preferences would be unlikely to raise U.S. imports by more than $300 million per year; they would be temporary anyway if we succeeded in winning multilateral a-greement to eliminate all tariffs over 10 to 20 years; and we would get some offsetting additional exports in return. Our trade balance would probably benefit from multilateral untying of bilateral aid, especially now that our competitive position has been dramatically improved by the two devalua-tions. It makes negligible difference to the financing of the U.S. govern-ment whether our aid loans are for 25 years at 3 percent or for 40 years at 1 percent. "Link" financing can be provided to the Third World with no cost to us.

Many of these steps have long since been agreed to in principle by the major countries. The Nixon Administration has taken initiatives on many of them—global trade negotiations, liberal tariff preferences, untying of aid, multilateralization of aid. *The Nixon Doctrine explicitly envisages a process in which U.S. help for other countries would evolve from direct involvement through support for their own security capacity to general support for the economic base on which they can construct their own security capability, a close parallel to the process called for here. But the Administration has attached inadequate priority to these issues, generally retreated in the face of domestic political opposition, and repeatedly demonstrated its own structural bureaucratic weaknesses in dealing on a sustained basis with matters which it perceives to be of secondary importance.* And the Congress has failed to counterbalance the absence of decisive Administration leadership.

The rationale for U.S. involvement I have outlined suggests pinpointing some U.S. programs, such as bilateral aid and debt reschedulings, on those countries which could most affect U.S. economic interests. In so doing, it could lead to results opposite from the present pinpointing. For instance, Chile would be viewed, at least in part, as the world's major copper producer rather than as an ideological foe whose internal politics we disapproved of and which has confiscated U.S. property. Some other programs, such as trade policies and the distribution of international liquid-ity, could be applied to the Third World as a whole in an effort to create a constructive overall climate. The few oil "sinks" obviously need no aid, but several "normal" LDC's play an important role in the oil picture and even the "sinks" might well be susceptible to sincere efforts to provide them with roles of international responsibility commensurate with their wealth.

The main conclusion from this analysis is that the United States must, in its own national self-interest, adopt much more cooperative and responsive policies toward the Third World. This will clearly require cooperation on the part of the Third World as well, in which it accepts clear-cut responsibilities in return for the cooperation extended to it. But simple insurance principles suggest that the United States would be well advised to spend a modest amount of resources in an effort to avoid the risks discussed above, particularly since these risks could deeply affect the great power relationships which seem likely to dominate future U.S. foreign policy.

The principles of *Realpolitik* lead to the same conclusion. U.S. leverage over countries with which it has a significant level of transactions is far greater than over those with which it has none or few. Both the stick of denial and the carrot of new assistance are then far more likely to be credible—as is abundantly clear whether we wish to negotiate about sky-jacking with Cuba, naval piracy with Barbary pirates or North Korea, or terrorism with Palestinian guerrillas. We would be able far better to avoid the risks of confrontation, and to "win" confrontations if they did occur, if we had long ago taken some of the measures proposed here.

None of the specific steps suggested, nor even the whole set taken together, should be expected to guarantee a Third World hospitable to all U.S. national interests. The United States cannot buy economic concessions any more than, in the past, it could buy political allegiance. Indeed, hard bargaining on numerous specific issues is likely in light of the sharp increase in Third World independence and power. But U.S. policy must seek to contain such bargaining within a framework of generally cooperative relations, rather than a framework of confrontation and hostility.

In the early 1960s, virtually all observers in the United States, and most abroad, erroneously projected the perpetuation of an American hegemony over the non-Communist world which was in fact already being permanently eroded by the economic miracles of Europe and Japan. In the early 1970s, most observers project an American-European-Japanese tripartite hegemony which may become obsolete before it is ever enthroned because of the economic progress of the Third World. The future will not be so simple. It will encompass an array of actors whose significance differs across an array of issues. The Third World will play an important role in that world, and thus deserves a much higher place among the priorities of contemporary American foreign policy.

Notes

1. As Isaiah Berlin has recently suggested, "It is lack of recognition that, more than any other cause, seems to lead to nationalist excesses."

"The Bent Twig: A Note on Nationalism," *Foreign Affairs,* October 1972, p.30.

2. See Edward P. Morgan, "Stockholm: The Clean (But Impossible) Dream," *Foreign Policy* 8 (Fall 1972).

3. Feeling no responsibility for the system, they hold their assets in whichever national currency appears most likely to appreciate in value and/or has the highest yield at the moment—switching rapidly among currencies (and even buying gold in the free market) as the situation changes. Some of those oil countries which are members of the IMF have even opted out of the SDR scheme, which was a first step toward reducing such problems. For the problems involved, see C. Fred Bergsten, "Reforming the Dollar: An International Monetary Policy for the United States," *Council on Foreign Relations Paper on International Affairs No. 2* (New York, Council on Foreign Relations, September 1972), esp. pp. 9-13 [chapter 4 in this volume].

4. As argued by Theodore H. Moran, "Coups and Costs," *Foreign Policy* 8 (Fall 1972).

5. The author's specific proposal was outlined in *Foreign Policy* 10 (Spring 1973), pp. 185-187.

28 The Response to the Third World

The threat from the Third World to a number of vital interests of the United States has deepened over the past year, and has broadened into new areas of critical importance.

—The oil cartel cut production significantly for several months, embargoed its political adversaries, and raised prices dramatically—and might do so again.

—Commodity cartels have been set up, or accelerated their activities, for eight primary products in addition to oil,[1] and a dozen more could follow.

—Most countries in the Third World are moving speedily and effectively to harness the "powerful" multinational firms to actively promote their own national interests, and thereby are levying increasingly significant economic costs on the United States.[2]

—Many countries in the Third World are successfully penetrating U.S. markets for manufactured products through exchange-rate depreciations and export subsidies.

—The Third World is threatening to block urgently needed reforms of the international economic order by using its collective veto power in the existing institutions.

In addition to these and many other economic issues (such as Turkey's renewal of opium production), the threat from the Third World has expanded dangerously into the security sphere. The Third World has become the focal point of potential nuclear proliferation. India has attained nuclear capability, and is helping Argentina to do so. Brazil is almost certain to go nuclear. Israel already has a major capability; both it and Egypt are to get expanded U.S. help. Iran is buying reactors from France, and the Shah has reportedly stated his intention to become a nuclear power. And there seems a high probability that some of the oil producers in the Middle East will also seek to do so.

With or without nuclear weapons, the incidence of armed conflict within the Third World could well accelerate. "Local leviathans" such as Brazil, Iran, India, and Nigeria are clearly seeking regional dominance, and indeed a place on the world stage.[3] But they face serious competition: from Argentina, Mexico, and Venezuela in Latin America; from Saudi Arabia

Originally published in *Foreign Policy* 17, Winter 1974-75.

and Iraq in the Persian Gulf; from China and Pakistan in the Asian subcontinent; from Zaire in Africa; and from each other where their regions overlap, as with India and Iran. These new threats to peace come at a time of ongoing hostilities between Israel and the Arabs in the Middle East, and between Communists and non-Communists in Southeast Asia. In addition to the human tragedies of such conflicts, they could involve the superpowers and hence threaten both vital U.S. national interests and world peace.

While these developments threaten key interests of the United States, they are, of course, providing major new sources of wealth and power for the countries of the Third World. And most of the steps undertaken by the Third World are both fully understandable and at least partially just.

The terms of trade did turn against most primary producers, including the oil countries, for most of the postwar period. The industrialized countries were slow to negotiate commodity agreements when their chief purpose was to prevent disastrous declines in Third World earnings. The industrialized countries have moved too slowly to provide access to their markets for the developing countries, even for processed raw materials, let alone finished manufactures. The home countries of multinational firms have been unwilling even to discuss surveillance of the activities of the firms in poorer host countries, let alone limitations on their actions.

The Third World has been excluded from much of the discussion on the international economic rules and institutions which vitally affect its national interests. The rich countries have been niggardly with their foreign aid over the past decade. The companies and governments of the rich countries have provided ample demonstrations of the utility of exercising monopoly leverage to maximize earnings and political power; indeed, the few countries which consume the lion's share of world resources sound a bit disingenuous in railing against the "unfairness" of a few countries' being in a position to produce the lion's share of world resources. Thus, the Third World is quite right to call for the creation of a new international economic order, which more fully responds to its needs and in which it plays a role commensurate with its ability to affect that order.

Unfortunately, the United States has continued to view developing countries primarily as pawns in its ongoing superpower competition with the Soviet Union (and, to a lesser extent, China)—as objects, rather than subjects, of world politics. The United States alone, or virtually alone, among the industrialized countries, has failed to implement tariff preferences for the manufactured products of the Third World, reduced its foreign aid, opposed all commodity agreements, and opposed linking the creation of international monetary reserves to development assistance. The policies of the United States have thus contributed significantly to the radicalization of Third World policies, and even to its tilting against the United States in favor of industrial competitors in some instances.

As a result of their shabby treatment in the past, and skepticism about meaningful change in the attitudes of the rich, the countries of the Third World are unlikely to recant quickly the policies based on that new power which has so sharply boosted their pocketbooks and prestige. Indeed, it may be impossible to persuade them to do so even with the most forthcoming measures.

The United States must therefore prepare to defend itself through new national policies, including efforts to break up the solidarity of the Third World itself, and seek to coordinate those policies with the other industrialized countries to reduce the threat of increasing tension with them. But such policies are both very risky and very costly, and might not succeed in any event. Hence primary focus must be placed on cooperative measures with the Third World to promote jointly the interests of both groups. However, the Third World will certainly not change unless it is offered the alternative of a truly new international economic order in which its legitimate interests in both adequate economic return and full political participation are met. An effective response to the Third World thus requires both decisive national actions by the United States and the creation of an entirely new framework for international economic cooperation.

The Response: Conceptual Bases

Such U.S. policies must be based on a whole new set of far-reaching changes in international security and economic relationships. An understanding of these new conceptual foundations for policy is a necessary basis for proposing specific measures, and is more important than any particular proposals.

First, the fundamental nature of the international system has changed dramatically from a bipolar world of rigid alliances grouped around the nuclear superpowers to a multipolar world of shifting alliances, in which different coalitions face each other on different issues.[4] This is especially true on economic issues, where the gap between others' power and that of the United States is much narrower than in the security arena. Thus, the United States cannot, on economic issues, now count on the support of either its industrialized allies or its former clients in the Third World, whose interests on these issues often differ from its own.[5]

Second, economic issues have risen rapidly toward the top of the agenda of world politics. The impact of external events on the economies of virtually all countries is becoming increasingly important. And governments, responding to the demands of their electorates, are accepting responsibility for an increasing array of economic objectives.

Third, and closely related, is the intense and accelerating politicization of international economics. During the first postwar period, broad security concerns largely determined the structure of international economic relations. Within that structure, the day-to-day management of economic and security issues was largely compartmentalized. Each was kept pretty much within its own bureaucratic and institutional channels, and linkage between the two was unusual.[6] In addition, the international rules and institutions created at the beginning of the postwar period—the International Monetary Fund (IMF) for monetary issues, the General Agreement on Tariffs and Trade (GATT) for trade—permitted the settlement of most economic disputes on a largely technical, nonpolitical basis.

Repoliticization of the international economy began in the mid-1960's, when General De Gaulle challenged the dollar-based monetary system for reasons more political than economic. It accelerated after 1967, as the rules and institutional bases of the old structure began to disintegrate: the devaluation of sterling heralded the end of fixed exchange rates, the agreement to create Special Drawing Rights (SDR's) provided a potential substitute for the dollar, and the Kennedy Round completed the steady trend of postwar trade-liberalizing negotiations. In August 1971, the United States too decided that the system—which it had created, and which only it could maintain—no longer served its interests, and so violated both of the fundamental rules of the game: it used its economic power to force economic change, without even seeking to achieve the needed reforms of the monetary and trading systems through negotiation first, and it politicized the economics to a significant degree. The final coup de grâce to the old order came in October 1973, when the Arab oil producers explicitly and overtly employed their economic power to pursue security objectives.

Fourth, this use and politicization of economic power is legitimized by the structural asymmetries which now dot the international landscape.[7] In the past, most countries possessed roughly equal military and economic strength. The United States was a superpower on both counts. The less-developed countries were weak on both. Western Europe and Japan were in the middle on both.

Now, however, some countries possess tremendous economic strength but virtually no military power, and vice versa. This asymmetry appeared for Japan and Germany, and a few other European countries, in the 1960's. The oil countries now represent the most extreme cases, but a large number of other Third World countries with global economic clout have, at most, local military capabilities. At the other end of the spectrum lie India and perhaps China, coupling extreme economic poverty with nuclear capability—the nuclear "have-nots."

The economically powerful are highly likely to use their economic power overtly to pursue their overall national objectives, including security objectives, if they are unsuccessful in achieving their goals through more pacific means. Even more ominously, it must be feared that the militarily powerful will use that power, if necessary, to shore up their economic weaknesses.[8] Yet it is extremely difficult, even in principle, to challenge these applications of comparative bargaining advantage. These asymmetries virtually foreordain a continuing use of economic, and even military power to pursue economic objectives, and of economic power to pursue security objectives, in the absence of sweeping systemic reform.

Fifth, the previous Third World has now split into two groups. One is the new Third World of countries not yet fully industrialized, but with major economic attributes: possession of key raw materials (e.g., Venezuela, Malaysia), a highly competitive manufacturing sector (e.g., Korea, Taiwan), a large and rapidly growing market (e.g., Indonesia), or all three (e.g., Brazil, Iran). This group includes all the large countries of Latin America, most of the Middle East, all of East Asia (except perhaps Indochina), and a few countries in Africa.

These countries still face serious problems, to be sure, and therein lies part of the need for new international arrangements. But they have, in effect, become the world's new middle class. Many of their economies continue to boom while the economies of most industrialized countries are stagnating. They have the indigenous talent needed to determine where their interests lie, and to go about promoting those interests effectively.

The major goals of these countries now include political independence and meaningful participation in the ordering of the world, as well as continued economic progress. At the same time, their increasing economic success increases their dependence on other countries—though it changes the form of that dependence. And they should be adopting more responsible policies to promote world economic order. In this sense, they are replicating the transition of Japan in the 1960's from a developing to an industrial country. And, like Japan during that period, most of them have been slow to seize the responsibility for the world system which should accompany their new roles, though the First World has been even slower to recognize their ascendance than the earlier ascendance of Japan, and thus has provided little leadership in helping them do so.

The second group is the new Fourth World of countries which possess relatively few economic attributes. They are now the real "have-not" nations, which suffered from extreme poverty even before the crushing additional blows of dramatically higher prices for food and fuel. They include the Indian subcontinent, much of Africa, and, to a lesser extent, some of the smaller countries of Central America and the Caribbean.[9] They present a much different set of problems from those of the new Third World, whose members possess many of the attributes needed for self-sustaining economic progress and political independence.

Sixth, the underlying nature of the international economic problem appears to have been reversed. From at least the late 1920's through the early 1970's, unemployment was at virtually all times the primary economic problem faced by virtually all countries. The postwar economic rules and institutions were born of the interwar depression and were reinforced by the pervasive fears of unemployment in the early years after 1945. Hence they were aimed at avoiding unemployment and preventing countries from trying to export unemployment to each other. Economists devoted most of their attention to the problems of unemployment and growth.

Now, however, inflation has replaced unemployment as the primary economic problem in most industrial countries, and has become the primary political problem in many as well. Many countries are thus seeking to export inflation to each other through export controls and competitive *up*valuations of exchange rates, despite the slowdown in global growth, with its rising rates of unemployment. This greatly enhances the power of countries which possess resources needed to fight inflation, including low-wage labor (as embodied in products manufactured in developing countries) and raw materials.

In my view, severe recessions are unlikely, and inflation will probably remain the world's dominant economic problem for the foreseeable future. If it does, this reversal in the orientation of international economic issues will persist and grow even more pronounced. At a minimum, inflation is almost certain to rank much more closely with unemployment as a policy problem than it has for 40 years, which is enough to sharply alter the priorities traditionally attached to the different economic targets and concerns of nations. If inflation and high unemployment were to persevere together, the international problem could be even more complicated, because countries might try to export both inflation and unemployment by applying different kinds of trade controls in different sectors of their economies.

The Policy Framework

These changes have produced, in just a few years, a startlingly different world in which the United States must fashion its policies.

The United States, in fact, faces the wholly unanticipated specter of a Third World which is often far more unified on key issues than the erstwhile First World of rich, industrial countries. This dramatic change is seen most obviously in the stark contrast between the continuing scrambles for special deals by the oil consumers and the effective cartelization of the oil producers. But it is now being repeated in a host of other commodities. And developing countries which host multinational firms are increasingly sharing their experiences to enhance their national bargaining positions, while the United States, the largest home country, sits idly by.

The destitutes of the Fourth World also importantly affect this new international milieu. They are desperately poor, may face periodic famines with millions starving, and have little economic power to participate in the fierce competition and negotiation engaged in by the rest of the world. Most of them can appeal only to the humanitarian impulses of the outside world for help, and they know only too well that those pleas often go largely unheeded.

But the biggest of them, India, has attained nuclear capacity. Driven by desperation, others may well do the same, and they may regard superpower deterrence as being as inapplicable to their use of nuclear weapons on the local level as it has proved to be against their use of conventional arms. The use of economic power to attain political objectives conjures up unhappy scenarios, one of which (the oil crisis) we are still living through and have yet to overcome. But the use of military power to pursue economic goals, even without any direct involvement of the superpowers, is terrifying. Hence both the power of the Third World and the poverty of the Fourth World pose major threats to fundamental interests of the United States. And the collapse of the international economic order, which governed most economic relations among nations with a high degree of effectiveness during the first postwar generation, leaves an exceedingly dangerous vacuum into which descend all the present international economic problems.

The world position of the United States, as it forms its policies, has also changed in fundamental ways. Exports now represent over 7 percent of the GNP, as do imports. Almost one-fourth of all new investment by U.S. firms now takes place overseas, and foreign investments provide a roughly equivalent share of U.S. corporate profits. All these ratios are rising rapidly.

In addition, the dollar devaluations of 1971-73 accounted for at least one-fourth of the increase in our rate of inflation. Foreign demand for U.S. output (particularly farm products) and price increases by foreign sellers (particularly oil) added a great deal more. The U.S. effort to use price controls to fight inflation was subverted in a large part by exports of controlled goods, in response to higher prices abroad and the close ties among world markets. Some fear that flexible exchange rates and flows of petrodollars will undermine the U.S. banking system, heretofore regarded as impregnable. The old refrain of American isolationists—"let trade wars come, we'll win them"—now sounds as ludicrous as Mao's famous dictum that China will emerge "victorious" from the ashes of a nuclear holocaust.

At the same time, the United States remains the strongest country. It is the only nation which is both a military and economic superpower. It is far more self-sufficient than any other non-Communist economy. It has the largest market in the world. The dollar remains the leading world currency. U.S.-based firms continue to lead the world in many key industries.

Thus, the United States retains a great deal of negative international economic power—the power to hurt others, and block their initiatives. This combination, in fact, dictates the proper U.S. response to the Third and Fourth Worlds: a combination of carrots and sticks, in which the United States employs tough national measures to defend its interests and seeks new international arrangements to create a more just, and therefore more stable, economic order. Precisely such a combination is in fact being applied by countries of the Third World themselves: the carrots of preferential commodity sales to favored countries and tax benefits to pliant multinationals, the sticks of commodity denial and expropriation to the uncooperative.

Most of the other industrial countries are pursuing solely national approaches. The bilateral deals with individual oil producers sought by Japan and several European countries are the most obvious examples, and the United States has flirted with a similar strategy. Europe has made bilateral arrangements with its overseas associates, including a number of former members of the British Commonwealth. Indeed, one major reason for U.S. multilateral initiatives is the need to halt the proliferation of such bilateral deals, which further strengthen the Third World and weaken the industrial countries.

The Response to Commodity Power

At present, the United States and the other consuming countries are in a relatively weak bargaining position vis-à-vis the oil exporters and their emulators in other commodities. As under the "massive retaliation" strategic doctrine of the Eisenhower years, the United States has no capability for flexible response, at least in the short run, either to the withholding of supplies or to major price increases. Widespread rationing is simply not viable, and market forces alone are not likely to reduce demand much in the short run. U.S. government stockpiles do exist for a few commodities, but even they cannot, under present law, be used to combat the economic actions of supplying countries. And new production, either in the United States or in "safe" foreign areas (if any can be found), takes time to develop.

Thus, at present, the United States can respond to raw materials problems only by military or economic retaliation. But either would raise enormous problems—in humanitarian, systemic, and domestic political terms. By contrast, the commodity producers possess a high degree of flexibility: they can raise prices slowly or swiftly, hold back supplies a little (often under the guise of technical problems) or a lot, announce their steps publicly or proceed sub rosa. Thus, the present imbalance of power between producers and consumers extends to tactics as well as to the fundamentals.

One obvious alternative is to do nothing. Such a policy would be quite rational if the costs of acting, and preparing for action, exceeded the damages caused by the foreign measures. It would be particularly attractive if one culd be confident that market forces would by themselves rectify the problem within a reasonable period of time.

Unfortunately, it is quite possible that the costs of inaction would be severe. Renewed production cutbacks and further price rises are quite possible in oil. No other single commodity is nearly as important, but the dozen or more which could experience similar developments could produce important economic costs and major political confrontations. Furthermore, inaction has the adverse effect of encouraging producing countries to intensify their use of commodity power. The inaction of the oil-consuming countries has clearly encouraged OPEC to push on, and has encouraged the creation of "one, two, many OPEC's." Indeed, the major objective of U.S. policy in this area should be deterrence of aggressive action by producing countries and unilateral scrambles by individual consuming countries.

Another alternative is for the United States to join the scramble for special deals. This is almost inevitable in the absence of more constructive policies. And the United States, with its huge market and vast reservoir of technology and capital, has much to offer the producing countries. Wouldn't the United States avoid any commodity problems if it could "lock up" Saudi Arabia, Canada, Australia, and Brazil? Or how about a Fortress Western Hemisphere?

Unfortunately (from a purely U.S. standpoint) it is simply not possible to "lock up" countries with enough commodity power. It is precisely those countries which gain most from playing off consumers against each other, and which would most resent the implications of dependence inherent in such a bilateral relationship. The major Latin-American countries epitomize both factors. As a result, any U.S. quest for special deals would simply reinforce the strength of the producers and encourage them to push harder—indeed, even to toughen their positions to avoid any appearance of "selling out to the Americans"—as the U.S. overtures toward Saudi Arabia seem already to have done. In addition, this approach would further increase the likelihood of conflict among the consuming countries.

The most straightforward response to individual commodity problems, and the simplest to execute, is the creation and maintenance of national stockpiles to defend the economic security of the United States. Stockpiles now exist for a number of commodities, such as bauxite and tin, where cartel action is likely. But present law permits use of these stocks, and decisions on stockpile levels, solely on traditional considerations of military security.

Indeed, large sales have recently taken place, or have been requested by the Administration, because the much shorter wars envisaged now (compared to the early 1950's, when stockpile policy was developed) require smaller holdings in terms of those traditional arguments. The result has been U.S. sales of key materials from the stockpile at a time when larger stocks are needed to deter cartel action. New legislation is required to make current stocks available for use in defending the economic security of the United States, and to authorize the building of stocks of materials where threats exist.

Such national stockpiles might be a sufficient defense for the United States against price gouging or denial in many commodities. It is clear from the historical record that stocks can have a decisive effect on commodity prices if they are large enough. For example, the huge grain reserves held by the United States in the mid-1960's prevented significant increases in food prices despite sudden, massive increases in shipments to the Soviet Union and India, in contrast to the dramatic increase in prices triggered by Soviet purchases in 1972, when stocks were much lower. And world tin shot through the price ceiling of the International Tin Agreement recently when its buffer stock was exhausted.

But building adequate stockpiles could be costly, depending on the nature of the particular commodity markets. And such a defense for the United States would not eliminate the threat of scrambles among the other consuming countries—most of whom are more dependent than the United States on imports of most commodities—unless they too built national stockpiles, or unless they were confident that the United States would make its stocks available to them in a crisis.[10] Finally, the large-scale purchases needed to build a credible stockpile would boost the prices of the commodities in question for some time.

These considerations all point to the desirability of an international, rather than a purely national, approach to the commodity problem. At a minimum, the consuming countries—particularly Western Europe, Japan, and perhaps some of the poorer consuming countries, along with the United States—should create and maintain joint stockpiles in order to spread costs and minimize national differences if the stockpile deterrents had to be used. They have been moving in this direction for oil, through the Integrated Emergency Program which evolved from the Washington Energy Conference of February 1974.

Beyond stockpiling, there are several other steps which the consuming countries could take to buttress their joint positions. They could develop standby measures to enable them to quickly reduce demand, at least for a while. They could improve their skill in recycling renewable resources, which include most of the minerals where supply is threatened. For the longer run, they could seek a steady reduction of demand. And they should develop a basis for increasing domestic production, or production within the countries of the consuper group, in order to boost total world supply. The United States is in a particularly strong position to lead in the development of such policies, because it is less dependent than most consuming countries on imports of commodities, and thus can contribute more to an international program.

If the consumers could agree to such measures, their substantive, and hence tactical, position vis-à-vis the producing countries would be strengthened immensely—both because each could defend itself far better, and because the risk of scrambles among them would be much reduced. Once such steps are taken, the next move should be the active pursuit —among the major consuming and supplying countries—of commodity agreements which would encompass guaranteed floor prices for the producers and guaranteed ceiling prices for the consumers. These price commitments would automatically protect the consumers against supply cutoffs and the producers against drastic reductions in foreign demand.

The consumers could spend part of the money allocated to building national stocks to maintain the agreed floor prices. In the process, a buffer stock would develop which would provide insurance to the consuming countries against violations of the agreement by the producing countries. The suppliers, by accepting a ceiling price and thereby guaranteeing access to their supplies, would reduce the threat of stockpiles and consumer policies of checking demand and developing substitutes. Such deals would also reduce the vulnerability of producers to the fluctuations in commodity prices, which are inherently possible in these markets, and which could even reduce their commodity power as suddenly as it has risen. Some countries, like the United States, both import and export commodities, and could benefit on both sides of the equation, as well as play a critical role in promoting the entire process.

Thus, there would appear to be a firm basis for a wide range of commodity agreements which would promote the economic security and welfare of both the producing and consuming countries, once it becomes clear that the consumers are willing to take the national actions—preferably together—to redress the current imbalance of commodity power favoring the producers. Widespread participation in the agreements by both producers and consumers should be promoted by denying their benefits to nonmembers. A general commodity code, which would detail the principles against which individual agreements would be negotiated, and which would elevate the whole issue of commodity trade to its rightful place in international economic arrangements, should also be sought.

Some observers would reject this approach on the grounds that most commodity agreements attempted in the past have not worked. In my view, those earlier attempts are simply not relevant to the current situation. Most of them were based on pleas by producers to consumers to keep prices from collapsing. They were unequal treaties, and were viewed by consuming countries as adjuncts to foreign aid rather than as integral to their own economic interests. To be sure, commodity agreements are more certain to hold prices up than to check them, for the simple reason that stocks can always be accumulated but may prove inadequate to meet sharp increases in demand. The creation of an adequate buffer stock would be a key requirement for participation by consuming countries, and would be cheaper for each than building up adequate national stockpiles alone.

Unlike past efforts, new commodity agreements would be based on the new balance of power among producers and consumers. This balance, rooted in fundamental changes in world economic and security relationships, and in world commodity markets per se, is one of the real uncertainties which both producers and consumers face. Hence both groups would go to the bargaining table on an equal basis, and both would have deep vested interests in preserving any new agreements which could be negotiated.

The negotiations to determine agreed price ranges and rules of access would be very tough. But they need not produce a highly politicized confrontation between North and South, if only because a number of key commodity producers (Canada, Australia, the United States, and France) are in the North and a number of large commodity consumers are in the South. If it were clear that the consumers were determined to move unilaterally or in concert in the absence of such agreements, deals should be possible.

In addition to, or instead of, a general commodity code, new international trade rules are needed to restrain export controls and other limitations on access to supplies, like the restraints that have applied to import controls and other limitations on access to markets throughout the postwar period. Such rules would provide for multinational retaliation against unjustified national restrictions. They would reinforce the commodity arrangements in assuring supplies of commodities where specific agreements could be negotiated, and would reduce the risk of interruptions in supplies of all other products. Such a "GATT for export controls" should be an integral part of any new producer-consumer relationship, in manufactured products as well as in commodities. Since virtually every country depends on imports for many of its vital necessities, all should have an interest in reducing the risks of trade wars of export controls.

The Response to Investment Threats

The same combination of national and international measures is needed to counter the threat to U.S. economic interests of growing host country success—in the Third World as well as in the industrial countries and even in the Fourth World—in tilting in their direction the benefits brought by foreign direct investment. It is becoming increasingly anomalous that major U.S. national interests—such as jobs, exports, technology, and capital flows—are negotiated solely between multinational firms and governments of host countries. There are three results of this process: (1) economic benefits are increasingly being transferred from the United States to the host countries; (2) those opposed to all foreign investment by U.S. firms are presented a new and far stronger argument than they had before; and (3) there is conflict between home and host countries, and among host countries, as they compete to provide the locus of world production for an increasing number of important products.

As a first step, the United States needs to adopt policies which stop the transfer of investments to the Third World through host-country subsidies, in cases where such transfers hurt U.S. economic interests. Along with the firms' needs for national resources, low-cost but readily trainable labor, and the more ready acceptance of pollution in the Third World, these subsidies induce the firms to keep investing despite the increasingly tough conditions levied on them by host governments. Just as the United States (and most other countries) has for many years applied countervailing duties on imports to offset export subsidies by foreign governments, so should it (as well as other home countries of multinational firms) offset, through tax action or direct controls, tax benefits and other subsidies offered by foreign governments to attract direct investment in cases where the resulting investment proves injurious to other U.S. interests.[11]

It is more difficult to deal with the requirements which host countries levy on firms to promote their national objectives: job quotas, export quotas, value-added, capital inflows and limitations on repatriation of earnings, infusion of modern technology (whether or not economically appropriate), upgrading of the local labor force, etc. Many of these requirements are fully justified, to countervail the proclivities of the firms to violate accepted norms of market behavior (e.g., by denying their local subsidiaries access to the latest technology, and evading local taxes through transfer pricing). Other requirements may promote home-country as well as host-country interests, e.g., by increasing world competition by forbidding firms to allocate markets among their different subsidiaries. Most importantly, the goals of the host countries—more jobs, better balance-of-payments positions, modernization and industrialization of their societies—are fully legitimate, and deserve the full support of the United States. Indeed, the United States should alter its policies to provide positive incentives for U.S. firms to meet the legitimate interests of host countries.

But many host-country practices are unjustified, and there are many ways for the United States to support Third World goals which are far more effective and far less risky than letting them dictate the activities of local subsidiaries.

An escape clause for investment, analogous to the traditional escape clause for trade, would enable the United States to deal on a case-by-case basis with the problems caused both by subsidies and by host-country requirements. Under the trade escape clause, any U.S. interest which feels injured or threatened by imports can petition for relief and, if the case is accepted, the government will place temporary limits on the imports, and/or help the injured party—through financial and technical assistance—adjust to the new circumstances. A similar procedure is needed whereby U.S. interests injured by foreign investments can petition for relief and, if the case is upheld, get help through temporary limitations on the investment itself and/or adjustment assistance. Needless to say, the United States would not support such investments through tax benefits and government guarantees.

But, as in the case of raw materials, these national policies would not alone solve the problem. Indeed, they might trigger at least three types of new international conflicts: (1) between the United States and the host countries as they jousted for the locus of production, with the hosts adopting increasingly subtle policies in an effort to evade U.S. retaliation, and the United States extending its net in response; (2) between the Ud ited States and other home countries, if the latter adopted more lenient attitudes toward host-country policies and hence received favored treatment from hosts on overall investment policy (and perhaps in other areas as well); and (3) between the United States and the hosts again, due to their favoritism toward other home countries. Another very serious aspect of the whole process would probably be an undermining of the very real gains to the world economy, and to the United States, which derive from most foreign direct investments by U.S.-based firms.

There is thus a compelling need for new international rules and institutions to govern international investment. Indeed, it is anomalous that no such rules exist. The trade wars of the 1930's were caused by national use of import controls to try to maximize the benefits to each of the primary mode of international exchange at that time. It is universally agreed that those measures helped no country but rather exacerbated the Great Depression. International rules and institutional arrangements to prevent the renewal of trade wars were thus set up for the postwar period, and have been quite effective.

Now, international investment and intracorporate trade have replaced traditional, arm's length trade as the primary mode of international exchange. The economic problems faced by most host countries virtually assure that they will try to use national policies to seize increasing shares of the benefits of that investment. And the increased economic and political power of many provides them with the ability to try. The same cycles of policy emulation and retaliation that marked international trade in the 1930's are thus almost certain to mark international investment in the 1980's, if not before, unless the world learns the lesson of the past and creates new international rules to deal with the problem.

As with commodities, the interests of countries on both sides of the transactions in avoiding such conflict suggest a high potential for negotiating new international rules—if the legitimate needs of the Third and, in this case, Fourth Worlds can be met in more constructive ways. (This requires, inter alia, that the rules provide an international counter to the ability of many transnational enterprises to evade the national jurisdictions of all countries on some key issues.) As with trade, where all countries both export and import, many countries must increasingly face investment issues as a two-way phenomenon, as traditional home countries (Britain, France, the United States) become host countries as well, and traditional host countries (Brazil, India) become home countries too. As with commodities, the United States occupies a unique middle position, as both the largest home country and the second largest (to Canada) host country, and hence could more readily than others adopt a leadership role. And, as in the case of commodities, negotiations on this issue need not produce North-South confrontation, if only because many countries from the North remain primarily host rather than home countries.

A Strategy of Interdependence

The needed response to these two specific threats from the Third World, in raw materials and investment, already adds up to an ambitious set of policies. Some of the proposals, such as wide-ranging commodity agreements and explicit surveillance of foreign investments by the U.S. government, deviate sharply from traditional U.S. approaches.

The responses proposed so far, however, are largely defensive and negative. They aim at preventing international conflict, and hence are essential. But they may be inadequate to deal with one of the key sources of the current problem: the wholly inadequate response by the United States, and most of the other industrial countries, to the legitimate aspirations of the developing countries. To be equitable and hence salable, such a package must include more positive support by the rich countries for primary policy objectives of the Third World.

Of critical importance is the desire of most countries in the Third World—even those with few resources other than their new commodity power, like the desert oil countries—to diversify and modernize their economies, which in most cases means industrialization. This in turn usually requires export-oriented strategies, because efficient economies of scale cannot be supported by the domestic markets of most countries (or even by regional associations, where they are feasible).

The United States should improve the access of the Third World to its market in two major ways. First, it should extend generalized tariff preferences to the manufactured exports of these countries on a far more generous basis than proposed in the Trade Reform Act, returning instead to the original U.S. proposals of 1969-70: no quota ceilings on preferential imports, a far wider list of eligible products, and liberal rules determining country and product eligibility. Unlike in 1969-70, however, this effort should not be viewed as an adjunct to the U.S. foreign aid program, but rather as one step in evolving a set of cooperative multilateral economic relationships.

Second, all tariff and nontariff barriers to world trade should be sharply reduced, and eliminated wherever possible, in the forthcoming Multilateral Trade Negotiations (MTN). Since the highest barriers usually persist in precisely those industries the Third World is entering, such reductions would go far toward meeting its needs. The MTN provides an apt forum for addressing the several key trade issues among which linkage is needed: reduction of tariff and nontariff barriers, liberalization of the several national schemes which extend generalized tariff preferences, commodity agreements on a product-by-product or sector basis, perhaps a new general commodity code, and new rules to limit future use of both export controls and import controls.

There are numerous other measures which the United States should take as part of this strategy. In order to provide additional outlets for exports from the developing countries, the United States should revive its earlier support for the formation of free trade areas and customs unions among developing countries, with supporting payments unions where they would be helpful. In the monetary area, it should support the link between the creation of international reserves and development assistance,[12] increases in the quotas of many Third World countries in the IMF, and better access for them to the world's private capital markets.

Such a strategy of interdependence, including the proposals made above on commodities, could play a major role in the battle against world inflation, as well as provide a constructive response to the Third World. It would both provide a check on commodity prices and reduce their instability. It would marry the reservoirs of under-utilized labor in the Third World with the anti-inflationary imperatives of the industrial world. Commodity agreements and new ground rules for multinational corporations could spur additional output of raw materials and of food, where developing countries provide the main potential locus for rapid expansion of desperately needed supply.

The far-reaching economic interdependence of all nations becomes clear at this point. The need of the rich, industrial countries for assured access to supplies of primary products and cheaper manufactured goods is matched by the need of the middle-class, industrializing countries for access to markets for both those primary products and their manufactures, and in some cases for foreign investment and technical assistance to help them take advantage of that access. A far-reaching strategy of interdependence could thus bolster the true independence of all countries: the industrial countries by enhancing their economic security and helping them fight inflation, the new middle class by enhancing their prospects for further development and modernization. Indeed, the European Community and Japan have already begun to link quite closely their aid, trade, investment, and commodity policies toward the Third World, and the United States will slip even further behind in this phase of its competition with them if it does not do so as well.

But the increased imports, which would reduce the costs of many of our material inputs and consumer products, and provide a needed competitive spur to some of our highly concentrated industries, could displace workers and hurt individual firms. Indeed, this very real concern is probably *the most serious obstacle* to U.S. adoption of the proposed approach. A strategy of interdependence would thus require a U.S. willingness to spend adequate funds—perhaps as much as $300 million to $500 million per year—to compensate injured parties (mainly workers) and to help them find new employment.

The final major component of the needed new order is as much political as economic: effective participation by the Third World in the decision-making process on international economic issues. These countries quite rightly reject the imposition on them of rules and institutional arrangements created solely by the industrialized nations, including those which survive from a period when the United States and Western Europe dominated the world economy. Inclusion of more countries in the decision-making process may make it more difficult, but there is no prospect of a viable system without it.

A start in this direction was made with the creation of the Committee of Twenty to try to negotiate world monetary reform, and continues with its successor ''interim committee'' within the IMF and with the Ministerial Committee of the Fund and World Bank on the transfer of real resources. Each of these groups has major representation from the developing world. And the increase in Third World quotas at the IMF, as suggested above, would automatically give them a larger voice in that institution. In addition, the Third World must have a major voice in each of the key aspects of the forthcoming trade negotiations, and in the development of new international conventions to deal with multinational enterprises.

The need is not for new institutions—except, perhaps, in cases where none now exist to cover an issue at all, such as investment—but rather for the formation of informal steering groups and, even more important, new processes through which all important participants are actively consulted at all stages of the evolution of international arrangements which affect their national interests. The final proof of the pudding will still be whether the industrial countries meet Third World requirements sufficiently to enable them to achieve their legitimate aspirations in constructive ways. But the sense of meaningful participation, in and of itself, would go far to meet a separate and very critical concern of the Third World.

Foreign aid has not been mentioned as part of this strategy. Most countries of the Third World no longer need the traditional types of help for specific projects or general budgetary and balance-of-payments support. Many no longer want such aid anyway, preferring to tap the private international capital markets—even at somewhat higher rates of interest—when they need foreign exchange.

However, many countries in the Third World do need access to modern science and technology, management and marketing skills, to further their modernization efforts. Some of these assets can be bought commercially or imported through transnational enterprises. But help can be provided through governmental programs, both bilaterally and through multilateral channels, where research is needed to develop new technologies adapted to Third World problem areas.

The United States is in an extremely good position to provide such assistance. It could best do so by creating the International Development Institute proposed in 1970-71 by former President Nixon, on the recommendation of his Task Force on International Development, chaired by Rudolph Peterson. Such assistance would round out a strategy in which the United States would help the countries of the Third World pursue their national objectives, in return for Third World actions which would help the United States to pursue its national objectives.

The Response to the Fourth World

As noted earlier, a new Fourth World of resource-poor, low-income countries is now clearly distinguishable from the Third World of resource "haves" and rapid industrializers. These countries pose three kinds of issues for the United States: (1) humanitarian concern over their abject poverty, and even mass starvation; (2) the risk that their desperation will drive them to threaten, or even to take, military action in efforts to relieve their economic straits (or divert attention from them), a risk of inordinate consequence concerning the one nuclear power (India) in the group and others which might follow; and (3) the ever present possibility that the resources, or other potential sources of economic power which they possess, will someday catapult them into the Third World, perhaps with even greater lust for revenge against the rich.

All three problems derive fundamentally from the poverty of this Fourth World. The poverty is, in turn, fed by the rapid growth of their populations, which the recent World Population Conference in Bucharest agreed is likely to slow only when their economic conditions improve significantly. Some of the steps suggested above toward the Third World—commodity agreements, reduction of trade barriers, access to private capital markets, technical assistance—would help. But few of the poorest could really take much advantage of these opportunities, especially in competition with the rising Third World countries.

Hence, an effective U.S. response to them must comprise significant amounts of foreign aid, carried out primarily through institutional methods which respect the zeal for autonomy even of the poorest. Thus, U.S. foreign aid should focus on the Fourth World. Its explicit purpose should be to foster its economic development, defined on whatever terms individual recipient countries suggest—maximum growth per se, reductions in unemployment, redistribution of internal income. At the present time, and perhaps for the next few years, much of the aid would aim simply at avoiding a sharp deterioration of conditions, even starvation, and would thus amount to emergency relief from the increase in prices of fuel, food, and fertilizers.

The United States should channel most of this assistance through multilateral lending institutions, to reduce the likelihood of bilateral political problems and to maximize the total flow of funds. Any remaining bilateral aid is best handled through consortia of the traditional type. New forms of assistance—linking the creation of world reserves to real development needs, allocating a share of the benefits from exploiting the seas' riches—should play an important role in the process. Other rich countries, notably the oil producers, should contribute both to the relief needed now and the long-run effort to reduce poverty. *But it is in the national interest of the United States to pursue such programs whether other potential donors do so or not.*

The United States should not expect the restoration of even a generous program of foreign aid to deter India, or others, from developing a nuclear capability. The objective of the program, in addition to its obvious humanitarian content, would be threefold: (1) to reduce the likelihood that Fourth World countries would, over time, be driven to desperate ''wars of redistribution,'' by supporting economic development which would both limit population growth and provide them with more resources; (2) to make clear that the United States is making every effort to help them achieve their legitimate national objectives; and (3) to tilt the Fourth World toward supporting U.S. policies vis-à-vis both the Third World and its industrial competitors, in cases—such as the creation of commodity cartels—where doing so is in their objective national interests and has been precluded mainly by the antagonisms produced by the wholly inadequate U.S. policies toward them.

Conclusions

The proposed program would obviously represent a major new initiative by the U.S. government. It could not be developed in detail and implemented simply as a stopgap answer to any individual short-run problem, nor purely out of compassion (however high-minded) for citizens of less-affluent countries. It could only be based on a recognition that such measures were needed to promote two sets of fundamental U.S. national interests: its economic interests in combating inflation, achieving economic security, and restoring cooperative international economic relations; and its foreign policy interests in nuclear nonproliferation and avoiding tensions among nations.

It might be asked why the United States should support the objectives of the Third World through the measures proposed, instead of simply letting them exercise their new power through commodity cartels, controlling transnational enterprises, export subsidies, and the like. The answer is both economic and political. The proposals made here would help fight inflation; most unilateral Third World efforts would accelerate it. The proposals here would begin to restore a functioning international economic order; most unilateral Third World efforts, and most unilateral responses to them by industrial countries, will further weaken the very fragile order that now exists. My proposals would begin to restore the economic security of nations and hence promote overall national security; unilateral initiatives and responses will heighten national, and hence international, insecurity. My proposals would seek to build a political base within the United States of positive support for Third World interests; aggressive Third World initiatives would lead instead to outrage and efforts to retaliate.

To be sure, the proposed program does not accept a number of the positions advanced most fervently by the Third World. It rejects "indexing" of the terms of trade, which would guarantee the developing countries that the prices they pay for imports (mainly manufactured goods) would not rise faster than the prices they receive for exports (mainly commodities). It rejects the "responsibility" of the industrial countries to extend foreign aid equal to 1 percent of their GNP's, or government aid equal to 0.7 percent. It rejects the Third World opposition to flexible exchahge rates, and direct linkage between the creation of SDR's and development assistance. It rejects the siren call of immediate cooperation between producers and consumers of oil and other raw materials, before the consumers have taken sufficient domestic measures to equalize the bargaining situation.

But the proposed program would make a massive contribution to the needs of the Third and Fourth Worlds. If offered sincerely and implemented faithfully, it should induce them to respond constructively and cooperatively in the search for a new international economic order. If they do not, the industrialized countries would then simply have no alternative to very tough reactions, such as declaring all countries which join commodity cartels ineligible for all forms of foreign assistance, and using the leverage afforded by their huge markets to discriminate between countries which cooperate and countries which do not.

After such a U.S. program was conceived in detail, a tremendous effort would be required to sell it domestically and implement it internationally. Powerful domestic interests—particularly groups of workers and perhaps the AFL-CIO as a whole, those who benefit from volatile commodity prices, multinational firms that want to avoid governmental intervention in their affairs, opponents of the needed budgetary expenditures—would oppose important parts of it.

Our society is not organized to prepare and implement such far-reaching programs, particularly when they depend on forging a consensus from a host of disparate elements, and cross the traditional dividing line between government and the private sector. Sustained leadership would be required, frequently by the President and at least one top official in the government. This would call for constant and active collaboration between those responsible for economic and foreign policy, and probably new machinery within the government to coordinate the many phases of the operation. One is tempted to call for a "Kissinger for foreign economic policy," but the task is even more difficult than the brilliant technical negotiations engineered by Kissinger, because it links so many more domestic interests and so many more foreign countries, and because it requires detailed attention to a host of issues sustained for many years.

But what is the alternative? There can be no "fortress America" in today's interdependent world economy. One need look only at oil, jobs in the factory and on the farm, and U.S. corporate profits to reject such nonsense. Nor can the United States force others—oil producers and "export platforms," Europeans and Japanese—to bend to its will. And today's international economic order is obviously inadequate to accomplish even the minimal task of assuring us all against a relapse into economic ruin and political fragmentation, let alone to constructively resolve the manifold problems confronting us.

The U.S. response to the Third (and Fourth) World should thus comprise a comprehensive, interlocking, and carefully orchestrated series of carrots and sticks. The United States should take steps to defend itself effectively—unilaterally, if necessary. But the fundamental strategy of interdependence should pursue a new international economic order within which the legitimate interests of all sets of nations would be served. Devising and implementing such a strategy is a worthy challenge for the economic and foreign policy-makers of the United States, and indeed could provide its primary focus for the rest of the 1970's.

Notes

1. Bananas, bauxite, coffee, copper, iron ore, mercury, phosphates, tin. For an analysis of these developments, and why they are likely to persist and proliferate, see C. Fred Bergsten, "The New Era in World Commodity Markets," *Challenge,* September/October 1974 [chapter 18 in this volume].

2. This thesis is developed in C. Fred Bergsten, "Coming Investment Wars?" *Foreign Affairs,* October 1974 [chapter 16 in this volume].

3. Samuel P. Huntington, "After Containment," *Annals,* March 1973.

4. Seyom Brown, *New Forces in World Politics* (Washington, D.C.: The Brookings Institution, 1974).

5. See Stanley Hoffman, "Choices," *Foreign Policy* 12. In "The Threat from the Third World," *Foreign Policy* 11, p. 124, I concluded that "In the early 1970's, most observers project an American-European-Japanese tripartite hegemony which may become obsolete before it is ever enthroned because of the economic progress of the Third World."

6. This has been characterized as a "two-track" system by Richard N. Cooper, "Trade Policy is Foreign Policy," *Foreign Policy* 9.

7. For a pathbreaking analysis of these asymmetries, see Robert O. Keohane and Joseph S. Nye, "World Politics and the International Economic System," in C. Fred Bergsten, *The Future of the International Economic Order: An Agenda for Research* (Lexington, Mass.: Lexington Books, D.C. Heath and Co., 1973).

8. Nuclear "wars of redistribution" are anticipated by Robert Heilbroner, *An Inquiry into the Human Prospect* (New York: W.W. Norton, 1974).

9. Some observers would include China in this grouping, but its preference for autarky has insulated it from the severity of recent world economic disturbances and renders highly unlikely its seeking outside help even for those problems which do result for it. China is an ardent cheer-

leader for Third World economic initiatives against the industrial countries, but due to its poverty and autarky has nothing to offer the new wielders of economic power, and hence is largely relegated to the sidelines.

10. Conversely, the scrambles could also be intensified if some countries built national stockpiles, as Japan is now doing, and the United States did not.

11. The present U.S. countervailing duty law is flawed because it does not condition application of such duties on injury to other U.S. interests. There is no reason for the U.S. government to deny U.S. consumers the benefits of export subsidies financed by foreign governments if no other Americans are injured, and there is no reason to deny U.S. firms the benefits of foreign investment subsidies if no other Americans are injured. But both kinds of subsidies should be countervailed if there is such injury.

12. The United States should do this in ways which will not undermine financial confidence in SDR's, as I proposed in *Foreign Policy* 10, pp. 185-187.

29

The Fourth Replenishment of the International Development Association

The U.S. Position in the World Economy of the 1970s

The proposed U.S. participation in the fourth replenishment of funds for the International Development Association (IDA), and expansion of the special funds of the Asian Development Bank (ADB), must be judged within the context of the dramatic changes which have transformed the U.S. position in the world economy within a very short period of time. The keynotes of that new U.S. position are *dependence* and *competition*.

Until quite recently, most Americans regarded our country as free to operate largely independent of external events. Now the energy crisis has brought crashingly home how dependent we have come to be. The energy crisis, however, is not an isolated event. The United States already depends on impots for over half its supply of six of the thirteen basic raw materials, and projections by the Department of the Interior indicate that the number will rise to nine a decade hence.[1] This represents the culmination of a long-term trend: the United States changed from a net exporter of raw materials to a net importer in the 1920s, and our dependence on foreign sources has been growing ever since.

Our dependence ranges far beyond raw materials. Almost five million U.S. jobs depend on exports. Our battle against inflation depends critically on imports of a wide range of manufactured foods and foodstuffs, as well as raw materials. A large and rapidly growing share of total U.S. corporate profits derive from foreign investments, and earnings on those investments are a major source of strength for the dollar and our balance of payments.

Until quite recently, most Americans also viewed the United States as internationally omnipotent, in two senses. First, we regarded ourselves as the most productive and efficient economy in the world, with unchallenged competitive superiority. Second, we thought we could unilaterally prompt any needed changes in international economic arrangements. Both views were largely true throughout the 1950s; the latter was even true into the late 1960s, as the United States pushed through both the Kennedy Round of trade negotiations and major changes in the international monetary system,

Originally presented as testimony to the Subcommittee on International Finance of the House Banking and Currency Committee in its hearings on *Providing for Additional U.S. Contributions to the Asian Development Bank and the International Development Association*, December 6, 1973.

and the notion of American competitive superiority remained imbued in the American mentality beyond its time because our internal economic situation was so favorable until the very end of the 1960s.

Both views are now clearly relics of the past. Per capita income in several European countries matches our own, and Japan will be there soon. U.S. international monetary reserves, relative to the level of our international transactions, are among the lowest of the industrialized countries and are far lower than the equivalent ratio for many developing countries. Germany and Japan have run far larger trade surpluses than ever achieved by the United States. And a series of events in the last two or three years, both at home and abroad, have clearly demonstrated that we can no longer force changes in international monetary and trading arrangements. In short, active competition among near equals has replaced U.S. dominance as the power base of the world economy.

The Threat From the Third World

Both new determinants of U.S. foreign economic policy—dependence and competition—are central to the focus of these hearings, U.S. relations with the developing countries. In a recent article,[2] I outlined in detail how many developing countries could use their new leverage to hurt U.S. interests. They could drive up our prices of raw materials through cartelization and hence further exacerbate inflation, or even deny us those materials. They could take over our investments, or at least sharply increase their take —and reduce ours—from both existing and new investments. They could deny us markets. They could block changes which we seek in the international monetary and trading rules and institutions.

The developing countries could take such steps against the industrialized world as a whole. Or they could use their leverage against the United States alone, playing on the U.S.-Europe-Japan economic competition of the present as they placed on the U.S.-U.S.S.R.-China political competition in the past, perhaps simply by giving our major economic rivals preferred access to their output or markets. They can thus hurt U.S. national interests both directly and indirectly.

Until recently, and even when I published the article just mentioned, few people recognized the seriousness of these threats. Four factors have made them very real. First, inflation and shortages of supply have replaced unemployment and shortages of demand as the dominant forces in the world economy for the first time in over forty years. The power balance has thus shifted from purchasers toward suppliers, particularly of raw materials but also of manufactured goods—witness the unilateral cuts of import barriers and currency *up*valuations by country after industrialized country to fight inflation in the last two years. Second, the end of the Cold War has removed the security blanket and ideological rigidities which kept individual developing countries tied to individual industrialized countries, particularly the United States. Third, the developmental progress of many countries in the Third World, while far from satisfying fully their aspirations, has brought them both new indigenous talent to carry out bolder policies and the self-confidence to actually do so. Fourth, the success of OPEC in oil has provided a dramatic demonstration of the potential for strong, concentrated Third World action; indeed, the beginnings of similar action can already be detected at least in copper and coffee.

OPEC has carried out many of the steps noted above. It has boosted oil prices astronomically. Many of its Arab members have now effectively denied supplies, and favored certain consuming countries over others. Some of its members have steadily expropriated foreign-owned companies.

While the oil situation itself must be the focus of policy attention at the moment, we must recognize its far broader implications for the longer run. In my view, similar action with regard to other commodities by other countries is in some senses *more* likely than could have been expected from OPEC:

—A successful OPEC required close collaboration among a relatively large number of countries. Effective cartelization would require fewer countries for several key commodities.

—The disparity between the highly sophisticated, rich and technologically advanced companies and the "backward producers" seemed far greater in oil than it now appears for most other commodities.

—The national economies of most of the OPEC countries relied heavily (or even solely) on oil, whereas potential cartelizers of some of the other key commodities are more diversified. For example, Brazil's willingness to hold an umbrella over the coffee market, which prompted the supplying countries to let the International Coffee Agreement lapse rather than accept the proposals of consuming countries, was made possible by the diversification of both its internal economy and export earnings.

—It is true that the major *Arab* oil producers were united in their antagonism toward Israel. But the cartel could exist only with cooperation from non-Arab countries, including such a staunch friend of Israel—and enemy of Iraq and Kuwait—as Iran. And there are even sharp differences among the Arabs: between conservative Saudi Arabia (and, before 1969, Libya) and radical Iraq (and, after 1969, Libya), to the extent that two of the most radical states (Iraq and Libya) are not "cooperating" in the production cutbacks even at the present time. By contrast, there are few if any sources of hostility among the potential cartelizers of, e.g., tin (Malaysia, Thailand, Bolivia) or bauxite (Jamaica, Surinam, Guinea, perhaps Australia).

At the same time, there are aspects of the OPEC situation which are *not* replicated elsewhere. Oil is more important than the other commodities. Foreign exchange earnings had reached the point in some OPEC countries where the threat of denial became credible. Anti-Israel sentiment was a binding tie for some of its key members. The small populations and primitive economies of some OPEC members make them invulnerable to economic retaliation by their victims. But it is by no means clear that similar patterns are *less* likely to emerge in other key commodities and—by groups of countries or individual countries—on the other ''threat'' issues.

Perhaps the broadest lesson to be learned from the oil situation is the reminder that countries will adopt extreme—even wholly irrational —policies when frustrated repeatedly in achieving their most cherished aspirations.[3] Fortunately, the aspirations of most countries in the Third World focus on economic and social development rather than territorial gains. But they could well adopt policies similar to those of OPEC if their aspirations are frustrated, and the United States thus has a major interest in helping them achieve their developmental goals.

The Response to the Third World

There are three broad classes of U.S. response to these threats. One is simply to accept whatever happens. The second is retaliation, which can take either economic or military form. The third is preemption, which takes primarily economic form.

Passive acceptance can be very costly, as we had seen in oil even before the recent production cutbacks triggered abject appeasement throughout the world and turned the issue into a security problem. To be sure, the costs of a new producer cartel for tin or expropriations by a few ''host'' countries might be far less. But they could exact a cost, and policy must compare those costs, weighted by the probability that they will actually occur, with the costs of action to deal with them, weighted by the probability that it would do so effectively.

Economic retaliation may in some instances be an effective response and the risk of economic retaliation an effective deterrent, depending on the vulnerability of the country concerned on a wide range of criteria. At a minimum, new international rules (along the lines proposed by Senator Mondale earlier this week) are needed to bring the whole issue of export controls under international surveillance, and to provide for international sanctions against unjustified acts.

The history of economic sanctions is replete with failures, however, and their effectiveness as a general proposition is highly dubious. In addition, their use would of course generate sizable costs of its own. (The costs of military retaliation are so immense that I mention it only for logical completeness.) And any mode of retaliation implies acceptance of the costs of the triggering action for a transitional period, which could be rather long. So retaliation is not a very attractive option.

In principle, preemption—as usual—thus looks like the best approach. The trick is (a) how to convince policy-makers to take the long-term view needed to do it, which has been the effort in this statement until now, and (b) to figure out how to do it. This brings us directly to the topic of these hearings.

IDA and U.S. Policy Toward the Third World

The primary motivation for countries to undertake the kinds of actions cited above would usually be economic: a desire for increased foreign exchange earnings, reduced unemployment, diversification of their economies, limiting foreign interference with their internal decision-making, increased weight in international councils. Security concerns will occasionally enter into their calculations directly, but oil is probably an exception in this sense.

Action to preempt the threat from the Third World, including its threat to the U.S. position vis-a-vis Europe and Japan, should thus focus on helping developing countries meet these needs in alternative ways. Such alternatives represent sound U.S. policy if their costs to us are less than the costs of the actions which are preempted.

There are a number of such policies which I would propose. One of the most important is U.S. cooperation in, indeed leadership of, a sizable and steady increase in the lending capacity of the international financial institutions, such as IDA and ADB.

Three or four policy issues have become crucial to relations between the industrialized countries and the developing countries as a whole. In the trade field, it is generalized tariff preferences. In the monetary field, it is the "link" between reserve creation and development assistance. In the foreign assistance field, it is both the level of a country's aid (with respect to the "target" for each 1% of GNP, including 0.7% of GNP for public aid) and its contributions to the international lending institutions. *On every one of these issues,* the United States has lagged behind virtually every other industrialized country in recent years. In fact, Japan and most European countries have steadily catered to the Third World on precisely these issues. A failure to reverse that performance runs the serious risk of accelerating, rather than preempting, the likelihood of actions adverse to U.S. interests.

Contributions to IDA and the ADB (along with the Inter-American

Development Bank) are an essential element in such a strategy. These institutions have now become the biggest single source of development finance. Their money is not tied to procurement in particular donor countries, and hence provides at least 10-30 percent more development per dollar than does most bilateral aid. They encompass fewer restrictions and obviate the most sensitive political problems of donor-recipient relations; hence they are the *kind* of assistance which is sought by the developing world. The developing countries have an important voice in their management. A successful IDA will go far toward meeting the aspirations of the Third World, and hence preempting the onset of frustration, which could prove exceedingly costly to U.S. interests.

In addition, IDA and the regional lending organizations provide an institutional framework within which effective relations can evolve between the industrialized world and the developing countries. The rules and institutions which governed the monetary and trading systems during the first postwar generation, embodied in the IMF and GATT, have collapsed and we do not know what will take their place.[4] As a result, relations among the industrialized countries have deteriorated markedly. Fortunately, however, the international lending institutions—which are the chief fora in which the industrialized and developing countries now meet on key operational issues—have flourished.

The United States has a major stake in such institutional arrangements. In view of our deep involvement in the world economy, we badly need an international economic order which will provide a stable and predictable basis for international economic policies and transactions. In view of our continued world leadership, we need an economic order which will promote the course of peace.

In addition, it is extremely important to us that other countries meet *their* international obligations. As indicated earlier, we want the developing countries to supply us with raw materials at reasonable prices, honor our investments, and provide us with markets. But history shows that countries are far more likely to fulfill their obligations in a world of effective international rules and institutions, wherein both we and they are held accountable for any actions we take which deviate from accepted norms. U.S. leadership on such institutional issues is critical, because we remain by far the largest single country and because of our historical role in promoting the development of international institutions.

The United States thus has a very direct national interest in the further success of IDA and the regional development banks. Indeed, its IDA role provides the United States with a unique opportunity to start restoring its relationship with the Third World. As IDA's largest and (lately) most recalcitrant donor, every dollar which we are willing to contribute raises total IDA funding by three times as much. A generous U.S. effort would thus go at least some distance toward limiting the adverse impact of our declining level of bilateral aid. A resumption of true U.S. leadership in IDA, which was exercised as recently as 1969, would greatly help our relations with the Third World. A similar U.S. role in the ADB would further help our relations in Asia, where lie many of the most important developing countries.

U.S. policy efforts within IDA are also important. When we seek to force on an international institution a rigid and unilateral interpretation of delicate issues such as the fairness of compensation for an expropriation, or idiosyncrasies such as our own audit of an institution's books, we are in essence seeking to bilateralize multilateral aid. This is the wrong approach, and it further erodes our relationship with developing countries.

This brings me to my final point. In addition to its efforts to improve overall U.S.-Third World relations, the United States is going to have to pinpoint its policies on those particular developing countries which can most affect our national interests. For example, when we awaken to an oil crisis we realize how vital to us are Nigeria, Indonesia, and Ecuador.

Many of these interests are best pursued through bilateral policies. However, such bilateral efforts have well-known shortcomings. We thus need to use our influence within IDA, and the other regional institutions, to foster these interests. We could do so by promoting more IDA activity in countries which might otherwise seek to improve their economic fortunes in ways less coincident with our interests. Such U.S. efforts would often coincide with the interests of the other major donor countries, who in broad terms join us as consumers of raw materials and as investors and sellers in the Third World, and need not lead to conflict within the institution. At a minimum, we should avoid futile hostility to IDA loans to countries whose help we need, which simply provides an opportunity for our major competitors to improve *their* relations with the countries in question at our expense.

However, one cannot push too far this targeting of assistance on particular countries whose leverage now looks impressive. We do not know for sure where our dependence may show up in the years ahead, in terms either of commodities or supplier countries. Hence the assistance net should be cast as widely as possible in the effort to preempt the risk of foreign actions inimical to the interests of the United States. IDA, as the single most important *global* developmental institution, is uniquely positioned to pursue that objective.

IDA: A Good Investment

I conclude that the proposed funding for IDA and the ADB represent extremely good investments from the standpoint of the United States. Like any insurance policy, we cannot be wholly sure that they are necessary —but the odds are high that they are, and those odds are getting higher every day. At the other extreme, they are almost certainly not enough to do the *whole* job—but they are an integral part of what *is* necessary, and they provide us with a unique opportunity to get on with it.

I therefore recommend that this Subcommittee promptly authorize the full amounts proposed by the President for IDA replenishment and increase special funds for the ADB, urge the other bodies of the Congress (including the appropriations committees) to do so as well, and avoid restrictions which would undermine the ability of the U.S. Government to pursue the kind of policies I have suggested. In doing so, you will make a major contribution, at very low cost, to dealing with one of the most critical problems facing our society over the next decade and perhaps beyond.

Notes

1. *First Annual Report of the Secretary of the Interior Under the Mining and Minerals Policy Act of 1970,* March 1972, esp. pp. 63-64.

2. C. Fred Bergsten, "The Threat From the Third World," *Foreign Policy* 11 (Summer 1973), pp. 102-24 [chapter 26 in this volume].

3. I regard the oil embargoes and huge price increases as irrational from the economic standpoint of OPEC countries because they have pushed the industrialized countries (especially the United States) to adopt conservation measures and develop alternative sources of energy, which will significantly reduce the demand for Arab oil over the longer and even medium term, which otherwise might never have been undertaken. A profit-maximizing oligopolist would have raised prices more slowly and would never have interrupted supply. If the embargoes push the consumers to military intervention, the irrationality of the action would of course be even clearer.

4. See C. Fred Bergsten, *The Future of the International Economic Order* (Lexington, Mass.: Lexington Books, D.C. Heath and Company, 1973), esp. pp. 2-8. [chapter 2 in this volume].

30 Relations between the United States and Latin America to 1980

The U.S. Economic Interest in Latin America

The sweeping changes in world economic conditions outlined in the previous chapters imply a sharp increase in U.S. economic interests in Latin America.

Latin America can make a major contribution to the U.S. battle against inflation, and to the U.S. quest for economic security. It can supply large and increasing quantities of a wide variety of the primary products, both industrial raw materials and some foods, needed by the United States.

Oil is the most obvious example. Venezuela is the leading Latin supplier, and has been cutting down its output—hence depriving the United States and raising world prices. But, Ecuador, Bolivia and several other Latin countries will play an increasingly important role in the world oil picture.

But Latin American countries play equally, and often more, important roles in some of the other primary products where shortages—and cartelization a la OPEC[1]—are distinctly possible. Chile and Peru are among the four dominant copper exporters. Guyana, Jamaica and Surinam are key members of the new International Bauxite Association. Venezuela and Brazil are among the leading producers of iron ore. Brazil, with help from Colombia, is holding up the coffee price. Seven Latin countries have just joined together to force up U.S. banana prices. Bolivia is the second leading tin producer. So Latin American countries play an important role in virtually every primary product where "new OPECs," or other actions to force up the returns to producing countries, are now taking place or are imminent.

The prices at which Latin American countries make these commodities available, and the security of those supplies, must be of major concern to the United States. The other industrialized countries have launched major efforts to achieve such objectives for themselves, including in Latin America—so U.S. access to these supplies will importantly affect our international competitive position as well as the performance of our internal economy. Indeed, *securing assured access to Latin American primary*

Excerpted from a paper prepared for a meeting of the Commission on U.S.-Latin American relations in New York in June 1974 and published in *The Americas in a Changing World* (New York: Quadrangle Books, 1975).

431

products, especially raw materials, at reasonable prices should be the primary objective of U.S. economic policy toward Latin America. Achieving this objective will of course require agreement on what constitutes "reasonable prices" and a quid pro quo to Latin America in return for "assured access," to which we turn in the concluding section of this paper.

The anti-inflationary efforts of the United States would also be promoted by increased imports of manufactured goods from Latin America. Increasing U.S. imports of manufactures from Latin America is of course more controversial than increasing U.S. imports of primary products, because at least some of the Latin manufactures would compete with U.S. production and hence would preempt U.S. jobs or even create new unemployment. They would almost certainly be opposed by the AFL-CIO, because the skewed distribution of its membership—which is highly misrepresentative of the overall U.S. labor force[2] —compels it to seek to avoid even gradual shifts in the composition of U.S. production.

As already indicated, however, the scope of this risk is limited because even the maximum conceivable increase in Latin sales would be small relative to U.S. consumption in virtually every industry.[3] Nevertheless, an effective and generous U.S. program of trade adjustment assistance, to meet the real social costs which might result and the political opposition which will certainly be raised against the proposal, is a necessary concomitant of any such policy.[4] The costs of such adjustment assistance —which is desirable in terms of overall U.S. trade policy anyway —stemming from its application to imports from Latin America would undoubtedly be far less than the benefits to the U.S. economy of liberalizing imports of manufactured goods from Latin America.[5]

The U.S. anti-inflationary interest in Latin American commodites and manufactures should not, however, be seen solely in the context of intrahemispheric trade. Increased global sales by Latin America serve to reduce world prices, with indirect benefits to the United States. For example, increased Venezuelan oil sales to Europe which derived from increased Venezuelan production would both place downward pressure on world oil prices and make more Middle East oil available to the United States. At the other extreme, even a U.S. "special deal" which assured it access to Venezuelan oil might provide no help on prices—though providing the U.S. with more secure supplies—if Venezuela concomitantly cut back its sales to Europe and left world supply unchanged. Thus the United States cannot pragmatically view its desire for stepped-up purchases in purely bilateral U.S.-Latin terms, but must consider the overall production level of the goods in question and *world* market developments for them.

This consideration leads directly to the U.S. interest in U.S. and other foreign investments in Latin America. The best of all worlds from the U.S. standpoint would be one in which the maximum feasible production increases in Latin America, both in primary products and manufactured goods, were assured to the U.S. in whatever quantities it needed and were developed by U.S. firms. In this situation, the U.S. would get both the real resources and the balance-of-payments benefits of whatever share of the production profits were permitted by the Latin American governments to leave their countries.

It must be recognized, however, that the profits are the decidedly secondary interest—and that the multinational firms, far from promoting U.S. consumer interests, may at least tacitly add to the strength of producer-country cartels in some industries. At the extreme, U.S. interests would be better served by foreign (including local Latin) production of the resources which better assured U.S. access to them, than by production by U.S. firms which was limited by local governments and/or sold at least in part to countries other than the United States—which is in fact the traditional practice of most U.S. firms in Latin America.

At the same time, the United States does have a major interest in maximum access to Latin America for U.S. (and foreign-based) multinational firms, because they must still play a major role in developing the needed expansion of both primary products and manufactured output for some time to come. This in turn requires policies on the part of U.S. firms and the U.S. Government which respond to the Latin American goal of reaping a greater share of the benefits brought by the firms, such as increasing the degree of domestic processing of materials and value-added. It also requires Latin policies which recognize the legitimate demands of the firms for a stable and profitable environment in which to operate. So, as in trade, convergent measures need to be negotiated to achieve the goals of the several parties to the problem.

U.S. economic interests in Latin America also encompass the traditional goal of maintaining Latin markets for U.S. exports, to help support the exchange rate of the dollar and U.S. jobs. This goal now is subsidiary to those outlined above, and Latin America remains a less important market for aggregate U.S. exports than Canada, Europe, or Japan—though Latin America is a more important market for U.S. machinery, and some other items, than are the other industrial areas. Nevertheless, it is probably more important in absolute terms than ever before due to the increased wealth and income of many Latin countries, and must remain an important objective of U.S. economic policy in the hemisphere.

U.S. interests in Latin American monetary policy are more ambiguous. In the previous days of dollar-based fixed exchange rates, the U.S.—to the extent that it concerned itself at all with the effect of Latin American monetary policies on the U.S. economy—wanted the Latins to avoid depreciations, which would both raise at least marginal doubts about the fixed-rate system and hurt U.S. trade competitiveness in the region (in part by promoting further U.S. direct investment to produce there instead). There was also concern that the capital flows from the United States which were often necessary to avoid Latin depreciation would wind up financing imports from Europe, and hence increase the "dollar overhang" threat to the U.S. gold stock. Indeed, in the middle 1960s the United States sought special Latin investments (mainly from Venezuela and Mexico) in "long-term" U.S. securities to both window-dress the U.S. payments data and reduce the risk of such "pass-throughs."

In the present world of flexible rates, however, these concerns of the past have largely disappeared. Latin devaluations now cheapen the cost of at least their manufactured goods, further enhancing their anti-inflationary benefits for the United States. It should be noted, however, that Latin devaluations probably have little impact on U.S. exports to the region because the devaluations occur vis-à-vis the currencies of our European and Japanese competitors as well as against the dollar.

As noted above, however, many Latin American countries are pegging their exchange rates to the dollar rather than floating them freely à la most of the industrial countries. (Even Brazil and others who periodically alter their parities vis-à-vis the dollar maintain a close market link to the dollar at the prevailing parity at all times.) To do so, they at some periods accumulate dollars rather than letting their exchange rates rise in value. The United States would certainly prefer that they do so, rather than converting the dollars into Deutschemarks or some other national currency, because their so doing would generate downward pressure on the dollar in the exchange markets and accelerate our domestic inflation.

However, too much dollar accumulation by Latin (or any other) countries would harken back to the earlier dollar standard, whereby countries avoided upvaluing their currencies to such an extent that U.S. deficits because unacceptably large both at home and abroad. There is some danger that Brazil, particularly, will be "the new Japan" not only in terms of its economic strength but in failing to recognize the adverse effects on the world economic system of its nationalistic actions—which is a fair characterization of its contining minidevaluations at a time when its reserves are rising sharply and have become the ninth highest in the world.

Extreme action in this area would work only if the United States (and perhaps the other industrial countries) decided to use their external policies *wholly* to fight inflation, while the Latin American (and perhaps other) developing countries sought to use their external policies wholly to fight unemployment. In that instance, both sides would be happy with an over-valued dollar and undervalued Latin currencies. Such a pattern should not be ruled out, and need not have large trade effects if restricted to the DC-LDC framework, i.e., Japan or Italy did not take advantage of the renewed U.S. permissiveness and did not undervalue vis-à-vis the dollar.

But it is extremely difficult to maintain within proper limits and would raise some political problems—from labor in the United States, and from consumers in Latin America—even in so doing.

The Position of Latin America

In facing these U.S. interests, what is the position of Latin America? What are *its* goals? (One cannot of course speak heterogenously of "Latin America," but I do so in this chapter in full cognizance of the need to disaggregate carefully among countries when developing policy proposals in detail.)

First and most important, Latin America's position is incomparably stronger than before for the reasons stressed throughout this paper. In some senses, they are now the "have" nations.

The shift over the past decade is perhaps best demonstrated by the case of coffee. In the early 1960s, Brazil and the other coffee producers literally begged the U.S. and other coffee consumers to create together the International Coffee Agreement to keep coffee prices from plummeting. In 1973, Brazil and the other producers let that same Agreement expire because they felt that they alone could drive the coffee price higher; cooperation from the consuming countries was no longer needed. So far at least, the producers have been proven right. A key reason is that Brazil, like Saudi Arabia in oil, is now wealthy enough (and, better than Saudi Arabia, economically diversified enough) that it can actually *import* huge amounts of coffee—the whole Salvadorean crop and even much of the Colombian crop this year—to maintain the price umbrella over the world coffee market.

This new economic power of most South American countries reduces the Continent's need for foreign aid of the traditional type. As indicated, it reduces *their* need to plead for commodity agreements (though, as we will see later, it does not necessarily reduce their interest in negotiating such agreements). Indeed, "concessional" help from the United States is no longer important for most Latin countries.

But this by no means signals an end to Latin problems, nor an end to their interests in seeking new economic arrangements with the United States. It does signal a change in the focus and form thereof.

A chief Latin goal remains the modernization and diversification of their economies, via industrialization, including increasing processing of their raw materials. Such evolution could contribute significantly to easing the unemployment which remains of cardinal importance in many Latin countries, and to strengthening their external financial positions. So most Latin countries are much more likely to use the resurgent strength of their commodity positions to achieve these industrialization/modernization goals than they are to regard those goals as no longer necessary.

This is partly because the commodity outlook is always somewhat uncertain. It is possible, though in my view quite unlikely, that the current commodity boom will bust in the near future. But its longer run future is quite uncertain, as higher prices induce conservation of demand and the development of substitutes (e.g., tin for copper and ore-bearing clays for bauxite). Thus the commodity-producing countries in Latin America (and elsewhere) might welcome new kinds of commodity deals in which they would assure access for the consuming countries in return for guaranteed prices for their output. They would be particularly likely to show such interest if the consuming countries would agree to relate these prices to the overall terms of trade of the producing countries, both limiting fluctuations and providing steady secular improvement therein.

This kind of arrangement might be possible now particularly because discussions thereof would be initiated by the consuming countries—a role reversal from the scenario of even the recent past (e.g., the continued producer efforts to get a cocoa agreement). This extra attraction stems from a second fundamental goal of Latin America today: independence of decision-making, and avoidance of any remnant of *dependencia*.

Another specific policy manifestation of this pervasive sentiment concerns U.S. investment in Latin America. Latin countries will simply insist on a greater share of control over the decisions of the multinational firms, and on getting a greater share of the benefits which they generate—which will in turn require increased tolerance both by the U.S. Government, since the result may sometimes be transfers of jobs and exports to the host country, and by these enterprises.

At the same time, Latin America's needs for capital and especially technology suggest that it will certainly continue to want foreign investment. But the terms must be right: the investment must be perceived by the host countries to promote their goals of industrialization, better balance-of-payments positions, reduced unemployment, technological advance, and the like.

A third manifestation of the new Latin emphasis on "independence within interdependence" relates to any "foreign aid" programs which continue. They will simply have to operate in less politicized forms than in the past, to obviate any semblance of the former donor-client syndrome. Thia need not obviate bilateral aid, though it would require significant alteration in the style of bilateral aid—particularly with regard to Congressionally directed limitations. In particular, debt relief provides a possible alternative to conventional aid which would be far superior to it on several counts. But it does suggest an increased focus on multilateral aid and particularly on assistance obtained through, e.g., the SDR link and the use of revenues from exploitation of the seabeds.

The foregoing discussion has stressed the new economic strength of Latin America, and hence the dramatic improvement in its bargaining position vis-à-vis the United States. But it has also laid out the continued needs of the Latins for external markets, especially for their manufactured products, and for infusions of capital and technology.

In the newly pluralistic world economy, these Latin needs can be met from a variety of industrial countries. Indeed, one of the elements of Latin America's new strength is its ability to go to different sources—and even play them off against each other—for imports available only from the United States in an earlier era. Japan and several European countries have concluded that they must fashion their own "resources diplomacy" as centerpieces of their own foreign polities,[6] and hence Latin America is in some senses a new battleground for competition among the industrialized countries.

But there are certain commodities where the Latins do not produce sufficiently to meet their needs, and which are available only from a small number of other countries. Oil fits this category for a few Latin countries, particularly Brazil. So do foodstuffs and feedgrains, especially wheat, corn and other commodities of which the United States and Canada are the world's primary suppliers. Indeed, food problems—both of security of supply and price—may loom at least as large in Latin America in the future as raw materials problems loom in the United States. Both the North and South Americans will doubtlessly seek to enhance their security by diversifying their sources but obvious possibilities for reciprocal arrangements guaranteeing access to their respective supplies thus emerge between the Northern and Southern halves of the hemisphere.

A final issue concerning the Latin American economic position is whether it should maintain and/or accelerate its various regional efforts: LAFTA, the Andean Pact, CACM, CARIFTA, etc. In today's pluralistic world, units of different sizes seem best equipped to deal with different problems. As already noted, the European Common Market seemed ideal for dealing with a range of both economic and political problems at one point in recent history, but no longer does so for many. Latin America may be at a stage somewhat similar to that of Europe twenty years ago; hence it might benefit from a similar all-out effort toward regional economic unity.

It seems more likely, however, that pragmatic answers to the regional questions are called for. Different groups of similarly placed countries within the region may find it desirable to get together on particular issues, primarily to permit their new manufacturing industries to serve economies of adequate scale and to strengthen their bargaining positions on, e.g., increasing foreign investments. Some Latin countries may find it desirable to link with non-Latin countries on particular issues, e.g., Brazil with Korea on textiles and Chile with Zaire on copper. An all-LDC focus may be optimal for some issues, e.g., international monetary reform, with or without Latin American caucuses inside the bigger group. Latin America-wide groups, such as CECLA, may be best on some issues. Hemisphere-wide coordination will prove best on still others, as in the Inter-American Development Bank.

The likelihood of such differentiated responses to specific issues is reinforced by the very real, if largely latent, potential for intra-Latin American conflict. Brazil is now becoming a global economic force, Venezuela a wielder of vast oil and financial wealth, and Mexico and Argentina have hardly abandoned their visions of leadership of the Continent. So intra-Latin tension and overt competition can certainly not be ruled out. In addition, the long-standing territorial issues between some of the Latin countries (Venezuela and Guyana, Venezuela and Colombia, Bolivia and Chile) may well become more heated as considerations of mineral wealth add to the political characteristics of the disputes. And the reduced profile of the United States throughout the region lifts the hemispheric security blanket as well.

The lesson is that overlapping and even criss-crossing patterns of association appear to prove most desirable for individual Latin American countries at this point in time. This is natural and predictable, in view of the highly pluralistic and shifting world structure outlined in the first section of this paper—especially for a region whose new-found strength is not yet adequately reflected in the traditional international institutions.

Two implications emerge for U.S.-Latin American relations in the near future. First, there is no call for a U.S. push for Latin integration like the push of the early and mid-1960s. The breakdown of the drive toward European unity—the implicit model of that early period—of course adds weight to that conclusion. Second, any push for a comprehensive hemispheric "special relationship" seems to run counter to global interests and options which Latin America, as well as the United States, now enjoys. It would thus have to carry a powerful new rationale, far beyond those advanced in the past, to merit consideration at this point in history.

Policy Possibilities for the Years Ahead

It is not the function of this paper to lay out detailed policy proposals for the United States or for Latin America. However, the environment and objectives of each sketched out in the previous sections suggest several possible directions for action.

First, a reciprocal deal appears highly feasible to encompass the U.S. desire for assured access to key primary products at reasonable prices, to fight its inflation, and Latin America's desire for increased sales of manufactured products, to reduce its unemployment and to speed and diversify its economic and social modernization. Latin America would guarantee U.S. access to its raw materials, probably through assuring a certain negotiated volume of output "needed by the United States." The United States would probably guarantee a floor price at the same time, so commodity deals arranged on a commodity-by-commodity basis could provide part of the package. Simultaneously, the United States would guarantee Latin America access to the U.S. market for manufactured products through a far more liberal set of tariff preferences than presently proposed, plus—more importantly—a general reduction of tariff and non-tariff barriers which reduced (or eliminated) particularly the high effective tariffs on processed goods of greatest concern to the Latins.

Various permutations on this theme might of course be negotiated. The volume-for-price floor commodity deals might be adequate by themselves, although the United States would then probably have to guarantee higher floor prices than if it also made "concessions" on imports of manufactures. In my view, the U.S. interest would be better served to use the opportunity to fight its inflation doubly, by reducing its barriers to the manufactured goods and using the benefits which would derive therefrom to Latin America to negotiate lower floor prices for the Latins' primary products.

A critical issue is whether any such arrangement should be couched solely in purely hemispheric terms, in view of the "spheres of influence" implications thereof. The same concept could be applied either by the United States alone toward all developing countries, or by the industrial countries together toward the developing countries together.

There are arguments in favor of both approaches.[7] The hemispheric approach might prove easier to negotiate initially and to manage subsequently, if only because fewer countries are involved. The United States might thus steal a march on its main industrial competitors, since Latin America is clearly the most advanced and resource-rich of the developing regions; any efforts by Europe and Japan to form rival North-South blocs would leave them worse off, except in the highly unlikely circumstance that one of them could line up exclusive access to Middle East oil. A regional initiative in the Western Hemisphere might be the only way to jar Europe sufficiently to get it to back away from its own expanding network of special North-South ties.[8]

But there are also strong arguments for the more global approach. As noted earlier in the paper, only increases in *global* output can really give assurance of adequate supply at reasonable prices; a Latin Qaddafi or a thoughtless move by the U.S. Congress could break off any new "special relationship'' and leave the United States worse off than before. Deals in most commodities would be hard to work out without the cooperation of non-Latin countries (Malaysia on tin, Australia on bauxite, Zaire on copper, etc.). Any U.S. move to form such a regional bloc would (rightly) be regarded by Europe and Japan as an act of economic aggression, and undermine the delicate structure of interdependence among them with potentially huge costs to U.S. economic and security interests—including the vital interests of many of the same U.S. firms which might benefit from a special hemispheric relationship.

From the Latin standpoint, such a deal—though its terms would clearly manifest its new economic strength—would appear to many to represent a throwback to the days of abject reliance on the United States. Worse, this would occur just at a time when new global options were opening to Latin America and the "new nationalism" rejects such binding ties, thus fueling internal political opposition to consummation of the arrangement. Pragmatically, it would undermine Latin America's possibilities for allying with Western Europe and/or Japan against the United States on the numerous issues where it may prove to be in the Latin interest to do so. And it would reduce the opportunity for Latin America to use its new power to affect the reform of the global economic order, which as outlined at the outset must now undergo thorough reform.

There is probably no single answer to whether this whole array of new arrangements should be pursued bilaterally, hemispherically, or globally. A U.S.-Venezuela deal on oil is an obvious possibility. The hemisphere might be the right focus for food commitments. A pluralism of types of approaches in fact meshes most appropriately with the pluralistic world economic and political environment outlined in the early sections of this paper.

But the most promising approach to achieving the overall commodities-for-manufactures exchange might be within the framework of the forthcoming multilateral trade negotiation (MTN). The United States and Latin America already have a number of common interests which they should pursue jointly in those negotiations: e.g., a reduction in agricultural protectionism in Europe, elimination of Europe's preferential deals with the developing states associated with the Common Market, elimination of Europe's continuing import quotas against Japan (which induce the Japanese to focus their export drives excessively on the United States and, increasingly, Latin American markets).

In addition, careful U.S.-Latin coordination to pursue the high-level tradeoff suggested here could dramatically focus the MTN on the most serious international economic issues of the foreseeable future. The United States could seek to develop a joint offer of the industrial countries covering floor prices for particular commodities, liberalized tariff preferences (in terms of both commodity coverage and safeguard provisions), and across-the-board reductions of especially those tariffs and NTBs which limit the manufactured exports of developing countries. The Latin Americans could seek agreement among the commodity producers to guarantee access to their supplies for the consuming countries, to accept new international rules limiting recourse to export controls like the traditional GATT limits on import controls, and to decide what floor (and ceiling?) prices and other industrial-country concessions would be acceptable to them.

The goal would be a wholly new, cooperative and relatively stable economic relationship between the United States and Latin America, within the framework of a cooperative and stable new relationship between North and South globally. "Regionalism within globalism" would supplement "independence within interdependence" as new themes for U.S.-Latin relations. Institutional innovations would of course be needed to implement effectively such a new set of hemispheric arrangements.

Trade would be the focus of this approach, since all of the other key aspects of international economic relationships in this post-aid era—investment and monetary relationships—serve largely to generate trade and affect the direction of its flow. These other issues are also important for U.S.-Latin relations in their own right, however. Several other new policy directions are thus needed as well.

Second, the United States should gear its policies toward foreign direct investment in Latin America to the clear Latin desire for independence and a fair share of the benefits brought by the MNEs, in return for guarantees of a stable environment for the firms themselves. For example, OPIC might sharply modify its policies to insure only those investments that appear viable in the light of host-country attitudes, such as their insistence on increased domestic processing of primary products—and even push U.S. firms to accept conditions which make them so. The Andean Code need not be fought, though its faithful implementation must be assured. The Hickenlooper and Gonzales Amendments must go. These are only among the more obvious examples; investment relations call for perhaps the most creative new thinking of any of the economic policy issues. Indeed, there may well prove to be ways in which the United States could serve its own national interests while at the same time meeting legitimate Latin American (and other LDC) interests in "decoupling" the *packages* of technology, capital, marketing organization, etc. now usually available only through multinational firms.

The direction of foreign assistance policies is clearer. Large amounts of concessional aid are not needed, so style and purpose become much more important. Concessional aid should be pinpointed on those poorest countries which really need it—and perhaps provided jointly by the United States and the richer Latin Americans. The form should also be pinpointed;

e.g., debt relief may prove far superior to new loans for many countries, and any needed assistance—perhaps including both U.S. Government and IDB guarantees—for Latin access to private capital markets (both in the United States and abroad) might become an important part of the program. The bilateral program must eliminate most of its bureaucratic strings and political overtones or be jettisoned. The multilateral approach, particularly through the IDB—the institution which Latin America rightly regards as "its own"—should be emphasized. Still better would be steady movement toward developing forms of assistance, such as the SDR link (which, depending on a variety of factors, could provide between a few hundred million and over a billion dollars annually for Latin America) and proceeds from exploitation of the seabeds.

Most of these approaches can only be carried out by the United States in cooperation with other industrial countries, and with other developing countries along with Latin America as beneficiaries. Hence they reinforce the preference for the global as opposed to the hemispheric approach developed in the discussion on trade.

They also highlight the wide array of options available to the United States and to Latin America in evolving their new economic relationship. As outlined in previous sections, each has a number of major economic interests in the other—some traditional, some quite new. The United States wants assured access to primary products at reasonable prices, more manufactured goods at least in areas of domestic shortage, markets for its own exports, reasonable treatment for its investments, and cooperative monetary policies. Latin American countries want assurances that their commodity prices do not again collapse, new markets for their manufactures, capital on acceptable terms, technology, assured supplies of food and other needed imports, a greater voice in international decision-making and perhaps some concessional aid. At least a few political issues must of course be considered as well. From these lengthy agendas of each, it is obvious that there are myriad possibilities for specific tradeoffs.

Thus there is clearly ample ground for the United States and Latin America to carry on a "special relationship." But it now needs to be a new kind of special relationship, in which each works together in many different ways—sometimes bilaterally, sometimes hemispherically, sometimes within the broader grouping of countries with which each also has special ties to promote global programs of joint benefit to both: regionalism within globalism. A vision of such expanded and diversified progress together should animate U.S.-Latin American economic relations in the new world economy and polity of the late 1970s and beyond. And since economic issues will almost certainly lie at the heart of overall U.S.-Latin relations for the foreseeable future, the realization of such progress could provide the basis for stability and progress throughout the Western Hemisphere for some time to come.

Notes

1. See C. Fred Bergsten, "The Threat From the Third World," *Foreign Policy* 11 (Summer 1973) [chapter 27 in this volume] and "The Threat is Real," *Foreign Policy* 14 (Spring 1974).

2. For example, the share of U.S. textile and shoe workers is four times greater in the AFL-CIO than in the U.S. labor force as a whole, while the share of workers in most export-oriented and service-oriented industries is far less. For the details see C. Fred Bergsten, "The Costs of Import Restrictions to American Consumers," American Importers Association, 1972 [chapter 33 in this volume].

3. All studies of the effects of tariff preferences indicate that the maximum additional flow from *all* LDCs under the original, liberal U.S. plan was $200-300 million. The amounts would of course be higher if non-tariff barriers were also eliminated and agricultural products were also covered.

4. For such a program see "Economic Adjustment to Liberal Trade: A New Approach," proposed by the Task Force on Adjustment Assistance of the U.S. Chamber of Commerce, chaired by C. Fred Bergsten, in *Trade Reform,* Hearings before the House Ways and Means Committee on the Trade Reform Act of 1973, Part 3, pp. 895-906 [chapter 15 in this volume].

5. The most detailed estimates of the costs of adjustment assistance for workers likely to be dislocated by imports from *all* sources ranges from $150-500 million annually. By contrast, conservative estimates of the cost to U.S. inflation of *all* present trade barriers exceed $10 billion.

6. E.g., see "The Struggle for the World Product," *Foreign Affairs,* April 1974, by Helmut Schmidt—then Minister of Finance and now Chancellor of the Federal Republic of Germany.

7. If the essentially liberal world economic order of today were to break down, regional arrangements to salvage at least some of the benefits of economic interdependence would of course look much more desirable —and perhaps even necessary—even to those, such as most Latin Americans, who would deplore the "dependencia" implications thereof.

8. Some Europeans (notably the French) might, however, to the contrary welcome such a move as justifying their own approach and undermining the persistent U.S. efforts to interfere with their own "special relationships." For a good, recent study of the whole issue of North-South arrangements, which concludes that special deals are being pursued only by Europe although the potential exists for Japan as well, see Ernest Preeg, *Economic Blocs and U.S. Foreign Policy* (Washington: National Planning Association, 1973).

31

U.S. Policy Toward Latin America in the 1970s and Tariff Preferences

The Policy Context

U.S. trade policy toward Latin America in the 1970s must be viewed in the context of the dramatic changes which have occurred in the structure of the world economy, and the effect of those changes on the international position of the United States.

The U.S. hegemony of the first postwar generation has given way to the attainment of nuclear parity by the Soviet Union and the attendant thawing of the Cold War, and by the achievement of equal economic status by Japan and the expanded European Community. Two implications relevant for our present topic follow. One is that the developing countries (including Latin America) no longer need ally themselves blindly to the United States for security reasons; the removal of this security blanket in turn exposes economic conflicts which had long remained suppressed. The second is that the developing countries (especially Latin America) can now pursue new economic options: Europe and Japan offer markets, credits and advice which fully rival our own. The new pluralism of both world politics and world economics has opened up a wide variety of new opportunities for the countries of the Third World.

This new pluralism is an extremely healthy and favorable development for world peace and, if properly managed, for world prosperity. But it raises major new problems as well, especially for the United States. We have become at the same time more dependent on the developing countries and less able to influence their policies. To meet our own interests there, we must now compete actively with our economic equals from Europe and Japan. Indeed, we must view our whole range of policies toward the Third World—especially our policy toward Latin America—as an essential component of our effort to compete effectively with Europe and Japan in the new world economy of the 1970s and beyond.

There are numerous areas in which the United States is increasingly dependent on the developing countries.[1] Let me cite two here. The United States is increasingly dependent on Third World sources of raw materials; oil is just the beginning. A number of these sources are in Latin America:

Originally presented as testimony to the Subcommittee on Inter-American Affairs of the House Foreign Affairs Committee in its hearings on *Trade Preferences: Latin America and the Caribbean* on June 25, 1973.

Venezuela and a few smaller suppliers for oil; Guyana, Surinam, and Jamaica for bauxite; Chile and Peru for copper; Bolivia for tin; Brazil, potentially, for several items. At a time when inflation has become our cardinal economic problem, and appears likely to continue as such into the indefinite future, we must be deeply concerned about both maintaining our access to these raw materials and minimizing the inevitable rises in their prices. Yet each of the suppliers mentioned is a member of an existing or potential producers' cartel, which—learning from the overwhelming success of the oil producers—could easily withhold the critical marginal supplies and/or insist on unjustifiably higher prices to the detriment of the United States: perhaps along with all other consuming countries, or perhaps in a discriminatory way. Their proclivity to do so will obviously relate in large part to the extent to which they perceive that the United States, both in absolute terms and relative to Europe and Japan, is helping them achieve their chief policy objectives, primarily rapid economic and social development without excessive dependence on outsiders.

Another example relates to U.S. direct investment. In Latin America alone, these investments were valued conservatively at more than $15 billion at the end of 1971, returning about $1.5 billion annually to our investors at that time. These earnings represent a significant share of total U.S. corporate profits. They are a strategic element in our balance of payments, where they can play a crucial and growing role in helping meet the increasing bill for energy and other imports. Yet they face increasing hostility in most of Latin America, on both economic and political grounds. Thus they are extremely vulnerable to takeovers by disgruntled host countries—and, as we have already seen in Chile, Europeans and Japanese are waiting in the wings to step in quickly and replace the capital, management and other resources which the host country might have in the past expected to lose as the result of such action. This is an area where the United States is particularly vulnerable, relative to Europe and Japan, because we account for the bulk of foreign direct investment in Latin America.

Thus the United States has a major national interest, largely on economic grounds, in preserving amicable and cooperative relations with the nations of the Third World, especially in Latin America where our economic stake is already so great. Europe and Japan have long since recognized that they have such interests, and have made the achievement and maintenance of such relations an element of high priority in their foreign policies.

By contrast, U.S. policy since the late 1960s has virtually ignored the Third World and some of our policies have run directly counter to Third World interests, playing directly into the hands of our European and Japanese competitors. Our aid has declined, while the aid of all other donors has risen; the United States now contributes the next-to-lowest share of its GNP of any industrialized country. Our trade barriers have risen, while the barriers of others have declined. We have held up the lending of several of the international lending institutions, and brought to a standstill the current negotiations to replenish IDA. We have tried to bilateralize multilateral aid, by blocking international loans to countries which have expropriated U.S. firms even when they have provided full compensation. It is in this context that we must view U.S. trade policy toward the developing world (including Latin America), including tariff preferences.

U.S. Trade Policy and Latin America

Tariff preferences are not the central issue of U.S. trade policy toward the Third World. Even under a far more liberal scheme than has been proposed by the Administration, preferences could not be expected to raise U.S. imports from all developing countries by more than $300 million annually when they took full effect after several years of transition. Far more critical to the developing countries is assurance of continued access to the U.S. market for the approximately $15 billion of goods which they now sell here, and the increase of at least $1 billion annually without any preferences which they can confidently expect *in the absence of new trade barriers*.

The importance of assured market access for Latin American countries is highlighted by the fact that a significant share of our present imports from them are already limited by high tariffs and a wide variety of non-tariff barriers (''voluntary'' export restraints on cotton textiles and apparel, quotas until quite recently on petroleum and meat, marketing orders on a variety of fruits and vegetables, etc.), which are holding those imports well below Latin American capacities to sell here. Overall U.S. trade policy, relative to tariff preferences, is even more important for Latin America than for most developing countries—since most of our southern neighbors are among the most advanced countries in the Third World, and hence have greater opportunity to sell in the overall U.S. market.

The political importance of this economic problem is heightened by the perception held throughout the Third World, with a great deal of justification, that the present trade policies of the United States (and, in this case, most of the other industrialized countries as well) discriminate against them. Tariffs on products of interest to developing countries are much higher than those traded primarily within the industrialized world. Effective tariff rates are quite high in absolute terms, belying the frequently held view that ''tariffs are no longer important.'' The tariff cuts of the Kennedy

Round intensified these disparities, cutting duties on developed-country exports by much more than duties of developing-country exports.

This is not the place to discuss in detail the trade legislation now pending before another committee of this House. But it should be noted that, in terms of the interests of the developing countries, it is probably the most important piece of U.S. legislation in many years. Developing countries rely on exports for over 80% of the crucial foreign exchange which enables them to implement their development programs. Any relapse toward widespread protectionism in the major markets of the world economy could derail such programs, and force developing countries to adopt inward-oriented strategies of import substitution, along the lines disastrously pursued in Latin America in the 1950s and decisively rejected ever since, instead of the outward-oriented global marketing strategies which have propelled such countries as Brazil, Korea, and Taiwan into such spectacular growth rates in recent years.

The trade bill is particularly crucial for Latin America, with its heavy reliance on the U.S. market, and hence for U.S. policy toward that area of the world. Those interested in U.S. policy toward Latin America should thus exert a major effort to oppose any calls for new U.S. import restrictions, and to improve the trade bill submitted by the Administration. For example, its "market disruption" clause, in addition to opening wide the gate to import restrictions in general, could hit developing countries particularly hard. This is because their exports might most easily fall prey to two of its three criteria—"a rapid rise" in imports, to which they would be susceptible because of the low base from which many of their export increases would have to be judged, and "prices substantially below those of comparable domestic articles," which reflect the lower quality of their output—whose fulfillment would constitute a *prima facie* case that imports had been the cause of injury to a U.S. industry.

The risk of frequent recourse to import restrictions under the Administration's bill is heightened by the weakness of its proposals for adjustment assistance to workers and firms who are injured by imports, which is the only viable (and far superior) alternative to such restrictions. The inclusion of the "market disruption" formula and the weakening of adjustment assistance, taken together, have generated suspicions in the minds of many that the U.S. trade policy which would result might be aimed in large part at limiting imports of the very products which the Third World might otherwise expect to develop over the coming years. Passage of such legislation could thus *intensify* the Third World view that U.S. trade policy discriminates against it, instead of moving to eliminate the discrimination which already exists. Fortunately, detailed proposals for improving the adjustment assistance program have been presented to the Congress. I urge members of this Committee to support those proposals, and to seek to eliminate the dangerous "market disruption" formula.

Tariff Preferences

Finally, let me address directly the issue of tariff preferences. All I have said suggests strongly that the United States should implement preferences as soon as possible. Europe and Japan have long since done so. Trade growth is crucial to the developing countries, especially for the manufactured products which would be the prime beneficiaries of the scheme. The developing countries at present view preferences as the acid test of whether individual industrialized countries want to cooperate with them; thus it is perhaps the most important political issue on the agenda of U.S. relations toward the Third World. It is one of the few issues on which the countries of Latin America have presented a solid front in requesting U.S. action, in response to the frequent U.S. request (most recently by Secretary Rogers on his trip to Latin America) that they do so. Continued U.S. abstinence from extending preferences would deepen the rift between us and them, and thrust them further toward Europe and Japan.

Indeed, I would view the preferences legislation as a major opportunity for the United States to once again seize a leading role in the Third World. In 1969 and 1970, the U.S. did seize leadership on the preferences issue by pushing the other donor countries to table schemes far more liberal than they had previously planned. That U.S. effort of course lost all credibility when the Administration decided not even to submit its own preferences proposal to the Congress, when it applied a surcharge on all imports in August 1971, and when the preferences legislation which it has now submitted is far less liberal than its own proposals of 1969-70. But the preferences plans implemented by Europe and Japan—while obviously far superior to our own total absence of action—are extremely restrictive. The U.S. could thus not only recoup for the delay of at least three years in fulfilling its commitment to extend preferences, but could again seize leadership on the issue and bring effective pressure on Europe and Japan to liberalize their own schemes in response.

There are several specific ways in which the plan proposed by the Administration could be liberalized with very little "cost" to the United States in terms of total imports:

—The Administration proposal would suspend tariff preferences when imports of any article from any individual supplying country reached 50% of total U.S. imports or $25 million. This so-called "competitive need" test would apparently bar more than one-half of existing imports of eligible articles from preferential treatment! It should be abandoned or greatly liberalized. It would appear that the standard escape clause, particularly as modified in the Administration's overall trade proposals even without the "market disruption" formula, would suffice to deal with any disruption to U.S. industry caused by preferential imports—as was indeed stated to be the case under the Administration's original preferences proposal of

1969-70. If any cutoff is needed, it should be based on the share of preferential imports in total domestic consumption—not their share of imports, which could reach 50% in a product where total imports are virtually non-existent and thus be suspended despite the absence of any injury to U.S. producers. And the ten-year limit now proposed for the entire preferences scheme should be eliminated if any "competitive need" formula is retained, since such a formula would take care of disqualifying countries as their competitive position progressed. Latin America would be hit harder than most other countries by this "competitive need" limitation, in view of its greater existing presence in the U.S. market, so would benefit most by the proposed changes.

—The Administration proposal exempts from preferences all items now under quantitative restriction, such as textiles. These are often products on which the developing countries could benefit most from preferences. And it is precisely those items which could *most* readily be made eligible for preferences, since the volume of their sales to the United States—and hence their impact on our domestic industry and workers—is already rigidly controlled. The effect of eliminating duties on these products would be (a) to transfer U.S. customs duties to exporting countries (and perhaps partly to U.S. consumers), and (b) to help developing countries compete against industrialized countries within the quantitative limits. Both objectives would promote U.S. economic as well as foreign policy interests.

—The Administration proposal could produce very tight "rules of origin," limiting the application of preferential treatment by requiring a very high percentage of value-added in the exporting country. To be sure, it is necessary to avoid transhipments of, say, Italian exports through an LDC entrepot to take advantage of the preferences. But the value-added requirement should be modest, and should cover value-added in all *developing countries* rather than just the country of origin of the final product.

Such steps would enable preferences to play a significant role in restoring a cooperative U.S. policy toward the Third World, including Latin America. Much more is needed to construct a really forthcoming U.S. trade policy toward the Third World, however, since even a preference scheme liberalized along the lines proposed here would have a modest impact in improving the prospects for Third World exports of manufactured goods to the United States.[2] One such possibility would be for the U.S. to support accelerated—perhaps immediate—application to developing-country exports of any tariff cuts which emerge from the forthcoming multilateral trade negotiations. This would also serve the purpose of muting the opposition already expressed by some of those countries to such negotiations on the grounds that multi-lateral tariff cuts would erode their newly won preferences—a view which is extremely short-sighted, however, because the developing countries have a far greater stake in a liberal world trading order, which a new multilateral negotiation is essential to restore, than in tariff preferences.

A Special Relationship?

You will note that I have referred throughout to U.S. policy toward Latin America as simply one aspect of U.S. policy toward the developing countries as a whole. This is because I see no merit in any "special relationship" between the United States and Latin America in the economic field, from the standpoint of either.

To be sure, there are issues on which U.S. and Latin American interests will coincide and where they should work together. An example is the network of special preferential arrangements maintained by the European Communities, which discriminate against both U.S. and Latin American exports. But there are issues on which Latin America can best promote its interests by siding with Europe or Japan against the United States, e.g., to avoid a restrictive new all-fiber international textile agreement and, instead, to roll back the present "voluntary" limitations on exports of cotton textiles. Indeed, the great promise of the new world pluralism is the opportunity it provides for precisely such shifting of alliances, which by avoiding rigid and continuing confrontations can make a major contribution to world peace and prosperity.

Indeed, I can foresee no circumstances in which special trade preferences (reciprocal or non-reciprocal) between the United States and Latin America would represent good policy for either. Even in a world economy rent by trade protectionism, I find it inconceivable that Europe or Japan would discriminate broadly against Latin America—or that Latin America would wish to give them cause (or to do so. Even in a world of floating exchange rates in which some Latin American countries choose to peg their currencies to the dollar to minimize financial and trade instability, I see no reason for spillover into trade preferences.

And, under either scenario, I can see no reason why the United States, with its global economic as well as security interests, would wish to tip the world toward aligning by North-South blocs. It is certainly true that Europe is busy creating such a bloc. But it is equally true that Japan has neither a national interest in doing so, nor receptivity throughout Asia to any such designs it might even harbor. Thus the United States can either tip the balance toward blocs, or hold the line against them. We should certainly do the latter.

Notes

1. See C. Fred Bergsten, "The Threat From the Third World," *Foreign Policy* 11 (Summer 1973) [chapter 26 in this volume].

2. Indeed, the likelihood of such modest efforts has caused some observers to oppose the whole concept of preferences due to a fear that, by raising expectations that could not be fulfilled, it would have a negative effect on relations between the industrialized and developing countries. See, e.g., Richard N. Cooper, "Third World Tariff Tangle," *Foreign Policy* 4, Fall 1971. There is now widespread realization in the Third World of the likely real outcome, however, so such an outcome is unlikely.

Part IX
United States Management
of Foreign Economic Policy:
Domestic Constituencies
and Governmental
Organization

32

The International Economy and American Business

The Thesis

My thesis is very simple:

—American business has probably been the greatest single beneficiary of the liberal international trading and payments system which has underpinned the phenomenal prosperity of the postwar world.

—American business has an overwhelming interest in preserving such an international system, and should be willing to devote sizable resources to the task of doing so.

—The liberal monetary and trading systems which governed international economic relations during the first postwar generation have collapsed, and we do not know what will take their place. As a result, new restrictions and distortions of international trade flows and capital movements have been proliferating at a rapid and accelerating pace. A wide variety of deeply rooted pressures are seeking to reverse the evolution of history by basing the new international economic order on protectionism, blocs, and the "new mercantilism."

—But American business, with the notable and praiseworthy exceptions of a few individual firms, remains largely supine in the face of these fundamental threats to its continued prosperity. Continued ineffectual efforts by the business community court international economic disaster, with far-reaching consequences for our entire American society, and indeed the entire world, as well as for the narrowly conceived interests of business itself. There are a number of specific steps which business should undertake, quickly and decisively, to avert such an outcome.

The Postwar Economic System and American Business

American multinational corporations rode an international gravy train in the 1950s and 1960s. Fixed exchange rates and world reliance on the dollar provided an environment of international economic stability and predictability within which foreign trade and investment could flourish. An increasingly overvalued dollar in fact subsidized US foreign investment at the

This paper was originally presented as part of the Key Issues Lecture Series at New York University in May 1973 and published in Jules Backman, ed., *Business Problems for the Seventies* (New York: New York University Press, 1973), pp. 86-102.

expense of other sectors of our society. World trade was steadily liberalized through a series of international negotiations triggered by US initiatives, and those impediments to trade which did exist usually took the readily recognizable form of tariffs. International investment remained largely free of serious impediments from either capital-exporting or capital-importing countries. Large foreign aid programs boosted the purchasing power of first Europe and then the Third World, and enabled them to open their economies to foreign participation. I will note shortly that every one of these vital elements of the international economic framework of the past two decades has now collapsed.

More basic than any of these specific phenomena, however, though built largely upon them, was the intellectual and emotional milieu which pervaded this postwar international economic order. There was global confidence in the existing monetary and trading systems. There was global confidence that international economic cooperation among the major non-Communist countries, and even most minor countries, would prevail. New evidence for this comfortable feeling was provided with the resolution of each succeeding monetary crisis and the steady liberalization of world trade. There were problems and some setbacks to these trends, to be sure. But the overriding perception of the world economy, in virtually all quarters, was confidence in its continued success.

This perception ranged far beyond economics. The economic stability imparted by the Bretton Woods and GATT systems promoted overall harmony between the United States and its major allies, in Europe and Japan, which in turn contributed significantly to the avoidance of armed conflict between major powers—either within Europe itself, as has occurred once per generation during the previous three-quarters of a century, or between East and West. Indeed, a major objective of postwar US foreign economic policy was to avoid replication of the experience of the 1930s, when a breakdown of the international economic order deeply exacerbated national economic difficulties and hence contributed importantly to the rise of the totalitarian regimes in Europe which soon thereafter plunged the world into global conflagration. That policy clearly succeeded. And the peaceful environment which ensued, in part because of that policy, provided the optimum environment for American business as well as for the world as a whole.

Finally, the domestic politics underlying US foreign economic policy remained tranquil as a result of the success of the postwar international economic system. To be sure, a few individual industries sought protection against liberal trade in the 1950s and early 1960s. But there was a broad national consensus, shared by labor and the vast bulk of American business, that a liberal international economic order promoted US national interests. Thus there was little rancor over the issue, between labor and business or within the business community itself, to deflect American business from pursuing maximum global expansion. There was seldom any cause for business to even consider the effects of its foreign involvement other than on its own growth and profits, except as it may have been forced to do so by countries which were hosts to its foreign investment. There were no real constraints from US policy, either legal or through the dynamics of our internal politics.

I have focused so far on the advantages of the postwar economic system to US *multinational* firms. They have certainly been its major beneficiaries: foreign investments now return a large (perhaps 15%) and rapidly growing share of total US corporate profits, and a large and growing number of US firms receive more than half their total income from overseas.

But the international economy is of critical importance to "purely domestic" US business as well. Export sales and imported inputs are essential for many firms. Even more important for these firms, however, are two broad aspects of the international economy.

One is its success, or lack thereof, in maintaining equilibrium exchange rates. It is clear that a significant part of the inroads made by imports against US production in the late 1960s was due to the growing overevaluation of the dollar which accompanied our Vietnam-related inflation. The steel and textile industries are particular cases in point. Both are now receiving sizable orders for *exports* in the wake of the two devaluations of the dollar—which have boosted our competitive position by almost 40% vis-à-vis our major competitors in Germany and Japan. So American business, though it often fails to realize it, has a vital interest in an effectively functioning international monetary system.

Second, the postwar system of liberal trade has played an important role in fighting US inflation and helping to preserve the competitive character of our economy. There are many well-known cases in which imports alone spurred particular US industries to modernize, cut costs, and hence contribute much more than they would otherwise have done to our national productivity. Perhaps most important, because of the critical impact of the industries involved to our entire price-cost structure, were the impetus provided by imports to adoption of the process and continuous casting (and more competitive pricing) by the US steel industry, and to the production of compact and subcompact automobiles by Detroit.

To be sure, particular American firms (and groups of workers) have occasionally been adversely affected by imports. But American business as a whole has benefited greatly from the increased competition which imports have provided, whether their interests are viewed narrowly in terms

458

of corporate profits or broadly as leading participants in a dynamic process of continuous change and improvement.

The Collapse of the System

The international economic system which provided this optimum environment for American business has now collapsed. It probably reached its zenith in 1967, with the successful conclusion of the Kennedy Round of trade negotiations and the agreement among all IMF members to create Special Drawing Rights, a truly international money, as the first step toward reforming the international monetary system. It started to break down shortly thereafter: the devaluation of sterling in late 1967 heralded the end of fixed exchange rates, the abolition of the gold pool in early 1968 essentially ended the gold convertibility of the dollar and sharply accelerated the precipitous decline of its ability to remain the world's key currency, and the United States began almost immediately erecting new import barriers in major industries (steel and meat in 1968, efforts on synthetic and woolen textiles beginning in 1969). The ultimate collapse was sealed by the US adoption of explicit dollar inconvertibility and its infamous import surcharge in August 1971.

It is impossible to return to these "good old days," even if one wished to do so. The monetary system can no longer be based on fixed exchange rates or the dollar. International trade has been subjected to a mounting array of barriers, is now controlled and influenced by a wide range of policies far more subtle and difficult to check than the tariffs and quotas of the past, and increasingly risks wholesale rejection of the most-favored-nation principle as the European Community increasingly expands its trading bloc. International capital flows have been subjected to a tightening web of national controls.[1] Regulation of foreign direct investment is rising rapidly. US policy almost wholly neglects fundamental interests of the Third World across a whole range of economic issues, contributing to the emotional and nationalistic policies which increasingly emerge from those countries.[2]

Any sober appraisal of the future of the world economy must start from these rather ominous trends. At the same time, it must recognize that the trends are of relatively short duration—no more than five or six years. They might simply represent an understandable backlash to the exceedingly rapid pace of recent international change, compounded in the United States by the twin difficulties of unemployment and inflation which we may hope will be less severe in the years ahead than in the years just past. World trade and capital movements have continued to rise rapidly. And major systemic readjustments are to be expected during a period in which the power structure underlying the world economy is changing rapidly, with the emergence of the European Community and Japan to equal or even surpass the United States in many regards, and when the security blanket which smothered most intra-alliance economic disputes is nudged aside as the result of the thawing of the Cold War.

All of these factors help explain why recent events have occurred. And they point up fairly clearly the options which the world faces: continued deterioration in international economic relations along the trend line of the past five or so years, or the creation of a new and relatively stable order based on the new underlying structure. But they give us little clue as to what will actually replace the system which has collapsed, and the implications for American business of that new regime. Such forecasts require a more detailed look at the individual issues.

The Outlook for International Trade Policy

International trade is probably the most uncertain policy area for the future. The multiplicity and growth of economic and social policy objectives in virtually every country renders governments increasingly dubious of risking disturbances from external sources over which they cannot exercise control. Protection of declining industries is one result. "The new mercantilist" support for new, particularly high-technology, industries is another. The collapse of the international framework of rules and institutions to govern national trade policies permit such tendencies to flourish.

In my view, the single most likely trigger for a rapid deterioration of international economic relations is a major protectionist move by a major country in the trade field. Indeed, the continued protectionism of Japan into the early 1970s, far beyond any conceivable justification for such a policy, is one of the most important elements in the deterioration we have witnessed to date.

One particularly worrisome possibility for the future is the apparent European effort to build a Community-wide "industrial policy," which would support the development of high-technology industries through policies discriminating against outside (mainly US) firms and perhaps even against the European subsidiaries of outside (mainly US) firms. Such a policy would focus on such industries as computers and aircraft, wherein lies much of the comparative advantage of the United States. Europe's agricultural policy already hits one central area of our comparative advantage; the significance of any such new European industrial policy is that it would replicate in industry what has already occurred in agriculture. This could in turn unite American business and agriculture (along with labor) against Europe, and virtually assure sharp US retaliation at least on economic issues. It might even render impossible the efforts of any President to maintain active security relations. So such a move by Europe could readily unravel the entire international economic order.

Of even greater concern is the threat of major protectionist policies in the United States. Some observers seem to believe that the present protectionist push by the AFL-CIO relates solely to "temporary" problems: our high rate of aggregate unemployment, continuing inflationary pressures, the deterioration of the trade balance and the balance of payments. To be sure, all of these "temporary" elements—if they are temporary—both intensify the legitimate concerns of labor and generate sympathy in the Congress and the public for their policy proposals. But any simple relationship can be readily dismissed by noting the inverse correlation between the decline of aggregate unemployment from 6.7 percent in 1961 to 3.5 percent in 1969 and the shift of the AFL-CIO from supporting the Trade Expansion Act in the former year to its virulent call for full-scale protectionism in the latter.

I am afraid that the problems run far deeper.[3] The entry of most of organized US labor into the middle class appears to have changed its views on a range of economic issues, including trade. At the higher levels of income now reached by most workers, job stability appears worth the price of forgoing further marginal gains in wages and other financial benefits. Since trade flows may in fact be one of the faster paced sources of change in our economy, and since "the foreigners" are far more susceptible to political attack than other Americans and can—erroneously—be portrayed as the sole party against which protectionism is aimed, trade policy is one of the first issues on which this new attitude of American labor is manifest.

A related issue is the structural weakness of American society in dealing with the dislocations which trade flows (and countless other sources of change, of course) bring to some workers. Individual firms, supported by their government, provide for the workers in Japan. National governments, through generous social security systems, national health insurance, manpower programs, etc., do so in Europe. But, with the notable exception of a few firms and some government benefits, workers in the United States are far less protected against dislocation.

Thus it is understandable that American labor is more inclined to protectionism than its foreign counterparts. It was not protectionist in the 1950s, because then the US faced little real international competition. It was not protectionist for much of the 1960s, because the American economy was booming. But it will certainly be so in the 1970s and beyond, since we are quite likely to continue to face serious economic problems at home and we are certain to continue to face real international competition from abroad—the first time we have experienced that combination for a sustained period since the Depression.

Finally, the bureaucratic politics of the AFL-CIO strongly reinforce the protectionist implications of these underlying developments. Virtually any structural change in the US economy means shifts of workers from traditional, highly unionized old-line manufacturing industries into modern, largely non-unionized high-technology and services industries. Thus it undermines the basic membership and power structure of the AFL-CIO. This pattern appears particularly true for changes induced by trade flows: import-competing industries are highly over-represented (relative to their share in the total labor force) in the AFL-CIO, while exporting industries and, particularly, the services industries whose workers' interest in trade is largely as consumers, are significantly underrepresented.[4] When combined with some foreign investment issues to which we turn shortly, these several considerations strongly suggest that the AFL-CIO is protectionist to stay—and that, as a result, US trade policy will remain under severe pressure to move steadily in this direction into the foreseeable future.

At the same time, the main source of support for the liberal US trade policy of the first postwar generation—US foreign policy—has declined sharply. Every major trade policy initiative has been motivated essentially by the US objective of avoiding economic cleavages in its alliance systems and hence strengthening those systems vis-à-vis the Communist countries. Now, however, there is much less concern both about the Communist threat and about the importance of rigid alliances in combatting that threat. Indeed, the present Administration seems to believe in the desirability of periodic confrontation with its allies, to nudge them toward "equal participation in a new balance-of-power world," especially on "secondary" issues like international economic policies. And no Administration is likely to stress international political harmony as much in formulating trade policy as has previously been true throughout the postwar period; candidate McGovern's call to "Come Home, America" is much more likely to represent the pressure point of the future. So foreign policy is no longer likely to provide a strong underpinning for a liberal US trade policy.

All of this could lead to a major protectionist swing. Even if the Burke-Hartke bill is too extreme to ever become law in its entirety, the whole debate over trade policy has shifted dramatically. The "Trade Reform Act" of the present Administration—which is ideologically committed to free enterprise (in most cases) and to an active foreign policy—represents the liberal end of the trade policy spectrum now before the Congress, whereas it would have been regarded as highly protectionist just a decade ago. The loosening of the escape clause proposed in that bill, particularly due to the inclusion of its "market disruption" formula, would open the door to import protection for a vast number of US industries *even if enacted into law precisely as proposed by the President*. In fact, of course, the Congress—if it passes any trade bill at all—is almost certain to add to the protectionist tendency of the escape clause, perhaps by inserting quantitative criteria under which industries could qualify automatically. Congress did in fact add such provisions, which would have covered over $7 billion of US imports at the time, *over Administration opposition* to the "Mills bill" of 1970 which passed the House and died only as the Congressional session expired.

The likelihood of increasingly frequent import restrictions is further increased by the Administration's failure to propose a viable alternative to restrictions. There are only two ways to deal with the dislocation for firms and workers which imports cause: to check the imports, or to assist those who are dislocated to adjust. The Congress voted in 1962 to provide an adjustment alternative, although the program proved largely ineffectual because its eligibility criteria were too light and its administrative machinery cumbersome and slow.

Rather than build on that precedent and the experience gained to date, and the variety of well-conceived and feasible alternatives which are available, however, the Administration has essentially proposed to eliminate the program. It would do so explicitly for firms. It would do so implicitly for workers, by failing to provide new machinery to administer the adjustment provisions and—perhaps more important, politically—by rolling back the level of benefits available to workers during the period of unemployment they suffer as a result of import increases, when there is virtually universal agreement that those benefit levels were already far too low. Unless the Congress seizes the initiative to add such a program to the trade legislation, the absence of a viable alternative to import restrictions sharply increases the probability that such restrictions will become much more pervasive.

The international repercussions of such a US policy shift are readily ascertainable. Other countries might well retaliate against some of the import restrictions which the US would then adopt. But they would more likely emulate this stance, in response to the pleas of their own protectionists. Indeed, the Administration appears to envisage internationalization of its new escape clause approach, so that all countries could adopt it quite legally. Whether legal or illegal, the foreign emulation of the proposed US approach would clearly add to the steady proliferation of restrictions over international trade—with marked effects on the interests of American business in such trade.

In addition, it is difficult to envisage a successful international negotiation to reduce trade barriers, of the type now scheduled to begin in late 1973, in such an environment. The Congress may not authorize the Administration to enter meaningfully into such a negotiation, but it is unclear in any event that the Administration is willing to make the concessions needed to do so—for example, abolition of our dairy import quotas or even cuts in our industrial tariffs, leading to a net increase in labor-intensive manufactured goods, to compensate other countries for reducing their barriers to our agricultural exports which the Administration has indicated is the *sine qua non* of the negotiations for the United States. Indeed, the Administration might scuttle the negotiations even before they start by insisting on non-reciprocal concessions in order to help the trade *balance*.

Yet engagement of the major countries in a new international trade negotiation is probably essential to protect politicians in each against protectionism. The major contribution of the Kennedy Round to freer trade was not its tariff cuts, but the defense it provided—as "a major international enterprise which could not be undercut"—against protectionist steps. History clearly indicates that special interests succeed in winning protection in the absence of some major enterprise pursued on behalf of the general interest in more liberal trade. The success of a variety of US industries in winning protection immediately after the end of the Kennedy Round provides only the latest empirical support. If such defenses were necessary during 1962-67, when the US economy was booming, they will be much more necessary in the mid-1970s. So the uncertain outlook for trade negotiations adds to the likelihood of continued protectionist advances in the years ahead.

The Outlook for International Investment Policy

The outlook for national policies toward foreign investment adds significantly to this picture of proliferating restraints on international economic transactions, with further adverse effects on American business—in this case, particularly on multinational corporations. We all know that host countries have frequently caused problems for such investment, and indeed are now becoming more sophisticated in their efforts to maximize their gains from foreign firms. In addition, however, a major new dimension has been added to the picture for the first time: serious political concern in the home countries of the multinational firms, particularly the United States, that the activities of the firms run counter to *their* national interests.

There are now at least six major lines of serious attack against the multinationals in terms of their impact on US national interests. Organized labor views foreign investment as exporting jobs, and the limited empirical work on the subject so far suggests that this is certainly true in specific cases and might very well be true in the aggregate.[5] Even more important to labor, in my view, is the real and psychological disadvantage it faces as an intentionally immobile factor of production in negotiating across the table with capital and management, which are highly mobile in their abilities to cross national borders. Indeed, the AFL-CIO has been noticeably silent about encouraging investment in the US by foreign-based multinationals, which it should regard as "importing jobs" on the same logic that it sees US multinationals "exporting jobs," in large part because it wants to avoid negotiating with a California subsidiary of Datsun as much as with a Ford Motor Company which can build its next plant in Germany or Brazil instead of Detroit. This particular labor view is felt intensely, and seems impossible to dislodge.

But the attack on multinationals goes far beyond organized labor. Tax reformers are after the present "loopholes which favor foreign investment," both on equity grounds and to provide new sources of revenue in a tight budgetary situation. Many different groups attack the multinationals for "speculating in the foreign exchange markets," hence contributing importantly to the recent monetary crisis and indeed "selling out their own currency." In the international monetary area, there is also the very real concern that multinationals foil successful balance of payments adjustment, including exchange rate changes, because they do not respond to price changes, at least in the short run, as the more atomistic economic men of economic theory are supposed to do. And many people, including some in the US Government, continue to favor restrictions on foreign investment—not just on the financing of such investment, as in the past—to help reduce our balance of payments deficit, in view of the unfavorable effect of the investment in the short run and its uncertain effects in the long run.

A fifth line of attack comes from those who view multinationals as distorting and endangering US foreign policy, as highlighted by the hearings of the Church Subcommittee. And a sixth centers simply on their bigness: serious observers see the multinationals either as dominating the entire world economy, or at least as oligopolizing it in a number of key industries—and hence adding significantly to world inflation.

All of these pressures, taken together, add up to a politically potent attack on multinationals. And there is feedback between the attacks on them in host and home countries: the more that a host country extracts from its negotiations with a multinational, the less the gain to the home country from the deal (even if the firm is largely unaffected or even benefited.) For example, Canada has induced at least one major US computer company to invest in Canada by denying government procurement contracts to foreigners and by extending cash grants to the company. The company has undoubtedly profited from the deal but jobs, taxes on profits and technology have been exported from the United States to Canada through devices which clearly distorted market forces. The US Government can be expected to take an increasingly dim view of the benefits of foreign investment to US national interests as such situations proliferate, as they are.

These projections strongly suggest a continuation of the recent trends toward increased controls over international trade and investment. As such, they represent a major threat to American business.

But such trends could also deteriorate into real economic conflict among nations. The world was very close to that brink in late 1971, after three months of unresolved crisis triggered by the US actions of August 15; investment plans plummeted around the world and the British Prime Minister refused to meet the President of the United States at the summit until the US initiated steps to resolve it. In a world without functioning international rules or institutions, and without a leader to guide its course such as the US provided for the first postwar generation, such an outcome is certainly possible. It would of course represent disaster for American business. Indeed, given the reliance of US firms on foreign investment as well as on trade flows, it might well represent a greater disaster for American business than for European or Japanese business (although a smaller disaster for American than foreign labor, given the importance of investment in the US picture)—though the relative degree of disaster is quite unimportant anyway to the firms which suffer its absolute costs.

The Response of American Business

So there is a very serious risk of creeping international economic paralysis, and a real possibility of a sharp breakdown of economic cooperation among nations. Confidence in that cooperation has already been greatly eroded, as evidenced in the continuing speculation against currencies and, implicitly, against the stability of the entire monetary system.

American business is thus faced with a potentially explosive setback to its own central interests. It would thus seem incumbent on the business community to take whatever action is needed to prevent such developments. Some firms are doing so. Unfortunately, most are not. And the business community as a whole, through its industrial organizations, has performed dismally in dealing with these imminent problems.

Business needs to respond in two ways: intellectually, to refute the blandishments of those who seek to build walls around our economy, and through political actions. It has done neither.

Intellectually, business has done very little to apply the traditional case for liberal trade to modern circumstances. That case has become even stronger than in the past due to the increased importance of the world economy to the US economy, as noted at the outset; to our increased national need to utilize all available policy tools to combat the structural causes of seemingly endemic inflation; and because of the central—if altered in substance—role which international economic issues will clearly be playing in US foreign policy in the years ahead. But the business community has failed to appreciate and/or seek to draw public attention to these trends and their clear implications for US trade policy.

The failure of business to do so may be partly because it has focused most of its attention on investment. But here too, with the exceptions of a few firms, it has provided very little useful material. It is wholly unpersuasive to argue that US firms have not "exported jobs" because their domestic employment has risen faster than the average rate of domestic employment. Since the firms involved are by definition the largest and most dynamic in the country, I would certainly hope that all aspects of their operation are growing faster than in the national average—if not, something is vitally wrong! And it is nonsense to say that wages were not a factor in investments in Europe and Canada; wages are significantly *lower* there than in the United States, even though they are of course not "low wage" in the sense of a Korea or Taiwan. It is equally irrelevant to argue that foreign investment helps the US balance of payments because the annual return on the *stock* of all outstanding investments exceeds the outward *flow* of capital to add to that outstanding stock. At least a large part of the return on present holdings would of course continue even if new outflows were halted completely.

In all these cases, the need is for comparisons between what has actually happened and what would have happened in the absence of the foreign investments. This is difficult, and cannot be done precisely, but it is certainly possible. Union Carbide has done it fairly well.[6] Upjohn is trying to do it. Until it is done, multinational firms will probably find it impossible to convince a broad spectrum of American opinion that their activities serve the US *national* interest. Indeed, as already indicated, these firms are now widely suspect of activities injurious to the US national interest. They will only deepen the stigma if they, like those government officials involved in the Watergate episode, appear to be hiding their activities from the public and fail to face honestly the problems which they are accused of causing—which means meaningful discussions on such issues as transfer pricing, tax shifting, and activities in the foreign exchange markets. To be sure, the AFL-CIO and its protectionist allies have done at least as poor an intellectual job, relying almost entirely on anecdotes and blaming imports for layoffs which have occurred for a variety of reasons. In such a confrontation of poor cases, however, labor probably gets a greater degree of public sympathy and may well come out on top.

Business has also been extremely derelict in pursuing the political action needed to avert international economic breakdown. To be sure, the organizations comprised solely of multinational firms (especially ECAT) are highly effective at this level; but their potential is limited by the obviously self-serving nature of their efforts, especially now that foreign investment has entered the picture so directly.

It is the broader-based business groups which should be leading the battle. Instead, they find it difficult even to organize themselves. The Chamber of Commerce and the National Association of Manufacturers, for example, spend much of their time competing with each other rather than pursuing their common interest. The business "community," such as it is, has failed to forge effective working ties even with its natural allies, as on trade policy with farm and consumer groups.

Beyond these tactical points lies substance. The issue on which the whole future of US trade (and perhaps investment) policy may rest is how we decide, as a nation, to deal with the real dislocations to workers and firms caused by import competition. There are only two choices: to limit the imports themselves, or to help the dislocated workers and firms adjust to the new competition. Import limitation will reduce the competitiveness of our own economy and trigger foreign retaliation or emulation; effective adjustment to imports will help us fight both inflation and unemployment, and avoid the risk of international economic warfare. American business, in its own narrow interest, as well as the broader national interest, should thus wholeheartedly support a liberal, effective program of adjustment assistance. The issue is politically crucial, because the several major unions which have deserted the AFL-CIO leadership on the Burke-Hartke bill—the Communications Workers of America, the International Paperworkers Union, and the United Auto Workers—have done so only on the assumption that an effective adjustment assistance program will give them a meaningful answer to the concerns of their members about imports. Avoidance of a monolithic labor position in favor of import restrictions thus requires such a program.

But American business, again with a few notable exceptions, has not supported meaningful adjustment assistance. The NAM published a staff report which effectively recommended abolition of the concept altogether. The Chamber of Commerce, because of failure of the majority of its membership to take sufficiently vigorous action to overcome the outmoded procedures and non-representative structure of its Board of Directors, failed to adopt a proposed program recommended unanimously to it by three component bodies of the Chamber—putting it in the position, as one of its directors commented during the debate, of "fiddling while Washington burns." As a result, the American business community has *no* position; it stands largely impotent on this most central determining issue of the future of US foreign economic policy, and perhaps of world economic relations for the foreseeable future.

It is not enough in 1973 to *say* that one is for a liberal trade and payments system, and it will not be enough in the years ahead. One must be willing to *pay* to maintain such a system. The American business community should be especially willing to pay, since that community is the major beneficiary of such a system. Yet key Congressional staffers have informed me that not a single one of the deluge of corporate letters opposing Burke-Hartke even attempted to outline in the most general terms an alternative which would provide a constructive answer to the dislocations caused by international trade and investment. Without such leadership from business, a relapse of both US foreign economic policy and international economic cooperation looms as a real possibility. American business should grasp the seriousness of the problem which now confronts it, and act accordingly to preserve both its own interests and those of the United States as a whole.

Notes

1. See "Controls on Capital Flows: The Recent Escalation," *OECD Economic Outlook* (December 1972), pp. 71-75.

2. See C. Fred Bergsten, "The Threat From the Third World," *Foreign Policy II* (Summer 1973) [chapter 26 in this volume].

3. For a more elaborate treatment see C. Fred Bergsten, "Crisis in U.S. Trade Policy," *Foreign Affairs* (July 1971), pp. 619-635 [chaper 12 in this volume].

4. See C. Fred Bergsten, "The Cost of Import Restrictions to American Consumers," in Robert E. Baldwin and J. David Richardson, eds., *International Trade and Finance* (Boston: Little, Brown and Co., 1974) [chapter 33 in this volume].

5. Robert G. Hawkins, "Job Displacement and the Multinational Firm: A Methodological Review," Occasional Paper No. 3 (New York: New York University Center for Multinational Studies, June 1972), esp. p. 26.

6. Union Carbide, *Union Carbide's International Investment Benefits the U.S. Economy* (New York: October 1972).

33
The Cost of Import Restrictions to American Consumers

The American consumer has been one of the primary beneficiaries of the steady liberalization of the world trading order throughout the postwar period. The liberal trade policy of the United States has made such progress possible. Since 1968, however, the AFL-CIO has joined with a growing number of U.S. industries to demand quota protection for domestic companies and workers. A shift by the United States to protectionist trade policies would reverse the postwar trend, foster trade restrictions throughout the world, and levy major new costs on consumers—on top of the billions of dollars they already pay as a result of present U.S. trade restrictions. Such a shift now would come at the worst possible time, since American consumers are already burdened by the most rapid inflation since the Korean War.

The Effects of Restrictions

Consumers suffer from restrictions on international trade in several ways. Tariffs raise the prices of imported goods. Quotas and "voluntary" export restraint agreements under which other countries yield to pressure by the U.S. Government to limit their exports to the United States, generally to avoid the imposition of import quotas by the United States, reduce the quantity of foreign goods available. Thus they too raise prices.

The economic effects of "voluntary" export restraints and import quotas are virtually identical. "Voluntary" restraints may have even greater price effects than quotas, however, because they are administered by the exporting countries and are thus more likely to lead to market-sharing and price-supporting arrangements among foreign firms. Quotas and voluntary restraints also limit significantly the range of consumer choice by making some goods totally unavailable, both because of the low levels set by the quotas themselves and because foreign sellers can often reduce their losses from the imposition of quantitative controls by discontinuing lower priced items in favor of those with higher unit prices. Low-income consumers generally suffer most, both because they are most sensitive to any

Originally prepared for the American Importers Association, March 1972 and published in Robert E. Baldwin and J. David Richardson, eds., *International Trade and Finance* (Boston: Little, Brown and Co., 1974).

increases in prices and because low-price goods from abroad are the primary targets of U.S. import restriction.[1]

Both tariffs and quotas reduce the competitive pressures on U.S. domestic industries, permitting them to charge higher prices and reduce the quality of their products. Such competition from abroad is particularly important in industries dominated by a few large firms, and hence unresponsive to the usual price pressures of the market. Only the Volkswagen forced Detroit to make a compact car, and only foreign success with the oxygen process forced U.S. steel firms to modernize. So the consumer costs of import restrictions go far beyond the increased prices of the imports themselves, because they raise the prices of goods produced at home as well.

Protectionist trade policies have the same effects in all countries. Indeed, consumers elsewhere suffer even more from trade restrictions than do American consumers, relative to their total incomes, because most countries rely more heavily on international trade than does the United States. At the same time, the great size of the United States means that it has a bigger impact on world trade policy and practices than any other country. The liberal trade policy of the U.S. has thus made possible the relatively liberal trading order of the entire world, with its attendant benefits for people in all countries. Overall U.S. foreign policy has of course benefitted greatly from this economic approach.

The United States is the largest single exporter and importer in the world, so American consumers reap the largest gains in total dollar terms from free flows of international trade. Therefore, even the present level of U.S. trade restrictions places a heavy cost on consumers. Tariffs average 7-8% on industrial imports, and are much higher on many important consumer products, such as textiles and watches. As a result, consumer prices are increased by at least $2 billion annually.[2] The 10% surcharge imposed by the President from August 15, 1971 to December 20 would have roughly doubled this cost to consumers had it become permanent.)

The U.S. now has an array of quotas and "voluntary" export restraints which have an even greater price effect than tariffs.[3] Indeed, they cover commodities which represent about $100 billion of U.S. consumption and make up 15-20% of the entire Consumer Price Index.[4]

The quotas on oil imports carry the greatest consumer costs. According to the Cabinet Task Force on Oil Import Control, this cost totaled $5 billion in 1969 and is rising by about $300 million annually under the present program.[5] Standard Oil of New Jersey places the present cost slightly lower, due to temporary factors, but suggests even higher costs over the longer run.[6] The quotas raise oil prices by an estimated 60%.[7]

Apparel prices are raised significantly by the "voluntary" export restraints on cotton textiles maintained since 1962, and the similar restraints on woolen and synthetic textiles negotiated in October 1971. Tariffs on these items average about 25%, and the "voluntary" restraints boost the consumer cost by another 10% or so.[8] Analysis by the staff of the Federal Reserve Board, as reported by Governor Andrew Brimmer, suggests that consumer apparel costs will be over $1 billion higher as a result,[9] and that the new restrictions alone will cost consumers about $300 million.[10] The limitations on imports of textile fabrics raise the consumer bill further. It is no comfort to note that cotton textile prices have risen less than the overall price level, despite the "voluntary" restraints, because they would otherwise have risen even less and helped curb inflation. Indeed, the Federal Reserve analysis concluded that apparel prices would have fallen between now and 1975 in the absence of import restraints.[11]

Sugar imports are also subject to quotas, and U.S. sugar prices have generally been about twice as high as world market prices in recent years. The annual consumer cost is about $500 million.[12] "Voluntary" restraints by the major foreign suppliers of fresh and frozen meat (Australia, New Zealand, Ireland, Mexico, and several Central American countries) probably cost U.S. consumers about $350 million annually,[13] and hit low-income families with particular severity because most meat imports are used in the manufacture of lower cost items such as frankfurters and hamburgers. President Nixon actually liberalized these controls in 1970 in recognition of their serious price effects. Tight quotas on imports of all dairy products add about $500 million more to the annual consumer bill.[14]

"Voluntary" steel restraints have existed since 1969, and raise import prices by an estimated 10%.[15] Their total price effect is particularly hard to estimate because steel is an intermediate input to many manufactured products, such as cars and home appliances, but its great importance cannot be doubted. The output of the domestic industry exceeds 4% of total GNP, and changes in steel prices have more strategic impact on the entire price-cost structure of American industry than any other. It is thus highly significant that, in the first three years of the import controls, the U.S. steel industry raised its prices five times as much as in the previous eight years—in the face of declining production and the idleness of 25-50% of the industry's producing capacity.[16] The acceleration of inflation in the late 1960s was obviously related closely to the sharp increases in steel prices, which were in turn related closely to the import controls instituted in response to pressures from that industry. In view of the small number of companies in the steel industry, both domestically and abroad, the steel restraints probably promote monopolistic pricing practices on a global basis more than any of the other present import restrictions.

Finally, special protective devices raise costs on additional specific items. The American Selling Price system of customs valuation sharply raises the effective tariff on benzenoid chemicals and a few other products, by applying the duty to prices charged by U.S. manufacturers of the product rather than the lower prices of foreign exporters. Additional duties under escape clause actions raise prices on carpets and glass. There are tariff quotas on imports of stainless steel flatware. "Buy American" preferences for U.S. firms under procurement contracts let by the Federal Government and some states generate unnecessarily higher costs and thus increase their budget deficits. Marketing orders by the Department of Agriculture limit the access of American consumers to some foreign fruits and vegetables, such as tomatoes. United States law calls for levying countervailing duties on foreign goods subsidized by their governments, even if no U.S. firms or workers are injured. There are many more special devices which raise costs.

The total consumer cost of all these tariff and non-tariff restrictions cannot be quantified precisely. However, including the effects on competing domestic production, it clearly reaches $10 billion annually and may exceed $15 billion.

The current pressures for additional protectionist legislation would add sharply to these already high costs. The Federal Reserve Board staff estimated that H.R. 16920 (the "Mills Bill"), passed by the House of Representatives and by the Senate Finance Committee in 1970, would have added almost $2 billion to consumer costs for footwear alone, raising the average shoe price by 32% and particularly affecting lower-income groups. Together with the apparel restraints, a large part of which eventuated without the bill, they would have raised the overall consumer price index by almost a full percentage point.[17]

In addition, the so-called "basket provision" of H.R. 16920 would have imposed quotas at the 1967-69 level on most items where imports accounted for 15% or more of domestic consumption, and where the ratio between imports and consumption was rising rapidly. Tight controls could have resulted on additional billions of dollars of imports of such items as radios, phonographs, television sets, sewing machines, calculators, chinaware, glassware, stainless steel flatware, gloves, and many sporting goods.[18] This provision was the most recent proof that protection for a specific industry breeds protection for other industries, on "equity" grounds, rapidly multiplying the consumer (and other) costs of the initially limited action.

The "Foreign Trade and Investment Act of 1972," (the "Burke-Hartke Bill"), introduced into the Congress in the fall of 1971, would if enacted have far more drastic effects on consumers than would H.R. 16920. It carries the "equity" case to its logical extreme and would place virtually all U.S. imports under quotas, basically excepting only those not produced at all domestically. All covered imports would be limited to the average import level of 1965-69. The result would be a tremendous cutback in total imports, and a drastic rise in consumer prices. The price effects of such legislation could by themselves offset completely the success of Phase 2 predicted by the Administration—a reduction of U.S. inflation by 1½-2 percentage points—and require tightening and prolonged extension of the entire price and wage control program.

The Fallacy of the Argument for Import Restrictions

In view of these extremely high costs, why is there support in the United States for new trade barriers? The reason most often expressed is that such barriers increase the number of U.S. jobs, and hence can play a critical role in combatting unemployment, along with inflation the most urgent economic problem now faced by the United States.

This argument is totally erroneous. More barriers to imports will increase U.S. unemployment, rather than reduce it. This is because (1) a reduction in our imports from foreign countries means that their incomes drop, so they are unable to buy as much U.S. merchandise, and (2) other countries would retaliate against such increased United States barriers, directly or indirectly, on at least a dollar-for-dollar basis. There would thus be no net increase in the U.S. trade balance, and the level of both exports and imports would be lower. This would cost jobs, because U.S. exports are more labor-intensive than U.S. imports; a dollar's worth of exports produces more jobs here than a dollar's worth of imports eliminates.[19] In addition, the higher prices resulting from import barriers reduce the overall purchasing power of Americans, because a larger share of their incomes would have to be used to buy the restricted goods, and hence reduce demand for domestic production and jobs.[20]

The absence of retaliation against the import surcharge in late 1971 was due to widespread acceptance of the Administration's assertion that it was solely a temporary bargaining lever, and the widespread acceptance of the need for a realignment of exchange rates. The absence of retaliation against the new "voluntary" textile restraints is due to their very special place in overall US-Japan relations since 1969. No such tolerance by other trading nations could be expected in the face of legislation anything like the "Foreign Trade and Investment Act of 1972," or even H.R. 16920 of 1970, especially in light of the surcharge and textile actions.

In addition to creating more jobs, U.S. exports generate much higher wages than U.S. import-competing industries.[21] This is because the United States exports largely high-productivity, advanced products and imports low-productivity, standardized products. Import restrictions and the resulting loss of export opportunities would thus significantly reduce total American incomes and national wealth. The competitiveness of our entire economy, which is its chief driving force toward greater economic efficiency and maintaining a low level of unemployment, would decrease perceptibly if our textile firms had to pay much more for their foreign machinery or if our auto manufacturers had to pay much more for the foreign components in their compact cars—assuming they could get them at all—and if U.S. firms no longer had to compete at all in the world marketplace.

The fallacy of the employment argument for protectionism is best exposed by simply referring to the situation of 1968 and 1969, when there coexisted the lowest rate of unemployment since the Korean War and the lowest trade surpluses in the 1960s. (To be sure, inflation was accelerating and the overall economic situation was far from perfect at that time; nevertheless, the correlation between fullemployment and a small trade surplus was clear.) Imports were rising dramatically while unemployment was falling, equally dramatically. The high rate of activity of the U.S. economy, which generated such job growth, also generated major pressures on the price level which were mitigated at least partially by the surge of imports. And it was this high rate of domestic economic activity, rather than any fundamental decline in U.S. competitiveness or "unfair foreign trade practices," including export subsidies, which caused imports to grow so rapidly. U.S. exports continued to grow rapidly throughout this period, though not as rapidly as imports. The trade surplus in capital goods such as electrical machinery, machine tools, computers, tractors, and aircraft—in which the U.S. retains a strong comparative advantage—continued to grow impressively despite the decline in the overall trade surplus.[22]

The Case for Import Liberalization

Indeed, the United States badly needs a liberal trade policy at this time to help achieve the twin objectives of full employment and price stability. Because of structural changes in the labor force, much higher rates of inflation are now associated with a given rate of unemployment than was true even a decade ago. U.S. inflation is now likely to run at about 4¾% annually when the rate of unemployment is 4%, the "full employment" norm of the 1960s. Around 1960, inflation ran at only 3¼% annually when unemployment was 4%. So inflation is now 1½ per year higher at "full employment."[23] It has thus become much harder to achieve the traditional employment objectives without at the same time spurring unacceptable rates of price increase. In addition to this structural problem, the present cyclical economic situation combines unacceptably high unemployment and unacceptably high rates of inflation, exacerbating the policy dilemma.

Both fiscal and monetary policy must therefore be aimed at restoring and maintaining full employment; indeed, if they succeeded in doing so there would be far less clamor for using trade policy to increase jobs. As a corollary, however, selective policies must be found to moderate inflation. The wage-price freeze, and its successor stabilization effort, is such a policy. Another is a more liberal trade policy, as pointed out and proposed by Federal Reserve Board Chairman Arthur Burns in early 1971, for the reasons outlined at the outset of this paper. Proper domestic policies can achieve full employment now, as they did in the 1960s. Protectionist trade policies cannot help do so, but liberal trade policies can contribute significantly to the corollary battle against inflation.

Numerous other countries have in fact followed such an approach. Germany and Canada are among those which have cut tariffs unilaterally to increase their imports and thus fight inflation. Partly for the same reason, Germany, Canada, Switzerland, Austria and the Netherlands upvalued their exchange rates (long before August 15, 1971) to make imports cost less.

Labor and Trade Policy

The strongest political force urging quota legislation upon the Congress is the AFL-CIO. However, workers are also consumers, and most consumer organizations have long been linked with organized labor and sympathized with its viewpoints. Why then does the Executive Council of the AFL-CIO now support protectionist trade policies, reversing its traditional liberal trade stance?

The answer is simply that the AFL-CIO does not accurately represent the overall American labor force. Not only do its constituent unions represent less than 20% of all American workers; even this sample is highly skewed. Workers in the services industries (excluding contract construction, a special case) account for almost 70% of the total labor force, but only about 40% of the membership of the AFL-CIO. Traditional manufacturing industries, such as textiles and steel, make up almost three times as great a share of AFL-CIO membership as they do of the total labor force. Other proponents of protectionism, such as shoe and glass workers, are also over-represented. The high technology industries, such as chemicals and nonelectrical machinery, rely much more heavily on exports than most U.S. industries and are under-represented within the Federation. Table 33-1 demonstrates the unrepresentative character of the AFL-CIO, and indeed organized labor as a whole, by comparing the share of each industry group in the total labor force with its share in (1) the AFL-CIO and (2) organized labor as a whole.

The trade policy implications of this skewness are obvious. It is the

Table 33-1

Composition of Labor Unions, and Total U.S. Labor Force, by Industry Group

(ranked from most over-represented in AFL-CIO to least represented, as shown in column 4)

Industry Group	% of AFL-CIO membership (1)	% of all unions'' membership (2)	% of total labor force (3)	Representation ratio in AFL-CIO (4) = (1)/(3)	Representation ratio in all unions (5) = (2)/(3)	Number of workers (6) (Total labor force in thousands)
Contract construction	15.8	12.6	4.9	322%	257%	3,502
Ordinance and Accessories	0.9	0.8	0.3	300%	267%	194
Apparel and other finished products made from fabrics	5.5	4.3	1.9	289%	226%	1,353
Primary metals industries	4.4	3.8	1.7	259%	224%	1,190
Paper and allied products	2.5	2.2	0.1	250%	220%	970
Lumber and wood products (except furniture)	2.0	1.5	0.8	250%	187%	800
Transportation	9.7	12.4	4.2	230%	295%	2,962
Electrical machinery, equipment, and supplies	5.2	5.0	2.5	208%	200%	1,778
Tobacco manufactures	0.2	0.2	0.1	200%	200%	74
Petroleum refining and related industries	0.6	0.5	0.3	200%	167%	193

Leather and leather products	0.8	0.6	0.4	200%	150%	316
Stone, clay, glass and concrete products	1.7	1.5	0.9	189%	167%	644
Rubber and misc. plastic products	1.5	1.2	0.8	188%	150%	590
Electric, gas, sanitary services	1.8	1.6	1.0	180%	160%	733
AVERAGE, ALL MANUFACTURING	43.4	45.6	26.0	167%	175%	18,717
Telephone and telegraph	2.7	2.4	1.6	156%	150%	1,146
Printing, publishing and allied industries	2.3	1.9	1.5	153%	127%	1,086
Federal gov.	5.7	6.7	3.8	150%	176%	2,678
Fabricated metal products, exc. ordinance machinery and transport equipment	2.8	2.7	1.9	147%	142%	1,335
Furniture and fixtures	0.9	0.8	0.7	129%	114%	465
Food and beverages	3.4	4.4	2.7	126%	163%	1,899
Chemical and allied products	1.6	1.9	1.4	114%	136%	1,014
Non-electrical machinery	2.7	3.4	2.5	108%	136%	1,768
Mining and quarrying	0.9	1.7	0.9	100%	188%	626
Transportation equipment	2.1	6.6	2.4	88%	275%	1,706
Textile mill products	1.2	1.0	1.4	86%	71%	963
AVERAGE, ALL NON-MANUFACTURING	56.6	54.4	74.0	77%	74%	52,196

Table 33-1 (continued)

Industry Group	% of AFL-CIO membership (1)	% of all unions'' membership (2)	% of total labor force (3)	Representation ratio in AFL-CIO (4) = (1)/(3)	Representation ratio in all unions (5) = (2)/(3)	Number of workers (6) (Total labor force in thousands)
AVERAGE, ALL NON-MANUFACTURING (Excluding Contract Construction)	40.8	41.8	69.1	59%	60%	48,694
Professional, scientific and controlling instruments	0.3	0.3	0.6	50%	50%	434
Misc. service industries (e.g., health, education, lodging places, personal services)	6.3	5.4	16.8	38%	32%	11,943
State and local government	5.1	4.0	13.6	37%	29%	9,630
Wholesale and retail trade	7.8	6.9	21.3	37%	32%	15,112
Misc. manufacturing	0.8	1.0	2.6	31%	38%	427
Finance, insurance real estate	0.3	0.2	5.4	6%	4%	3,864

Data for union membership are for 1968, for total labor force July or August 1971.

Sources: Department of Labor, Bureau of Labor Statistics, Directory of National and International Labor Unions in the United States 1969, Bulletin 1665. Department of Labor, Bureau of Labor Statistics, *Employment and Earnings*, Vol. 18, No. 3 (Sept. 1971).

traditional manufacturing industries which are most threatened by imports, and seek protection against them. It is the high-technology industries which are most reliant on exports, whose competitiveness is hurt by import restrictions on their material inputs, and which thus support a liberal trade policy. It is the services workers whose product does not compete internationally, and who have the greatest interest in liberal trade as consumers. So the AFL-CIO cannot be regarded as accurately representing American labor on the trade issue. Instead, it seeks primarily to protect the traditional industries (which have lost much of their competitive ability) and to freeze the present structure of production, avoiding any changes in the composition of the labor force, rather than boost the level of overall employment and overall wages.

To be sure, liberal trade policies require the labor force, and business firms, to shift from one set of occupations to another—as does purely domestic competition. And they must now do so at increasing speed due to the rapid acceleration of global transportation and communications, abetted by the wide-ranging activities of multinational corporations. However, such structural shifts in the huge United States economy have always been required due to technological advances, changes in consumer tastes and, more recently, changes in defense activities and environmental concerns. (Changes in military and military-related spending affected 2 million jobs in 1968-71, for example, whereas changes in imports seldom affect more than 100,000-200,000 jobs annually.) But a new economic transition program is clearly needed to cushion the costs of adjustment to trade, and perhaps to these other causes of structural change as well.[24]

Another requirement for the maintenance of liberal trade is an international monetary system which keeps exchange rates in equilibrium. Otherwise a country's currency can become overvalued in relation to its true competitive position, and disadvantage its export and import-competing industries. Just such a situation developed for the dollar as a result of our domestic inflation of the late 1960s, at least vis-a-vis the Japanese yen, the German mark, and the Canadian dollar—the currencies of the three countries whose trade gains mirrored our trade losses in that period.

The Administration has recently succeeded in a major effort to eliminate this overvaluation through a sizeable realignment of exchange rates. The devaluation of the dollar will help greatly to restore the U.S. competitive position, by making our exports cheaper in other countries and by making imports more expensive here—for example, after a 10% dollar devaluation, U.S. "widgets" would cost about $90 rather than $100 in Germany, and German "widgets" would cost almost $100 instead of $90 here.[25] Every one percent devaluation of the dollar is expected to build our trade surplus by about $800 million.[26] In the process, it creates about 60,000-70,000 new jobs.[27] The recent realignment should thus recover the

500,000-700,000 jobs which may have been lost in recent years due to the overvaluation of the dollar and the failure of domestic economic policy to compensate for them.

This approach stands in direct contrast to trade restrictions, which achieve no gain in the trade balance and actually cost jobs. In addition, the transitional problems of American labor are eased if we restore our trade surplus by increasing exports rather than by limiting imports. This is because the composition of U.S. exports approximates the composition of overall U.S. production much more closely than does the composition of imports, which means that workers can shift more readily into producing more exports than into producing goods to replace imports.[28]

The administration is also seeking reforms in the international monetary system which would protect the United States against a new overvaluation of the dollar, and the accompanying job losses, in the future. Passage of protectionist trade legislation, by destroying the basic framework of international economic cooperation and triggering retaliation on a wide scale, would make such progress impossible—and undercut the opportunity to provide new jobs through continued expansion of foreign trade.

Consumers have been hurt by the devaluation of the dollar, of course, because import prices are now higher. However, improvement had to be made in the U.S. balance of payments and consumers are hurt much less by devaluation than they would be by the import quotas sought by the AFL-CIO. "Since such quotas would not bring any *net* gain to the U.S. payments position, for reasons outlined above, consumers would in fact face the cost of *both* devaluation and quotas if the latter were adopted." This is because they share the adjustment costs of devaluation with exporters, foreign investors and others throughout the economy—all of whom are affected by the new exchange rate. In addition, U.S. importers and foreign exporters must still compete for U.S. markets after a devaluation, whereas they can raise prices easily when they are protected by quotas or "voluntary" export restraints.

The Need for Action

Consumers thus have a major interest in stopping any new import restrictions, and indeed in liberalizing present trade policy. The dollar impact of such measures on consumers is large, and much greater than the impact of numerous other policies which they already oppose vigorously. Protectionist trade policies cannot reduce unemployment; liberal trade policies can do so, and fight inflation at the same time. Consumers need not avoid the trade issue out of concern for its employment effects. The present domestic economic situation, and the present international negotiating efforts of the Administration, make this a particularly dangerous time for protectionism from the standpoint of American consumers. Consumers need to mobilize a major effort on this issue, to make their keen interest in it heard both within the Administration and on Capitol Hill.

Notes

1. Norman S. Fieleke, "The Cost of Tariffs to Consumers," *New England Economic Review,* Sept.-Oct. 1971, pp. 13-18, estimates tariffs absorb a 10% greater share of the budget outlays of low-income consumers than of middle-income consumers, and a 20% greater share of the budget of low-income consumers than of high-income consumers. This is because internationally traded items weigh more heavily in the consumption patterns of lower income consumers, and because tariff rates appear to be higher on lower quality goods, which are purchased more heavily by lower income groups.

2. U.S. customs receipts totaled $2.4 billion in fiscal year 1970 and $2.6 billion in fiscal 1971. (*The Budget of the United States Government, Fiscal Year 1973,* p. 496). These receipts are the tariff payments by American importers, and thus a rough measure of their cost to consumers. The $2 billion estimate in the text recognizes that some consumption may be deterred by the higher prices, so that foreign suppliers lower their prices and the net price impact of the tariff on American consumers is less than the tariff itself. The estimate is very conservative, however, because it makes no allowance for the increased prices of domestically produced goods which compete with the dutiable imports and are protected from them by the tariff.

Fieleke, *op. cit.,* in fact implicitly estimates that U.S. tariffs in 1972 (after completion of the Kennedy Round cuts) will cost consumers about $10 billion—1.5% on total consumption of about $700 billion. He recognizes that his estimates are too high, however, and the objective of his analysis was to compare the differential effects of tariffs on different income groups rather than their absolute magnitude. Nevertheless, his estimates may be regarded as a plausible maximum cost of tariffs to American consumers.

3. A current listing includes:

- animal feeds containing milk or milk derivatives
- brooms of broom corn
- cattle
- cotton—raw, waste, etc.

- crude petroleum & petroleum products
- dairy products
- fish & fish products (fresh, frozen or filleted)
- meat & meat products
- peanuts
- potatoes, white or Irish
- sugar & sugar-containing products or mixtures incl. candy & confectionery
- textiles & apparel of cotton, man-made fibers & wool
- stainless steel flatware
- steel
- wheat & wheat flour

4. The latest (1963) weighting of items included in the Consumer Price Index (Bureau of Labor Statistics, *The Consumer Price Index: Technical Notes, 1959-63,* Bulletin No. 1554) includes the following items subject to import quotas or "voluntary" export restraint agreements:

Meat (excluding lamb)	5.0%
Dairy products	4.5%
Fresh fruit	.7%
Sugar	.5%
Fuel oil	.5%
Automobile gasoline and oil	2.5%
Men's and boys' apparel	2.8%
Women's and girls' apparel	3.7%
Steel products (in automobiles and home appliances)	1.3%
Total	21.5%

This figure can only be regarded as an approximation, both because some items included in these broad categories may not actually be under quota and because some items covered by quotas are not specified in the CPI. A conservative estimate of 15-20% is thus cited in the text. U.S. personal consumption expenditures were running at an annual rate of $672.5 billion in the third quarter of 1971 (*Survey of Current Business,* November 1971, p. S-1), so this 15-20% represents at least $100 billion of U.S. consumption at this time.

5. Cabinet Task Force on Oil Import Control, *The Oil Import Question,* pp. 20-30.

6. *Ibid.* p. 26.

7. Harry H. Bell, "Some Domestic Price Implications of U.S. Protective Measures," in *United States International Economic Policy in an*

Interdependent World, papers submitted to the (Williams) Commission on International Trade and Investment Policy, July 1971, Volume I, p. 483.

8. *Ibid.,* p. 487. The American Retail Federation has estimated that retail prices averaged 34% more than prices of comparable imports of 22 selected cotton items in 1970—including the effects of both the U.S. tariff and the "voluntary" export restraints. See Exhibit A, attached to Gardner Ackley's testimony on behalf of the American Retail Federation, in "Tariff and Trade Proposals," Hearings before the Ways and Means Committee, Part 3, May 18, 1970, p. 927. Richard Wood, Director, Foreign Buying, Montgomery Ward Co. "Remarks to Republican Task Force on International Trade," Jan. 25, 1972, reports that this price differential—which may amount to $2.50-$4.00 per dozen units—is often added through the sale of quota allocations from one exporter to another.

9. Andrew F. Brimmer, "Import Controls and Domestic Inflation," a paper presented before the Economics Seminar, University of Maryland, November 11, 1970; especially pp. 17-19 and Table 2. Brimmer concluded that the textile quotas of the Mills Bill of 1970 would raise apparel costs by $1.8 billion (in constant 1969 dollars) in 1975. The much lower figure in the text reflects the later base period, narrower product coverage, and slightly higher growth factor of the "voluntary" restraints compared with the Mills Bill.

10. Andrew F. Brimmer, "Imports and Economic Welfare in the United States," remarks before the Foreign Policy Association, New York, Feb. 16, 1972, pp., 22-23.

11. Brimmer, "Import Controls and Domestic Inflation," p. 19.

12. U.S. sugar consumption totaled 11.3 million short tons in 1970. From 1966 to 1970, the U.S. domestic price averaged about 4¢ per pound more than the world price. (U.S. Department of Agriculture, *Sugar Reports,* November 1971.) The elimination of U.S. import quotas would reduce this difference, but still save U.S. consumers $50-60 per ton. The total cost of the present controls compared with 1966-70 is thus $500-750 million. Brimmer, "Imports and Economic Welfare in the United States," p. 21, compares the present situation with the 1968-1971 period, when U.S. wholesale prices exceeded estimated import prices by 3¢ (instead of the 4¢ differential for 1966-1970), and concludes that the sugar quotas cost U.S. consumers $300-500 million. He also notes that industry experts regard the recent sharp rise in world prices as a temporary phenomenon which should pass soon.

13. It is estimated that each 100 million pounds of meat imports reduce domestic prices by ½¢ per pound, and that the present restrictions are restraining imports by about 300 million pounds. U.S. consumption of beef and veal reached 23.5 billion pounds in 1970. The total consumer cost is thus about $350 million.

---

14. Manufactured milk production now amounts to about $3 billion in the U.S. Costs in New Zealand, the most efficient world producer, are about 1/3 less. However, New Zealand could not supply anywhere near the total U.S. demand for dairy products, and other foreign suppliers are not as efficient as New Zealand (though some are more efficient than the U.S.). The $500 million cited in the text is thus an estimated order of magnitude.

15. Bell, *op. cit.*, pp. 485-86.

16. See the testimony of Walter Adams before the Senate Monopoly Subcommittee, November 12, 1971.

17. Brimmer, "Import Controls and Domestic Inflation," pp. 22-25.

18. List prepared by the Tariff Commission as published in the *National Journal,* August 22, 1970, p. 1850.

19. Lawrence B. Krause, "How Much of Current Unemployment Did We Import?" *Brookings Papers on Economic Activity 2, 1971,* especially pp. 421-5, concludes that each $1 billion of *additional* exports from the first quarter of 1970 to the first quarter of 1971 created 111,000 jobs, while each $1 billion of *additional* imports over the same period displaced 88,600 jobs. Brimmer, "Imports and Economic Welfare in the United States," pp. 11-17, updates earlier Department of Labor data and concludes that each $1 billion of exports in 1971 produced an *average* of 66,000 jobs while each $1 billion of imports resulted in *average* cutbacks of just under 65,000 jobs. The marginal analysis of Krause is of course more relevant, since policy issues deal with changes from current levels. See in addition the enormous literature since 1953 on this so-called "Leontief paradox."

20. Brimmer, "Imports and Economic Welfare in the United States," estimates that the present level of competitive imports ($40 billion in 1971) creates about 360,000 U.S. jobs through this price effect. Based on an assumption that imports are about 10% cheaper than domestic goods, he concludes that consumers have about $4 billion more to spend and, since about 90,000 domestic jobs are created for every $1 billion of consumer expenditures, that 360,000 jobs are created.

21. Again, see the enormous literature on the Leontief paradox. The latest broad analysis of the issue is William H. Branson and Helen B. Junz, "Trends in U.S. Trade and Comparative Advantage," *Brookings Papers on Economic Activity 2, 1971,* esp. pp. 322-334.

22. Branson and Junz, *op. cit.*, esp. Table 6 on p. 308 and Table 7 on pp. 310-315.

23. George L. Perry, "Changing Labor Markets and Inflation," *Brookings Papers on Economic Activity 3, 1970,* pp. 411-441; Charles L. Schultze, "Has the Phillips Curve Shifted? Some Additional Evidence," *Brookings Papers on Economic Activity 2, 1971,* pp. 452-467.

24. See, for example, the proposals in *U.S. Foreign Economic Policy for the 1970s: A New Approach to New Realities,* a policy report by an Advisory Committee of the National Planning Association, Nov. 1971, pp. 20-22.

25. The United States agreed in December 1971 to devalue the dollar by 8.57% in terms of gold. In addition, several countries—notably Japan and Germany—agreed to upvalue their currencies against gold, and hence by more than 8.57% against the dollar. The economic significance of the exchange rate realignment for the United States lies in the effective changes in exchange rates between the dollar and other currencies, which exceeds 13% in the case of the deutschemark and almost 17% in the case of the yen. The overall depreciation of the dollar, in terms of the changes of all major exchange rates, and weighted by the share of each individual foreign country in U.S. trade, amounts to about 10.4%.

26. Based on public statements by the Administration during the recent monetary negotiations, and corroborated by the analyses of the International Monetary Fund and Organization for Economic Cooperation and Development.

27. Krause, *op. cit.,* esp. Table 2 on pp. 422-423. His estimates imply that, for each $1 billion of trade growth from the first quarter of 1970 to the first quarter of 1971, U.S. jobs *rose* by 111,000 through exports and were displaced by 88,600 through imports, although he recognizes that the absolute magnitude of his figures may be slightly too high. Krause's figure accords closely with the 1966 estimates of import effects by the Department of Labor ("Foreign Trade and Employment," *United States International Economic Policy in an Interdependent World,* p. 501), which found a mean of 80,400 and an average of 76,618 jobs per $1 billion of imports in 1966.

28. Daniel J. B. Mitchell, "The Occupational Structure of U.S. Exports and Imports," *Quarterly Review of Economics and Business,* Vol. 10, No. 4 (Winter 1970), pp. 17-30.

34

Organizing for Foreign Economic Policy

Abolish CIEP

I recommend the abolition of the Council on International Economic Policy (CIEP) instead of its permanent authorization as proposed in the legislation under consideration. My recommendations are based solely on an analysis of the organizational structures involved in the issue, and should not —repeat not—be construed as reflecting on the individuals now or recently incumbent in those structures.

The CIEP was created in early 1971 for two reasons. First, no White House official at the highest staff level was exercising effective responsibility for U.S. foreign economic policy. That responsibility had traditionally been exercised by the Assistant to the President for National Security Affairs, but Dr. Kissinger chose not to do so. No other top-level White House staffer had authority in his stead. Thus there was a management vacuum at the top level of the White House, which must be the locus for coordinating U.S. foreign economic policy because of the wide variety of interests engaged on almost every issue.

Second, the management of U.S. trade policy was completely ineffectual because of the impotence of the Office of the Special Representative for Trade Negotiations (STR). There were a variety of reasons for this impotence, including successful attempts by other parts of the bureaucracy to undercut STR and the absence of Presidential support for it. The result was a vacuum at both the coordinating and operating levels for trade policy.

The CIEP was created to fill these two vacuums. Both vacuums, however, represented temporary aberrations from a relatively stable organizational situation that had prevailed for a decade. In such a situation, there was some logic in the creation of CIEP.

In practice, however, CIEP never filled either vacuum. Shortly after its inception, Secretary of the Treasury Connally took command of overall U.S. foreign economic policy. STR was rebuilt and again effectively operated U.S. trade policy.

The only role for CIEP was then to coordinate the various facets of foreign economic policy en route to the decision-making level. But it has

Originally presented as testimony to the Subcommittee on International Finance of the Senate Committee on Banking, Housing and Urban Affairs in its hearings on the *Extension of the Council on International Economic Policy*, May 14, 1973.

played no noticeable role in monetary policy, foreign economic aid, energy matters, foreign investment or any of the other issues which it might have coordinated with trade policy. The operation of U.S. international monetary policy remained with the Treasury Department, as it always has and probably always will, and policy recommendations in that area went directly from an interagency group chaired by the Under Secretary for Monetary Affairs to the Secretary rather than via CIEP. Economic aid fell into a sorry vacuum at the White House. Energy was given to another part of the White House. Nobody picked up the ball on investment. CIEP clearly devoted the bulk of its attention to trade policy, duplicating the responsibilities delegated to STR by the Trade Expansion Act of 1962 and which STR can certainly handle. So there is no reason to suspect that the proposed legislation, and the administrative actions which the Administration has indicated it would then take, would have any effect in achieving the praiseworthy objective of assuring that "trade negotiations will proceed in the fullest organizational harmony with other, related aspects of international economi policy" as asserted in the letter transmitting the Administration proposals.

The two temporary conditions which motivated the creation of CIEP in 1971 clearly do not exist at this time. First, the President has clearly designated Secretary of the Treasury Shultz, who is also Assistant to the President for Economic Affairs, to coordinate U.S. foreign economic policy and be the channel for recommendations to the President in this field. A Council on Economic Policy has been created to provide a mechanism through which Secretary Shultz can exercise that authority, and the Administration has indicated that it would use the proposed legislation to install the Secretary as chairman of the CIEP as well. In addition, the Administration's own proposal "to free the President from statutory membership and chairmanship" of the CIEP indicates the termination of any effort to imbue the Executive Director of CIEP with Presidential authority to coordinate foreign economic policy. The top-level White House staff vacuum which existed in 1969-1970 has clearly been filled, and not by CIEP.

Second, STR has been rejuvenated and is now an effective instrument for coordinating and operating U.S. trade policy. In recognition of that fact, the President has delegated Deputy STR William Pearce to manage his trade legislation and STR William Eberle to handle the international trade negotiations in which that legislation seeks to authorize U.S. participation. Secretary Shultz has reportedly assured European leaders, when discussing with them the negotiations scheduled to begin this fall, that Ambassador Eberle "is the President's man on trade." CIEP seems to have no central role in operating U.S. trade policy.

Both functions originally intended for CIEP are thus being exercised elsewhere. It has proven ineffective in pulling together the different aspects of foreign economic policy, as could readily have been predicted at the time it was created. Its continued existence appears redundant and anomalous.

Indeed, its existence could even prove quite costly. It could impede the decision-making process, either simply because of the delay caused by the additional layer or because of the inherent rivalry between redundant trade bureaucracies. The existence of overlapping bureaucracies on trade dilutes the competence of both by further dividing up the scarce pool of talented personnel, and by inducing them to waste time combatting each other. Such redundancy obviously wastes money. The negotiating effectiveness of STR could be reduced as a result of its being simply an operating arm of CIEP twice-removed from the President. And the cost could be exceedingly high if the proposed downgrading of STR, and/or a battle over the issue, impeded constructive Congressional action on the pending trade legislation, which is overwhelmingly more important to the future of U.S. foreign economic policy than the organizational charts within the White House. On structural grounds, the case for the abolition of CIEP seems clear.

The Longer Term

One should, of course, step back from current considerations in making structural decisions of this type. In doing so, three considerations are paramount.

One is that foreign economic policy is inherently very messy. Every issue in this field encompasses domestic economic (and therefore political) considerations and overall foreign policy (including U.S. security concerns). The weight of each of these considerations shifts from issue to issue. It is clear, however, that every policy decision is rooted in both. Any Administration's chief economic policy official and chief foreign policy official have to address foreign economics, and together either resolve problems or submit them to the President for decision. It is probably futile to seek to install any individual and/or mechanism *outside* the two components of foreign economic policy to intercede between the two officials in charge of two of the most important areas of the President's overall responsibilities and the President himself.

In this context, the experiment with CIEP may prove to have been very useful. Numerous well-meaning observers continually seek a "single coordinating mechanism" for foreign economic policy on the mistaken analogy that such an area of public policy, seeking multiple and often conflicting goals, can be organized like a firm seeking relatively simple targets like higher profits or a greater market share. The CIEP effort has demonstrated once more that powerful forces inherently pull the locus of decision-making back to where real power lies: with those who manage the domestic economy, those who manage overall foreign policy (even in the case of Dr. Kissinger, who was instrumental in bringing the fall 1971 crisis to a negotiated resolution), and ultimately the President himself. There is little room for real power to reside in a hybrid intermediary standing somewhere among those three poles of power, and the CIEP experience has provided fresh evidence thereof.

An important corollary is that serious imbalances in foreign economic policy will result if it is dominated by *either* domestic economic officials or foreign policy officials. The key organizational issues are (a) how the few critical issues which require Presidential decision are presented to him, and (b) who manages the rest. Foreign policy is bound to suffer if the President hears only from his economic officials and if they have autonomy in managing the field, and vice-versa. The latest (and a classic) case in point was the so-called New Economic Policy of August 1971, which incredibly was undertaken and implemented for three months with zero apparent input from the foreign policy community despite its immense importance for U.S. foreign policy for years (perhaps decades) to come.

The second key consideration, in light particularly of this inherent messiness of the subject, is that every President will want to create his own machinery for handling it. Presidents Eisenhower, Kennedy and Johnson, essentially viewing foreign economic policy as part of overall U.S. foreign policy, used the Department of State (as through Under Secretary Douglas Dillon) and the National Security Council staff (as with Deputy Assistant to the President for National Security Affairs Francis Bator) to coordinate overall policy. They used State and, from 1962 through mid-1967, STR to implement trade policy. President Nixon, apparently viewing foreign economic policy as part of U.S. economic policy (at least since August 1971), now uses his Treasury Secretary-Assistant for Economic Affairs for economic policy.

It is really a matter of indifference whether foreign economic policy is nominally managed by the chief economic or foreign policy official as long as *both* are active in the process. Under Eisenhower and the Democrats, the economic policy-makers had a major input. A major problem in the present Administration is the inadequate input of the foreign policy community, due to the general impotence of the Department of State and the continued neglect of Dr. Kissinger (which could be remedied either by his greater personal attention or by the delegation of a large measure of Presidential authority to a deputy of his, as was done under his predecessors).[1]

But any President should be permitted to choose his own mechanism in this area, and will in fact do so in any event. This means that the Congress should not deny the President the authority to have a CIEP if he really wants it, even if it agrees with my own judgment that CIEP should be abolished instead. But this respect for Presidential prerogative also recommends against any authorization for CIEP running beyond the incumbency of the present Administration.

A third factor is that personalities will dominate organizational charts, whatever the charts may say. Despite its statutory authority, STR failed to coordinate U.S. trade policy in 1968-70. Despite the widespread maligning of the Department of State for "selling out U.S. economic interests," Assistant Secretary for Economic Affairs Anthony M. Solomon was the dominant government official on trade policy from late 1967 through 1968—and was supported in that role by key Congressmen and the U.S. business community. Treasury Secretary Connally of course obliterated all functions assigned to CIEP (or anyone else) for several months in late 1971. The State Department would overnight regain much of its clout in this area (and many others) if Mr. Connally, or even Dr. Kissinger, became Secretary. So one should not overemphasize the *real* importance of whatever structural decisions are made either by the President or by the Congress. (The President may of course create structures in order to buttress the position of his preferred individuals, as with the recent creation of a Council on Economic Policy chaired by the Secretary of the Treasury to strengthen Secretary Shultz, but the structure is clearly the *dependent* variable.)

Conclusion

Foreign economic policy is a messy area, any President should be free to organize it as he wishes, and personalities will dominate organizational charts. So I would not deny the President the right to have a CIEP now if he really wants it. Nor would I preclude setting up another CIEP in the future if, for example, personality or bureaucratic factors required it to entice into government the men whom the President wanted to do the job.

But it is objectively inescapable that CIEP is redundant, both structurally and under present circumstances. Foreign economic policy is rooted in domestic economic policy and overall foreign policy, and an intermediary between the two is unlikely to succeed. Secretary Shultz clearly has Presidential authority to manage foreign economic policy at present, STR can effectively coordinate and implement trade policy, and CIEP is having no impact in pulling together the strands of foreign economic policy at the staff level. So I recommend the abolition of CIEP, and would certainly not force any President to inherit the mechanism.

Any Administration organizational structure for foreign economic policy, however, must be clearly and directly responsible to the Congress. Foreign economic policy, particularly trade and investment policy but increasingly international monetary policy as well, is intensely political and requires full consideration of the wide range of viewpoints which only constant Congressional input can assure. The Secretary of the Treasury is so responsible (and so is the Secretary of State). The STR is. It would thus be particularly anomalous for an official ranking between them, as the Executive Director of CIEP now does, not to be fully responsible to Congress. If CIEP were to be authorized, and regarded as a meaningful part of the decision-making process of the present Administration, its Executive Director should certainly be subject to Senate confirmation and fully accountable to the Congress.

Note

1. To maximize its effectiveness on foreign economic issues, the Department of State needs either to abolish its Bureau of Economic Affairs and integrate economic with security issues at all levels in a Bureau of Advanced Nations Affairs (handling Europe, Japan, Canada, and Australia-New Zealand) or at least integrate those issues under an Under Secretary for Advanced Nations Affairs. The National Security Council should again do the same, as it did to some extent under Presidents Kennedy and Johnson.

35 Organizing for a World of Resource Shortages

Introduction

I strongly support the creation of new governmental machinery to monitor the availability to the U.S. economy of primary products and manufactured goods at reasonable prices, and to propose policy measures to alleviate threatened shortages thereof.

Inflation is presently the cardinal economic problem facing the United States, and may continue to be so for some time to come. Resource shortages at all stages of the production process, from the availability of raw materials through intermediate processing to final manufacture, play a vital role in fueling inflation. These shortages cannot be combatted effectively without far better information than is now available, and without a far more systematic process for developing policy options to work toward alleviating the shortages in a timely and cost-effective manner. Hence legislation of the type now under consideration by your committees —which encompasses systematic compilation of data analysis of their implications for the economy, and the establishment of a focal point to recommend action programs to deal with threatened shortages—could make a major contribution to the national welfare.

However, such legislation is obviously far-reaching. Indeed, it would represent adoption by the Federal Government of a major new responsibility for managing the U.S. economy. I will focus on three aspects of the legislation in my testimony: the philosophy underlying such increased government involvement, the need to view the shortages problem in a global rather than purely national context, and the organizational implications which will flow from the discussion of those two points.

The Basic Philosophy

In the last quarter of the twentieth century, we need no longer debate the propriety of active government participation in the U.S. economy. The core economic issues under discussion today are too important to be "left

Originally presented as testimony to the Senate Commerce and Government Operations Committees in their Hearings on Legislation to Establish New Machinery to Monitor and Alleviate Product and Material Shortages on April 9, 1974.

493

to the market," even if "the market" functioned as effectively as economic textbooks suggest it should.

But we know, particularly with regard to natural resources, that "the market" often consists of a few vertically integrated oligopolists. The capital investments and technology needed to find and exploit new materials raise formidable barriers to entry of private firms, even under the incentive of much higher prices as now exist for petroleum. The governments of producing countries are playing an increasingly active role in seeking to increase their take from the exploitation of resources within their territory, including the creation of internationlnal organizations modeled on OPEC in copper, bauxite, phosphate rock, coffee, bananas, etc.[1] So both private and host-country oligopolists distort "the market" for many raw materials, and for some manufactured goods as well. This situation fully justifies—indeed requires—countervailing intervention by the government of consuming countries such as the United States.

But the question immediately arises as to why such intervention should deal only with the problem of material shortages. To be sure, such shortages and their consequences for both inflation and employment are among our primary economic problems today.

But tomorrow, as in the recent past, our primary concern may again be with inadequate demand for U.S. output rather than inadequate supply. One result of that situation would, as in the past, be unemployment and a reduction in our rate of national growth. Should not any "early warning system" of the type contemplated by the legislation before the Committees seek to forecast and head off developments of that type as well?

Let me illustrate with an example which has arisen repeatedly in the Congressional and public debate on U.S. trade policy over the last decade, and particularly in the past five years. Foreign imports may in some instances grow rapidly enough to capture a sizable share of some of our domestic markets. Such penetration was in fact felt acutely by several U.S. industries during the late 1960s and early 1970s, largely due to the overvaluation of the dollar in the exchange markets. The result was growing unemployment in some of these industries, and insistent calls for the erection of new import barriers by the AFL-CIO and some of the industries themselves—which, if enacted, would among other things have had severe inflationary consequences and made our present problem of shortages even worse.

The point here, however, is that our economy was no more prepared for the sharp unemployment effects of increased imports of consumer electronic products than it was for the sharp inflationary effects of increased wheat exports or skyrocketing oil prices. Having studied the problem carefully, international trade experts have unanimously called for an "early warning system" to enable our economy to begin to adjust to increased imports in a timely manner.[2] Similar problems of course arise from changes in defense procurement and other purely domestic sources of economic activity.

Thus I am afraid that your Committees must fact the issue of whether the objectives of the new machinery which you quite properly envisage should be broadened, to provide for better data, forecasting, and policy proposals on the broader range of economic problems which the United States is likely to face at different times, or even simultaneously. One answer would of course be simply to proceed on your present course, with its focus on the crucial problem of materials shortages, with an intent to use the experience gleaned in that process over the next few years to broaden the scope of the activity as time passes. I certainly do not wish to discourage the legislation you are now considering, but only to point out the potential which it in fact encompasses for dealing with even broader problems than occupy our attention today.

A Global Focus

It should now be clear to all observers that materials shortages, and the economic problems which they spawn, are a global problem which are not susceptible to purely national solutions. This is now abundantly true even for the United States, the least exposed to external forces of any non-Communist country. Let me enumerate a few of the ways in which external events contribute to our domestic problems, over which any new institution of the type proposed in the bills before you would have to maintain surveillance:

—An undervalued exchange rate both inflates the costs of U.S. imports and thereby reduces their availability, and drains resources from our economy by unduly encouraging exports.

—Export limitations by foreign countries, as practiced in recent months by a large number of nations, both industrialized and developed, can deny us resources. Such export limitations are undertaken for both economic reasons, as the producing country seeks to fight its own inflation (as we did with soybeans) or improve its export prices (as Brazil is doing with coffee), and for political reasons as in the Middle East.

—Surges of exports into the United States, as mentioned above, can generate strong social and political pressure for import limitations (higher tariffs, quotas, "voluntary" export restraints forced on foreign suppliers, countervailing and anti-dumping duties) which would in turn create shortages and accelerate our inflation. One good current example is meat: by merely suspending the import quotas mandated by the Meat Import Act of 1964 rather than repealing the Act itself, and hence preserving uncertainty in the minds of foreign producers about their future access to our market, we by our own action discourage the expansion of cattle breeding around the world which is absolutely vital to meet our own (and world) demand for meat in the years ahead. An effective program of trade adjustment assistance, to help deal with the real problems faced by the small number of workers and firms adversely affected by imports which are in the overall national interest, is thus an integral part of an effective anti-inflationary program (and is one reason for affirmative Congressional action on the pending Trade Reform Act). This example also demonstrates the interrelationship between inflation and unemployment, in social and political terms, and hence the need to forecast and deal more effectively with the broad range of economic problems as outlined in the first part of my testimony.

—By exempting exports from price control, our own Economic Stabilization Program stimulated exports and hence undermined its own purpose.[3] Petrochemical prices in foreign markets, for example, reached a level triple the level permitted here; our industry thus quite naturally took a dim view of domestic sales. Conversely, price controls in foreign countries could either help our own battle against shortages, if they too exempted exports, or hurt us by limiting export prices even more severely than domestic prices.

These are just a few of the ways in which foreign developments can dramatically affect our own access to materials and efforts to fight inflation. More broadly, we must recognize that, in a world of limited resources, we face a constant scramble with the other consuming countries to get what *is* available. A number of other major countries, such as Germany and Japan, in fact regard this scramble as a cardinal focus of their overall foreign policy.[4] France, the United Kingdom, Italy, Iran (for commodities other than oil, e.g., iron ore from India) and others are actively seeking deals to try to assure themselves access to critical raw materials over the longer haul.

So far, the United States has not done so. It is simply unrealistic to think that control of foreign production by U.S. *companies* will necessarily produce materials for *the United States,* and the control exercised by those companies is waning fast anyway. Our policy neglect of most of the key producing countries is now coming home to roost.[5] In short, we may be losing out in a competition which is vital for the future of our economic welfare and security.

At the same time, we as a nation of course have great strengths and great potential to assure ourselves the needed materials. But my point is that both our information systems and our action programs in this area must often be conceived on a global, rather than a purely national, basis. This implies that our basic policy thrust must be to expand *global* output of whatever items appear at any moment to be headed for short supply, so that both we and the other countries on which we now so heavily depend can avoid commodity wars and prosper together. Our economic interdependence with many countries around the world, particularly in Western Europe, suggest that the gains to our economy would be short-lived even if we were successful in "bidding away" resources from them. A purely national approach, as was implied by our own export embargoes of last summer and excessive devaluation of the dollar, will be self-defeating.

Inflation and shortages have simply outrun the capacity of even the United States to respond on a solely national basis. As a matter which is more important than just terminology, I would hope that you will not in the end label your legislation the "*Domestic* Supply Information Act," the title now attached to S. 2966.

Organization

The foregoing comments suggest several amendments to the organizational approaches proposed in the several bills before you.

First, political factors abroad may be as important as "purely economic" factors—if there are any such things—in determining supply availabilities. Producing countries are combining to form new "OPECs." Host countries are tightening the terms on which they will permit multinational firms to produce, and especially to exploit raw materials, in their territories. Hence any National Information System (as in S. 3209) will have to include international *political* data, and data gathered by the foreign policy community—the State Department, the Central Intelligence Agency, and perhaps even the Department of Defense—will have to be made available to any Office of Domestic Supply (as in S. 2966).

Second, international monetary and trade policies, both our own and those of other countries, can obviously play vital roles in the process, as outlined above. Ways must therefore be found to engage the Treasury Department and the Office of the Special Representative for Trade Negotiations (STR), the agencies responsible for those two aspects of U.S. foreign economic policy, in the analysis of material shortages and what to do about them. Indeed, in periods such as the present it might make sense to use our international economic policy explicitly to counter shortages and fight inflation—by overvaluing the dollar, unilaterally liberalizing imports, and avoiding any artificial inducements to exports (e.g., the DISC tax incentive).[6] It is even possible that our trade policy could now be doubly effective in fighting internal inflation by reducing our barriers to imports of manufactured goods from the developing countries, whose high rates of unemployment require them to continue to focus on expanding exports of labor-intensive products, in return for assured access for us to the primary products of those countries at reasonable prices.

Third, U.S. foreign economic policy as a whole must take full account of the materials needs projected by your new machinery and coordinate closely with the action recommendations proposed to remedy them. As already noted, several important foreign countries have already made "resources diplomacy" a centerpiece of their foreign policy. Whatever agency maintains overall responsibility for U.S. foreign economic policy—be it the Treasury Department as recently under Secretaries Connally and then Shultz, or the Council on International Economic Policy as is nominally the case now, or the National Security Council as in the Kennedy-Johnson and early Nixon Administrations—must therefore also fully engage in the national effort which you are launching.

Notes

1. I have argued elsewhere that OPEC is only the first of the producer-country cartels which will exacerbate the problem of shortages of raw materials. See my "The Threat From the Third World," *Foreign Policy* 11 (Summer 1973) [chapter 26 in this volume] and "The Threat Is Real," *Foreign Policy* 14 (Spring 1974) [excerpted in chapter 19 in this volume].

2. See for example *Economic Adjustment to Liberal Trade: A New Approach,* a report by a special task force of the U.S. Chamber of Commerce which I had the privilege to chair and which can be found in *Trade Reform,* Hearings before the House Ways and Means Committee on the Trade Reform Act of 1973, pp. 894-906 [chapter 15 in this volume].

3. The increased exports, however, also contributed to an appreciation of the exchange rate of the dollar which offset some of the inflationary effects of the exports themselves. The net impact would depend on a variety of factors, including the importance of the controlled product to our overall price picture.

4. See, for example, "The Struggle for the World Product," *Foreign Affairs* (April 1974), by Helmut Schmidt—then Minister of Finance and now Chancellor of the Federal Republic of Germany.

5. For an analysis see C. Fred Bergsten, "The Threat From the Third World," *Foreign Policy* 11 (Summer 1973) [chapter 26 in this volume].

6. See my testimony of April 3, 1974 to the Senate Finance Committee on the Trade Reform Act. [chapter 14 in this volume].

36 Mr. Kissinger: No Economic Superstar

Economics are now clearly central to U.S. foreign policy. They represent the bulk of our relations with Japan, Canada and the Third World. They are an integral component of our relations with Europe, with direct links to our security ties. Much of the Soviet motivation for detente appears based on a desire for American technology, credits and food. Future U.S. leverage in both Hanoi and Saigon depends importantly on its ability to provide economic assistance.

Thus those who seek to run U.S. foreign policy can do so effectively only if they are able to play an equal role, along with those responsible for domestic policy, in formulating U.S. policy on international economic issues. This is true particularly since these issues have also become central to many of our domestic concerns, as exemplified most graphically by the energy crisis, and hence generate heavy pressures for actions which ignore our global relationships.

But Henry Kissinger's record on economics is dismal. On most issues, he has totally abstained. This is true even on the most critical matters of international monetary relations and trade, such as those which led directly to the collapse of the postwar economic system in late 1971 and the recent outbreak of vicious export controls both by (soybeans) and against (oil) the United States. It is true even on the issues most obviously related to foreign policy, such as restoring a viable U.S. foreign assistance program.

Where Mr. Kissinger did reluctantly get involved in economic issues, he usually bungled badly. He botched the textile negotiations with Japan, which badly soured U.S.-Japan relations, on several occasions. He contributed to the giveaway of wheat to the Soviet Union in the pellmell rush to reach concrete agreements at the Moscow summit. He ignored the economic issues which are central to U.S.-European relations in his call for a new Atlantic charter. For a time, he blocked Congressional action on the trade bill, in an inherently futile effort to avoid restrictions on U.S.-Soviet economic relations, jeopardizing the whole outlook for the trade negotiations which are key to alliance relations and through them to U.S.-Soviet relations. He recently sought to keep George Shultz from even going to the Loire to discuss urgent monetary matters with the key Europeans and Japanese. And his emasculation of the traditional foreign policy machinery

Originally appeared in the *New York Times*, December 12, 1973.

in Washington has precluded any meaningful foreign policy input to major international economic decisions.

Why has Mr. Kissinger, the "superstar" of foreign policy, performed so poorly on such a central issue of foreign policy? Ignorance of the subject, which he readily admits, can be as readily dismissed as an explanation. Mr. Kissinger was no expert on Chou En-lai before 1969. He engineered a quick solution of the 1971 monetary crisis when he finally realized that it was threatening to shatter U.S. alliance relationships. And he performed admirably in negotiating that solution with Mr. Pompidou at the Azores. (John Connally worked out the details at the Smithsonian.)

The explanation runs far deeper into the Kissinger style and substantive point of view. Economic issues cannot be handled by superstar solos. They require both political and bureaucratic consensus at home, sustained attention, and messy negotiation with a variety of leaders abroad, because the issues fuse a wide variety of interests on a wide variety of negotiating fronts. Mr. Kissinger has yet to demonstrate the ability to develop a domestic consensus on any issue, let alone those of economics where vested interests clash sharply. His major foreign sorties have been to totalitarian opposite numbers who could, alone, speak to him for their governments. He is reluctant to engage with lots of bureaucratic adversaries on issues in which he is not recognized as the leading authority in town, as would be true in the economic area, especially in the absence of administrative machinery which he can control. After all, this is the man who told the Italian journalist Oriana Fallaci that "my success . . . stems from the fact that I've always acted alone," a posture which precludes serious involvement in economic issues.

Substantively, Mr. Kissinger apparently seeks a balance-of-power world in which Western Europe and Japan would play leading roles. Yet neither seems able or willing to fill the bill. So why not kick them around a bit, to get them to "stand up like men"—particularly on "minor issues like economics"—and, incidentally, to demonstrate to Moscow and Peking that this Administration really does believe in fluid international relationships. John Connally went too far, even for Henry Kissinger, but there is no reason to suspect that Mr. Kissinger would have objected to the rough treatment of old allies in the "New Economic Policy" even if he had been at Camp David in August 1971.

Finally come bureaucratic issues. Before he became a superstar, Mr. Kissinger feared that the liberal position suggested by foreign policy concerns on most economic matters, which would sometimes have pitted him against the interests of major Nixon political supporters and contributors, would have endangered him further with the Haldeman-Ehrlichman-Colson wing of the White House, whose intense resentment of his growing role might here find the issue on which to deep-six Henry. With the daily headlines trumpeting his ascendance over State and Defense, Mr. Kissinger also wanted to avoid the additional bureaucratic explosions which would inevitably emit from Treasury, Commerce, Agriculture, etc. if he forayed into economics.

Many of these considerations have changed dramatically. Haldeman et al. are blessedly gone, the contributors need no longer be solicited, and Mr. Nixon needs Mr. Kissinger more than vice-versa. Mr. Kissinger's bureaucratic position (as "merely a White House aide") no longer requires him to move surreptitiously, avoiding overt engagement in politics at home and negotiations abroad, and gives him no excuse to do so. Indeed, the Secretary of State must seek domestic support for U.S. foreign policy and negotiate with the major foreign countries.

Mr. Kissinger himself has placed heavy emphasis on developing a "new consensus" and "an open foreign policy." He has told the Senate Foreign Relations Committee, "I have learned by experience the crucial importance of economic affairs and the intricate connection between the solution of economic issues and political issues . . ." It is to be hoped that he will move in the directions indicated by his recent statements. However, there is yet no evidence that he will do so. And his deep-seated hostility toward openness and economics in the past raise more than a few doubts about the "new Kissinger," both in substance and in style.

The central questions are whether Kissinger will grasp the substantive importance of international economic issues for U.S. foreign policy in the 1970's and beyond, whether he will seek and use the right advice as to how to deal with them and whether he will be able to alter his personal style to do so effectively. Affirmative answers to these questions could make Kissinger a great Secretary of State. Negative answers could render him an anachronism.

**Part X
Bibliography of the Writings
of C. Fred Bergsten through
1974**

Bibliography
Writings of C. Fred Bergsten (in reverse chronological order, through 1974)

Overviews of the International Economic Order

"The International Economy in the Post-Postwar Era," in Wilfred L. Kohl, ed., *Foreign Economic Policies of Industrial States*, New York: Columbia University Press, 1975.

"International Economics and World Politics: A Framework for Analysis," in C. Fred Bergsten and Lawrence B. Krause, eds., *World Politics and International Economics*, a special issue of *International Organization*, Winter 1975 (with Robert O. Keohane and Joseph S. Nye).

"New Era: New Issues," *Economic Impact*, January 1975.

"Interdependence: Now A Cold Reality," *Washington Post*, January 13, 1974.

The Future of the International Economic Order: An Agenda for Research, Lexington, Mass.: Lexington Books, D.C. Heath and Company, 1973.

"World Leaders Will Pursue Economic Peace in 1973," *Washington Post*, January 1973.

"International Economics Changed Drastically in 1971," *Washington Post*, January 9, 1972.

Co-author, *Reshaping the International Economic Order*, A Tripartite Report by Twelve Economists from North America, the European Community, and Japan, The Brookings Institution, December 1971.

"The Changed International Outlook," *Washington Post*, August 20, 1971.

The International Monetary System

The Dilemmas of the Dollar: The Economics and Politics of United States International Monetary Policy, New York: Council on Foreign Relations, forthcoming 1975.

"Oil and the Cash Flow," *New York Times* (Op-Ed), June 3, 1974.

"Outlook for the Dollar," *The Conference Board Record*, Vol. X, No. 11 (November 1973).

"The Dollar Overhang," *New York Times* (Op-Ed), August 31, 1973.

"Convertibility for the Dollar and International Monetary Reform," in C. Fred Bergsten and William G. Tyler, eds., *Leading Issues in International Economic Policy: Essays in Honor of George N. Halm*, Lexington, Mass: Lexington Books, D.C. Heath and Company, 1973.

"International Monetary Reform: A Viewpoint from the United States," in Alexander Swoboda, ed., *Europe and the Evolution of the International Monetary System*, Leiden: A.W. Sitjhoff, 1973.

"Statement" and subsequent testimony in *To Amend the Par Value Modification Act*, International Finance Subcommittee of the House Banking and Currency Committee, March 7, 1973.

"The World's Next Monetary System," *New York Times* (Sunday), February 18, 1973.

"European Monetary Unification and U.S. Foreign Policy" in Lawrence B. Krause and Walter Salant, eds., *European Monetary Unification and its Meaning for the United States* (Washington, D.C.: The Brookings Institution, 1973).

"A New International Monetary Policy and World Public Order," *Proceedings (September 1972) of the American Society of International Law.*

Reforming the Dollar: An International Monetary Policy for the United States, Council on Foreign Relations Occasional Paper No. 2, September 1972.

"International Monetary Reform and the U.S. Balance of Payments," in National Planning Association, *U.S. Foreign Economic Policy in the 1970s,* November 1971.

"Statement" and subsequent testimony in *The Balance of Payments Myth*, Subcommittee on International Exchange and Payments of The Joint Economic Committee, June 23, 1971.

"The United States Balance of Payments in Mid-1971 and International Flows of Short-Term Capital," *Euromoney*, June 1971.

Statements in Randall Hinshaw, ed., *The Economics of International Adjustment*, Baltimore: The Johns Hopkins Press, 1971.

"The United States and Greater Flexibility of Exchange Rates" in Bergsten, et al. *Approaches to Greater Flexibility of Exchange Rates: The Bürgenstock Papers*, Princeton, N.J.: Princeton University Press, 1970.

"Toward A Dollar Zone," *Interplay*, March 1969.

"Taking the Monetary Initiative," *Foreign Affairs*, July 1968.

"A New Monetary System?" *The Reporter*, April 19, 1968 (reprinted in *Atlantic Community Quarterly*, Summer 1968).

World Trade

"On the Non-Equivalence of Import Quotas and 'Voluntary' Export Re-
straints," in C. Fred Bergsten, ed., *Toward A New World Trade Policy:
The Maidenhead Papers*, Lexington, Mass.: Lexington Books, D.C.
Heath and Company, 1975.

*Completing the GATT: Toward New International Rules to Govern Export
Controls*, British-North American Committee, October 1974.

"The Case Against Export Controls," *Washington Post*, August 1974.

"The Future of World Trade," in Herbert Giersch, ed., *The International
Division of Labour: Problems and Perspectives*, Tubingen: J.C.S.
Mohr, 1974.

"Statement" and subsequent testimony in *The Trade Reform Act*, Part 4,
Senate Finance Committee, April 3, 1974.

"Future Directions for U.S. Trade," *American Journal of Agricultural
Economics*, Vol. 55, No. 2, May 1973 (also Brookings Reprint 275).

"Economic Adjustment to Liberal Trade: A New Approach," in *Trade
Reform*, Hearings before the Ways and Means Committee on H.R. 6767,
Part 3, pp. 894-906, May 1973.

"Comments on the Welfare Effects of Restrictions on U.S. Trade,"
Brookings Papers on Economic Activity 1: 1973.

"Trade Policy at the Crossroads: Which Route for Negotiations?"
Columbia Journal of Transnational Law. Fall 1972.

"The Cost of Import Restrictions to American Consumers," American
Importers Association, March 1972, reprinted in Robert E. Baldwin and
J. David Richardson, eds., *Selected Topics in International Trade and
Finance*, Boston: Little, Brown and Co., 1974.

"The Costs and Benefits of Trade Adjustment Assistance" and subsequent
testimony in *Trade Adjustment Assistance*, Subcommittee on Foreign
Economic Policy, House Foreign Affairs Committee, April 25, 1972.

"American Jobs and Foreign Trade: Two Views," *Washington Post Sunday Outlook*, March 1972.

"Crisis in U.S. Trade Policy," *Foreign Affairs*, July 1971.

Foreign Investment and Transnational Enterprises

"Coming Investment Wars? *Foreign Affairs*, October 1974.

"Comment on the Balance of Payments and International Investment,"
Journal of Finance, May 1974.

"Comment on the Political Economy of Multinational Enterprises," *Journal of Finance*, May 1974.

"Statement" and subsequent testimony in *Foreign Investment in the United States*, International Finance Subcommittee of the Senate Banking, Housing and Urban Affairs Committee, February 21, 1974.

"The International Economy and American Business," in Jules Backman, ed., *Business Problems of the Seventies*, New York: NYU Press, 1973.

"The Role of the Multinational Corporation" in Helen Hughes, ed., *Prospects for Partnership: Industrialization and Trade Policies in the 1970s* (Washington, D. C.: IBRD, 1973).

"Comment on the Multinational Corporation," *Journal of Finance*, May 1973.

Natural Resources

"The New Era in World Commodity Markets," *Challenge*, September/October 1974 (also Brookings Reprint 297).

"Commodity Power is Here to Stay," *Brookings Bulletin*, July 1974.

"Statement" and subsequent testimony in *Global Scarcities in an Interdependent World*, Foreign Economic Policy Subcommittee of the House Foreign Affairs Committee, May 15, 1974 (reprinted in *Washington Post*, May 20, 1974.)

"The Threat is Real," *Foreign Policy* 14 (Spring 1974), reprinted in *Growth and Its Implications for the Future*, Appendix to Hearings before the Senate Subcommittee on Fisheries and Wildlife Conservation and the Environment, May 1, 1974.

Testimony in *Oversight Hearings on Mineral Scarcity*, Subcommittee on Mines and Mining, House Interior and Insular Affairs Committee, March 29, 1974.

"The World May Have to Live with 'Shortages'," *New York Times* (Week in Review), January 27, 1974.

U.S. Economic Relations

Global

"Statement" and subsequent testimony in Hearings on the *Annual Report of the Council on International Economic Policy*, Subcommittee on International Finance, House Committee on Banking and Currency, May 2, 1973.

"The New Economics and U.S. Foreign Policy," *Foreign Affairs*, January 1972 (also Brookings Reprint 231).

"Statement" and subsequent testimony in *The International Implications of the New Economic Policy*, Subcommittee on Foreign Economic Policy, House Foreign Affairs Committee, September 21, 1971.

Europe

"Prospects for the Atlantic World: An American Perspective," *SAIS Review*, Summer 1974, and (in German) *Europa-Archiv*, No. 16/1974.

"U.S. Foreign Economic Policy and Europe: The Ascendance of Germany and the Stagnation of the Common Market" in *American Interest in the European Community*. Subcommittees on Europe and Foreign Economic Policy, House Foreign Affairs Committee, November 8, 1973, and (in German) *Europa-Archiv*, No. 4/1974.

The Third World

"The Response to the Third World," *Foreign Policy* 17 (Winter 1974-75).

"Statement" and subsequent testimony in *The Fourth Replenishment of the International Development Association*, International Finance Subcommittee of the House Banking and Currency Committee, December 6, 1973.

"The Threat From the Third World," *Foreign Policy* 11, Summer 1973 (also Brookings Reprint 268 and reprinted in Richard N. Cooper, ed., *A Reordered World: Emerging International Economic Problems*, Washington, D.C.: Potomac Associates, 1973).

"An Urgency in Multilateral Aid," *Washington Post*, October 15, 1971.

Latin America

"U.S.-Latin American Relations to 1980: The International Framework and Some Possible New Approaches," in *The Americas in a Changing World* (New York: Quadrangle Books, 1975).

"U.S. Policy Toward Latin America in the 1970s and Tariff Preferences" in *Trade Preferences: Latin America and the Caribbean*, Subcommittee on Inter-American Affairs of the House Foreign Affairs Committee, June 25-26, 1973.

Organization of the U.S. Government to Conduct Foreign Economic Policy

"Statement" and subsequent testimony on "Monitoring Resource Shortages," Senate Commerce and Government Operations Committees, April 9, 1974.

"Mr. Kissinger: No Economic Superstar," *New York Times* (Op-Ed), December 12, 1973.

"Statement" and subsequent testimony in *Extension of the Council on International Economic Policy*, International Finance Subcommittee of the Senate Banking, Housing and Urban Affairs Committee, May 14, 1973.

Index

Index

516

61-73, 102-3, 155. *See also* International Monetary Fund
International Paperworkers Union, 467
International Petroleum Company, 388
International Tin Agreement, 287, 408
International Trade Organization, 108-9, 125
Investment, foreign, 9, 225-310; in Third World, 381-452 *passim*; in U.S., *see* Foreign direct investment
Iran, 8, 10, 154, 261, 294, 296, 299, 301, 386, 399, 400, 403, 425
Iraq, 299, 301, 400, 425
Iron ore, 6, 226, 288, 431
Israel, 291-92, 299, 301, 399, 400, 425
Italy, 8, 173, 261, 316, 318, 342, 363, 386

Jamaica, 6, 134, 150, 154, 155, 287, 290, 291, 292, 295-96, 425, 431, 446
Japan, 3, 6, 14, 15, 16, 19, 21, 22, 28, 31, 32-33, 37-38, 51, 52, 80, 81, 85, 88, 99, 102, 108, 109, 113, 121-22, 123, 130, 132, 136, 141, 143, 149, 154, 157-89 *passim*, 195, 201, 202, 203, 206, 207, 214, 218, 219, 220, 226, 234, 235, 267, 279-80, 284, 295, 307, 310, 314, 343-54, 358, 359, 363, 369, 370, 373, 375, 383, 393, 402, 403, 415, 424, 427, 434, 439, 440, 445, 451. *See also* Yen
Javits, Jacob, 363
Javits-Mondale-Harris bill, 374
Job Development Credit, 351
Job quotas, for nationals, 261-63, 271
Job security. *See* Compensation benefits; Fringe benefits; Workers, protection of
Jobert, Michel, 314, 320
Johnson, D. Gale, 211
Johnson, Harry, 290
Johnson, Lyndon B., 490
Johnson administration, 193
"Joint European float," 325-26

Kennan, George, 322
Kennedy, John F., 195, 199, 203, 490
Kennedy Round, 171, 193, 202, 206, 210, 214, 217, 223, 345, 348, 369, 402, 423, 447-48, 458, 463
Kissinger, Henry, 281, 314, 316, 320, 419, 490, 491, 499-501
Korea, 15, 105, 136, 159, 161, 163, 170, 173, 175, 202, 403, 438, 448
Korean War, 108, 115, 295
Krasner, Stephen, 299, 300
Krause, Lawrence, 196
Kuwait, 99, 113, 135, 145, 301, 303, 425

LAFTA, 437
LDCs (less-developed countries). *See* Developing countries; Fourth World; Third World
Labor, 196-97, 203, 475-80. *See also* AFL-CIO; Burke-Hartke bill; United Auto Workers; Workers, protection of
Laqueur, Walter, 322
Latin America, 109, 112, 177, 204, 262, 403; relations with U.S., 431-43, 445-52
Lead, 100
League of Nations, 108
Leather, 109, 113, 226
Libya, 99, 113, 135, 145, 301, 303, 425
Liquidity. *See* International monetary system
Long-Term Arrangement on Cotton Textiles (LTA), 158, 169, 175

MITI (Ministry of Industry and International Trade), 166
Magee, Stephen P., 168
Malaya, 156
Malaysia, 151, 155, 291, 292, 300
Manganese, 290
Manley, Michael N., 290
Manpower programs, 244
Mansfield, Mike, 38-39, 345-46
Mansfield Amendment, 359
Mao Tse-tung, 405
Mark. *See* Deutschemark
"Market convertibility," 44, 45
Market disruption, 132, 134, 160-61, 181, 448
Market intervention, 81-82
Marshall Plan, 69, 195, 375
Matsunaga, Spark M., 105
McGovern, George, 461
Meat, 100, 105, 136, 161, 210, 226, 228, 232, 495-96; VERs on, 158, 159-60, 162, 175, 471
Meat Import Act, 1964, 158, 176, 193, 495
Mercantilism, 17, 22, 35, 37, 204
Mercury, 288
Metal scrap, 109
Mexico, 139, 202, 262, 399, 434, 438. *See also* Sisal combine, Mexican
Middle East, 20, 108, 129, 131, 292, 339, 399-400, 432
Mills, Wilbur, 47, 193, 346
Mills bill, 1970, 174, 176, 193-94, 199, 204-5, 210, 472
Ministerial Committee (IMF), 415
Mintz, Ilse, 168
Mondale, Walter F., 108, 426
Mondale Amendments, 8, 122, 139-40, 155

About the Author

C. Fred Bergsten is a Senior Fellow at the Brookings Institution. From January 1969 until May 1971, he was Assistant for International Economic Affairs on the Senior Staff of the National Security Council. He remains a consultant to several government agencies. Dr. Bergsten was a Visiting Fellow at the Council on Foreign Relations in 1968 and again in 1971. From 1963 to 1967, he was in the Office of International Monetary Affairs at the Department of State. He has published several books and numerous articles on a wide range of international economic issues. He received the master's and Ph.D. degrees from the Fletcher School of Law and Diplomacy.